About the Authors

Kenneth C. Laudon is a Professor of Information Systems at New York University's Stern School of Business. He holds a B.A. in Economics from Stanford and a Ph.D. from Columbia University. He has authored twelve books dealing with electronic commerce, information systems, organizations, and society. Professor Laudon has also written over forty articles concerned with the social, organizational, and management impacts of information systems, privacy, ethics, and multimedia technology.

Professor Laudon's current research is on the planning and management of large-scale information systems and multimedia information technology. He has received grants from the National Science Foundation to study the evolution of national information systems at the Social Security Administration, the IRS, and the FBI. Ken's research focuses on enterprise system implementation, computer-related organizational and occupational changes in large organizations, changes in management ideology, changes in public policy, and understanding productivity change in the knowledge sector.

Ken Laudon has testified as an expert before the United States Congress. He has been a researcher and consultant to the Office of Technology Assessment (United States Congress), Department of Homeland Security, and to the Office of the President, several executive branch agencies, and Congressional Committees. Professor Laudon also acts as an in-house educator for several consulting firms and as a consultant on systems planning and strategy to several Fortune 500 firms.

At NYU's Stern School of Business, Ken Laudon teaches courses on Managing the Digital Firm, Information Technology and Corporate Strategy, Professional Responsibility (Ethics), and Electronic Commerce and Digital Markets. Ken Laudon's hobby is sailing.

Jane Price Laudon is a management consultant in the information systems area and the author of seven books. Her special interests include systems analysis, data management, MIS auditing, software evaluation, and teaching business professionals how to design and use information systems.

Jane received her Ph.D. from Columbia University, her M.A. from Harvard University, and her B.A. from Barnard College. She has taught at Columbia University and the New York University Graduate School of Business. She maintains a lifelong interest in Oriental languages and civilizations.

The Laudons have two daughters, Erica and Elisabeth, to whom this book is dedicated.

Brief Contents

Complete Contents

Chapter 3   Information Systems, Organizations, and Strategy 108

Chapter 6

Foundations of Business Intelligence: Databases and Information Management 238

Part Three   Key System Applications for the Digital Age 365

BUSINESS CASES AND INTERACTIVE SESSIONS

Here are some of the business firms you will find described in the cases and Interactive Sessions of this book:

Chapter 1: Information Systems in Global Business Today
Efficiency in Wood Harvesting with Information Systems
Running the Business from the Palm of Your Hand
UPS Competes Globally with Information Technology
Mashaweer

Chapter 2: Global E-Business and Collaboration
Telus Embraces Social Learning
Schiphol International Hub
Piloting Procter & Gamble from Decision Cockpits
Modernization of NTUC Income

Chapter 3: Information Systems, Organizations, and Strategy
Will Sears's Technology Strategy Work This Time?
Technology Helps Starbucks Find New Ways to Compete
Automakers Become Software Companies
Can This Bookstore Be Saved?

Chapter 4: Ethical and Social Issues in Information Systems
Ethical Issues Facing the use of Technologies for the Aged Community
Life on the Grid: iPhone Becomes iTrack
Monitoring in the Workplace
Facebook: It's About the Money

Chapter 5: IT Infrastructure and Emerging Technologies
Reforming the Regulatory System for Construction Permits
Should You Use Your iPhone for Work?
Nordea Goes Green with IT
Should Businesses Move to the Cloud?

Chapter 6: Foundations of Business Intelligence: Databases and Information Management
BAE Systems
Big Data, Big Rewards
Controversy Whirls Around the Consumer Product Safety Database
Lego: Embracing Change by Combining BI with a Flexible Information System

Chapter 7: Telecommunications, the Internet and Wireless Technology
RFID and Wireless Technology Speed Up Production at Continental Tires
The Battle Over Net Neutrality
Monitoring Employees on Networks: Unethical or Good Business?
Apple, Google, and Microsoft Battle for your Internet Experience

Preface

We wrote this book for business school students who wanted an in-depth look at how today's business firms use information technologies and systems to achieve corporate objectives. Information systems are one of the major tools available to business managers for achieving operational excellence, developing new products and services, improving decision making, and achieving competitive advantage. Students will find here the most up-to-date and comprehensive overview of information systems used by business firms today.

When interviewing potential employees, business firms often look for new hires who know how to use information systems and technologies for achieving bottom-line business results. Regardless of whether you are an accounting, finance, management, operations management, marketing, or information systems major, the knowledge and information you find in this book will be valuable throughout your business career.

WHAT'S NEW IN THIS EDITION

CURRENCY

The 13th edition features many new opening, closing, and Interactive Session cases. The text, figures, tables, and cases have been updated through November 2012 with the latest sources from industry and MIS research.

NEW FEATURES

- Chapter-opening cases have been expanded and new case study questions have been added.
- More online cases: MIS Classic Cases, consisting of five outstanding cases from previous editions on companies such as Kmart or Blockbuster/Netflix, will be available on the book's Web site. In addition, some of the chapter-ending cases from the previous edition (MIS12e) will be available online.
- New Video Cases collection: 30 video cases (2 per chapter) and additional instructional videos covering key concepts and experiences in the MIS world.
- Learning Tracks: over 40 Learning Tracks are for additional coverage of selected topics.

NEW TOPICS

- **Social Business:** Extensive coverage of social business, introduced in Chapter 2 and discussed in throughout the text. Detailed discussions of enterprise (internal corporate) social networking as well as social networking in e-commerce.
- **Big Data:** Chapter 6 on Databases and Information Management rewritten to provide in-depth coverage of Big Data and new data management

technologies, including Hadoop, in-memory computing, non-relational databases, and analytic platforms.

- **Cloud Computing:** Expanded and updated coverage of cloud computing in Chapter 5 (IT Infrastructure), with more detail on types of cloud services, private and public clouds, hybrid clouds, managing cloud services, and a new chapter-ending case on Amazon's cloud services. Cloud computing also covered in Chapter 6 (databases in the cloud); Chapter 8 (cloud security); Chapter 9 (cloud-based CRM); and Chapter 13 (cloud-based systems development and component-based development).

- **Ethical and Social issues:** expanded and updated coverage in Chapter 4 (Ethical and Social Issues) of the social and ethical issues that surround the rapid expansion of the mobile platform, including privacy, patent and copyright, behavioral and smartphone tracking, data quality, due process, and quality of life.

- Social graph
- Social marketing
- Social search
- Social CRM
- Consumerization of IT and BYOD
- Mobile device management
- Mobile application development
- Responsive Web design
- Cyberlockers
- Expanded coverage of business analytics
- Machine learning
- Windows 8, Android, iOS, and Chrome operating systems
- Apps
- HTML5
- IPv6
- Microblogging
- Multitouch interface
- Siri
- Software-defined networking
- Tablet computers
- 3-D printing

WHAT'S NEW IN MIS

Plenty. In fact, there's a whole new world of doing business using new technologies for managing and organizing. What makes the MIS field the most exciting area of study in schools of business is the continuous change in technology, management, and business processes. (Chapter 1 describes these changes in more detail.)

A continuing stream of information technology innovations is transforming the traditional business world. Examples include the emergence of cloud computing, the growth of a mobile digital business platform based on smartphones, tablets, and ultrabooks, and not least, the use of social networks by managers to achieve business objectives. Most of these changes have occurred in the last few years. These innovations are enabling entrepreneurs and innovative traditional firms to create new products and services, develop new business models, and transform the day-to-day conduct of business. In the process, some old businesses, even industries, are being destroyed while new businesses are springing up.

For instance, the rapid growth of online content stores such as iTunes and Amazon, based on cloud storage services—driven by millions of consumers who prefer smartphones and tablet computers as the center of their media world—has forever changed the older business models of distributing music, television, and movies on physical discs, such as CDs and DVDs. Cloud-based content delivered on the Internet is beginning to challenge the dominance of cable television networks for the delivery of television shows.

E-commerce is growing rapidly again following a deep recession, generating over $362 billion in revenues in 2012, and is estimated to grow to over $542 billion in 2016. With nearly 122 million Americans accessing the Internet with their smartphones, mobile commerce in 2012 has grown to $30 billion in a few years, and is growing by double digits each year. Amazon's revenues grew 41 percent in 2011, despite the recession, while offline retail grew by 5 percent. E-commerce is changing how firms design, produce and deliver their products and services. E-commerce has reinvented itself again, disrupting the traditional marketing and advertising industry and putting major media and content firms in jeopardy. Facebook and other social networking sites such as YouTube, Twitter, and Tumblr, and new graphical social sites such as Pinterest, exemplify the new face of e-commerce in the 21st Century. They sell services. When we think of e-commerce we tend to think of an online store selling physical products. While this iconic vision of e-commerce is still very powerful and the fastest growing form of retail sales in the U.S., growing up alongside is a whole new value stream based on selling services, not goods. It's a services model of e-commerce. Information systems and technologies are the foundation of this new services-based e-commerce.

Likewise, the management of business firms has changed: With new mobile smartphones, high-speed wireless Wi-Fi networks, and wireless laptop and tablet computers, remote salespeople on the road are only seconds away from their managers' questions and oversight. Managers on the move arc in direct, continuous contact with their employees. The growth of enterprise-wide information systems with extraordinarily rich data means that managers no longer operate in a fog of confusion, but instead have online, nearly instant, access to the really important information they need for accurate and timely decisions. In addition to their public uses on the Web, private social networks, wikis and blogs are becoming important corporate tools for communication, collaboration, and information sharing.

THE 13TH EDITION: THE COMPREHENSIVE SOLUTION FOR THE MIS CURRICULUM

Since its inception, this text has helped to define the MIS course around the globe. This edition continues to be authoritative, but is also more customizable, flexible, and geared to meeting the needs of different colleges, universities, and individual instructors. This book is now part of a complete learning package that includes the core text and an extensive offering of supplemental materials on the Web.

The core text consists of 15 chapters with hands-on projects covering essential topics in MIS. An important part of the core text is the Video Case Study and Instructional Video package: 30 video case studies (2 per chapter) plus many instructional videos that illustrate business uses of information systems, explain new technologies, and explore concepts. Video cases are keyed to the topics of each chapter.

In addition, for students and instructors who want to go deeper into selected topics, there are over 40 online Learning Tracks that cover a variety of MIS topics in greater depth.

MyMISLab provides more in-depth coverage of chapter topics, career resources, additional case studies, supplementary chapter material, and data files for hands-on projects.

THE CORE TEXT

The core text provides an overview of fundamental MIS concepts using an integrated framework for describing and analyzing information systems. This framework shows information systems composed of management, organization, and technology elements and is reinforced in student projects and case studies.

A diagram accompanying each chapter-opening case graphically illustrates how management, organization, and technology elements work together to create an information system solution to the business challenges discussed in the case.

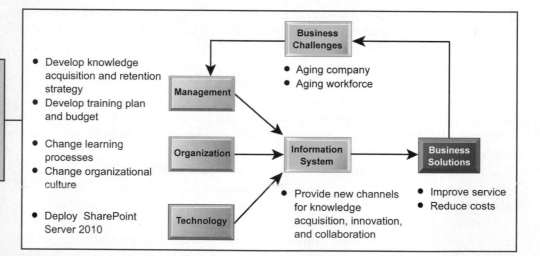

Chapter Organization

Each chapter contains the following elements:
- A chapter-opening case describing a real-world organization to establish the theme and importance of the chapter
- A diagram analyzing the opening case in terms of the management, organization, and technology model used throughout the text
- A series of learning objectives
- Two Interactive Sessions with Case Study Questions
- A Learning Tracks section identifying supplementary material in MyMISLab
- A Review Summary section keyed to the learning objectives
- A list of key terms that students can use to review concepts
- Review questions for students to test their comprehension of chapter material
- Discussion questions raised by the broader themes of the chapter
- A series of Hands-on MIS Projects consisting of two Management Decision Problems, a hands-on application software project, and a project to develop Internet skills
- A pointer to the chapter's video cases
- A Collaboration and Teamwork project to develop teamwork and presentation skills, with options for using open source collaboration tools

- A chapter-ending case study for students to learn about how real business firms use information systems, and to apply chapter concepts

KEY FEATURES

We have enhanced the text to make it more interactive, leading-edge, and appealing to both students and instructors. The features and learning tools are described in the following sections.

Business-Driven with Real-World Business Cases and Examples

The text helps students see the direct connection between information systems and business performance. It describes the main business objectives driving the use of information systems and technologies in corporations all over the world: operational excellence; new products and services; customer and supplier intimacy; improved decision making; competitive advantage; and survival. In-text examples and case studies show students how specific companies use information systems to achieve these objectives.

We use current examples from business and public organizations throughout the text to illustrate the important concepts in each chapter. The case studies describe companies or organizations that are familiar to students, such as Starbucks, Google, Groupon, Facebook, Amazon, L'Oréal, and Procter & Gamble.

Interactivity

There's no better way to learn about MIS than by doing MIS. We provide different kinds of hands-on projects where students can work with real-world business scenarios and data, and learn first hand what MIS is all about. These projects heighten student involvement in this exciting subject.

- **Online Video Case Package.** Students can watch short videos online, either in-class or at home or work, and then apply the concepts of the book to the analysis of the video. Every chapter contains at least two business video cases (30 videos in all) that explain how business firms and managers are using information systems, describe new management practices, and explore concepts discussed in the chapter. Each video case consists of a video about a real-world company, a background text case, and case study questions. These video cases enhance students' understanding of MIS topics and the relevance of MIS to the business world.   In addition, there are many Instructional Videos that describe developments and concepts in MIS keyed to respective chapters.

- **Interactive Sessions.** Two short cases in each chapter have been redesigned as Interactive Sessions to be used in the classroom (or on Internet discussion boards) to stimulate student interest and active learning. Each case concludes with case study questions. The case study questions provide topics for class discussion, Internet discussion, or written assignments.

Each chapter contains two Interactive Sessions focused on management, organizations, or technology using real-world companies to illustrate chapter concepts and issues.

INTERACTIVE SESSION: ORGANIZATIONS

BURTON SNOWBOARDS SPEEDS AHEAD WITH NIMBLE BUSINESS PROCESSES

When we hear "snowboarding", we tend to think of snow-covered slopes, acrobatic jumps, and high-flying entertainment. We don't usually think of improving business process efficiency. But snowboarding is business for Burton Snowboards, an industry pioneer and market leader. Founded in 1977 by Jake Burton Carpenter and headquartered in Burlington, Vermont, Burton designs, manufactures, and markets equipment, clothing, and related accessories for snowboarders. Today, Burton is a global enterprise that serves customers in 27 countries and has offices in Japan, Austria, and throughout the United States.

At its peak, Burton controlled over 40 percent of the U.S. snowboarding market, and it remains the market leader amidst a growing number of competitors. Now, as Burton continues to expand into a global company, it has a new set of problems: improving its systems for inventory, supply chain, purchasing, and customer service.

Stocking and managing inventory is a difficult problem for Burton, whose inventory changes dramatically depend on product line updates and the time of the year. Burton takes feedback from its

SAP Enterprise Resource Planning (ERP) software. Rather than buying new software to solve IT problems, Burton decided that it would explore basic functionalities of SAP ERP software that it had not used yet. Often, Burton could resolve problems this way without adding new layers of complexity to its IT infrastructure, and the company gained proficiency with SAP enterprise software in the process. Burton aims for a standard, traditional version of software whenever possible, realizing that with more bells and whistles comes increased maintenance costs and steeper learning curves to understanding the software.

SAP analysts helped Burton identify the top five transactions that were the most critical to its business operations and that needed optimization from a systems standpoint. Burton had to identify unnecessarily complicated processes, backlogs, and design gaps in the flow of its business processes. For example, the available-to-promise process was taking hours to complete. (Available to promise, in response to customer order inquiries, reports on available quantities of a requested product and delivery due dates.) Burton wanted to

Case study questions encourage students to apply chapter concepts to real-world companies in class discussions, student presentations, or writing assignments.

CASE STUDY QUESTIONS

1. Analyze Burton using the value chain and competitive forces models.
2. Why are the business processes described in this case such an important source of competitive advantage for Burton?

3. Explain exactly how these process improvements enhance Burton's operational performance and decision making.

- **Hands-on MIS Projects.** Every chapter concludes with a Hands-on MIS Projects section containing three types of projects: two Management Decision Problems, a hands-on application software exercise using Microsoft Excel, Access, or Web page and blog creation tools, and a project that develops Internet business skills. A Dirt Bikes USA running case in MyMISLab provides additional hands-on projects for each chapter.

Two real-world business scenarios per chapter provide opportunities for students to apply chapter concepts and practice management decision making.

Management Decision Problems

1. Dealerships for Subaru and other automobile manufacturers keep records of the mileage of cars they sell and service. Mileage data are used to remind customers of when they need to schedule service appointments, but they are used for other purposes as well. What kinds of decisions does this piece of data support at the local level and at the corporate level? What would happen if this piece of data were erroneous, for example, showing mileage of 130,000 instead of 30,000? How would it affect decisionmaking? Assess its business impact.
2. Applebee's is the largest casual dining chain in the world, with over 1800 locations throughout the U.S. and also in 20 other countries. The menu features beef, chicken, and pork items, as well as burgers, pasta, and seafood. Applebee's CEO wants to make the restaurant more profitable by developing menus that are tastier and contain more items that customers want and are willing to pay for despite rising costs for gasoline and agricultural products. How might business intelligence help management implement this strategy? What pieces of data would Applebee's need to collect? What kinds of reports would be useful to help management make decisions on how to improve menus and profitability?

⊞ Store & Region Sales Database								
Il ▾	Store N ▾	Sales Region ▾	Item N ▾	Item Descriptic ▾	Unit Pric ▾	Units Sol ▾	Week Ending ▾	Click to Add ▾
1	1	South	2005	17" Monitor	$229.00	28	10/27/2012	
2	1	South	2005	17" Monitor	$229.00	30	11/24/2012	
3	1	South	2005	17" Monitor	$229.00	9	12/29/2012	
4	1	South	3006	101 Keyboard	$19.95	30	10/27/2012	
5	1	South	3006	101 Keyboard	$19.95	35	11/24/2012	
6	1	South	3006	101 Keyboard	$19.95	39	12/29/2012	
7	1	South	6050	PC Mouse	$8.95	28	10/27/2012	
8	1	South	6050	PC Mouse	$8.95	3	11/24/2012	
9	1	South	6050	PC Mouse	$8.95	38	12/29/2012	
10	1	South	8500	Desktop CPU	$849.95	25	10/27/2012	
11	1	South	8500	Desktop CPU	$849.95	27	11/24/2012	
12	1	South	8500	Desktop CPU	$849.95	33	12/29/2012	
13	2	South	2005	17" Monitor	$229.00	8	10/27/2012	
14	2	South	2005	17" Monitor	$229.00	8	11/24/2012	
15	2	South	2005	17" Monitor	$229.00	10	12/29/2012	
16	2	South	3006	101 Keyboard	$19.95	8	10/27/2012	

Record: H ◀ 1 of 96 ▶ H ▶ꭍ | ☒ No Filter | Search

> Students practice using software in real-world settings for achieving operational excellence and enhancing decision making.

Improving Decision Making: Using Web Tools to Configure and Price an Automobile

Software skills: Internet-based software
Business skills: Researching product information and pricing

In this exercise, you will use software at car Web sites to find product information about a car of your choice and use that information to make an important purchase decision. You will also evaluate two of these sites as selling tools.

You are interested in purchasing a new Ford Escape (or some other car of your choice). Go to the Web site of CarsDirect (www.carsdirect.com) and begin your investigation. Locate the Ford Escape. Research the various Escape models, choose one you prefer in terms of price, features, and safety ratings. Locate and read at least two reviews. Surf the Web site of the manufacturer, in this case Ford (www.ford.com). Compare the information available on Ford's Web site with that of CarsDirect for the Ford Escape. Try to locate the lowest price for the car you want in a local dealer's inventory. Suggest improvements for CarsDirect.com and Ford.com.

> Each chapter features a project to develop Internet skills for accessing information, conducting research, and performing online calculations and analysis.

- **Collaboration and Teamwork Projects.** Each chapter features a collaborative project that encourages students working in teams to use Google Sites, Google Docs, and other open-source collaboration tools. The first team project in Chapter 1 asks students to build a collaborative Google site.

Assessment and AACSB Assessment Guidelines

The Association to Advance Collegiate Schools of Business (AACSB) is a not-for-profit corporation of educational institutions, corporations and other organizations that seeks to improve business education primarily by accrediting university business programs. As a part of its accreditation activities, the AACSB has developed an Assurance of Learning Program designed to ensure that schools do in fact teach students what they promise. Schools are required to state a clear mission, develop a coherent business program, identify student learning objectives, and then prove that students do in fact achieve the objectives.

We have attempted in this book to support AACSB efforts to encourage assessment-based education. On the Laudon Web site is a more inclusive and detailed assessment matrix that identifies the learning objectives of each chapter and points to all the available assessment tools for ensuring students in fact do achieve the learning objectives. Because each school is different and may have different missions and learning objectives, no single document can satisfy all situations. The authors will provide custom advice on how to use this text in their colleges with different missions and assessment needs. Please e-mail the authors or contact your local Pearson Education representative for contact information.

For more information on the AACSB Assurance of Learning Program, and how this text supports assessment-based learning, please visit the Web site for this book.

Customization and Flexibility: New Learning Track Modules

Our Learning Tracks feature gives instructors the flexibility to provide in-depth coverage of the topics they choose. There are over 40 Learning Tracks available to instructors and students. A Learning Tracks section at the end of each chapter directs students to short essays or additional chapters in MyMISLab. This supplementary content takes students deeper into MIS topics, concepts and debates; reviews basic technology concepts in hardware, software, database design, telecommunications, and other areas; and provide additional hands-on software instruction. The 13th Edition includes new Learning Tracks on E-Commerce Payment Systems, LAN Topologies, and the Occupational and Career Outlook for Information Systems Majors 2012–2018.

AUTHOR-CERTIFIED TEST BANK AND SUPPLEMENTS

- **Author-Certified Test Bank.** The authors have worked closely with skilled test item writers to ensure that higher level cognitive skills are tested. The test bank includes multiple-choice questions on content, but also includes many questions that require analysis, synthesis, and evaluation skills.

- **New Annotated Interactive PowerPoint Lecture Slides.** The authors have prepared a comprehensive collection of over five hundred PowerPoint slides to be used in lectures. Ken Laudon uses many of these slides in his MIS classes and executive education presentations. Each of the slides is annotated with teaching suggestions for asking students questions, developing in-class lists that illustrate key concepts, and recommending other firms as examples in addition to those provided in the text. The annotations are like an Instructor's Manual built into the slides and make it easier to teach the course effectively.

STUDENT LEARNING-FOCUSED

Student learning objectives are organized around a set of study questions to focus student attention. Each chapter concludes with a review summary and review questions organized around these study questions.

MYMISLAB

MyMISLab is a Web-based assessment and tutorial tool that provides practice and testing while personalizing course content and providing student and class assessment and reporting. Your course is not the same as the course taught down the hall. Now, all the resources that instructors and students need for course success are in one place—flexible and easily organized and adapted for an individual course experience. Visit www.pearsonglobaleditions.com/mymislab to see how you can teach, learn, and experience MIS.

CAREER RESOURCES

The Instructor's Resource section of the Laudon Web site also provides extensive Career Resources, including job-hunting guides and instructions on how to build a Digital Portfolio demonstrating the business knowledge, application software proficiency, and Internet skills acquired from using the text. The portfolio can be included in a resume or job application or used as a learning assessment tool for instructors.

INSTRUCTIONAL SUPPORT MATERIALS

Instructor Resource Center

Most of the support materials described in the following sections are conveniently available for adopters on the online Instructor Resource Center (IRC). The IRC includes the Image Library (a very helpful lecture tool), Instructor's Manual, Lecture Notes, Test Item File and TestGen, and PowerPoint slides.

Image Library

The Image Library is an impressive resource to help instructors create vibrant lecture presentations. Almost every figure and photo in the text is provided and organized by chapter for convenience. These images and lecture notes can be imported easily into PowerPoint to create new presentations or to add to existing ones.

Instructor's Manual

The Instructor's Manual features not only answers to review, discussion, case study, and group project questions, but also in-depth lecture outlines, teaching objectives, key terms, teaching suggestions, and Internet resources.

Test Item File

The Test Item File is a comprehensive collection of true-false, multiple-choice, fill-in-the-blank, and essay questions. The questions are rated by difficulty level and the answers are referenced by section. The Test Item File also contains questions tagged to the AACSB learning standards. An electronic version of the Test Item File is also available in TestGen.

PowerPoint Slides

Electronic color slides created by the authors are available in PowerPoint. The slides illuminate and build on key concepts in the text.

Video Cases and Instructional Videos

Instructors can download the video cases from MyMISLab at www.pearsonglobaleditions.com/mymislab. See page 28 for a list of video cases and instructional videos available at the time of publication.

Learning Track Modules

Over 40 Learning Tracks provide additional coverage topics for students and instructors. See page 29 for a list of the Learning Tracks available for this edition.

Video Cases and Instructional Videos

Chapter	Video
Chapter 1: Information Systems In Global Business Today	Case 1: UPS Global Operations with the DIAD IV Case 2: Google: Google Data Center Efficiency Best Practices
Chapter 2: Global E-business and Collaboration	Case 1: IS in Action: Walmart's Retail Link Supply Chain Case 2: Saleforce.com: The Emerging Social Enterprise Case 3: How FedEx Works: Inside the Memphis Super Hub Instructional Video 1: US Foodservice Grows Market with Oracle CRM on Demand
Chapter 3: Information Systems, Organizations, and Strategy	Case 1: National Basketball Association: Competing on Global Delivery With Akamai OS Streaming Case 2: IT and Geo-Mapping Help a Small Business Succeed Case 3: Materials Handling Equipment Corp: Enterprise Systems Drive Strategy Instructional Video 1: SAP BusinessOne ERP: From Orders to Final Delivery and Payment
Chapter 4: Ethical and Social Issues in Information Systems	Case 1: What Net Neutrality Means For You Case 2: Privacy: Social Network Data Mining Case 3: Data Mining for Terrorists and Innocents. Instructional Video 1: The Right to be Forgotten
Chapter 5: IT Infrastructure: and Emerging Technologies	Case 1: ESPN: Getting to eXtreme Scale On the Web Case 2: Salsesforce.com: Managing by Smartphone Case 3: Hudson's Bay Company and IBM: Virtual Blade Platform Instructional Video 1: Google and IBM Produce Cloud Computing Instructional Video 2: IBM Blue Cloud is Ready-to-Use Computing
Chapter 6: Foundations of Business Intelligence: Databases and Information Management	Case 1: Dubuque Uses Cloud Computing and Sensors to Build a Smarter City Case 2: Data Warehousing at REI: Understanding the Customer Case 3: Maruti Suzuki Business Intelligence and Enterprise Databases
Chapter 7: Telecommunications, the Internet, and Wireless Technology	Case 1: Telepresence Moves Out of the Boardroom and Into the Field Case 2: Unified Communications Systems: Virtual Collaboration With Lotus Sametime Instructional Video 1: CNN Telepresence
Chapter 8: Securing Information Systems	Case 1: Stuxnet and Cyber Warfare Case 2: Cyber Espionage: The Chinese Threat Case 3: UBS Access Key: IBM Zone Trusted Information Channel Instructional Video 1: Sony PlayStation Hacked; Data Stolen from 77 Million Users Instructional Video 2: Zappos Working To Correct Online Security Breach Instructional Video 3: Meet the Hackers: Annonymous Video Statement on Hacking SONY Instructional Video 4: Dick Hardt: Identity 2.0
Chapter 9: Achieving Operational Excellence and Customer Intimacy: Enterprise Applications	Case 1: Workday: Enterprise Software as a Service Case 2: Evolution Homecare Manages Patients with Microsoft CRM Case 3: Sinosteel Strengthens Business Management with ERP Applications Instructional Video 1: Zara's: Wearing Today's Fashions With Supply Chain Management
Chapter 10: E-commerce: Digital Markets, Digital Goods	Case 1: Deals Galore at Groupon Case 2: Etsy: A Marketplace and Community Case 3: Ford AutoXchange B2B Marketplace
Chapter 11: Managing Knowledge	Case 1: How IBM's Watson Became a Jeopardy Champion Case 2: Alfresco: Open Source Document Management and Collaboration Case 3 L'Oréal: Knowledge Management Using Microsoft SharePoint Instructional Video 1: Analyzing Big Data: IBM Watson: Watson After Jeopardy Instructional Video 2: Teamwork and Collaboration: John Chambers on Collaboration vs. Command and Control in Web 2.0 Instructional Video 3: FreshDirect's Secret Sauce: Customer Data From the Website Instructional Video 4: Oracle's Mobile Business Intelligence App
Chapter 12: Enhancing Decision Making	Case 1: FreshDirect Uses Business Intelligence to Manage Its Online Grocery Case 2: Business Intelligence: Decision Making at the Cincinnati Zoo
Chapter 13: Building Information Systems	Case 1: IBM: SaaS Business Process Management Case 2: IBM Helps the City of Madrid With Real-Time BPM Software Instructional Video 1: IBM BPM Business Process Management Customer Story: Besthome Store Instructional Video 2: Workflow Management: Visualized
Chapter 14: Managing Projects	Case 1: Blue Cross Blue Shield: Smarter Computing Project Case 2: NASA: Project Management Challenges Instructional Video: Software Project Management in 15 Minutes
Chapter 15: Managing Global Systems	Case 1 Daum Runs Oracle Apps on Linux Case 2: Lean Manufacturing and Global ERP: Humanetics and Global Shop Case 3: Monsanto, Cisco ANS, and Microsoft SharePoint

Learning Track Modules

Chapter	Learning Tracks
Chapter 1: Information Systems in Global Business Today	How Much Does IT Matter? Information Systems and Your Career The Mobile Digital Platform
Chapter 2: Global E-Business and Collaboration	Systems From a Functional Perspective IT Enables Collaboration and Teamwork Challenges of Using Business Information Systems Organizing the Information Systems Function Occupational and Career Outlook for Information Systems Majors 2012-2018
Chapter 3: Information Systems, Organizations, and Strategy	The Changing Business Environment for IT
Chapter 4: Ethical and Social Issues in Information Systems	Developing a Corporate Code of Ethics for IT
Chapter 5: IT Infrastructure and Emerging Technologies	How Computer Hardware Works How Computer Software Works Service Level Agreements The Open Source Software Initiative Comparing Stages in IT Infrastructure Evolution Cloud Computing
Chapter 6: Foundations of Business Intelligence: Databases and Information Management	Database Design, Normalization, and Entity-Relationship Diagramming Introduction to SQL Hierarchical and Network Data Models
Chapter 7: Telecommunications, the Internet, and Wireless Technology	LAN Topologies Broadband Network Services and Technologies Cellular System Generations Wireless Applications for Customer Relationship Management, Supply Chain Management, and Healthcare Introduction to Web 2.0
Chapter 8: Securing Information Systems	The Booming Job Market in IT Security The Sarbanes-Oxley Act Computer Forensics General and Application Controls for Information Systems Management Challenges of Security and Control Software Vulnerability and Reliability
Chapter 9: Achieving Operational Excellence and Customer Intimacy: Enterprise Applications	SAP Business Process Map Business Processes in Supply Chain Management and Supply Chain Metrics Best-Practice Business Processes in CRM Software
Chapter 10: E-commerce: Digital Markets, Digital Goods	E-Commerce Challenges: The Story of Online Groceries Build an E-Commerce Business Plan Hot New Careers in E-Commerce E-commerce Payment Systems
Chapter 11: Managing Knowledge	Challenges of Knowledge Management Systems
Chapter 12: Enhancing Decision Making	Building and Using Pivot Tables
Chapter 13: Building Information Systems	Unified Modeling Language Primer on Business Process Design and Documentation Primer on Business Process Management
Chapter 14: Managing Projects	Capital Budgeting Methods for Information Systems Investments Information Technology Investments and Productivity Enterprise Analysis (Business Systems Planning) and Critical Success Factors

ACKNOWLEDGEMENTS

The production of any book involves valued contributions from a number of persons. We would like to thank all of our editors for encouragement, insight, and strong support for many years. We thank Bob Horan for guiding the development of this edition and Karalyn Holland for her role in managing the project.

Our special thanks go to our supplement authors for their work. We are indebted to William Anderson for his assistance in the writing and production of the text and to Megan Miller for her help during production. We thank Diana R. Craig for her assistance with database and software topics.

Special thanks to my colleagues at the Stern School of Business at New York University; to Professor Lawrence Andrew of Western Illinois University; to Professor Detlef Schoder of the University of Cologne; to Professor Walter Brenner of the University of St. Gallen; to Professor Lutz Kolbe of the University of Gottingen; to Professor Donald Marchand of the International Institute for Management Development; and to Professor Daniel Botha of Stellenbosch University who provided additional suggestions for improvement. Thank you to Professor Ken Kraemer, University of California at Irvine, and Professor John King, University of Michigan, for more than a decade's long discussion of information systems and organizations. And a special remembrance and dedication to Professor Rob Kling, University of Indiana, for being my friend and colleague over so many years.

We also want to especially thank all our reviewers whose suggestions helped improve our texts. Reviewers for this edition include the following:

Brad Allen, Plymouth State University
Anne Formalarie, Plymouth State University
Bin Gu, University of Texas – Austin
Essia Hamouda, University of California – Riverside

Kimberly L. Merritt, Oklahoma Christian University
James W. Miller, Dominican University
Fiona Nah, University of Nebraska – Lincoln
Thomas Schambach, Illinois State University

Pearson gratefully acknowledges and thanks the following people for their work on the Global Edition:

Global Edition Contributors

Ahmed Elragal, German University in Cairo
Niveen Ezzat, Cairo University
Bee Hua Goh, National University of Singapore
Jonas Hedman, Copenhagen Business School
Ari Heiskanen, University of Oulu
Stefan Henningsson, Copenhagen Business School
Andy Jones, Staffordshire University
Faouzi Kamoun, Zayed University

Patricia Lago, VU University Amsterdam
Lesley Land, University of New South Wales
Daniel Ortiz-Arroyo, Aalborg University
Neerja Sethi, Nanyang Technological University
Vijay Sethi Nanyang, Technological University
Upasana Singh, University of KwaZulu-Natal
Damian A. Tamburri, VU University Amsterdam
Robert Manderson, University of Roehampton

Global Edition Reviewers

James Collins, Aalto University School of Business
Navonil Mustafee, Swansea University
Karsten Boye Rasmussen, University of Southern Denmark

Abdul Razak bin Rahmat, Universiti Utara Malaysia
Bernd Schenk, University of Liechtenstein

K.C.L.
J.P.L.

PART ONE

Organizations, Management, and the Networked Enterprise

Part One introduces the major themes of this book, raising a series of important questions: What is an information system and what are its management, organization, and technology dimensions? Why are information systems so essential in businesses today? Why are systems for collaboration and social business so important? How can information systems help businesses become more competitive? What broader ethical and social issues are raised by widespread use of information systems?

Chapter 1

Information Systems in Global Business Today

EFFICIENCY IN WOOD HARVESTING WITH INFORMATION SYSTEMS

Finland is a leader in the timber machine industry. The Finnish company Ponsse is one of the largest manufacturers of rubber-wheel cut-to-length forest machines. The timber industry uses two cutting methods: the cut-to-length method and the tree-length method. With the cut-to-length method, tree trunks are cut in the forest into various sized logs for different uses, such as saw logs or pulpwood. With the tree-length method, trunks are cut in the forest and transported to the mill whole or almost whole. At the mill, trunk pieces are separated according to use. Approximately 45 percent of the world's harvest is harvested with cut-to-length machines, like those produced by Ponsse, and 35 percent of this yield is harvested using the cut-to-length method.

Ponsse's main products are harvesters, harvester cutting heads, forwarders, and cranes. A harvester is a tractor-like machine used for cutting logs. It has a crane with a cutting head, which grasps the tree at the stem and uses its saw to make the first cut. Then the head moves the cut tree trunk in its "jaws" and finds the next cutting points. During the movement, the cutting head removes the branches of the tree. A forwarder is a special forest tractor with a crane that is designed for efficient trunk collection and transportation.

Ponsse also offers its clients an integrated set of sophisticated information systems. "Ponsse wants to know the business of its clients, because it sells forest machines and information systems to all partners in the logistic chain," says Information Systems Product Manager Hanna Vilkman. These information systems support the entire wood procurement chain. The first step in this chain is to estimate the demand for different types and sizes of timber. Typically, this is done in the field office of a wood purchasing organization. With the help of information systems, a cutting plan is created that will optimize the cutting yield for a particular logging area. Data on similar areas that were logged previously are used in order to optimize the cutting plan. A map

© Ponsse

of the logging area is also produced, as well as working instructions for the harvester driver. The map describes the borders of the logging area as well as areas to be protected. Should a single tree need to be left uncut, it is marked manually with a plastic stripe.

The harvester driver gets the map and working instructions via a dedicated e-mail system that transfers data between the harvester's information system and the wood purchase organization. Instructions and maps are presented on a display located in the harvester cabin. A special feature in the harvester's information system enables it to optimize the cutting of a log into pieces during the cutting process. This means that the system is able to calculate the optimal cutting places when the log is moving through the cutting head, after being first cut from the stem. After the trees have been cut according to the instructions, the driver sends the harvest information to the field office via a dedicated e-mail system. The assortment typically contains 10 different types of cut logs of five different lengths. The harvester marks each type with a different color spot in order to help the forwarder to sort each log into its correct pile.

Forwarders (special forest tractors) use a map application and GPS positioning to transport the cut logs from the forest to the roadside. This facilitates work and improves safety, because the system warns the operator when the machine is approaching dangerous hazards, such as power lines. Piles of cut logs are then transported from the roadside to factories by trucks that also use information systems, for example, to find optimal routes.

Drivers of harvesters and foresters can learn the skills required to operate their machines by using 3D simulators that simulate real-world conditions. A driver can sit in a simulated machine and control the machine using the levers, just like they would in the field. The forest landscape is reflected as a 3D image on a canvas, and the operator can move freely within the harvesting area and view the forest from different angles.

Sources: Quotes and other information from interview with Simo Tauriainen, 2010, Software Chief Designer, Ponsse, www.ponsse.com.

Case contributed by Ari Heiskanen, University of Oulu

Ponsse has well-functioning, cooperative information systems that link together the various parties of the wood production and procurement chain, such as the forest owner, the wood-purchasing organization, the forest machine owner and operator, and the manufacturing plant that uses the wood cut from the forest. The systems benefit all parties. Some of the information systems provided by Ponsse are integral parts of forest machinery, like those embedded in harvesters and forwarders; others are products that can be purchased. Information flows between these parties automatically. The availability of these kinds of information systems boosts the selling of Ponsse's main products, the forest machines. The harvester information system guides the machine and gathers exact information on how the machine is being operated and the details of the yield. The company that owns the forest machine can monitor the machine's utilization and the distribution of working hours and sequences, for example. The harvester driver can adjust the harvester operating settings according to his or her own preferences. The forest field office gets information from several sources, such as harvester operations in the forest, the trucks, or the factory. All of this makes the management of the various phases of the wood procurement chain more efficient. Harvester and forwarder information systems also enhance the ecological treatment of forests by highlighting areas to be avoided.

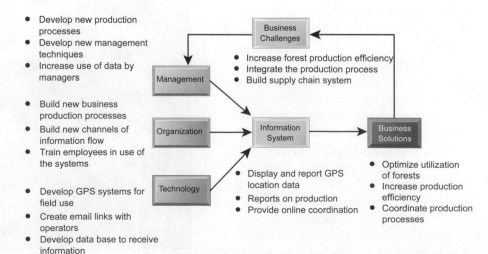

1.1 THE ROLE OF INFORMATION SYSTEMS IN BUSINESS TODAY

It's not business as usual in America anymore, or the rest of the global economy. In 2012, American businesses will spend over $540 billion on information systems hardware, software, and telecommunications equipment. In addition, they will spend another $650 billion on business and management consulting and services—much of which involves redesigning firms' business operations to take advantage of these new technologies. Figure 1.1 shows that between 1980 and 2011, private business investment in information technology consisting of hardware, software, and communications equipment grew from 32 percent to 52 percent of all invested capital.

As managers, most of you will work for firms that are intensively using information systems and making large investments in information technology. You will certainly want to know how to invest this money wisely. If you make wise choices, your firm can outperform competitors. If you make poor choices, you will be wasting valuable capital. This book is dedicated to helping you make wise decisions about information technology and information systems.

HOW INFORMATION SYSTEMS ARE TRANSFORMING BUSINESS

You can see the results of this massive spending around you every day by observing how people conduct business. More wireless cell phone accounts were opened in 2012 than telephone landlines installed. Smartphones, texting, e-mail, and online conferencing have all become essential tools of business. One hundred twenty-two million people in the United States access the Internet using mobile devices in 2012, which is half of the total Internet user population

FIGURE 1.1 INFORMATION TECHNOLOGY CAPITAL INVESTMENT

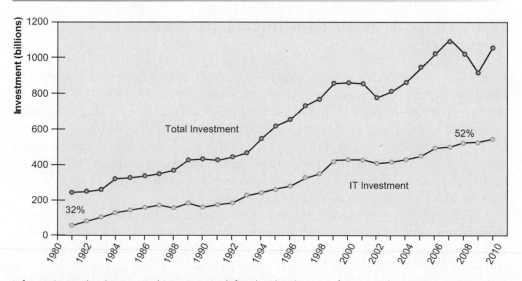

Information technology capital investment, defined as hardware, software, and communications equipment, grew from 32 percent to 52 percent of all invested capital between 1980 and 2011.

Source: Based on data in U.S. Department of Commerce, Bureau of Economic Analysis, *National Income and Product Accounts,* 2012.

(eMarketer, 2010). There are 242 million cell phone subscribers in the United States, and nearly 5 billion worldwide (ITU, 2011).

By June 2012, more than 104 million businesses worldwide had dot-com Internet sites registered (Whois, 2012). Today, 184 million Americans shop online, and 150 million have purchased online. Every day about 67 million Americans go online to research a product or service.

In 2012, FedEx moved over 9 million packages daily worldwide (6 million in the United States), mostly overnight, and the United Parcel Service (UPS) moved over 15 million packages daily worldwide. Businesses sought to sense and respond to rapidly changing customer demand, reduce inventories to the lowest possible levels, and achieve higher levels of operational efficiency. Supply chains have become more fast-paced, with companies of all sizes depending on just-in-time inventory to reduce their overhead costs and get to market faster.

As newspaper readership continues to decline, more than 150 million people read a newspaper online, and millions more read other news sites. About 67 million people watch a video online every day, 76 million read a blog, and 26 million post to blogs, creating an explosion of new writers and new forms of customer feedback that did not exist five years ago (Pew, 2012). Social networking site Facebook attracted 162 million monthly visitors in 2012 in the United States, and over 900 million worldwide. Google+ has attracted over 100 million users in the United States. Businesses are starting to use social networking tools to connect their employees, customers, and managers worldwide. Many Fortune 500 companies now have Facebook pages, Twitter accounts, and Tumblr sites.

Despite the economic slowdown, e-commerce and Internet advertising continue to expand. Google's online ad revenues surpassed $36 billion in 2011, and Internet advertising continues to grow at more than 10 percent a year, reaching more than $39.5 billion in revenues in 2012.

New federal security and accounting laws, requiring many businesses to keep e-mail messages for five years, coupled with existing occupational and health laws requiring firms to store employee chemical exposure data for up to 60 years, are spurring the annual growth of digital information at the estimated rate of 5 exabytes annually, equivalent to 37,000 new Libraries of Congress.

WHAT'S NEW IN MANAGEMENT INFORMATION SYSTEMS?

Lots! What makes management information systems the most exciting topic in business is the continual change in technology, management use of the technology, and the impact on business success. New businesses and industries appear, old ones decline, and successful firms are those that learn how to use the new technologies. Table 1.1 summarizes the major new themes in business uses of information systems. These themes will appear throughout the book in all the chapters, so it might be a good idea to take some time now and discuss these with your professor and other students.

There are three interrelated changes in the technology area: (1) the emerging mobile digital platform, (2) the growing business use of "big data," and (3) the growth in "cloud computing," where more and more business software runs over the Internet.

IPhones, iPads, BlackBerrys, and Android tablets and smartphones are not just gadgets or entertainment outlets. They represent new emerging computing platforms based on an array of new hardware and software technologies.

TABLE 1.1 WHAT'S NEW IN MIS

CHANGE	BUSINESS IMPACT
TECHNOLOGY	
Cloud computing platform emerges as a major business area of innovation	A flexible collection of computers on the Internet begins to perform tasks traditionally performed on corporate computers. Major business applications are delivered online as an Internet service (Software as a Service, or SaaS).
Big data	Businesses look for insights from huge volumes of data from Web traffic, e-mail messages, social media content, and machines (sensors) that require new data management tools to capture, store, and analyze.
A mobile digital platform emerges to compete with the PC as a business system	The Apple iPhone and Android mobile devices are able to download hundreds of thousands of applications to support collaboration, location-based services, and communication with colleagues. Small tablet computers, including the iPad, Google Nexus, and Kindle Fire, challenge conventional laptops as platforms for consumer and corporate computing.
MANAGEMENT	
Managers adopt online collaboration and social networking software to improve coordination, collaboration, and knowledge sharing	Google Apps, Google Sites, Microsoft Windows SharePoint Services, and IBM Lotus Connections are used by over 100 million business professionals worldwide to support blogs, project management, online meetings, personal profiles, social bookmarks, and online communities.
Business intelligence applications accelerate	More powerful data analytics and interactive dashboards provide real-time performance information to managers to enhance decision making.
Virtual meetings proliferate	Managers adopt telepresence videoconferencing and Web conferencing technologies to reduce travel time, and cost, while improving collaboration and decision making.
ORGANIZATIONS	
Social business	Businesses use social networking platforms, including Facebook, Twitter, and internal corporate social tools, to deepen interactions with employees, customers, and suppliers. Employees use blogs, wikis, e-mail texting, and messaging to interact in online communities.
Telework gains momentum in the workplace	The Internet, wireless laptops, smartphones, and tablet computers make it possible for growing numbers of people to work away from the traditional office. Fifty-five percent of U.S. businesses have some form of remote work program.
Co-creation of business value	Sources of business value shift from products to solutions and experiences, and from internal sources to networks of suppliers and collaboration with customers. Supply chains and product development become more global and collaborative; customer interactions help firms define new products and services.

More and more business computing is moving from PCs and desktop machines to these mobile devices. Managers are increasingly using these devices to coordinate work, communicate with employees, and provide information for decision making. We call these developments the "emerging mobile digital platform."

Managers routinely use online collaboration and social technologies in order to make better, faster decisions. As management behavior changes, how work gets organized, coordinated, and measured also changes. By connecting employees working on teams and projects, the social network is where works gets done, where plans are executed, and where managers manage. Collaboration spaces are where employees meet one another—even when they are separated by continents and time zones.

The strength of cloud computing and the growth of the mobile digital platform allow organizations to rely more on telework, remote work, and distributed decision making. This same platform means firms can outsource more work, and rely on markets (rather than employees) to build value. It also means that firms can collaborate with suppliers and customers to create new products, or make existing products more efficiently.

You can see some of these trends at work in the Interactive Session on Management. Millions of managers rely heavily on the mobile digital platform to coordinate suppliers and shipments, satisfy customers, and manage their employees. A business day without these mobile devices or Internet access would be unthinkable. As you read this case, note how the emerging mobile platform greatly enhances the accuracy, speed, and richness of decision making.

GLOBALIZATION CHALLENGES AND OPPORTUNITIES: A FLATTENED WORLD

In 1492, Columbus reaffirmed what astronomers were long saying: the world was round and the seas could be safely sailed. As it turned out, the world was populated by peoples and languages living in isolation from one another, with great disparities in economic and scientific development. The world trade that ensued after Columbus's voyages has brought these peoples and cultures closer. The "industrial revolution" was really a world-wide phenomenon energized by expansion of trade among nations.

In 2005, journalist Thomas Friedman wrote an influential book declaring the world was now "flat," by which he meant that the Internet and global communications had greatly reduced the economic and cultural advantages of developed countries. Friedman argued that the U.S. and European countries were in a fight for their economic lives, competing for jobs, markets, resources, and even ideas with highly educated, motivated populations in low-wage areas in the less developed world (Friedman, 2007). This "globalization" presents both challenges and opportunities for business firms

A growing percentage of the economy of the United States and other advanced industrial countries in Europe and Asia depends on imports and exports. In 2012, more than 33 percent of the U.S. economy resulted from foreign trade, both imports and exports. In Europe and Asia, the number exceeded 50 percent. Many Fortune 500 U.S. firms derive half their revenues from foreign operations. For instance, 85 percent of Intel's revenues in 2011 came from overseas sales of its microprocessors. Eighty percent of the toys sold in the United States are manufactured in China, while about 90 percent of the PCs manufactured in China use American-made Intel or Advanced Micro Design (AMD) chips.

It's not just goods that move across borders. So too do jobs, some of them high-level jobs that pay well and require a college degree. In the past decade, the United States lost several million manufacturing jobs to offshore, low-wage

TABLE 1.1 WHAT'S NEW IN MIS

CHANGE	BUSINESS IMPACT
TECHNOLOGY	
Cloud computing platform emerges as a major business area of innovation	A flexible collection of computers on the Internet begins to perform tasks traditionally performed on corporate computers. Major business applications are delivered online as an Internet service (Software as a Service, or SaaS).
Big data	Businesses look for insights from huge volumes of data from Web traffic, e-mail messages, social media content, and machines (sensors) that require new data management tools to capture, store, and analyze.
A mobile digital platform emerges to compete with the PC as a business system	The Apple iPhone and Android mobile devices are able to download hundreds of thousands of applications to support collaboration, location-based services, and communication with colleagues. Small tablet computers, including the iPad, Google Nexus, and Kindle Fire, challenge conventional laptops as platforms for consumer and corporate computing.
MANAGEMENT	
Managers adopt online collaboration and social networking software to improve coordination, collaboration, and knowledge sharing	Google Apps, Google Sites, Microsoft Windows SharePoint Services, and IBM Lotus Connections are used by over 100 million business professionals worldwide to support blogs, project management, online meetings, personal profiles, social bookmarks, and online communities.
Business intelligence applications accelerate	More powerful data analytics and interactive dashboards provide real-time performance information to managers to enhance decision making.
Virtual meetings proliferate	Managers adopt telepresence videoconferencing and Web conferencing technologies to reduce travel time, and cost, while improving collaboration and decision making.
ORGANIZATIONS	
Social business	Businesses use social networking platforms, including Facebook, Twitter, and internal corporate social tools, to deepen interactions with employees, customers, and suppliers. Employees use blogs, wikis, e-mail texting, and messaging to interact in online communities.
Telework gains momentum in the workplace	The Internet, wireless laptops, smartphones, and tablet computers make it possible for growing numbers of people to work away from the traditional office. Fifty-five percent of U.S. businesses have some form of remote work program.
Co-creation of business value	Sources of business value shift from products to solutions and experiences, and from internal sources to networks of suppliers and collaboration with customers. Supply chains and product development become more global and collaborative; customer interactions help firms define new products and services.

More and more business computing is moving from PCs and desktop machines to these mobile devices. Managers are increasingly using these devices to coordinate work, communicate with employees, and provide information for decision making. We call these developments the "emerging mobile digital platform."

Managers routinely use online collaboration and social technologies in order to make better, faster decisions. As management behavior changes, how work gets organized, coordinated, and measured also changes. By connecting employees working on teams and projects, the social network is where works gets done, where plans are executed, and where managers manage. Collaboration spaces are where employees meet one another—even when they are separated by continents and time zones.

The strength of cloud computing and the growth of the mobile digital platform allow organizations to rely more on telework, remote work, and distributed decision making. This same platform means firms can outsource more work, and rely on markets (rather than employees) to build value. It also means that firms can collaborate with suppliers and customers to create new products, or make existing products more efficiently.

You can see some of these trends at work in the Interactive Session on Management. Millions of managers rely heavily on the mobile digital platform to coordinate suppliers and shipments, satisfy customers, and manage their employees. A business day without these mobile devices or Internet access would be unthinkable. As you read this case, note how the emerging mobile platform greatly enhances the accuracy, speed, and richness of decision making.

GLOBALIZATION CHALLENGES AND OPPORTUNITIES: A FLATTENED WORLD

In 1492, Columbus reaffirmed what astronomers were long saying: the world was round and the seas could be safely sailed. As it turned out, the world was populated by peoples and languages living in isolation from one another, with great disparities in economic and scientific development. The world trade that ensued after Columbus's voyages has brought these peoples and cultures closer. The "industrial revolution" was really a world-wide phenomenon energized by expansion of trade among nations.

In 2005, journalist Thomas Friedman wrote an influential book declaring the world was now "flat," by which he meant that the Internet and global communications had greatly reduced the economic and cultural advantages of developed countries. Friedman argued that the U.S. and European countries were in a fight for their economic lives, competing for jobs, markets, resources, and even ideas with highly educated, motivated populations in low-wage areas in the less developed world (Friedman, 2007). This "globalization" presents both challenges and opportunities for business firms

A growing percentage of the economy of the United States and other advanced industrial countries in Europe and Asia depends on imports and exports. In 2012, more than 33 percent of the U.S. economy resulted from foreign trade, both imports and exports. In Europe and Asia, the number exceeded 50 percent. Many Fortune 500 U.S. firms derive half their revenues from foreign operations. For instance, 85 percent of Intel's revenues in 2011 came from overseas sales of its microprocessors. Eighty percent of the toys sold in the United States are manufactured in China, while about 90 percent of the PCs manufactured in China use American-made Intel or Advanced Micro Design (AMD) chips.

It's not just goods that move across borders. So too do jobs, some of them high-level jobs that pay well and require a college degree. In the past decade, the United States lost several million manufacturing jobs to offshore, low-wage

INTERACTIVE SESSION: MANAGEMENT

RUNNING THE BUSINESS FROM THE PALM OF YOUR HAND

Can you run your company from the palm of your hand? Perhaps not entirely, but there are many functions today that can be performed using an iPhone, iPad, BlackBerry, or other mobile handheld device.

The BlackBerry used to be the favorite mobile handheld for business because it was optimized for e-mail and messaging, with strong security and tools for accessing internal corporate systems. Now that's changing. Companies large and small are starting to deploy Apple's iPhone and iPad as well as Android mobile devices to conduct more of their work. They are enhancing their security systems so that mobile users can remotely accessing proprietary corporate resources with confidence.

For some, these handhelds have become indispensible. Eric Jackson is a champion kayaker who spends half of each year following competitions and events throughout North America. He's also president of Jackson Kayak, the leading whitewater kayak manufacturer. It's essential that he participate in athletic events, monitor industry trends in the field, and meet directly with dealers and customers. Jackson's strong customer focus has helped the company expand successfully worldwide, with distributors on six continents. With the iPhone and iPad, Jackson claims he can run the entire 120-person company from afar.

Jackson's Wi-Fi-equipped RV connects wirelessly to the company headquarters in Sparta, Tennessee. When Jackson's not on Wi-Fi, he uses his iPad 3G cellular connection. The iPad gives him instant access to his entire operation, so he can analyze customer data, refresh Web site content, or approve new designs. Jackson's iPad includes calendars, e-mail, contact management, and the ability to create and edit documents, spreadsheets, and presentations—all the tools this executive needs to communicate with the home office, dealers, and customers.

Back at the shop, Jackson Kayak's managers and employees find iPad and iPhone equally invaluable. In the factory, Chief Operations Officer John Ratliff can compare Jackson Kayak's manufacturing equipment side-by-side with images of replacement parts on the iPad to make sure he's getting the correct pieces. The iPhone and iPad have become so indispensable that the company outfitted its entire workforce, from customer service, to design, to quality control, with iPhones. Many have iPads as well.

Using handhelds to run the business is not limited to small companies. General Electric (GE) is one of the world's largest companies, producing aircraft engines, locomotives and other transportation equipment, kitchen and laundry appliances, lighting, electric distribution and control equipment, generators and turbines, and medical imaging equipment. GE is also a leading provider of financial services, aviation, clean energy, media, and health care technology. This giant multinational was an early adopter of mobile technology. GE employees use their iPads to access e-mail, contacts, documents, and electronic presentations. GE's Mobile Center of Excellence has developed dozens of iPhone and iPad applications, including industry-specific diagnostic and monitoring tools and business intelligence tools that help decision makers find patterns and trends in large volumes of data. The company's Transformer Monitoring app helps manage gas turbine inventory and electronic transformers throughout the world, with the ability to zoom in from a global map to a specific transformer and read all of the key performance indicators. A PDS Movement Planner lets service personnel monitor railway tracks and obtain diagnostic information on locomotives.

With operations in 60 countries, Dow Corning offers more than 7,000 products and services for consumer and industrial applications, from adhesives to lubricants, delivered as fluids, solids, gels, and powders. The Roambi Visualizer app lets Dow Corning executives use their iPhones to quickly view and analyze real-time data from their core corporate system, including sales figures, trends, and projections. It presents managers with simple, intuitive dashboards of complex data. According to Executive Vice President and Chief Financial Officer Don Sheets, in 15 seconds he can get a sense of whether there's a financial performance issue he needs to get involved with.

Dow Corning's Analytics App for the iPhone monitors Web site traffic and online sales for the company's XIAMETER brand of standard silicone products. Analytics App interfaces with Google Analytics. When Dow Corning rolls out XIAMETER Web sites across the globe, executives can monitor what content is and isn't being used whether they are home, traveling, or at the office.

Sunbelt Rentals, based in Fort Mill, South Carolina, is one of the largest equipment rental companies in the United States, with a $2 billion inventory of rental equipment. More than 1,200 company employees, including sales staff, field personnel, and executives, are equipped with iPhones to interact with contacts and stay abreast of calendar events. In addition to using iPhones for e-mail, scheduling, and contact management, Sunbelt deployed a custom application called Mobile SalesPro, which ties multiple systems and databases into a single package for the sales team.

This application connects the corporate point-of-sale system, inventory control and management system, and enterprise system, which integrates data from many different business functions. Users are able to share sales quotes based on the most up-to-date information on rental rates and equipment availability. With this application, Sunbelt's sales team can respond immediately to customer requests while they are at a job site.

Sources: "Apple IPhone in Business" and "Apple iPad in Business," www.apple.com, accessed September 6, 2012; Erik Eckel, "What the IPhone5 Will Offer Business Users," *TechRepublic*, September 5, 2012; and Doug Henschen, "Mobilizing Enterprise Apps: The Next Big Leap," *Information Week*, February 12, 2011.

CASE STUDY QUESTIONS

1. What kinds of applications are described here? What business functions do they support? How do they improve operational efficiency and decision making?

2. Identify the problems that businesses in this case study solved by using mobile digital devices.

3. What kinds of businesses are most likely to benefit from equipping their employees with mobile digital devices such as iPhones and iPads?

4. One company deploying iPhones has said: The iPhone is not a game changer, it's an industry changer. It changes the way that you can interact with your customers and with your suppliers. Discuss the implications of this statement.

iPhone and iPad
Business Applications:

1. Salesforce Mobile

2. Cisco WebEx

3. iSchedule

4. iWork

5. Documents To Go

6. PDF Reader Pro

7. BizXpenseTracker

8. Dropbox

© STANCA SANDA / Alamy

Whether it's attending an online meeting, checking orders, working with files and documents, or obtaining business intelligence, Apple's iPhone and iPad offer unlimited possibilities for business users. Both devices have a stunning multitouch display, full Internet browsing, digital camera, and capabilities for messaging, voice transmission, and document management. These features make each an all-purpose platform for mobile computing.

producers. But manufacturing is now a very small part of U.S. employment (less than 12 percent and declining). In a normal year, about 300,000 service jobs move offshore to lower wage countries. Many of the jobs are in less-skilled information system occupations, but some are "tradable service" jobs in architecture, financial services, customer call centers, consulting, engineering, and even radiology.

On the plus side, the U.S. economy creates over 3.5 million new jobs in a normal, non-recessionary year. However, only 1.1 million private sector jobs were created due to slow recovery in 2011. Employment in information systems and the other service occupations is expanding, and wages are stable. Outsourcing has actually accelerated the development of new systems in the United States and worldwide.

The challenge for you as a business student is to develop high-level skills through education and on-the-job experience that cannot be outsourced. The challenge for your business is to avoid markets for goods and services that can be produced offshore much less expensively. The opportunities are equally immense. Throughout this book, you will find examples of companies and individuals who either failed or succeeded in using information systems to adapt to this new global environment.

What does globalization have to do with management information systems? That's simple: everything. The emergence of the Internet into a full-blown international communications system has drastically reduced the costs of operating and transacting on a global scale. Communication between a factory floor in Shanghai and a distribution center in Rapid Falls, South Dakota, is now instant and virtually free. Customers can now shop in a worldwide marketplace, obtaining price and quality information reliably 24 hours a day. Firms producing goods and services on a global scale achieve extraordinary cost reductions by finding low-cost suppliers and managing production facilities in other countries. Internet service firms, such as Google and eBay, are able to replicate their business models and services in multiple countries without having to redesign their expensive fixed-cost information systems infrastructure. Half of the revenue of eBay (as well as General Motors) in 2011 will originate outside the United States. Briefly, information systems enable globalization.

THE EMERGING DIGITAL FIRM

All of the changes we have just described, coupled with equally significant organizational redesign, have created the conditions for a fully digital firm. A digital firm can be defined along several dimensions. A **digital firm** is one in which nearly all of the organization's *significant business relationships* with customers, suppliers, and employees are digitally enabled and mediated. *Core business processes* are accomplished through digital networks spanning the entire organization or linking multiple organizations.

Business processes refer to the set of logically related tasks and behaviors that organizations develop over time to produce specific business results and the unique manner in which these activities are organized and coordinated. Developing a new product, generating and fulfilling an order, creating a marketing plan, and hiring an employee are examples of business processes, and the ways organizations accomplish their business processes can be a source of competitive strength. (A detailed discussion of business processes can be found in Chapter 2.)

Key corporate assets—intellectual property, core competencies, and financial and human assets—are managed through digital means. In a digital firm, any piece of information required to support key business decisions is available at any time and anywhere in the firm.

Digital firms sense and respond to their environments far more rapidly than traditional firms, giving them more flexibility to survive in turbulent times. Digital firms offer extraordinary opportunities for more flexible global organization and management. In digital firms, both time shifting and space shifting are the norm. *Time shifting* refers to business being conducted continuously, 24/7, rather than in narrow "work day" time bands of 9 a.m. to 5 p.m. *Space shifting* means that work takes place in a global workshop, as well as within national boundaries. Work is accomplished physically wherever in the world it is best accomplished.

Many firms, such as Cisco Systems, 3M, and IBM, are close to becoming digital firms, using the Internet to drive every aspect of their business. Most other companies are not fully digital, but they are moving toward close digital integration with suppliers, customers, and employees. Many firms, for example, are replacing traditional face-to-face meetings with "virtual" meetings using videoconferencing and Web conferencing technology. (See Chapter 2.)

STRATEGIC BUSINESS OBJECTIVES OF INFORMATION SYSTEMS

What makes information systems so essential today? Why are businesses investing so much in information systems and technologies? In the United States, more than 21 million managers and 154 million workers in the labor force rely on information systems to conduct business. Information systems are essential for conducting day-to-day business in the United States and most other advanced countries, as well as achieving strategic business objectives.

Entire sectors of the economy are nearly inconceivable without substantial investments in information systems. E-commerce firms such as Amazon, eBay, Google, and E*Trade simply would not exist. Today's service industries—finance, insurance, and real estate, as well as personal services such as travel, medicine, and education—could not operate without information systems. Similarly, retail firms such as Walmart and Sears and manufacturing firms such as General Motors and General Electric require information systems to survive and prosper. Just as offices, telephones, filing cabinets, and efficient tall buildings with elevators were once the foundations of business in the twentieth century, information technology is a foundation for business in the twenty-first century.

There is a growing interdependence between a firm's ability to use information technology and its ability to implement corporate strategies and achieve corporate goals (see Figure 1.2). What a business would like to do in five years often depends on what its systems will be able to do. Increasing market share, becoming the high-quality or low-cost producer, developing new products, and increasing employee productivity depend more and more on the kinds and quality of information systems in the organization. The more you understand about this relationship, the more valuable you will be as a manager.

Specifically, business firms invest heavily in information systems to achieve six strategic business objectives: operational excellence; new products, services, and business models; customer and supplier intimacy; improved decision making; competitive advantage; and survival.

FIGURE 1.2   THE INTERDEPENDENCE BETWEEN ORGANIZATIONS AND INFORMATION SYSTEMS

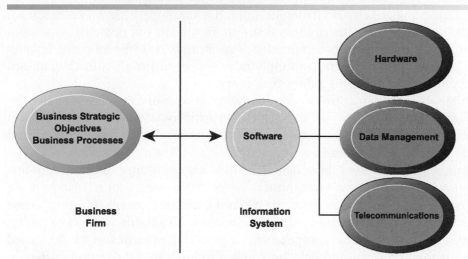

In contemporary systems, there is a growing interdependence between a firm's information systems and its business capabilities. Changes in strategy, rules, and business processes increasingly require changes in hardware, software, databases, and telecommunications. Often, what the organization would like to do depends on what its systems will permit it to do.

Operational Excellence

Businesses continuously seek to improve the efficiency of their operations in order to achieve higher profitability. Information systems and technologies are some of the most important tools available to managers for achieving higher levels of efficiency and productivity in business operations, especially when coupled with changes in business practices and management behavior.

Walmart, the largest retailer on earth, exemplifies the power of information systems coupled with brilliant business practices and supportive management to achieve world-class operational efficiency. In fiscal year 2012, Walmart achieved $460 billion in sales—nearly one-tenth of retail sales in the United States—in large part because of its Retail Link system, which digitally links its suppliers to every one of Walmart's stores. As soon as a customer purchases an item, the supplier monitoring the item knows to ship a replacement to the shelf. Walmart is the most efficient retail store in the industry, achieving sales of more than $28 per square foot, compared to its closest competitor, Target, at $23 a square foot. Other retail firms producing less than $12 a square foot.

New Products, Services, and Business Models

Information systems and technologies are a major enabling tool for firms to create new products and services, as well as entirely new business models. A **business model** describes how a company produces, delivers, and sells a product or service to create wealth.

Today's music industry is vastly different from the industry a decade ago. Apple Inc. transformed an old business model of music distribution based on vinyl records, tapes, and CDs into an online, legal distribution model based on its own iPod technology platform. Apple has prospered from a continuing stream of iPod innovations, including the iTunes music service, the iPad, and the iPhone.

Customer and Supplier Intimacy

When a business really knows its customers, and serves them well, the customers generally respond by returning and purchasing more. This raises revenues and profits. Likewise with suppliers: the more a business engages its suppliers, the better the suppliers can provide vital inputs. This lowers costs. How to really know your customers, or suppliers, is a central problem for businesses with millions of offline and online customers.

The Mandarin Oriental in Manhattan and other high-end hotels exemplify the use of information systems and technologies to achieve customer intimacy. These hotels use computers to keep track of guests' preferences, such as their preferred room temperature, check-in time, frequently dialed telephone numbers, and television programs, and store these data in a large data repository. Individual rooms in the hotels are networked to a central network server computer so that they can be remotely monitored or controlled. When a customer arrives at one of these hotels, the system automatically changes the room conditions, such as dimming the lights, setting the room temperature, or selecting appropriate music, based on the customer's digital profile. The hotels also analyze their customer data to identify their best customers and to develop individualized marketing campaigns based on customers' preferences.

JCPenney exemplifies the benefits of information systems-enabled supplier intimacy. Every time a dress shirt is bought at a JCPenney store in the United States, the record of the sale appears immediately on computers in Hong Kong at the TAL Apparel Ltd. supplier, a contract manufacturer that produces one in eight dress shirts sold in the United States. TAL runs the numbers through a computer model it developed and then decides how many replacement shirts to make, and in what styles, colors, and sizes. TAL then sends the shirts to each JCPenney store, bypassing completely the retailer's warehouses. In other words, JCPenney's shirt inventory is near zero, as is the cost of storing it.

Improved Decision Making

Many business managers operate in an information fog bank, never really having the right information at the right time to make an informed decision. Instead, managers rely on forecasts, best guesses, and luck. The result is over- or underproduction of goods and services, misallocation of resources, and poor response times. These poor outcomes raise costs and lose customers. In the past decade, information systems and technologies have made it possible for managers to use real-time data from the marketplace when making decisions.

For instance, Verizon Corporation, one of the largest telecommunication companies in the United States, uses a Web-based digital dashboard to provide managers with precise real-time information on customer complaints, network performance for each locality served, and line outages or storm-damaged lines. Using this information, managers can immediately allocate repair resources to affected areas, inform consumers of repair efforts, and restore service fast.

Competitive Advantage

When firms achieve one or more of these business objectives—operational excellence; new products, services, and business models; customer/supplier intimacy; and improved decision making—chances are they have already achieved a competitive advantage. Doing things better than your competitors, charging less for superior products, and responding to customers and suppliers in real time all add up to higher sales and higher profits that your competitors cannot match. Apple Inc., Walmart, and UPS, described later in this chapter, are industry leaders because they know how to use information systems for this purpose.

Survival

Business firms also invest in information systems and technologies because they are necessities of doing business. Sometimes these "necessities" are driven by industry-level changes. For instance, after Citibank introduced the first automated teller machines (ATMs) in the New York region in 1977 to attract customers through higher service levels, its competitors rushed to provide ATMs to their customers to keep up with Citibank. Today, virtually all banks in the United States have regional ATMs and link to national and international ATM networks, such as CIRRUS. Providing ATM services to retail banking customers is simply a requirement of being in and surviving in the retail banking business.

There are many federal and state statutes and regulations that create a legal duty for companies and their employees to retain records, including digital records. For instance, the Toxic Substances Control Act (1976), which regulates the exposure of U.S. workers to more than 75,000 toxic chemicals, requires firms to retain records on employee exposure for 30 years. The Sarbanes-Oxley Act (2002), which was intended to improve the accountability of public firms and their auditors, requires certified public accounting firms that audit public companies to retain audit working papers and records, including all e-mails, for five years. Many other pieces of federal and state legislation in health care, financial services, education, and privacy protection impose significant information retention and reporting requirements on U.S. businesses. Firms turn to information systems and technologies to provide the capability to respond to these challenges.

1.2 PERSPECTIVES ON INFORMATION SYSTEMS

So far we've used *information systems* and *technologies* informally without defining the terms. **Information technology (IT)** consists of all the hardware and software that a firm needs to use in order to achieve its business objectives. This includes not only computer machines, storage devices, and handheld mobile devices, but also software, such as the Windows or Linux operating systems, the Microsoft Office desktop productivity suite, and the many thousands of computer programs that can be found in a typical large firm. "Information systems" are more complex and can be best be understood by looking at them from both a technology and a business perspective.

WHAT IS AN INFORMATION SYSTEM?

An **information system** can be defined technically as a set of interrelated components that collect (or retrieve), process, store, and distribute information to support decision making and control in an organization. In addition to supporting decision making, coordination, and control, information systems may also help managers and workers analyze problems, visualize complex subjects, and create new products.

Information systems contain information about significant people, places, and things within the organization or in the environment surrounding it. By **information** we mean data that have been shaped into a form that is meaningful and useful to human beings. **Data**, in contrast, are streams of raw facts representing events occurring in organizations or the physical environment before they have been organized and arranged into a form that people can understand and use.

A brief example contrasting information and data may prove useful. Supermarket checkout counters scan millions of pieces of data from bar codes, which describe each product. Such pieces of data can be totaled and analyzed to provide meaningful information, such as the total number of bottles of dish detergent sold at a particular store, which brands of dish detergent were selling the most rapidly at that store or sales territory, or the total amount spent on that brand of dish detergent at that store or sales region (see Figure 1.3).

Three activities in an information system produce the information that organizations need to make decisions, control operations, analyze problems, and create new products or services. These activities are input, processing, and output (see Figure 1.4). **Input** captures or collects raw data from within the organization or from its external environment. **Processing** converts this raw input into a meaningful form. **Output** transfers the processed information to the people who will use it or to the activities for which it will be used. Information systems also require **feedback**, which is output that is returned to appropriate members of the organization to help them evaluate or correct the input stage.

For example, in Disney World's systems for controlling crowds, the raw input consists of data from airline bookings and hotel reservations, satellite weather data, historic attendance data for the date being analyzed, and images of crowds from video cameras stationed at key locations throughout the park. Computers store these data and process them to calculate projected total attendance for a specific date as well as attendance figures and wait times for each ride and restaurant at various times during the day. The systems indicate which rides or attractions are too overcrowded, which have spare capacity, and which can add capacity. The system provides meaningful information such as the number of

FIGURE 1.3   DATA AND INFORMATION

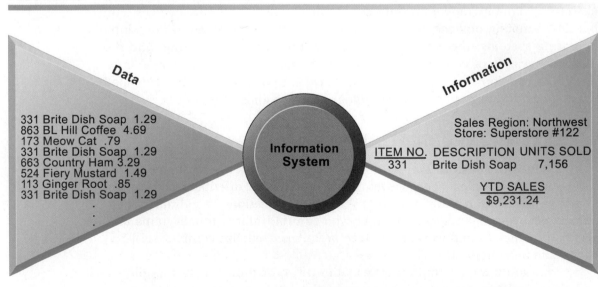

Raw data from a supermarket checkout counter can be processed and organized to produce meaningful information, such as the total unit sales of dish detergent or the total sales revenue from dish detergent for a specific store or sales territory.

FIGURE 1.4   FUNCTIONS OF AN INFORMATION SYSTEM

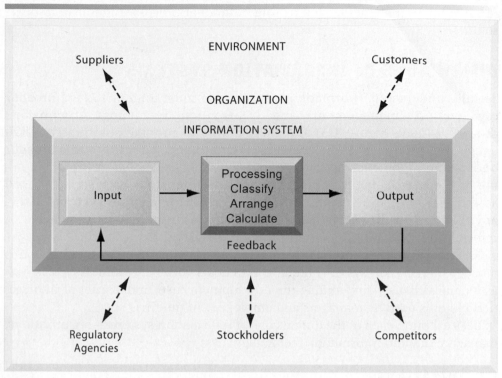

An information system contains information about an organization and its surrounding environment. Three basic activities—input, processing, and output—produce the information organizations need. Feedback is output returned to appropriate people or activities in the organization to evaluate and refine the input. Environmental actors, such as customers, suppliers, competitors, stockholders, and regulatory agencies, interact with the organization and its information systems.

guests attending on a particular day or time period, the average wait time per ride, the average number of restaurant and shop visits, the average number of rides guests squeezed into a single day's visit, and the average amount spent per customer during a specific time period. Such information helps Disney management gauge the theme park's overall efficiency and profitability.

Although computer-based information systems use computer technology to process raw data into meaningful information, there is a sharp distinction between a computer and a computer program on the one hand, and an information system on the other. Electronic computers and related software programs are the technical foundation, the tools and materials, of modern information systems. Computers provide the equipment for storing and processing information. Computer programs, or software, are sets of operating instructions that direct and control computer processing. Knowing how computers and computer programs work is important in designing solutions to organizational problems, but computers are only part of an information system.

A house is an appropriate analogy. Houses are built with hammers, nails, and wood, but these do not make a house. The architecture, design, setting, landscaping, and all of the decisions that lead to the creation of these features are part of the house and are crucial for solving the problem of putting a roof over one's head. Computers and programs are the hammers, nails, and lumber of computer-based information systems, but alone they cannot produce the information a particular organization needs. To understand information systems, you must understand the problems they are designed to solve, their architectural and design elements, and the organizational processes that lead to these solutions.

DIMENSIONS OF INFORMATION SYSTEMS

To fully understand information systems, you must understand the broader organization, management, and information technology dimensions of systems (see Figure 1.5) and their power to provide solutions to challenges and problems in the business environment. We refer to this broader understanding of information systems, which encompasses an understanding of the management and organizational dimensions of systems as well as the technical dimensions of systems, as **information systems literacy**. **Computer literacy**, in contrast, focuses primarily on knowledge of information technology.

The field of **management information systems (MIS)** tries to achieve this broader information systems literacy. MIS deals with behavioral issues as well as technical issues surrounding the development, use, and impact of information systems used by managers and employees in the firm.

Let's examine each of the dimensions of information systems—organizations, management, and information technology.

Organizations

Information systems are an integral part of organizations. Indeed, for some companies, such as credit reporting firms, there would be no business without an information system. The key elements of an organization are its people, structure, business processes, politics, and culture. We introduce these components of organizations here and describe them in greater detail in Chapters 2 and 3.

FIGURE 1.5   INFORMATION SYSTEMS ARE MORE THAN COMPUTERS

Using information systems effectively requires an understanding of the organization, management, and information technology shaping the systems. An information system creates value for the firm as an organizational and management solution to challenges posed by the environment.

Organizations have a structure that is composed of different levels and specialties. Their structures reveal a clear-cut division of labor. Authority and responsibility in a business firm are organized as a hierarchy, or a pyramid structure. The upper levels of the hierarchy consist of managerial, professional, and technical employees, whereas the lower levels consist of operational personnel.

Senior management makes long-range strategic decisions about products and services as well as ensures financial performance of the firm. **Middle management** carries out the programs and plans of senior management, and **operational management** is responsible for monitoring the daily activities of the business. **Knowledge workers**, such as engineers, scientists, or architects, design products or services and create new knowledge for the firm, whereas **data workers**, such as secretaries or clerks, assist with scheduling and communications at all levels of the firm. **Production or service workers** actually produce the product and deliver the service (see Figure 1.6).

Experts are employed and trained for different business functions. The major **business functions**, or specialized tasks performed by business organizations, consist of sales and marketing, manufacturing and production, finance and accounting, and human resources (see Table 1.2). Chapter 2 provides more detail on these business functions and the ways in which they are supported by information systems.

An organization coordinates work through its hierarchy and through its business processes, which are logically related tasks and behaviors for accomplishing work. Developing a new product, fulfilling an order, and hiring a new employee are examples of business processes.

Most organizations' business processes include formal rules that have been developed over a long time for accomplishing tasks. These rules guide employees in a variety of procedures, from writing an invoice to responding to customer complaints. Some of these business processes have been written down, but others

FIGURE 1.6   LEVELS IN A FIRM

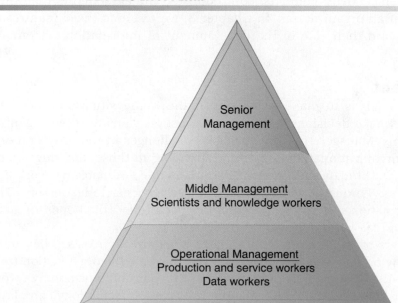

Business organizations are hierarchies consisting of three principal levels: senior management, middle management, and operational management. Information systems serve each of these levels. Scientists and knowledge workers often work with middle management.

TABLE 1.2 MAJOR BUSINESS FUNCTIONS

FUNCTION	PURPOSE
Sales and marketing	Selling the organization's products and services
Manufacturing and production	Producing and delivering products and services
Finance and accounting	Managing the organization's financial assets and maintaining the organization's financial records
Human resources	Attracting, developing, and maintaining the organization's labor force; maintaining employee records

are informal work practices, such as a requirement to return telephone calls from coworkers or customers, that are not formally documented. Information systems automate many business processes. For instance, how a customer receives credit or how a customer is billed is often determined by an information system that incorporates a set of formal business processes.

Each organization has a unique **culture**, or fundamental set of assumptions, values, and ways of doing things, that has been accepted by most of its members. You can see organizational culture at work by looking around your university or college. Some bedrock assumptions of university life are that professors know more than students, the reasons students attend college is to learn, and that classes follow a regular schedule.

Parts of an organization's culture can always be found embedded in its information systems. For instance, UPS's first priority is customer service, which is an aspect of its organizational culture that can be found in the company's package tracking systems, which we describe later in this section.

Different levels and specialties in an organization create different interests and points of view. These views often conflict over how the company should be run and how resources and rewards should be distributed. Conflict is the basis for organizational politics. Information systems come out of this cauldron of differing perspectives, conflicts, compromises, and agreements that are a natural part of all organizations. In Chapter 3, we examine these features of organizations and their role in the development of information systems in greater detail.

Management

Management's job is to make sense out of the many situations faced by organizations, make decisions, and formulate action plans to solve organizational problems. Managers perceive business challenges in the environment; they set the organizational strategy for responding to those challenges; and they allocate the human and financial resources to coordinate the work and achieve success. Throughout, they must exercise responsible leadership. The business information systems described in this book reflect the hopes, dreams, and realities of real-world managers.

But managers must do more than manage what already exists. They must also create new products and services and even re-create the organization from time to time. A substantial part of management responsibility is creative work driven by new knowledge and information. Information technology can play a powerful role in helping managers design and deliver new products and services and redirecting and redesigning their organizations. Chapter 12 treats management decision making in detail.

Information Technology

Information technology is one of many tools managers use to cope with change. **Computer hardware** is the physical equipment used for input, processing, and output activities in an information system. It consists of the following: computers of various sizes and shapes (including mobile handheld devices); various input, output, and storage devices; and telecommunications devices that link computers together.

Computer software consists of the detailed, preprogrammed instructions that control and coordinate the computer hardware components in an information system. Chapter 5 describes the contemporary software and hardware platforms used by firms today in greater detail.

Data management technology consists of the software governing the organization of data on physical storage media. More detail on data organization and access methods can be found in Chapter 6.

Networking and telecommunications technology, consisting of both physical devices and software, links the various pieces of hardware and transfers data from one physical location to another. Computers and communications equipment can be connected in networks for sharing voice, data, images, sound, and video. A **network** links two or more computers to share data or resources, such as a printer.

The world's largest and most widely used network is the **Internet**. The Internet is a global "network of networks" that uses universal standards (described in Chapter 7) to connect millions of different networks with nearly 2.3 billion users in over 230 countries around the world.

The Internet has created a new "universal" technology platform on which to build new products, services, strategies, and business models. This same technology platform has internal uses, providing the connectivity to link different systems and networks within the firm. Internal corporate networks based on Internet technology are called **intranets**. Private intranets extended to authorized users outside the organization are called **extranets**, and firms use such networks to coordinate their activities with other firms for making purchases, collaborating on design, and other interorganizational work. For most business firms today, using Internet technology is both a business necessity and a competitive advantage.

The **World Wide Web** is a service provided by the Internet that uses universally accepted standards for storing, retrieving, formatting, and displaying information in a page format on the Internet. Web pages contain text, graphics, animations, sound, and video and are linked to other Web pages. By clicking on highlighted words or buttons on a Web page, you can link to related pages to find additional information and links to other locations on the Web. The Web can serve as the foundation for new kinds of information systems such as UPS's Web-based package tracking system described in the following Interactive Session.

All of these technologies, along with the people required to run and manage them, represent resources that can be shared throughout the organization and constitute the firm's **information technology (IT) infrastructure**. The IT infrastructure provides the foundation, or *platform*, on which the firm can build its specific information systems. Each organization must carefully design and manage its IT infrastructure so that it has the set of technology services it needs for the work it wants to accomplish with information systems. Chapters 5 through 8 of this book examine each major technology component of information technology infrastructure and show how they all work together to create the technology platform for the organization.

The Interactive Session on Technology describes some of the typical technologies used in computer-based information systems today. UPS invests heavily in information systems technology to make its business more efficient and customer oriented. It uses an array of information technologies, including bar code scanning systems, wireless networks, large mainframe computers, handheld computers, the Internet, and many different pieces of software for tracking packages, calculating fees, maintaining customer accounts, and managing logistics.

Let's identify the organization, management, and technology elements in the UPS package tracking system we have just described. The organization element anchors the package tracking system in UPS's sales and production functions (the main product of UPS is a service—package delivery). It specifies the required procedures for identifying packages with both sender and recipient information, taking inventory, tracking the packages en route, and providing package status reports for UPS customers and customer service representatives.

The system must also provide information to satisfy the needs of managers and workers. UPS drivers need to be trained in both package pickup and delivery procedures and in how to use the package tracking system so that they can work efficiently and effectively. UPS customers may need some training to use UPS in-house package tracking software or the UPS Web site.

UPS's management is responsible for monitoring service levels and costs and for promoting the company's strategy of combining low cost and superior service. Management decided to use computer systems to increase the ease of sending a package using UPS and of checking its delivery status, thereby reducing delivery costs and increasing sales revenues.

The technology supporting this system consists of handheld computers, bar code scanners, desktop computers, wired and wireless communications networks, UPS's data center, storage technology for the package delivery data, UPS in-house package tracking software, and software to access the World Wide Web. The result is an information system solution to the business challenge of providing a high level of service with low prices in the face of mounting competition.

IT ISN'T JUST TECHNOLOGY: A BUSINESS PERSPECTIVE ON INFORMATION SYSTEMS

Managers and business firms invest in information technology and systems because they provide real economic value to the business. The decision to build or maintain an information system assumes that the returns on this investment will be superior to other investments in buildings, machines, or other assets. These superior returns will be expressed as increases in productivity, as increases in revenues (which will increase the firm's stock market value), or perhaps as superior long-term strategic positioning of the firm in certain markets (which produce superior revenues in the future).

We can see that from a business perspective, an information system is an important instrument for creating value for the firm. Information systems enable the firm to increase its revenue or decrease its costs by providing information that helps managers make better decisions or that improves the execution of business processes. For example, the information system for analyzing supermarket checkout data illustrated in Figure 1.3 on page 46 can increase firm profitability by helping managers make better decisions as to which products to stock and promote in retail supermarkets.

INTERACTIVE SESSION: TECHNOLOGY

UPS COMPETES GLOBALLY WITH INFORMATION TECHNOLOGY

United Parcel Service (UPS) started out in 1907 in a closet-sized basement office. Jim Casey and Claude Ryan—two teenagers from Seattle with two bicycles and one phone—promised the "best service and lowest rates." UPS has used this formula successfully for more than a century to become the world's largest ground and air package-delivery company. It's a global enterprise with over 400,000 employees, 93,000 vehicles, and the world's ninth largest airline.

UPS delivers 15.6 million packages and documents each day in the United States and more than 220 other countries and territories. The firm has been able to maintain leadership in small-package delivery services despite stiff competition from FedEx and Airborne Express by investing heavily in advanced information technology. UPS spends more than $1 billion each year to maintain a high level of customer service while keeping costs low and streamlining its overall operations.

It all starts with the scannable bar-coded label attached to a package, which contains detailed information about the sender, the destination, and when the package should arrive. Customers can download and print their own labels using special software provided by UPS or by accessing the UPS Web site. Before the package is even picked up, information from the "smart" label is transmitted to one of UPS's computer centers in Mahwah, New Jersey, or Alpharetta, Georgia, and sent to the distribution center nearest its final destination.

Dispatchers at this center download the label data and use special software to create the most efficient delivery route for each driver that considers traffic, weather conditions, and the location of each stop. UPS estimates its delivery trucks save 28 million miles and burn 3 million fewer gallons of fuel each year as a result of using this technology. To further increase cost savings and safety, drivers are trained to use "340 Methods" developed by industrial engineers to optimize the performance of every task from lifting and loading boxes to selecting a package from a shelf in the truck.

The first thing a UPS driver picks up each day is a handheld computer called a Delivery Information Acquisition Device (DIAD), which can access a wireless cell phone network. As soon as the driver logs on, his or her day's route is downloaded onto the handheld. The DIAD also automatically captures customers' signatures along with pickup and delivery information. Package tracking information is then transmitted to UPS's computer network for storage and processing. From there, the information can be accessed worldwide to provide proof of delivery to customers or to respond to customer queries. It usually takes less than 60 seconds from the time a driver presses "complete" on the DIAD for the new information to be available on the Web.

Through its automated package tracking system, UPS can monitor and even re-route packages throughout the delivery process. At various points along the route from sender to receiver, bar code devices scan shipping information on the package label and feed data about the progress of the package into the central computer. Customer service representatives are able to check the status of any package from desktop computers linked to the central computers and respond immediately to inquiries from customers. UPS customers can also access this information from the company's Web site using their own computers or mobile phones. UPS now has mobile apps and a mobile Web site for iPhone, BlackBerry, and Android smartphone users.

Anyone with a package to ship can access the UPS Web site to track packages, check delivery routes, calculate shipping rates, determine time in transit, print labels, and schedule a pickup. The data collected at the UPS Web site are transmitted to the UPS central computer and then back to the customer after processing. UPS also provides tools that enable customers, such Cisco Systems, to embed UPS functions, such as tracking and cost calculations, into their own Web sites so that they can track shipments without visiting the UPS site.

A Web-based Post Sales Order Management System (OMS) manages global service orders and inventory for critical parts fulfillment. The system enables high-tech electronics, aerospace, medical equipment, and other companies anywhere in the world that ship critical parts to quickly assess their critical parts inventory, determine the most optimal routing strategy to meet customer needs, place orders online, and track parts from the warehouse to the end user. An automated e-mail or fax feature keeps customers informed of each shipping milestone and can provide notification of any changes to flight schedules for commercial airlines carrying their parts.

UPS is now leveraging its decades of expertise managing its own global delivery network to manage logistics and supply chain activities for other companies. It created a UPS Supply Chain Solutions division that provides a complete bundle of standardized services to subscribing companies at a fraction of what it would cost to build their own systems and infrastructure. These services include supply chain design and management, freight forwarding, customs brokerage, mail services, multimodal transportation, and financial services, in addition to logistics services.

In 2006, UPS started running the supply chains of medical device and pharmaceutical companies. For example, at UPS headquarters in Louisville, Kentucky, company pharmacists fill 4,000 orders a day for insulin pumps and other supplies from customers of Medtronic Inc., the Minneapolis-based medical-device company. UPS pharmacists in Louisville log into Medtronic's system, fill the orders with devices stocked on site, and arrange for UPS to ship them to patients. UPS's service has allowed Medtronic to close its own distribution warehouse and significantly reduce the costs of processing each order. UPS and other parcel delivery companies are investing in giant warehouses that service multiple pharmaceutical companies at once, with freezers for medicines and high-security vaults for controlled substances.

UPS has partnered with Pratt & Whitney, a world leader in the design, manufacture, and service of aircraft engines, space propulsion systems, and industrial gas turbines, to run its Georgia Distribution Center, which processes 98 percent of the parts used to overhaul Pratt & Whitney jet engines for shipment around the world. UPS and Pratt & Whitney employees together keep track of about 25,000 different kinds of parts and fulfill up to 1,400 complex orders each day—ranging from a few nuts and bolts to kits comprising all the parts needed to build an entire engine. On the receiving side of the 250,000-square-foot building, UPS quality inspectors check newly arrived parts against blueprints.

Sources: Jennifer Levitz and Timothy W. Martin, "UPS, Other Big Shippers, Carve Health Care Niches," *The Wall Street Journal*, June 27, 2012; "Logistics in action: At Pratt & Whitney Facility, Silence Is Golden," *UPS Compass*, August 2012; Bob DuBois, "UPS Mobile Goes Global," *UPS Compass*, January 27, 2011; Jennifer Levitz, "UPS Thinks Out of the Box on Driver Training," *The Wall Street Journal*, April 6, 2010; Agam Shah, "UPS Invests $1 Billion in Technology to Cut Costs," *Bloomberg Businessweek*, March 25, 2010.

CASE STUDY QUESTIONS

1. What are the inputs, processing, and outputs of UPS's package tracking system?

2. What technologies are used by UPS? How are these technologies related to UPS's business strategy?

3. What strategic business objectives do UPS's information systems address?

4. What would happen if UPS's information systems were not available?

Using a handheld computer called a Delivery Information Acquisition Device (DIAD), UPS drivers automatically capture customers' signatures along with pickup, delivery, and time card information. UPS information systems use these data to track packages while they are being transported.

Every business has an information value chain, illustrated in Figure 1.7, in which raw information is systematically acquired and then transformed through various stages that add value to that information. The value of an information system to a business, as well as the decision to invest in any new information system, is, in large part, determined by the extent to which the system will lead to better management decisions, more efficient business processes, and higher firm profitability. Although there are other reasons why systems are built, their primary purpose is to contribute to corporate value.

From a business perspective, information systems are part of a series of value-adding activities for acquiring, transforming, and distributing information that managers can use to improve decision making, enhance organizational performance, and, ultimately, increase firm profitability.

The business perspective calls attention to the organizational and managerial nature of information systems. An information system represents an organizational and management solution, based on information technology, to a challenge or problem posed by the environment. Every chapter in this book begins with a short case study that illustrates this concept. A diagram at the beginning of each chapter illustrates the relationship between a business challenge and resulting management and organizational decisions to use IT as a solution to challenges generated by the business environment. You can use this diagram as a starting point for analyzing any information system or information system problem you encounter.

Review the diagram at the beginning of this chapter. The diagram shows how the Ponsse wood production firm systems solved the business problem presented by the need to integrate its production and manufacturing processes.

FIGURE 1.7 THE BUSINESS INFORMATION VALUE CHAIN

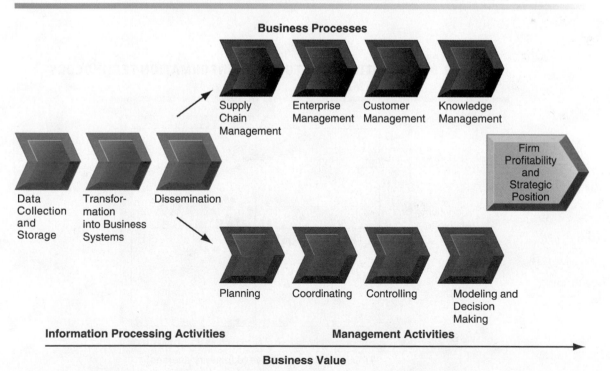

From a business perspective, information systems are part of a series of value-adding activities for acquiring, transforming, and distributing information that managers can use to improve decision making, enhance organizational performance, and, ultimately, increase firm profitability.

These systems provide a solution that takes advantage of new interactive digital technology and opportunities created by a host of technologies such as GPS. The firm developed new ways to coordinate production, manufacturing, and sales. The diagram also illustrates how management, technology, and organizational elements work together to create system solutions.

COMPLEMENTARY ASSETS: ORGANIZATIONAL CAPITAL AND THE RIGHT BUSINESS MODEL

Awareness of the organizational and managerial dimensions of information systems can help us understand why some firms achieve better results from their information systems than others. Studies of returns from information technology investments show that there is considerable variation in the returns firms receive (see Figure 1.8). Some firms invest a great deal and receive a great deal (quadrant 2); others invest an equal amount and receive few returns (quadrant 4). Still other firms invest little and receive much (quadrant 1), whereas others invest little and receive little (quadrant 3). This suggests that investing in information technology does not by itself guarantee good returns. What accounts for this variation among firms?

The answer lies in the concept of complementary assets. Information technology investments alone cannot make organizations and managers more effective unless they are accompanied by supportive values, structures, and behavior patterns in the organization and other complementary assets. Business firms need to change how they do business before they can really reap the advantages of new information technologies.

Some firms fail to adopt the right business model that suits the new technology, or seek to preserve an old business model that is doomed by new technology. For instance, recording label companies refused to change their

FIGURE 1.8 **VARIATION IN RETURNS ON INFORMATION TECHNOLOGY INVESTMENT**

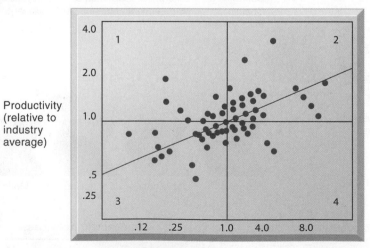

Although, on average, investments in information technology produce returns far above those returned by other investments, there is considerable variation across firms.

Source: Based on Brynjolfsson and Hitt (2000).

old business model, which was based on physical music stores for distribution rather than adopt a new online distribution model. As a result, online legal music sales are dominated not by record companies but by a technology company called Apple Computer.

Complementary assets are those assets required to derive value from a primary investment (Teece, 1988). For instance, to realize value from automobiles requires substantial complementary investments in highways, roads, gasoline stations, repair facilities, and a legal regulatory structure to set standards and control drivers.

Research indicates that firms that support their technology investments with investments in complementary assets, such as new business models, new business processes, management behavior, organizational culture, or training, receive superior returns, whereas those firms failing to make these complementary investments receive less or no returns on their information technology investments (Brynjolfsson, 2003; Brynjolfsson and Hitt, 2000; Davern and Kauffman, 2000; Laudon, 1974). These investments in organization and management are also known as **organizational and management capital**.

Table 1.3 lists the major complementary investments that firms need to make to realize value from their information technology investments. Some of this investment involves tangible assets, such as buildings, machinery, and tools. However, the value of investments in information technology depends to a large extent on complementary investments in management and organization.

Key organizational complementary investments are a supportive business culture that values efficiency and effectiveness, an appropriate business model, efficient business processes, decentralization of authority, highly distributed decision rights, and a strong information system (IS) development team.

TABLE 1.3 COMPLEMENTARY SOCIAL, MANAGERIAL, AND ORGANIZATIONAL ASSETS REQUIRED TO OPTIMIZE RETURNS FROM INFORMATION TECHNOLOGY INVESTMENTS

Organizational assets	Supportive organizational culture that values efficiency and effectiveness
	Appropriate business model
	Efficient business processes
	Decentralized authority
	Distributed decision-making rights
	Strong IS development team
Managerial assets	Strong senior management support for technology investment and change
	Incentives for management innovation
	Teamwork and collaborative work environments
	Training programs to enhance management decision skills
	Management culture that values flexibility and knowledge-based decision making.
Social assets	The Internet and telecommunications infrastructure
	IT-enriched educational programs raising labor force computer literacy
	Standards (both government and private sector)
	Laws and regulations creating fair, stable market environments
	Technology and service firms in adjacent markets to assist implementation

Important managerial complementary assets are strong senior management support for change, incentive systems that monitor and reward individual innovation, an emphasis on teamwork and collaboration, training programs, and a management culture that values flexibility and knowledge.

Important social investments (not made by the firm but by the society at large, other firms, governments, and other key market actors) are the Internet and the supporting Internet culture, educational systems, network and computing standards, regulations and laws, and the presence of technology and service firms.

Throughout the book we emphasize a framework of analysis that considers technology, management, and organizational assets and their interactions. Perhaps the single most important theme in the book, reflected in case studies and exercises, is that managers need to consider the broader organization and management dimensions of information systems to understand current problems as well as to derive substantial above-average returns from their information technology investments. As you will see throughout the text, firms that can address these related dimensions of the IT investment are, on average, richly rewarded.

1.3 CONTEMPORARY APPROACHES TO INFORMATION SYSTEMS

The study of information systems is a multidisciplinary field. No single theory or perspective dominates. Figure 1.9 illustrates the major disciplines that contribute problems, issues, and solutions in the study of information systems. In general, the field can be divided into technical and behavioral approaches. Information systems are sociotechnical systems. Though they are composed of machines, devices, and "hard" physical technology, they require substantial social, organizational, and intellectual investments to make them work properly.

TECHNICAL APPROACH

The technical approach to information systems emphasizes mathematically based models to study information systems, as well as the physical technology and formal capabilities of these systems. The disciplines that contribute to the technical approach are computer science, management science, and operations research.

Computer science is concerned with establishing theories of computability, methods of computation, and methods of efficient data storage and access. Management science emphasizes the development of models for decision-making and management practices. Operations research focuses on mathematical techniques for optimizing selected parameters of organizations, such as transportation, inventory control, and transaction costs.

BEHAVIORAL APPROACH

An important part of the information systems field is concerned with behavioral issues that arise in the development and long-term maintenance of information systems. Issues such as strategic business integration, design, implementation, utilization, and management cannot be explored usefully with the models used

FIGURE 1.9   CONTEMPORARY APPROACHES TO INFORMATION SYSTEMS

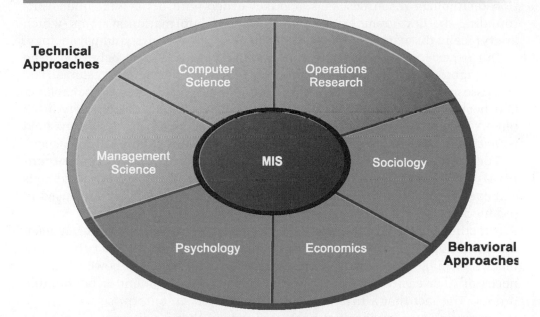

The study of information systems deals with issues and insights contributed from technical and behavioral disciplines.

in the technical approach. Other behavioral disciplines contribute important concepts and methods.

For instance, sociologists study information systems with an eye toward how groups and organizations shape the development of systems and also how systems affect individuals, groups, and organizations. Psychologists study information systems with an interest in how human decision makers perceive and use formal information. Economists study information systems with an interest in understanding the production of digital goods, the dynamics of digital markets, and how new information systems change the control and cost structures within the firm.

The behavioral approach does not ignore technology. Indeed, information systems technology is often the stimulus for a behavioral problem or issue. But the focus of this approach is generally not on technical solutions. Instead, it concentrates on changes in attitudes, management and organizational policy, and behavior.

APPROACH OF THIS TEXT: SOCIOTECHNICAL SYSTEMS

Throughout this book you will find a rich story with four main actors: suppliers of hardware and software (the technologists); business firms making investments and seeking to obtain value from the technology; managers and employees seeking to achieve business value (and other goals); and the contemporary legal, social, and cultural context (the firm's environment). Together these actors produce what we call *management information systems*.

The study of management information systems (MIS) arose to focus on the use of computer-based information systems in business firms and government agencies. MIS combines the work of computer science, management science, and operations research with a practical orientation toward developing system solutions to real-world problems and managing information technology resources. It is also concerned with behavioral issues surrounding the development, use, and impact of information systems, which are typically discussed in the fields of sociology, economics, and psychology.

Our experience as academics and practitioners leads us to believe that no single approach effectively captures the reality of information systems. The successes and failures of information are rarely all technical or all behavioral. Our best advice to students is to understand the perspectives of many disciplines. Indeed, the challenge and excitement of the information systems field is that it requires an appreciation and tolerance of many different approaches.

The view we adopt in this book is best characterized as the **sociotechnical view** of systems. In this view, optimal organizational performance is achieved by jointly optimizing both the social and technical systems used in production.

Adopting a sociotechnical systems perspective helps to avoid a purely technological approach to information systems. For instance, the fact that information technology is rapidly declining in cost and growing in power does not necessarily or easily translate into productivity enhancement or bottom-line profits. The fact that a firm has recently installed an enterprise-wide financial reporting system does not necessarily mean that it will be used, or used effectively. Likewise, the fact that a firm has recently introduced new business procedures and processes does not necessarily mean employees will be more productive in the absence of investments in new information systems to enable those processes.

In this book, we stress the need to optimize the firm's performance as a whole. Both the technical and behavioral components need attention. This means that technology must be changed and designed in such a way as to fit organizational and individual needs. Sometimes, the technology may have to be "de-optimized" to accomplish this fit. For instance, mobile phone users adapt this technology to their personal needs, and as a result manufacturers quickly seek to adjust the technology to conform with user expectations. Organizations and individuals must also be changed through training,

FIGURE 1.10 **A SOCIOTECHNICAL PERSPECTIVE ON INFORMATION SYSTEMS**

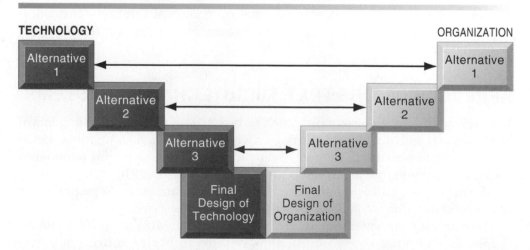

In a sociotechnical perspective, the performance of a system is optimized when both the technology and the organization mutually adjust to one another until a satisfactory fit is obtained.

learning, and planned organizational change to allow the technology to operate and prosper. Figure 1.10 illustrates this process of mutual adjustment in a sociotechnical system.

LEARNING TRACK MODULES

The following Learning Tracks provide content relevant to topics covered in this chapter:

1. How Much Does IT Matter?
2. Information Systems and Your Career
3. The Mobile Digital Platform

Review Summary

1. *How are information systems transforming business, and what is their relationship to globalization?*

E-mail, online conferencing, smartphones, and tablet computers have become essential tools for conducting business. Information systems are the foundation of fast-paced supply chains. The Internet allows many businesses to buy, sell, advertise, and solicit customer feedback online. Organizations are trying to become more competitive and efficient by digitally enabling their core business processes and evolving into digital firms. The Internet has stimulated globalization by dramatically reducing the costs of producing, buying, and selling goods on a global scale. New information system trends include the emerging mobile digital platform, online software as a service, and cloud computing.

2. *Why are information systems so essential for running and managing a business today?*

Information systems are a foundation for conducting business today. In many industries, survival and the ability to achieve strategic business goals are difficult without extensive use of information technology. Businesses today use information systems to achieve six major objectives: operational excellence; new products, services, and business models; customer/supplier intimacy; improved decision making; competitive advantage; and day-to-day survival.

3. *What exactly is an information system? How does it work? What are its management, organization, and technology components?*

From a technical perspective, an information system collects, stores, and disseminates information from an organization's environment and internal operations to support organizational functions and decision making, communication, coordination, control, analysis, and visualization. Information systems transform raw data into useful information through three basic activities: input, processing, and output.

From a business perspective, an information system provides a solution to a problem or challenge facing a firm and represents a combination of management, organization, and technology elements. The management dimension of information systems involves issues such as leadership, strategy, and management behavior. The technology dimension consists of computer hardware, software, data management technology, and networking/telecommunications technology (including the Internet). The organization dimension of information systems involves issues such as the organization's hierarchy, functional specialties, business processes, culture, and political interest groups.

4. *What are complementary assets? Why are complementary assets essential for ensuring that information systems provide genuine value for an organization?*

In order to obtain meaningful value from information systems, organizations must support their technology investments with appropriate complementary investments in organizations and management. These complementary assets include new business models and business processes, supportive organizational culture and management behavior, appropriate technology standards, regulations, and laws. New information technology investments are unlikely to produce high returns unless businesses make the appropriate managerial and organizational changes to support the technology.

5. *What academic disciplines are used to study information systems? How does each contribute to an understanding of information systems? What is a sociotechnical systems perspective?*

The study of information systems deals with issues and insights contributed from technical and behavioral disciplines. The disciplines that contribute to the technical approach focusing on formal models and capabilities of systems are computer science, management science, and operations research. The disciplines contributing to the behavioral approach focusing on the design, implementation, management, and business impact of systems are psychology, sociology, and economics. A sociotechnical view of systems considers both technical and social features of systems and solutions that represent the best fit between them.

Key Terms

Review Questions

1. How are information systems transforming business, and what is their relationship to globalization?

   - Describe how information systems have changed the way businesses operate and their products and services.

   - Identify three major new information system trends.

   - Describe the characteristics of a digital firm.

   - Describe the challenges and opportunities of globalization in a "flattened" world.

2. Why are information systems so essential for running and managing a business today?

   - List and describe six reasons why information systems are so important for business today.

3. What exactly is an information system? How does it work? What are its management, organization, and technology components?

   - Define an information system and describe the activities it performs.

   - List and describe the organizational, management, and technology dimensions of information systems.

   - Distinguish between data and information and between information systems literacy and computer literacy.

   - Explain how the Internet and the World Wide Web are related to the other technology components of information systems.

4. What are complementary assets? Why are complementary assets essential for ensuring that information systems provide genuine value for an organization?

   - Define complementary assets and describe their relationship to information technology.

   - Describe the complementary social, managerial, and organizational assets required to optimize returns from information technology investments.

5. What academic disciplines are used to study information systems? How does each contribute to an understanding of information systems? What is a sociotechnical systems perspective?

   - List and describe each discipline that contributes to a technical approach to information systems.

   - List and describe each discipline that contributes to a behavioral approach to information systems.

   - Describe the sociotechnical perspective on information systems.

Discussion Questions

1. Information systems are too important to be left to computer specialists. Do you agree? Why or why not?

2. If you were setting up the Web site for Disney World visitors, what management, organization, and technology issues might you encounter?

3. What are some of the organizational, managerial, and social complementary assets that help make UPS's information systems so successful?

Hands-On MIS Projects

The projects in this section give you hands-on experience in analyzing financial reporting and inventory management problems, using data management software to improve management decision making about increasing sales, and using Internet software for researching job requirements.

Management Decision Problems

1. Snyders of Hanover, which sells about 80 million bags of pretzels, snack chips, and organic snack items each year, had its financial department use spreadsheets and manual processes for much of its data gathering and reporting. Hanover's financial analyst would spend the entire final week of every month collecting spreadsheets from the heads of more than 50 departments worldwide. She would then consolidate and re-enter all the data into another spreadsheet, which would serve as the company's monthly profit-and-loss statement. If a department needed to update its data after submitting the spreadsheet to the main office, the analyst had to return the original spreadsheet, then wait for the department to re-submit its data before finally submitting the updated data in the consolidated document. Assess the impact of this situation on business performance and management decision making.

2. Dollar General Corporation operates deep-discount stores offering housewares, cleaning supplies, clothing, health and beauty aids, and packaged food, with most items selling for $1. Its business model calls for keeping costs as low as possible. The company has no automated method for keeping track of inventory at each store. Managers know approximately how many cases of a particular product the store is supposed to receive when a delivery truck arrives, but the stores lack technology for scanning the cases or verifying the item count inside the cases. Merchandise losses from theft or other mishaps have been rising and now represent over 3 percent of total sales. What decisions have to be made before investing in an information system solution?

Improving Decision Making: Using Databases to Analyze Sales Trends

Software skills: Database querying and reporting
Business skills: Sales trend analysis

In this project, you will start out with raw transactional sales data and use Microsoft Access database software to develop queries and reports that help managers make better decisions about product pricing, sales promotions, and inventory replenishment. In MyMISLab, you can find a Store and Regional Sales Database developed in Microsoft Access. The database contains raw data on weekly store sales of computer equipment in various sales regions. The database includes fields for store identification number, sales region, item number, item description, unit price, units sold, and the weekly sales period when the sales were made. Use Access to develop some reports and queries to make this information more useful for running the business. Sales and production managers want answers to the following questions:

- Which products should be restocked?
- Which stores and sales regions would benefit from a promotional campaign and additional marketing?
- When (what time of year) should products be offered at full price, and when should discounts be used?

You can easily modify the database table to find and report your answers. Print your reports and results of queries.

Improving Decision Making: Using the Internet to Locate Jobs Requiring Information Systems Knowledge

Software skills: Internet-based software
Business skills: Job searching

Visit a job-posting Web site such as Monster.com. Spend some time at the site examining jobs for accounting, finance, sales, marketing, and human resources. Find two or three descriptions of jobs that require some information systems knowledge. What information systems knowledge do these jobs require? What do you need to do to prepare for these jobs? Write a one- to two-page report summarizing your findings.

Video Cases

Video Cases and Instructional Videos illustrating some of the concepts in this chapter are available. Contact your instructor to access these videos.

Collaboration and Teamwork Project

In MyMISLab, you will find a Collaboration and Teamwork Project dealing with the concepts in this chapter. You will be able to use Google Sites, Google Docs, and other open-source collaboration tools to complete the assignment.

Mashaweer
CASE STUDY

Mashaweer is the first personal service company in Egypt. It's purely dedicated to saving its clients' time and effort acting as a personal assistant 24 hours a day. The personal assistant is a rider with a motorcycle who runs any errands for individual clients or corporations at any given time. The most common service they provide is buying groceries or other goods from stores, paying bills, and acting as a courier. Mashaweer's success relies heavily on their flexibility, and they have often received unusual requests that they have fulfilled in order to gain customer loyalty – including: going to the gym to tell someone to turn on the phone as someone is trying to reach them, delivering presents to a client's fiancée every 15 minutes, and carrying a client's shopping bags from the car to the house.

Mashaweer is an essential service for the Egyptians because traffic is a problem that everyone in Egypt faces, making it difficult for an individual to get a couple of errands done on the same day. Mashaweer's service has achieved such success in Alexandria and Cairo, where traffic is an issue, saving people one of the most valuable commodities out there; time. The service is able to give people more quality time to spend with family or friends, instead of taking care of the daily errands that usually take up half of one's day. They also act as a security or safety measure as they perform people's errands in unsafe times, such as the period after the revolution or simply late at night. Most individuals cannot afford having a full time assistant to perform their errands whenever needed. Mashaweer's agents act as full time assistants for every individual at a part time cost.

Since starting the company in Alexandria in 2010, Mashaweer has since expanded to Cairo and operates around 600 orders per day. They plan to expand even further geographically within Egypt and to other countries in the region as well as enhancing and increasing the services they provide.

The idea of Mashaweer was created by Mohamed Wahid (24 years old) and then co-founded with his partners, Ahmed El Kordy (25 years old) and Aly El Shazly (27 years old). They were all born and raised in Alexandria. Ahmed El Kordy and Mohamed Wahid met when they both transferred from different schools to IGCSE Academy (AAST) for high school. Ahmed El Kordy finished high school in 2 years and went on to

achieve his bachelor's degree in industrial engineering from The Arab Academy of Science and Technology (AAST), graduating in 2008. Part of his undergraduate degree was spent doing a year abroad in Carleton University in Ottawa, Canada. During the summers of his undergraduate years, Ahmed completed several internships in the United Kingdom and Ireland. Mohamed Wahid also went to AAST graduating in 2009 with a bachelor's degree in construction engineering. Aly El Shazly attended St. Marks School for his entire school career, he then went on to Alexandria University where he studied business and graduated in 2007. After college, Ahmed El Kordy went on to work at his father's import/export business. Mohamed Wahid went on to establish a company called X-trade for trade and contracting, followed by a marketing and advertising company called Green Media. Currently, he's a main shareholder in both, in addition to being the vice-chairman of Green Towers, a real estate company with a net worth of about $16 million.

Wahid thought of the idea of establishing Mashaweer while he was preparing for his wedding. His bride-to-be was overwhelmed with errands that she had to get done within a few days and he started wondering what she would have done if she couldn't afford having a full time driver who did all of her errands for her. While on his honeymoon, he kept thinking about this idea and how much time people could save and what a valuable service it could be, so he decided to call his friends to start transforming the idea into an actual business plan. After developing a business plan, the three entrepreneurs decided to go into the implementation phase and actually build this business. They started small and grew organically as the demand for the service increased. Each of the three entrepreneurs invested $5,000 into the project to total a starting capital of $15,000. They started with only 3 motorcycles, 6 riders, and a hotline.

As the three friends realized they had actually succeeded in Alexandria, they decided they wanted to move to the next phase by establishing Mashaweer in Cairo. When they decided to expand to Cairo, they decided to adopt a completely different strategy. They wanted to be able to cover all of Greater Cairo, as a whole, and not just specific areas, from the very beginning. During the Revolution in January 2011 they started gathering market research to expand in Cairo and started investing heavily. Since business all over the country had come to a standstill, they made several large purchases such as motorcycles and advertising space for fractions of the price. When others saw it as a time to slow down, the entrepreneurs saw it as an opportunity to start marketing for their business. By March they realized that they needed to increase the original investment so that they can grow large enough to capture the market in Cairo. To do so, they brought in other investors, mainly from their friends and family, to raise the capital investment up to $1.67 million. They planned to enter Cairo with full force so that there would be a high barrier of entry for any competitor they decided that their competitive advantage would have to be in investing in technology. They wanted to get an ERP (Enterprise Resource Planning) system but found quotations to be too high. To fix this they started their own information technology company, Innov8 (innovate), where they created a customized ERP system, which they then connected to their customized PDAs (Personal Digital Assistants) through a cloud computing system that was made by LinkDotNet and Mobinil. Each rider receives tasks one at a time on the PDA, which also includes a GPS to provide detailed directions. The GPS monitors the rider's location.

To reduce cost and ensure quality, Mashaweer does not rely on outsourcing in any of its stages as long as it can do the work with the same or better quality. This explains why Mashaweer founded Innov8 in order to build its system and manage its technical work. Now, Mashaweer only owns part of this company and is one of its numerous clients. One further example of Mashaweer's in house capabilities is its call center. The company preferred to have an internal call center after rejecting a number of offers for an outsourced one. The reason for this was to be able to monitor the performance of the agents and always work on improving the quality of their customer service. Investing in an innovative contact center and using CISCO, which supports up to 300IP phones, a reporting module and a recording system made it much easier for Mashaweer to track its received calls and work on any problems that might face its customer service agents.

Software components developed by Innov8 include the Mashaweer Server, Mashaweer API (Application Programmers' Interface), and Mashaweer PDA client.

The Mashaweer Server is a centralized application that manages the following elements:
- Orders (placement, editing, pricing, review, tracking and reports)
- Routes management and optimization
- Clients (management, reports, discounts)
- Packages tracking
- Contracts
- Call center
- Satellite offices
- Representatives
- Cash transactions and expenses tracking for representatives and satellite offices
- Asset tracking of vehicles, PDAs and mobile printers
- Management reports

The API is a method of integrating Mashaweer ordering system with third parties. This allows third parties to automate their delivery system and integrate Mashaweer into their existing CRM/dispatching systems, opening a wide opportunity for business expansion.

The Mashaweer PDA application is installed on each representative PDA and manages the following elements:
- Order items progress tracking
- Collection of order fees and other costs, against a printed invoice
- Package handling (barcode scanning and destinations)
- Messaging
- Cash and expenses tracking
- Synchronizing data periodically and at the beginning of each shift

When Mashaweer was first introduced in Egypt, it captured 100 percent of market share for such a service, because it was the first and only company of its nature. However, the market was not aware or used to such a service, so it started growing slowly in Alexandria until people grasped the idea and got accustomed to the fact that there is a company that can take over your errands. In contrast, when the company started operating in Cairo, it grew at surprisingly fast pace. There are several factors are expected to affect the target market and make it easier for Mashaweer to penetrate it aggressively.

At the beginning, people's assumption is that using Mashaweer is too luxurious and costly. When they use it for the first couple of times, this perception changes and they begin to rely on this convenient service. As more and more people get accustomed with the service, it creates a cultural change that significantly affects the demand on the service.

Another factor that is expected to facilitate working conditions and reduce costs is the technological advances that occur every day. Mashaweer heavily depends on technological tools, and would benefit from the advancements and price reductions that continuously take place. As a result, Mashaweer's total costs will decrease, enabling it to decrease its prices and further improve its quality to become even more convenient for a larger number of people.

Mashaweer is the only company of its kind in Egypt that operates on this scale. However, there is a company called Wassaly that was established in Cairo after Mashaweer's success in Alexandria. This company operates on a much smaller scale. Their indirect competitors include other courier services (e.g. DHL, UPS, TNT, and FedEx). However, they have positioned themselves as the flexible courier in contrast to the couriers available in the market today; they offer same day delivery rather than next day delivery. Mashaweer has several other advantages that make it very hard for others to compete:

- Database of thousands of loyal clients.
- Self-investment is manageable.
- Highly qualified and carefully selected riders due to the high salaries compared to the delivery sector in the Egypt.
- Various revenue streams.
- Being the owner of the IT company Innov8 fosters technology integration in Mashaweer.

Mashaweer has several unique selling propositions. The main two aspects are being the first in the market, and the only of its kind. Also the most important differentiator is the flexibility of their service, which addresses all of their customer's needs and requests.

Unlike new entrants or copycats in the market, Mashaweer have invested highly in the systems they use. They invested in PDAs to enable the operations process to be monitored accurately since it provides data like GPS tracking to track each order and the location or stage the messenger is located. Through this technology, Mashaweer decreases the amount of errors due to the fact that the messenger is tied to an automated process where he receives his tasks through the PDA handheld. Meanwhile, a SCADA (Supervisory Control and Data Acquisition) system presented on a big screen will be available at Mashaweer headquarters to monitor all live orders and measure the traffic in case of rush hours, thus enabling the operation team to react and try a preventive and corrective action.

Mashaweer's infrastructures includes the following.

Equipment: 130 motorcycles units and 10 cars.

Software: A logistics management solution system was developed specifically for Mashaweer, and served from a cloud-hosted server. The solution consists of a web-based portal where call center agents, logistics, and managers can add, edit, track, and view reports.

PDA: A PDA client was developed to connect to the server in order to allow Mashaweer representatives to view and update their assigned orders via an XML-based web service. Except for the PDA client, the solution is based on open source technologies (PHP, CodeIgniter, MySQL, jQuery, Ubuntu Linux). The PDA devices will be a main factor in integrating the operational team with the fleet of riders.

Hardware: Windows Mobile PDAs were used for viewing and updating orders on the move. Each PDA is paired to a Bluetooth mobile printer for printing receipts. The printer is also equipped with a swipe card reader module so that it can be used in the future for credit card payment collection, and for promotion cards. Mashaweer server is a Linux VM hosted on a cloud solution provided by Innov8, the sister company that developed the entire information technology system.

Head Quarters: The decision was made to buy a new headquarters instead of renting an existing one.

Mashaweer's future strategy is as follows:

Mashaweer Market: Mashaweer Market is an online supermarket that will enable people to do their grocery shopping through Mashaweer's website and get it delivered by its representatives within 30 minutes of placing the order. This will be made possible by having access to a large number of supermarkets around Cairo and Alexandria, so that representatives can pick the order from the closest outlet and deliver it to the customer as quickly as possible. All products will be displayed on the website.

Mashaweer is hoping to reach an average of 4000 orders daily in return for a delivery charge of 5 Egyptian pounds per order.

Call center: Mashaweer's call center is expected to make up an important revenue stream for the company in the near future, as the company starts introducing marketing campaigns. In addition, Mashaweer is planning to expand its call center to include other companies other than Mashaweer.

Geographical Expansion: Using the technology they have invested in building their infrastructure, Mashaweer now has the potential to easily enter and penetrate other markets in different regions at a very low initiation cost. They plan to expand to other regions within Egypt, in addition to expanding to other countries within the Middle East. In October 2013 they will open their first franchise in Beirut, Lebanon. They are also looking to expand to several countries in the Gulf.

Sources: Mashaweer web site, http://www.mashaweeronline.com/, accessed Novemeber 2012; interviews with Mashaweer owners, conducted November 2012.

CASE STUDY QUESTIONS

1. What kinds of applications are described in this case? What business functions do they support?

2. What are the benefits from equipping their riders with PDAs?

3. Was it a good decision to expand the business to Cairo? What are the implications of information systems?

4. Do you think that Mashaweer will be able to accomplish their future strategy and sustain its market share?

5. Do you think in near future, the competition between Mashaweer and Wassaly will be aggressive? Why?

Case contributed by Niveen Ezzat, Cairo University

Chapter 2

Global E-business and Collaboration

LEARNING OBJECTIVES

After reading this chapter, you will be able to answer the following questions:

1. What are business processes? How are they related to information systems?

2. How do systems serve the different management groups in a business?

3. How do systems that link the enterprise improve organizational performance?

4. Why are systems for collaboration and social business so important and what technologies do they use?

5. What is the role of the information systems function in a business?

Interactive Sessions:

Schiphol International Hub

Piloting Procter & Gamble from Decision Cockpits

CHAPTER OUTLINE

TELUS EMBRACES SOCIAL LEARNING

TELUS is a Canadian telecommunications company that has been around for a century, and it wants to ensure that every Canadian is connected to the rest of the world, whether that connection is through wireless devices, the Internet, television, or traditional telephone lines. The company has 12.7 million customer accounts.

Providing superior service is an important corporate goal. Management believes that good teamwork and employee learning are vital for achieving this goal. Until recently, most employee learning at TELUS took place in formal classroom settings outside the company. Much of what employees learned depended on knowledge presented by instructors, and this learning method was expensive. Employees would be better off learning from each other's expertise, management concluded. Moreover, 40 percent of the TELUS workforce was expected to retire within the next 10 years, making it essential for the company to find multiple ways of sharing and preserving employee experience and knowledge.

The company decided to focus on making team member education more "continuous, collaborative, and connected" through informal and social learning, using mentoring, coaching, job rotations, videos, blogs, and wikis. TELUS set a 2010 learning budget of $21 million, 40 percent of which was for informal and social learning and 60 percent for formal learning. (The year before, formal learning had accounted for 90 percent of the firm's $28.5 million learning budget.)

To support the new learning initiative, TELUS harnessed the capabilities of Microsoft SharePoint Server 2010, which provides team members with a single point of entry to shared knowledge within the company and the ability to search all the company's learning assets simultaneously. TELUS used the SharePoint MySites feature to enable team members to create their own Web pages that describe their areas of expertise and special skills. Team members are able to see their positions and those of others in the organizational hierarchy, connect with colleagues, and establish informal groups with other people with similar skills. An Expert Search capability provides ranked search results identifying TELUS employees with expertise in specific areas. MySites also offers blogging tools for team members to build their own blogs and contribute to those of others. Through these blogs, a team member can locate an expert, discuss his or her experiences, share advice, and find the answers to questions without having to take a class or interrupt a colleague.

TELUS used SharePoint to develop team sites called My Communities, where project teams, departments, and other groups can work together and share documents and other content. They are able to create categories for classifying and tagging user-generated content. TELUS Tube allows team members to post and view user-generated video of their accomplishments on the job or questions to ask colleagues. Over 1,000 videos have been posted. A new learning management system working closely with SharePoint Server 2010 enables team members to track and display the formal learning courses they have taken as well as the courses other team members have taken.

TELUS recognized that moving from formal learning to acquiring knowledge through employee collaboration and participation required a shift in company culture. "This is not a scenario in which we can flip a switch and have everyone change their work habits overnight," observed Dan Pontefract, Senior Director of Learning for TELUS. To encourage acceptance of and participation in the new social learning processes, the company set up an internal site showing tangible examples of the new collaboration tools and launched a wiki to facilitate employee discussion. Pontefract includes information about the new learning initiative on his blog to help prepare team members for the shift.

The new SharePoint system gives TELUS team members much faster access to the specific skills and knowledge areas where they need help—they don't need to wait for the next formal learning class. Instead, team members can immediately reach out to colleagues who have expertise in a specific area, or they can read wikis and blogs, watch videos, and participate in discussions to find answers.

Implementing SharePoint reduced the TELUS learning budget to $21 million in 2010. The company was able to trim this budget by 20 percent the following year as it continued its shift to informal and social learning. Further cost savings will occur as the new learning solutions take hold. In the TELUS three-year plan, formal learning will comprise just 50 percent of the total learning budget.

Sources: Sharon Gaudin, "Telus Links Social, Traditional Training," *Computerworld*, March 27, 2012; "TELUS Telecom Company Embraces Social Computing, Streamlines Formal Learning," www.microsoft.com, accessed April 5, 2012; Barb Mosher, "Sharepoint 2010 Case Study: Informal and Social Learning at TELUS," *CMSWire*, June 30, 2010, and www.telus.com, accessed April 6, 2012.

The experience of TELUS illustrates how much organizations today rely on information systems to improve their performance and remain competitive. It also shows how much systems supporting collaboration and teamwork make a difference in an organization's ability to execute, provide superior customer service, and grow profits.

The chapter-opening diagram calls attention to important points raised by this case and this chapter. TELUS is an "old" company that wanted to continue changing with the times and remain customer-focused. It also needed to find a way to capture and preserve employee knowledge and expertise as 40 percent of its workforce neared retirement age.

TELUS management decided that the best solution was to deploy new technology to move from a formal learning environment to one in which team members contributed to and obtained knowledge from colleagues. The company implemented Microsoft SharePoint Server 2010 as a company-wide platform for collaboration, knowledge acquisition, and knowledge transfer, and it took advantage of the software's new "social" tools to facilitate employee collaboration and engagement. TELUS now relies on its internal enterprise social network for much of employee learning and problem-solving, and SharePoint integrates all of the ways employees learn and share knowledge—formal training classes, podcasts, blogs, wikis, videos, and corporate social networking. The company more effectively shares institutional knowledge and has reduced its costs.

New technology alone would not have solved TELUS's problem. To make the solution effective, TELUS had to change its organizational culture and business processes for knowledge dissemination and employee learning.

Here are some questions to think about: How are collaboration and employee learning keeping TELUS competitive? What are the benefits of each of the collaboration and social tools discussed in this case?

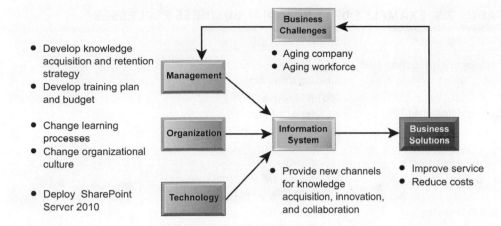

- Develop knowledge acquisition and retention strategy
- Develop training plan and budget

- Change learning processes
- Change organizational culture

- Deploy SharePoint Server 2010

Management

Organization

Technology

Business Challenges
- Aging company
- Aging workforce

Information System

- Provide new channels for knowledge acquisition, innovation, and collaboration

Business Solutions
- Improve service
- Reduce costs

2.1 BUSINESS PROCESSES AND INFORMATION SYSTEMS

In order to operate, businesses must deal with many different pieces of information about suppliers, customers, employees, invoices, and payments, and of course their products and services. They must organize work activities that use this information to operate efficiently and enhance the overall performance of the firm. Information systems make it possible for firms to manage all their information, make better decisions, and improve the execution of their business processes.

BUSINESS PROCESSES

Business processes, which we introduced in Chapter 1, refer to the manner in which work is organized, coordinated, and focused to produce a valuable product or service. Business processes are the collection of activities required to produce a product or service. These activities are supported by flows of material, information, and knowledge among the participants in business processes. Business processes also refer to the unique ways in which organizations coordinate work, information, and knowledge, and the ways in which management chooses to coordinate work.

To a large extent, the performance of a business firm depends on how well its business processes are designed and coordinated. A company's business processes can be a source of competitive strength if they enable the company to innovate or to execute better than its rivals. Business processes can also be liabilities if they are based on outdated ways of working that impede organizational responsiveness and efficiency. The chapter-opening case describing TELUS's improvements in employee learning processes clearly illustrates these points, as do many of the other cases in this text.

Every business can be seen as a collection of business processes, some of which are part of larger encompassing processes. For instance, uses of mentoring, wikis, blogs, and videos are all part of the overall knowledge management process. Many business processes are tied to a specific functional area. For example, the sales and marketing function is responsible for identifying customers, and the human resources function is responsible for hiring employees. Table 2.1 describes some typical business processes for each of the functional areas of business.

TABLE 2.1 EXAMPLES OF FUNCTIONAL BUSINESS PROCESSES

FUNCTIONAL AREA	BUSINESS PROCESS
Manufacturing and production	Assembling the product Checking for quality Producing bills of materials
Sales and marketing	Identifying customers Making customers aware of the product Selling the product
Finance and accounting	Paying creditors Creating financial statements Managing cash accounts
Human resources	Hiring employees Evaluating employees' job performance Enrolling employees in benefits plans

Other business processes cross many different functional areas and require coordination across departments. For instance, consider the seemingly simple business process of fulfilling a customer order (see Figure 2.1). Initially, the sales department receives a sales order. The order passes first to accounting to ensure the customer can pay for the order either by a credit verification or request for immediate payment prior to shipping. Once the customer credit is established, the production department pulls the product from inventory or produces the product. Then the product is shipped (and this may require working with a logistics firm, such as UPS or FedEx). A bill or invoice is generated by the accounting department, and a notice is sent to the customer indicating that the product has shipped. The sales department is notified of the shipment and prepares to support the customer by answering calls or fulfilling warranty claims.

FIGURE 2.1   THE ORDER FULFILLMENT PROCESS

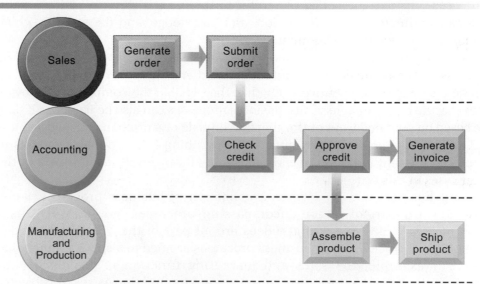

Fulfilling a customer order involves a complex set of steps that requires the close coordination of the sales, accounting, and manufacturing functions.

What at first appears to be a simple process, fulfilling an order, turns out to be a very complicated series of business processes that require the close coordination of major functional groups in a firm. Moreover, to efficiently perform all these steps in the order fulfillment process requires a great deal of information. The required information must flow rapidly both within the firm from one decision maker to another; with business partners, such as delivery firms; and with the customer. Computer-based information systems make this possible.

HOW INFORMATION TECHNOLOGY IMPROVES BUSINESS PROCESSES

Exactly how do information systems improve business processes? Information systems automate many steps in business processes that were formerly performed manually, such as checking a client's credit, or generating an invoice and shipping order. But today, information technology can do much more. New technology can actually change the flow of information, making it possible for many more people to access and share information, replacing sequential steps with tasks that can be performed simultaneously, and eliminating delays in decision making. New information technology frequently changes the way a business works and supports entirely new business models. Downloading a Kindle e-book from Amazon, buying a computer online at Best Buy, and downloading a music track from iTunes are entirely new business processes based on new business models that would be inconceivable without today's information technology.

That's why it's so important to pay close attention to business processes, both in your information systems course and in your future career. By analyzing business processes, you can achieve a very clear understanding of how a business actually works. Moreover, by conducting a business process analysis, you will also begin to understand how to change the business by improving its processes to make it more efficient or effective. Throughout this book, we examine business processes with a view to understanding how they might be improved by using information technology to achieve greater efficiency, innovation, and customer service.

2.2   TYPES OF INFORMATION SYSTEMS

Now that you understand business processes, it is time to look more closely at how information systems support the business processes of a firm. Because there are different interests, specialties, and levels in an organization, there are different kinds of systems. No single system can provide all the information an organization needs.

A typical business organization has systems supporting processes for each of the major business functions—sales and marketing, manufacturing and production, finance and accounting, and human resources. You can find examples of systems for each of these business functions in the Learning Tracks for this chapter. Functional systems that operate independently of each other are becoming a thing of the past because they cannot easily share information to support cross-functional business processes. Many have been replaced with large-scale cross-functional systems that integrate the activities of related business processes and organizational units. We describe these integrated cross-functional applications later in this section.

A typical firm also has different systems supporting the decision-making needs of each of the main management groups we described in Chapter 1. Operational management, middle management, and senior management each use systems to support the decisions they must make to run the company. Let's look at these systems and the types of decisions they support.

SYSTEMS FOR DIFFERENT MANAGEMENT GROUPS

A business firm has systems to support different groups or levels of management. These systems include transaction processing systems and systems for business intelligence.

Transaction Processing Systems

Operational managers need systems that keep track of the elementary activities and transactions of the organization, such as sales, receipts, cash deposits, payroll, credit decisions, and the flow of materials in a factory. **Transaction processing systems (TPS)** provide this kind of information. A transaction processing system is a computerized system that performs and records the daily routine transactions necessary to conduct business, such as sales order entry, hotel reservations, payroll, employee record keeping, and shipping.

The principal purpose of systems at this level is to answer routine questions and to track the flow of transactions through the organization. How many parts are in inventory? What happened to Mr. Smith's payment? To answer these kinds of questions, information generally must be easily available, current, and accurate.

At the operational level, tasks, resources, and goals are predefined and highly structured. The decision to grant credit to a customer, for instance, is made by a lower-level supervisor according to predefined criteria. All that must be determined is whether the customer meets the criteria.

Figure 2.2 illustrates a TPS for payroll processing. A payroll system keeps track of money paid to employees. An employee time sheet with the employee's name, social security number, and number of hours worked per week represents a single transaction for this system. Once this transaction is input into the system, it updates the system's master file (or database—see Chapter 6) that permanently maintains employee information for the organization. The data in the system are combined in different ways to create reports of interest to management and government agencies and to send paychecks to employees.

Managers need TPS to monitor the status of internal operations and the firm's relations with the external environment. TPS are also major producers of information for the other systems and business functions. For example, the payroll system illustrated in Figure 2.2, along with other accounting TPS, supplies data to the company's general ledger system, which is responsible for maintaining records of the firm's income and expenses and for producing reports such as income statements and balance sheets. It also supplies employee payment history data for insurance, pension, and other benefits calculations to the firm's human resources function, and employee payment data to government agencies such as the U.S. Internal Revenue Service and Social Security Administration.

Transaction processing systems are often so central to a business that TPS failure for a few hours can lead to a firm's demise and perhaps that of other firms linked to it. Imagine what would happen to UPS if its package tracking system were not working! What would the airlines do without their computerized reservation systems?

FIGURE 2.2   A PAYROLL TPS

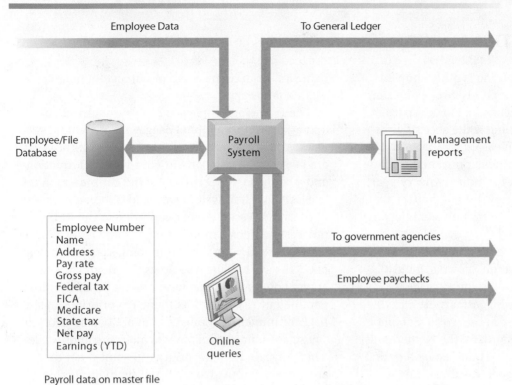

A TPS for payroll processing captures employee payment transaction data (such as a time card). System outputs include online and hard-copy reports for management and employee paychecks.

The Interactive Session on Technology describes the impact on airline travel when automated baggage handling systems are not working properly. As you read this case, try to identify the transactions being processed and how the data generated from these systems impact business performance.

Systems for Business Intelligence

Firms also have business intelligence systems that focus on delivering information to support management decision making. **Business intelligence** is a contemporary term for data and software tools for organizing, analyzing, and providing access to data to help managers and other enterprise users make more informed decisions. Business intelligence addresses the decision-making needs of all levels of management. This section provides a brief introduction to business intelligence. You'll learn more about this topic in Chapters 6 and 12.

Business intelligence systems for middle management help with monitoring, controlling, decision-making, and administrative activities. In Chapter 1, we defined management information systems as the study of information systems in business and management. The term **management information systems (MIS)** also designates a specific category of information systems serving middle management. MIS provide middle managers with reports on the organization's current performance. This information is used to monitor and control the business and predict future performance.

MIS summarize and report on the company's basic operations using data supplied by transaction processing systems. The basic transaction data from TPS are compressed and usually presented in reports that are produced on a regular

INTERACTIVE SESSION: TECHNOLOGY

SCHIPHOL INTERNATIONAL HUB

Theoretically, baggage-handling is quite simple. Baggage input is connected to merely two events: an airplane lands or a person checks in. However, it's risky business. Baggage handling is the second most important factor in having a pleasant trip, according to a 2009 IATA CATS survey. Moreover, mishandled baggage is a $2.5 billion problem for industry every year. Just think that this problem may annually affect about 51 million passengers travelling through Schiphol airport alone.

In 2004, IBM Corporation, Vanderlande Industries and later Grenzebach Automation Systems, jointly took up the challenge of renewing the Baggage Control System for one of the biggest airport hubs in Europe, and one of the busiest in the world: Schiphol International Airport, in Amsterdam, the Netherlands. With an investment of around $1 billion over a period of about 10 years, Schiphol's goal was threefold: (a) realize a monumental 1% maximum loss of transfer baggage (against the initial 22 million lost baggage); (b) increase capacity from 40 to 70 million bags; (c) reduce cost per bag without increasing wait-times.

Most of the job involved Schiphol's gigantic baggage conveyor network: 21 kilometers of transport tracks, 6 robotic units, and 9,000 storage capacitors, all behaving as one system. Also, extending the system with more surfaces is not possible, given the land conditions surrounding the airport. The baggage conveyor network has a simple goal: the right bag must be at the right place at the right time. To pursue this goal the network must perform several key roles: move bags from the check-in area to the departure gate, move bags from gate to gate, move bags from the arrival gate to the baggage claim, and plan and control peripheral hardware and software. In addition, these roles involve a wide variety of sensors, actuators, mechanical devices, and computers. The network uses over 3 million lines of source code. Some of the advanced technology used in baggage-handling systems includes destination-coded vehicles (DCVs), automatic bar code scanners, radio-frequency identification (RFID) tags, and high-tech conveyors equipped with sorting machines. Baggage should move from its current location to its destination before travellers do. To add further complications, all of this must be available and robust, i.e. operate 99.99% of times while

being able to minimize loss or damage in that 0.01% of time it doesn't!

The following simple scenario summarizes the operations of the Schiphol baggage conveyors network. You arrive at check-in desk, and your bags are tagged. The tags contain your flight information and a bar-code/RFID that all of the computers in the baggage-handling system can read. When computers in the system scan the bar code/detect the RFID, they process the information it contains and determine where to send your bag. After being scanned (at least) once, the system always knows where your bag is at any point, and is able to redirect it based on three parameters: (a) time of its flight; (b) priority; (c) size. Bags for immediate embarkation are considered "hot". These are sent immediately to aircraft stands while "cold" baggage (i.e. low priority, distant flight time) are quickly rerouted away from the main "highway" tracks, directed towards various storage points in the network. DCVs are unmanned carts that can load and unload bags without stopping movement. These carts move on tracks like miniature roller coasters along the main "highway" tracks that span the airport. Buffers and hot/cold storage areas are used to avoid overcrowding. Computers throughout the system keep track of the location of each bag, its destination, and the time it is needed at that destination. The system can optimize the routes taken by the carts to get the bags needed most urgently to their destinations fastest. Because DCVs move at high speed and do not come to a full stop to receive baggage, the conveyors must be extremely precise, depositing bags where they are needed at just the right time for maximum efficiency. Once bags reach the gate, they enter a sorting station where airline employees use computer terminals to send bags to the correct plane. To make sure that baggage is not lost, the system "reconciles" baggage with its owner, i.e. it checks if the baggage and the owner are actually on the same plane!

However beautiful and harmonious this process may seem, there are still many things that can go wrong. For example, what if baggage is mis-tagged? What if the tag is unreadable? What about schedule changes?

Baggage handling systems can be extremely expensive, but if implemented successfully, they pay for themselves — imagine saving around 0.1% of $2.5 billion. It's a lot of money!

The new baggage system at Schiphol is not flawless. In November 2012, a special warrant by local Police was issued that required stopping the tracks at Schiphol as part of a drug-smuggling investiga-

tion. Some of the 140,000 passengers that were being served by the international Hub at the time suffered baggage loss.

Sources: Based on data available online. Partly acquired from Amsterdam Airport Schiphol Case Study Video, available online.

CASE STUDY QUESTIONS

1. How many levels of complexity can you identify in Schiphol's baggage conveyor network?

2. What are the management, organization, and technology components of Schiphol's baggage conveyor network?

3. What is the problem that Schiphol is trying to solve? Discuss the business impact of this problem.

4. Think of the data that the network uses. What kinds of management reports can be generated from that data?

Case contributed by Damian A. Tamburri and Patricia Lago, VU University Amsterdam

schedule. Today, many of these reports are delivered online. Figure 2.3 shows how a typical MIS transforms transaction-level data from inventory, production, and accounting into MIS files that are used to provide managers with reports. Figure 2.4 shows a sample report from this system.

MIS typically provide answers to routine questions that have been specified in advance and have a predefined procedure for answering them. For instance, MIS reports might list the total pounds of lettuce used this quarter by a fast-food chain or, as illustrated in Figure 2.4, compare total annual sales figures for specific products to planned targets. These systems generally are not flexible and have little analytical capability. Most MIS use simple routines, such as summaries and comparisons, as opposed to sophisticated mathematical models or statistical techniques.

Other types of business intelligence systems support more non-routine decision making. **Decision-support systems (DSS)** focus on problems that are unique and rapidly changing, for which the procedure for arriving at a solution may not be fully predefined in advance. They try to answer questions such as these: What would be the impact on production schedules if we were to

FIGURE 2.3   **HOW MANAGEMENT INFORMATION SYSTEMS OBTAIN THEIR DATA FROM THE ORGANIZATION'S TPS**

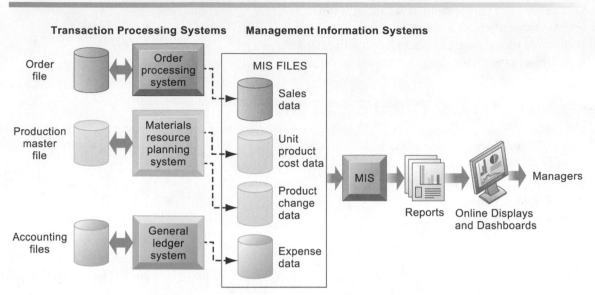

In the system illustrated by this diagram, three TPS supply summarized transaction data to the MIS reporting system at the end of the time period. Managers gain access to the organizational data through the MIS, which provides them with the appropriate reports.

double sales in the month of December? What would happen to our return on investment if a factory schedule were delayed for six months?

Although DSS use internal information from TPS and MIS, they often bring in information from external sources, such as current stock prices or product prices of competitors. These systems are employed by "super-user" managers and business analysts who want to use sophisticated analytics and models to analyze data.

FIGURE 2.4   **SAMPLE MIS REPORT**

Consolidated Consumer Products Corporation Sales by Product and Sales Region: 2013

PRODUCT CODE	PRODUCT DESCRIPTION	SALES REGION	ACTUAL SALES	PLANNED	ACTUAL versus PLANNED
4469	Carpet Cleaner	Northeast	4,066,700	4,800,000	0.85
		South	3,778,112	3,750,000	1.01
		Midwest	4,867,001	4,600,000	1.06
		West	4,003,440	4,400,000	0.91
	TOTAL		16,715,253	17,550,000	0.95
5674	Room Freshener	Northeast	3,676,700	3,900,000	0.94
		South	5,608,112	4,700,000	1.19
		Midwest	4,711,001	4,200,000	1.12
		West	4,563,440	4,900,000	0.93
	TOTAL		18,559,253	17,700,000	1.05

This report, showing summarized annual sales data, was produced by the MIS in Figure 2.3.

An interesting, small, but powerful DSS is the voyage-estimating system of a large global shipping company that transports bulk cargoes of coal, oil, ores, and finished products. The firm owns some vessels, charters others, and bids for shipping contracts in the open market to carry general cargo. A voyage-estimating system calculates financial and technical voyage details. Financial calculations include ship/time costs (fuel, labor, capital), freight rates for various types of cargo, and port expenses. Technical details include a myriad of factors, such as ship cargo capacity, speed, port distances, fuel and water consumption, and loading patterns (location of cargo for different ports).

The system can answer questions such as the following: Given a customer delivery schedule and an offered freight rate, which vessel should be assigned at what rate to maximize profits? What is the optimal speed at which a particular vessel can optimize its profit and still meet its delivery schedule? What is the optimal loading pattern for a ship bound for the U.S. West Coast from Malaysia? Figure 2.5 illustrates the DSS built for this company. The system operates on a powerful desktop personal computer, providing a system of menus that makes it easy for users to enter data or obtain information.

The voyage-estimating DSS we have just described draws heavily on models. Other business intelligence systems are more data-driven, focusing instead on extracting useful information from massive quantities of data. For example, Intrawest—the largest ski operator in North America—collects and stores large amounts of customer data from its Web site, call center, lodging reservations, ski schools, and ski equipment rental stores. It uses special software to analyze these data to determine the value, revenue potential, and loyalty of each customer so managers can make better decisions on how to target their marketing programs. The system segments customers into seven categories based on needs, attitudes, and behaviors, ranging from "passionate experts" to "value-minded family vacationers." The company then e-mails video clips that would appeal to each segment to encourage more visits to its resorts.

FIGURE 2.5   **VOYAGE-ESTIMATING DECISION-SUPPORT SYSTEM**

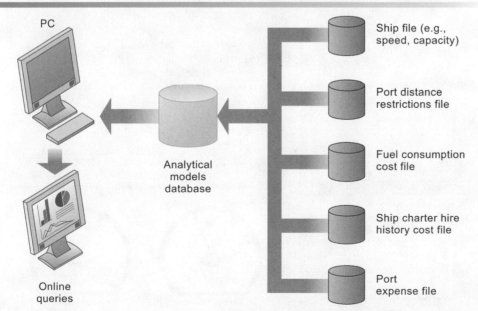

This DSS operates on a powerful PC. It is used daily by managers who must develop bids on shipping contracts.

Business intelligence systems also address the decision-making needs of senior management. Senior managers need systems that focus on strategic issues and long-term trends, both in the firm and in the external environment. They are concerned with questions such as: What will employment levels be in five years? What are the long-term industry cost trends? What products should we be making in five years?

Executive support systems (ESS) help senior management make these decisions. They address non-routine decisions requiring judgment, evaluation, and insight because there is no agreed-on procedure for arriving at a solution. ESS present graphs and data from many sources through an interface that is easy for senior managers to use. Often the information is delivered to senior executives through a **portal**, which uses a Web interface to present integrated personalized business content.

ESS are designed to incorporate data about external events, such as new tax laws or competitors, but they also draw summarized information from internal MIS and DSS. They filter, compress, and track critical data, displaying the data of greatest importance to senior managers. Increasingly, such systems include business intelligence analytics for analyzing trends, forecasting, and "drilling down" to data at greater levels of detail.

For example, the CEO of Leiner Health Products, the largest manufacturer of private-label vitamins and supplements in the United States, has an ESS that provides on his desktop a minute-to-minute view of the firm's financial performance as measured by working capital, accounts receivable, accounts payable, cash flow, and inventory. The information is presented in the form of a **digital dashboard**, which displays on a single screen graphs and charts of key performance indicators for managing a company. Digital dashboards are becoming an increasingly popular tool for management decision makers.

A digital dashboard delivers comprehensive and accurate information for decision making often using a single screen. The graphical overview of key performance indicators helps managers quickly spot areas that need attention.

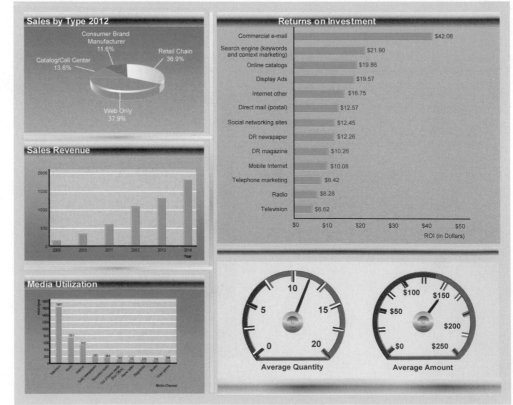

Contemporary business intelligence and analytics technology have promoted data-driven management, where decision makers rely heavily on analytical tools and data at their fingertips to guide their work. Data captured at the factory or sales floor level are immediately available for high-level or detailed views in executive dashboards and reports. It's real-time management. The Interactive Session on Management illustrates information-driven management at work in Procter & Gamble (P&G), a world-class corporation.

SYSTEMS FOR LINKING THE ENTERPRISE

Reviewing all the different types of systems we have just described, you might wonder how a business can manage all the information in these different systems. You might also wonder how costly it is to maintain so many different systems. And you might wonder how all these different systems can share information and how managers and employees are able to coordinate their work. In fact, these are all important questions for businesses today.

Enterprise Applications

Getting all the different kinds of systems in a company to work together has proven a major challenge. Typically, corporations are put together both through normal "organic" growth and through acquisition of smaller firms. Over a period of time, corporations end up with a collection of systems, most of them older, and face the challenge of getting them all to "talk" with one another and work together as one corporate system. There are several solutions to this problem.

One solution is to implement **enterprise applications**, which are systems that span functional areas, focus on executing business processes across the business firm, and include all levels of management. Enterprise applications help businesses become more flexible and productive by coordinating their business processes more closely and integrating groups of processes so they focus on efficient management of resources and customer service.

There are four major enterprise applications: enterprise systems, supply chain management systems, customer relationship management systems, and knowledge management systems. Each of these enterprise applications integrates a related set of functions and business processes to enhance the performance of the organization as a whole. Figure 2.6 on page 86 shows that the architecture for these enterprise applications encompasses processes spanning the entire organization and, in some cases, extending beyond the organization to customers, suppliers, and other key business partners.

Enterprise Systems Firms use **enterprise systems**, also known as enterprise resource planning (ERP) systems, to integrate business processes in manufacturing and production, finance and accounting, sales and marketing, and human resources into a single software system. Information that was previously fragmented in many different systems is stored in a single comprehensive data repository where it can be used by many different parts of the business.

For example, when a customer places an order, the order data flow automatically to other parts of the company that are affected by them. The order transaction triggers the warehouse to pick the ordered products and schedule shipment. The warehouse informs the factory to replenish whatever has been depleted. The accounting department is notified to send the

INTERACTIVE SESSION: MANAGEMENT

PILOTING PROCTER & GAMBLE FROM DECISION COCKPITS

Procter & Gamble (P&G) is one of the biggest consumer goods companies in the world, with 127,000 employees across 180 countries, 300 brands, and $82 billion in revenues in 2011. P&G is regularly ranked near the top of lists of "most admired companies" for its ability to create, market, and sell major consumer product brands. A major reason for P&G's success has been its robust information technology and willingness to pursue new IT innovations to maintain a competitive advantage in its industry.

To that end, P&G has made it its goal to digitize its processes from end to end and to fundamentally change the way it gathers, reports, and interprets data. While P&G is trimming costs from other areas of the business, its Global Business Services division is building analytics expertise and undertaking new analytical solutions such as Business Sufficiency, Business Sphere, and Decision Cockpits.

These solutions eliminate time spent debating different data sets, and instead use a system that allows leaders to focus on immediate business decisions using the most accurate data available at that precise moment.

The solutions are based on a transformation in the way P&G uses data for decision making across the company, from executives, to brand managers, to lower-level employees. P&G's old decision-making model was to figure out what reports people wanted, capture the data, and then deliver them to the key decision makers days or weeks later. The new model is more instantaneous, with people huddling together in person or via video and pulling in the right experts to fix a problem the moment it arises. More real-time data and analytics expertise are required.

The Business Sufficiency program, launched in 2010, furnishes executives with predictions about P&G market share and other key performance metrics six months to one year into the future. It is based on a series of analytic models showing what's occurring in the business right now (shipments, sales, market share), why it's happening, and what actions P&G can take. The "why" models highlight sales data at the country, territory, product line, and store levels, along with drivers such as advertising and consumer consumption, factoring in specific economic data at the regional and country levels. The "actions"

show ways that P&G can adjust pricing, advertising, and product mix to respond to the predictions.

For example, when CEO Bob McDonald meets with his executive committee each Monday, they examine the top categories of products and country markets (such as Italy and hair care) that are responsible for 60 percent of sales. Data visualizations show changes in sales and market share. Executives may want more detailed data: Is the sales dip in detergent in Germany because of one large retailer? Is that retailer buying less only in Germany or across Europe? Did a rival take away market share because P&G raised prices or cut promotions, or is the product category overall losing sales?

P&G's Business Sphere is an interactive system designed to reveal insights, trends, and opportunities for P&G's leaders and prompt them to ask focused business questions that can be addressed with data on the spot. Two giant 32-foot by 8-foot concave display screens physically surround these managers with the data on sales, market share, and ad spending required to make actionable decisions. Thousands of algorithms and analytical models aggregate data, organizing it by country, territory, product line, store level, and other categories, and monitor trends like response to advertising and consumer consumption within individual regions and countries. Everyone in the meeting sees the same information.

The program analyzes 200 terabytes of P&G data, equivalent to 200,000 copies of the Encyclopedia Britannica, and displays information quickly and clearly. The Business Sphere allows top executives to answer their own specific business questions, and to visualize data in a more intuitive way than a simple report allows. The Business Sphere was envisioned as a kind of command center, where top managers gather either in person or via high-quality videoconferencing technology like Cisco TelePresence, and immediately determine the biggest problems facing the business and who can fix those problems as soon as they arise. P&G now has more than 50 Business Spheres around the world.

P&G can now obtain the same data about point of sale, inventory, ad spending, and shipment data that it did years ago—it just obtains that data much faster and at more frequent time intervals. The improved analytics tools at the company's disposal means that the same information is presented with more granularity and specificity than ever before.

The Business Sphere is mostly used by upper-level P&G managers and executives, but the company was determined to extend the same principles deeper within the business. That's where the Decision Cockpits come in. P&G has started to give more of its employees access to the same common data sources—over 58,000 employees now use the technology. These cockpits are dashboards displaying easy-to-read charts illustrating business status and trends. The cockpits feature automated alerts when important events occur, control charts, statistical analyses in real time, and the ability to "drill down" to more detailed levels of data.

One of the major goals of the Decision Cockpits was to eliminate time spent by P&G employees debating the validity of competing versions of data found in e-mails, spreadsheets, letters, and reports. By providing a one-stop source of accurate and detailed real-time business data, all P&G employees are able to focus instead on decisions for improving the business. Both the Business Sphere and Decision Cockpits encourage P&G employees and managers to "manage by exception." This means that by looking at the data

and taking note of the exceptions, such as regions that are losing market share the fastest, or areas that are booming and require more resources, P&G can devote time and energy where it is most needed.

Managers and employees are now able to make faster and better decisions than were previously possible. Other benefits of the project have been the reduced complexity involved in generating a statistical report, as well as cost reductions from maintaining one standardized set of data across the enterprise instead of duplicated, redundant data. P&G has seen the number of e-mails generated by employees drop sharply, as more workers can answer their own questions and obtain their own information using Decision Cockpits. Better messaging and video will help employees pull in anyone needed to make a decision. The company is also able to better anticipate future events affecting the business and more quickly respond to market stimuli.

Sources: Shirish Netke and Ravi Kalakota, "Procter & Gamble — A Case Study in Business Analytics," SmartAnalytics, March 5, 2012; Chris Murphy, "Hard Calls, Big Risks, and Heated Debate," *Information Week*, August 13, 2012; Brian P. Watson, "Data Wrangling: How Procter and Gamble Maximizes Business Analytics," *CIO Insight*, January 30, 2012; Chris Murphy, "Procter & Gamble CIO Filippo Passerini: 2010 Chief Of The Year," *InformationWeek*, December 4, 2010.

CASE STUDY QUESTIONS

1. What management, organization, and technology issues had to be addressed when implementing Business Sufficiency, Business Sphere, and Decision Cockpits?

2. How did these decision-making tools change the way the company ran its business? How effective are they? Why?

3. How are these systems related to P&G's business strategy?

customer an invoice. Customer service representatives track the progress of the order through every step to inform customers about the status of their orders. Managers are able to use firmwide information to make more precise and timely decisions about daily operations and longer-term planning.

Supply Chain Management Systems Firms use **supply chain management (SCM) systems** to help manage relationships with their suppliers. These systems help suppliers, purchasing firms, distributors, and logistics companies share information about orders, production, inventory levels, and delivery of products and services so they can source, produce, and deliver goods and services efficiently. The ultimate objective is to get the right amount of their products from their source to their point of consumption in the least amount of time and at the lowest cost. These systems increase firm profitability by

FIGURE 2.6   ENTERPRISE APPLICATION ARCHITECTURE

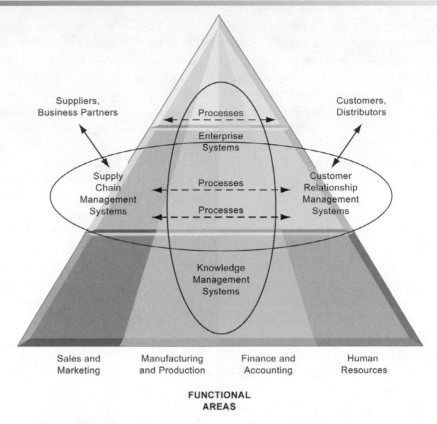

Enterprise applications automate processes that span multiple business functions and organizational levels and may extend outside the organization.

lowering the costs of moving and making products and by enabling managers to make better decisions about how to organize and schedule sourcing, production, and distribution.

Supply chain management systems are one type of **interorganizational system** because they automate the flow of information across organizational boundaries. You will find examples of other types of interorganizational information systems throughout this text because such systems make it possible for firms to link electronically to customers and to outsource their work to other companies.

Customer Relationship Management Systems Firms use **customer relationship management (CRM) systems** to help manage their relationships with their customers. CRM systems provide information to coordinate all of the business processes that deal with customers in sales, marketing, and service to optimize revenue, customer satisfaction, and customer retention. This information helps firms identify, attract, and retain the most profitable customers; provide better service to existing customers; and increase sales.

Knowledge Management Systems Some firms perform better than others because they have better knowledge about how to create, produce, and deliver products and services. This firm knowledge is unique, difficult to imitate, and can be leveraged into long-term strategic benefits. **Knowledge management systems (KMS)** enable organizations to better manage processes for capturing and applying knowledge and expertise. These systems collect all relevant knowledge and experience in the firm, and make it available wherever and whenever it is needed to improve business processes and management decisions. They also link the firm to external sources of knowledge.

We examine enterprise systems and systems for supply chain management and customer relationship management in greater detail in Chapter 9. We discuss collaboration systems that support knowledge management in this chapter and cover other types of knowledge management applications in Chapter 11.

Intranets and Extranets

Enterprise applications create deep-seated changes in the way the firm conducts its business, offering many opportunities to integrate important business data into a single system. They are often costly and difficult to implement. Intranets and extranets deserve mention here as alternative tools for increasing integration and expediting the flow of information within the firm, and with customers ad suppliers.

Intranets are simply internal company Web sites that are accessible only by employees. The term "intranet" refers to an internal network, in contrast to the Internet, which is a public network linking organizations and other external networks. Intranets use the same technologies and techniques as the larger Internet, and they often are simply a private access area in a larger company Web site. Likewise with extranets. Extranets are company Web sites that are accessible to authorized vendors and suppliers, and are often used to coordinate the movement of supplies to the firm's production apparatus.

For example, Six Flags, which operates 19 theme parks throughout North America, maintains an intranet for its 2,500 full-time employees that provides company-related news and information on each park's day-to-day operations, including weather forecasts, performance schedules, and details about groups and celebrities visiting the parks. The company also uses an extranet to broadcast information about schedule changes and park events to its 30,000 seasonal employees. We describe the technology for intranets and extranets in more detail in Chapter 7.

E-BUSINESS, E-COMMERCE, AND E-GOVERNMENT

The systems and technologies we have just described are transforming firms' relationships with customers, employees, suppliers, and logistic partners into digital relationships using networks and the Internet. So much business is now enabled by or based upon digital networks that we use the terms "electronic business" and "electronic commerce" frequently throughout this text.

Electronic business, or **e-business**, refers to the use of digital technology and the Internet to execute the major business processes in the enterprise. E-business includes activities for the internal management of the firm and for coordination with suppliers and other business partners. It also includes **electronic commerce**, or **e-commerce**.

E-commerce is the part of e-business that deals with the buying and selling of goods and services over the Internet. It also encompasses activities supporting those market transactions, such as advertising, marketing, customer support, security, delivery, and payment.

The technologies associated with e-business have also brought about similar changes in the public sector. Governments on all levels are using Internet technology to deliver information and services to citizens, employees, and businesses with which they work. **E-government** refers to the application of the Internet and networking technologies to digitally enable government and public sector agencies' relationships with citizens, businesses, and other arms of government.

In addition to improving delivery of government services, e-government makes government operations more efficient and also empowers citizens by giving them easier access to information and the ability to network electronically with other citizens. For example, citizens in some states can renew their driver's licenses or apply for unemployment benefits online, and the Internet has become a powerful tool for instantly mobilizing interest groups for political action and fund-raising.

2.3 SYSTEMS FOR COLLABORATION AND SOCIAL BUSINESS

With all these systems and information, you might wonder how is it possible to make sense of them? How do people working in firms pull it all together, work towards common goals, and coordinate plans and actions? Information systems can't make decisions, hire or fire people, sign contracts, agree on deals, or adjust the price of goods to the marketplace. In addition to the types of systems we have just described, businesses need special systems to support collaboration and teamwork.

WHAT IS COLLABORATION?

Collaboration is working with others to achieve shared and explicit goals. Collaboration focuses on task or mission accomplishment and usually takes place in a business, or other organization, and between businesses. You collaborate with a colleague in Tokyo having expertise on a topic about which you know nothing. You collaborate with many colleagues in publishing a company blog. If you're in a law firm, you collaborate with accountants in an accounting firm in servicing the needs of a client with tax problems.

Collaboration can be short-lived, lasting a few minutes, or longer term, depending on the nature of the task and the relationship among participants. Collaboration can be one-to-one or many-to-many.

Employees may collaborate in informal groups that are not a formal part of the business firm's organizational structure or they may be organized into formal teams. **Teams** have a specific mission that someone in the business assigned to them. Team members need to collaborate on the accomplishment of specific tasks and collectively achieve the team mission. The team mission might be to "win the game," or "increase online sales by 10 percent." Teams are often short-lived, depending on the problems they tackle and the length of time needed to find a solution and accomplish the mission.

Collaboration and teamwork are more important today than ever for a variety of reasons.

- *Changing nature of work*. The nature of work has changed from factory manufacturing and pre-computer office work where each stage in the production process occurred independently of one another, and was coordinated by supervisors. Work was organized into silos. Within a silo, work passed from one machine tool station to another, from one desktop to another, until the finished product was completed. Today, jobs require much closer coordination and interaction among the parties involved in producing the service or product. A recent report from the consulting firm McKinsey & Company argued that 41 percent of the U.S. labor force is now composed of jobs where interaction (talking, e-mailing, presenting, and persuading) is the primary value-adding activity. Even in factories, workers today often work in production groups, or pods.

- *Growth of professional work.* "Interaction" jobs tend to be professional jobs in the service sector that require close coordination and collaboration. Professional jobs require substantial education, and the sharing of information and opinions to get work done. Each actor on the job brings specialized expertise to the problem, and all the actors need to take one another into account in order to accomplish the job.

- *Changing organization of the firm.* For most of the industrial age, managers organized work in a hierarchical fashion. Orders came down the hierarchy, and responses moved back up the hierarchy. Today, work is organized into groups and teams, and the members are expected to develop their own methods for accomplishing the task. Senior managers observe and measure results, but are much less likely to issue detailed orders or operating procedures. In part, this is because expertise and decision-making power have been pushed down in organizations.

- *Changing scope of the firm.* The work of the firm has changed from a single location to multiple locations—offices or factories throughout a region, a nation, or even around the globe. For instance, Henry Ford developed the first mass-production automobile plant at a single Dearborn, Michigan factory. In 2012, Ford employed over 166,000 people at around 90 plants and facilities worldwide. With this kind of global presence, the need for close coordination of design, production, marketing, distribution, and service obviously takes on new importance and scale. Large global companies need to have teams working on a global basis.

- *Emphasis on innovation.* Although we tend to attribute innovations in business and science to great individuals, these great individuals are most likely working with a team of brilliant colleagues. Think of Bill Gates and Steve Jobs (founders of Microsoft and Apple), both of whom are highly regarded innovators, and both of whom built strong collaborative teams to nurture and support innovation in their firms. Their initial innovations derived from close collaboration with colleagues and partners. Innovation, in other words, is a group and social process, and most innovations derive from collaboration among individuals in a lab, a business, or government agencies. Strong collaborative practices and technologies are believed to increase the rate and quality of innovation.

- *Changing culture of work and business.* Most research on collaboration supports the notion that diverse teams produce better outputs, faster, than individuals working on their own. Popular notions of the crowd ("crowdsourcing," and the "wisdom of crowds") also provide cultural support for collaboration and teamwork.

WHAT IS SOCIAL BUSINESS?

Many firms today enhance collaboration by embracing **social business**—the use of social networking platforms, including Facebook, Twitter, and internal corporate social tools—to engage their employees, customers, and suppliers. These tools enable workers to set up profiles, form groups, and "follow" each other's status updates. The goal of social business is to deepen interactions with groups inside and outside the firm to expedite and enhance information-sharing, innovation, and decision making.

A key word in social business is "conversations." Customers, suppliers, employees, managers, and even oversight agencies continually have conversations about firms, often without the knowledge of the firm or its key actors (employees and managers).

Supporters of social business argue that, if firms could tune into these conversations, they would strengthen their bonds with consumers, suppliers, and employees, increasing their emotional involvement in the firm.

All of this requires a great deal of information transparency. People need to share opinions and facts with others quite directly, without intervention from executives or others. Employees get to know directly what customers and other employees think; suppliers will learn very directly the opinions of supply chain partners; and even managers presumably will learn more directly from their employees how well they are doing. Nearly everyone involved in the creation of value will know much more about everyone else.

If such an environment could be created, it is likely to drive operational efficiencies, spur innovation, and accelerate decision making. If product designers can learn directly about how their products are doing in the market in real time, based on consumer feedback, they can speed up the redesign process. If employees can use social connections inside and outside the company to capture new knowledge and insights, they will be able to work more efficiently and solve more business problems.

Table 2.2 describes important applications of social business inside and outside the firm. This chapter focuses on enterprise social business—its internal corporate uses. Chapters 7 and 10 describe social business applications relating to customers and suppliers outside the company.

BUSINESS BENEFITS OF COLLABORATION AND SOCIAL BUSINESS

Although many articles and books have been written about collaboration, nearly all of the research on this topic is anecdotal. Nevertheless, there is a general belief among both business and academic communities that the more a business firm is "collaborative," the more successful it will be, and that collaboration within and among firms is more essential than in the past. A recent global survey of business and information systems managers found that investments in collaboration technology produced organizational improvements that returned over four times the amount of the investment, with the greatest benefits for sales, marketing, and research and development functions (Frost and White, 2009).

TABLE 2.2 APPLICATIONS OF SOCIAL BUSINESS

SOCIAL BUSINESS APPLICATION	DESCRIPTION
Social networks	Connect through personal and business profiles
Crowdsourcing	Harness collective knowledge to generate new ideas and solutions
Shared workspaces	Coordinate projects and tasks; co-create content
Blogs and wikis	Publish and rapidly access knowledge; discuss opinions and experiences
Social commerce	Share opinions about purchasing or purchase on social platforms
File sharing	Upload, share, and comment on photos, videos, audio, text documents
Social marketing	Use social media to interact with customers; derive customer insights
Communities	Discuss topics in open forums; share expertise

TABLE 2.3 **BUSINESS BENEFITS OF COLLABORATION AND SOCIAL BUSINESS**

BENEFIT	RATIONALE
Productivity	People interacting and working together can capture expert knowledge and solve problems more rapidly than the same number of people working in isolation from one another. There will be fewer errors.
Quality	People working collaboratively can communicate errors, and corrective actions faster than if they work in isolation. Collaborative and take social technologies help reduce time delays in design and production.
Innovation	People working collaboratively can come up with more innovative ideas for products, services, and administration than the same number working in isolation from one another. Advantages to diversity and the "wisdom of crowds."
Customer service	People working together using collaboration and social tools can solve customer complaints and issues faster and more effectively than if they were working in isolation from one another.
Financial performance (profitability, sales, and sales growth)	As a result of all of the above, collaborative firms have superior sales, sales growth, and financial performance.

Another study of the value of collaboration also found that the overall economic benefit of collaboration was significant: for every word seen by an employee in e-mails from others, $70 of additional revenue was generated (Aral, Brynjolfsson, and Van Alstyne, 2007). McKinsey & Company consultants predict that social technologies used within and across enterprises could potentially raise the productivity of interaction workers by 20 to 25 percent (McKinsey, 2012).

Table 2.3 summarizes some of the benefits of collaboration and social business that have been identified. Figure 2.7 graphically illustrates how collaboration is believed to impact business performance.

BUILDING A COLLABORATIVE CULTURE AND BUSINESS PROCESSES

Collaboration won't take place spontaneously in a business firm, especially if there is no supportive culture or business processes. Business firms, especially large firms, had a reputation in the past for being "command and control" organizations where the top leaders thought up all the really important matters, and then ordered lower-level employees to execute senior management plans. The job of middle management supposedly was to pass messages back and forth, up and down the hierarchy.

Command and control firms required lower-level employees to carry out orders without asking too many questions, with no responsibility to improve processes, and with no rewards for teamwork or team performance. If your work group needed help from another work group, that was something for the bosses to figure out. You never communicated horizontally, always vertically, so management could control the process. Together, the expectations of management and employees formed a culture, a set of assumptions about common goals and how people should behave. Many business firms still operate this way.

A collaborative business culture and business processes are very different. Senior managers are responsible for achieving results, but rely on teams of employees to achieve and implement the results. Policies, products, designs,

FIGURE 2.7 **REQUIREMENTS FOR COLLABORATION**

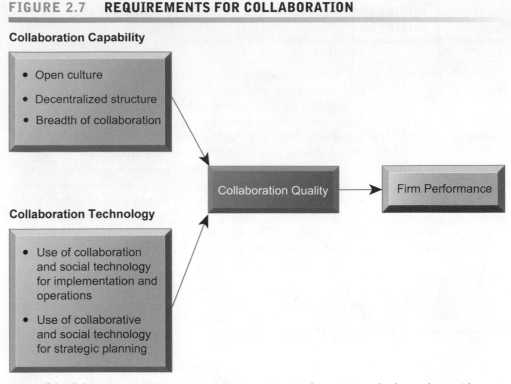

Collaboration Capability

- Open culture
- Decentralized structure
- Breadth of collaboration

Collaboration Technology

- Use of collaboration and social technology for implementation and operations
- Use of collaborative and social technology for strategic planning

Collaboration Quality → Firm Performance

Successful collaboration requires an appropriate organizational structure and culture, along with appropriate collaboration technology.

processes, and systems are much more dependent on teams at all levels of the organization to devise, to create, and to build. Teams are rewarded for their performance, and individuals are rewarded for their performance in a team. The function of middle managers is to build the teams, coordinate their work, and monitor their performance. The business culture and business processes are more "social." In a collaborative culture, senior management establishes collaboration and teamwork as vital to the organization, and it actually implements collaboration for the senior ranks of the business as well.

TOOLS AND TECHNOLOGIES FOR COLLABORATION AND SOCIAL BUSINESS

A collaborative, team-oriented culture won't produce benefits without information systems in place to enable collaboration and social business. Hundreds of tools are designed to deal with the fact that, in order to succeed in our jobs, we must depend on one another—our fellow employees, customers, suppliers, and managers. Some high-end tools like IBM Lotus Notes are expensive, but powerful enough for global firms. Others are available online for free (or with premium versions for a modest fee) and are suitable for small businesses. Let's look more closely at some of these tools.

E-mail and Instant Messaging (IM)

E-mail and instant messaging (including text messaging) have been major communication and collaboration tools for interaction jobs. Their software operates on computers, cell phones, and other wireless handheld devices and includes features for sharing files as well as transmitting messages. Many instant messaging systems allow users to engage in real-time conversations with multiple participants simultaneously. In recent years, e-mail use has declined, with messaging and social media becoming preferred channels of communication.

Wikis

Wikis are a type of Web site that makes it easy for users to contribute and edit text content and graphics without any knowledge of Web page development or programming techniques. The most well-known wiki is Wikipedia, the largest collaboratively edited reference project in the world. It relies on volunteers, makes no money, and accepts no advertising.

Wikis are very useful tools for storing and sharing corporate knowledge and insights. Enterprise software vendor SAP AG has a wiki that acts as a base of information for people outside the company, such as customers and software developers who build programs that interact with SAP software. In the past, those people asked and sometimes answered questions in an informal way on SAP online forums, but that was an inefficient system, with people asking and answering the same questions over and over.

Virtual Worlds

Virtual worlds, such as Second Life, are online 3-D environments populated by "residents" who have built graphical representations of themselves known as avatars. Organizations such as IBM and Insead, an international business school with campuses in France and Singapore, are using this virtual world to house online meetings, training sessions, and "lounges." Real-world people represented by avatars meet, interact, and exchange ideas at these virtual locations using gestures, chat box conversations, and voice communication (which requires microphones).

Collaboration and Social Business Platforms

There are now suites of software products providing multi-function platforms for collaboration and social business among teams of employees who work together from many different locations. The most widely used are Internet-based audio conferencing and videoconferencing systems, online software services such as Google Apps/Google Sites, cyberlockers, corporate collaboration systems such as Lotus Notes and Microsoft SharePoint, and enterprise social networking tools such as Salesforce Chatter, Microsoft Yammer, Jive, and IBM Connections and SmartCloud for Business.

Virtual Meeting Systems In an effort to reduce travel expenses, many companies, both large and small, are adopting videoconferencing and Web conferencing technologies. Companies such as Heinz, General Electric, Pepsico, and Wachovia are using virtual meeting systems for product briefings, training courses, strategy sessions, and even inspirational chats.

A videoconference allows individuals at two or more locations to communicate simultaneously through two-way video and audio transmissions. High-end videoconferencing systems feature **telepresence** technology, an integrated audio and visual environment that allows a person to give the appearance of being present at a location other than his or her true physical location. Free or low-cost Internet-based systems such as Skype group videoconferencing, Zoom.us, and ooVoo are of lower quality, but still useful for smaller companies. Apple's FaceTime and Google video chat tools are useful tools for one-to-one videoconferencing.

Companies of all sizes are finding Web-based online meeting tools such as Cisco WebEx, Microsoft Live Meeting, and Adobe Connect especially helpful for training and sales presentations. These products enable participants to share documents and presentations in conjunction with audio conferencing and live video via Webcam.

Google Apps/Google Sites and Cloud Collaboration Services One of the most widely used "free" online services for collaboration is Google Apps/Google Sites. Google Sites allows users to quickly create online group-editable Web sites. Google Sites is one part of the larger Google Apps suite of tools. Google Sites users can design and populate Web sites in minutes and can, without any advanced technical skills, post a variety of files including calendars, text, spreadsheets, and videos for private, group, or public viewing and editing.

Google Apps work with Google Sites and include the typical desktop productivity office software tools (word processing, spreadsheet, presentation, contact management, messaging, and mail). A Premier edition charging businesses $50 per year for each user offers 25 gigabytes of mail storage, a 99.9 percent uptime guarantee for e-mail, tools to integrate with the firm's existing infrastructure, and 24/7 phone support. Table 2.4 describes some of the capabilities of Google Apps/GoogleSites.

Google Drive is an example of a cloud-based **cyberlocker**. Cyberlockers are online file-sharing services that allow users to upload files to secure online storage sites from which the files can be shared with others. Google Drive offers 5 free gigabytes of online storage, with additional monthly charges for more storage up to 16 terabytes. This service works on multiple operating systems, browsers, and mobile devices. Users can create and edit some types of documents online, synchronize these files with all of their devices, and share them with other people. Google Docs is built into Google Drive, enabling users to work in real-time on documents, spreadsheets, and presentations and receive notifications when there are comments.

Other cyberlocker services used for collaboration include Dropbox and Microsoft SkyDrive, with both free and paid services, depending on the amount of storage space required. Users are able to synchronize their files stored online

TABLE 2.4 GOOGLE APPS/GOOGLE SITES COLLABORATION FEATURES

GOOGLE APPS/GOOGLE SITES CAPABILITY	DESCRIPTION
Google Calendar	Private and shared calendars; multiple calendars.
Google Gmail	Google's free online e-mail service, with mobile access capabilities
Google Talk	Instant messaging; text, voice, and voice chat
Google Docs	Online word processing, electronic presentation software, spreadsheets; drawings; online editing, sharing, publishing
Google Sites	Team collaboration sites for sharing of documents, schedules, calendars, searching documents; creation of group wikis
Google Drive	Offers 5 free gigabytes of online storage for 30 types of documents as well as images and HD video; users can create and edit some types of documents online and synchronize these files with all of their devices; ability to view, comment, or edit files based on different usage rights and to keep the files private

with their local PCs and many other kinds of devices, with options for making the files private or public and sharing them with designated contacts. Microsoft SkyDrive offers 7 gigabytes of free online storage for Office documents and other files and works with Microsoft's Web versions of Word, Excel, PowerPoint, and OneNote called Office Web Apps. Dropbox (offering 2 gigabytes of free storage) itself does not include tools for document creation and editing.

Microsoft SharePoint Microsoft SharePoint is a browser-based collaboration and document management platform, combined with a powerful search engine that is installed on corporate servers. SharePoint has a Web-based interface and close integration with everyday tools such as Microsoft Office desktop software products. SharePoint software makes it possible for employees to share their documents and collaborate on projects using Office documents as the foundation.

SharePoint can be used to host internal Web sites that organize and store information in one central workspace to enable teams to coordinate work activities, collaborate on and publish documents, maintain task lists, implement workflows, and share information via wikis and blogs. Users are able to control versions of documents and document security. Because SharePoint stores and organizes information in one place, users can find relevant information quickly and efficiently while working together closely on tasks, projects, and documents. Enterprise search tools help locate people, expertise, and content. As noted in the chapter-opening case, SharePoint has recently added social tools.

ICA is a large Mexican construction company specializing in infrastructure projects, with operations in North, South, and Central America and Europe. The company implemented Microsoft SharePoint Server 2010 to organize the 500,000 documents used by its 3,000 employees daily. ICA employees can now immediately locate the documents and internal expertise they need to finish projects on time and within budget. Project documentation is far more secure, and ICA has created online communities where it can capture the knowledge of internal experts (Microsoft, 2011).

Lotus Notes Lotus Notes was an early example of groupware, a collaborative software system with capabilities for sharing calendars, collective writing and editing, shared database access, and electronic meetings, with each participant able to see and display information from others and other activities. Notes software installed on desktop or laptop computers obtains applications stored on an IBM Lotus Domino server. Lotus Notes is now Web-enabled with a scripting and application development environment so that users can build custom applications to suit their unique needs.

Notes software installed on the user's client computer allows the machine to be used as a platform for e-mail, instant messaging (working with Lotus Sametime), Web browsing, and calendar/resource reservation work, as well as for interacting with collaborative applications. Today, Notes also has capabilities for blogs, microblogs, wikis, RSS aggregators, help desk systems, voice and videoconferencing, and online meetings.

Large firms adopt IBM Lotus Notes because Notes promises high levels of security and reliability, and the ability to retain control over sensitive corporate information. For example, the Magnum AS Group, which specializes in wholesale and retail sales of pharmaceuticals and medical supplies throughout the Baltic States, uses Lotus Notes to manage more than 500,000 documents and meet strict regulatory requirements. The software provides a central document repository with full version control for all company documentation, which includes written documents, spreadsheets, images, PDF files, and e-mails. Users are able to find the latest version of a document with a single search. Documents can only be edited by authorized users, enhancing security and simplifying compliance with the stringent regulations and audit requirements of the international pharmaceuticals industry (IBM, 2010).

Two related IBM Lotus products provide more specialized teamwork and social networking tools and are able to access information from Lotus Notes. IBM Lotus Quickr helps teams of people share documents and information using team spaces, content libraries, discussion forums, and wikis. IBM Connections supports internal corporate social networking with capabilities for searchable profiles, communities, blogs, activities, wikis, and forums.

Roland Corporation, a Japanese manufacturer of electric musical instruments, musical amplifiers, professional video and audio, and computer music equipment, uses Lotus Quickr and IBM Connections to foster creativity and collaboration among its 3,100 employees worldwide. It now has an "electronic public square" that facilitates sharing of concepts and ideas as they develop. Lotus Quickr helps the company manage and track projects, such as a new product launch where 90 percent of the 200 employees involved worked overseas. The software gathered and stored all the product launch information and made it much easier to set up Web sites for the accompanying sales activities. Connections increased the visibility of the specialists and expertise within the company and helped employees informally share information and ideas (IBM, 2011).

Enterprise Social Networking Tools The tools we have just described include capabilities for supporting social business, but there are also more specialized social tools for this purpose, such as Salesforce Chatter, Microsoft's Yammer, Jive, and IBM Connections. Enterprise social networking tools create business value by connecting the members of an organization through profiles, updates, and notifications, similar to Facebook features, but tailored to internal corporate uses. IBM recently introduced a set of social business tools running on a cloud platform called SmartCloud for Social Business, featuring user profiles, communities, e-mail, instant messaging, Web meetings, calendars, personal dashboards, and file sharing.

Table 2.5 provides more detail about these internal social capabilities.

TABLE 2.5 ENTERPRISE SOCIAL NETWORKING SOFTWARE CAPABILITIES

SOCIAL SOFTWARE CAPABILITY	DESCRIPTION
Profiles	Ability to set up member profiles describing who individuals are, educational background, interests. Includes work-related associations and expertise (skills, projects, teams).
Content sharing	Share, store, and manage content including documents, presentations, images, and videos.
Feeds and notifications	Real-time information streams, status updates, and announcements from designated individuals and groups.
Groups and team workspaces	Establish groups to share information, collaborate on documents, and work on projects, with the ability to set up private and public groups and to archive conversations to preserve team knowledge.
Tagging and social bookmarking	Indicate preferences for specific pieces of content, similar to the Facebook Like button. Tagging lets people add keywords to identify content they like.
Permissions and privacy	Ability to make sure private information stays within the right circles, as determined by the nature of relationships. In enterprise social networks, there is a need to establish who in the company has permission to see what information.

Dallas-based 7-Eleven Inc. has about 2,000 employees who have used Yammer since May 2011. The convenience store chain deployed the application to help field consultants, who work with local franchise owners, share their knowledge and learn best practices from one another. For example, someone might post a picture of a display that worked particularly well in one franchise location for others to see and try in their locations. The social software creates a "virtual water cooler" environment where people are able to talk about what's going on in an informal way yet have formal documentation to keep track of best practices.

Although 7-Eleven and other companies have benefited from enterprise social networking, internal social networking has not caught on as quickly as consumer uses of Facebook, Twitter, and other public social networking products.

Checklist for Managers: Evaluating and Selecting Collaboration and Social Software Tools

With so many collaboration and social business tools and services available, how do you choose the right collaboration technology for your firm? To answer this question, you need a framework for understanding just what problems these tools are designed to solve. One framework that has been helpful for us to talk about collaboration tools is the time/space collaboration matrix developed in the early 1990s by a number of collaborative work scholars (Figure 2.8).

The time/space matrix focuses on two dimensions of the collaboration problem: time and space. For instance, you need to collaborate with people in different time zones and you cannot all meet at the same time. Midnight in New York is noon in Bombay, so this makes it difficult to have a videoconference (the people in New York are too tired). Time is clearly an obstacle to collaboration on a global scale.

FIGURE 2.8   THE TIME/SPACE COLLABORATION AND SOCIAL TOOL MATRIX

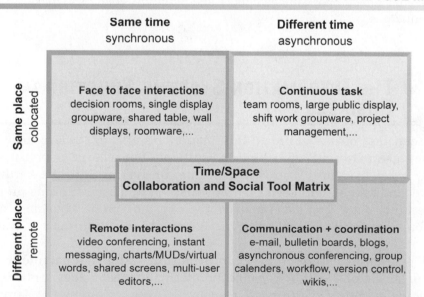

Collaboration and social technologies can be classified in terms of whether they support interactions at the same or different time or place, and whether these interactions are remote or colocated.

Place (location) also inhibits collaboration in large global or even national and regional firms. Assembling people for a physical meeting is made difficult by the physical dispersion of distributed firms (firms with more than one location), the cost of travel, and the time limitations of managers.

The collaboration and social technologies we have just described are ways of overcoming the limitations of time and space. Using this time/space framework will help you to choose the most appropriate collaboration and teamwork tools for your firm. Note that some tools are applicable in more than one time/place scenario. For example, Internet collaboration suites such as Lotus Notes have capabilities for both synchronous (instant messaging, electronic meeting tools) and asynchronous (e-mail, wikis, document editing) interactions.

Here's a "to-do" list to get started. If you follow these six steps, you should be led to investing in the correct collaboration software for your firm at a price you can afford, and within your risk tolerance.

1. What are the collaboration challenges facing the firm in terms of time and space? Locate your firm in the time/space matrix. Your firm can occupy more than one cell in the matrix. Different collaboration tools will be needed for each situation.

2. Within each cell of the matrix where your firm faces challenges, exactly what kinds of solutions are available? Make a list of vendor products.

3. Analyze each of the products in terms of their cost and benefits to your firm. Be sure to include the costs of training in your cost estimates, and the costs of involving the information systems department, if needed.

4. Identify the risks to security and vulnerability involved with each of the products. Is your firm willing to put proprietary information into the hands of external service providers over the Internet? Is your firm willing to risk its important operations to systems controlled by other firms? What are the financial risks facing your vendors? Will they be here in three to five years? What would be the cost of making a switch to another vendor in the event the vendor firm fails?

5. Seek the help of potential users to identify implementation and training issues. Some of these tools are easier to use than others.

6. Make your selection of candidate tools, and invite the vendors to make presentations.

2.4 THE INFORMATION SYSTEMS FUNCTION IN BUSINESS

We've seen that businesses need information systems to operate today and that they use many different kinds of systems. But who is responsible for running these systems? Who is responsible for making sure the hardware, software, and other technologies used by these systems are running properly and are up to date? End users manage their systems from a business standpoint, but managing the technology requires a special information systems function.

In all but the smallest of firms, the **information systems department** is the formal organizational unit responsible for information technology services. The information systems department is responsible for maintaining the hardware, software, data storage, and networks that comprise the firm's IT infrastructure. We describe IT infrastructure in detail in Chapter 5.

THE INFORMATION SYSTEMS DEPARTMENT

The information systems department consists of specialists, such as programmers, systems analysts, project leaders, and information systems managers. **Programmers** are highly trained technical specialists who write the software instructions for computers. **Systems analysts** constitute the principal liaisons between the information systems groups and the rest of the organization. It is the systems analyst's job to translate business problems and requirements into information requirements and systems. **Information systems managers** are leaders of teams of programmers and analysts, project managers, physical facility managers, telecommunications managers, or database specialists. They are also managers of computer operations and data entry staff. Also, external specialists, such as hardware vendors and manufacturers, software firms, and consultants, frequently participate in the day-to-day operations and long-term planning of information systems.

In many companies, the information systems department is headed by a **chief information officer (CIO)**. The CIO is a senior manager who oversees the use of information technology in the firm. Today's CIOs are expected to have a strong business background as well as information systems expertise and to play a leadership role in integrating technology into the firm's business strategy. Large firms today also have positions for a chief security officer, chief knowledge officer, and chief privacy officer, all of whom work closely with the CIO.

The **chief security officer (CSO)** is in charge of information systems security for the firm and is responsible for enforcing the firm's information security policy (see Chapter 8). (Sometimes this position is called the chief information security officer [CISO] where information systems security is separated from physical security.) The CSO is responsible for educating and training users and information systems specialists about security, keeping management aware of security threats and breakdowns, and maintaining the tools and policies chosen to implement security.

Information systems security and the need to safeguard personal data have become so important that corporations collecting vast quantities of personal data have established positions for a **chief privacy officer (CPO)**. The CPO is responsible for ensuring that the company complies with existing data privacy laws.

The **chief knowledge officer (CKO)** is responsible for the firm's knowledge management program. The CKO helps design programs and systems to find new sources of knowledge or to make better use of existing knowledge in organizational and management processes.

End users are representatives of departments outside of the information systems group for whom applications are developed. These users are playing an increasingly large role in the design and development of information systems.

In the early years of computing, the information systems group was composed mostly of programmers who performed highly specialized but limited technical functions. Today, a growing proportion of staff members are systems analysts and network specialists, with the information systems department acting as a powerful change agent in the organization. The information systems department suggests new business strategies and new information-based products and services, and coordinates both the development of the technology and the planned changes in the organization.

In the next five years, employment growth in IS/MIS jobs will be about 50 percent greater than the average job growth in other fields. Out of 114 occupations, MIS is ranked 15th in terms of salaries. While all IS occupations show above-average growth, the fastest growing occupations are computer support specialists (30%), systems analysts (21%), software engineers and programmers (20%), and information systems managers (17%) (Bureau of Labor Statistics, 2012). With businesses and government agencies increasingly relying on the Internet for computing and communication resources, system and network security management positions are especially in demand. See the Learning Track for this chapter titled "Occupational and Career Outlook for Information Systems Majors 2012–2018" for more details on IS job opportunities.

ORGANIZING THE INFORMATION SYSTEMS FUNCTION

There are many types of business firms, and there are many ways in which the IT function is organized within the firm. A very small company will not have a formal information systems group. It might have one employee who is responsible for keeping its networks and applications running, or it might use consultants for these services. Larger companies will have a separate information systems department, which may be organized along several different lines, depending on the nature and interests of the firm. Our Learning Track describes alternative ways of organizing the information systems function within the business.

The question of how the information systems department should be organized is part of the larger issue of IT governance. **IT governance** includes the strategy and policies for using information technology within an organization. It specifies the decision rights and framework for accountability to ensure that the use of information technology supports the organization's strategies and objectives. How much should the information systems function be centralized? What decisions must be made to ensure effective management and use of information technology, including the return on IT investments? Who should make these decisions? How will these decisions be made and monitored? Firms with superior IT governance will have clearly thought out the answers (Weill and Ross, 2004).

LEARNING TRACK MODULES

The following Learning Tracks provide content relevant to topics covered in this chapter:

1. Systems from a Functional Perspective
2. IT Enables Collaboration and Teamwork
3. Challenges of Using Business Information Systems
4. Organizing the Information Systems Function
5. Occupational and Career Outlook for Information Systems Majors 2012–2018

Review Summary

1. *What are business processes? How are they related to information systems?*

   A business process is a logically related set of activities that defines how specific business tasks are performed, and it represents a unique way in which an organization coordinates work, information, and knowledge. Managers need to pay attention to business processes because they determine how well the organization can execute its business, and they may be a source of strategic advantage. There are business processes specific to each of the major business functions, but many business processes are cross-functional. Information systems automate parts of business processes, and they can help organizations redesign and streamline these processes.

2. *How do systems serve the different management groups in a business?*

   Systems serving operational management are transaction processing systems (TPS), such as payroll or order processing, that track the flow of the daily routine transactions necessary to conduct business. Management information systems (MIS) produce reports serving middle management by condensing information from TPS, and these are not highly analytical. Decision-support systems (DSS) support management decisions that are unique and rapidly changing using advanced analytical models. All of these types of systems provide business intelligence that helps managers and enterprise employees make more informed decisions. These systems for business intelligence serve multiple levels of management, and include executive support systems (ESS) for senior management that provide data in the form of graphs, charts, and dashboards delivered via portals using many sources of internal and external information.

3. *How do systems that link the enterprise improve organizational performance?*

   Enterprise applications are designed to coordinate multiple functions and business processes. Enterprise systems integrate the key internal business processes of a firm into a single software system to improve coordination and decision making. Supply chain management systems help the firm manage its relationship with suppliers to optimize the planning, sourcing, manufacturing, and delivery of products and services. Customer relationship management (CRM) systems coordinate the business processes surrounding the firm's customers. Knowledge management systems enable firms to optimize the creation, sharing, and distribution of knowledge. Intranets and extranets are private corporate networks based on Internet technology that assemble information from disparate systems. Extranets make portions of private corporate intranets available to outsiders.

4. *Why are systems for collaboration and social business so important and what technologies do they use?*

   Collaboration is working with others to achieve shared and explicit goals. Social business is the use of internal and external social networking platforms to engage employees, customers, and suppliers, and it can enhance collaborative work. Collaboration and social business have become increasingly important in business because of globalization, the decentralization of decision making, and growth in jobs where interaction is the primary value-adding activity. Collaboration and social business enhance innovation, productivity, quality, and customer service. Tools for collaboration and social business include e-mail and instant messaging, wikis, virtual meeting systems, virtual worlds, cyberlockers, collaboration platforms such as Google Sites/Google Apps, Microsoft SharePoint, and Lotus Notes, and enterprise social networking tools such as Chatter, Yammer, Jive, and IBM Connections.

5. *What is the role of the information systems function in a business?*

   The information systems department is the formal organizational unit responsible for information technology services. It is responsible for maintaining the hardware, software, data storage, and networks that comprise the firm's IT infrastructure. The department consists of specialists, such as programmers, systems analysts, project leaders, and information systems managers, and is often headed by a CIO.

Key Terms

Business intelligence, 77
Chief information officer (CIO), 99
Chief knowledge officer (CKO), 99
Chief privacy officer (CPO), 99
Chief security officer (CSO), 99
Collaboration, 88
Customer relationship management (CRM) systems, 86
Cyberlockers, 94
Decision-support systems (DSS), 79
Digital dashboard, 82
Electronic business (e-business), 87
Electronic commerce (e-commerce), 87
E-government, 87
End users, 99
Enterprise applications, 83

Enterprise systems, 83
Executive support systems (ESS), 82
Information systems department, 98
Information systems managers, 99
Interorganizational system, 86
IT governance, 100
Knowledge management systems (KMS), 86
Management information systems (MIS), 77
Portal, 82
Programmers, 99
Social business, 89
Supply chain management (SCM) systems, 85
Systems analysts, 99
Teams, 88
Telepresence, 93
Transaction processing systems (TPS), 76

Review Questions

1. What are business processes? How are they related to information systems?

- Define business processes and describe the role they play in organizations.
- Describe the relationship between information systems and business processes.

2. How do systems serve the different management groups in a business?

- Describe the characteristics of transaction processing systems (TPS) and the roles they play in a business.
- Describe the characteristics of management information systems (MIS) and explain how MIS differ from TPS and from DSS.
- Describe the characteristics of decision-support systems (DSS) and how they benefit businesses.
- Describe the characteristics of executive support systems (ESS) and explain how these systems differ from DSS.

3. How do systems that link the enterprise improve organizational performance?

- Explain how enterprise applications improve organizational performance.
- Define enterprise systems, supply chain management systems, customer relationship

management systems, and knowledge management systems and describe their business benefits.

- Explain how intranets and extranets help firms integrate information and business processes.

4. Why are systems for collaboration and social business so important and what technologies do they use?

- Define collaboration and social business, and explain why they have become so important in business today.
- List and describe the business benefits of collaboration and social business.
- Describe a supportive organizational culture and business processes for collaboration.
- List and describe the various types of collaboration and social business tools.

5. What is the role of the information systems function in a business?

- Describe how the information systems function supports a business.
- Compare the roles played by programmers, systems analysts, information systems managers, the chief information officer (CIO), chief security officer (CSO), and chief knowledge officer (CKO).

Discussion Questions

1. How could information systems be used to support the order fulfillment process illustrated in Figure 2.1? What are the most important pieces of information these systems should capture? Explain your answer.

2. Identify the steps that are performed in the process of selecting and checking out a book from your college library and the information that flows among these activities. Diagram the process. Are there any ways this process could be improved to improve the performance of your library or your school? Diagram the improved process.

3. Use the Time/Space Collaboration and Social Tool Matrix to classify the collaboration and social technologies used by TELUS.

Hands-On MIS Projects

The projects in this section give you hands-on experience analyzing opportunities to improve business processes with new information system applications, using a spreadsheet to improve decision making about suppliers, and using Internet software to plan efficient transportation routes.

Management Decision Problems

1. Don's Lumber Company on the Hudson River features a large selection of materials for flooring, decks, moldings, windows, siding, and roofing. The prices of lumber and other building materials are constantly changing. When a customer inquires about the price on pre-finished wood flooring, sales representatives consult a manual price sheet and then call the supplier for the most recent price. The supplier in turn uses a manual price sheet, which has been updated each day. Often, the supplier must call back Don's sales reps because the company does not have the newest pricing information immediately on hand. Assess the business impact of this situation, describe how this process could be improved with information technology, and identify the decisions that would have to be made to implement a solution.

2. Henry's Hardware is a small family business in Sacramento, California. The owners, Henry and Kathleen, must use every square foot of store space as profitably as possible. They have never kept detailed inventory or sales records. As soon as a shipment of goods arrives, the items are immediately placed on store shelves. Invoices from suppliers are only kept for tax purposes. When an item is sold, the item number and price are rung up at the cash register. The owners use their own judgment in identifying items that need to be reordered. What is the business impact of this situation? How could information systems help Henry and Kathleen run their business? What data should these systems capture? What decisions could the systems improve?

Improving Decision Making: Using a Spreadsheet to Select Suppliers

Software skills: Spreadsheet date functions, data filtering, DAVERAGE function
Business skills: Analyzing supplier performance and pricing

In this exercise, you will learn how to use spreadsheet software to improve management decisions about selecting suppliers. You will filter transactional data on suppliers based on several different criteria to select the best suppliers for your company.

You run a company that manufactures aircraft components. You have many competitors who are trying to offer lower prices and better service to customers, and you are trying to determine whether you can benefit from better supply chain management. In MyMISLab, you will find a spreadsheet file that contains a list of all of the items that your firm has ordered from its suppliers during the past three months. The fields in the spreadsheet file include vendor name, vendor identification number, purchaser's order number, item identification number and item description (for each item ordered from the vendor), cost per item, number of units of the item ordered (quantity), total cost of each order, vendor's accounts payable terms, order date, and actual arrival date for each order.

Prepare a recommendation of how you can use the data in this spreadsheet database to improve your decisions about selecting suppliers. Some criteria to consider for identifying preferred suppliers include the supplier's track record for on-time deliveries, suppliers offering the best accounts payable terms, and suppliers offering lower pricing when the same item can be provided by multiple suppliers. Use your spreadsheet software to prepare reports to support your recommendations.

Achieving Operational Excellence: Using Internet Software to Plan Efficient Transportation Routes

Software skills: Internet-based software
Business skills: Transportation planning

In this exercise, you will use MapQuest software to map out transportation routes for a business and select the most efficient route.

You have just started working as a dispatcher for Cross-Country Transport, a new trucking and delivery service based in Cleveland, Ohio. Your first assignment is to plan a delivery of office equipment and furniture from Elkhart, Indiana (at the corner of E. Indiana Ave. and Prairie Street) to Hagerstown, Maryland (corner of Eastern Blvd. N. and Potomac Ave.).To guide your trucker, you need to know the most efficient route between the two cities. Use MapQuest to find the route that is the shortest distance between the two cities. Use MapQuest again to find the route that takes the least time. Compare the results. Which route should Cross-Country use?

Video Cases

Video Cases and Instructional Videos illustrating some of the concepts in this chapter are available. Contact your instructor to access these videos.

Collaboration and Teamwork Project

In MyMISLab, you will find a Collaboration and Teamwork Project dealing with the concepts in this chapter. You will be able to use Google Sites, Google Docs, and other open-source collaboration tools to complete the assignment.

Modernization of NTUC Income
CASE STUDY

NTUC Income ("Income"), one of Singapore's largest insurers, has over 1.8 million policy holders with total assets of S$21.3 billion. The insurer employs about 3,400 insurance advisors and 1,200 office staff, with the majority located across an eight-branch network. On June 1, 2003, Income succeeded in the migration of its legacy insurance systems to a digital web-based system. The Herculean task required not only the upgrading of hardware and applications, it also required Income to streamline its decade-old business processes and IT practices.

Until a few years ago, Income's insurance processes were very tedious and paper-based. The entire insurance process started with customers meeting an agent, filling in forms and submitting documents. The agent would then submit the forms at branches, from where they were sent by couriers to the Office Services department. The collection schedule could introduce delays of two to three days. Office Services would log documents, sort them, and then send them to departments for underwriting. Proposals were allocated to underwriting staff, mostly at random. Accepted proposals were sent for printing at the Computer Services department and then redistributed. For storage, all original documents were packed and sent to warehouses where, over two to three days, a total of seven staff would log and store the documents. In all, paper policies comprising 45 million documents were stored in over 16,000 cartons at three warehouses. Whenever a document needed to be retrieved, it would take about two days to locate and ship it by courier. Refiling would again take about two days.

In 2002, despite periodic investments to upgrade the HP 3000 mainframe that hosted the core insurance applications as well as the accounting and management information systems, it still frequently broke down. When a system breakdown did occur, work had to be stopped while data was restored. Additionally, the HP 3000 backup system could only restore the data to the version from the previous day. This meant that backups had to be performed at the end of every day in a costly and tedious process, or the company would risk losing important data. In one of the hardware crashes, it took several months to recover the lost data. In all, the HP 3000 system experienced a total of three major hardware failures, resulting in a total of six days of complete downtime.

That was not enough. The COBOL programs that were developed in the early 1980s and maintained by Income's in-house IT team also broke multiple times, halted the systems, and caused temporary interruptions. In addition, the IT team found developing new products in COBOL to be quite cumbersome and the time taken to launch new products ranged from a few weeks to months.

At the same time, transaction processing for policy underwriting was still a batch process and information was not available to agents and advisors in real-time. As a result, when staff processed a new customer application for motor insurance, they did not know if the applicant was an existing customer of Income, which led to the loss of opportunities for cross-product sales, as staff had to pass physical documents between each other and there was no means of viewing an up-to-date report on a customer's history on demand. Furthermore, compatibility issues between the HP 3000 and employees' notebooks caused ongoing problems, especially with a rise in telecommuting.

All this changed in June 2003, when Income switched to the Java based eBao LifeSystem from eBao Technology. The software comprised three sub-systems - Policy Administration, Sales Management and Supplementary Resources — and fulfilled many of the company's requirements, from customer-orientated design to barcode technology capabilities, and the ability to support changes in business processes.

Implementation work started in September 2002 and the project was completed in nine months. By May 2003, all the customization, data migration of Income's individual and group life insurance businesses and training were completed.

The new system was immediately operational on a high-availability platform. All applications resided on two or more servers, each connected by two or more communication lines, all of which were "load balanced." This robust architecture minimized downtime occurrence due to hardware or operating system failures.

As part of eBao implementation, Income decided to replace its entire IT infrastructure with a more robust, scalable architecture. For example, all servicing branches were equipped with scanners; monitors were changed to 20 inches; PC RAM size was upgraded to 128 MB; and new hardware and software for application servers, database servers, web servers, and disk storage systems were installed. Furthermore, the LAN cables were replaced with faster cables, a fiber-optic backbone, and wireless capability.

In addition, Income also revamped its business continuity and disaster-recovery plans. A real-time hot backup disaster-recovery center was implemented, where the machines were always running and fully operational. Data was transmitted immediately on the fly from the primary datacenter to the backup machines' data storage. In the event of the datacenter site becoming unavailable, the operations could be switched quickly to the disasterrecovery site without the need to rely on restoration of previous day data.

Moving to a paperless environment, however, was not easy. Income had to throw away all paper records, including legal paper documents. Under the new system, all documents were scanned and stored on "trusted" storage devices - secured, reliable digital vaults that enabled strict compliance with stringent statutory requirements. Income had to train employees who had been accustomed to working with paper to use the eBao system and change the way they worked.

As a result of adopting eBao Life System, about 500 office staff and 3,400 insurance advisors could access the system anytime, anywhere. Staff members who would telecommute enjoyed faster access to information, almost as fast as those who accessed the information in the office.

This allowed Income to view a summary of each customer over different products and business areas. As a result, cross-selling became easier, and customer service could be improved. Simplified workflows cut policy processing time and cost by half, and greatly reduced the time required to design and launch new products from months to days.

Additionally, the systems allowed for online support of customers, agents and brokers.

Sources: Melanie Liew, Computerworld, July 2004; "NTUC Income of Singapore Successfully Implemented eBaoTech Lifesystem," ebaotech.com, accessed November 2008; Neerja Sethi & D G Allampallai, "NTUC Income of Singapore (A): Re-architecting Legacy Systems," asiacase.com, October 2005.

CASE STUDY QUESTIONS

1. What were the problems faced by Income in this case? How were the problems resolved by the new digital system?

2. What types of information systems and business processes were used by Income before migrating to the fully digital system?

3. Describe the Information systems and IT infrastructure at Income after migrating to the fully digital system?

4. What benefits did Income reap from the new system?

5. How well is Income prepared for the future? Are the problems described in the case likely to be repeated?

Case contributed by Neerja Sethi and Vijay Sethi, Nanyang Technological University.

Chapter 3

Information Systems, Organizations, and Strategy

LEARNING OBJECTIVESS

After reading this chapter, you will be able to answer the following questions:

1. Which features of organizations do managers need to know about to build and use information systems successfully? What is the impact of information systems on organizations?

2. How does Porter's competitive forces model help companies develop competitive strategies using information systems?

3. How do the value chain and value web models help businesses identify opportunities for strategic information system applications?

4. How do information systems help businesses use synergies, core competencies, and network-based strategies to achieve competitive advantage?

5. What are the challenges posed by strategic information systems and how should they be addressed?

Interactive Sessions:

Technology Helps Starbucks Find New Ways to Compete

Automakers Become Software Companies

CHAPTER OUTLINE

3.1 ORGANIZATIONS AND INFORMATION SYSTEMS
What Is an Organization?
Features of Organizations

3.2 HOW INFORMATION SYSTEMS IMPACT ORGANIZATIONS AND BUSINESS FIRMS
Economic Impacts
Organizational and Behavioral Impacts
The Internet and Organizations
Implications for the Design and Understanding of Information Systems

3.3 USING INFORMATION SYSTEMS TO ACHIEVE COMPETITIVE ADVANTAGE
Porter's Competitive Forces Model
Information System Strategies for Dealing with Competitive Forces
The Internet's Impact on Competitive Advantage
The Business Value Chain Model
Synergies, Core Competencies, and Network-Based Strategies

3.4 USING SYSTEMS FOR COMPETITIVE ADVANTAGE: MANAGEMENT ISSUES
Sustaining Competitive Advantage
Aligning IT with Business Objectives
Managing Strategic Transitions

LEARNING TRACK MODULE
The Changing Business Environment for Information Technology

WILL SEARS'S TECHNOLOGY STRATEGY WORK THIS TIME?

Sears, Roebuck used to be the largest retailer in the United States, with sales representing 1 to 2 percent of the U.S. gross national product for almost 40 years after World War II. Since then, Sears has steadily lost ground to discounters such as Walmart and Target and to competitively priced specialty retailers such as Home Depot and Lowe's. Even the merger with Kmart in 2005 to create Sears Holding Company failed to stop the downward spiral in sales and market share.

Over the years, Sears had invested heavily in information technology. At one time it spent more on information technology and networking than all other non-computer firms in the United states except the Boeing Corporation. Sears used its huge customer databases of 60 million past and present Sears credit card holders to target groups such as tool buyers, appliance buyers, and gardening enthusiasts with special promotions. These efforts did not translate into competitive advantage because Sears's cost structure was one of the highest in its industry.

The company has been slow to reduce operating costs, keep pace with current merchandising trends, and remodel its 2,172 stores, many of which are run-down and in undesirable locations. It is still struggling to find a viable business strategy that will pull it out of its rut. The Sears company tried to use new technology strategies to revive flagging sales: online shopping, mobile apps, and an Amazon.com-like marketplace with other vendors for 18 million products, along with heavy in-store promotions. So far, these efforts have not paid off, and sales have declined since the 2005 merger. The company posted a loss of $3.1 billion in 2011.

Sears Holdings CEO Lou D'Ambrosio, thinks he has an answer—even more intensive use of technology and mining of customer data. The expectation is that deeper knowledge of customer preferences and buying patterns will make promotions, merchandising, and selling much more effective. Customers will flock to Sears stores because they will be carrying exactly what they want.

A customer loyalty program called Shop Your Way Rewards promises customers generous free deals for repeat purchases if they agree to share their personal shopping data with the company. Sears would not disclose how many customers have signed up for Shop Your Way Rewards, but loyalty-markcting firm Colloquy estimates around 50 million people are members.

Shoppers who use their smartphones to "check in" to some Sears stores will be greeted by Sears employees, who find them using the global-positioning systems on their mobile devices and then direct them to the flat-panel televisions and French Connection ankle jeans they searched for earlier online. "It's the equivalent of walking into a coffee shop and not having to say anything as someone prepares your coffee with just the right amount of cream and sugar," notes Michael Archer of Kurt Salmon management consultants, who had helped design Citibank's American Airlines loyalty cards.

The data Sears is collecting are changing how its sales floors are arranged and how promotions are designed to attract

© OleksiyMaksymenko/Alamy

shoppers. For example, work wear has been moved closer to where tools are sold. After data analysis showed that many jewelry customers were men who bought tools, the company created a special Valentine's Day offer for Shop Your Way Rewards members that offered $100 credit for $400 spent on jewelry. According to D'Ambrosio, what people are spending using their loyalty points "has exceeded our expectations."

Sears spent several hundred million dollars improving its stores in 2011, including technological enhancements. Woodfield Mall Sears, one of several hundred that was recently remodeled, reflects the new approach. Outdoor clothing from Lands, End dominates the area near the main mall entrance, while pastel-colored women's tops from Covington line the main hall. (Sears owns both of these brands.) Workers use iPads and iPod Touches to access online reviews for customers and check whether items are in stock. Ron Boire, who oversees Sears merchandising and store formats believes that with a little more time and customer information, he can make the store experience much better.

But retail industry experts are skeptical. The Sears Shop Your Way Rewards program is not very different from what Target, Macy's, and other retail chains already offer, and these programs alone cannot turn a company around. Jim Sullivan, a partner at loyalty marketing firm Colloquy, observes that a good loyalty program can be a strategic advantage if the program gives a company better intelligence about what its customers really want. But "even the best loyalty programs can't fix a fundamentally broken brand."

Sources: Miguel Bustillo, "The Plan to Rescue Sears," *The Wall Street Journal*, March 12, 2012; Miguel Bustillo and Dana Mattioli, "In Retreat, Sears Set to Unload Stores," *The Wall Street Journal*, February 24, 2012, and Stephanie Clifford, "A Tough Sell at Sears," *The New York Times*, December 21, 2010.

The story of Sears illustrates some of the ways that information systems help businesses compete, and it reveals the challenges of sustaining a competitive advantage. Retailing today is extremely crowded, with many large and powerful players and competition from the Internet as well as other physical stores. At one time, Sears was the top retailer in the United States, but the company is struggling with all of these competitive pressures and is searching for a competitive strategy to regain its footing.

The chapter-opening diagram calls attention to important points raised by this case and this chapter. By all accounts, Sears is a fading brand saddled with too many nonperforming physical stores in undesirable locations. Over the years, it has tried many different competitive strategies-mergers, promotional campaigns, and store renovations, and various technology initiatives. None have been able to stem the tide of red ink. Sears's most recent initiative uses a blend of technology and loyalty-rewards programs in the hope that more aggressive mining of customer data will enable stores to offer the stock customers want and deliver buying superior experiences. The case study shows how clearly difficult this will be to achieve. Both regaining competitive momentum and sustaining a competitive advantage may not be possible for Sears, given its history of missteps and its damaged brand image. Technology alone won't be able to solve Sears's problems until it repairs its tarnished brand image and creates a more robust business model.

Here are some questions to think about: 1. How do the competitive forces and value chain models apply to Sears? 2. Visit a nearby Sears store and observe sales activity. Do you think Sears's new strategy has been implemented there? How effective is it?

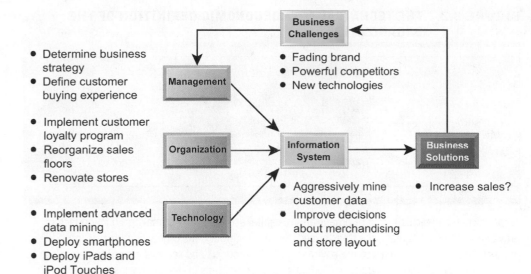

- Determine business strategy
- Define customer buying experience

- Implement customer loyalty program
- Reorganize sales floors
- Renovate stores

- Implement advanced data mining
- Deploy smartphones
- Deploy iPads and iPod Touches

Business Challenges

- Fading brand
- Powerful competitors
- New technologies

Management

Organization

Information System

Technology

- Aggressively mine customer data
- Improve decisions about merchandising and store layout

Business Solutions

- Increase sales?

ORGANIZATIONS AND INFORMATION SYSTEMS

Information systems and organizations influence one another. Information systems are built by managers to serve the interests of the business firm. At the same time, the organization must be aware of and open to the influences of information systems to benefit from new technologies.

The interaction between information technology and organizations is complex and is influenced by many mediating factors, including the organization's structure, business processes, politics, culture, surrounding environment, and management decisions (see Figure 3.1). You will need to understand how information systems can change social and work life in your firm. You will not be able to design new systems successfully or understand existing systems without understanding your own business organization.

FIGURE 3.1 **THE TWO-WAY RELATIONSHIP BETWEEN ORGANIZATIONS AND INFORMATION TECHNOLOGY**

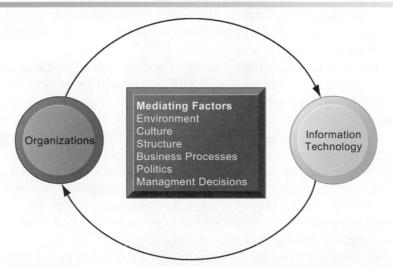

This complex two-way relationship is mediated by many factors, not the least of which are the decisions made—or not made—by managers. Other factors mediating the relationship include the organizational culture, structure, politics, business processes, and environment.

FIGURE 3.2   THE TECHNICAL MICROECONOMIC DEFINITION OF THE ORGANIZATION

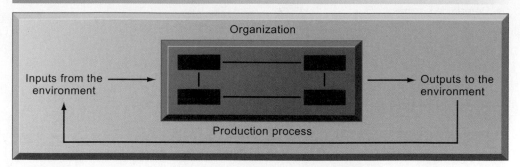

In the microeconomic definition of organizations, capital and labor (the primary production factors provided by the environment) are transformed by the firm through the production process into products and services (outputs to the environment). The products and services are consumed by the environment, which supplies additional capital and labor as inputs in the feedback loop.

As a manager, you will be the one to decide which systems will be built, what they will do, and how they will be implemented. You may not be able to anticipate all of the consequences of these decisions. Some of the changes that occur in business firms because of new information technology (IT) investments cannot be foreseen and have results that may or may not meet your expectations. Who would have imagined fifteen years ago, for instance, that e-mail and instant messaging would become a dominant form of business communication and that many managers would be inundated with more than 200 e-mail messages each day?

WHAT IS AN ORGANIZATION?

An **organization** is a stable, formal social structure that takes resources from the environment and processes them to produce outputs. This technical definition focuses on three elements of an organization. Capital and labor are primary production factors provided by the environment. The organization (the firm) transforms these inputs into products and services in a production function. The products and services are consumed by environments in return for supply inputs (see Figure 3.2).

An organization is more stable than an informal group (such as a group of friends that meets every Friday for lunch) in terms of longevity and routineness. Organizations are formal legal entities with internal rules and procedures that must abide by laws. Organizations are also social structures because they are a collection of social elements, much as a machine has a structure—a particular arrangement of valves, cams, shafts, and other parts.

This definition of organizations is powerful and simple, but it is not very descriptive or even predictive of real-world organizations. A more realistic behavioral definition of an organization is a collection of rights, privileges, obligations, and responsibilities delicately balanced over a period of time through conflict and conflict resolution (see Figure 3.3).

In this behavioral view of the firm, people who work in organizations develop customary ways of working; they gain attachments to existing relationships; and they make arrangements with subordinates and superiors about how work will be done, the amount of work that will be done, and under what conditions

FIGURE 3.3   THE BEHAVIORAL VIEW OF ORGANIZATIONS

The behavioral view of organizations emphasizes group relationships, values, and structures.

work will be done. Most of these arrangements and feelings are not discussed in any formal rulebook.

How do these definitions of organizations relate to information systems technology? A technical view of organizations encourages us to focus on how inputs are combined to create outputs when technology changes are introduced into the company. The firm is seen as infinitely malleable, with capital and labor substituting for each other quite easily. But the more realistic behavioral definition of an organization suggests that building new information systems, or rebuilding old ones, involves much more than a technical rearrangement of machines or workers—that some information systems change the organizational balance of rights, privileges, obligations, responsibilities, and feelings that have been established over a long period of time.

Changing these elements can take a long time, be very disruptive, and requires more resources to support training and learning. For instance, the length of time required to implement a new information system effectively is much longer than usually anticipated simply because there is a lag between implementing a technical system and teaching employees and managers how to use the system.

Technological change requires changes in who owns and controls information, who has the right to access and update that information, and who makes decisions about whom, when, and how. This more complex view forces us to look at the way work is designed and the procedures used to achieve outputs.

The technical and behavioral definitions of organizations are not contradictory. Indeed, they complement each other: The technical definition tells us how thousands of firms in competitive markets combine capital, labor, and information technology, whereas the behavioral model takes us inside the individual firm to see how that technology affects the organization's inner workings. Section 3.2 describes how each of these definitions of organizations can help explain the relationships between information systems and organizations.

FEATURES OF ORGANIZATIONS

All modern organizations share certain characteristics. They are bureaucracies with clear-cut divisions of labor and specialization. Organizations arrange specialists in a hierarchy of authority in which everyone is accountable to someone and authority is limited to specific actions governed by abstract rules or procedures. These rules create a system of impartial and universal decision making. Organizations try to hire and promote employees on the basis of technical qualifications and professionalism (not personal connections). The organization is devoted to the principle of efficiency: maximizing output using limited inputs. Other features of organizations include their business processes, organizational culture, organizational politics, surrounding environments, structure, goals, constituencies, and leadership styles. All of these features affect the kinds of information systems used by organizations.

Routines and Business Processes

All organizations, including business firms, become very efficient over time because individuals in the firm develop **routines** for producing goods and services. Routines—sometimes called *standard operating procedures*—are precise rules, procedures, and practices that have been developed to cope with virtually all expected situations. As employees learn these routines, they become highly productive and efficient, and the firm is able to reduce its costs over time as efficiency increases. For instance, when you visit a doctor's office, receptionists have a well-developed set of routines for gathering basic information from you; nurses have a different set of routines for preparing you for an interview with a doctor; and the doctor has a well-developed set of routines for diagnosing you. *Business processes*, which we introduced in Chapters 1 and 2, are collections of such routines. A business firm, in turn, is a collection of business processes (Figure 3.4).

Organizational Politics

People in organizations occupy different positions with different specialties, concerns, and perspectives. As a result, they naturally have divergent viewpoints about how resources, rewards, and punishments should be distributed. These differences matter to both managers and employees, and they result in political struggle for resources, competition, and conflict within every organization. Political resistance is one of the great difficulties of bringing about organizational change—especially the development of new information systems. Virtually all large information systems investments by a firm that bring about significant changes in strategy, business objectives, business processes, and procedures become politically charged events. Managers who know how to work with the politics of an organization will be more successful than less-skilled managers in implementing new information systems. Throughout this book, you will find many examples where internal politics defeated the best-laid plans for an information system.

Organizational Culture

All organizations have bedrock, unassailable, unquestioned (by the members) assumptions that define their goals and products. Organizational culture encompasses this set of assumptions about what products the organization should produce, how it should produce them, where, and for whom. Generally, these cultural assumptions are taken totally for granted and are

FIGURE 3.4   ROUTINES, BUSINESS PROCESSES, AND FIRMS

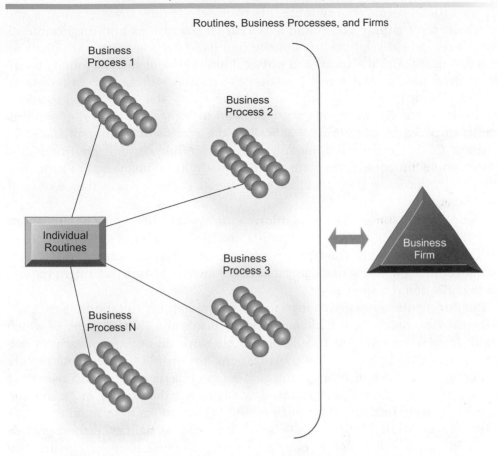

Routines, Business Processes, and Firms

All organizations are composed of individual routines and behaviors, a collection of which make up a business process. A collection of business processes make up the business firm. New information system applications require that individual routines and business processes change to achieve high levels of organizational performance.

rarely publicly announced or discussed. Business processes—the actual way business firms produce value—are usually ensconced in the organization's culture.

You can see organizational culture at work by looking around your university or college. Some bedrock assumptions of university life are that professors know more than students, the reason students attend college is to learn, and classes follow a regular schedule. Organizational culture is a powerful unifying force that restrains political conflict and promotes common understanding, agreement on procedures, and common practices. If we all share the same basic cultural assumptions, agreement on other matters is more likely.

At the same time, organizational culture is a powerful restraint on change, especially technological change. Most organizations will do almost anything to avoid making changes in basic assumptions. Any technological change that threatens commonly held cultural assumptions usually meets a great deal of resistance. However, there are times when the only sensible way for a firm to move forward is to employ a new technology that directly opposes an existing organizational culture. When this occurs, the technology is often stalled while the culture slowly adjusts.

Organizational Environments

Organizations reside in environments from which they draw resources and to which they supply goods and services. Organizations and environments have a reciprocal relationship. On the one hand, organizations are open to, and dependent on, the social and physical environment that surrounds them. Without financial and human resources—people willing to work reliably and consistently for a set wage or revenue from customers—organizations could not exist. Organizations must respond to legislative and other requirements imposed by government, as well as the actions of customers and competitors. On the other hand, organizations can influence their environments. For example, business firms form alliances with other businesses to influence the political process; they advertise to influence customer acceptance of their products.

Figure 3.5 illustrates the role of information systems in helping organizations perceive changes in their environments and also in helping organizations act on their environments. Information systems are key instruments for *environmental scanning*, helping managers identify external changes that might require an organizational response.

Environments generally change much faster than organizations. New technologies, new products, and changing public tastes and values (many of which result in new government regulations) put strains on any organization's culture, politics, and people. Most organizations are unable to adapt to a rapidly changing environment. Inertia built into an organization's standard operating procedures, the political conflict raised by changes to the existing order, and the threat to closely held cultural values inhibit organizations from making significant changes. Young firms typically lack resources to sustain even short periods of troubled times. It is not surprising that only 10 percent of the Fortune 500 companies in 1919 still exist today.

FIGURE 3.5   ENVIRONMENTS AND ORGANIZATIONS HAVE A RECIPROCAL RELATIONSHIP

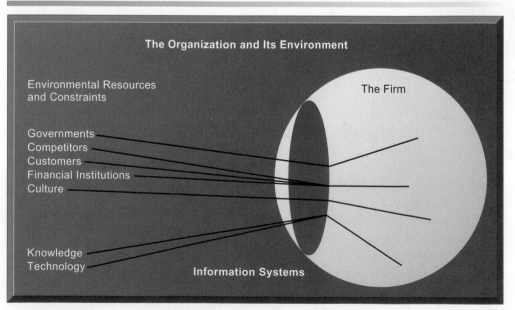

Environments shape what organizations can do, but organizations can influence their environments and decide to change environments altogether. Information technology plays a critical role in helping organizations perceive environmental change and in helping organizations act on their environment.

Disruptive Technologies: Riding the Wave. Sometimes a technology and resulting business innovation comes along to radically change the business landscape and environment. These innovations are loosely called "disruptive." (Christensen, 2003). What makes a technology disruptive? In some cases, **disruptive technologies** are substitute products that perform as well as or better (often much better) than anything currently produced. The car substituted for the horse-drawn carriage; the word processor for typewriters; the Apple iPod for portable CD players; digital photography for process film photography.

In these cases, entire industries were put out of business. In other cases, disruptive technologies simply extend the market, usually with less functionality and much less cost, than existing products. Eventually they turn into low-cost competitors for whatever was sold before. Disk drives are an example: Small hard disk drives used in PCs extended the market for disk drives by offering cheap digital storage for small files. Eventually, small PC hard disk drives became the largest segment of the disk drive marketplace.

Some firms are able to create these technologies and ride the wave to profits; others learn quickly and adapt their business; still others are obliterated because their products, services, and business models become obsolete. They may be very efficient at doing what no longer needs to be done! There are also cases where no firms benefit, and all the gains go to consumers (firms fail to capture any profits). Table 3.1 describes just a few disruptive technologies from the past.

Disruptive technologies are tricky. Firms that invent disruptive technologies as "first movers" do not always benefit if they lack the resources to exploit the technology or fail to see the opportunity. The MITS Altair 8800 is widely regarded as the first PC, but its inventors did not take advantage of their first mover status. Second movers, so-called "fast followers" such as IBM and

TABLE 3.1 DISRUPTIVE TECHNOLOGIES: WINNERS AND LOSERS

TECHNOLOGY	DESCRIPTION	WINNERS AND LOSERS
Microprocessor chips (1971)	Thousands and eventually millions of transistors on a silicon chip	Microprocessor firms win (Intel, Texas Instruments) while transistor firms (GE) decline.
Personal computers (1975)	Small, inexpensive, but fully functional desktop computers	PC manufacturers (HP, Apple, IBM), and chip manufacturers prosper (Intel), while mainframe (IBM) and minicomputer (DEC) firms lose.
Digital photography (1975)	Using CCD (charge-coupled device) image sensor chips to record images	CCD manufacturers and traditional camera companies win, manufacturers of film products lose.
World Wide Web (1989)	A global database of digital files and "pages" instantly available	Owners of online content, news benefit while traditional publishers (newspapers, magazines, and broadcast television) lose.
Internet music, video, TV services (1998)	Repositories of downloadable music, video, TV broadcasts on the Web	Owners of Internet platforms, telecommunications providers owning Internet backbone (ATT, Verizon), local Internet service providers win, while content owners and physical retailers lose (Tower Records, Blockbuster).
PageRank algorithm	A method for ranking Web pages in terms of their popularity to supplement Web search by key terms	Google is the winner (they own the patent), while traditional key word search engines (Alta Vista) lose.
Software as Web service	Using the Internet to provide remote access to online software	Online software services companies (Salesforce.com) win, while traditional "boxed" software companies (Microsoft, SAP, Oracle) lose.

Microsoft, reaped the rewards. Citibank's ATMs revolutionized retail banking, but they were copied by other banks. Now all banks use ATMs, with the benefits going mostly to the consumers.

Organizational Structure

All organizations have a structure or shape. Mintzberg's classification, described in Table 3.2, identifies five basic kinds of organizational structure (Mintzberg, 1979).

The kind of information systems you find in a business firm—and the nature of problems with these systems—often reflects the type of organizational structure. For instance, in a professional bureaucracy such as a hospital, it is not unusual to find parallel patient record systems operated by the administration, another by doctors, and another by other professional staff such as nurses and social workers. In small entrepreneurial firms, you will often find poorly designed systems developed in a rush that often quickly outgrow their usefulness. In huge multidivisional firms operating in hundreds of locations, you will often find there is not a single integrating information system, but instead each locale or each division has its set of information systems.

Other Organizational Features

Organizations have goals and use different means to achieve them. Some organizations have coercive goals (e.g., prisons); others have utilitarian goals (e.g., businesses). Still others have normative goals (universities, religious groups). Organizations also serve different groups or have different constituencies, some primarily benefiting their members, others benefiting clients, stockholders, or the public. The nature of leadership differs greatly from one organization to another—some organizations may be more democratic or authoritarian than others. Another way organizations differ is by the tasks they perform and the technology they use. Some organizations perform primarily

TABLE 3.2 ORGANIZATIONAL STRUCTURES

ORGANIZATIONAL TYPE	DESCRIPTION	EXAMPLES
Entrepreneurial structure	Young, small firm in a fast-changing environment. It has a simple structure and is managed by an entrepreneur serving as its single chief executive officer.	Small start-up business
Machine bureaucracy	Large bureaucracy existing in a slowly changing environment, producing standard products. It is dominated by a centralized management team and centralized decision making.	Midsize manufacturing firm
Divisionalized bureaucracy	Combination of multiple machine bureaucracies, each producing a different product or service, all topped by one central headquarters.	Fortune 500 firms, such as General Motors
Professional bureaucracy	Knowledge-based organization where goods and services depend on the expertise and knowledge of professionals. Dominated by department heads with weak centralized authority.	Law firms, school systems, hospitals
Adhocracy	Task force organization that must respond to rapidly changing environments. Consists of large groups of specialists organized into short-lived multidisciplinary teams and has weak central management.	Consulting firms, such as the Rand Corporation

routine tasks that can be reduced to formal rules that require little judgment (such as manufacturing auto parts), whereas others (such as consulting firms) work primarily with nonroutine tasks.

3.2 HOW INFORMATION SYSTEMS IMPACT ORGANIZATIONS AND BUSINESS FIRMS

Information systems have become integral, online, interactive tools deeply involved in the minute-to-minute operations and decision making of large organizations. Over the last decade, information systems have fundamentally altered the economics of organizations and greatly increased the possibilities for organizing work. Theories and concepts from economics and sociology help us understand the changes brought about by IT.

ECONOMIC IMPACTS

From the point of view of economics, IT changes both the relative costs of capital and the costs of information. Information systems technology can be viewed as a factor of production that can be substituted for traditional capital and labor. As the cost of information technology decreases, it is substituted for labor, which historically has been a rising cost. Hence, information technology should result in a decline in the number of middle managers and clerical workers as information technology substitutes for their labor.

As the cost of information technology decreases, it also substitutes for other forms of capital such as buildings and machinery, which remain relatively expensive. Hence, over time we should expect managers to increase their investments in IT because of its declining cost relative to other capital investments.

IT also affects the cost and quality of information and changes the economics of information. Information technology helps firms contract in size because it can reduce transaction costs—the costs incurred when a firm buys on the marketplace what it cannot make itself. According to **transaction cost theory**, firms and individuals seek to economize on transaction costs, much as they do on production costs. Using markets is expensive because of costs such as locating and communicating with distant suppliers, monitoring contract compliance, buying insurance, obtaining information on products, and so forth (Coase, 1937; Williamson, 1985). Traditionally, firms have tried to reduce transaction costs through vertical integration, by getting bigger, hiring more employees, and buying their own suppliers and distributors, as both General Motors and Ford used to do.

Information technology, especially the use of networks, can help firms lower the cost of market participation (transaction costs), making it worthwhile for firms to contract with external suppliers instead of using internal sources. As a result, firms can shrink in size (numbers of employees) because it is far less expensive to outsource work to a competitive marketplace rather than hire employees.

For instance, by using computer links to external suppliers, the Chrysler Corporation can achieve economies by obtaining more than 70 percent of its parts from the outside. Information systems make it possible for companies such as Cisco Systems and Dell Inc. to outsource their production to contract manufacturers such as Flextronics instead of making their products themselves.

As transaction costs decrease, firm size (the number of employees) should shrink because it becomes easier and cheaper for the firm to contract for the purchase of goods and services in the marketplace rather than to make the product or offer the service itself. Firm size can stay constant or contract even as the company increases its revenues. For example, when Eastman Chemical Company split off from Kodak in 1994, it had $3.3 billion in revenue and 24,000 full-time employees. In 2011, it generated over $7.2 billion in revenue with only 10,000 employees.

Information technology also can reduce internal management costs. According to **agency theory**, the firm is viewed as a "nexus of contracts" among self-interested individuals rather than as a unified, profit-maximizing entity (Jensen and Meckling, 1976). A principal (owner) employs "agents" (employees) to perform work on his or her behalf. However, agents need constant supervision and management; otherwise, they will tend to pursue their own interests rather than those of the owners. As firms grow in size and scope, agency costs or coordination costs rise because owners must expend more and more effort supervising and managing employees.

Information technology, by reducing the costs of acquiring and analyzing information, permits organizations to reduce agency costs because it becomes easier for managers to oversee a greater number of employees. By reducing overall management costs, information technology enables firms to increase revenues while shrinking the number of middle managers and clerical workers. We have seen examples in earlier chapters where information technology expanded the power and scope of small organizations by enabling them to perform coordinating activities such as processing orders or keeping track of inventory with very few clerks and managers.

Because IT reduces both agency and transaction costs for firms, we should expect firm size to shrink over time as more capital is invested in IT. Firms should have fewer managers, and we expect to see revenue per employee increase over time.

ORGANIZATIONAL AND BEHAVIORAL IMPACTS

Theories based in the sociology of complex organizations also provide some understanding about how and why firms change with the implementation of new IT applications.

IT Flattens Organizations

Large, bureaucratic organizations, which primarily developed before the computer age, are often inefficient, slow to change, and less competitive than newly created organizations. Some of these large organizations have downsized, reducing the number of employees and the number of levels in their organizational hierarchies.

Behavioral researchers have theorized that information technology facilitates flattening of hierarchies by broadening the distribution of information to empower lower-level employees and increase management efficiency (see Figure 3.6). IT pushes decision-making rights lower in the organization because lower-level employees receive the information they need to make decisions without supervision. (This empowerment is also possible because of higher educational levels among the workforce, which give employees the capabilities to make intelligent decisions.) Because managers now receive so much more accurate information on time, they become much faster at making decisions, so fewer managers are required. Management costs decline as a percentage of revenues, and the hierarchy becomes much more efficient.

FIGURE 3.6   **FLATTENING ORGANIZATIONS**

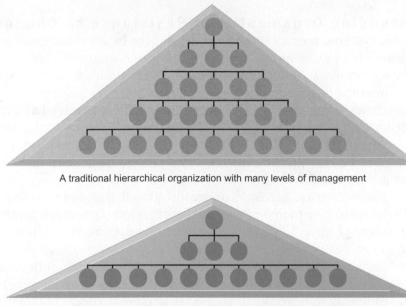

A traditional hierarchical organization with many levels of management

An organization that has been "flattened" by removing layers of management

Information systems can reduce the number of levels in an organization by providing managers with information to supervise larger numbers of workers and by giving lower-level employees more decision-making authority.

These changes mean that the management span of control has also been broadened, enabling high-level managers to manage and control more workers spread over greater distances. Many companies have eliminated thousands of middle managers as a result of these changes.

Postindustrial Organizations

Postindustrial theories based more on history and sociology than economics also support the notion that IT should flatten hierarchies. In postindustrial societies, authority increasingly relies on knowledge and competence, and not merely on formal positions. Hence, the shape of organizations flattens because professional workers tend to be self-managing, and decision making should become more decentralized as knowledge and information become more widespread throughout the firm (Drucker, 1988).

Information technology may encourage task force-networked organizations in which groups of professionals come together—face to face or electronically— for short periods of time to accomplish a specific task (e.g., designing a new automobile); once the task is accomplished, the individuals join other task forces. The global consulting service Accenture is an example. Many of its 246,000 employees move from location to location to work on projects at client locations in more than 120 different countries.

Who makes sure that self-managed teams do not head off in the wrong direction? Who decides which person works on which team and for how long? How can managers evaluate the performance of someone who is constantly rotating from team to team? How do people know where their careers are headed? New approaches for evaluating, organizing, and informing workers are required, and not all companies can make virtual work effective.

Understanding Organizational Resistance to Change

Information systems inevitably become bound up in organizational politics because they influence access to a key resource—namely, information. Information systems can affect who does what to whom, when, where, and how in an organization. Many new information systems require changes in personal, individual routines that can be painful for those involved and require retraining and additional effort that may or may not be compensated. Because information systems potentially change an organization's structure, culture, business processes, and strategy, there is often considerable resistance to them when they are introduced.

There are several ways to visualize organizational resistance. Research on organizational resistance to innovation suggests that four factors are paramount: the nature of the IT innovation, the organization's structure, the culture of people in the organization, and the tasks impacted by the innovation (see Figure 3.7). Here, changes in technology are absorbed, interpreted, deflected, and defeated by organizational task arrangements, structures, and people. In this model, the only way to bring about change is to change the technology, tasks, structure, and people simultaneously. Other authors have spoken about the need to "unfreeze" organizations before introducing an innovation, quickly implementing it, and "refreezing" or institutionalizing the change (Kolb, 1970).

Because organizational resistance to change is so powerful, many information technology investments flounder and do not increase productivity. Indeed, research on project implementation failures demonstrates that the most common reason for failure of large projects to reach their objectives is not the failure of the technology, but organizational and political resistance to change. Chapter 14 treats this issue in detail. Therefore, as a manger involved in future IT investments, your ability to work with people and organizations is just as important as your technical awareness and knowledge.

FIGURE 3.7 ORGANIZATIONAL RESISTANCE TO INFORMATION SYSTEM INNOVATIONS

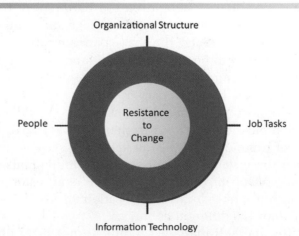

Implementing information systems has consequences for task arrangements, structures, and people. According to this model, to implement change, all four components must be changed simultaneously.

THE INTERNET AND ORGANIZATIONS

The Internet, especially the World Wide Web, has an important impact on the relationships between many firms and external entities, and even on the organization of business processes inside a firm. The Internet increases the accessibility, storage, and distribution of information and knowledge for organizations. In essence, the Internet is capable of dramatically lowering the transaction and agency costs facing most organizations. For instance, brokerage firms and banks in New York can now deliver their internal operating procedures manuals to their employees at distant locations by posting them on the corporate Web site, saving millions of dollars in distribution costs. A global sales force can receive nearly instant product price information updates using the Web or instructions from management sent by e-mail. Vendors of some large retailers can access retailers' internal Web sites directly to find up-to-the-minute sales information and to initiate replenishment orders instantly.

Businesses are rapidly rebuilding some of their key business processes based on Internet technology and making this technology a key component of their IT infrastructures. If prior networking is any guide, one result will be simpler business processes, fewer employees, and much flatter organizations than in the past.

IMPLICATIONS FOR THE DESIGN AND UNDERSTANDING OF INFORMATION SYSTEMS

To deliver genuine benefits, information systems must be built with a clear understanding of the organization in which they will be used. In our experience, the central organizational factors to consider when planning a new system are the following:

- The environment in which the organization must function
- The structure of the organization: hierarchy, specialization, routines, and business processes
- The organization's culture and politics
- The type of organization and its style of leadership
- The principal interest groups affected by the system and the attitudes of workers who will be using the system
- The kinds of tasks, decisions, and business processes that the information system is designed to assist

3.3 USING INFORMATION SYSTEMS TO ACHIEVE COMPETITIVE ADVANTAGE

In almost every industry you examine, you will find some firms do better than most others. There's almost always a stand-out firm. In the automotive industry, Toyota is considered a superior performer. In pure online retail, Amazon is the leader; in off-line retail, Walmart, the largest retailer on earth, is the leader. In online music, Apple's iTunes is considered the leader with more than 70 percent of digital music sold worldwide, and in the related industry of digital music players, the iPod is the leader. In Web search, Google is considered the leader.

Firms that "do better" than others are said to have a competitive advantage over others: They either have access to special resources that others do not, or they are able to use commonly available resources more efficiently—usually because of superior knowledge and information assets. In any event, they do better in terms of revenue growth, profitability, or productivity growth (efficiency), all of which ultimately in the long run translate into higher stock market valuations than their competitors.

But why do some firms do better than others and how do they achieve competitive advantage? How can you analyze a business and identify its strategic advantages? How can you develop a strategic advantage for your own business? And how do information systems contribute to strategic advantages? One answer to that question is Michael Porter's competitive forces model.

PORTER'S COMPETITIVE FORCES MODEL

Arguably, the most widely used model for understanding competitive advantage is Michael Porter's **competitive forces model** (see Figure 3.8). This model provides a general view of the firm, its competitors, and the firm's environment. Earlier in this chapter, we described the importance of a firm's environment and the dependence of firms on environments. Porter's model is all about the firm's general business environment. In this model, five competitive forces shape the fate of the firm.

Traditional Competitors

All firms share market space with other competitors who are continuously devising new, more efficient ways to produce by introducing new products and services, and attempting to attract customers by developing their brands and imposing switching costs on their customers.

New Market Entrants

In a free economy with mobile labor and financial resources, new companies are always entering the marketplace. In some industries, there are very low barriers to entry, whereas in other industries, entry is very difficult. For

FIGURE 3.8   PORTER'S COMPETITIVE FORCES MODEL

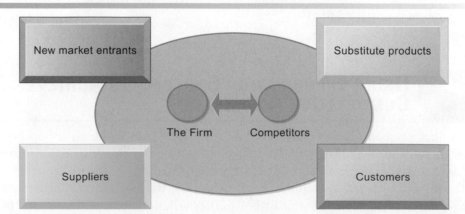

In Porter's competitive forces model, the strategic position of the firm and its strategies are determined not only by competition with its traditional direct competitors but also by four other forces in the industry's environment: new market entrants, substitute products, customers, and suppliers.

instance, it is fairly easy to start a pizza business or just about any small retail business, but it is much more expensive and difficult to enter the computer chip business, which has very high capital costs and requires significant expertise and knowledge that is hard to obtain. New companies have several possible advantages: They are not locked into old plants and equipment, they often hire younger workers who are less expensive and perhaps more innovative, they are not encumbered by old worn-out brand names, and they are "more hungry" (more highly motivated) than traditional occupants of an industry. These advantages are also their weakness: They depend on outside financing for new plants and equipment, which can be expensive; they have a less-experienced workforce; and they have little brand recognition.

Substitute Products and Services

In just about every industry, there are substitutes that your customers might use if your prices become too high. New technologies create new substitutes all the time. Even oil has substitutes: Ethanol can substitute for gasoline in cars; vegetable oil for diesel fuel in trucks; and wind, solar, coal, and hydro power for industrial electricity generation. Likewise, the Internet telephone service can substitute for traditional telephone service, and fiber-optic telephone lines to the home can substitute for cable TV lines. And, of course, an Internet music service that allows you to download music tracks to an iPod is a substitute for CD-based music stores. The more substitute products and services in your industry, the less you can control pricing and the lower your profit margins.

Customers

A profitable company depends in large measure on its ability to attract and retain customers (while denying them to competitors), and charge high prices. The power of customers grows if they can easily switch to a competitor's products and services, or if they can force a business and its competitors to compete on price alone in a transparent marketplace where there is little **product differentiation**, and all prices are known instantly (such as on the Internet). For instance, in the used college textbook market on the Internet, students (customers) can find multiple suppliers of just about any current college textbook. In this case, online customers have extraordinary power over used-book firms.

Suppliers

The market power of suppliers can have a significant impact on firm profits, especially when the firm cannot raise prices as fast as can suppliers. The more different suppliers a firm has, the greater control it can exercise over suppliers in terms of price, quality, and delivery schedules. For instance, manufacturers of laptop PCs almost always have multiple competing suppliers of key components, such as keyboards, hard drives, and display screens.

INFORMATION SYSTEM STRATEGIES FOR DEALING WITH COMPETITIVE FORCES

What is a firm to do when it is faced with all these competitive forces? And how can the firm use information systems to counteract some of these forces? How do you prevent substitutes and inhibit new market entrants? There are four generic strategies, each of which often is enabled by using information technology and systems: low-cost leadership, product differentiation, focus on market niche, and strengthening customer and supplier intimacy.

Supermarkets and large retail stores such as Walmart use sales data captured at the checkout counter to determine which items have sold and need to be reordered. Walmart's continuous replenishment system transmits orders to restock directly to its suppliers. The system enables Walmart to keep costs low while fine-tuning its merchandise to meet customer demands.

© Bonnie Kamin/Photoedit

Low-Cost Leadership

Use information systems to achieve the lowest operational costs and the lowest prices. The classic example is Walmart. By keeping prices low and shelves well stocked using a legendary inventory replenishment system, Walmart became the leading retail business in the United States. Walmart's continuous replenishment system sends orders for new merchandise directly to suppliers as soon as consumers pay for their purchases at the cash register. Point-of-sale terminals record the bar code of each item passing the checkout counter and send a purchase transaction directly to a central computer at Walmart headquarters. The computer collects the orders from all Walmart stores and transmits them to suppliers. Suppliers can also access Walmart's sales and inventory data using Web technology.

Because the system replenishes inventory with lightning speed, Walmart does not need to spend much money on maintaining large inventories of goods in its own warehouses. The system also enables Walmart to adjust purchases of store items to meet customer demands. Competitors, such as Sears, have been spending 24.9 percent of sales on overhead. But by using systems to keep operating costs low, Walmart pays only 16.6 percent of sales revenue for overhead. (Operating costs average 20.7 percent of sales in the retail industry.)

Walmart's continuous replenishment system is also an example of an **efficient customer response system**. An efficient customer response system directly links consumer behavior to distribution and production and supply chains. Walmart's continuous replenishment system provides such an efficient customer response.

Product Differentiation

Use information systems to enable new products and services, or greatly change the customer convenience in using your existing products and services. For instance, Google continuously introduces new and unique search services on its Web site, such as Google Maps. By purchasing PayPal, an electronic payment system, in 2003, eBay made it much easier for customers to pay sellers and expanded use of its auction marketplace. Apple created the iPod, a unique portable digital music player, plus a unique online Web music service where songs can be purchased for $.69 to $1.29 each. Apple has continued to innovate with its multimedia iPhone, iPad tablet computer, and iPod video player.

Manufacturers and retailers are using information systems to create products and services that are customized and personalized to fit the precise specifications of individual customers. For example, Nike sells customized sneakers through its NIKEiD program on its Web site. Customers are able to select the type of shoe, colors, material, outsoles, and even a logo of up to eight characters. Nike transmits the orders via computers to specially equipped plants in China and Korea. The sneakers cost only $10 extra and take about three weeks to reach the customer. This ability to offer individually tailored products or services using the same production resources as mass production is called **mass customization**.

Table 3.3 lists a number of companies that have developed IT-based products and services that other firms have found difficult to copy, or at least a long time to copy.

Focus on Market Niche

Use information systems to enable a specific market focus, and serve this narrow target market better than competitors. Information systems support this strategy by producing and analyzing data for finely tuned sales and marketing techniques. Information systems enable companies to analyze customer buying patterns, tastes, and preferences closely so that they efficiently pitch advertising and marketing campaigns to smaller and smaller target markets.

The data come from a range of sources—credit card transactions, demographic data, purchase data from checkout counter scanners at supermarkets and retail stores, and data collected when people access and interact with Web sites. Sophisticated software tools find patterns in these large pools of data and infer rules from them to guide decision making. Analysis of such data drives one-to-one marketing that creates personal messages based on individualized preferences. For example, Hilton Hotels' OnQ system analyzes detailed data collected on active guests in all of its properties to determine the preferences of each guest and each guest's profitability. Hilton uses this information to give its most profitable customers additional privileges, such as late

TABLE 3.3 IT-ENABLED NEW PRODUCTS AND SERVICES PROVIDING COMPETITIVE ADVANTAGE

Amazon: One-click shopping	Amazon holds a patent on one-click shopping that it licenses to other online retailers.
Online music: Apple iPod and iTunes	The iPod is an integrated handheld player backed up with an online library of over 13 million songs.
Golf club customization: Ping	Customers can select from more than 1 million different golf club options; a build-to-order system ships their customized clubs within 48 hours.
Online person-to-person payment: PayPal	PayPal enables the transfer of money between individual bank accounts and between bank accounts and credit card accounts.

checkouts. Contemporary customer relationship management (CRM) systems feature analytical capabilities for this type of intensive data analysis (see Chapters 2 and 9).

Credit card companies are able to use this strategy to predict their most profitable cardholders. The companies gather vast quantities of data about consumer purchases and other behaviors and mine these data to construct detailed profiles that identify cardholders who might be good or bad credit risks. We discuss the tools and technologies for data analysis in Chapters 6 and 12.

Strengthen Customer and Supplier Intimacy

Use information systems to tighten linkages with suppliers and develop intimacy with customers. Chrysler Corporation uses information systems to facilitate direct access by suppliers to production schedules, and even permits suppliers to decide how and when to ship supplies to Chrysler factories. This allows suppliers more lead time in producing goods. On the customer side, Amazon keeps track of user preferences for book and CD purchases, and can recommend titles purchased by others to its customers. Strong linkages to customers and suppliers increase **switching costs** (the cost of switching from one product to a competing product), and loyalty to your firm.

Table 3.4 summarizes the competitive strategies we have just described. Some companies focus on one of these strategies, but you will often see companies pursuing several of them simultaneously. Starbucks, discussed in the Interactive Session on Organizations, is an example.

THE INTERNET'S IMPACT ON COMPETITIVE ADVANTAGE

Because of the Internet, the traditional competitive forces are still at work, but competitive rivalry has become much more intense (Porter, 2001). Internet technology is based on universal standards that any company can use, making it easy for rivals to compete on price alone and for new competitors to enter the market. Because information is available to everyone, the Internet raises the bargaining power of customers, who can quickly find the lowest-cost provider

TABLE 3.4 FOUR BASIC COMPETITIVE STRATEGIES

STRATEGY	DESCRIPTION	EXAMPLE
Low-cost leadership	Use information systems to produce products and services at a lower price than competitors while enhancing quality and level of service	Walmart
Product differentiation	Use information systems to differentiate products, and enable new services and products	Google, eBay, Apple, Lands' End
Focus on market niche	Use information systems to enable a focused strategy on a single market niche; specialize	Hilton Hotels, Harrah's
Customer and supplier intimacy	Use information systems to develop strong ties and loyalty with customers and suppliers	Chrysler Corporation, Amazon

INTERACTIVE SESSION: ORGANIZATIONS

TECHNOLOGY HELPS STARBUCKS FIND NEW WAYS TO COMPETE

Starbucks is the world's largest specialty coffee retailer, with over 1,700 coffee shops in 55 countries. For years, Starbucks grew throughout the United States and internationally, opening franchises at an impressive rate. From 2002 to 2007 alone, the company tripled the number of stores it operated worldwide. Starbucks offers a unique experience: high-end specialty coffees and beverages, friendly and knowledgeable servers, and customer-friendly coffee shops. This was a winning formula for many years and enabled Starbucks to charge premium prices.

During the economic downturn beginning in 2008, profits plunged. Customers complained that the company had lost its hip, local feel and had become more like a fast-food chain. Many coffee drinkers went in search of cheaper alternatives from McDonald's and Dunkin' Donuts for their coffee fixes. Starbucks stock lost over 50 percent of its value by the end of 2008. Major changes were in order.

Starbucks seized the opportunity to overhaul its business by using several different strategies simultaneously. First, the company has revamped its in-store technology and sought to integrate its business processes with wireless technology and the mobile digital platform. Also, rather than copy the practices of competitors, Starbucks pursued a more aggressive product differentiation strategy, intended to emphasize the high quality of their drinks and efficient and helpful customer service. At the same time, however, Starbucks also focused on becoming 'lean', like many of their competitors, eliminating inefficiency wherever possible.

When Starbucks set out to improve its customer experience, it found that more than a third of its customers are active users of smartphones. The company set out to implement several features and improvements that would appeal to this segment of its customer base. First, Starbucks implemented a technology that allows customers to pay using a smartphone app. The app is integrated with the Starbucks Card system, which allows regular customers to pay with a pre-paid and rechargeable card at any Starbucks branch. When customers make a purchase using the app, a cashier scans a bar code displayed on the phone, and the resulting sale is charged to the customer's Starbucks Card

account. Customers report that paying using this app, available for all major smartphone operating systems, is much faster than traditional forms of payment. In its first 15 months of use, the Starbucks mobile payment system processed 42 million transactions.

Many of Starbucks' most loyal customers regularly spend time using the free Wi-Fi wireless network offered in each store. A majority of these customers also use mobile devices to connect to the in-store Wi-Fi networks. Recognizing this, Starbucks launched what it calls the "Starbucks Digital Network," a portal designed specifically for mobile devices as opposed to traditional Web browsers. The site is optimized for all major smartphone operating systems (iOS, Android, and BlackBerry), and responds to the multi-touch capability of devices like the iPad.

The Starbucks Digital Network site was developed in partnership with Yahoo and functions as a content portal. Starbucks customers using the site will receive free Wall Street Journal access, select free iTunes downloads, and a wide variety of other content. The site will integrate with Foursquare, a location-based social networking site for mobile devices. This arrangement will allow users to check in and receive award points using Starbucks' site. Because Starbucks has the most Foursquare check-ins of any company to date, this feature has been popular with customers.

Rather than serve ads on the site, Starbucks has opted to offer the site free of advertising, hoping that striking deals with content providers will make it a profitable venture. Even if the Starbucks Digital Network is not highly profitable, analysts suggest that the site is an effective way for Starbucks to improve its relationship with its most valuable customers and a creative use of the mobile digital platform to enhance customer satisfaction.

In addition to revamping their business to better serve the needs of their mobile users, Starbucks has made a concerted effort to become more efficient, reduce waste, and use the time saved to provide better customer service. Starbucks set out to streamline the business processes used in each of its stores so that baristas do not need to bend down to scoop coffee, cutting down on idle time while waiting for coffee to drain, and finding ways to reduce the amount of time each employee spends making a drink. Starbucks created a 10 person "lean team" whose job is to travel the country visiting franchises and coaching them in lean techniques made famous by automaker Toyota's production system.

Store labor costs Starbucks about $2.5 billion, amounting to 24 percent of its annual revenue. If Starbucks is able to reduce the time each employee spends making a drink, the company can make more drinks with the same number of workers or with fewer workers. Alternatively, Starbucks could use this time savings to give baristas more time to interact with customers and hopefully improve the Starbucks experience.

Wireless technology enhanced Starbucks' business process simplification effort. Starbucks district managers use the in-store wireless networks to run store operations and to connect to the company's private corporate network and systems. Starbucks district managers were equipped with Wi-Fi enabled laptops for this purpose. Before the in-store wireless networks were implemented, a district manager who oversaw around 10 stores had to visit each store, review its operations, develop a list of items on which to follow up, and then drive to a Starbucks regional office to file reports and send e-mail. Instead of running the business from cubicles in regional headquarters, Starbucks district managers can do most of their work sitting at a table in one of the stores they oversee. The time saved from going back and forth to regional offices can be used to observe how employees are serving customers and improve their training. Implementing Wi-Fi technology enabled Starbucks to increase the in-store presence of district managers by 25 percent without adding any extra managers.

In 2008 and 2009, the weakened economy forced Starbucks to close 900 stores, renegotiate some rents, cut prices on some of their big ticket items, and begin offering price-reduced specials, such as a breakfast sandwich and a drink for $3.95. Cost reductions from procedural changes made it possible for Starbucks to offer these lower prices.

Major fast food chains already used these techniques. While some baristas have resisted the changes, and analysts were skeptical that the changes would take hold, Starbucks attributes much of its recent uptick in profits to its efforts to go lean. Starbucks CEO Howard Schultz said that "the majority of cost reductions we've achieved come from a new way of operating and serving our customers," and also added that the time and money saved was also allowing the company to improve its customer engagement. By 2011, Starbucks had returned to profitability and continuing growth, with plans to open 500 new stores, in large part because of the success of each these changes.

Sources: "Starbucks Corporation," *The New York Times*, January 26, 2012; Mark Raby, "Starbucks Mobile Payments Hit 42 Million," Mark Raby, "Starbucks Mobile Payments Hit 42 Million," SlashGear, April 9, 2012; Trefis Team, "Starbucks Brews Up Smartphone Payment Platform," *Forbes*, February 7, 2011; http://blogs.forbes.com/greatspeculations/2011/02/17/starbucks-brews-up-smartphone-payment-platform/; Ryan Kim, "Starbucks' New Portal Designed with Mobile in Mind," *Businessweek*, September 2, 2010; Starbucks Form 10-K for Fiscal Year ended October 2, 2011; Julie Jargon, "Latest Starbucks Buzzword: 'Lean' Japanese Techniques," *The Wall Street Journal*, August 4, 2009.

CASE STUDY QUESTIONS

1. Analyze Starbucks using the competitive forces and value chain models.

2. What is Starbucks' business strategy? Assess the role played by technology in this business strategy.

3. How much has technology helped Starbucks compete? Explain your answer.

on the Web. Profits have been dampened. Table 3.5 summarizes some of the potentially negative impacts of the Internet on business firms identified by Porter.

The Internet has nearly destroyed some industries and has severely threatened more. For instance, the printed encyclopedia industry and the travel agency industry have been nearly decimated by the availability of substitutes

TABLE 3.5 IMPACT OF THE INTERNET ON COMPETITIVE FORCES AND INDUSTRY STRUCTURE

COMPETITIVE FORCE	IMPACT OF THE INTERNET
Substitute products or services	Enables new substitutes to emerge with new approaches to meeting needs and performing functions
Customers' bargaining power	Availability of global price and product information shifts bargaining power to customers
Suppliers' bargaining power	Procurement over the Internet tends to raise bargaining power over suppliers; suppliers can also benefit from reduced barriers to entry and from the elimination of distributors and other intermediaries standing between them and their users
Threat of new entrants	Internet reduces barriers to entry, such as the need for a sales force, access to channels, and physical assets; it provides a technology for driving business processes that makes other things easier to do
Positioning and rivalry among existing competitors	Widens the geographic market, increasing the number of competitors, and reducing differences among competitors; makes it more difficult to sustain operational advantages; puts pressure to compete on price

over the Internet. Likewise, the Internet has had a significant impact on the retail, music, book, retail brokerage, software, telecommunications, and newspaper industries.

However, the Internet has also created entirely new markets, formed the basis for thousands of new products, services, and business models, and provided new opportunities for building brands with very large and loyal customer bases. Amazon, eBay, iTunes, YouTube, Facebook, Travelocity, and Google are examples. In this sense, the Internet is "transforming" entire industries, forcing firms to change how they do business.

For most forms of media, the Internet has posed a threat to business models and profitability. Growth in book sales other than textbooks and professional publications has been sluggish, as new forms of entertainment continue to compete for consumers' time. Newspapers and magazines have been hit even harder, as their readerships diminish, their advertisers shrink, and more people get their news for free online. The television and film industries have been forced to deal with pirates who are robbing them of some of their profits. The chapter-ending case explores the impact of the Internet on retail bookstores and book publishers.

THE BUSINESS VALUE CHAIN MODEL

Although the Porter model is very helpful for identifying competitive forces and suggesting generic strategies, it is not very specific about what exactly to do, and it does not provide a methodology to follow for achieving competitive advantages. If your goal is to achieve operational excellence, where do you start? Here's where the business value chain model is helpful.

The **value chain model** highlights specific activities in the business where competitive strategies can best be applied (Porter, 1985) and where information systems are most likely to have a strategic impact. This model identifies specific, critical leverage points where a firm can use information technology most effectively to enhance its competitive position. The value chain model views the firm as a series or chain of basic activities that add a margin of value to a firm's products or services. These activities can be categorized as either primary activities or support activities (see Figure 3.9 on p. 132).

FIGURE 3.9 **THE VALUE CHAIN MODEL**

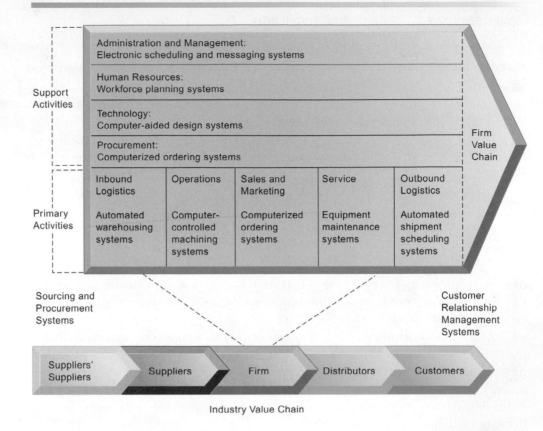

This figure provides examples of systems for both primary and support activities of a firm and of its value partners that can add a margin of value to a firm's products or services.

Primary activities are most directly related to the production and distribution of the firm's products and services, which create value for the customer. Primary activities include inbound logistics, operations, outbound logistics, sales and marketing, and service. Inbound logistics includes receiving and storing materials for distribution to production. Operations transforms inputs into finished products. Outbound logistics entails storing and distributing finished products. Sales and marketing includes promoting and selling the firm's products. The service activity includes maintenance and repair of the firm's goods and services.

Support activities make the delivery of the primary activities possible and consist of organization infrastructure (administration and management), human resources (employee recruiting, hiring, and training), technology (improving products and the production process), and procurement (purchasing input).

Now you can ask at each stage of the value chain, "How can we use information systems to improve operational efficiency, and improve customer and supplier intimacy?" This will force you to critically examine how you perform value-adding activities at each stage and how the business processes might be improved. You can also begin to ask how information systems can be used to improve the relationship with customers and with suppliers who lie outside the firm's value chain but belong to the firm's extended value chain where they are absolutely critical to your success. Here, supply chain management systems that coordinate the flow of resources into your firm, and customer relationship management systems that coordinate your sales and support employees with customers, are two of the most common system applications that result from a business value chain analysis. We discuss these enterprise applications in detail later in Chapter 9.

Using the business value chain model will also cause you to consider benchmarking your business processes against your competitors or others in related industries, and identifying industry best practices. **Benchmarking** involves comparing the efficiency and effectiveness of your business processes against strict standards and then measuring performance against those standards. Industry **best practices** are usually identified by consulting companies, research organizations, government agencies, and industry associations as the most successful solutions or problem-solving methods for consistently and effectively achieving a business objective.

Once you have analyzed the various stages in the value chain at your business, you can come up with candidate applications of information systems. Then, once you have a list of candidate applications, you can decide which to develop first. By making improvements in your own business value chain that your competitors might miss, you can achieve competitive advantage by attaining operational excellence, lowering costs, improving profit margins, and forging a closer relationship with customers and suppliers. If your competitors are making similar improvements, then at least you will not be at a competitive disadvantage—the worst of all cases!

In the Interactive Session on Technology, we can see how value chain analysis might have helped automakers refine their competitive strategies. Ford, GM, and other leading automakers are adding more value to their products by offering software interfaces and applications for improving vehicle performance, providing entertainment, and integrating with other systems for maintenance and future traffic control.

Extending the Value Chain: The Value Web

Figure 3.9 shows that a firm's value chain is linked to the value chains of its suppliers, distributors, and customers. After all, the performance of most firms depends not only on what goes on inside a firm but also on how well the firm coordinates with direct and indirect suppliers, delivery firms (logistics partners, such as FedEx or UPS), and, of course, customers.

How can information systems be used to achieve strategic advantage at the industry level? By working with other firms, industry participants can use information technology to develop industry-wide standards for exchanging information or business transactions electronically, which force all market participants to subscribe to similar standards. Such efforts increase efficiency, making product substitution less likely and perhaps raising entry costs—thus discouraging new entrants. Also, industry members can build industry-wide, IT-supported consortia, symposia, and communications networks to coordinate activities concerning government agencies, foreign competition, and competing industries.

Looking at the industry value chain encourages you to think about how to use information systems to link up more efficiently with your suppliers, strategic partners, and customers. Strategic advantage derives from your ability to relate your value chain to the value chains of other partners in the process. For instance, if you are Amazon.com, you want to build systems that:

INTERACTIVE SESSION: TECHNOLOGY

AUTOMAKERS BECOME SOFTWARE COMPANIES

As the smartphone market continues to expand and initiatives like smart electric grids continue to pick up steam, another industry has begun getting "smarter" with software and apps: the automobile industry. Ford, BMW, and other automobile companies are enhancing their vehicles with onboard software that improves the customer experience, and the auto industry is working on technology that will allow cars to be managed via the cloud.

Automakers are finding that software is a way of adding more "value" and freshness to their products without having to invest so heavily in new vehicle production. It takes Ford Motor Company, for example, about two and one-half years to plan, design, and build a new car. Design and production, including metal stamping equipment and assembly line setup, must be finalized long before the car rolls off the line. But the auto makers can create a new software interface for a car within months and update it again and again over the life of the car without much lead time. This enables Ford and other automakers to significantly improve the passenger experience and add new features to cars years after they are built.

Ford is perhaps the automaker doing the most to innovate with software and apps. Its MyFord Touch interface is an in-dash touch screen available for select vehicles with controls for navigation, music, phone integration, and temperature. Ford has upgraded this interface and the Sync software behind the interface, adding tablet and smartphone integration and better voice response. In 2010, Ford added support for the online music streaming service Pandora, which is very popular among young potential buyers. This update enables drivers to connect their tablets and smartphones to the Sync system to access music and other apps using voice commands.

Chairman Bill Ford Jr. has championed the use of software to alleviate urban congestion by investing in technology that responds to the problems created by traffic in the biggest cities. Theoretically, technology might help cars to avoid traffic jams, to reserve parking spaces in advance, and possibly to even drive themselves.

To manage vehicles in this way, cars need to be connected to some kind of central system, which would coordinate with public transit and other transportation methods, and to do this, cars need to be equipped with software that can monitor and enhance vehicle function at the most basic levels. The eventual system would require that cars feed increasing amounts of information to systems whose purpose would be to minimize highway congestion. The system would also require an industry standard, which does not exist as of yet. Ford has doubled its investment in vehicle-to-vehicle communication technologies and BMW is also continuing to develop ways for vehicles to communicate with one another on the road to avoid collisions.

With the inclusion of software in their cars, automakers are entering uncharted territory. They must now devote resources to updating and testing their software, as well as establishing ways to provide the updated software to their customers. Car companies need to coordinate their car development cycles more closely with their software development cycles. Also, many of the technologies included in automobile software packages raise the same privacy concerns surrounding location tracking that have often plagued smartphone manufacturers and app developers.

Ford is grappling with the best way to roll out software upgrades to its customers. The company has been mailing USB sticks to 250,000 customers whose cars have an advanced touch screen control panel running the MyFord Touch interface. The stick contains a software upgrade that will improve navigation controls, the music and phone features, as well as the ability to control car temperature. The upgrade also contains code that will upgrade system speed and improve the interface based on common criticisms from Ford owners.

Although Ford says it plans to continue issuing software upgrades this way, the company hopes that customers will get into the habit of checking the Ford Web site for software upgrades on their own. Though most car owners are used to the technology in their cars remaining constant throughout the life of the car, newer cars are poised to change all of that.

Ford has hired "human-machine interface engineers," whose job is to analyze how their customers interact with the software in their cars. Often, these engineers use customer feedback to make changes to the software. Customers complained that too much information was available on each screen of the interface, so Ford moved the most commonly used features to more prominent positions on screen and increased their font size, relegating the rest to submenus. Feedback has been positive. Ford has also asked dealers to dedicate more time and personnel to hands-on technology training to help customers master its interface.

GM, Daimler, and other companies are all developing new features for their cars that operate online in the cloud. Users will be able to remotely track their cars (you'll never forget where you parked again) and diagnose problems with the car, like low tire pressure or the need for an oil change. Corporations will be able to track employee use of company cars by interpreting car sensors and engine readouts. Manufacturers will be able to aggregate and analyze the data from customers' cars to identify quality problems and, if necessary, quickly issue recalls. Just as with apps, the possibilities are limited only by the imagination of automakers.

GM will allow its app developers to access its computer systems to improve app function, which raises a familiar set of privacy concerns. Auto analysts believe that automakers will make mistakes as they learn how to properly handle sensitive customer data and to provide robust privacy options. On the other hand, automakers are hoping that younger customers who have grown up using Facebook are less likely to care about privacy, and features that collect highly targeted information about a car's location and driving habits.

BMW is also investing a whopping $100 million in mobile apps, hoping to market them to their customers as "premium services." Some analysts are skeptical of the decision to invest that much money, but BMW believes that mobile apps will become an increasingly attractive selling point for customers of its BMWi electric and hybrid cars. Although the future of cars sharing information with other nearby cars is still years away, automakers are excited by the possibilities afforded by smart software and apps.

Sources: Ian Sherr, "Cars Pump Up IQ To Get Edge," *The Wall Street Journal*, January 13, 2012; Chris Murphy, "4 Ways Ford Is Exploring Next-Gen Car Tech," *Information Week*, July 27, 2012; Mike Ramsey, "Avoiding Gridlock with Smart Autos," *The Wall Street Journal*, February 27, 2012; Joseph B. White, "New Driver's Ed: Tutors to Decode High-Tech Dashboards," *The Wall Street Journal*, May 8, 2012; Chris Murphy, "Ford is Now a Software Company," *Information Week*, November 28, 2011 and "Why BMW Suddenly Loves Mobile Apps," *Information Week*, March 2, 2011; and Chuck Squatriglia, "Ford Brings SmartPhone Apps to Your Dashboard," *Wired*, April 20, 2010.

CASE STUDY QUESTIONS

1. How is software adding value to automakers' products?

2. How are the automakers benefiting from software-enhanced cars? How are customers benefiting?

3. What value chain activities are involved in enhancing cars with software?

4. How much of a competitive advantage is software providing for automakers? Explain your answer.

- Make it easy for suppliers to display goods and open stores on the Amazon site
- Make it easy for customers to pay for goods
- Develop systems that coordinate the shipment of goods to customers
- Develop shipment tracking systems for customers

Internet technology has made it possible to create highly synchronized industry value chains called value webs. A **value web** is a collection of independent firms that use information technology to coordinate their value chains to produce a product or service for a market collectively. It is more customer driven and operates in a less linear fashion than the traditional value chain.

FIGURE 3.10 THE VALUE WEB

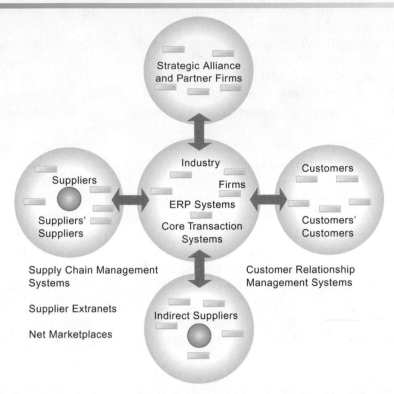

The value web is a networked system that can synchronize the value chains of business partners within an industry to respond rapidly to changes in supply and demand.

Figure 3.10 shows that this value web synchronizes the business processes of customers, suppliers, and trading partners among different companies in an industry or in related industries. These value webs are flexible and adaptive to changes in supply and demand. Relationships can be bundled or unbundled in response to changing market conditions. Firms will accelerate time to market and to customers by optimizing their value web relationships to make quick decisions on who can deliver the required products or services at the right price and location.

SYNERGIES, CORE COMPETENCIES, AND NETWORK-BASED STRATEGIES

A large corporation is typically a collection of businesses. Often, the firm is organized financially as a collection of strategic business units and the returns to the firm are directly tied to the performance of all the strategic business units. Information systems can improve the overall performance of these business units by promoting synergies and core competencies.

Synergies

The idea of synergies is that when the output of some units can be used as inputs to other units, or two organizations pool markets and expertise, these relationships lower costs and generate profits. Recent bank and financial firm mergers, such as the merger of JPMorgan Chase and Bank of New York as well as Bank of America and Countrywide Financial Corporation occurred precisely for this purpose.

One use of information technology in these synergy situations is to tie together the operations of disparate business units so that they can act as a whole. For example, acquiring Countrywide Financial enabled Bank of America to extend its mortgage lending business and to tap into a large pool of new customers who might be interested in its credit card, consumer banking, and other financial products. Information systems would help the merged companies consolidate operations, lower retailing costs, and increase cross-marketing of financial products.

Enhancing Core Competencies

Yet another way to use information systems for competitive advantage is to think about ways that systems can enhance core competencies. The argument is that the performance of all business units will increase insofar as these business units develop, or create, a central core of competencies. A **core competency** is an activity for which a firm is a world-class leader. Core competencies may involve being the world's best miniature parts designer, the best package delivery service, or the best thin-film manufacturer. In general, a core competency relies on knowledge that is gained over many years of practical field experience with a technology. This practical knowledge is typically supplemented with a long-term research effort and committed employees.

Any information system that encourages the sharing of knowledge across business units enhances competency. Such systems might encourage or enhance existing competencies and help employees become aware of new external knowledge; such systems might also help a business leverage existing competencies to related markets.

For example, Procter & Gamble, a world leader in brand management and consumer product innovation, uses a series of systems to enhance its core competencies. An intranet called InnovationNet helps people working on similar problems share ideas and expertise. InnovationNet connects those working in research and development (R&D), engineering, purchasing, marketing, legal affairs, and business information systems around the world, using a portal to provide browser-based access to documents, reports, charts, videos, and other data from various sources. It includes a directory of subject matter experts who can be tapped to give advice or collaborate on problem solving and product development, and links to outside research scientists and entrepreneurs who are searching for new, innovative products worldwide.

Network-Based Strategies

The availability of Internet and networking technology have inspired strategies that take advantage of firms' abilities to create networks or network with each other. Network-based strategies include the use of network economics, a virtual company model, and business ecosystems.

Network Economics. Business models based on a network may help firms strategically by taking advantage of **network economics**. In traditional economics—the economics of factories and agriculture—production experiences diminishing returns. The more any given resource is applied to production, the lower the marginal gain in output, until a point is reached where the additional inputs produce no additional outputs. This is the law of diminishing returns, and it is the foundation for most of modern economics.

In some situations, the law of diminishing returns does not work. For instance, in a network, the marginal costs of adding another participant are about zero, whereas the marginal gain is much larger. The larger the number of subscribers in a telephone system or the Internet, the greater the value to all participants because each user can interact with more people. It is not much more expensive to operate a television station with 1,000 subscribers than with 10 million subscribers. The value of a community of people grows with size, whereas the cost of adding new members is inconsequential.

From this network economics perspective, information technology can be strategically useful. Internet sites can be used by firms to build communities of users—like-minded customers who want to share their experiences. This builds customer loyalty and enjoyment, and builds unique ties to customers. EBay, the giant online auction site, and iVillage, an online community for women, are examples. Both businesses are based on networks of millions of users, and both companies have used the Web and Internet communication tools to build communities. The more people offering products on eBay, the more valuable the eBay site is to everyone because more products are listed, and more competition among suppliers lowers prices. Network economics also provides strategic benefits to commercial software vendors. The value of their software and complementary software products increases as more people use them, and there is a larger installed base to justify continued use of the product and vendor support.

Virtual Company Model. Another network-based strategy uses the model of a virtual company to create a competitive business. A **virtual company**, also known as a virtual organization, uses networks to link people, assets, and ideas, enabling it to ally with other companies to create and distribute products and services without being limited by traditional organizational boundaries or physical locations. One company can use the capabilities of another company without being physically tied to that company. The virtual company model is useful when a company finds it cheaper to acquire products, services, or capabilities from an external vendor or when it needs to move quickly to exploit new market opportunities and lacks the time and resources to respond on its own.

Fashion companies, such as GUESS, Ann Taylor, Levi Strauss, and Reebok, enlist Hong Kong-based Li & Fung to manage production and shipment of their garments. Li & Fung handles product development, raw material sourcing, production planning, quality assurance, and shipping. Li & Fung does not own any fabric, factories, or machines, outsourcing all of its work to a network of more than 15,000 suppliers in 40 countries all over the world. Customers place orders to Li & Fung over its private extranet. Li & Fung then sends instructions to appropriate raw material suppliers and factories where the clothing is produced. The Li & Fung extranet tracks the entire production process for each order. Working as a virtual company keeps Li & Fung flexible and adaptable so that it can design and produce the products ordered by its clients in short order to keep pace with rapidly changing fashion trends.

Business Ecosystems: Keystone and Niche Firms. The Internet and the emergence of digital firms call for some modification of the industry competitive forces model. The traditional Porter model assumes a relatively static industry environment; relatively clear-cut industry boundaries; and a relatively stable set of suppliers, substitutes, and customers, with the focus on industry players in a market environment. Instead of participating in a single industry, some of today's firms are much more aware that they participate in industry sets—collections of industries that provide related services and products (see Figure 3.11). **Business ecosystem** is another term for these loosely coupled but interdependent networks of suppliers, distributors, outsourcing

FIGURE 3.11 AN ECOSYSTEM STRATEGIC MODEL

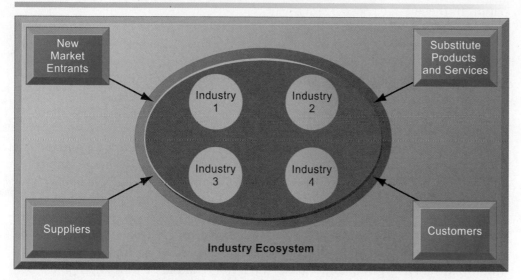

The digital firm era requires a more dynamic view of the boundaries among industries, firms, customers, and suppliers, with competition occurring among industry sets in a business ecosystem. In the ecosystem model, multiple industries work together to deliver value to the customer. IT plays an important role in enabling a dense network of interactions among the participating firms.

firms, transportation service firms, and technology manufacturers (Iansiti and Levien, 2004).

The concept of a business ecosystem builds on the idea of the value web described earlier, the main difference being that cooperation takes place across many industries rather than many firms. For instance, both Microsoft and Walmart provide platforms composed of information systems, technologies, and services that thousands of other firms in different industries use to enhance their own capabilities. Microsoft has estimated that more than 40,000 firms use its Windows platform to deliver their own products, support Microsoft products, and extend the value of Microsoft's own firm. Walmart's order entry and inventory management system is a platform used by thousands of suppliers to obtain real-time access to customer demand, track shipments, and control inventories.

Business ecosystems can be characterized as having one or a few keystone firms that dominate the ecosystem and create the platforms used by other niche firms. Keystone firms in the Microsoft ecosystem include Microsoft and technology producers such as Intel and IBM. Niche firms include thousands of software application firms, software developers, service firms, networking firms, and consulting firms that both support and rely on the Microsoft products.

Information technology plays a powerful role in establishing business ecosystems. Obviously, many firms use information systems to develop into keystone firms by building IT-based platforms that other firms can use. In the digital firm era, we can expect greater emphasis on the use of IT to build industry ecosystems because the costs of participating in such ecosystems will fall and the benefits to all firms will increase rapidly as the platform grows.

Individual firms should consider how their information systems will enable them to become profitable niche players in larger ecosystems created by keystone firms. For instance, in making decisions about which products to build or which services to offer, a firm should consider the existing business ecosystems related to these products and how it might use IT to enable participation in these larger ecosystems.

A powerful, current example of a rapidly expanding ecosystem is the mobile Internet platform. In this ecosystem there are four industries: device makers (Apple iPhone, RIM BlackBerry, Motorola, LG, and others), wireless telecommunication firms (AT&T, Verizon, T-Mobile, Sprint, and others), independent software applications providers (generally small firms selling games, applications, and ring tones), and Internet service providers (who participate as providers of Internet service to the mobile platform).

Each of these industries has its own history, interests, and driving forces. But these elements come together in a sometimes cooperative, and sometimes competitive, new industry we refer to as the mobile digital platform ecosystem. More than other firms, Apple has managed to combine these industries into a system. It is Apple's mission to sell physical devices (iPhones) that are nearly as powerful as today's personal computers. These devices work only with a high-speed broadband network supplied by the wireless phone carriers. In order to attract a large customer base, the iPhone had to be more than just a cell phone. Apple differentiated this product by making it a "smart phone," one capable of running 700,000 different, useful applications. Apple could not develop all these applications itself. Instead it relies on generally small, independent software developers to provide these applications, which can be purchased at the iTunes store. In the background is the Internet service provider industry, which makes money whenever iPhone users connect to the Internet.

3.4   USING SYSTEMS FOR COMPETITIVE ADVANTAGE: MANAGEMENT ISSUES

Strategic information systems often change the organization as well as its products, services, and operating procedures, driving the organization into new behavioral patterns. Successfully using information systems to achieve a competitive advantage is challenging and requires precise coordination of technology, organizations, and management.

SUSTAINING COMPETITIVE ADVANTAGE

The competitive advantages that strategic systems confer do not necessarily last long enough to ensure long-term profitability. Because competitors can retaliate and copy strategic systems, competitive advantage is not always sustainable. Markets, customer expectations, and technology change; globalization has made these changes even more rapid and unpredictable. The Internet can make competitive advantage disappear very quickly because virtually all companies can use this technology. Classic strategic systems, such as American Airlines's SABRE computerized reservation system, Citibank's ATM system, and FedEx's package tracking system, benefited by being the first in their industries. Then rival systems emerged. Amazon was an e-commerce leader but now faces competition from eBay, Yahoo, and Google. Information systems alone cannot provide an enduring business advantage. Systems originally intended to be strategic frequently become tools for survival, required by every firm to stay in business, or they may inhibit organizations from making the strategic changes essential for future success.

ALIGNING IT WITH BUSINESS OBJECTIVES

The research on IT and business performance has found that (a) the more successfully a firm can align information technology with its business goals, the more profitable it will be, and (b) only one-quarter of firms achieve alignment of IT with the business. About half of a business firm's profits can be explained by alignment of IT with business (Luftman, 2003).

Most businesses get it wrong: Information technology takes on a life of its own and does not serve management and shareholder interests very well. Instead of business people taking an active role in shaping IT to the enterprise, they ignore it, claim not to understand IT, and tolerate failure in the IT area as just a nuisance to work around. Such firms pay a hefty price in poor performance. Successful firms and managers understand what IT can do and how it works, take an active role in shaping its use, and measure its impact on revenues and profits.

Management Checklist: Performing a Strategic Systems Analysis

To align IT with the business and use information systems effectively for competitive advantage, managers need to perform a strategic systems analysis. To identify the types of systems that provide a strategic advantage to their firms, managers should ask the following questions:

1. What is the structure of the industry in which the firm is located?

   • What are some of the competitive forces at work in the industry? Are there new entrants to the industry? What is the relative power of suppliers, customers, and substitute products and services over prices?

   • Is the basis of competition quality, price, or brand?

   • What are the direction and nature of change within the industry? From where are the momentum and change coming?

   • How is the industry currently using information technology? Is the organization behind or ahead of the industry in its application of information systems?

2. What are the business, firm, and industry value chains for this particular firm?

   • How is the company creating value for the customer—through lower prices and transaction costs or higher quality? Are there any places in the value chain where the business could create more value for the customer and additional profit for the company?

   • Does the firm understand and manage its business processes using the best practices available? Is it taking maximum advantage of supply chain management, customer relationship management, and enterprise systems?

   • Does the firm leverage its core competencies?

   • Is the industry supply chain and customer base changing in ways that benefit or harm the firm?

   • Can the firm benefit from strategic partnerships and value webs?

   • Where in the value chain will information systems provide the greatest value to the firm?

3. Have we aligned IT with our business strategy and goals?

   • Have we correctly articulated our business strategy and goals?

   • Is IT improving the right business processes and activities to promote this strategy?

   • Are we using the right metrics to measure progress toward those goals?

MANAGING STRATEGIC TRANSITIONS

Adopting the kinds of strategic systems described in this chapter generally requires changes in business goals, relationships with customers and suppliers, and business processes. These sociotechnical changes, affecting both social and technical elements of the organization, can be considered **strategic transitions**—a movement between levels of sociotechnical systems.

Such changes often entail blurring of organizational boundaries, both external and internal. Suppliers and customers must become intimately linked and may share each other's responsibilities. Managers will need to devise new business processes for coordinating their firms' activities with those of customers, suppliers, and other organizations. The organizational change requirements surrounding new information systems are so important that they merit attention throughout this text. Chapter 14 examines organizational change issues in more detail.

LEARNING TRACK MODULE

The following Learning Track provides content relevant to topics covered in this chapter.

1. The Changing Business Environment for Information Technology

Review Summary

1. *Which features of organizations do managers need to know about to build and use information systems successfully? What is the impact of information systems on organizations?*

    All modern organizations are hierarchical, specialized, and impartial, using explicit routines to maximize efficiency. All organizations have their own cultures and politics arising from differences in interest groups, and they are affected by their surrounding environment. Organizations differ in goals, groups served, social roles, leadership styles, incentives, types of tasks performed, and type of structure. These features help explain differences in organizations' use of information systems.

    Information systems and the organizations in which they are used interact with and influence each other. The introduction of a new information system will affect organizational structure, goals, work design, values, competition between interest groups, decision making, and day-to-day behavior. At the same time, information systems must be designed to serve the needs of important organizational groups and will be shaped by the organization's structure, business processes, goals, culture, politics, and management. Information technology can reduce transaction and agency costs, and such changes have been accentuated in organizations using the Internet. New systems disrupt established patterns of work and power relationships, so there is often considerable resistance to them when they are introduced.

2. *How does Porter's competitive forces model help companies develop competitive strategies using information systems?*

    In Porter's competitive forces model, the strategic position of the firm, and its strategies, are determined by competition with its traditional direct competitors, but they are also greatly affected by new market entrants, substitute products and services, suppliers, and customers. Information systems help companies compete by maintaining low costs, differentiating products or services, focusing on market niche, strengthening ties with customers and suppliers, and increasing barriers to market entry with high levels of operational excellence.

3. *How do the value chain and value web models help businesses identify opportunities for strategic information system applications?*

   The value chain model highlights specific activities in the business where competitive strategies and information systems will have the greatest impact. The model views the firm as a series of primary and support activities that add value to a firm's products or services. Primary activities are directly related to production and distribution, whereas support activities make the delivery of primary activities possible. A firm's value chain can be linked to the value chains of its suppliers, distributors, and customers. A value web consists of information systems that enhance competitiveness at the industry level by promoting the use of standards and industry-wide consortia, and by enabling businesses to work more efficiently with their value partners.

4. *How do information systems help businesses use synergies, core competencies, and network-based strategies to achieve competitive advantage?*

   Because firms consist of multiple business units, information systems achieve additional efficiencies or enhance services by tying together the operations of disparate business units. Information systems help businesses leverage their core competencies by promoting the sharing of knowledge across business units. Information systems facilitate business models based on large networks of users or subscribers that take advantage of network economics. A virtual company strategy uses networks to link to other firms so that a company can use the capabilities of other companies to build, market, and distribute products and services. In business ecosystems, multiple industries work together to deliver value to the customer. Information systems support a dense network of interactions among the participating firms.

5. *What are the challenges posed by strategic information systems and how should they be addressed?*

   Implementing strategic systems often requires extensive organizational change and a transition from one sociotechnical level to another. Such changes are called strategic transitions and are often difficult and painful to achieve. Moreover, not all strategic systems are profitable, and they can be expensive to build. Many strategic information systems are easily copied by other firms so that strategic advantage is not always sustainable.

Key Terms

Agency theory, 120
Benchmarking, 133
Best practices, 133
Business ecosystem, 138
Competitive forces model, 124
Core competency, 137
Disruptive technologies, 117
Efficient customer response system, 126
Mass customization, 127
Network economics, 137
Organization, 112

Primary activities, 132
Product differentiation, 125
Routines, 114
Strategic transitions, 142
Support activities, 132
Switching costs, 128
Transaction cost theory, 119
Value chain model, 131
Value web, 135
Virtual company, 138

Review Questions

1. Which features of organizations do managers need to know about to build and use information systems successfully? What is the impact of information systems on organizations?

   - Define an organization and compare the technical definition of organizations with the behavioral definition.

   - Identify and describe the features of organizations that help explain differences in organizations' use of information systems.

   - Describe the major economic theories that help explain how information systems affect organizations.

- Describe the major behavioral theories that help explain how information systems affect organizations.
- Explain why there is considerable organizational resistance to the introduction of information systems.
- Describe the impact of the Internet and disruptive technologies on organizations.

2. How does Porter's competitive forces model help companies develop competitive strategies using information systems?
   - Define Porter's competitive forces model and explain how it works.
   - Describe what the competitive forces model explains about competitive advantage.
   - List and describe four competitive strategies enabled by information systems that firms can pursue.
   - Describe how information systems can support each of these competitive strategies and give examples.
   - Explain why aligning IT with business objectives is essential for strategic use of systems.

3. How do the value chain and value web models help businesses identify opportunities for strategic information system applications?
   - Define and describe the value chain model.
   - Explain how the value chain model can be used to identify opportunities for information systems.

- Define the value web and show how it is related to the value chain.
- Explain how the value web helps businesses identify opportunities for strategic information systems.
- Describe how the Internet has changed competitive forces and competitive advantage.

4. How do information systems help businesses use synergies, core competences, and network-based strategies to achieve competitive advantage?
   - Explain how information systems promote synergies and core competencies.
   - Describe how promoting synergies and core competencies enhances competitive advantage.
   - Explain how businesses benefit by using network economics.
   - Define and describe a virtual company and the benefits of pursuing a virtual company strategy.

5. What are the challenges posed by strategic information systems and how should they be addressed?
   - List and describe the management challenges posed by strategic information systems.
   - Explain how to perform a strategic systems analysis.

Discussion Questions

1. It has been said that there is no such thing as a sustainable strategic advantage. Do you agree? Why or why not?

2. It has been said that the advantage that leading-edge retailers such as Dell and Walmart have over their competition isn't technology; it's their management. Do you agree? Why or why not?

3. What are some of the issues to consider in determining whether the Internet would provide your business with a competitive advantage?

Hands-On MIS Projects

The projects in this section give you hands-on experience identifying information systems to support a business strategy and to solve a customer retention problem, using a database to improve decision making about business strategy, and using Web tools to configure and price an automobile.

Management Decision Problems

1. Macy's, Inc., through its subsidiaries, operates approximately 800 department stores in the United States. Its retail stores sell a range of merchandise, including apparel, home furnishings, and housewares. Senior management has decided that Macy's needs to tailor merchandise more to local tastes, and that the colors, sizes, brands, and styles of clothing and other merchandise should be based on the sales patterns in each individual Macy's store. How could information systems help Macy's management implement this new strategy? What pieces of data should these systems collect to help management make merchandising decisions that support this strategy?

2. Despite aggressive campaigns to attract customers with lower mobile phone prices, T-Mobile has been losing large numbers of its most lucrative two-year contract subscribers. Management wants to know why so many customers are leaving T-Mobile and what can be done to entice them back. Are customers deserting because of poor customer service, uneven network coverage, wireless service charges, or competition from carriers with Apple iPhone service? How can the company use information systems to help find the answer? What management decisions could be made using information from these systems?

Improving Decision Making: Using a Database to Clarify Business Strategy

Software skills: Database querying and reporting; database design
Business skills: Reservation systems; customer analysis

In this exercise, you will use database software to analyze the reservation transactions for a hotel and use that information to fine-tune the hotel's business strategy and marketing activities.

In MyMISLab, you will find a database for hotel reservation transactions developed in Microsoft Access with information about The President's Inn in Cape May, New Jersey. At the Inn, 10 rooms overlook side streets, 10 rooms have bay windows that offer limited views of the ocean, and the remaining 10 rooms in the front of the hotel face the ocean. Room rates are based on room choice, length of stay, and number of guests per room. Room rates are the same for one to four guests. Fifth and sixth guests must pay an additional $20 charge each per person per day. Guests staying for seven days or more receive a 10 percent discount on their daily room rates.

The owners currently use a manual reservation and bookkeeping system, which has caused many problems. Use the database to develop reports on average length of stay, average visitors per room, base revenue per room (i.e., length of visit multiplied by the daily rate), and strongest customer base. After answering these questions write a brief report about the Inn's current business situation and suggest future strategies.

Improving Decision Making: Using Web Tools to Configure and Price an Automobile

Software skills: Internet-based software
Business skills: Researching product information and pricing

In this exercise, you will use software at car Web sites to find product information about a car of your choice and use that information to make an important purchase decision. You will also evaluate two of these sites as selling tools.

You are interested in purchasing a new Ford Escape (or some other car of your choice). Go to the Web site of CarsDirect (www.carsdirect.com) and begin your investigation. Locate the Ford Escape. Research the various Escape models, choose one you prefer in terms of price, features, and safety ratings. Locate and read at least two reviews. Surf the Web site of the manufacturer, in this case Ford (www.ford.com). Compare the information available on Ford's Web site with that of CarsDirect for the Ford Escape. Try to locate the lowest price for the car you want in a local dealer's inventory. Suggest improvements for CarsDirect.com and Ford.com.

Video Cases

Video Cases and Instructional Videos illustrating some of the concepts in this chapter are available. Contact your instructor to access these videos.

Collaboration and Teamwork Project

In MyMISLab, you will find a Collaboration and Teamwork Project dealing with the concepts in this chapter. You will be able to use Google Sites, Google Docs, and other open-source collaboration tools to complete the assignment.

Can This Bookstore Be Saved?
CASE STUDY

Barnes & Noble (B&N) has been portrayed in the past as a big bully that drove small independent bookstores out of business with aggressive pricing tactics and an unbeatable inventory of books. Today, B&N finds its role reversed as the company fights a fierce battle to survive in the inevitable era of e-books. Booksellers were one of the many industries disrupted by the Internet and, more specifically, the rise of e-books and e-readers. B&N hopes to change its business model to adapt to this new environment before it suffers a similar fate as many of its competitors, like Borders, B. Dalton, and Crown Books, or their peers in other industries, like Blockbuster, Circuit City, and Eastman Kodak.

More than ever, consumers are reading books on electronic gadgets—e-readers, iPods, tablets, and PCs—instead of physical books. Although B&N still depends on its physical, brick-and-mortar stores to drive its business (B&N operates 691 bookstores in 50 states, as well as 641 college bookstores), the company has thrown its energies behind development and marketing of the Nook series of e-readers and tablets. Once simply a bookseller, B&N now styles itself as a seller of e-books, devices to read them on, and apps that enhance the reading experience. The company has had success gaining market share, but at a steep cost, and to stay afloat, it will need to contend with increased competition from Amazon, Apple, and Google—not exactly feeble opposition. B&N has a market capitalization of $1 billion. Amazon, B&N's current top competitor, has a market capitalization of $98 billion. How can B&N compete against these tech titans?

The answer remains to be seen. B&N was likely the only bookseller big enough to complete the considerable task of developing an e-reader, marketing it, and setting up manufacturing and retail operations for the device. Even if its competitors had been faster to react to consumer demand for e-books, it's unlikely they would have made the inroads that B&N has achieved into the e-book space. Reaction to the Nook has been positive, as B&N has grabbed a significant market share from Amazon and Apple in the e-book marketplace. In 2011, analysts estimated that B&N controlled approximately 27 percent of the digital book market (Amazon held 60 percent).

B&N's progress with e-books has come at a steep cost, however. The company incurred a loss of $73.9 million in 2011, compared to a $36.7 million profit the previous year. The investment required to launch and promote the Nook was the primary reason for the shortfall, and expenditures are expected to continue to climb. In response, B&N canceled its stock dividend. The key questions for B&N are whether the Nook will eventually bring in revenues that justify its steep development and marketing costs, as well as whether the Nook can help drive traffic to B&N's brick-and-mortar stores.

The economics of e-book sales are very different from traditional book sales. Customers who visit B&N's Web site buy three digital books for every one physical book, but booksellers still make more money on print books than e-books. Still, B&N's Nook business has been growing rapidly, and traditional bookstores are not. Total e-book sales were nearly $970 million in 2011, more than double from the previous year, and the percentage of e-books within the total number of books sold is still on the rise, measuring 14 percent that same year. Ironically, one of the first companies to realize the potential of e-books was B&N itself. As early as 1998, the company had partnered with software companies like NuvoMedia to develop prototype e-reader called the Rocket, but in 2003 it nixed the project because there didn't appear to be any money in it. At the time, B&N was right, but technology has come a long way since 2003, and so too have e-books.

B&N clearly took notice of the fate of Borders, its chief rival. Borders stubbornly refused to adapt to the Internet, first handing over its entire Internet operations to Amazon, and waiting to relaunch its own Web site until 2008, at which point the company was already on the road to bankruptcy. Borders had a devoted following, but it wasn't enough to combat the company's $350 million debt and dwindling profitability. B&N is the only national bookstore chain remaining in the United States, and while the company saw a bump in store traffic in the immediate aftermath of the Borders collapse, it also knew it would need to shake things up to avoid a similar fate.

Other companies also have a stake in B&N's transformation. Publishing companies have been forced to adjust their allocations of printed books and new titles for stores, and books are beginning to be released as apps in addition to physical books. Apps for books are adding more features all the time, including the ability to manipulate and enlarge images, flip through photo albums, watch videos, read instant messages, and listen to the music of characters within the book. These books, called "enhanced e-books," are considered to be the next step in the growth of digital books, but thus far, the performance of enhanced e-books has been mixed.

Publishers and e-reader manufacturers both are teaming up on enhanced e-book projects. Penguin will release 50 enhanced e-books over the course of 2012. Apple is working with publishers to create interactive digital versions of textbooks. But do readers really need these features? Some publishers believe that these apps cost more money than they are worth, and worry that there is not a big enough market for enhanced e-books to justify the expenditure of time and money. However, this is the same line of thought that was used about e-books themselves in the early 2000s, and e-book skeptics turned out to be dead wrong.

Publishers are doing anything they can to support B&N's efforts to stay afloat, because the survival of physical book retailers is important to effectively market and sell books. Bookstores spur publisher sales with the "browsing effect." Surveys have shown that only one-third of the people who visit a bookstore and walk out with a book actually arrived with the specific desire to purchase one. According to Madeline McIntosh, Random House president of sales, operations, and digital, a bookstore's display space is "one of the most valuable places that exists in this country for communicating to the consumer that a book is a big deal." Brick-and-mortar retail stores are not only essential for selling physical books, but also stimulate sales of e-books and audio books. The more visibility a book has, the more likely readers will want to purchase it. With the demise of B. Dalton, Crown Books, and Borders, B&N is the only retailer offering an extensive inventory of physical books. Book publishers need a physical presence.

Without B&N, the likely candidate to fill the void is Amazon, and publishers are not eager for that to happen. Amazon's goal for e-books is to cut out the publishers and publish books directly, selling books at an extremely steep discount to drive sales of its Kindle devices. Editors, publicists, and other entities within the publishing business view Amazon as an enemy. Selling books at Amazon's prices is not a tenable business model for publishers in the long-term.

Publishers received even worse news in April 2012, as the U.S. Department of Justice (DOJ) sued Apple and five of the country's largest publishing houses for colluding to fix e-book prices. In response to Amazon's aggressive pricing strategy, publishers and Apple had agreed to an "agency pricing" model, in which publishers set the price and retailers take a commission. (Under the wholesale arrangement with Amazon, the publishers received half of the list price, but this gave them no control over the pricing of their product.) Many books would be sold by Apple for about $13, with Apple taking a 30 percent cut. By increasing the price of e-books by a dollar or two, publishers stood to gain an extra $100 million. Even Amazon was under investigation for striking deals with publishers that forbade them from offering the same level of discounts provided by other e-reader manufacturers. The bottom line is that the DOJ action is bad news for publishers, who need B&N now more than ever.

Because the Nook was booming and brick-and-mortar stores had been stagnating, B&N has been considering spinning off its digital business from its fading bookstore business. On April 30, 2012, Microsoft announced that it would invest $300 million for a 17.6 percent stake in a new company consisting of B&N's Nook tablet and e-reader business and its College division. As part of the deal, a Nook application would be included in Microsoft's Windows 8 operating system. This arrangement will provide B&N with additional points of distribution from hundreds of millions of Windows users around the world, and both companies will share revenues from sales of e-books and other content. B&N might eventually spin off this new company.

The deal also furthers Microsoft's strategy of investing in new businesses to move beyond its Windows and Office software franchises. A Nook e-reading app could also enhance Microsoft efforts to establish a digital storefront to market e-books, apps, and other content for Windows 8, which is critical to plans for entering the tablet market.

B&N has also experimented with ways to drive traffic to their physical stores using apps on the Nook. Although this is a seemingly impossible task, they are at least coming up with some inventive ideas. For example, if you connect to a Wi-Fi network in a B&N store with your Nook, you can get free extras in many apps and games like Angry Birds, where you can unlock a bonus character that normally costs a dollar. Other companies are using similar techniques to promote board games, toys, movies, and of course, physical books. B&N has also expanded its store space for toys and games and added new display space for its Nook devices. There are also plans to experiment with slightly smaller stores.

These promotional campaigns probably won't be enough to stop B&N's dwindling in-store sales. What will the future hold? Will B&N be able to succeed as a digital company, and is there a future for its brick-and-mortar stores? Is there a way for e-books to help sell print books, just as print books have stimulated demand for their digital versions? Although B&N has made a spirited effort to revamp its business and go toe-to-toe with several tech titans, it's possible that it might be too tall an order for the storied bookseller.

Sources: Michael J. De La Merced and Julie Bosman, "Microsoft Deal Adds to Battle over E-Books," *The New York Times*, May 1, 2012; Shira Ovide and Jeffrey A. Trachtenberg, "Microsoft Hooks Onto Nook," *The Wall Street Journal*, May 1, 2012; Julie Bosnan, "The Bookstore's Last Stand," *The New York Times*, January 29, 2012; Paul Vigna, "E-Books, Apple, Amazon: The Deadly Hallows for Publishers," *The New York Times*, April 11, 2012; Brian X. Chen, "Barnes & Noble Uses Apps to Lure Customers Into Stores," *The New York Times*, January 27, 2012; Alter, Alexandra,

"Blowing Up the Book," *The Wall Street Journal*, January 20, 2012; Rick Newman, "4 Lessons from the Demise of Borders," *U.S. News and World Report*, July 20, 2011; Chunka Mui, "Borders and Kodak are Facing Doomsday: Who's Next?" *Forbes*, July 22, 2011; and Jeffrey A. Trachtenberg and Martin Peers, "Barnes and Noble: The Next Chapter," *The Wall Street Journal*, January 6, 2011.

CASE STUDY QUESTIONS

1. Use the value chain and competitive forces models to evaluate the impact of the Internet on book publishers and book retail stores such as B&N.

2. How are B&N and the book publishers changing their business models to deal with the Internet and e-book technology?

3. Will B&N's new strategy be successful? Explain your answer.

4. Is there anything else B&N and the book publishers should be doing to stimulate more business?

Chapter 4

Ethical and Social Issues in Information Systems

Interactive Sessions:

Life on the Grid: iPhone Becomes iTrack

Monitoring in the Workplace

ETHICAL ISSUES FACING THE USE OF TECHNOLOGIES FOR THE AGED COMMUNITY

The Australian government takes a strong interest in the use of IT for the direct and indirect care of the aged community. Indirect care includes the administrative aspects of aged care in nursing and aged care communities. No doubt, IT has the potential to improve the quality of lifestyle for the aged. For example, access to the Internet makes the aged feel more in touch with the rest of the world and, in many cases, can assist with day-to-day living such as online grocery purchases, online bill payment and checking bank statements. However, this is conditional upon various factors such as their feeling comfortable with computers, having the computer knowledge and skill and, of course, a trust in online transactions.

Increasingly, new ideas are generated through research and development in an effort to enhanceet chronic illnesses like heart conditions, and diabetes. It is particularly the use of these technologies that poses a plethora of ethical issues of concern to healthcare providers and consumers. The 'Smart House' is a Sydney initiative, designed to allow future generations to remain in their own homes while ageing. It uses a range of 'telecare' sensor technology.

"This Smart House technology includes passive infrared detectors and a door-entry system, which will allow the resident to see who is at the door, via their TV, and open the door remotely. The technology also features emergency pendants and pull cords to trigger an emergency monitoring system, along with bed and chair sensors. Future incorporations into the Smart House will include central locking systems, electric windows and doors, electric curtain and blind openers and other devices." (BCS, 2006).

A recurring ethical issue in the use of such technology is invasion of the aged consumers' privacy. Many may not feel comfortable about being monitored in their own homes, 24-hours a day, even though they may see the benefits of such systems. There is also the question of awareness, consent, ownership, and access of any data collected from these aged consumers. Health-related data is particularly very sensitive and, thus, should not be given public access without prior privacy, security, and safety considerations. Socially and culturally, these systems may also not be acceptable as a replacement for traditional human carers (most often close family members) who can produce a much more personalised level of care. In Australia, a number of aged care providers focus on different minority groups (for example Chinese and Koreans) and there is increasing awareness that the technology adopted for them must be socially acceptable and culturally competent, with the facility to adapt to the social and cultural needs of these minority groups (for example, use of appropriate language - voice or textual - interface, or exhibiting understanding of the living habits and preferences in the design of the technology).

© Ocean/Corbis

Sources: BCS (2006). Smart House holds key to future aged care needs, Baptist Community Services NSW & ACT, Media Release, 1st May 2006, http://www.bcs.org.au/resource/R0058Corp.pdf.

Case contributed by Dr. Lesley Land, University of New South Wales

The opening case highlights a number of ethical issues that are specific to healthcare for the ageing population. However, some of these are recurring issues in other healthcare domains, or in organizations in general (such as privacy and security). For example, the data collected from the monitoring and tracking of consumers can be both beneficial from a business viewpoint (in the opening case, it can improve the quality of life, and/or the clinical care of the aged), but at the same time, it also creates opportunities for ethical abuse by invading the privacy of consumers. Such ethical dilemmas arise in the building of new information systems that potentially promise increased efficiency and effectiveness in business processes. In this chapter, we wish to highlight the need to be aware of the negative impact of information systems, alongside the positive benefits. In many cases, management needs to create an acceptable trade-off through the creation of appropriate policies and standards, as agreed upon by all stakeholders, prior to system implementation.

The following part of the case is contributed by Robert Manderson, University of Roehampton

The chapter-opening diagram highlights critical points raised by this case and this chapter. Sydney's 'Smart House' initiative demonstrates some of the potential for sensor-driven 'telecare' technology in its indirect, administrative, and direct, in-home, IT forms. Both administrators and consumers experienced the limitations of the current technology in the form of administration burden due to unintegrated systems, and lack of IT skills in both cases. In order to achieve increased efficiency in the delivery of 'telecare' technology and, at the same time, improve the consumer's in-home quality of care, further development of the health care technologies is required. However, as sensor technology, and information systems which make use of the data from these, evolve and become more integrated using the Internet and the developments in cloud computing, it has become increasingly apparent that major ethical considerations need to be taken into account which address the concerns of consumers, particularly in relation to privacy, security, safety, and increasingly cultural aspects.

The traditional approach to caring for the aged community within the healthcare system has been to increasingly support individuals through the use of health care professionals in dedicated health care facilities. Whilst this is expected to be a continuing practice into the foreseeable future, Sydney's 'telecare' initiative is an example of how technologies can support aged individuals in their own home for longer than has been possible hitherto, enabling an increase in the health care provider's quality of care and a reduction in the administration burden. As 'telecare' technologies continue to be developed, and increasingly used, major ethical and social issues need to be addressed to satisfy the concerns of the individuals in the aged community who will be offered these technologies to live normally at home. The Sydney 'Smart House' 'telecare' initiative has identified a number of processes that should be included in future information systems developments to address the ethical issues, including user-involvement in the design of the information systems to incorporate features with the ethical concerns in-mind, redesign business processes which take account of the ethical concerns, allocate sufficient resources to include in the design the ethics informed features, and deploy new technologies to meet user needs.

Here are some questions to think about: What 'Smart Home' 'telecare' technologies were used as part of the Sydney initiative and how were they deployed to support the aged community at home? What were the ethical concerns associated with each 'telecare' technology and how were these being addressed?

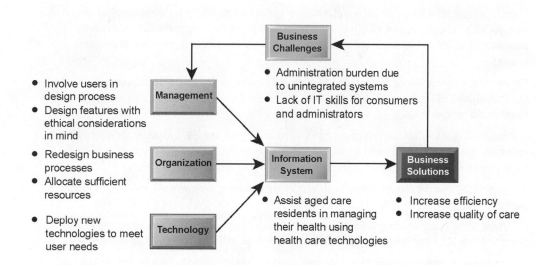

4.1 UNDERSTANDING ETHICAL AND SOCIAL ISSUES RELATED TO SYSTEMS

In the past 10 years, we have witnessed, arguably, one of the most ethically challenging periods for U.S. and global business. Table 4.1 provides a small sample of recent cases demonstrating failed ethical judgment by senior and middle managers. These lapses in ethical and business judgment occurred across a broad spectrum of industries.

In today's new legal environment, managers who violate the law and are convicted will most likely spend time in prison. U.S. federal sentencing guidelines adopted in 1987 mandate that federal judges impose stiff sentences

TABLE 4.1 RECENT EXAMPLES OF FAILED ETHICAL JUDGMENT BY SENIOR MANAGERS

Barclays Bank PLC (2012)	One of the world's largest banks admitted to manipulating its submissions for the LIBOR benchmark interest rates in order to benefit its trading positions and the media's perception of the bank's financial health. Fined $160 million.
GlaxoSmithKline LLC (2012)	The global health care giant admitted to unlawful and criminal promotion of certain prescription drugs, its failure to report certain safety data, and its civil liability for alleged false price reporting practices. Fined $3 billion, the largest health care fraud settlement in U.S. history and the largest payment ever by a drug company.
Walmart Inc. (2012)	Walmart executives in Mexico accused of paying millions in bribes to Mexican officials in order to receive building permits. Under investigation by the Department of Justice.
Minerals Management Service (U.S. Department of the Interior) (2010)	Government managers accused of accepting gifts and other favors from oil companies, letting oil company rig employees write up inspection reports, and failing to enforce existing regulations on offshore Gulf drilling rigs. Employees systematically falsified information record systems.
Pfizer, Eli Lilly, and AstraZeneca (2009)	Major pharmaceutical firms paid billions of dollars to settle U.S. federal charges that executives fixed clinical trials for antipsychotic and pain killer drugs, marketed them inappropriately to children, and claimed unsubstantiated benefits while covering up negative outcomes. Firms falsified information in reports and systems.
Galleon Group (2011)	Founder of the Galleon Group sentenced to 11 years in prison for trading on insider information. Found guilty of paying $250 million to Wall Street banks, and in return received market information that other investors did not get.
Siemens (2009)	The world's largest engineering firm paid over $4 billion to German and U.S. authorities for a decades-long, worldwide bribery scheme approved by corporate executives to influence potential customers and governments. Payments concealed from normal reporting accounting systems.
IBM (2011)	IBM settled SEC charges that it paid off South Korean and Chinese government officials with bags of cash over a 10-year period.
McKinsey & Company (2011)	CEO Rajat Gupta heard on tapes leaking insider information. The former CEO of prestigious management consulting firm McKinsey & Company was found guilty in 2012 and sentenced to two years in prison.
Tyson Foods (2011)	World's largest producer of poultry, beef, and pork agreed to pay $5 million in fines for bribing Mexican officials to ignore health violations.

on business executives based on the monetary value of the crime, the presence of a conspiracy to prevent discovery of the crime, the use of structured financial transactions to hide the crime, and failure to cooperate with prosecutors (U.S. Sentencing Commission, 2004).

Although business firms would, in the past, often pay for the legal defense of their employees enmeshed in civil charges and criminal investigations, firms are now encouraged to cooperate with prosecutors to reduce charges against the entire firm for obstructing investigations. These developments mean that, more than ever, as a manager or an employee, you will have to decide for yourself what constitutes proper legal and ethical conduct.

Although these major instances of failed ethical and legal judgment were not masterminded by information systems departments, information systems were instrumental in many of these frauds. In many cases, the perpetrators of these crimes artfully used financial reporting information systems to bury their decisions from public scrutiny in the vain hope they would never be caught.

We deal with the issue of control in information systems in Chapter 8. In this chapter, we talk about the ethical dimensions of these and other actions based on the use of information systems.

Ethics refers to the principles of right and wrong that individuals, acting as free moral agents, use to make choices to guide their behaviors. Information systems raise new ethical questions for both individuals and societies because they create opportunities for intense social change, and thus threaten existing distributions of power, money, rights, and obligations. Like other technologies, such as steam engines, electricity, the telephone, and the radio, information technology can be used to achieve social progress, but it can also be used to commit crimes and threaten cherished social values. The development of information technology will produce benefits for many and costs for others.

Ethical issues in information systems have been given new urgency by the rise of the Internet and electronic commerce. Internet and digital firm technologies make it easier than ever to assemble, integrate, and distribute information, unleashing new concerns about the appropriate use of customer information, the protection of personal privacy, and the protection of intellectual property.

Other pressing ethical issues raised by information systems include establishing accountability for the consequences of information systems, setting standards to safeguard system quality that protects the safety of the individual and society, and preserving values and institutions considered essential to the quality of life in an information society. When using information systems, it is essential to ask, "What is the ethical and socially responsible course of action?"

A MODEL FOR THINKING ABOUT ETHICAL, SOCIAL, AND POLITICAL ISSUES

Ethical, social, and political issues are closely linked. The ethical dilemma you may face as a manager of information systems typically is reflected in social and political debate. One way to think about these relationships is shown in Figure 4.1. Imagine society as a more or less calm pond on a summer day, a delicate ecosystem in partial equilibrium with individuals and with social and political institutions. Individuals know how to act in this pond because social institutions (family, education, organizations) have developed well-honed rules of behavior, and these are supported by laws developed in the political sector that prescribe behavior and promise sanctions for violations. Now toss a rock into the center of the pond. What happens? Ripples, of course.

Imagine instead that the disturbing force is a powerful shock of new information technology and systems hitting a society more or less at rest. Suddenly, individual actors are confronted with new situations often not covered by the old rules. Social institutions cannot respond overnight to these ripples—it may take years to develop etiquette, expectations, social responsibility, politically correct attitudes, or approved rules. Political institutions also require time before developing new laws and often require the demonstration of real harm before they act. In the meantime, you may have to act. You may be forced to act in a legal gray area.

We can use this model to illustrate the dynamics that connect ethical, social, and political issues. This model is also useful for identifying the main moral dimensions of the information society, which cut across various levels of action—individual, social, and political.

FIVE MORAL DIMENSIONS OF THE INFORMATION AGE

The major ethical, social, and political issues raised by information systems include the following moral dimensions:

FIGURE 4.1 **THE RELATIONSHIP BETWEEN ETHICAL, SOCIAL, AND POLITICAL ISSUES IN AN INFORMATION SOCIETY**

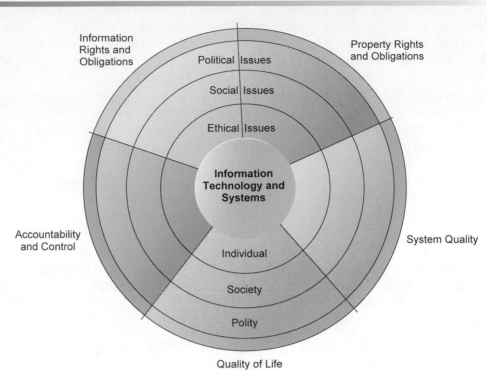

The introduction of new information technology has a ripple effect, raising new ethical, social, and political issues that must be dealt with on the individual, social, and political levels. These issues have five moral dimensions: information rights and obligations, property rights and obligations, system quality, quality of life, and accountability and control.

- *Information rights and obligations.* What **information rights** do individuals and organizations possess with respect to themselves? What can they protect?

- *Property rights and obligations.* How will traditional intellectual property rights be protected in a digital society in which tracing and accounting for ownership are difficult and ignoring such property rights is so easy?

- *Accountability and control.* Who can and will be held accountable and liable for the harm done to individual and collective information and property rights?

- *System quality.* What standards of data and system quality should we demand to protect individual rights and the safety of society?

- *Quality of life.* What values should be preserved in an information- and knowledge-based society? Which institutions should we protect from violation? Which cultural values and practices are supported by the new information technology?

We explore these moral dimensions in detail in Section 4.3.

KEY TECHNOLOGY TRENDS THAT RAISE ETHICAL ISSUES

Ethical issues long preceded information technology. Nevertheless, information technology has heightened ethical concerns, taxed existing social arrangements, and made some laws obsolete or severely crippled. There are

TABLE 4.2 TECHNOLOGY TRENDS THAT RAISE ETHICAL ISSUES

TREND	IMPACT
Computing power doubles every 18 months	More organizations depend on computer systems for critical operations.
Data storage costs rapidly decline	Organizations can easily maintain detailed databases on individuals.
Data analysis advances	Companies can analyze vast quantities of data gathered on individuals to develop detailed profiles of individual behavior.
Networking advances	Copying data from one location to another and accessing personal data from remote locations are much easier.
Mobile device growth Impact	Individual cell phones may be tracked without user consent or knowledge.

four key technological trends responsible for these ethical stresses and they are summarized in Table 4.2.

The doubling of computing power every 18 months has made it possible for most organizations to use information systems for their core production processes. As a result, our dependence on systems and our vulnerability to system errors and poor data quality have increased. Social rules and laws have not yet adjusted to this dependence. Standards for ensuring the accuracy and reliability of information systems (see Chapter 8) are not universally accepted or enforced.

Advances in data storage techniques and rapidly declining storage costs have been responsible for the multiplying databases on individuals—employees, customers, and potential customers—maintained by private and public organizations. These advances in data storage have made the routine violation of individual privacy both cheap and effective. Very large data storage systems capable of working with terabytes of data are inexpensive enough for large firms to use in identifying customers.

Advances in data analysis techniques for large pools of data are another technological trend that heightens ethical concerns because companies and government agencies are able to find out highly detailed personal information about individuals. With contemporary data management tools (see Chapter 6), companies can assemble and combine the myriad pieces of information about you stored on computers much more easily than in the past.

Think of all the ways you generate computer information about yourself—credit card purchases, telephone calls, magazine subscriptions, video rentals, mail-order purchases, banking records, local, state, and federal government records (including court and police records), and visits to Web sites. Put together and mined properly, this information could reveal not only your credit information but also your driving habits, your tastes, your associations, what you read and watch, and your political interests.

Companies with products to sell purchase relevant information from these sources to help them more finely target their marketing campaigns. Chapters 5 and 10 describe how companies can analyze large pools of data from multiple sources to rapidly identify buying patterns of customers and suggest individual responses. The use of computers to combine data from multiple sources and create electronic dossiers of detailed information on individuals is called **profiling**.

For example, several thousand of the most popular Web sites allow DoubleClick (owned by Google), an Internet advertising broker, to track the

Credit card purchases can make personal information available to market researchers, telemarketers, and direct mail companies. Advances in information technology facilitate the invasion of privacy.

© Corbis/Alamy

activities of their visitors in exchange for revenue from advertisements based on visitor information DoubleClick gathers. DoubleClick uses this information to create a profile of each online visitor, adding more detail to the profile as the visitor accesses an associated DoubleClick site. Over time, DoubleClick can create a detailed dossier of a person's spending and computing habits on the Web that is sold to companies to help them target their Web ads more precisely.

ChoicePoint gathers data from police, criminal, and motor vehicle records, credit and employment histories, current and previous addresses, professional licenses, and insurance claims to assemble and maintain electronic dossiers on almost every adult in the United States. The company sells this personal information to businesses and government agencies. Demand for personal data is so enormous that data broker businesses such as ChoicePoint are flourishing. In 2011, the two largest credit card networks, Visa Inc. and MasterCard Inc., were planning to link credit card purchase information with consumer social network and other information to create customer profiles that could be sold to advertising firms. In 2012, Visa will process more than 45 billion transactions a year and MasterCard will process more than 23 billion transactions. Currently, this transactional information is not linked with consumer Internet activities.

A new data analysis technology called **nonobvious relationship aware-ness (NORA)** has given both the government and the private sector even more powerful profiling capabilities. NORA can take information about people from many disparate sources, such as employment applications, telephone records, customer listings, and "wanted" lists, and correlate relationships to find obscure hidden connections that might help identify criminals or terrorists (see Figure 4.2).

NORA technology scans data and extracts information as the data are being generated so that it could, for example, instantly discover a man at an airline ticket counter who shares a phone number with a known terrorist before that person boards an airplane. The technology is considered a valuable tool for homeland security but does have privacy implications because it can provide such a detailed picture of the activities and associations of a single individual.

FIGURE 4.2   NONOBVIOUS RELATIONSHIP AWARENESS (NORA)

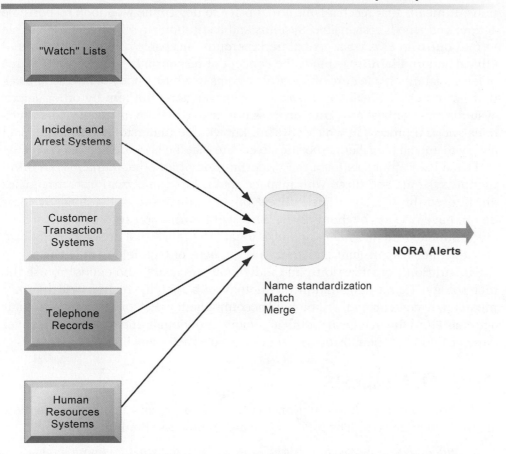

NORA technology can take information about people from disparate sources and find obscure, nonobvious relationships. It might discover, for example, that an applicant for a job at a casino shares a telephone number with a known criminal and issue an alert to the hiring manager.

Finally, advances in networking, including the Internet, promise to greatly reduce the costs of moving and accessing large quantities of data and open the possibility of mining large pools of data remotely using small desktop machines, permitting an invasion of privacy on a scale and with a precision heretofore unimaginable.

4.2   ETHICS IN AN INFORMATION SOCIETY

Ethics is a concern of humans who have freedom of choice. Ethics is about individual choice: When faced with alternative courses of action, what is the correct moral choice? What are the main features of ethical choice?

BASIC CONCEPTS: RESPONSIBILITY, ACCOUNTABILITY, AND LIABILITY

Ethical choices are decisions made by individuals who are responsible for the consequences of their actions. **Responsibility** is a key element of ethical action. Responsibility means that you accept the potential costs, duties, and obligations for the decisions you make. **Accountability** is a feature of systems and social institutions: It means that mechanisms are in place to determine who took responsible action, and who is responsible. Systems and institutions in which it is impossible to find out who took what action are inherently incapable of ethical analysis or ethical action. **Liability** extends the concept of responsibility further to the area of laws. Liability is a feature of political systems in which a body of laws is in place that permits individuals to recover the damages done to them by other actors, systems, or organizations. **Due process** is a related feature of law-governed societies and is a process in which laws are known and understood, and there is an ability to appeal to higher authorities to ensure that the laws are applied correctly.

These basic concepts form the underpinning of an ethical analysis of information systems and those who manage them. First, information technologies are filtered through social institutions, organizations, and individuals. Systems do not have impacts by themselves. Whatever information system impacts exist are products of institutional, organizational, and individual actions and behaviors. Second, responsibility for the consequences of technology falls clearly on the institutions, organizations, and individual managers who choose to use the technology. Using information technology in a socially responsible manner means that you can and will be held accountable for the consequences of your actions. Third, in an ethical, political society, individuals and others can recover damages done to them through a set of laws characterized by due process.

ETHICAL ANALYSIS

When confronted with a situation that seems to present ethical issues, how should you analyze it? The following five-step process should help:

1. *Identify and describe the facts clearly.* Find out who did what to whom, and where, when, and how. In many instances, you will be surprised at the errors in the initially reported facts, and often you will find that simply getting the facts straight helps define the solution. It also helps to get the opposing parties involved in an ethical dilemma to agree on the facts.

2. *Define the conflict or dilemma and identify the higher-order values involved.* Ethical, social, and political issues always reference higher values. The parties to a dispute all claim to be pursuing higher values (e.g., freedom, privacy, protection of property, and the free enterprise system). Typically, an ethical issue involves a dilemma: two diametrically opposed courses of action that support worthwhile values. For example, the chapter-ending case study illustrates two competing values: the need to improve health care record keeping and the need to protect individual privacy.

3. *Identify the stakeholders.* Every ethical, social, and political issue has stakeholders: players in the game who have an interest in the outcome, who have invested in the situation, and usually who have vocal opinions. Find out the identity of these groups and what they want. This will be useful later when designing a solution.

4. *Identify the options that you can reasonably take.* You may find that none of the options satisfy all the interests involved, but that some options do a better job than others. Sometimes arriving at a good or ethical solution may not always be a balancing of consequences to stakeholders.

5. *Identify the potential consequences of your options.* Some options may be ethically correct but disastrous from other points of view. Other options may work in one instance but not in other similar instances. Always ask yourself, "What if I choose this option consistently over time?"

CANDIDATE ETHICAL PRINCIPLES

Once your analysis is complete, what ethical principles or rules should you use to make a decision? What higher-order values should inform your judgment? Although you are the only one who can decide which among many ethical principles you will follow, and how you will prioritize them, it is helpful to consider some ethical principles with deep roots in many cultures that have survived throughout recorded history:

1. Do unto others as you would have them do unto you (the **Golden Rule**). Putting yourself into the place of others, and thinking of yourself as the object of the decision, can help you think about fairness in decision making.

2. If an action is not right for everyone to take, it is not right for anyone **(Immanuel Kant's Categorical Imperative)**. Ask yourself, "If everyone did this, could the organization, or society, survive?"

3. If an action cannot be taken repeatedly, it is not right to take at all **(Descartes' rule of change)**. This is the slippery-slope rule: An action may bring about a small change now that is acceptable, but if it is repeated, it would bring unacceptable changes in the long run. In the vernacular, it might be stated as "once started down a slippery path, you may not be able to stop."

4. Take the action that achieves the higher or greater value **(Utilitarian Principle)**. This rule assumes you can prioritize values in a rank order and understand the consequences of various courses of action.

5. Take the action that produces the least harm or the least potential cost **(Risk Aversion Principle).** Some actions have extremely high failure costs of very low probability (e.g., building a nuclear generating facility in an urban area) or extremely high failure costs of moderate probability (speeding and automobile accidents). Avoid these high-failure-cost actions, paying greater attention to high-failure-cost potential of moderate to high probability.

6. Assume that virtually all tangible and intangible objects are owned by someone else unless there is a specific declaration otherwise. (This is the **ethical "no free lunch" rule.)** If something someone else has created is useful to you, it has value, and you should assume the creator wants compensation for this work.

Actions that do not easily pass these rules deserve close attention and a great deal of caution. The appearance of unethical behavior may do as much harm to you and your company as actual unethical behavior.

PROFESSIONAL CODES OF CONDUCT

When groups of people claim to be professionals, they take on special rights and obligations because of their special claims to knowledge, wisdom, and respect. Professional codes of conduct are promulgated by associations of professionals, such as the American Medical Association (AMA), the American Bar Association (ABA), the Association of Information Technology Professionals (AITP), and the Association for Computing Machinery (ACM). These professional groups take responsibility for the partial regulation of their professions by determining entrance qualifications and competence. Codes of ethics are promises by professions to regulate themselves in the general interest of society. For example, avoiding harm to others, honoring property rights (including intellectual property), and respecting privacy are among the General Moral Imperatives of the ACM's Code of Ethics and Professional Conduct.

SOME REAL-WORLD ETHICAL DILEMMAS

Information systems have created new ethical dilemmas in which one set of interests is pitted against another. For example, many of the large telephone companies in the United States are using information technology to reduce the sizes of their workforces. Voice recognition software reduces the need for human operators by enabling computers to recognize a customer's responses to a series of computerized questions. Many companies monitor what their employees are doing on the Internet to prevent them from wasting company resources on non-business activities. Facebook monitors its subscribers and then sells the information to advertisers and app developers (see the chapter-ending case study).

In each instance, you can find competing values at work, with groups lined up on either side of a debate. A company may argue, for example, that it has a right to use information systems to increase productivity and reduce the size of its workforce to lower costs and stay in business. Employees displaced by information systems may argue that employers have some responsibility for their welfare. Business owners might feel obligated to monitor employee e-mail and Internet use to minimize drains on productivity. Employees might believe they should be able to use the Internet for short personal tasks in place of the telephone. A close analysis of the facts can sometimes produce compromised solutions that give each side "half a loaf." Try to apply some of the principles of ethical analysis described to each of these cases. What is the right thing to do?

4.3 THE MORAL DIMENSIONS OF INFORMATION SYSTEMS

In this section, we take a closer look at the five moral dimensions of information systems first described in Figure 4.1. In each dimension, we identify the ethical, social, and political levels of analysis and use real-world examples to illustrate the values involved, the stakeholders, and the options chosen.

INFORMATION RIGHTS: PRIVACY AND FREEDOM IN THE INTERNET AGE

Privacy is the claim of individuals to be left alone, free from surveillance or interference from other individuals or organizations, including the state. Claims to privacy are also involved at the workplace: Millions of employees are subject to electronic and other forms of high-tech surveillance. Information technology and systems threaten individual claims to privacy by making the invasion of privacy cheap, profitable, and effective.

The claim to privacy is protected in the U.S., Canadian, and German constitutions in a variety of different ways and in other countries through various statutes. In the United States, the claim to privacy is protected primarily by the First Amendment guarantees of freedom of speech and association, the Fourth Amendment protections against unreasonable search and seizure of one's personal documents or home, and the guarantee of due process.

Table 4.3 describes the major U.S. federal statutes that set forth the conditions for handling information about individuals in such areas as credit reporting, education, financial records, newspaper records, and electronic communications. The Privacy Act of 1974 has been the most important of

TABLE 4.3 FEDERAL PRIVACY LAWS IN THE UNITED STATES

GENERAL FEDERAL PRIVACY LAWS	PRIVACY LAWS AFFECTING PRIVATE INSTITUTIONS
Freedom of Information Act of 1966 as Amended (5 USC 552)	Fair Credit Reporting Act of 1970
Privacy Act of 1974 as Amended (5 USC 552a)	Family Educational Rights and Privacy Act of 1974
Electronic Communications Privacy Act of 1986	Right to Financial Privacy Act of 1978
Computer Matching and Privacy Protection Act of 1988	Privacy Protection Act of 1980
Computer Security Act of 1987	Cable Communications Policy Act of 1984
Federal Managers Financial Integrity Act of 1982	Electronic Communications Privacy Act of 1986
Driver's Privacy Protection Act of 1994	Video Privacy Protection Act of 1988
E-Government Act of 2002	The Health Insurance Portability and Accountability Act of 1996 (HIPAA)
	Children's Online Privacy Protection Act (COPPA) of 1998
	Financial Modernization Act (Gramm-Leach-Bliley Act) of 1999

these laws, regulating the federal government's collection, use, and disclosure of information. At present, most U.S. federal privacy laws apply only to the federal government and regulate very few areas of the private sector.

Most American and European privacy law is based on a regime called **Fair Information Practices (FIP)** first set forth in a report written in 1973 by a federal government advisory committee and updated most recently in 2010 to take into account new privacy-invading technology (FTC, 2010; U.S. Department of Health, Education, and Welfare, 1973). FIP is a set of principles governing the collection and use of information about individuals. FIP principles are based on the notion of a mutuality of interest between the record holder and the individual. The individual has an interest in engaging in a transaction, and the record keeper—usually a business or government agency—requires information about the individual to support the transaction. Once information is gathered, the individual maintains an interest in the record, and the record may not be used to support other activities without the individual's consent. In 1998, the FTC restated and extended the original FIP to provide guidelines for protecting online privacy. Table 4.4 describes the FTC's Fair Information Practice principles.

TABLE 4.4 FEDERAL TRADE COMMISSION FAIR INFORMATION PRACTICE PRINCIPLES

1. Notice/awareness (core principle). Web sites must disclose their information practices before collecting data. Includes identification of collector; uses of data; other recipients of data; nature of collection (active/inactive); voluntary or required status; consequences of refusal; and steps taken to protect confidentiality, integrity, and quality of the data.

2. Choice/consent (core principle). There must be a choice regime in place allowing consumers to choose how their information will be used for secondary purposes other than supporting the transaction, including internal use and transfer to third parties.

3. Access/participation. Consumers should be able to review and contest the accuracy and completeness of data collected about them in a timely, inexpensive process.

4. Security. Data collectors must take responsible steps to assure that consumer information is accurate and secure from unauthorized use.

5. Enforcement. There must be in place a mechanism to enforce FIP principles. This can involve self-regulation, legislation giving consumers legal remedies for violations, or federal statutes and regulations.

The FTC's FIP principles are being used as guidelines to drive changes in privacy legislation. In July 1998, the U.S. Congress passed the Children's Online Privacy Protection Act (COPPA), requiring Web sites to obtain parental permission before collecting information on children under the age of 13. The FTC has recommended additional legislation to protect online consumer privacy in advertising networks that collect records of consumer Web activity to develop detailed profiles, which are then used by other companies to target online ads. In 2010, the FTC added three practices to its framework for privacy. Firms should adopt "privacy by design," building products and services that protect privacy. Firms should increase the transparency of their data practices. And firms should require consumer consent and provide clear options to opt out of data collection schemes (FTC, 2010). Other proposed Internet privacy legislation focuses on protecting the online use of personal identification numbers, such as social security numbers; protecting personal information collected on the Internet that deals with individuals not covered by COPPA; and limiting the use of data mining for homeland security.

Beginning in 2009 and continuing through 2012, the FTC extended its FIP doctrine to address the issue of behavioral targeting. The FTC held hearings to discuss its program for voluntary industry principles for regulating behavioral targeting. The online advertising trade group Network Advertising Initiative (discussed later in this section), published its own self-regulatory principles that largely agreed with the FTC. Nevertheless, the government, privacy groups, and the online ad industry are still at loggerheads over two issues. Privacy advocates want both an opt-in policy at all sites and a national Do Not Track list. The industry opposes these moves and continues to insist on an opt-out capability being the only way to avoid tracking. In May 2011, Senator Jay D. Rockefeller (D-WV), Chairman of the Senate Commerce Subcommittee on Consumer Protection, Product Safety, and Insurance, held hearings to discuss consumer privacy concerns and to explore the possible role of the federal government in protecting consumers in the mobile marketplace. Rockefeller supports the Do-Not-Track Online Act of 2011, which requires firms to notify consumers they are being tracked and allows consumers to opt out of the tracking (U.S. Senate, 2011). Nevertheless, there is an emerging consensus among all parties that greater transparency and user control (especially making opt-out of tracking the default option) is required to deal with behavioral tracking.

Privacy protections have also been added to recent laws deregulating financial services and safeguarding the maintenance and transmission of health information about individuals. The Gramm-Leach-Bliley Act of 1999, which repeals earlier restrictions on affiliations among banks, securities firms, and insurance companies, includes some privacy protection for consumers of financial services. All financial institutions are required to disclose their policies and practices for protecting the privacy of nonpublic personal information and to allow customers to opt out of information-sharing arrangements with nonaffiliated third parties.

The Health Insurance Portability and Accountability Act (HIPAA) of 1996, which took effect on April 14, 2003, includes privacy protection for medical records. The law gives patients access to their personal medical records maintained by health care providers, hospitals, and health insurers, and the right to authorize how protected information about themselves can be used or disclosed. Doctors, hospitals, and other health care providers must limit the disclosure of personal information about patients to the minimum amount necessary to achieve a given purpose.

The European Directive on Data Protection

In Europe, privacy protection is much more stringent than in the United States. Unlike the United States, European countries do not allow businesses to use personally identifiable information without consumers' prior consent. On October 25, 1998, the European Commission's Directive on Data Protection went into effect, broadening privacy protection in the European Union (EU) nations. The directive requires companies to inform people when they collect information about them and disclose how it will be stored and used. Customers must provide their informed consent before any company can legally use data about them, and they have the right to access that information, correct it, and request that no further data be collected. **Informed consent** can be defined as consent given with knowledge of all the facts needed to make a rational decision. EU member nations must translate these principles into their own laws and cannot transfer personal data to countries, such as the United States, that do not have similar privacy protection regulations. In 2009, the European Parliament passed new rules governing the use of third-party cookies for behavioral tracking purposes. These new rules were implemented in May 2011 and require that Web site visitors must give explicit consent to be tracked by cookies. Web sites will be required to have highly visible warnings on their pages if third-party cookies are being used (European Parliament, 2009).

In January 2012, the E.U. issued significant proposed changes to its data protection rules, the first overhaul since 1995 (European Commission, 2012). The new rules would apply to all companies providing services in Europe, and require Internet companies like Amazon, Facebook, Apple, Google, and others to obtain explicit consent from consumers about the use of their personal data, delete information at the user's request (based on the "right to be forgotten"), and retain information only as long as absolutely necessary. The proposed rules provide for fines up to 2% of the annual gross revenue of offending firms. In the case of Google, for instance, with annual revenue of $38 billion, a maximum fine would amount to $760 million. The requirement for user consent includes the use of cookies and super cookies used for tracking purposes across the Web (third-party cookies), and not for cookies used on a Web site. Like the FTC's proposed framework, the EU's new proposed rules have a strong emphasis on regulating tracking, enforcing transparency, limiting data retention periods, and obtaining user consent.

Working with the European Commission, the U.S. Department of Commerce developed a safe harbor framework for U.S. firms. A **safe harbor** is a private, self-regulating policy and enforcement mechanism that meets the objectives of government regulators and legislation but does not involve government regulation or enforcement. U.S. businesses would be allowed to use personal data from EU countries if they develop privacy protection policies that meet EU standards. Enforcement would occur in the United States using self-policing, regulation, and government enforcement of fair trade statutes.

Internet Challenges to Privacy

Internet technology has posed new challenges for the protection of individual privacy. Information sent over this vast network of networks may pass through many different computer systems before it reaches its final destination. Each of these systems is capable of monitoring, capturing, and storing communications that pass through it.

Web sites track searches that have been conducted, the Web sites and Web pages visited, the online content a person has accessed, and what items that person has inspected or purchased over the Web. This monitoring and tracking of Web site visitors occurs in the background without the visitor's knowledge. It is conducted not just by individual Web sites but by advertising networks such as Microsoft Advertising, Yahoo, and DoubleClick that are capable of tracking personal browsing behavior across thousands of Web sites. Both Web site publishers and the advertising industry defend tracking of individuals across the Web because doing so allows more relevant ads to be targeted to users, and it pays for the cost of publishing Web sites. In this sense, it's like broadcast television: advertiser-supported content that is free to the user. The commercial demand for this personal information is virtually insatiable.

Cookies are small text files deposited on a computer hard drive when a user visits Web sites. Cookies identify the visitor's Web browser software and track visits to the Web site. When the visitor returns to a site that has stored a cookie, the Web site software will search the visitor's computer, find the cookie, and know what that person has done in the past. It may also update the cookie, depending on the activity during the visit. In this way, the site can customize its content for each visitor's interests. For example, if you purchase a book on Amazon.com and return later from the same browser, the site will welcome you by name and recommend other books of interest based on your past purchases. DoubleClick, described earlier in this chapter, uses cookies to build its dossiers with details of online purchases and to examine the behavior of Web site visitors. Figure 4.3 illustrates how cookies work.

Web sites using cookie technology cannot directly obtain visitors' names and addresses. However, if a person has registered at a site, that information can be combined with cookie data to identify the visitor. Web site owners can also combine the data they have gathered from cookies and other Web site monitoring tools with personal data from other sources, such as offline data collected from surveys or paper catalog purchases, to develop very detailed profiles of their visitors.

There are now even more subtle and surreptitious tools for surveillance of Internet users. So-called "super cookies" or Flash cookies cannot be easily

FIGURE 4.3   HOW COOKIES IDENTIFY WEB VISITORS

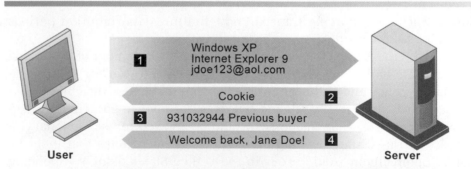

1. The Web server reads the user's Web browser and determines the operating system, browser name, version number, Internet address, and other information.
2. The server transmits a tiny text file with user identification information called a cookie, which the user's browser receives and stores on the user's computer hard drive.
3. When the user returns to the Web site, the server requests the contents of any cookie it deposited previously in the user's computer.
4. The Web server reads the cookie, identifies the visitor, and calls up data on the user.

Cookies are written by a Web site on a visitor's hard drive. When the visitor returns to that Web site, the Web server requests the ID number from the cookie and uses it to access the data stored by that server on that visitor. The Web site can then use these data to display personalized information.

deleted and can be installed whenever a person clicks on a Flash video. These so-called "Local Shared Object" files are used by Flash to play videos and are put on the user's computer without their consent. Marketers use Web beacons as another tool to monitor online behavior. **Web beacons**, also called *Web bugs* (or simply "tracking files"), are tiny software programs that keep a record of users' online clickstream and report this data back to whomever owns the tracking file invisibly embedded in e-mail messages and Web pages that are designed to monitor the behavior of the user visiting a Web site or sending e-mail. Web beacons are placed on popular Web sites by third-party firms who pay the Web sites a fee for access to their audience. So how common is Web tracking? In a path-breaking series of articles in the *Wall Street Journal* in 2010 and 2011, researchers examined the tracking files on 50 of the most popular U.S Web sites. What they found revealed a very widespread surveillance system. On the 50 sites, they discovered 3,180 tracking files installed on visitor computers. Only one site, Wikipedia, had no tracking files. Some popular sites such as Dictionary. com, MSN, and Comcast, installed more than 100 tracking files! Two-thirds of the tracking files came from 131 companies whose primary business is identifying and tracking Internet users to create consumer profiles that can be sold to advertising firms looking for specific types of customers. The biggest trackers were Google, Microsoft, and Quantcast, all of whom are in the business of selling ads to advertising firms and marketers. A follow-up study in 2012 found the situation had worsened: tracking on the 50 most popular sites had risen nearly five fold! The cause: growth of online ad auctions where advertisers buy the data about users' Web browsing behavior.

Other **spyware** can secretly install itself on an Internet user's computer by piggybacking on larger applications. Once installed, the spyware calls out to Web sites to send banner ads and other unsolicited material to the user, and it can report the user's movements on the Internet to other computers. More information is available about intrusive software in Chapter 8.

About 75 percent of global Internet users use Google Search and other Google services, making Google the world's largest collector of online user data. Whatever Google does with its data has an enormous impact on online privacy. Most experts believe that Google possesses the largest collection of personal information in the world—more data on more people than any government agency. The nearest competitor is Facebook.

After Google acquired the advertising network DoubleClick in 2007, Google has been using behavioral targeting to help it display more relevant ads based on users' search activities and to target individuals as they move from one site to another in order to show them display or banner ads. Google allows tracking software on its search pages, and using DoubleClick, it is able to track users across the Internet. One of its programs enables advertisers to target ads based on the search histories of Google users, along with any other information the user submits to Google such as age, demographics, region, and other Web activities (such as blogging). Google's AdSense program enables Google to help advertisers select keywords and design ads for various market segments based on search histories, such as helping a clothing Web site create and test ads targeted at teenage females. A recent study found that 88 percent of 400,000 Web sites had at least one Google tracking bug.

Google has also been scanning the contents of messages received by users of its free Web-based e-mail service called Gmail. Ads that users see when they read their e-mail are related to the subjects of these messages. Profiles are developed on individual users based on the content in their e-mail. Google now displays targeted ads on YouTube and on Google mobile applications, and its DoubleClick ad network serves up targeted banner ads.

The United States has allowed businesses to gather transaction information generated in the marketplace and then use that information for other marketing purposes without obtaining the informed consent of the individual whose information is being used. An **opt-out** model of informed consent permits the collection of personal information until the consumer specifically requests that the data not be collected. Privacy advocates would like to see wider use of an **opt-in** model of informed consent in which a business is prohibited from collecting any personal information unless the consumer specifically takes action to approve information collection and use. Here, the default option is no collection of user information.

The online industry has preferred self-regulation to privacy legislation for protecting consumers. The online advertising industry formed the Online Privacy Alliance to encourage self-regulation to develop a set of privacy guidelines for its members. The group promotes the use of online seals, such as that of TRUSTe, certifying Web sites adhering to certain privacy principles. Members of the advertising network industry, including Google's DoubleClick, have created an additional industry association called the Network Advertising Initiative (NAI) to develop its own privacy policies to help consumers opt out of advertising network programs and provide consumers redress from abuses.

Individual firms like Microsoft, Mozilla Foundation, Yahoo, and Google have recently adopted policies on their own in an effort to address public concern about tracking people online. Microsoft has promised to ship its new Internet Explorer 10 Web browser with the opt-out option as the default in 2012. AOL established an opt-out policy that allows users of its site to not be tracked. Yahoo follows NAI guidelines and also allows opt-out for tracking and Web beacons (Web bugs). Google has reduced retention time for tracking data.

In general, most Internet businesses do little to protect the privacy of their customers, and consumers do not do as much as they should to protect themselves. For commercial Web sites that depend on advertising to support themselves, most revenue derives from selling customer information. Of the companies that do post privacy polices on their Web sites, about half do not monitor their sites to ensure they adhere to these policies. The vast majority of online customers claim they are concerned about online privacy, but less than half read the privacy statements on Web sites. In general, Web site privacy policies require a law degree to understand and are ambiguous about key terms (Laudon and Traver, 2013).

In one of the more insightful studies of consumer attitudes towards Internet privacy, a group of Berkeley students conducted surveys of online users, and of complaints filed with the FTC involving privacy issues. Here are some of their results: people feel they have no control over the information collected about them, and they don't know who to complain to. Web sites collect all this information, but do not let users have access, the Web site policies are unclear, and they share data with "affiliates" but never identify who the affiliates are and how many there are. Web bug trackers are ubiquitous and users are not informed of trackers on the pages users visit. The results of this study and others suggest that consumers are not saying "Take my privacy, I don't care, send me the service for free." They are saying "We want access to the information, we want some controls on what can be collected, what is done with the information, the ability to opt out of the entire tracking enterprise, and some clarity on what the policies really are, and we don't want those policies changed without our participation and permission." (The full report is available at knowprivacy.org.)

Technical Solutions

In addition to legislation, there are a few technologies that can protect user privacy during interactions with Web sites. Many of these tools are used for encrypting e-mail, for making e-mail or surfing activities appear anonymous, for preventing client computers from accepting cookies, or for detecting and eliminating spyware. For the most part, technical solutions have failed to protect users from being tracked as they move from one site to another.

Because of growing public criticism of behavioral tracking and targeting of ads, and the failure of industry to self-regulate, attention has shifted to browsers. Many browsers have Do Not Track options. For users who have selected the Do Not Track browser option, their browser will send a request to Web sites requesting the user's behavior not be tracked. Both Internet Explorer 9 and Mozilla's Firefox browsers implement this opt-out option. However, these browsers are shipped with tracking turned on as the default. And most consumers never visit the Options Privacy tab in their browser. The online advertising industry has bitterly opposed Microsoft's plans and warns that Web sites are not obligated to follow users' requests to Do Not Track. There is no online advertising industry agreement on how to respond to Do Not Track requests, and currently no legislation requiring Web sites to stop tracking.

The Interactive Session on Technology, *Life on the Grid: iPhone Becomes iTrack*, describes how mobile phones are used to track the location of individuals.

PROPERTY RIGHTS: INTELLECTUAL PROPERTY

Contemporary information systems have severely challenged existing laws and social practices that protect private intellectual property. **Intellectual property** is considered to be intangible property created by individuals or corporations. Information technology has made it difficult to protect intellectual property because computerized information can be so easily copied or distributed on networks. Intellectual property is subject to a variety of protections under three different legal traditions: trade secrets, copyright, and patent law.

Trade Secrets

Any intellectual work product—a formula, device, pattern, or compilation of data—used for a business purpose can be classified as a **trade secret**, provided it is not based on information in the public domain. Protections for trade secrets vary from state to state. In general, trade secret laws grant a monopoly on the ideas behind a work product, but it can be a very tenuous monopoly.

Software that contains novel or unique elements, procedures, or compilations can be included as a trade secret. Trade secret law protects the actual ideas in a work product, not only their manifestation. To make this claim, the creator or owner must take care to bind employees and customers with nondisclosure agreements and to prevent the secret from falling into the public domain.

The limitation of trade secret protection is that, although virtually all software programs of any complexity contain unique elements of some sort, it is difficult to prevent the ideas in the work from falling into the public domain when the software is widely distributed.

INTERACTIVE SESSION: TECHNOLOGY

LIFE ON THE GRID: IPHONE BECOMES ITRACK

Do you like your smartphone? Living on the grid has its advantages. You can access the Internet, visit your Facebook page, get Twitter feeds, watch video, and listen to music all with the same "communication and media device." Less well known is that living on the grid means near continuous tracking of your whereabouts, locations, habits, and friends. At first, the Web made it possible for you to search for and find products, and some friends. Now the mobile Web grid tracks you and your friends to sell you products and services.

New technologies found on smartphones can identify where you are located within a few yards. And there's a great deal of money to be made knowing where you are. Performing routine actions using your smartphone makes it possible to locate you throughout the day, to report this information to corporate databases, retain and analyze the information, and then sell it to advertisers. A number of firms have adopted business models based on the ability of smartphones to report on your whereabouts, whether or not you choose to do so. Most of the popular apps report your location. Law enforcement agencies certainly have an interest in knowing the whereabouts of criminals and suspects. There are, of course, many times when you would like to report your location either automatically or on your command. If you were injured, for instance, you might like your cell phone to be able to automatically report your location to authorities, or, if you were in a restaurant, you might want to notify your friends where you are and what you are doing. But what about occasions when you don't want anyone to know where you are, least of all advertisers and marketers?

Location data gathered from cell phones has extraordinary commercial value because advertising companies can send you highly targeted advertisements, coupons, and flash bargains, based on where you are located. This technology is the foundation for many location-based services, which include smartphone maps and charts, shopping apps, and social apps that you can use to let your friends know where you are and what you are doing. Revenues from the global location-based services market are projected to reach $3.8 billion by the end of 2012, and will rise to $10.3 billion in 2015, according to Gartner.

But where does the location data come from, who collects it, and who uses it? In April 2011,

the Wall Street Journal published the results of its research on smartphone tracking technology and individual private location data. They discovered that both Apple's iPhone and Google's Android phones were collecting personal, private location data, for a variety of reasons. Both firms are building massive databases that can pinpoint your location, and although Google is already a leader in search across most platforms, Apple is also trying to establish itself in the mobile advertising marketplace. Advertising firms will pay Apple and Google for that information and for distributing their mobile ads.

Apple transmits your location data back to central servers once every 12 hours, and it also stores a copy of your locations on the iPhone. Android phones transmit your location data continuously. Apple's files on the iPhone device can be stored for many months. Both Apple and Google have denied that they share this information with third parties, as well as that the information can identify individuals (as opposed to cell phones), and claim the information is being used only to identify the location of cell phones for Wi-Fi–connected phones, and to improve the customer experience of location-based services. Apple's technology reads the signal strength of nearby Wi-Fi transmitters, identifies and maps their location, and then calculates the location of the iPhone device. The result is a very large database of Wi-Fi hotspots in the United States, and a method for locating iPhones that is not dependent on global positioning system (GPS) signals. Both companies say the location information is needed for them to improve their services. And location tracking is itself improving: newer tracking technologies can automatically detect the places you visit, know when you arrive or leave, track how many times you've been to that location, and even know whether you've been sitting, walking, or driving. Several companies, including Alohar Mobile, Skyhook, Wifarer, and Broadcom, are developing this type of next-generation tracking technology, which will add even more value to the data you generate by using your smartphone.

Smartphone apps that provide location-based services are also sources of personal, private location information based on the smartphone GPS capability. Foursquare is a popular mobile social application that allows users to "check in" to a restaurant or other location, and the app automatically lets friends on Facebook and other programs learn where you are. If you're in a new town, the app transmits your location and sends you popular spots close by, with reviews from other Foursquare users. After starting up Foursquare on a smartphone, you'll see a list of local bars and restaurants based on your cell phone's GPS position, select a location, and "check in," which sends a message to your friends. Foursquare has a widely accepted loyalty program. Each check-in awards users points and badges, which can be used later for discounts at various venues. Visitors to places compete to become "Mayors" of the venue based on how many times they have checked in over a month's time. Mayors receive special offers.

As the popularity of location-based services like Foursquare has grown, so too have concerns about the privacy of individual subscribers, and their friends on Facebook and Twitter who may not be members. Many observers fear these services will operate automatically, without user permission or awareness. The revelation in 2011 that Apple and Google were surreptitiously and continuously collecting personal, private, and location data spurred privacy groups and Congress to launch investigations. Most cell phone users are unaware that their locations and travels are readily available to law enforcement agencies through a simple e-mail request, and without judicial review, and at the expense of the carriers. In June 2012, a U.S. District Judge in California ruled that Apple must defend against a lawsuit accusing it of secretly tracking location data on millions of its iPhone and iPad users, and the Supreme Court ruled that law enforcement may not use GPS devices planted on a car to track suspects without a warrant.

To date, wireless location-based services remain largely unregulated. In 2011, the Federal

Communications Commission in cooperation with the Federal Trade Commission sponsored a forum to discuss with industry and privacy groups the social impact of location-based services, both positive and negative. Industry representatives from Facebook, Google, and Foursquare argued that existing apps as well as corporate policies were adequate to protect personal privacy because they rely on user permissions to share location data (opt-in services). The industry argued as well that consumers get real benefits from sharing location data, otherwise they would not voluntarily share this data. Privacy experts asked if consumers knew they were sharing their location information and what kind of "informed consent" was obtained. Privacy advocates pointed out that 22 of the top 30 paid apps have no privacy policy, that most of the popular apps transmit location data to their developers after which the information is not well controlled, and that these services are creating a situation where government agencies, marketers, creditors, and telecommunications firms will end up knowing nearly everything about citizens including their whereabouts. The biggest danger they described are services that locate people automatically and persistently without users having a chance to go off the grid, and without being able to turn off the location features of their phones.

Sources: "Apple Fails to Fend Off Mobile Tracking Lawsuit," Reuters, June 14, 2012; Christina DesMarais, "Location Tracking of Mobile Devices Gets Really Nosy," *PC World*, June 2, 2012; "This Smart Phone Tracking Tech Will Give You the Creeps," *PC World*, May 22, 2012; Andy Greenberg, "Reminder to Congress: Cops' Cell Phone Tracking Can Be Even More Precise than GPS," Forbes.com, May 17, 2012; Noam Cohen, "It's Tracking Your Every Move and You May Not Even Know," *The New York Times*, March 26, 2011; Robert Hotz, "The Really Smart Phone," *The Wall Street Journal*, April 23, 2011; Peter Swire, "Wrap Up on Privacy and Location Based Services" and Matt Blaze, "Technology and Privacy," FCC Forum: "Helping Consumers Harness the Potential of Location Based Services," June 28, 2011; Julia Angwin and Jennifer Valentino-Devries, "Apple, Google Collect User Data," *The Wall Street Journal*, April 22, 2011; "When a Cell Phone Is More Than a Phone: Protecting Your Privacy in the Age of the Smartphone," Privacy Rights Clearinghouse, http://www.privacyrights.org.

CASE STUDY QUESTIONS

1. Why do mobile phone manufacturers (Apple, Google, and BlackBerry) want to track where their customers go?
2. Do you think mobile phone customers should be able to turn tracking off? Should customers be

informed when they are being tracked? Why or why not?
3. Do you think mobile phone tracking is a violation of a person's privacy? Why or why not?

Copyright

Copyright is a statutory grant that protects creators of intellectual property from having their work copied by others for any purpose during the life of the author plus an additional 70 years after the author's death. For corporate-owned works, copyright protection lasts for 95 years after their initial creation. Congress has extended copyright protection to books, periodicals, lectures, dramas, musical compositions, maps, drawings, artwork of any kind, and motion pictures. The intent behind copyright laws has been to encourage creativity and authorship by ensuring that creative people receive the financial and other benefits of their work. Most industrial nations have their own copyright laws, and there are several international conventions and bilateral agreements through which nations coordinate and enforce their laws.

In the mid-1960s, the Copyright Office began registering software programs, and in 1980, Congress passed the Computer Software Copyright Act, which clearly provides protection for software program code and for copies of the original sold in commerce, and sets forth the rights of the purchaser to use the software while the creator retains legal title.

Copyright protects against copying of entire programs or their parts. Damages and relief are readily obtained for infringement. The drawback to copyright protection is that the underlying ideas behind a work are not protected, only their manifestation in a work. A competitor can use your software, understand how it works, and build new software that follows the same concepts without infringing on a copyright.

"Look and feel" copyright infringement lawsuits are precisely about the distinction between an idea and its expression. For instance, in the early 1990s, Apple Computer sued Microsoft Corporation and Hewlett-Packard for infringement of the expression of Apple's Macintosh interface, claiming that the defendants copied the expression of overlapping windows. The defendants countered that the idea of overlapping windows can be expressed only in a single way and, therefore, was not protectable under the merger doctrine of copyright law. When ideas and their expression merge, the expression cannot be copyrighted.

In general, courts appear to be following the reasoning of a 1989 case—*Brown Bag Software v. Symantec Corp*—in which the court dissected the elements of software alleged to be infringing. The court found that similar concept, function, general functional features (e.g., drop-down menus), and colors are not protectable by copyright law (*Brown Bag Software v. Symantec Corp.*, 1992).

Patents

A **patent** grants the owner an exclusive monopoly on the ideas behind an invention for 20 years. The congressional intent behind patent law was to ensure that inventors of new machines, devices, or methods receive the full financial and other rewards of their labor and yet make widespread use of the invention possible by providing detailed diagrams for those wishing to use the idea under license from the patent's owner. The granting of a patent is determined by the United States Patent and Trademark Office and relies on court rulings.

The key concepts in patent law are originality, novelty, and invention. The Patent Office did not accept applications for software patents routinely until a 1981 Supreme Court decision that held that computer programs could be a part of a patentable process. Since that time, hundreds of patents have been granted and thousands await consideration.

The strength of patent protection is that it grants a monopoly on the underlying concepts and ideas of software. The difficulty is passing stringent criteria of nonobviousness (e.g., the work must reflect some special understanding and contribution), originality, and novelty, as well as years of waiting to receive protection.

In what some call the patent trial of the century, in 2011, Apple sued Samsung for violating its patents for iPhones, iPads, and iPods. On August 24, 2012, a California jury in federal district court delivered a decisive victory to Apple and a stunning defeat to Samsung. The jury awarded Apple $1 billion in damages. The decision established criteria for determining just how close a competitor can come to an industry-leading and standard-setting product like Apple's iPhone before it violates the design and utility patents of the leading firm. The same court ruled that Samsung could not sell its new tablet computer (Galaxy 10.1) in the United States. This was not just a loss for Samsung but a warning shot across the bow for Google, which developed the Android operating system, and all other makers of Android phones, including Google's newly purchased Motorola Mobile Devices, makers of Motorola Mobility phones.

Challenges to Intellectual Property Rights

Contemporary information technologies, especially software, pose severe challenges to existing intellectual property regimes and, therefore, create significant ethical, social, and political issues. Digital media differ from books, periodicals, and other media in terms of ease of replication; ease of transmission; ease of alteration; difficulty in classifying a software work as a program, book, or even music; compactness—making theft easy; and difficulties in establishing uniqueness.

The proliferation of electronic networks, including the Internet, has made it even more difficult to protect intellectual property. Before widespread use of networks, copies of software, books, magazine articles, or films had to be stored on physical media, such as paper, computer disks, or videotape, creating some hurdles to distribution. Using networks, information can be more widely reproduced and distributed. The Ninth Annual Global Software Piracy Study conducted by International Data Corporation and the Business Software Alliance reported that the rate of global software piracy climbed to 42 percent in 2011, representing $63 billion in global losses from software piracy. Worldwide, for every $100 worth of legitimate software sold that year, an additional $75 worth was obtained illegally (Business Software Alliance, 2012).

The Internet was designed to transmit information freely around the world, including copyrighted information. With the World Wide Web in particular, you can easily copy and distribute virtually anything to thousands and even millions of people around the world, even if they are using different types of computer systems. Information can be illicitly copied from one place and distributed through other systems and networks even though these parties do not willingly participate in the infringement.

Individuals have been illegally copying and distributing digitized MP3 music files on the Internet for a number of years. File-sharing services such as Napster, and later Grokster, Kazaa, and Morpheus, sprung up to help users locate and swap digital music files, including those protected by copyright. Illegal file sharing became so widespread that it threatened the viability of the music recording industry and, at one point, consumed 20 percent of Internet bandwidth. The recording industry won the legal battles for shutting these services down, but it has not been able to halt illegal file sharing entirely.

While illegal file sharing still goes on, it has actually declined since the opening of the iTunes Store in 2001. As legitimate online music stores expanded, and more recently as Internet radio services like Pandora expanded, illegal file sharing has declined. Technology has radically altered the prospects for intellectual property protection from theft, at least for music, videos, and television shows (less so for software). The Apple iTunes Store legitimated paying for music and entertainment, and created a closed environment where music and videos could not be easily copied and widely distributed unless played on Apple devices. Amazon's Kindle also protects the rights of publishers and writers because its books cannot be copied to the Internet and distributed. Streaming of Internet radio, on services such as Pandora and Spotify, and Hollywood movies (at sites such as Hulu and Netflix) also inhibits piracy because the streams cannot be easily recorded on separate devices. Moreover, the large Web distributors like Apple, Google, and Amazon do not want to encourage piracy in music or videos simply because they need these properties to earn revenue.

The Digital Millennium Copyright Act (DMCA) of 1998 also provides some copyright protection. The DMCA implemented a World Intellectual Property Organization Treaty that makes it illegal to circumvent technology-based protections of copyrighted materials. Internet service providers (ISPs) are required to take down sites of copyright infringers they are hosting once the ISPs are notified of the problem. Microsoft and other major software and information content firms are represented by the Software and Information Industry Association (SIIA), which lobbies for new laws and enforcement of existing laws to protect intellectual property around the world. The SIIA runs an antipiracy hotline for individuals to report piracy activities, offers educational programs to help organizations combat software piracy, and has published guidelines for employee use of software.

ACCOUNTABILITY, LIABILITY, AND CONTROL

Along with privacy and property laws, new information technologies are challenging existing liability laws and social practices for holding individuals and institutions accountable. If a person is injured by a machine controlled, in part, by software, who should be held accountable and, therefore, held liable? Should a public bulletin board or an electronic service, such as America Online, permit the transmission of pornographic or offensive material (as broadcasters), or should they be held harmless against any liability for what users transmit (as is true of common carriers, such as the telephone system)? What about the Internet? If you outsource your information processing, can you hold the external vendor liable for injuries done to your customers? Some real-world examples may shed light on these questions.

Computer-Related Liability Problems

For a week in October 2011, millions of BlackBerry users around the world began experiencing disruption to their e-mail service, the most vital service provided by the smartphone maker Research in Motion (RIM). The three-day blackout of e-mail involved users in Asia, Europe, the Middle East, and the Americas, a substantial part of BlackBerry's installed base of 70 million users. The BlackBerry, until recently, had the dominant position in the corporate smartphone market because it provided excellent e-mail security, and integrated well with corporate mail servers. The iPhone and Android smartphones championed by employees now account for more than half of all new corporate mobile devices. The outage is expected to encourage more corporations to abandon the BlackBerry. On the positive side, police departments around the world reported a significant drop in urban car accidents during the outage because drivers could no longer text or telephone using their BlackBerry (Austen, 2011).

After the outage, Research in Motion CTO for Software David Yach said a backlog of messages to Europe created a cascading outage effect around the world.

The company determined the root cause of the initial European BlackBerry e-mail service and said there was no evidence that a hack or security breach was involved.

RIM customers in Europe had been suffering from major outages for days, but it wasn't until the Americas caught the bug that BlackBerry customers started complaining on Twitter of mail delays and lack of access to their BlackBerry devices. Yach described the initial outage as a failure of one of RIM's core switches. However, the real trouble began when RIM's redundant systems failed as well. "The failover did not function as expected," Yach said, "despite the fact that we regularly test failover systems." This led to a significant backup of mail.

Who is liable for any economic harm caused to individuals or businesses that could not access their e-mail during this three-day period? If consumers pay for cell phone service, come to rely on it, and then are denied service for a significant period of time, is the cell phone provider liable for damages?

This case reveals the difficulties faced by information systems executives who ultimately are responsible for any harm done by systems they have selected and installed. Beyond IT managers, insofar as computer software is part of a machine, and the machine injures someone physically or economically, the producer of the software and the operator can be held liable for damages. Insofar as the software acts like a book, storing and displaying information, courts have been reluctant to hold authors, publishers, and booksellers liable for contents (the exception being instances of fraud or defamation), and hence courts have been wary of holding software authors liable for software.

In general, it is very difficult (if not impossible) to hold software producers liable for their software products that are considered to be like books, regardless of the physical or economic harm that results. Historically, print publishers, books, and periodicals have not been held liable because of fears that liability claims would interfere with First Amendment rights guaranteeing freedom of expression.

What about software as a service? ATM machines are a service provided to bank customers. Should this service fail, customers will be inconvenienced and perhaps harmed economically if they cannot access their funds in a timely manner. Should liability protections be extended to software publishers and operators of defective financial, accounting, simulation, or marketing systems?

Software is very different from books. Software users may develop expectations of infallibility about software; software is less easily inspected than a book, and it is more difficult to compare with other software products for quality; software claims actually to perform a task rather than describe a task, as a book does; and people come to depend on services essentially based on software. Given the centrality of software to everyday life, the chances are excellent that liability law will extend its reach to include software even when the software merely provides an information service.

Telephone systems have not been held liable for the messages transmitted because they are regulated common carriers. In return for their right to provide telephone service, they must provide access to all, at reasonable rates, and achieve acceptable reliability. But broadcasters and cable television stations are subject to a wide variety of federal and local constraints on content and facilities. In the United States, with few exceptions, Web sites are not held liable for content posted on their sites regardless if it was placed their by the Web site owners or users.

SYSTEM QUALITY: DATA QUALITY AND SYSTEM ERRORS

The debate over liability and accountability for unintentional consequences of system use raises a related but independent moral dimension: What is an acceptable, technologically feasible level of system quality? At what point should system managers say, "Stop testing, we've done all we can to perfect this software. Ship it!" Individuals and organizations may be held responsible for avoidable and foreseeable consequences, which they have a duty to perceive and correct. And the gray area is that some system errors are foreseeable and correctable only at very great expense, an expense so great that pursuing this level of perfection is not feasible economically—no one could afford the product.

For example, although software companies try to debug their products before releasing them to the marketplace, they knowingly ship buggy products because the time and cost of fixing all minor errors would prevent these products from ever being released. What if the product was not offered on the marketplace, would social welfare as a whole not advance and perhaps even decline? Carrying this further, just what is the responsibility of a producer of computer services—should it withdraw the product that can never be perfect, warn the user, or forget about the risk (let the buyer beware)?

Three principal sources of poor system performance are (1) software bugs and errors, (2) hardware or facility failures caused by natural or other causes, and (3) poor input data quality. A Chapter 8 Learning Track discusses why zero defects in software code of any complexity cannot be achieved and why the seriousness of remaining bugs cannot be estimated. Hence, there is a technological barrier to perfect software, and users must be aware of the potential for catastrophic failure. The software industry has not yet arrived at testing standards for producing software of acceptable but imperfect performance.

Although software bugs and facility catastrophes are likely to be widely reported in the press, by far the most common source of business system failure is data quality. Few companies routinely measure the quality of their data, but individual organizations report data error rates ranging from 0.5 to 30 percent.

QUALITY OF LIFE: EQUITY, ACCESS, AND BOUNDARIES

The negative social costs of introducing information technologies and systems are beginning to mount along with the power of the technology. Many of these negative social consequences are not violations of individual rights or property crimes. Nevertheless, these negative consequences can be extremely harmful to individuals, societies, and political institutions. Computers and information technologies potentially can destroy valuable elements of our culture and society even while they bring us benefits. If there is a balance of good and bad consequences of using information systems, who do we hold responsible for the bad consequences? Next, we briefly examine some of the negative social consequences of systems, considering individual, social, and political responses.

Balancing Power: Center Versus Periphery

An early fear of the computer age was that huge, centralized mainframe computers would centralize power in the nation's capital, resulting in a Big Brother society, as was suggested in George Orwell's novel *1984*. The shift toward highly decentralized computing, coupled with an ideology of empowerment of thousands of workers, and the decentralization of decision making to lower organizational levels, have reduced the fears of power centralization in government institutions. Yet much of the empowerment described in popular business magazines is trivial. Lower-level employees may be empowered to make minor decisions, but the key policy decisions may be as centralized as in the past. At the same time, corporate Internet behemoths like Google, Apple, Yahoo, Amazon, and Microsoft have come to dominate the collection and analysis of personal private information of all citizens. In this sense, power has become more centralized into the hands of a few private oligopolies.

Rapidity of Change: Reduced Response Time to Competition

Information systems have helped to create much more efficient national and international markets. Today's more efficient global marketplace has reduced the normal social buffers that permitted businesses many years to adjust to competition. Time-based competition has an ugly side: The business you work for may not have enough time to respond to global competitors and may be wiped out in a year, along with your job. We stand the risk of developing a "just-in-time society" with "just-in-time jobs" and "just-in-time" workplaces, families, and vacations.

Maintaining Boundaries: Family, Work, and Leisure

Parts of this book were produced on trains and planes, as well as on vacations and during what otherwise might have been "family" time. The danger to ubiquitous computing, telecommuting, nomad computing, mobile computing, and the "do anything anywhere" computing environment is that it is actually coming true. The traditional boundaries that separate work from family and just plain leisure have been weakened.

Although authors have traditionally worked just about anywhere (typewriters have been portable for nearly a century), the advent of information systems, coupled with the growth of knowledge-work occupations, means that more and more people are working when traditionally they would have been playing or communicating with family and friends. The work umbrella now extends far beyond the eight-hour day into commuting time, vacation time, and leisure time.

Even leisure time spent on the computer threatens these close social relationships. Extensive Internet use, even for entertainment or recreational purposes, takes people away from their family and friends. Among middle school and teenage children, it can lead to harmful anti-social behavior, such as the recent upsurge in cyberbullying.

Weakening these institutions poses clear-cut risks. Family and friends historically have provided powerful support mechanisms for individuals, and they act as balance points in a society by preserving private life, providing a place for people to collect their thoughts, allowing people to think in ways contrary to their employer, and dream.

Dependence and Vulnerability

Today, our businesses, governments, schools, and private associations, such as churches, are incredibly dependent on information systems and are, therefore, highly vulnerable if these systems fail. Secondary schools, for instance, increasingly use and rely on educational software. Test results are often stored off campus. If these systems were to shut down, there is no backup educational structure or content that can make up for the loss of the system. With systems now as ubiquitous as the telephone system, it is startling to remember that there are no regulatory or standard-setting forces in place that are similar to telephone, electrical, radio, television, or other public utility technologies. The absence of standards and the criticality of some system applications will probably call forth demands for national standards and perhaps regulatory oversight.

Computer Crime and Abuse

New technologies, including computers, create new opportunities for committing crime by creating new valuable items to steal, new ways to steal them, and new ways to harm others. **Computer crime** is the commission of illegal acts through the use of a computer or against a computer system. Computers or computer systems can be the object of the crime (destroying a company's computer center or a company's computer files), as well as the instrument of a crime (stealing computer lists by illegally gaining access to a computer system using a home computer). Simply accessing a computer system without authorization or with intent to do harm, even by accident, is now a federal crime. How common is computer crime? One source of information is the Internet Crime Complaint Center ("IC3"), a partnership between the National White Collar Crime Center and the Federal Bureau of Investigation. The IC3 data is useful for gauging the types of e-commerce crimes most likely to be reported by consumers. In 2011, the IC3 processed almost 315,000 Internet crime complaints, the second-highest number in its 11-year history. Over half the complainants reported a financial loss, with the total reported amount at almost $500 million. The average amount of loss for those who reported a financial loss was more than $4,100. The most common complaints were for scams involving the FBI, identity theft, and advance fee fraud (National White Collar Crime Center and the Federal Bureau of Investigation, 2012). The Computer Security Institute's annual *Computer Crime and Security Survey* is another source of information. In 2011, the survey was based on the responses of 351 security practitioners in U.S. corporations, government agencies, financial institutions, medical institutions, and universities. The survey reported that 46 percent of responding organizations experienced a computer security incident within the past year. The most common type of attack experienced was a malware infection (67%), followed by phishing fraud (39%), laptop and mobile hardware theft (34%), attacks by botnets (29%), and insider abuse (25%). The true cost of all computer crime is estimated to be in the billions of dollars.

Although some people enjoy the convenience of working at home, the "do anything anywhere" computing environment can blur the traditional boundaries between work and family time.

© MBI/Alamy

INTERACTIVE SESSION: ORGANIZATIONS

MONITORING IN THE WORKPLACE

There may be only 11 players on the pitch during a match, but the Blackburn Rovers Football Club in the UK employs more than 800 people. As with any modern organization, computers are at the heart of running an efficient business. Most of the club's computers are housed with the administration department at the Ewood Park office, but others can be found at the club's training center and soccer academy.

The club decided to install a software product called Spector 360, which it obtained from the Manchester-based company Snapguard. According to Snapguard's sales literature, the product enables company-wide monitoring of employee PC and Internet usage. Previously, the club had tried to introduce an acceptable use policy (AUP), but initial discussions with employees stalled, and the policy was never implemented. Early trials of Spector 360 showed that some employees were abusing the easygoing nature of the workplace to spend most of their day surfing the Web, using social networking sites, and taking up a huge amount of bandwidth for downloads.

Before officially implementing the monitoring software, the AUP was resurrected. It was sent out as an e-mail attachment and added to the staff handbook. The policy was also made part of the terms and conditions of employment. Understandably, some employees were annoyed at the concept of being watched, but the software was installed anyway. According to Ben Hayler, senior systems administrator at Blackburn Rovers, Spector 360 has definitely restored order, increasing productivity and reducing activity on non-business apps.

Reports provided by Spector 360 can show managers the following: excessive use of Facebook, Twitter, and other social networking sites; visits to adult sites or shopping sites; use of chat services; the printing or saving of confidential information; and staff login and logout times. Managers can also use the software to drill-down to look at patterns of usage, generate screen snapshots, or even log individual keystrokes.

The software can also be used to benefit employees. For example, because it can log exactly what an employee is doing, the system can help in staff training and troubleshooting, because it is easy to track exactly what caused a particular problem to occur.

Another important benefit of the software is that it helps the club to stay compliant with the Payment Card Industry (PCI) Data Security Standard. PCI standards require access to credit card information. As Spector 360 tracks and records all data to do with credit card transactions, the information can be easily recovered.

However, what is the wider view of the monitoring of employees in the workplace? According to the Citizens Advice Bureau (a free information and advice service for UK residents), the following are some of the ways that employers monitor their employees in the workplace: recording the workplace on CCTV cameras; opening mail or e-mail; using automated software to check e-mail; checking telephone logs or recording telephone calls; checking logs of Web sites visited; videoing outside the workplace; getting information from credit reference agencies; and collecting information from point-of-sale terminals.

Although this list may look formidable, there is no argument that the employer has a right to ensure that his or her employees are behaving in a manner that is not illegal or harmful to the company. However, under UK data protection law the employer must ensure that the monitoring is justified and take into account any negative effects the monitoring may have on staff. Monitoring for the sake of it is not allowed. Secret monitoring without employees' knowledge is usually illegal.

In a case that went before the European Court of Human Rights in 2007 (Copeland v the United Kingdom), Ms. Copeland, who was an employee of Carmarthenshire College, claimed that her privacy had been violated. She was a personal assistant to the principal and also worked closely with the deputy principal, who instigated monitoring and analysis of her telephone bills, Web sites visited, and e-mail communication. The deputy principal wanted to determine whether Copeland was making excessive use of the college's services. The European Court ruled in her favor, stating that her personal Internet usage was deemed to be under the definitions of the Convention for the Protection of Rights, covered as "private life." Note that although this case came to the court in 2007, the monitoring took place in 1999, prior to the introduction into English and Welsh law of the Regulation of Investigatory Powers Act 2000 and the Telecommunications (Lawful Business Practice) Regulations 2001, which seek to clarify regulations about the interception of communications.

The major fault of Carmarthenshire College was in not having a usage policy in place. Employers and employees should have an agreed-upon policy as part of the contract of employment that clarifies what is and is not acceptable computer usage in the workplace. The employer can then follow normal disciplinary procedures if an employee is using workplace equipment in a manner that is not permitted in the contract of employment.

Whatever the legal situation, it is clear where potential problems can occur in the workplace regarding information technology use. An e-mail, once sent, becomes a legally published document that can be produced as evidence in court cases involving issues of libel, breach of contract, and so on. Most businesses rely on their company data to keep ahead of the competition. Therefore, the loss, theft, or sabotage of data is potentially more dangerous than similar problems with hardware. If a stick is lost in a bar parking lot, replacing the hardware will cost a few dollars, but if it contains the company's confidential data, then its loss could put the company out of business!

Many companies place great focus on employee productivity. It is relatively easy to block access to certain sites (e.g., YouTube, Facebook, etc.), but a blanket blocking of such sites could cause problems if an employee has a legitimate need to access a site. In addition, should sites be blocked during lunch hour? In any case, blocking such sites on the desktop computer is becoming less of a guarantee of increased productivity nowadays (if it ever was), as more and more employees will just use their smartphones to access these sites anyway.

Sources: Information Commissioners Office, "Employment Practices Data Protection Code-Supplementary Guidance" (www.ico.gov.uk/upload/documents/library/data_protection/practical_application/coi_html/english/supplementary_guidance/monitoring_at_work_3.html, accessed October 25, 2010); "Spector 360 Helps Blackburn Rovers Show Red Card to PC and Internet Abuse," Snapguard (www.snapguard.co.uk/blackburn_fc.html, accessed October 25, 2010); "Citizens Advice Bureau Advice Guide, Basic Rights at Work," Adviceguide (www.adviceguide.org.uk/index/your_money/employment/basic_rights_at_work.htm, accessed October 25, 2010); "Employee Monitoring in the Workplace: What Constitutes 'Personal Data'?" Crowell and Moring (www.crowell.com/NewsEvents/ Newsletter.aspx?id=654, accessed October 25, 2010).

Case contributed by Andy Jones, Staffordshire University.

CASE STUDY QUESTIONS

1. Do you consider the approach taken by Blackburn Rovers to be too strict on employees, too lenient, or just right?

2. Consider the five moral dimensions described in the text. Which are involved in the case of Copeland v. the United Kingdom?

3. Consider the following scenario. Your 14-year-old son attends a soccer academy. While there, he downloads unsuitable images, which he later sells to his friends. He would not have been able to download the images at home, because you have installed parental control software. Who is to blame for his indiscretion?

4. Why is the digital divide problem an ethical dilemma?

Computer abuse is the commission of acts involving a computer that may not be illegal but that are considered unethical. The popularity of the Internet and e-mail has turned one form of computer abuse—spamming—into a serious problem for both individuals and businesses. **Spam** is junk e-mail sent by an organization or individual to a mass audience of Internet users who have expressed no interest in the product or service being marketed. Spammers tend to market pornography, fraudulent deals and services, outright scams, and other products not widely approved in most civilized societies. Some countries have passed laws to outlaw spamming or to restrict its use. In the United States, it is still legal if it does not involve fraud and the sender and subject of the e-mail are properly identified.

Spamming has mushroomed because it costs only a few cents to send thousands of messages advertising wares to Internet users. The percentage of all e-mail that is spam is estimated at around 72 percent in 2012 (Symantec, 2012). Most spam originates from bot networks, which consist of thousands of captured PCs that can initiate and relay spam messages. Spam volume has declined somewhat since authorities took down the Rustock botnet in 2011. Spam is seasonally cyclical, and varies monthly due to the impact of new technologies (both supportive and discouraging of spammers), new prosecutions, and seasonal demand for products and services. Spam costs for businesses are very high (estimated at over $50 billion per year) because of the computing and network resources consumed by billions of unwanted e-mail messages and the time required to deal with them.

Internet service providers and individuals can combat spam by using spam filtering software to block suspicious e-mail before it enters a recipient's e-mail inbox. However, spam filters may block legitimate messages. Spammers know how to skirt around filters by continually changing their e-mail accounts, by incorporating spam messages in images, by embedding spam in e-mail attachments and electronic greeting cards, and by using other people's computers that have been hijacked by botnets (see Chapter 8). Many spam messages are sent from one country while another country hosts the spam Web site.

Spamming is more tightly regulated in Europe than in the United States. On May 30, 2002, the European Parliament passed a ban on unsolicited commercial messaging. Electronic marketing can be targeted only to people who have given prior consent.

The U.S. CAN-SPAM Act of 2003, which went into effect on January 1, 2004, does not outlaw spamming but does ban deceptive e-mail practices by requiring commercial e-mail messages to display accurate subject lines, identify the true senders, and offer recipients an easy way to remove their names from e-mail lists. It also prohibits the use of fake return addresses. A few people have been prosecuted under the law, but it has had a negligible impact on spamming in large part because of the Internet's exceptionally poor security and the use of offshore servers and botnets. In 2008, Robert Soloway, the so-called Seattle "Spam King," was sentenced to 47 months in prison for sending over 90 million spam messages in just three months off two servers. In 2011, the so-called Facebook "Spam King," Sanford Wallace, was indicted for sending over 27 million spam messages to Facebook users. He is facing a 40-year sentence because of prior spamming convictions.

Another negative impact of computer technology is the growing use of information technology to conduct surveillance of employees and ordinary citizens not engaged in any illegal behavior but nevertheless considered worth watching. The Interactive Session on Organizations explores this topic.

Employment: Trickle-Down Technology and Reengineering Job Loss

Reengineering work is typically hailed in the information systems community as a major benefit of new information technology. It is much less frequently noted that redesigning business processes has caused millions of mid-level managers and clerical workers to lose their jobs. One economist has raised the possibility that we will create a society run by a small "high tech elite of corporate professionals . . . in a nation of the permanently unemployed" (Rifkin, 1993). In 2011, some economists have sounded new alarms about information and computer technology threatening middle-class, white-collar jobs (in addition to blue-collar factory jobs). Erik Brynjolfsson and Andrew P. McAfee argue that the pace of automation has picked up in recent years because of a combination of technologies including robotics, numerically controlled machines, computerized inventory control, pattern recognition, voice recognition, and online commerce. One result is that machines can now do a great many jobs heretofore reserved for humans including tech support, call center work, X-ray examiners, and even legal document review (Brynjolfsson and McAfee, 2011).

Other economists are much more sanguine about the potential job losses. They believe relieving bright, educated workers from reengineered jobs will result in these workers moving to better jobs in fast-growth industries. Missing from this equation are unskilled, blue-collar workers and older, less well-educated middle managers. It is not clear that these groups can be retrained easily for high-quality (high-paying) jobs. Careful planning and sensitivity to employee needs can help companies redesign work to minimize job losses.

Equity and Access: Increasing Racial and Social Class Cleavages

Does everyone have an equal opportunity to participate in the digital age? Will the social, economic, and cultural gaps that exist in the United States and other societies be reduced by information systems technology? Or will the cleavages be increased, permitting the better off to become even more better off relative to others?

These questions have not yet been fully answered because the impact of systems technology on various groups in society has not been thoroughly studied. What is known is that information, knowledge, computers, and access to these resources through educational institutions and public libraries are inequitably distributed along ethnic and social class lines, as are many other information resources. Several studies have found that poor and minority groups in the United States are less likely to have computers or online Internet access even though computer ownership and Internet access have soared in the past five years. Although the gap is narrowing, higher-income families in each ethnic group are still more likely to have home computers and Internet access than lower-income families in the same group.

A similar **digital divide** exists in U.S. schools, with schools in high-poverty areas less likely to have computers, high-quality educational technology programs, or Internet access availability for their students. Left uncorrected, the digital divide could lead to a society of information haves, computer literate and skilled, versus a large group of information have-nots, computer illiterate and unskilled. Public interest groups want to narrow this digital divide by making digital information services—including the Internet—available to virtually everyone, just as basic telephone service is now.

In recent years, ownership of computers and digital devices has broadened, but the digital divide still exists. Today's digital divide is not only based on access to digital technology but also on how that technology is being used.

Health Risks: RSI, CVS, and Technostress

The most common occupational disease today is **repetitive stress injury (RSI)**. RSI occurs when muscle groups are forced through repetitive actions often with high-impact loads (such as tennis) or tens of thousands of repetitions under low-impact loads (such as working at a computer keyboard).

The single largest source of RSI is computer keyboards. The most common kind of computer-related RSI is **carpal tunnel syndrome (CTS)**, in which pressure on the median nerve through the wrist's bony structure, called a carpal tunnel, produces pain. The pressure is caused by constant repetition of keystrokes: in a single shift, a word processor may perform 23,000 keystrokes. Symptoms of carpal tunnel syndrome include numbness, shooting pain, inability to grasp objects, and tingling. Millions of workers have been diagnosed with carpal tunnel syndrome.

RSI is avoidable. Designing workstations for a neutral wrist position (using a wrist rest to support the wrist), proper monitor stands, and footrests all contribute to proper posture and reduced RSI. Ergonomically correct keyboards are also an option. These measures should be supported by frequent rest breaks and rotation of employees to different jobs.

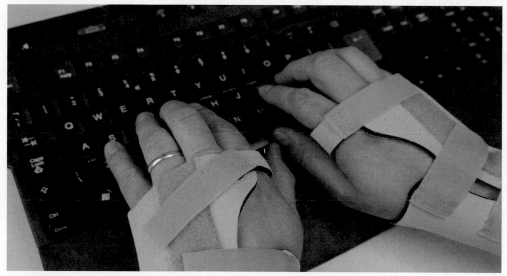

© Stephen Barnes/Alamy

Repetitive stress injury (RSI) is the leading occupational disease today. The single largest cause of RSI is computer keyboard work.

RSI is not the only occupational illness computers cause. Back and neck pain, leg stress, and foot pain also result from poor ergonomic designs of workstations. **Computer vision syndrome (CVS)** refers to any eyestrain condition related to display screen use in desktop computers, laptops, e-readers, smartphones, and handheld video games. CVS affects about 90 percent of people who spend three hours or more per day at a computer (Beck, 2010). Its symptoms, which are usually temporary, include headaches, blurred vision, and dry and irritated eyes.

The newest computer-related malady is **technostress**, which is stress induced by computer use. Its symptoms include aggravation, hostility toward humans, impatience, and fatigue. According to experts, humans working continuously with computers come to expect other humans and human institutions to behave like computers, providing instant responses, attentiveness, and an absence of emotion. Technostress is thought to be related to high levels of job turnover in the computer industry, high levels of early retirement from computer-intense occupations, and elevated levels of drug and alcohol abuse.

The incidence of technostress is not known but is thought to be in the millions and growing in the United States. Computer-related jobs now top the list of stressful occupations based on health statistics in several industrialized countries.

In addition to these maladies, computer technology may be harming our cognitive functions or at least changing how we think and solve problems. Although the Internet has made it much easier for people to access, create, and use information, some experts believe that it is also preventing people from focusing and thinking clearly.

The computer has become a part of our lives—personally as well as socially, culturally, and politically. It is unlikely that the issues and our choices will become easier as information technology continues to transform our world. The growth of the Internet and the information economy suggests that all the ethical and social issues we have described will be heightened further as we move into the first digital century.

LEARNING TRACK MODULE

The following Learning Track provides content relevant to topics covered in this chapter.

1. Developing a Corporate Code of Ethics for Information Systems

Review Summary

1. *What ethical, social, and political issues are raised by information systems?*

   Information technology is introducing changes for which laws and rules of acceptable conduct have not yet been developed. Increasing computing power, storage, and networking capabilities—including the Internet—expand the reach of individual and organizational actions and magnify their impacts. The ease and anonymity with which information is now communicated, copied, and manipulated in online environments pose new challenges to the protection of privacy and intellectual property. The main ethical, social, and political issues raised by information systems center around information rights and obligations, property rights and obligations, accountability and control, system quality, and quality of life.

2. *What specific principles for conduct can be used to guide ethical decisions?*

   Six ethical principles for judging conduct include the Golden Rule, Immanuel Kant's Categorical Imperative, Descartes' rule of change, the Utilitarian Principle, the Risk Aversion Principle, and the ethical "no free lunch" rule. These principles should be used in conjunction with an ethical analysis.

3. *Why do contemporary information systems technology and the Internet pose challenges to the protection of individual privacy and intellectual property?*

   Contemporary data storage and data analysis technology enables companies to easily gather personal data about individuals from many different sources and analyze these data to create detailed electronic profiles about individuals and their behaviors. Data flowing over the Internet can be monitored at many points. Cookies and other Web monitoring tools closely track the activities of Web site visitors. Not all Web sites have strong privacy protection policies, and they do not always allow for informed consent regarding the use of personal information. Traditional copyright laws are insufficient to protect against software piracy because digital material can be copied so easily and transmitted to many different locations simultaneously over the Internet.

4. *How have information systems affected everyday life?*

   Although computer systems have been sources of efficiency and wealth, they have some negative impacts. Computer errors can cause serious harm to individuals and organizations. Poor data quality is also responsible for disruptions and losses for businesses. Jobs can be lost when computers replace workers or tasks become unnecessary in reengineered business processes. The ability to own and use a computer may be exacerbating socioeconomic disparities among different racial groups and social classes. Widespread use of computers increases opportunities for computer crime and computer abuse. Computers can also create health problems, such as RSI, computer vision syndrome, and technostress.

Key Terms

Accountability, 160

Carpal tunnel syndrome (CTS), 182

Computer abuse, 180

Computer crime, 178

Computer vision syndrome (CVS), 183

Cookies, 166

Copyright, 172

Descartes' rule of change, 161

Digital divide, 181

Digital Millennium Copyright Act (DMCA), 174

Due process, 160

Ethical "no free lunch" rule, 161

Ethics, 155

Fair Information Practices (FIP), 163

Golden Rule, 161

Immanuel Kant's Categorical Imperative, 161

Information rights, 156

Informed consent, 165

Intellectual property, 169

Liability, 160

Nonobvious relationship awareness (NORA), 158

Opt-in, 168

Opt-out, 168

Patent, 172

Privacy, 162

Profiling, 157

Repetitive stress injury (RSI), 182

Responsibility, 159

Risk Aversion Principle, 161

Safe harbor, 165

Spam, 178

Spyware, 167

Technostress, 182

Trade secret, 169

Utilitarian Principle, 161

Web beacons, 167

Review Questions

1. What ethical, social, and political issues are raised by information systems?

   - Explain how ethical, social, and political issues are connected and give some examples.
   - List and describe the key technological trends that heighten ethical concerns.
   - Differentiate between responsibility, accountability, and liability.

2. What specific principles for conduct can be used to guide ethical decisions?

   - List and describe the five steps in an ethical analysis.
   - Identify and describe six ethical principles.

3. Why do contemporary information systems technology and the Internet pose challenges to the protection of individual privacy and intellectual property?

   - Define privacy and fair information practices.

   - Explain how the Internet challenges the protection of individual privacy and intellectual property.
   - Explain how informed consent, legislation, industry self-regulation, and technology tools help protect the individual privacy of Internet users.
   - List and define the three different regimes that protect intellectual property rights.

4. How have information systems affected everyday life?

   - Explain why it is so difficult to hold software services liable for failure or injury.
   - List and describe the principal causes of system quality problems.
   - Name and describe four quality-of-life impacts of computers and information systems.
   - Define and describe technostress and RSI and explain their relationship to information technology.

Discussion Questions

1. Should producers of software-based services, such as ATMs, be held liable for economic injuries suffered when their systems fail?

2. Should companies be responsible for unemployment caused by their information systems? Why or why not?

3. Discuss the pros and cons of allowing companies to amass personal data for behavioral targeting.

Hands-On MIS Projects

The projects in this section give you hands-on experience in analyzing the privacy implications of using online data brokers, developing a corporate policy for employee Web usage, using blog creation tools to create a simple blog, and using Internet newsgroups for market research.

Management Decision Problems

1. USAData's Web site is linked to massive databases that consolidate personal data on millions of people. Anyone with a credit card can purchase marketing lists of consumers broken down by location, age, income level, and interests. If you click on Consumer Lists to order a consumer mailing list, you can find the names, addresses, and sometimes phone numbers of potential sales leads residing in a specific location and purchase the list of those names. One could use this capability to obtain a list, for example, of everyone in Peekskill, New York, making $150,000 or more per year. Do data brokers such as USAData raise privacy issues? Why or why not? If your name and other personal information were in this database, what limitations on access would you want in order to preserve your privacy? Consider the following data users: government agencies, your employer, private business firms, other individuals.

2. As the head of a small insurance company with six employees, you are concerned about how effectively your company is using its networking and human resources. Budgets are tight, and you are struggling to meet payrolls because employees are reporting many overtime hours. You do not believe that the employees have a sufficiently heavy work load to warrant working longer hours and are looking into the amount of time they spend on the Internet.

Each employee uses a computer with Internet access on the job. Review a sample of your company's weekly report of employee Web usage, which can be found in MyMISLab.

- Calculate the total amount of time each employee spent on the Web for the week and the total amount of time that company computers were used for this purpose. Rank the employees in the order of the amount of time each spent online.
- Do your findings and the contents of the report indicate any ethical problems employees are creating? Is the company creating an ethical problem by monitoring its employees' use of the Internet?
- Use the guidelines for ethical analysis presented in this chapter to develop a solution to the problems you have identified.

Achieving Operational Excellence: Creating a Simple Blog

Software skills: Blog creation
Business skills: Blog and Web page design

In this project, you'll learn how to build a simple blog of your own design using the online blog creation software available at Blogger.com. Pick a sport, hobby, or topic of interest as the theme for your blog. Name the blog, give it a title, and choose a template for the blog. Post at least four entries to the blog, adding a label for each posting. Edit your posts, if necessary. Upload an image, such as a photo from your hard drive or the Web to your blog. Add capabilities for other registered users, such as team members, to comment on your blog. Briefly describe how your blog could be useful to a company selling products or services related to the theme of your blog. List the tools available to Blogger that would make your blog more useful for business and describe the business uses of each. Save your blog and show it to your instructor.

Improving Decision Making: Using Internet Newsgroups for Online Market Research

Software Skills: Web browser software and Internet newsgroups
Business Skills: Using Internet newsgroups to identify potential customers

This project will help develop your Internet skills in using newsgroups for marketing. It will also ask you to think about the ethical implications of using information in online discussion groups for business purposes.

You are producing hiking boots that you sell through a few stores at this time. You would like to use Internet discussion groups interested in hiking, climbing, and camping both to sell your boots and to make them well known. Visit groups.google.com, which stores discussion postings from many thousands of newsgroups. Through this site you can locate all relevant newsgroups and search them by keyword, author's name, forum, date, and subject. Choose a message and examine it carefully, noting all the information you can obtain, including information about the author.

- How could you use these newsgroups to market your boots?
- What ethical principles might you be violating if you use these messages to sell your boots? Do you think there are ethical problems in using newsgroups this way? Explain your answer.
- Next use Google or Yahoo to search the hiking boots industry and locate sites that will help you develop other new ideas for contacting potential customers.
- Given what you have learned in this and previous chapters, prepare a plan to use newsgroups and other alternative methods to begin attracting visitors to your site.

Video Cases

Video Cases and Instructional Videos illustrating some of the concepts in this chapter are available. Contact your instructor to access these videos.

Collaboration and Teamwork Project

In MyMISLab, you will find a Collaboration and Teamwork Project dealing with the concepts in this chapter. You will be able to use Google Sites, Google Docs, and other open source collaboration tools to complete the assignment.

Facebook: It's About the Money
CASE STUDY

Over the course of less than a decade, Facebook has morphed from a small, niche networking site for mostly Ivy League college students into a publicly traded company estimated to be worth at least $50 billion. Facebook boasts that it is free to join and always will be, so where's the money coming from to service 1 billion subscribers? Just like its fellow tech titan and rival Google, Facebook's revenue comes almost entirely from advertising. Facebook does not have a diverse array of hot new gadgets, a countrywide network of brick-and-mortar retail outlets, or a full inventory of software for sale; instead, it has your personal information, and the information of hundreds of millions of others with Facebook accounts.

Advertisers have long understood the value of Facebook's unprecedented trove of personal information. They can serve ads using highly specific details, like relationship status, location, employment status, favorite books, movies, or TV shows, and a host of other categories. For example, an Atlanta woman who posts that she has become engaged might be offered an ad for a wedding photographer on her Facebook page. When advertisements are served to finely targeted subsets of users, the response is much more successful than traditional types of advertising. A growing number of companies both big and small have taken notice: in 2011, Facebook made $3.2 billion in advertising revenue, which constituted 85 percent of its total revenue. The rest comes from the sale of virtual goods and services, principally Zynga games.

That was good news for Facebook, which launched its IPO (initial public stock offering) in May 2012 and is expected to continue to increase its revenue in coming years. But is it good news for you, the Facebook user? More than ever, companies like Facebook and Google, which made approximately $36.5 billion in advertising revenue in 2011, are using your online activity to develop a frighteningly accurate picture of your life. Facebook's goal is to serve advertisements that are more relevant to you than anywhere else on the Web, but the personal information they gather about you both with and without your consent can also be used against you in other ways.

Facebook has a diverse array of compelling and useful features. Facebook's partnership with the Department of Labor helps to connect job seekers and employers; Facebook has helped families find lost pets after natural disasters, such as when tornadoes hit the Midwest in 2012; Facebook allows active-duty soldiers to stay in touch with their families; it gives smaller companies a chance to further their e-commerce efforts and larger companies a chance to solidify their brands; and, perhaps most obviously, Facebook allows you to more easily keep in touch with your friends. These are the reasons why so many people are on Facebook.

However, Facebook's goal is to get its users to share as much data as possible, because the more Facebook knows about you, the more accurately it can serve relevant advertisements to you. Facebook CEO Mark Zuckerberg often says that people want the world to be more open and connected. It's unclear whether that is truly the case, but it is certainly true that Facebook wants the world to be more open and connected, because it stands to make more money in that world. Critics of Facebook are concerned that the existence of a repository of personal data of the size that Facebook has amassed requires protections and privacy controls that extend far beyond those that Facebook currently offers.

Facebook wanting to make more money is not a bad thing, but the company has a checkered past of privacy violations and missteps that raise doubts about whether it should be responsible for the personal data of hundreds of millions of people. There are no laws in the United States that give consumers the right to know what data companies like Facebook have compiled. You can challenge information in credit reports, but you can't even see what data Facebook has gathered about you, let alone try to change it. It's different in Europe: you can request Facebook to turn over a report of all the information it has about you. More than ever, your every move, every click, on social networks is being used by outside entities to assess your interests, and behavior, and then pitch you an ad based on this knowledge. Law enforcement agencies use social networks to gather evidence on tax evaders, and other criminals; employers use social networks to make decisions about prospective candidates for jobs; and data aggregators are gathering as much information about you as they can sell to the highest bidder.

In a recent study, *Consumer Reports* found that of 150 million Americans on Facebook, at least 4.8

million are willingly sharing information that could be used against them in some way. That includes plans to travel on a particular day, which burglars could use to time robberies, or Liking a page about a particular health condition or treatment, which insurers could use to deny coverage. 13 million users have never adjusted Facebook's privacy controls, which allow friends using Facebook applications to unwittingly transfer your data to a third party without your knowledge. Credit card companies and other similar organizations have begun engaging in "weblining", taken from the phrase redlining, by altering their treatment of you based on the actions of other people with profiles similar to yours.

Ninety-three percent of people polled believe that Internet companies should be forced to ask for permission before using your personal information, and 72 percent want the ability to opt out of online tracking. Why, then, do so many people share sensitive details of their life on Facebook? Often it's because users do not realize that their data are being collected and transmitted in this way. A Facebook user's friends are not notified if information about them is collected by that user's applications. Many of Facebook's features and services are enabled by default when they are launched without notifying users. And a study by Siegel + Gale found that Facebook's privacy policy is more difficult to comprehend than government notices or typical bank credit card agreements, which are notoriously dense. Next time you visit Facebook, click on Privacy Settings, and see if you can understand your options.

Facebook's value and growth potential is determined by how effectively it can leverage the personal data is aggregated about its users to attract advertisers. Facebook also stands to gain from managing and avoiding the privacy concerns raised by its users and government regulators. For Facebook users that value the privacy of their personal data, this situation appears grim. But there are some signs that Facebook might become more responsible with its data collection processes, whether by its own volition or because it is forced to do so. As a publicly traded company, Facebook now invites more scrutiny from investors and regulators because, unlike in the past, their balance sheets, assets, and financial reporting documents are readily available.

In August 2012, Facebook settled a lawsuit with the FTC in which they were barred from misrepresenting the privacy or security of users' personal information. Facebook was charged with deceiving its users by telling them they could keep their information on Facebook private, but then repeatedly

allowing it to be shared and made public. Facebook agreed to obtain user consent before making any change to that user's privacy preferences, and to submit to bi-annual privacy audits by an independent firm for the next 20 years. Privacy advocate groups like the Electronic Privacy Information Center (EPIC) want Facebook to restore its more robust privacy settings from 2009, as well as to offer complete access to all data it keeps about its users. Facebook has also come under fire from EPIC for collecting information about users who are not even logged into Facebook or may not even have accounts on Facebook. Facebook keeps track of activity on other sites that have Like buttons or "recommendations" widgets, and records the time of your visit and your IP address when you visit a site with those features, regardless of whether or not you click on them.

While U.S. Facebook users have little recourse to access data that Facebook has collected on them, users from other countries have made inroads in this regard. An Austrian law student was able to get a full copy of his personal information from Facebook's Dublin office, due to the more stringent consumer privacy protections in Ireland. The full document was 1,222 pages long and covered three years of activity on the site, including deleted Wall posts and messages with sensitive personal information and deleted e-mail addresses.

It isn't just text-based data that Facebook is stockpiling, either. Facebook is also compiling a biometric database of unprecedented size. The company stores more than 60 billion photos on its servers and that number grows by 250 million each day. A recent feature launched by Facebook called Tag Suggest scans photographs using facial recognition technology. When Tag Suggest was launched, it was enabled for many users without opting in. This database has value to law enforcement and other organizations looking to compile profiles of users for use in advertising. EPIC also has demanded that Facebook stop creating facial recognition profiles without user consent.

In 2012, as part of the settlement of another class-action lawsuit, Facebook agreed to allow users to opt in to its Sponsored Stories service, which serves advertisements that highlight products and businesses that your Facebook friends are using. Now, users can control and see which of their actions on Facebook generate advertisements that their friends will see. Sponsored Stories are one of the most effective forms of advertising on Facebook because they don't seem like advertisements at all to most users. Facebook had previously argued that users were giving "implied consent" every time they clicked a Like button on a page. Users are now confronted with an opt-in notice that analysts speculate may cost Facebook up to $103 million in advertising revenue.

Additionally, in response to the increased scrutiny brought about by its IPO, Facebook has improved its archive feature to include more categories of information that the company makes available to users that request copies of their personal data. In Europe, 40,000 Facebook users have already requested their data, and European law requires that Facebook respond to these requests within 40 days. Still, even after Facebook's improvements, they will offer users access to 39 data categories, while the company supposedly maintains at least 84 categories about each user. And, despite the increased emphasis on privacy and data disclosure, European lawmakers are unlikely to hamper Facebook's ability to offer highly customized advertisements, which is the backbone of Facebook's business model.

Perhaps sensing that privacy concerns represent a long-term threat to its profitability, Facebook is working to develop revenue streams beyond display advertising. Facebook is now a strong second to Google in the United States in display advertising, with 28 percent of all display ads served on Facebook, but the company hopes to become more of an online marketplace, facilitating the selling of goods and services, potentially challenging Amazon and eBay. Still, it's likely that the personal data of hundreds of millions of users will always be Facebook's most valuable asset. How responsibly it manages that asset will guide its path into the future.

Sources: "Selling You on Facebook," Julia Angwin and Jeremy Singer-Vine, *The Wall Street Journal*, April 7, 2012; Consumer Reports, "Facebook and Your Privacy," May 3, 2012; "Facebook Is Using You," Lori Andrews, *The New York Times*, Feb. 4, 2012; "Personal Data's Value? Facebook Set to Find Out," Somini Sengupta and Evelyn M. Rusli, *The New York Times*, Jan. 31, 2012; "Facebook, Eye on Privacy Laws, Offers More Disclosure to Users," Kevin J O'Brien, *The New York Times*, April 13, 2012; "To Settle Lawsuit, Facebook Alters Policy for Its 'Like' Button," Somini Sengupta, *The New York Times*, June 21, 2012.

CASE STUDY QUESTIONS

1. Perform an ethical analysis of Facebook. What is the ethical dilemma presented by this case?

2. What is the relationship of privacy to Facebook's business model?

3. Describe the weaknesses of Facebook's privacy policies and features. What management, organization, and technology factors have contributed to those weaknesss?

4. Will Facebook be able to have a successful business model without invading privacy? Explain your answer. Are there any measures Facebook could take to make this possible?

PART TWO

Information Technology Infrastructure

Part Two provides the technical foundation for understanding information systems by examining hardware, software, database, and networking technologies along with tools and techniques for security and control. This part answers questions such as: What technologies do businesses today need to accomplish their work? What do I need to know about these technologies to make sure they enhance the performance of the firm? How are these technologies likely to change in the future? What technologies and procedures are required to ensure that systems are reliable and secure?

Chapter 5

IT Infrastructure and Emerging Technologies

LEARNING OBJECTIVES

After reading this chapter, you will be able to answer the following questions:

1. What is IT infrastructure and what are its components?

2. What are the stages and technology drivers of IT infrastructure evolution?

3. What are the current trends in computer hardware platforms?

4. What are the current trends in software platforms?

5. What are the challenges of managing IT infrastructure and management solutions?

Interactive Sessions:

Should You Use Your iPhone for Work?

Nordea Goes Green with IT

CHAPTER OUTLINE

REFORMING THE REGULATORY SYSTEM FOR CONSTRUCTION PERMITS

The Singapore Government envisions a need to transform the building and construction industry through the Construction 21 Blueprint and a strategic vision to become a "World Class Builder in the Knowledge Age". The increased use of IT is critical for this government to realize its vision, primarily because of the symbiotic relationship between technology and knowledge. Clearly, in a knowledge-based industry, organizations must leverage technologies as a means to improve productivity, reduce costs and enhance the quality of products and services. Government efforts have to focus on developing a set of IT infrastructure projects to provide businesses and other organizations with the means to streamline business processes and workflow, and maximize the use of information to gain and sustain their competitive advantage.

The CORENET project (COnstruction and Real Estate NETwork) has come a long way, since its launch in 1995, to become a major IT initiative. Led by the Ministry of National Development and driven by the Building and Construction Authority with the purpose of re-engineering the business processes of the building and construction industry to achieve great improvements in turnaround time, productivity and quality. CORENET revolves around developing IT systems and key infrastructure to integrate the four major processes of a building project life cycle, namely, design, procurement, build, and maintenance. One of the goals of CORENET is to implement an appropriate IT infrastructure to facilitate participants of building projects, including the planning authorities, to exchange information seamlessly and speedily. In essence, putting in place a government-to-business (G2B) infrastructure enables businesses to make electronic building plan submissions for obtaining approvals and permits from the 16 government authorities across eight ministries that regulate activities of the industry. The internet-based system can handle project-related documents for the whole project life cycle, from processing of building plans and documents related to the issuance of development planning approvals, building plans approval, structural plans approvals, temporary occupation permits, fire safety certificates and certificates of statutory completion.

Traditionally, the whole construction process comprises four distinct sequential stages. They are design, tender documentation and selection, construction, and handover and maintenance. In the first stage, the key activities of design consist of developing concept and schematic designs, and obtaining planning approvals. As planning approvals are granted by the various regulatory bodies, the building owner needs to submit the building plans through the appointed design consultant (or the Qualified Person) to these bodies separately to apply for the approvals. The complex process of submitting the application, checking against planning requirements, evaluating the proposal, re-submission for non-compliance and issuing approval involves many parties and uses different channels of communication. In the traditional (or old) process, the 'Qualified Person' has to make multiple submissions of plans, documents and

© leungchopan/Shutterstock

applications to different authorities, resulting in voluminous paper documents generated, inefficient manual processing of submissions by the regulatory agencies, insufficient storage space for all the paper documents and disorganized exchange of project information among project team members.

How can an IT infrastructure help to improve the submissions process in this situation? CORENET's e-submission system provides a virtual one-stop 24/7 counter to facilitate electronic submission of building plans and documents to multiple regulatory agencies, online enquiry of submission status, integrated application with fee collection, quicker processing and turnaround time of an application, and elimination of (hardcopy) printing of plans, documents and application forms. In other words, by allowing industry players to submit their applications over the Internet, they do not need to make hardcopy prints of the plans and documents nor travel physically to the premises of the government agencies to submit them. The element of transparency is also enhanced as all parties involved are able to monitor online the status and progress of the planning applications made.

The Singapore Government ascertains the amount of cost savings derived from the use of the e-submission system as an estimated S$450 (equivalent to about US$368) for each submission. The amount is estimated from the reduction in hardcopy prints of plans and documents, as well as elimination of manual dispatching of documents to the various authorities concerned. Further results from an industry-wide survey of 754 companies show that the majority of them (77.1 percent) have found it to be beneficial to their work. This high percentage obtained helps to register a relatively firm adoption of the new system, as well as good success of its implementation.

Sources: Building and Construction Authority, "Construction and Real Estate Network (CORENET)". Website visited on November 1, 2012, athttp://www.corenet.gov.sg. Goh, B.H., "e-Government for Construction: The Case of Singapore's CORENET Project". In proceedings of the IFIP TC 8 WG 8.9 International Conference on Research and Practical Issues of Enterprise Information Systems, Beijing, China, October 14, 2007. Lim, B.H., "The CORENET Project in Singapore". Article retrieved on November 1, 2012, from http://www.buildingsmartsingapore.org/news/news-docs/20060228_CORENET_case_study.pdf

This case is contributed by Bee Hua Goh, National University of Singapore

The CORENET project illustrates a government's strategic plan and initiatives to transform the building and construction industry from one that is traditional into another that is more knowledge-based. An IT infrastructure is implemented to allow businesses and other organizations to collaborate with one another in order to share and exchange common building project information.

More specifically, it illustrates how the setting up of a G2B (internet-based) infrastructure can help the industry as a whole to rationalize its practice and processes for building plans submissions. Significant improvement in turnaround time for each application is evident which translates into measurable cost savings. In other words, without the IT infrastructure, the various private and public organizations would have to work in isolation, resulting in duplication of work, wastage of time and other resources, as well as a lack of integration and transparency of the application process.

The benefits, in terms of tangible and intangible, are obvious to everyone who participates in the process of obtaining and granting planning approvals and permits for construction work. But there is an added advantage for organizations in the construction industry. The accumulation of project information (or knowledge) that is stored digitally can be easily retrieved for subsequent use. Knowledge reuse is most valuable in construction projects as each project contains the relevant best practices that can be repeated in other projects to ensure better success in them.

Here are some questions to think about: How did CORENET's e-submission system facilitate businesses and other organizations in streamlining their business processes and workflow? How are the businesses and other organizations benefiting from CORENET's G2B infrastructure for building plans submission?

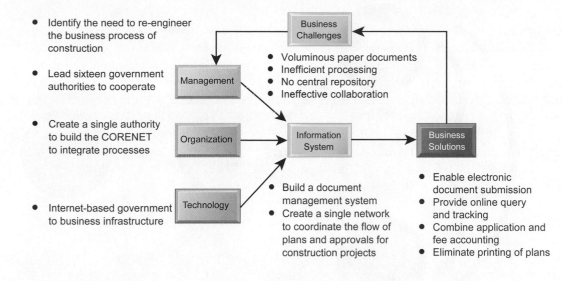

- Identify the need to re-engineer the business process of construction

- Lead sixteen government authorities to cooperate

- Create a single authority to build the CORENET to integrate processes

- Internet-based government to business infrastructure

Business Challenges

- Voluminous paper documents
- Inefficient processing
- No central repository
- Ineffective collaboration

Management

Organization

Technology

Information System

- Build a document management system
- Create a single network to coordinate the flow of plans and approvals for construction projects

Business Solutions

- Enable electronic document submission
- Provide online query and tracking
- Combine application and fee accounting
- Eliminate printing of plans

5.1   IT INFRASTRUCTURE

In Chapter 1, we defined *information technology (IT) infrastructure* as the shared technology resources that provide the platform for the firm's specific information system applications. An IT infrastructure includes investment in hardware, software, and services—such as consulting, education, and training—that are shared across the entire firm or across entire business units in the firm. A firm's IT infrastructure provides the foundation for serving customers, working with vendors, and managing internal firm business processes (see Figure 5.1).

Supplying firms worldwide with IT infrastructure (hardware and software) in 2012 is estimated to be a $3.6 trillion industry when telecommunications, networking equipment, and telecommunications services (Internet, telephone, and data transmission) are included. This does not include IT and related business process consulting services, which add another $400 billion. Investments in infrastructure account for between 25 and 50 percent of information technology expenditures in large firms, led by financial services firms where IT investment is well over half of all capital investment.

DEFINING IT INFRASTRUCTURE

An IT infrastructure consists of a set of physical devices and software applications that are required to operate the entire enterprise. But an IT infrastructure is also a set of firmwide services budgeted by management and comprising both human and technical capabilities. These services include the following:

- Computing platforms used to provide computing services that connect employees, customers, and suppliers into a coherent digital environment, including large mainframes, midrange computers, desktop and laptop computers, and mobile handheld and remote cloud computing services.

- Telecommunications services that provide data, voice, and video connectivity to employees, customers, and suppliers

FIGURE 5.1   CONNECTION BETWEEN THE FIRM, IT INFRASTRUCTURE, AND BUSINESS CAPABILITIES

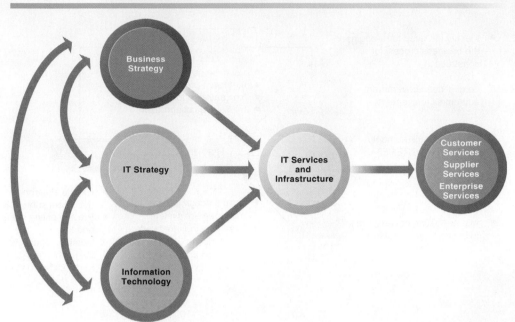

The services a firm is capable of providing to its customers, suppliers, and employees are a direct function of its IT infrastructure. Ideally, this infrastructure should support the firm's business and information systems strategy. New information technologies have a powerful impact on business and IT strategies, as well as the services that can be provided to customers.

- Data management services that store and manage corporate data and provide capabilities for analyzing the data
- Application software services, including online software services, that provide enterprise-wide capabilities such as enterprise resource planning, customer relationship management, supply chain management, and knowledge management systems that are shared by all business units
- Physical facilities management services that develop and manage the physical installations required for computing, telecommunications, and data management services
- IT management services that plan and develop the infrastructure, coordinate with the business units for IT services, manage accounting for the IT expenditure, and provide project management services
- IT standards services that provide the firm and its business units with policies that determine which information technology will be used, when, and how
- IT education services that provide training in system use to employees and offer managers training in how to plan for and manage IT investments
- IT research and development services that provide the firm with research on potential future IT projects and investments that could help the firm differentiate itself in the marketplace

This "service platform" perspective makes it easier to understand the business value provided by infrastructure investments. For instance, the real business value of a fully loaded personal computer operating at 3 gigahertz that costs about $1,000 and a high-speed Internet connection is hard to understand without knowing who will use it and how it will be used. When we look at the services provided by these tools, however, their value becomes more apparent: The new PC makes it possible for a high-cost employee making $100,000 a year to connect to all the company's major systems and the public Internet. The high-speed Internet service saves this employee about one hour per day in reduced wait time for Internet information. Without this PC and Internet connection, the value of this one employee to the firm might be cut in half.

EVOLUTION OF IT INFRASTRUCTURE

The IT infrastructure in organizations today is an outgrowth of over 50 years of evolution in computing platforms. There have been five stages in this evolution, each representing a different configuration of computing power and infrastructure elements (see Figure 5.2). The five eras are general-purpose mainframe and minicomputer computing, personal computers, client/server networks, enterprise computing, and cloud and mobile computing.

Technologies that characterize one era may also be used in another time period for other purposes. For example, some companies still run traditional mainframe systems or use mainframe computers as massive servers supporting large Web sites and corporate enterprise applications.

General-Purpose Mainframe and Minicomputer Era: (1959 to Present)

The introduction of the IBM 1401 and 7090 transistorized machines in 1959 marked the beginning of widespread commercial use of **mainframe** computers. In 1965, the mainframe computer truly came into its own with the introduction of the IBM 360 series. The 360 was the first commercial computer with a powerful operating system that could provide time sharing, multitasking, and virtual memory in more advanced models. IBM has dominated mainframe computing from this point on. Mainframe computers became powerful enough to support thousands of online remote terminals connected to the centralized mainframe using proprietary communication protocols and proprietary data lines.

The mainframe era was a period of highly centralized computing under the control of professional programmers and systems operators (usually in a corporate data center), with most elements of infrastructure provided by a single vendor, the manufacturer of the hardware and the software.

This pattern began to change with the introduction of **minicomputers** produced by Digital Equipment Corporation (DEC) in 1965. DEC minicomputers (PDP-11 and later the VAX machines) offered powerful machines at far lower prices than IBM mainframes, making possible decentralized computing, customized to the specific needs of individual departments or business units rather than time sharing on a single huge mainframe. In recent years, the minicomputer has evolved into a midrange computer or midrange server and is part of a network.

Personal Computer Era: (1981 to Present)

Although the first truly personal computers (PCs) appeared in the 1970s (the Xerox Alto, the MITS Altair 8800, and the Apple I and II, to name a few), these machines had only limited distribution to computer enthusiasts. The appearance of the IBM PC in 1981 is usually considered the beginning of the PC era because this machine was the first to be widely adopted by American businesses. At first using the DOS operating system, a text-based command language, and later the Microsoft Windows operating system, the **Wintel PC** computer (Windows operating system software on a computer with an Intel microprocessor) became the standard desktop personal computer. In 2012, there are an estimated 1.2 billion

FIGURE 5.2   **ERAS IN IT INFRASTRUCTURE EVOLUTION**

Stages in IT Infrastructure Evolution

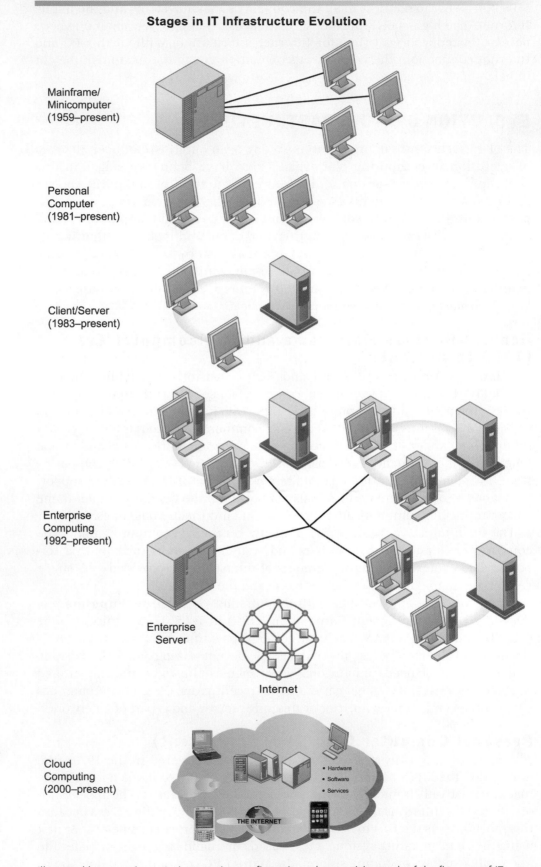

Mainframe/
Minicomputer
(1959–present)

Personal
Computer
(1981–present)

Client/Server
(1983–present)

Enterprise
Computing
1992–present)

Enterprise
Server

Internet

Cloud
Computing
(2000–present)

- Hardware
- Software
- Services

THE INTERNET

Illustrated here are the typical computing configurations characterizing each of the five eras of IT infrastructure evolution.

PCs in the world, and 300 million new PCs are sold each year. 90% are thought to run a version of Windows, and 10% run a Macintosh OS. The Wintel dominance as a computing platform is receding as iPhone and Android device sales increase. Nearly one billion people worldwide own smartphones, and most of these users access the Internet with their mobile devices.

Proliferation of PCs in the 1980s and early 1990s launched a spate of personal desktop productivity software tools—word processors, spreadsheets, electronic presentation software, and small data management programs—that were very valuable to both home and corporate users. These PCs were stand-alone systems until PC operating system software in the 1990s made it possible to link them into networks.

Client/Server Era (1983 to Present)

In **client/server computing**, desktop or laptop computers called **clients** are networked to powerful **server** computers that provide the client computers with a variety of services and capabilities. Computer processing work is split between these two types of machines. The client is the user point of entry, whereas the server typically processes and stores shared data, serves up Web pages, or manages network activities. The term "server" refers to both the software application and the physical computer on which the network software runs. The server could be a mainframe, but today, server computers typically are more powerful versions of personal computers, based on inexpensive chips and often using multiple processors in a single computer box., or in server racks.

The simplest client/server network consists of a client computer networked to a server computer, with processing split between the two types of machines. This is called a *two-tiered client/server architecture*. Whereas simple client/server networks can be found in small businesses, most corporations have more complex, **multitiered** (often called **N-tier**) **client/server architectures** in which the work of the entire network is balanced over several different levels of servers, depending on the kind of service being requested (see Figure 5.3).

For instance, at the first level, a **Web server** will serve a Web page to a client in response to a request for service. Web server software is responsible

FIGURE 5.3   A MULTITIERED CLIENT/SERVER NETWORK (N-TIER)

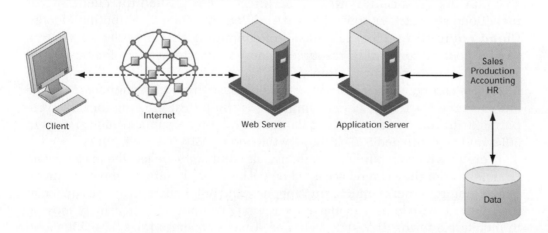

In a multitiered client/server network, client requests for service are handled by different levels of servers.

for locating and managing stored Web pages. If the client requests access to a corporate system (a product list or price information, for instance), the request is passed along to an **application server**. Application server software handles all application operations between a user and an organization's back-end business systems. The application server may reside on the same computer as the Web server or on its own dedicated computer. Chapters 6 and 7 provide more detail on other pieces of software that are used in multitiered client/server architectures for e-commerce and e-business.

Client/server computing enables businesses to distribute computing work across a series of smaller, inexpensive machines that cost much less than centralized mainframe systems. The result is an explosion in computing power and applications throughout the firm.

Novell NetWare was the leading technology for client/server networking at the beginning of the client/server era. Today, Microsoft is the market leader with its **Windows** operating systems (Windows Server, Windows 8, Windows 7, and Windows Vista).

Enterprise Computing Era (1992 to Present)

In the early 1990s, firms turned to networking standards and software tools that could integrate disparate networks and applications throughout the firm into an enterprise-wide infrastructure. As the Internet developed into a trusted communications environment after 1995, business firms began seriously using the *Transmission Control Protocol/Internet Protocol (TCP/IP)* networking standard to tie their disparate networks together. We discuss TCP/IP in detail in Chapter 7.

The resulting IT infrastructure links different pieces of computer hardware and smaller networks into an enterprise-wide network so that information can flow freely across the organization and between the firm and other organizations. It can link different types of computer hardware, including mainframes, servers, PCs, and mobile devices, and it includes public infrastructures such as the telephone system, the Internet, and public network services. The enterprise infrastructure also requires software to link disparate applications and enable data to flow freely among different parts of the business, such as enterprise applications (see Chapters 2 and 9) and Web services (discussed in Section 5.4).

Cloud and Mobile Computing Era (2000 to Present)

The growing bandwidth power of the Internet has pushed the client/server model one step further, towards what is called the "Cloud Computing Model." **Cloud computing** refers to a model of computing that provides access to a shared pool of computing resources (computers, storage, applications, and services) over a network, often the Internet. These "clouds" of computing resources can be accessed on an as-needed basis from any connected device and location. Currently, cloud computing is the fastest growing form of computing, with companies spending about $109 billion on public cloud services in 2012, and an estimated $207 billion by the end of 2016 (Gartner, 2012).

Thousands or even hundreds of thousands computers are located in cloud data centers, where they can be accessed by desktop computers, laptop computers, tablets, entertainment centers, smartphones, and other client machines linked to the Internet, with both personal and corporate computing increasingly moving to mobile platforms. IBM, HP, Dell, and Amazon operate huge, scalable cloud computing centers that provide computing power, data storage, and high-speed Internet connections to firms that want to maintain their IT infrastructures remotely. Software firms such as Google, Microsoft, SAP, Oracle, and Salesforce.com sell software applications as services delivered over the Internet.

We discuss cloud and mobile computing in more detail in Section 5.3. The Learning Tracks include a table titled Comparing Stages in IT Infrastructure Evolution, which compares each era on the infrastructure dimensions introduced.

TECHNOLOGY DRIVERS OF INFRASTRUCTURE EVOLUTION

The changes in IT infrastructure we have just described have resulted from developments in computer processing, memory chips, storage devices, telecommunications and networking hardware and software, and software design that have exponentially increased computing power while exponentially reducing costs. Let's look at the most important developments.

Moore's Law and Microprocessing Power

In 1965, Gordon Moore, the director of Fairchild Semiconductor's Research and Development Laboratories, an early manufacturer of integrated circuits, wrote in *Electronics* magazine that since the first microprocessor chip was introduced in 1959, the number of components on a chip with the smallest manufacturing costs per component (generally transistors) had doubled each year. This assertion became the foundation of **Moore's Law**. Moore later reduced the rate of growth to a doubling every two years.

This law would later be interpreted in multiple ways. There are at least three variations of Moore's Law, none of which Moore ever stated: (1) the power of microprocessors doubles every 18 months; (2) computing power doubles every 18 months; and (3) the price of computing falls by half every 18 months.

FIGURE 5.4   MOORE'S LAW AND MICROPROCESSOR PERFORMANCE

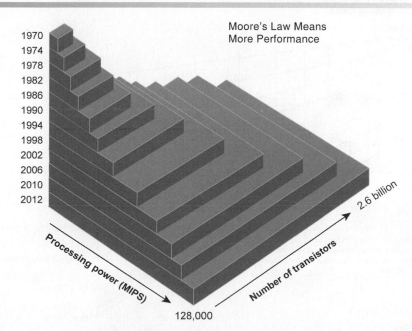

Packing over 2 billion transistors into a tiny microprocessor has exponentially increased processing power. Processing power has increased to over 128,000 MIPS (2.6 billion instructions per second).

Source: Authors' estimate.

Figure 5.4 illustrates the relationship between number of transistors on a microprocessor and millions of instructions per second (MIPS), a common measure of processor power. Figure 5.5 shows the exponential decline in the cost of transistors and rise in computing power. For instance, in 2012, you can buy an Intel i7 quad-core processor on Amazon for about $355, and you will be purchasing a chip with 2.5 billion transistors, which works out to about one ten-millionth of a dollar per transistor.

Exponential growth in the number of transistors and the power of processors coupled with an exponential decline in computing costs is likely to continue. Chip manufacturers continue to miniaturize components. Today's transistors should no longer be compared to the size of a human hair but rather to the size of a virus.

By using nanotechnology, chip manufacturers can even shrink the size of transistors down to the width of several atoms. **Nanotechnology** uses individual atoms and molecules to create computer chips and other devices that are thousands of times smaller than current technologies permit. Chip manufacturers are trying to develop a manufacturing process that could produce nanotube processors economically (Figure 5.6). IBM has just started making microprocessors in a production setting using this technology.

The Law of Mass Digital Storage

A second technology driver of IT infrastructure change is the Law of Mass Digital Storage. The amount of digital information is roughly doubling every year (Gantz and Reinsel, 2011; Lyman and Varian, 2003). Fortunately, the cost of storing digital information is falling at an exponential rate of 100 percent a year. Figure 5.7 shows that the number of megabytes that can be stored on magnetic media for $1 from 1950 to the present roughly doubled every 15 months. In 2012, a 500 gigabyte hard disk drive sells at retail for about $60.

FIGURE 5.5   FALLING COST OF CHIPS

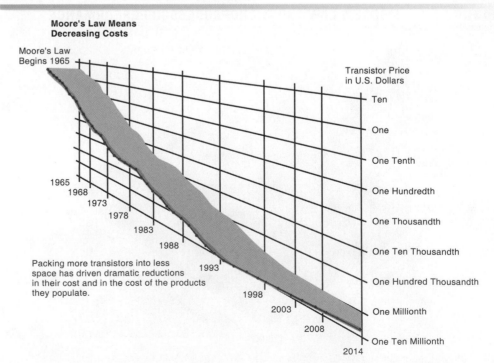

Packing more transistors into less space has driven down transistor costs dramatically as well as the cost of the products in which they are used.

Source: Authors' estimate.

FIGURE 5.6   EXAMPLE OF NANOTUBES

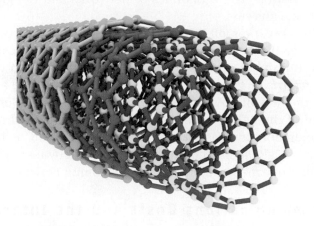

Nanotubes are tiny tubes about 10,000 times thinner than a human hair. They consist of rolled-up sheets of carbon hexagons and have the potential uses as minuscule wires or in ultrasmall electronic devices and are very powerful conductors of electrical current. © Tyler Boyes/Shutterstock.

FIGURE 5.7   THE AMOUNT OF STORAGE PER DOLLAR RISES EXPONENTIALLY, 1950–2012

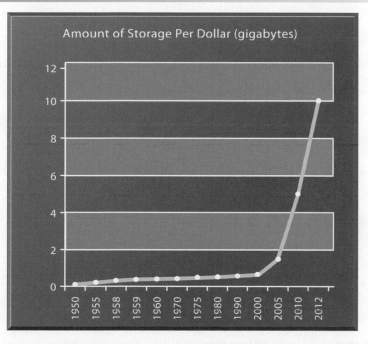

Since the first magnetic storage device was used in 1955, the amount of storage a dollar buys has risen exponentially, doubling the amount of digital storage for each dollar expended every 15 months on average.

Source: Authors' estimates.

Metcalfe's Law and Network Economics

Moore's Law and the Law of Mass Storage help us understand why computing resources are now so readily available. But why do people want more computing and storage power? The economics of networks and the growth of the Internet provide some answers.

Robert Metcalfe—inventor of Ethernet local area network technology—claimed in 1970 that the value or power of a network grows exponentially as a function of the number of network members. Metcalfe and others point to the *increasing returns to scale* that network members receive as more and more people join the network. As the number of members in a network grows linearly, the value of the entire system grows exponentially and continues to grow forever as members increase. Demand for information technology has been driven by the social and business value of digital networks, which rapidly multiply the number of actual and potential links among network members.

Declining Communications Costs and the Internet

A fourth technology driver transforming IT infrastructure is the rapid decline in the costs of communication and the exponential growth in the size of the Internet. An estimated 2.3 billion people worldwide now have Internet access (Internet World Stats, 2012). Figure 5.8 illustrates the exponentially declining cost of communication both over the Internet and over telephone networks (which increasingly are based on the Internet). As communication costs fall toward a very small number and approach 0, utilization of communication and computing facilities explode.

To take advantage of the business value associated with the Internet, firms must greatly expand their Internet connections, including wireless connectivity, and greatly expand the power of their client/server networks, desktop clients, and mobile computing devices. There is every reason to believe these trends will continue.

FIGURE 5.8   EXPONENTIAL DECLINES IN INTERNET COMMUNICATIONS COSTS

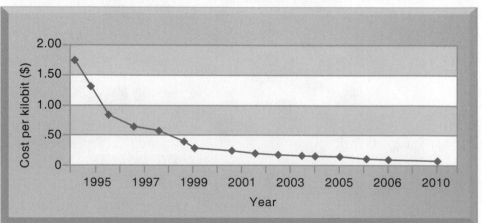

One reason for the growth in the Internet population is the rapid decline in Internet connection and overall communication costs. The cost per kilobit of Internet access has fallen exponentially since 1995. Digital subscriber line (DSL) and cable modems now deliver a kilobit of communication for a retail price of around 2 cents.

Source: Authors.

Standards and Network Effects

Today's enterprise infrastructure and Internet computing would be impossible—both now and in the future—without agreements among manufacturers and widespread consumer acceptance of **technology standards**. Technology standards are specifications that establish the compatibility of products and the ability to communicate in a network (Stango, 2004).

Technology standards unleash powerful economies of scale and result in price declines as manufacturers focus on the products built to a single standard. Without these economies of scale, computing of any sort would be far more expensive than is currently the case. Table 5.1 describes important standards that have shaped IT infrastructure.

Beginning in the 1990s, corporations started moving toward standard computing and communications platforms. The Wintel PC with the Windows operating system and Microsoft Office desktop productivity applications became the standard desktop and mobile client computing platform. (It now shares the spotlight with other standards, such as Apple's iOS and Macintosh operating systems and the Android operating system.) Widespread adoption of Unix-Linux as the enterprise server operating system of choice made possible the replacement of proprietary and expensive mainframe infrastructures. In telecommunications, the Ethernet standard enabled PCs to connect together in small local area networks (LANs; see Chapter 7), and the TCP/IP standard enabled these LANs to be connected into firmwide networks, and ultimately, to the Internet.

TABLE 5.1 SOME IMPORTANT STANDARDS IN COMPUTING

STANDARD	SIGNIFICANCE
American Standard Code for Information Interchange (ASCII) (1958)	Made it possible for computer machines from different manufacturers to exchange data; later used as the universal language linking input and output devices such as keyboards and mice to computers. Adopted by the American National Standards Institute in 1963.
Common Business Oriented Language (COBOL) (1959)	An easy-to-use software language that greatly expanded the ability of programmers to write business-related programs and reduced the cost of software. Sponsored by the Defense Department in 1959.
Unix (1969–1975)	A powerful multitasking, multiuser, portable operating system initially developed at Bell Labs (1969) and later released for use by others (1975). It operates on a wide variety of computers from different manufacturers. Adopted by Sun, IBM, HP, and others in the 1980s, it became the most widely used enterprise-level operating system.
Transmission Control Protocol/Internet Protocol (TCP/IP) (1974)	Suite of communications protocols and a common addressing scheme that enables millions of computers to connect together in one giant global network (the Internet). Later, it was used as the default networking protocol suite for local area networks and intranets. Developed in the early 1970s for the U.S. Department of Defense.
Ethernet (1973)	A network standard for connecting desktop computers into local area networks that enabled the widespread adoption of client/server computing and local area networks, and further stimulated the adoption of personal computers.
IBM/Microsoft/Intel Personal Computer (1981)	The standard Wintel design for personal desktop computing based on standard Intel processors and other standard devices, Microsoft DOS, and later Windows software. The emergence of this standard, low-cost product laid the foundation for a 25-year period of explosive growth in computing throughout all organizations around the globe. Today, more than 1 billion PCs power business and government activities every day.
World Wide Web (1989–1993)	Standards for storing, retrieving, formatting, and displaying information as a worldwide web of electronic pages incorporating text, graphics, audio, and video enables creation of a global repository of billions of Web pages.

5.2   INFRASTRUCTURE COMPONENTS

IT infrastructure today is composed of seven major components. Figure 5.9 illustrates these infrastructure components and the major vendors within each component category. These components constitute investments that must be coordinated with one another to provide the firm with a coherent infrastructure.

In the past, technology vendors supplying these components were often in competition with one another, offering purchasing firms a mixture of incompatible, proprietary, partial solutions. But increasingly the vendor firms have been forced by large customers to cooperate in strategic partnerships with one another. For instance, a hardware and services provider such as IBM cooperates with all the major enterprise software providers, has strategic relationships with system integrators, and promises to work with whichever database products its client firms wish to use (even though it sells its own database management software called DB2).

FIGURE 5.9   THE IT INFRASTRUCTURE ECOSYSTEM

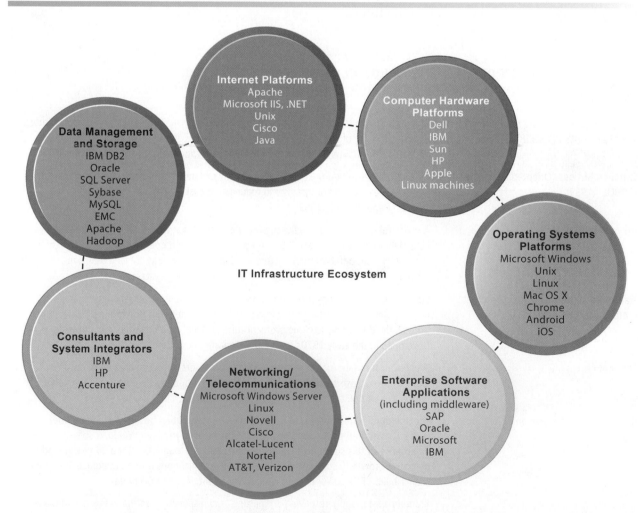

There are seven major components that must be coordinated to provide the firm with a coherent IT infrastructure. Listed here are major technologies and suppliers for each component.

COMPUTER HARDWARE PLATFORMS

Firms worldwide are expected to spend $448 billion on computer hardware in 2013, including servers and client devices. The server market uses mostly Intel or AMD processors in the form of blade servers in racks, but also includes Sun SPARC microprocessors and IBM chips specially designed for server use. **Blade servers**, which we discussed in the chapter-opening case, are computers consisting of a circuit board with processors, memory, and network connections that are stored in racks. They take up less space than traditional box-based servers. Secondary storage may be provided by a hard drive in each blade server or by external mass-storage drives.

The marketplace for computer hardware has increasingly become concentrated in top firms such as IBM, HP, Dell, and Sun Microsystems (acquired by Oracle), and three chip producers: Intel, AMD, and IBM. The industry has collectively settled on Intel as the standard processor for business computing, with major exceptions in the server market for Unix and Linux machines, which might use Sun or IBM processors.

Mainframes have not disappeared. Mainframes continue to be used to reliably and securely handle huge volumes of transactions, for analyzing very large quantities of data, and for handling large workloads in cloud computing centers. The mainframe is still the digital workhorse for banking and telecommunications networks. However, the number of providers has dwindled to one: IBM. IBM has also repurposed its mainframe systems so they can be used as giant servers for massive enterprise networks and corporate Web sites. A single IBM mainframe can run up to 17,000 instances of Linux or Windows Server software and is capable of replacing thousands of smaller blade servers (see the discussion of virtualization in Section 5.3).

OPERATING SYSTEM PLATFORMS

Microsoft Windows Server comprises about 35 percent of the server operating system market, with 65 percent of corporate servers using some form of the **Unix** operating system or **Linux**, an inexpensive and robust open source relative of Unix. Microsoft Windows Server is capable of providing enterprise-wide operating system and network services, and appeals to organizations seeking Windows-based IT infrastructures.

Unix and Linux are scalable, reliable, and much less expensive than mainframe operating systems. They can also run on many different types of processors. The major providers of Unix operating systems are IBM, HP, and Sun, each with slightly different and partially incompatible versions.

At the client level, 90 percent of PCs use some form of the Microsoft Windows **operating system** (such as Windows 8, Windows 7, or Windows Vista) to manage the resources and activities of the computer. However, there is now a much greater variety of operating systems than in the past, with new operating systems for computing on handheld mobile digital devices or cloud-connected computers.

Google's **Chrome OS** provides a lightweight operating system for cloud computing using netbooks. Programs are not stored on the user's PC but are used over the Internet and accessed through the Chrome Web browser. User data reside on servers across the Internet. **Android** is an open source operating system for mobile devices such as smartphones and tablet computers developed by the Open Handset Alliance led by Google. It has become the most popular smartphone platform worldwide, competing with iOS, Apple's mobile operating system for the iPhone, iPad, and iPod Touch.

Conventional client operating system software is designed around the mouse and keyboard, but increasingly becoming more natural and intuitive by using touch technology. **iOS**, the operating system for the phenomenally popular Apple iPad, iPhone, and iPod Touch, features a **multitouch** interface, where users employ one or more fingers to manipulate objects on a screen without a mouse or keyboard. Microsoft's **Windows 8,** which runs on tablets as well as PCs, has a user interface optimized for touch, but also works with a mouse and keyboard.

ENTERPRISE SOFTWARE APPLICATIONS

Firms worldwide are expected to spend about $301 billion in 2013 on software for enterprise applications that are treated as components of IT infrastructure. We introduced the various types of enterprise applications in Chapter 2, and Chapter 9 provides a more detailed discussion of each.

The largest providers of enterprise application software are SAP and Oracle (which acquired PeopleSoft). Also included in this category is middleware software supplied by vendors such as IBM and Oracle for achieving firmwide integration by linking the firm's existing application systems. Microsoft is attempting to move into the lower ends of this market by focusing on small and medium-sized businesses that have not yet implemented enterprise applications.

DATA MANAGEMENT AND STORAGE

Enterprise database management software is responsible for organizing and managing the firm's data so that they can be efficiently accessed and used. Chapter 6 describes this software in detail. The leading database software providers are IBM (DB2), Oracle, Microsoft (SQL Server), and Sybase (Adaptive Server Enterprise), which supply more than 90 percent of the U.S. database software marketplace. MySQL is a Linux open source relational database product now owned by Oracle Corporation, and Apache Hadoop is an open source software framework for managing massive data sets (see Chapter 6).

The physical data storage market is dominated by EMC Corporation for large-scale systems, and a small number of PC hard disk manufacturers led by Seagate and Western Digital.

Digital information is doubling every two years, with a staggering 1.8 zettabytes created in 2011 alone (IDC, 2011). All the tweets, blogs, videos, e-mails, and Facebook postings, as well as traditional corporate data, add up to thousands of Libraries of Congress.

With the amount of new digital information in the world growing so rapidly, the market for digital data storage devices has been growing at more than 15 percent annually over the last five years. In addition to traditional disk arrays and tape libraries, large firms are turning to network-based storage technologies. **Storage area networks (SANs)** connect multiple storage devices on a separate high-speed network dedicated to storage. The SAN creates a large central pool of storage that can be rapidly accessed and shared by multiple servers.

NETWORKING/TELECOMMUNICATIONS PLATFORMS

Companies worldwide are expected to spend $408 billion for telecommunications equipment in 2013 and another $1.7 billion on telecommunications services (Gartner, 2012). Chapter 7 is devoted to an in-depth description of the enterprise networking environment, including the Internet. Windows Server is predominantly used as a local area network operating system, followed by Linux and Unix. Large, enterprise wide area networks use some variant of Unix. Most local area networks, as well as wide area enterprise networks, use the TCP/IP protocol suite as a standard (see Chapter 7).

The leading networking hardware providers are Cisco, Alcatel-Lucent, Nortel, and Juniper Networks. Telecommunications platforms are typically provided by telecommunications/telephone services companies that offer voice and data connectivity, wide area networking, wireless services, and Internet access. Leading telecommunications service vendors include AT&T and Verizon. This market is exploding with new providers of cellular wireless, high-speed Internet, and Internet telephone services.

INTERNET PLATFORMS

Internet platforms overlap with, and must relate to, the firm's general networking infrastructure and hardware and software platforms. They include hardware, software, and management services to support a firm's Web site, including Web hosting services, routers, and cabling or wireless equipment. A **Web hosting service** maintains a large Web server, or series of servers, and provides fee-paying subscribers with space to maintain their Web sites.

The Internet revolution created a veritable explosion in server computers, with many firms collecting thousands of small servers to run their Internet operations. Since then there has been a steady push toward server consolidation, reducing the number of server computers by increasing the size and power of each and by using software tools that make it possible to run more applications on a single server. The Internet hardware server market has become increasingly concentrated in the hands of IBM, Dell, and Sun (Oracle), and HP, as prices have fallen dramatically.

The major Web software application development tools and suites are supplied by Microsoft (Microsoft Expression Studio and the Microsoft .NET family of development tools), Oracle-Sun (Sun's Java is the most widely used tool for developing interactive Web applications on both the server and client sides), and a host of independent software developers, including Adobe (Creative Suite) and Real Networks (media software). Chapter 7 describes the components of the firm's Internet platform in greater detail.

CONSULTING AND SYSTEM INTEGRATION SERVICES

Today, even a large firm does not have the staff, the skills, the budget, or the necessary experience to deploy and maintain its entire IT infrastructure. Implementing a new infrastructure requires (as noted in Chapters 3 and 14) significant changes in business processes and procedures, training and education, and software integration. Leading consulting firms providing this expertise include Accenture, IBM Global Services, HP, Infosys, and Wipro Technologies.

Software integration means ensuring the new infrastructure works with the firm's older, so-called legacy systems and ensuring the new elements of the infrastructure work with one another. **Legacy systems** are generally older transaction processing systems created for mainframe computers that continue to be used to avoid the high cost of replacing or redesigning them. Replacing these systems is cost prohibitive and generally not necessary if these older systems can be integrated into a contemporary infrastructure.

5.3 CONTEMPORARY HARDWARE PLATFORM TRENDS

The exploding power of computer hardware and networking technology has dramatically changed how businesses organize their computing power, putting more of this power on networks and mobile handheld devices. We look at eight hardware trends: the mobile digital platform, consumerization of IT, grid computing, virtualization, cloud computing, green computing, high-performance/power-saving processors, and autonomic computing.

THE MOBILE DIGITAL PLATFORM

Chapter 1 pointed out that new mobile digital computing platforms have emerged as alternatives to PCs and larger computers. Smartphones such as the iPhone, Android, and BlackBerry smartphones have taken on many functions of PCs, including transmission of data, surfing the Web, transmitting e-mail and instant messages, displaying digital content, and exchanging data with internal corporate systems. The new mobile platform also includes small, lightweight netbooks optimized for wireless communication and Internet access, **tablet computers** such as the iPad, and digital e-book readers such as Amazon's Kindle with Web access capabilities.

Smartphones and tablet computers are becoming an important means of accessing the Internet. These devices are increasingly used for business computing as well as for consumer applications. For example, senior executives at General Motors are using smartphone applications that drill down into vehicle sales information, financial performance, manufacturing metrics, and project management status.

CONSUMERIZATION OF IT AND BYOD

The popularity, ease of use, and rich array of useful applications for smartphones and tablet computers have created a groundswell of interest in allowing employees to use their personal mobile devices in the workplace, a phenomenon popularly called *"bring your own device" (BYOD)*. BYOD is one aspect of the **consumerization of IT**, in which new information technology that first emerges in the consumer market spreads into business organizations. Consumerization of IT includes not only mobile personal devices but also business uses of software services such as Google and Yahoo search, Gmail, Google Apps, Dropbox (see Chapter 2), and even Facebook and Twitter that originated in the consumer marketplace as well.

Consumerization of IT is forcing businesses, especially large enterprises, to rethink the way they obtain and manage information technology equipment and services. Historically, at least in large firms, the central IT department was responsible for selecting and managing the information technology and applications used by the firm and its employees. It furnished employees with desktops or laptops that were able to access corporate systems securely. The IT department maintained control over the firm's hardware and software to ensure that the business was being protected and that information systems served the purposes of the firm and its management. Today, employees and business departments are playing a much larger role in technology selection, in many cases demanding that employees be able to use their own personal computers, smartphones, and tablets to access the corporate network. It is more difficult for the firm to manage and control these consumer technologies, and make sure they serve the needs of the business. The Interactive Session on Management explores some of these management challenges created by BYOD and IT consumerization.

GRID COMPUTING

Grid computing involves connecting geographically remote computers into a single network to create a virtual supercomputer by combining the computational power of all computers on the grid. Grid computing takes advantage of the fact that most computers in the United States use their central processing units on average only 25 percent of the time for the work they have been assigned, leaving these idle resources available for other processing tasks. Grid computing was impossible until high-speed Internet connections enabled firms to connect remote machines economically and move enormous quantities of data. Grid computing requires software programs to control and allocate resources on the grid.

The business case for using grid computing involves cost savings, speed of computation, and agility. For example, Royal Dutch/Shell Group is using a scalable grid computing platform that improves the accuracy and speed of its scientific modeling applications to find the best oil reservoirs. This platform, which links 1,024 IBM servers running Linux, in effect creates one of the largest commercial Linux supercomputers in the world. The grid adjusts to accommodate the fluctuating data volumes that are typical in this seasonal business. Royal Dutch/Shell Group claims the grid has enabled the company to cut processing time for seismic data, while improving output quality and helping its scientists pinpoint problems in finding new oil supplies.

VIRTUALIZATION

Virtualization is the process of presenting a set of computing resources (such as computing power or data storage) so that they can all be accessed in ways that are not restricted by physical configuration or geographic location. Virtualization enables a single physical resource (such as a server or a storage device) to appear to the user as multiple logical resources. For example, a server or mainframe can be configured to run many instances of an operating system so that it acts like many different machines. Virtualization also enables multiple physical resources (such as storage devices or servers) to appear as a single logical resource, as would be the case with storage area networks or grid computing. Virtualization makes it possible for a company to handle its computer processing and storage using computing resources housed in remote locations. VMware is the leading virtualization software vendor for Windows and Linux servers.

By providing the ability to host multiple systems on a single physical machine, virtualization helps organizations increase equipment utilization rates, conserving data center space and energy usage. Most servers run at just 15–20 percent of capacity, and virtualization can boost server utilization rates to 70 percent or higher. Higher utilization rates translate into fewer computers required to process the same amount of work. Virtualization also facilitates centralization and consolidation of hardware administration. It is now possible for companies and individuals to perform all of their computing work using a virtualized IT infrastructure, as is the case with cloud computing.

INTERACTIVE SESSION: MANAGEMENT

SHOULD YOU USE YOUR IPHONE FOR WORK?

Look around. On the street, at restaurants, sports events, and stores, you'll find many people using their smartphones. And many people are starting to use these devices on the job as well. According to a Juniper Research report, the number of employees who use personal devices at work will increase to 350 million by 2014. About 150 million people use their own mobile phones and tablets at the workplace today.

If almost everyone has a personal smartphone, why not use it for work? Employees using their own smartphones would allow companies to enjoy all of the same benefits of a mobile workforce without spending their own money on these devices, but IT departments need to overcome several logistical hurdles to make that vision a reality. Using personal devices for business poses difficult problems for companies, including security, inventory management, support, integrating mobile devices into pre-existing IT functions and systems, and measuring return on investment. In other words, it's not that simple.

A significant portion of corporate IT resources is dedicated to managing and maintaining a large number of devices within an organization. In the past, companies tried to limit business smartphone use to a single platform. This made it easier to keep track of each mobile device and to roll out software upgrades or fixes, because all employees were using the same devices, or at the very least, the same operating system. The most popular employer-issued smartphone used to be Research in Motion's BlackBerry, because it was considered the "most secure" mobile platform available. (BlackBerry mobile devices access corporate e-mail and data using a proprietary software and networking platform that is company-controlled and protected from outsiders.) Today, the mobile digital landscape is much more complicated, with a variety of devices and operating systems on the market that do not have well-developed tools for administration and security.

If employees are allowed to work with more than one type of mobile device and operating system, companies need an effective way to keep track of all the devices employees are using. To access company information, the company's networks must be configured to receive connections from that device. When employees make changes to their personal phone, such as switching cellular carriers, changing their phone num-

ber, or buying a new mobile device altogether, companies will need to quickly and flexibly ensure that their employees are still able to remain productive. Firms need an efficient inventory management system that keeps track of which devices employees are using, where the device is located, whether it is being used, and what software it is equipped with. For unprepared companies, keeping track of who gets access to what data could be a nightmare.

With the variety of phones and operating systems available, providing adequate technical support for every employee could be difficult. When employees are not able to access critical data or encounter other problems with their mobile devices, they will need assistance from the information systems department. Companies that rely on desktop computers tend to have many of the same computers with the same specs and operating systems, making tech support that much easier. Mobility introduces a new layer of variety and complexity to tech support that companies need to be prepared to handle.

A firm's software development teams can benefit from having one person specifically focused on ensuring that new applications will be easily usable and useful on smartphones. Many companies are integrating these "mobility experts" into core IT functions and software development. Unless applications and software can be used on mobile devices to connect to the firm's existing IT platform and company-wide customer relationship management (CRM), supply chain management (SCM), and enterprise resource planning (ERP) systems, a business smartphone is just a phone, and mobility experts can help a company leverage mobility more effectively.

There are significant concerns with securing company information accessed with mobile devices. If a device is stolen or compromised, companies need ways to ensure that sensitive or confidential information isn't freely available to anyone. Mobility puts assets and data at greater risk than if they were only located within company walls and on company machines. Companies often use technologies that allow them to wipe data from devices remotely, or encrypt data so that if it is stolen, it cannot be used. You'll find a detailed discussion of mobile security issues in Chapter 8.

A number of software products have emerged to help companies manage diverse mobile platforms.

Sybase Afaria, Trellia, Microsoft Systems Center Device Manager, and Odyssey Software Athena have capabilities for configuring devices remotely, enforcing different sets of policies for different users and devices, and managing applications running on all of them.

Novo Nordisk, headquartered in Denmark, manufactures and markets pharmaceutical products and services throughout the world. Its 2,000-member sales force operates in 25 different countries, and uses a diverse assortment of mobile phones, smartphones, and mobile handhelds. To manage all of these devices centrally, Novo Nordisk implemented Sybase Afaria. Using Afaria, the company's internal IT department can deploy new applications to mobile devices quickly and without extensive end-user interaction. A new mobile phone user just needs to answer "yes" to Novo Nordisk's configuration process and the installation happens automatically. Afaria also has features for enabling individual countries or regions to provide their own local support, a necessity since each Novo Nordisk market has it own data connections, policies, and requirements.

Another approach to mobile device management is virtualization. Companies can install software such as Citrix Systems XenDesktop that runs Windows desktops and individual applications on any device, regardless of the operating system. Employees then use that software to access their entire desktop on their smartphones and mobile handhelds, and are thus able to use the same programs on the road that they use in the office. The virtualization software has built-in security features that allow corporations to prohibit saving data on local devices, to encrypt all corporate data without touching employees' personal applications and data, and to remotely erase the data in the event of a security breach. India's Anthem Group, a leading provider of pharmaceuticals and biotechnology services, implemented Citrix XenDesktop to enable employees to remotely access data because this virtualization solution runs on all devices with minimal bandwidth consumption.

In order to successfully deploy mobile devices, companies need to carefully examine their business processes and determine whether or not mobility makes sense for them. Not every firm will benefit from mobility to the same degree. Without a clear idea of how exactly mobile devices fit into the long-term plans for the firm, companies will end up wasting their money on unnecessary devices and programs. One of the biggest worries that managers have about mobility is the difficulty of measuring return on investment. Many workers swear by their mobile devices, and the benefits are too significant to ignore, but quantifying how much money is earned or saved by going mobile can be difficult.

Sources: Boonsri Dickinson, "Security Headaches: BYOD Users Expected to Double by 2014," *Information Week*, August 8, 2012; "Anthem Group Enables Secure Remove Access with Citrix XenDesktop and XenServer," expresscomputeronline.com, July 20, 2012; "So You Want to Use Your iPhone for Work: Uh-Oh," *The Wall Street Journal*, April 25, 2011. Samuel Greengard, "Managing Mobility in the Enterprise," *Baseline*, January 28, 2011; Dell Computer, "Management Madness: How to Manage Mobile Devices," mkting.cio.com, accessed July 18, 2011; and Dell Computer, "Is Your Infrastructure Mobile-Ready?" www.cio.com, accessed May 21, 2011.

CASE STUDY QUESTIONS

1. What are the advantages and disadvantages of allowing employees to use their personal smartphones for work?

2. What management, organization, and technology factors should be addressed when deciding whether to allow employees to use their personal smartphones for work?

3. Allowing employees to use their own smartphones for work will save the company money. Do you agree? Why or why not?

CLOUD COMPUTING

Cloud computing is a model of computing in which computer processing, storage, software, and other services are provided as a pool of virtualized resources over a network, primarily the Internet. These "clouds" of computing resources can be accessed on an as-needed basis from any connected device and location. Figure 5.10 illustrates the cloud computing concept.

FIGURE 5.10 CLOUD COMPUTING PLATFORM

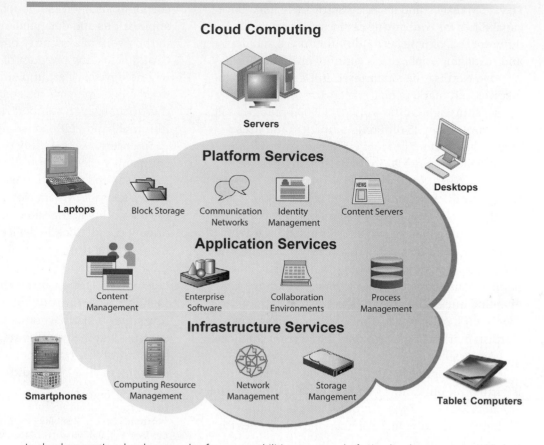

In cloud computing, hardware and software capabilities are a pool of virtualized resources provided over a network, often the Internet. Businesses and employees have access to applications and IT infrastructure anywhere, at any time, and on any device.

The U.S. National Institute of Standards and Technology (NIST) defines cloud computing as having the following essential characteristics (Mell and Grance, 2009):

- **On-demand self-service:** Consumers can obtain computing capabilities such as server time or network storage as needed automatically on their own.

- **Ubiquitous network access:** Cloud resources can be accessed using standard network and Internet devices, including mobile platforms.

- **Location-independent resource pooling:** Computing resources are pooled to serve multiple users, with different virtual resources dynamically assigned according to user demand. The user generally does not know where the computing resources are located.

- **Rapid elasticity:** Computing resources can be rapidly provisioned, increased, or decreased to meet changing user demand.

- **Measured service:** Charges for cloud resources are based on amount of resources actually used.

Cloud computing consists of three different types of services:

- **Cloud infrastructure as a service:** Customers use processing, storage, networking, and other computing resources from cloud service providers to run their information systems. For example, Amazon uses the spare capacity of its IT infrastructure to provide a broadly based cloud environment selling IT infrastructure services. These include its Simple Storage Service (S3) for storing customers' data and its Elastic Compute Cloud (EC2) service for running their applications. Users pay only for the amount of computing and storage capacity they actually use. (See the chapter-ending case study.)

- **Cloud platform as a service:** Customers use infrastructure and programming tools supported by the cloud service provider to develop their own applications. For example, IBM offers a Smart Business Application Development & Test service for software development and testing on the IBM Cloud. Another example is Salesforce.com's Force.com, which allows developers to build applications that are hosted on its servers as a service.

- **Cloud software as a service:** Customers use software hosted by the vendor on the vendor's cloud infrastructure and delivered over a network. Leading examples are Google Apps, which provides common business applications online and Salesforce.com, which also leases customer relationship management and related software services over the Internet. Both charge users an annual subscription fee, although Google Apps also has a pared-down free version. Users access these applications from a Web browser, and the data and software are maintained on the providers' remote servers.

A cloud can be private or public. A **public cloud** is owned and maintained by a cloud service provider, such as Amazon Web Services, and made available to the general public or industry group. A **private cloud** is operated solely for an organization. It may be managed by the organization or a third party and may exist on premise or off premise. Like public clouds, private clouds are able to allocate storage, computing power, or other resources seamlessly to provide computing resources on an as-needed basis. Companies that want flexible IT resources and a cloud service model while retaining control over their own IT infrastructure are gravitating toward these private clouds. (See the chapter-ending case study.)

Since organizations using public clouds do not own the infrastructure, they do not have to make large investments in their own hardware and software. Instead, they purchase their computing services from remote providers and pay only for the amount of computing power they actually use **(utility computing)** or are billed on a monthly or annual subscription basis. The term **on-demand computing** has also been used to describe such services.

Cloud computing has some drawbacks. Unless users make provisions for storing their data locally, the responsibility for data storage and control is in the hands of the provider. Some companies worry about the security risks related to entrusting their critical data and systems to an outside vendor that also works with other companies. Companies expect their systems to be available 24/7 and do not want to suffer any loss of business capability if cloud infrastructures malfunction. Another limitation of cloud computing is that users become dependent on the cloud computing provider, and this may not necessarily be desirable, as discussed in the chapter-ending case. Nevertheless, the trend is for companies to shift more of their computer processing and storage to some form of cloud infrastructure.

Cloud computing is more immediately appealing to small and medium-sized businesses that lack resources to purchase and own their own hardware and software. However, large corporations have huge investments in complex proprietary systems supporting unique business processes, some of which give them strategic advantages. The cost savings from switching to cloud services are not always easy to determine for large companies that already have their own IT infrastructures in place. Corporate data centers typically work with an IT budget that accounts for a mix of operational and capital expenses. Pricing for cloud services is usually based on a per-hour or other per-use charge. Even if a company can approximate the hardware and software costs to run a specific computing task on premises, it still needs to figure in how much of the firm's network management, storage management, system administration, electricity, and real estate costs should be allocated to a single on-premises IT service. An information systems department may not have the right information to analyze those factors on a service-by-service basis.

Large firms are most likely to adopt a **hybrid cloud** computing model where they use their own infrastructure for their most essential core activities and adopt public cloud computing for less-critical systems or for additional processing capacity during peak business periods. Cloud computing will gradually shift firms from having a fixed infrastructure capacity toward a more flexible infrastructure, some of it owned by the firm, and some of it rented from giant computer centers owned by computer hardware vendors. You can find out more about cloud computing in the Learning Tracks for this chapter.

GREEN COMPUTING

By curbing hardware proliferation and power consumption, virtualization has become one of the principal technologies for promoting green computing. **Green computing** or **green IT**, refers to practices and technologies for designing, manufacturing, using, and disposing of computers, servers, and associated devices such as monitors, printers, storage devices, and networking and communications systems to minimize the impact on the environment.

Reducing computer power consumption has been a very high "green" priority. Information technology is responsible for about 2 percent of total U.S. power demand and is believed to contribute about 2 percent of the world's greenhouse gases. Cutting power consumption in data centers has become both a serious business and environmental challenge. The Interactive Session on Organizations examines this problem.

HIGH-PERFORMANCE AND POWER-SAVING PROCESSORS

Another way to reduce power requirements and hardware sprawl is to use more efficient and power-saving processors. Contemporary microprocessors now feature multiple processor cores (which perform the reading and execution of computer instructions) on a single chip. A **multicore processor** is an integrated circuit to which two or more processor cores have been attached for enhanced performance, reduced power consumption, and more efficient simultaneous processing of multiple tasks. This technology enables two or more processing engines with reduced power requirements and heat dissipation to perform tasks faster than a resource-hungry chip with a single processing core. Today you'll find PCs with dual-core, quad-core, six-core, and eight core processors.

Intel and other chip manufacturers have developed microprocessors that minimize power consumption, which is essential for prolonging battery life in small mobile digital devices. Highly power-efficient microprocessors, such as ARM, Apple's A4 and A5 processors, and Intel's Atom are in netbooks, digital media players, and smartphones. The dual-core A5 processor used in the iPhone 4S and the iPad2 has about 1/50 to 1/30 the power consumption of a laptop dual-core processor.

INTERACTIVE SESSION: ORGANIZATIONS

NORDEA GOES GREEN WITH IT

One early morning in the fall of 2007, Dennis Jönsson was reading the latest reports on global warming and thought that someone ought to do something about it. Then he realized that he and his fellow coworkers at Nordea, all with airline gold cards and access to the airport lounges, were part of the problem—especially since Nordea employees occupied many of the seats on the 7:10 flight between Copenhagen and Helsinki every morning. Nordea is the largest bank group in the Nordic countries and the Baltic region. It has around 10 million customers, 1,400 branch offices, and a leading online banking position with 6.1 million e-customers. The bank has about 34,000 employees in 23 countries. Since its foundation in 1820, the organization that is now Nordea has incorporated some 250 banks, including Danish Unibank, Finish Merita, Swedish Nordbanken, and Norwegian Christiania Kreditkasse. The history of mergers has resulted in a geographically distributed organization that requires extensive travel between national branches.

Carbon dioxide emissions caused by one person traveling by airplane between two of the Nordic capitals is in the order of 200 kg—twice the amount a car with four passengers emits over the same distance. In total, short- and long-haul air travel makes up about a third of Nordea's total carbon dioxide emissions. Reducing travel is not only desirable from an environmental perspective, but from a cost-saving perspective, too. Every year a substantial amount of money is spent on air travel. In addition, for many Nordea employees who must travel frequently a reduction in travel days would mean more time home with friends and family.

In early 2008, Dennis Jönsson was himself one of the Nordea employees on the 7:10 flight to Helsinki. He had been called by the IT management group to give a presentation on "Nordea and Global Warming," focusing on what actions Nordea could take. The underlying question in the presentation was whether Nordea could use technology more efficiently to save costs and reduce its environmental impact at the same time. The presentation focused on two areas that the IT department was accountable for. The first was air travel between different Nordic branches. The second area was computer power consumption, which accounts for a substantial part of the total power consumption at IT-intensive organizations

such as banks. In the spring of 2008, Jönsson was appointed the green IT manager at Nordea. The initiative to use technology to reduce air travel consisted of two parts. First, meeting rooms at Nordea branches were equipped with special-purpose, high-quality videoconferencing equipment. Second, desktop and laptop computers with Web cameras, headsets, and software were provided to enable two-party video calls. It was hoped that videoconferencing and video calls would reduce travel needs as well as improve the quality of collaborative work at Nordea.

In the area of computer power consumption, Nordea works on both limiting the power needed to run the computer park and on innovative ways of cooling down computers in use. After launching a new component in its property management system that could document power use in the Nordea offices, Nordea discovered that power usage was surprisingly high at night. The reason was simple: many computers were never turned off. The Power-Off project resulted in power management software being installed on 23,100 computers at Nordea, forcing shutdown at night if the computers were not in use. Settings for turning off monitors and putting computers into sleep or standby mode were also fine-tuned. This saved 3.5 million kKh annually, which is equivalent to 647 tons of carbon dioxide. On the server side, the IT department worked with server virtualization to reduce the number of physical machines consuming power.

For an IT-intensive organization such as Nordea, the cooling of computers is a significant cost. The organization must pay to cool down its computer rooms at the same time it spends money heating other areas. The solution was to locate its computer halls in places where the excess heat could be used for heating purposes or to use a cooling method with a reduced environmental impact. Today, one of Nordea's major computer halls is located next to the sea. Cold, Nordic seawater is used to cool the hall. By lowering the power consumption for cooling, Nordea saves money and reduces its environmental impact. Nordea has noted that cutting costs and reducing its environmental impact often go hand in hand, because lowering the firm's environmental impact frequently means consuming fewer resources, and resources cost money. In other words, it is difficult to find the downside in the business case for green IT. The biggest obstacle to green IT is changing people's behavior and well-established practices.

Corporate social responsibility, of which low environmental impact is a part, is now an integrated part in Nordea's strategy to attract and retain both customers and skilled personnel. Guided by the European Union directive on energy use, Nordea has set out to reduce energy consumption by 15 percent, travel by 30 percent, and paper consumption by 50

percent. The directive suggests that 2020 would be a feasible deadline for achieving these goals, but Nordea has set itself a deadline of 2016. If the organization is to be successful in this, then IT in its various forms will definitely play a key role—both as part of the problem and as part of the solution.

Sources: Based on 15 personal interviews with representatives of Nordea during 2010; http://www.nordea.com.

CASE STUDY QUESTIONS

1. What business, personal, and social costs are involved when traveling by airplane between Copenhagen and Helsinki?

2. How can IT be both the culprit and the solution to environmental problems?

3. What are the arguments against corporate social responsibility?

4. Why should firms be engaged in making the world more sustainable?

Case contributed by Jonas Hedman and Stefan Henningsson, Copenhagen Business School

AUTONOMIC COMPUTING

With large systems encompassing many thousands of networked devices, computer systems have become so complex today that some experts believe they may not be manageable in the future. One approach to this problem is autonomic computing. **Autonomic computing** is an industry-wide effort to develop systems that can configure themselves, optimize and tune themselves, heal themselves when broken, and protect themselves from outside intruders and self-destruction.

You can glimpse a few of these capabilities in desktop systems. For instance, virus and firewall protection software are able to detect viruses on PCs, automatically defeat the viruses, and alert operators. These programs can be updated automatically as the need arises by connecting to an online virus protection service such as McAfee. IBM and other vendors are starting to build autonomic features into products for large systems.

5.4 CONTEMPORARY SOFTWARE PLATFORM TRENDS

There are four major themes in contemporary software platform evolution:

- Linux and open source software
- Java, HTML, and HTML5
- Web services and service-oriented architecture
- Software outsourcing and cloud services

LINUX AND OPEN SOURCE SOFTWARE

Open source software is software produced by a community of several hundred thousand programmers around the world. According to the leading open source professional association, OpenSource.org, open source software is free and can be modified by users. Works derived from the original code must also be free, and the software can be redistributed by the user without additional licensing. Open source software is by definition not restricted to any specific operating system or hardware technology, although most open source software is currently based on a Linux or Unix operating system.

The open source movement has been evolving for more than 30 years and has demonstrated that it can produce commercially acceptable, high-quality software. Popular open source software tools include the Linux operating system, the Apache HTTP Web server, the Mozilla Firefox Web browser, and the Apache OpenOffice desktop productivity suite. Open source tools are being used on netbooks as inexpensive alternatives to Microsoft Office. Major hardware and software vendors, including IBM, HP, Dell, Oracle, and SAP, now offer Linux-compatible versions of their products. You can find out more out more about the Open Source Definition from the Open Source Initiative and the history of open source software at the Learning Tracks for this chapter.

Linux

Perhaps the most well-known open source software is Linux, an operating system related to Unix. Linux was created by the Finnish programmer Linus Torvalds and first posted on the Internet in August 1991. Linux applications are embedded in cell phones, smartphones, netbooks, and consumer electronics. Linux is available in free versions downloadable from the Internet or in low-cost commercial versions that include tools and support from vendors such as Red Hat.

Although Linux is not used in many desktop systems, it is a major force in local area networks, Web servers, and high-performance computing work. IBM, HP, Intel, Dell, and Oracle have made Linux a central part of their offerings to corporations.

The rise of open source software, particularly Linux and the applications it supports, has profound implications for corporate software platforms: cost reduction, reliability and resilience, and integration, because Linux works on all the major hardware platforms from mainframes to servers to clients.

SOFTWARE FOR THE WEB: JAVA, HTML, AND HTML5

Java is an operating system-independent, processor-independent, object-oriented programming language that has become the leading interactive environment for the Web. Java was created by James Gosling and the Green Team at

Sun Microsystems in 1992. In November 13, 2006, Sun released much of Java as open source software under the terms of the GNU General Public License (GPL), completing the process on May 8, 2007.

The Java platform has migrated into cell phones, smartphones, automobiles, music players, game machines, and finally, into set-top cable television systems serving interactive content and pay-per-view services. Java software is designed to run on any computer or computing device, regardless of the specific microprocessor or operating system the device uses. Oracle Corporation estimates that 3 billion devices are running Java, and it is the most popular development platform for mobile devices running the Android operating system (Taft, 2012). For each of the computing environments in which Java is used, Sun created a Java Virtual Machine that interprets Java programming code for that machine. In this manner, the code is written once and can be used on any machine for which there exists a Java Virtual Machine.

Java developers can create small applet programs that can be embedded in Web pages and downloaded to run on a Web browser. A **Web browser** is an easy-to-use software tool with a graphical user interface for displaying Web pages and for accessing the Web and other Internet resources. Microsoft's Internet Explorer, Mozilla Firefox, and Google Chrome browser are examples. At the enterprise level, Java is being used for more complex e-commerce and e-business applications that require communication with an organization's back-end transaction processing systems.

HTML and HTML5

HTML (Hypertext Markup Language) is a page description language for specifying how text, graphics, video, and sound are placed on a Web page and for creating dynamic links to other Web pages and objects. Using these links, a user need only point at a highlighted keyword or graphic, click on it, and immediately be transported to another document.

HTML was originally designed to create and link static documents composed largely of text. Today, however, the Web is much more social and interactive, and many Web pages have multimedia elements—images, audio, and video. Third-party plug-in applications like Flash, Silverlight, and Java have been required to integrate these rich media with Web pages. However, these add-ons require additional programming and put strains on computer processing. This is one reason Apple dropped support for Flash on its mobile devices. The next evolution of HTML, called **HTML5**, solves this problem by making it possible to embed images, audio, video, and other elements directly into a document without processor-intensive add-ons. HTML5 will also make it easier for Web pages to function across different display devices, including mobile devices as well as desktops, and it will support the storage of data offline for apps that run over the Web. Web pages will execute more quickly, and look like smartphone apps. Although HTML5 is still under development, elements are already being used in a number of Internet tools, including Apple's Safari browsers, Google Chrome, and recent versions of the Firefox Web browser. Google's Gmail and Google Reader have adopted parts of the HTML5 standard as well. Web sites listed as "iPad ready" are making extensive use of HTML5 including CNN, The New York Times, and CBS.

WEB SERVICES AND SERVICE-ORIENTED ARCHITECTURE

Web services refer to a set of loosely coupled software components that exchange information with each other using universal Web communication standards and languages. They can exchange information between two different systems regardless of the operating systems or programming languages on which the systems are based. They can be used to build open standard Web-based applications linking systems of two different organizations, and they can also be used to create applications that link disparate systems within a single company. Web services are not tied to any one operating system or programming language, and different applications can use them to communicate with each other in a standard way without time-consuming custom coding.

The foundation technology for Web services is **XML**, which stands for **Extensible Markup Language**. This language was developed in 1996 by the World Wide Web Consortium (W3C, the international body that oversees the development of the Web) as a more powerful and flexible markup language than hypertext markup language (HTML) for Web pages. Whereas HTML is limited to describing how data should be presented in the form of Web pages, XML can perform presentation, communication, and storage of data. In XML, a number is not simply a number; the XML tag specifies whether the number represents a price, a date, or a ZIP code. Table 5.2 illustrates some sample XML statements.

By tagging selected elements of the content of documents for their meanings, XML makes it possible for computers to manipulate and interpret their data automatically and perform operations on the data without human intervention. Web browsers and computer programs, such as order processing or enterprise resource planning (ERP) software, can follow programmed rules for applying and displaying the data. XML provides a standard format for data exchange, enabling Web services to pass data from one process to another.

Web services communicate through XML messages over standard Web protocols. Companies discover and locate Web services through a directory much as they would locate services in the Yellow Pages of a telephone book. Using Web protocols, a software application can connect freely to other applications without custom programming for each different application with which it wants to communicate. Everyone shares the same standards.

The collection of Web services that are used to build a firm's software systems constitutes what is known as a service-oriented architecture. A **service-oriented architecture (SOA)** is set of self-contained services that communicate with each other to create a working software application. Business tasks are accomplished by executing a series of these services. Software

TABLE 5.2 EXAMPLES OF XML

PLAIN ENGLISH	XML
Subcompact	<AUTOMOBILETYPE="Subcompact">
4 passenger	<PASSENGERUNIT="PASS">4</PASSENGER>
$16,800	<PRICE CURRENCY="USD">$16,800</PRICE>

developers reuse these services in other combinations to assemble other applications as needed.

Virtually all major software vendors provide tools and entire platforms for building and integrating software applications using Web services. IBM includes Web service tools in its WebSphere e-business software platform, and Microsoft has incorporated Web services tools in its Microsoft .NET platform.

Dollar Rent A Car's systems use Web services for its online booking system with Southwest Airlines' Web site. Although both companies' systems are based on different technology platforms, a person booking a flight on Southwest.com can reserve a car from Dollar without leaving the airline's Web site. Instead of struggling to get Dollar's reservation system to share data with Southwest's information systems, Dollar used Microsoft .NET Web services technology as an intermediary. Reservations from Southwest are translated into Web services protocols, which are then translated into formats that can be understood by Dollar's computers.

Other car rental companies have linked their information systems to airline companies' Web sites before. But without Web services, these connections had to be built one at a time. Web services provide a standard way for Dollar's computers to "talk" to other companies' information systems without having to build special links to each one. Dollar is now expanding its use of Web services to link directly to the systems of a small tour operator and a large travel reservation system as well as a wireless Web site for cell phones and smartphones. It does not have to write new software code for each new partner's information systems or each new wireless device (see Figure 5.11).

FIGURE 5.11 HOW DOLLAR RENT A CAR USES WEB SERVICES

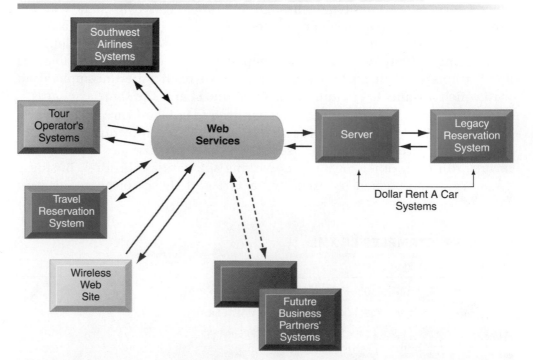

Dollar Rent A Car uses Web services to provide a standard intermediate layer of software to "talk" to other companies' information systems. Dollar Rent A Car can use this set of Web services to link to other companies' information systems without having to build a separate link to each firm's systems.

SOFTWARE OUTSOURCING AND CLOUD SERVICES

Today, many business firms continue to operate legacy systems that continue to meet a business need and that would be extremely costly to replace. But they will purchase or rent most of their new software applications from external sources. Figure 5.12 illustrates the rapid growth in external sources of software for U.S. firms.

There are three external sources for software: software packages from a commercial software vendor, outsourcing custom application development to an external vendor, (which may or may not be offshore), and cloud-based software services and tools.

Software Packages and Enterprise Software

We have already described software packages for enterprise applications as one of the major types of software components in contemporary IT infrastructures. A **software package** is a prewritten commercially available set of software programs that eliminates the need for a firm to write its own software programs for certain functions, such as payroll processing or order handling.

Enterprise application software vendors such as SAP and Oracle-PeopleSoft have developed powerful software packages that can support the primary business processes of a firm worldwide from warehousing, customer relationship management, and supply chain management, to finance and human resources. These large-scale enterprise software systems provide a single, integrated, worldwide software system for firms at a cost much less than they would pay if they developed it themselves. Chapter 9 discusses enterprise systems in detail.

FIGURE 5.12 CHANGING SOURCES OF FIRM SOFTWARE

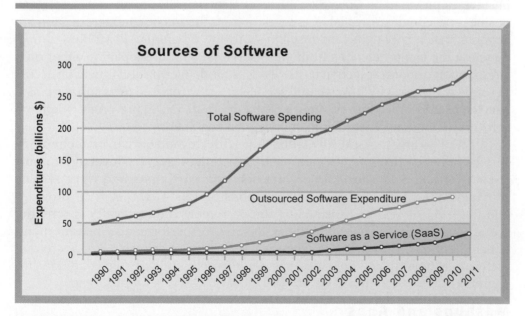

In 2012, U.S. firms will spend over $279 billion on software. About 35 percent of that ($98 billion) will originate outside the firm, either from enterprise software vendors selling firmwide applications or individual application service providers leasing or selling software modules. Another 4 percent ($11 billion) will be provided by SaaS vendors as an online cloud-based service.

Sources: BEA National Income and Product Accounts, 2012; authors' estimates.

Software Outsourcing

Software **outsourcing** enables a firm to contract custom software development or maintenance of existing legacy programs to outside firms, which often operate offshore in low-wage areas of the world. According to the industry analysts, spending on offshore IT outsourcing services was approximately $251 billion in 2012 (Gartner, 2012). The largest outsourcing expenditures are to domestic U.S. firms providing middleware, integration services, and other software support that are often required to operate larger enterprise systems.

For example, Cemex, Mexico's largest cement manufacturer, signed a 10-year $1 billion outsourcing deal with IBM in July 2012. Under the deal, IBM responsibilities include application development and maintenance as well as IT infrastructure management at Cemex company headquarters in Monterrey, Mexico, and around the globe. IBM will take over and run Cemex's finance, accounting, and human resources systems (McDougall, 2012).

Offshore software outsourcing firms have primarily provided lower-level maintenance, data entry, and call center operations, although more sophisticated and experienced offshore firms, particularly in India, have been hired for new-program development. However, as wages offshore rise, and the costs of managing offshore projects are factored in (see Chapter 13), some work that would have been sent offshore is returning to domestic companies.

Cloud-Based Software Services and Tools

In the past, software such as Microsoft Word or Adobe Illustrator came in a box and was designed to operate on a single machine. Today, you're more likely to download the software from the vendor's Web site, or to use the software as a cloud service delivered over the Internet.

Cloud-based software and the data it uses are hosted on powerful servers in massive data centers, and can be accessed with an Internet connection and standard Web browser. In addition to free or low-cost tools for individuals and small businesses provided by Google or Yahoo, enterprise software and other complex business functions are available as services from the major commercial software vendors. Instead of buying and installing software programs, subscribing companies rent the same functions from these services, with users paying either on a subscription or per-transaction basis. Services for delivering and providing access to software remotely as a Web-based service are now referred to as **software as a service (SaaS)**. A leading example is Salesforce.com, which provides on-demand software services for customer relationship management.

In order to manage their relationship with an outsourcer or technology service provider, firms need a contract that includes a **service level agreement (SLA)**. The SLA is a formal contract between customers and their service providers that defines the specific responsibilities of the service provider and the level of service expected by the customer. SLAs typically specify the nature and level of services provided, criteria for performance measurement, support options, provisions for security and disaster recovery, hardware and software ownership and upgrades, customer support, billing, and conditions for terminating the agreement. We provide a Learning Track on this topic.

Mashups and Apps

The software you use for both personal and business tasks may consist of large self-contained programs, or it may be composed of interchangeable components that integrate freely with other applications on the Internet. Individual users and entire companies mix and match these software components to create their own customized applications and to share information with others.

The resulting software applications are called **mashups**. The idea is to take different sources and produce a new work that is "greater than" the sum of its parts. You have performed a mashup if you've ever personalized your Facebook profile or your blog with a capability to display videos or slide shows.

Web mashups combine the capabilities of two or more online applications to create a kind of hybrid that provides more customer value than the original sources alone. For instance, ZipRealty uses Google Maps and data provided by online real estate database Zillow.com to display a complete list of multiple listing service (MLS) real estate listings for any zip code specified by the user. Amazon uses mashup technologies to aggregate product descriptions with partner sites and user profiles.

Apps are small pieces of software that run on the Internet, on your computer, or on your mobile phone or tablet and are generally delivered over the Internet. Google refers to its online services as apps, including the Google Apps suite of desktop productivity tools. But when we talk about apps today, most of the attention goes to the apps that have been developed for the mobile digital platform. It is these apps that turn smartphones and other mobile handheld devices into general-purpose computing tools.

An estimated 1 billion people used apps in 2012 worldwide, with about 200 million in the United States (eMarketer, 2012). By 2012, over 32 billion apps had been downloaded. Many are free or purchased for a small charge, much less than conventional software. There are already over 700,000 apps for the Apple iPhone and iPad platform and a similar number that run on devices using Google's Android operating system. The success of these mobile platforms depends in large part on the quantity and quality of the apps they provide. Apps tie the customer to a specific hardware platform: As the user adds more and more apps to his or her mobile phone, the cost of switching to a competing mobile platform rises.

Some downloaded apps do not access the Web but many do, providing faster access to Web content than traditional Web browsers. At the moment, the most commonly downloaded apps are games, news and weather, maps/navigation, social networking, music, and video/movies. But there are also serious apps for business users that make it possible to create and edit documents, connect to corporate systems, schedule and participate in meetings, track shipments, and dictate voice messages (see the Chapter 1 Interactive Session on Management). There are also a huge number of e-commerce apps for researching and buying goods and services online.

5.5 MANAGEMENT ISSUES

Creating and managing a coherent IT infrastructure raises multiple challenges: dealing with platform and technology change (including cloud and mobile computing), management and governance, and making wise infrastructure investments.

DEALING WITH PLATFORM AND INFRASTRUCTURE CHANGE

As firms grow, they often quickly outgrow their infrastructure. As firms shrink, they can get stuck with excessive infrastructure purchased in better times. How can a firm remain flexible when most of the investments in IT infrastructure are fixed-cost purchases and licenses? How well does the infrastructure scale? **Scalability** refers to the ability of a computer, product, or system to expand to serve a large number of users without breaking down. New applications, mergers and acquisitions, and changes in business volume all impact computer workload and must be considered when planning hardware capacity.

Firms using mobile computing and cloud computing platforms will require new policies and procedures for managing these platforms. They will need to inventory all of their mobile devices in business use and develop policies and tools for tracking, updating, and securing them and for controlling the data and applications that run on them. Firms using cloud computing and SaaS will need to fashion new contractual arrangements with remote vendors to make sure that the hardware and software for critical applications are always available when needed and that they meet corporate standards for information security. It is up to business management to determine acceptable levels of computer response time and availability for the firm's mission-critical systems to maintain the level of business performance they expect.

MANAGEMENT AND GOVERNANCE

A long-standing issue among information system managers and CEOs has been the question of who will control and manage the firm's IT infrastructure. Chapter 2 introduced the concept of IT governance and described some issues it addresses. Other important questions about IT governance are: Should departments and divisions have the responsibility of making their own information technology decisions or should IT infrastructure be centrally controlled and managed? What is the relationship between central information systems management and business unit information systems management? How will infrastructure costs be allocated among business units? Each organization will need to arrive at answers based on its own needs.

MAKING WISE INFRASTRUCTURE INVESTMENTS

IT infrastructure is a major investment for the firm. If too much is spent on infrastructure, it lies idle and constitutes a drag on the firm's financial performance. If too little is spent, important business services cannot be delivered and the firm's competitors (who spent just the right amount) will outperform the under-investing firm. How much should the firm spend on infrastructure? This question is not easy to answer.

A related question is whether a firm should purchase and maintain its own IT infrastructure components or rent them from external suppliers, including those offering cloud services. The decision either to purchase your own IT assets or rent them from external providers is typically called the *rent-versus-buy* decision.

Cloud computing may be a low-cost way to increase scalability and flexibility, but firms should evaluate this option carefully in light of security requirements and impact on business processes and workflows. In some instances, the cost of renting software adds up to more than purchasing and maintaining an application in-house. Yet there may be benefits to using cloud services, if this allows the company to focus on core business issues instead of technology challenges.

Total Cost of Ownership of Technology Assets

The actual cost of owning technology resources includes the original cost of acquiring and installing hardware and software, as well as ongoing administration costs for hardware and software upgrades, maintenance, technical support, training, and even utility and real estate costs for running and housing the technology. The **total cost of ownership (TCO)** model can be used to analyze these direct and indirect costs to help firms determine the actual cost of specific technology implementations. Table 5.3 describes the most important TCO components to consider in a TCO analysis.

When all these cost components are considered, the TCO for a PC might run up to three times the original purchase price of the equipment. Although the purchase price of a wireless handheld for a corporate employee may run several hundred dollars, the TCO for each device is much higher, ranging from $1,000 to $3,000, according to various consultant estimates. Gains in productivity and efficiency from equipping employees with mobile computing devices must be balanced against increased costs from integrating these devices into the firm's IT infrastructure and from providing technical support. Other cost components include fees for wireless airtime, end-user training, help desk support, and software for special applications. Costs are higher if the mobile devices run many different applications or need to be integrated into back-end systems such as enterprise applications.

Hardware and software acquisition costs account for only about 20 percent of TCO, so managers must pay close attention to administration costs to understand the full cost of the firm's hardware and software. It is possible to reduce some of these administration costs through better management. Many large firms are saddled with redundant, incompatible hardware and software because their departments and divisions have been allowed to make their own technology purchases.

In addition to switching to cloud services, these firms could reduce their TCO through greater centralization and standardization of their hardware and software resources. Companies could reduce the size of the information systems staff required to support their infrastructure if the firm minimizes the number of different computer models and pieces of software that employees are allowed

TABLE 5.3 TOTAL COST OF OWNERSHIP (TCO) COST COMPONENTS

INFRASTRUCTURE COMPONENT	COST COMPONENTS
Hardware acquisition	Purchase price of computer hardware equipment, including computers, terminals, storage, and printers
Software acquisition	Purchase or license of software for each user
Installation	Cost to install computers and software
Training	Cost to provide training for information systems specialists and end users
Support	Cost to provide ongoing technical support, help desks, and so forth
Maintenance	Cost to upgrade the hardware and software
Infrastructure	Cost to acquire, maintain, and support related infrastructure, such as networks and specialized equipment (including storage backup units)
Downtime	Cost of lost productivity if hardware or software failures cause the system to be unavailable for processing and user tasks
Space and energy	Real estate and utility costs for housing and providing power for the technology

to use. In a centralized infrastructure, systems can be administered from a central location and troubleshooting can be performed from that location.

Competitive Forces Model for IT Infrastructure Investment

Figure 5.13 illustrates a competitive forces model you can use to address the question of how much your firm should spend on IT infrastructure.

Market demand for your firm's services. Make an inventory of the services you currently provide to customers, suppliers, and employees. Survey each group, or hold focus groups to find out if the services you currently offer are meeting the needs of each group. For example, are customers complaining of slow responses to their queries about price and availability? Are employees complaining about the difficulty of finding the right information for their jobs? Are suppliers complaining about the difficulties of discovering your production requirements?

Your firm's business strategy. Analyze your firm's five-year business strategy and try to assess what new services and capabilities will be required to achieve strategic goals.

Your firm's IT strategy, infrastructure, and cost. Examine your firm's information technology plans for the next five years and assess its alignment with the firm's business plans. Determine the total IT infrastructure costs. You will want to perform a TCO analysis. If your firm has no IT strategy, you will need to devise one that takes into account the firm's five-year strategic plan.

FIGURE 5.13 COMPETITIVE FORCES MODEL FOR IT INFRASTRUCTURE

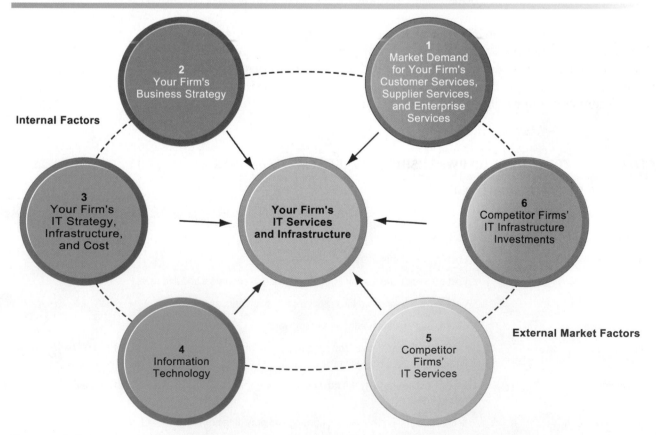

There are six factors you can use to answer the question, "How much should our firm spend on IT infrastructure?"

Information technology assessment. Is your firm behind the technology curve or at the bleeding edge of information technology? Both situations are to be avoided. It is usually not desirable to spend resources on advanced technologies that are still experimental, often expensive, and sometimes unreliable. You want to spend on technologies for which standards have been established and IT vendors are competing on cost, not design, and where there are multiple suppliers. However, you do not want to put off investment in new technologies or allow competitors to develop new business models and capabilities based on the new technologies.

Competitor firm services. Try to assess what technology services competitors offer to customers, suppliers, and employees. Establish quantitative and qualitative measures to compare them to those of your firm. If your firm's service levels fall short, your company is at a competitive disadvantage. Look for ways your firm can excel at service levels.

Competitor firm IT infrastructure investments. Benchmark your expenditures for IT infrastructure against your competitors. Many companies are quite public about their innovative expenditures on IT. If competing firms try to keep IT expenditures secret, you may be able to find IT investment information in public companies' SEC Form 10-K annual reports to the federal government when those expenditures impact a firm's financial results.

Your firm does not necessarily need to spend as much as, or more than, your competitors. Perhaps it has discovered much less-expensive ways of providing services, and this can lead to a cost advantage. Alternatively, your firm may be spending far less than competitors and experiencing commensurate poor performance and losing market share.

LEARNING TRACK MODULES

The following Learning Tracks provide content relevant to topics covered in this chapter:

1. How Computer Hardware and Software Work
2. Service Level Agreements
3. The Open Source Software Initiative
4. Comparing Stages in IT Infrastructure Evolution
5. Cloud Computing

Review Summary

1. What is IT infrastructure and what are its components?

IT infrastructure is the shared technology resources that provide the platform for the firm's specific information system applications. IT infrastructure includes hardware, software, and services that are shared across the entire firm. Major IT infrastructure components include computer hardware platforms, operating system platforms, enterprise software platforms, networking and telecommunications platforms, database management software, Internet platforms, and consulting services and systems integrators.

2. What are the stages and technology drivers of IT infrastructure evolution?

The five stages of IT infrastructure evolution are: the mainframe era, the personal computer era, the client/server era, the enterprise computing era, and the cloud and mobile computing era. Moore's Law deals with the exponential increase in processing power and decline in the cost of computer technology, stating that every 18 months the power of microprocessors doubles and the price of computing falls in half. The Law of Mass Digital Storage deals with the exponential decrease in the cost of storing data, stating that the number of kilobytes of data that can be stored on magnetic media for $1 roughly doubles every 15 months. Metcalfe's Law states that a network's value to participants grows exponentially as the network takes on more members. The rapid decline in costs of communication and growing agreement in the technology industry to use computing and communications standards is also driving an explosion of computer use.

3. What are the current trends in computer hardware platforms?

Increasingly, computing is taking place on a mobile digital platform. Grid computing involves connecting geographically remote computers into a single network to create a computational grid that combines the computing power of all the computers on the network. Virtualization organizes computing resources so that their use is not restricted by physical configuration or geographic location. In cloud computing, firms and individuals obtain computing power and software as services over a network, including the Internet, rather than purchasing and installing the hardware and software on their own computers. A multicore processor is a microprocessor to which two or more processing cores have been attached for enhanced performance. Green computing includes practices and technologies for producing, using, and disposing of information technology hardware to minimize negative impact on the environment. In autonomic computing, computer systems have capabilities for automatically configuring and repairing themselves. Power-saving processors dramatically reduce power consumption in mobile digital devices.

4. What are the current trends in software platforms?

Open source software is produced and maintained by a global community of programmers and is often downloadable for free. Linux is a powerful, resilient open source operating system that can run on multiple hardware platforms and is used widely to run Web servers. Java is an operating-system– and hardware-independent programming language that is the leading interactive programming environment for the Web. HTML5 makes it possible to embed images, audio, and video directly into a Web document without add-on programs. Web services are loosely coupled software components based on open Web standards that work with any application software and operating system. They can be used as components of Web-based applications linking the systems of two different organizations or to link disparate systems of a single company. Companies are purchasing their new software applications from outside sources, including software packages, by outsourcing custom application development to an external vendor (that may be offshore), or by renting online software services (SaaS). Mashups combine two different software services to create new software applications and services. Apps are small pieces of software that run on the Internet, on a computer, or on a mobile phone and are generally delivered over the Internet.

5. What are the challenges of managing IT infrastructure and management solutions?

Major challenges include dealing with platform and infrastructure change, infrastructure management and governance, and making wise infrastructure investments. Solution guidelines include using a competitive forces model to determine how much to spend on IT infrastructure and where to make strategic infrastructure investments, and establishing the total cost of ownership (TCO) of information technology assets. The total cost of owning technology resources includes not only the original cost of computer hardware and software but also costs for hardware and software upgrades, maintenance, technical support, and training.

Key Terms

Android, 207
Application server, 200
Apps, 225
Autonomic computing, 218
Blade servers, 207
Chrome OS, 207
Clients, 199
Client/server computing, 199
Cloud computing, 200
Consumerization of IT, 210
Extensible Markup Language (XML), 221
Green computing, 216
Grid computing, 211
HTML (Hypertext Markup Language), 220
HTML5, 220
Hybrid cloud, 216
iOS, 208
Java, 219
Legacy systems, 209
Linux, 207
Mainframe, 197
Mashup, 225
Minicomputers, 197
Moore's Law, 201
Multicore processor, 216
Multitiered (N-tier) client/server architecture, 199
Multitouch, 208

Nanotechnology, 202
On-demand computing, 215
Open source software, 219
Operating system, 207
Outsourcing, 224
Private cloud, 215
Public cloud, 215
SaaS (Software as a Service), 224
Scalability, 226
Service level agreement (SLA),224
Server, 199
Service-oriented architecture (SOA), 221
Software package, 223
Storage area network (SAN), 208
Tablet computers, 210
Technology standards, 205
Total cost of ownership (TCO), 227
Unix, 207
Utility computing, 215
Virtualization, 211
Web browser, 220
Web hosting service, 209
Web server, 199
Web services, 221
Windows, 200
Windows 8, 208
Wintel PC, 197

Review Questions

1. What is IT infrastructure and what are its components?

   - Define IT infrastructure from both a technology and a services perspective.

   - List and describe the components of IT infrastructure that firms need to manage.

2. What are the stages and technology drivers of IT infrastructure evolution?

   - List each of the eras in IT infrastructure evolution and describe its distinguishing characteristics.

   - Define and describe the following: Web server, application server, multitiered client/server architecture.

   - Describe Moore's Law and the Law of Mass Digital Storage.

   - Describe how network economics, declining communications costs, and technology standards affect IT infrastructure.

3. What are the current trends in computer hardware platforms?

   - Describe the evolving mobile platform, grid computing, and cloud computing.

   - Explain how businesses can benefit from autonomic computing, virtualization, green computing, and multicore processors.

4. What are the current trends in software platforms?

- Define and describe open source software and Linux and explain their business benefits.
- Define Java and HTML5 and explain why they are important.
- Define and describe Web services and the role played by XML.
- Name and describe the three external sources for software.
- Define and describe software mashups and apps.

5. What are the challenges of managing IT infrastructure and management solutions?
   - Name and describe the management challenges posed by IT infrastructure.
   - Explain how using a competitive forces model and calculating the TCO of technology assets help firms make good infrastructure investments.

Discussion Questions

1. Why is selecting computer hardware and software for the organization an important management decision? What management, organization, and technology issues should be considered when selecting computer hardware and software?

2. Should organizations use software service providers for all their software needs? Why or why not?

What management, organization, and technology factors should be considered when making this decision?

3. What are the advantages and disadvantages of cloud computing?

Hands-On MIS Projects

The projects in this section give you hands-on experience in developing solutions for managing IT infrastructures and IT outsourcing, using spreadsheet software to evaluate alternative desktop systems, and using Web research to budget for a sales conference.

Management Decision Problems

1. The University of Pittsburgh Medical Center (UPMC) relies on information systems to operate 19 hospitals, a network of other care sites, and international and commercial ventures. Demand for additional servers and storage technology was growing by 20 percent each year. UPMC was setting up a separate server for every application, and its servers and other computers were running a number of different operating systems, including several versions of Unix and Windows. UPMC had to manage technologies from many different vendors, including Hewlett-Packard (HP), Sun Microsystems, Microsoft, and IBM. Assess the impact of this situation on business performance. What factors and management decisions must be considered when developing a solution to this problem?

2. Qantas Airways, Australia's leading airline, faces cost pressures from high fuel prices and lower levels of global airline traffic. To remain competitive, the airline must find ways to keep costs low while providing a high level of customer service. Qantas had a 30-year-old data center. Management had to decide whether to replace its IT infrastructure with newer technology or outsource it. What factors should be considered by Qantas management when deciding whether to outsource? If Qantas decides to outsource, list and describe points that should be addressed in a service level agreement.

Improving Decision Making: Using a Spreadsheet to Evaluate Hardware and Software Options

Software skills: Spreadsheet formulas
Business skills: Technology pricing

In this exercise, you will use spreadsheet software to calculate the cost of desktop systems, printers, and software.

Use the Internet to obtain pricing information on hardware and software for an office of 30 people. You will need to price 30 PC desktop systems (monitors, computers, and keyboards) manufactured by Lenovo, Dell, and HP. (For the purposes of this exercise, ignore the fact that desktop systems usually come with preloaded software packages.) Also obtain pricing on 15 desktop printers manufactured by HP, Canon, and Dell. Each desktop system must satisfy the minimum specifications shown in tables which you can find in MyMISLab.

Also obtain pricing on 30 copies of the most recent versions of Microsoft Office, Lotus SmartSuite, and Apache OpenOffice (formerly Oracle Open Office), and on 30 copies of Microsoft Windows 7 Professional or Windows 8 Pro. Each desktop productivity package should contain programs for word processing, spreadsheets, database, and presentations. Prepare a spreadsheet showing your research results for the software and the desktop system, printer, and software combination offering the best performance and pricing per worker. Because every two workers share one printer (15 printers/30 systems), your calculations should assume only half a printer cost per worker.

Improving Decision Making: Using Web Research to Budget for a Sales Conference

Software skills: Internet-based software
Business skills: Researching transportation and lodging costs

The Foremost Composite Materials Company is planning a two-day sales conference for October 19–20, starting with a reception on the evening of October 18. The conference consists of all-day meetings that the entire sales force, numbering 120 sales representatives and their 16 managers, must attend. Each sales representative requires his or her own room, and the company needs two common meeting rooms, one large enough to hold the entire sales force plus a few visitors (200) and the other able to hold half the force. Management has set a budget of $150,000 for the representatives' room rentals. The company would like to hold the conference in either Miami or Marco Island, Florida, at a Hilton- or Marriott-owned hotel.

Use the Hilton and Marriott Web sites to select a hotel in whichever of these cities that would enable the company to hold its sales conference within its budget and meet its sales conference requirements. Then locate flights arriving the afternoon prior to the conference. Your attendees will be coming from Los Angeles (54), San Francisco (32), Seattle (22), Chicago (19), and Pittsburgh (14). Determine costs of each airline ticket from these cities. When you are finished, create a budget for the conference. The budget will include the cost of each airline ticket, the room cost, and $70 per attendee per day for food.

Video Cases

Video Cases and Instructional Videos illustrating some of the concepts in this chapter are available. Contact your instructor to access these videos.

Collaboration and Teamwork Project

In MyMISLab, you will find a Collaboration and Teamwork Project dealing with the concepts in this chapter. You will be able to use Google Sites, Google Docs, and other open source collaboration tools to complete the assignment.

Should Businesses Move to the Cloud?
CASE STUDY

Cloud computing has just begun to take off in the business world. The biggest player in the cloud computing marketplace is one you might not expect: Amazon. Under its Web Services division (AWS), Amazon has streamlined cloud computing and made it an affordable and sensible option for companies ranging from tiny Internet start-ups to established companies like FedEx.

AWS provides subscribing companies with flexible computing power and data storage, as well as data management, messaging, payment, and other services that can be used together or individually as the business requires. Anyone with an Internet connection and a little bit of money can harness the same computing systems that Amazon itself uses to run its now $48 billion a year retail business. To make the process of harnessing the cloud simpler, Amazon added an automated service called CloudFormation that helps customers get the right amount of computing resources. Customers provide the amount of server space, bandwidth, storage, and any other services they require, and AWS can automatically allocate those resources.

Since its launch in March 2006, AWS has continued to grow in popularity, with $1 billion in business in 2011 and hundreds of thousands of customers across the globe. In fact, Amazon believes that AWS will someday become more valuable than its vaunted retail operation. Amazon's sales pitch is that you don't pay a monthly or yearly fee to use their computing resources—instead, you pay for exactly what you use. For many businesses, this is an appealing proposition because it allows Amazon to handle all of the maintenance and upkeep of IT infrastructures, leaving businesses to spend more time on higher-value work.

The difference between cloud computing today and the cloud computing of the past is the scale of today's clouds and the amount of digital data requiring storage. This number has increased exponentially in the past few years. Web companies used to build dozens of data centers, often up to a half a billion dollars in cost per center. Leading cloud companies such as Amazon, Google, and Microsoft have built software that uses automated methods to spread data across the globe and control thousands of servers, and they have refined data center designs with the goal of increasing efficiency. Now, more than ever, companies are turning to cloud computing providers like these for their computing resources.

Zynga is a good example of a company using cloud computing to improve its business in a new way. Zynga is the developer of wildly popular Facebook applications like *FarmVille*, *Mafia Wars*, and many others. With over 290 million monthly active users, Zynga's computing demands are already significant. When Zynga releases a new game, however, it has no way of knowing what amount of computing resources to dedicate to the game. The game might be a mild success, or a smash hit that adds millions of new users. The ability to design applications that can scale up in the number of users quickly is one of Zynga's competitive advantages.

Because of the uncertainty surrounding resource usage for new game launches, Zynga uses Amazon's cloud computing platform to launch new offerings. That way, it can pay only for the resources it ends up using, and once game traffic stabilizes and reaches a steady number of users, Zynga moves the game onto its private zCloud, which is structurally similar to Amazon's cloud, but operates under Zynga's control in data centers on the East and West coasts. Zynga's own servers handle 80 percent of its games. (Zynga recently started selling extra capacity on zCloud to other game-makers.) To streamline the process of moving application data from Amazon to the zCloud, Zynga has automated many computing tasks, selected hardware and chip configurations that are very similar to Amazon's, and makes significant use of virtualization.

There are a few reasons why Zynga is well-suited to use this combination of public and private clouds. The first is its business model, which involves games that have a tendency to be boom or bust. Rather than spending on computing resources of its own before the launch of each game, it's much more cost-effective to use Amazon's cloud services until Zynga can more accurately predict the computing power it needs. As a recent start-up, Zynga lacks the accumulated legacy systems and infrastructure typically found in older companies. The more systems a company has, the tougher it is to integrate its applications and data with cloud systems.

Although the consequences for server downtime are not as catastrophic for Zynga as they would be for a financial services firm, Zynga still needs

99.9 percent uptime. On its own financial reports, Zynga recognized that a significant majority of its game traffic had been hosted by a single vendor and any failure or significant interruption in its network could negatively impact operations. Amazon Web Services had an outage for several hours in April 2011 that made it impossible for users to log into some of Zynga's games.

However, owning data centers also comes with risks. If the demand for Zynga's games were to drop dramatically, Zynga would have too much IT infrastructure on its hands and losses could result. The most likely scenario has Zynga owning part of its data centers and relying on external services such as Amazon for the rest.

Not all companies use cloud computing in the same way that Zynga does, but many do. Outback Steakhouse wasn't sure how popular an upcoming coupon promotion would be, so the company used Microsoft's Azure cloud to launch the promotion. Outback ended up selling an unexpectedly large 670,000 coupons. Using the cloud, it was able to avoid taxing in-house systems unnecessarily.

InterContinental Hotels has revamped its infrastructure to include both private and public cloud usage. To improve response time for customers, InterContinental moved its core room reservation transaction system onto a private cloud within its own data center, but it moved room availability and pricing Web site applications onto public cloud data centers on the East and West coasts. In fact, InterContinental hopes to put all of its publicly accessible information in these public clouds so that customers receive faster results to site queries. Customers receive data faster if the data are located on a server that is physically close to them, and cloud computing helps InterContinental to take advantage of this.

Start-up companies and smaller companies are finding that they no longer need to build a data center. With cloud infrastructures like Amazon's readily available, they have access to technical capability that was formerly only available to much larger businesses. For example, online crafts marketplace Etsy uses Amazon computers to analyze data from the 1 billion monthly views of its Web site. Etsy can then use its findings to create product recommendation systems that allow customers to rank which products they like best and to generate a list of 100 products they might enjoy. Etsy's engineers and managers are excited about their ability to handle these types of issues on someone else's computer systems.

IBM, Cisco, and other traditional data center giants realize that cloud computing is a threat to their technology infrastructure business. As a solution to rising computing costs, they have been steering their customers toward virtualization software, which allows them to run many more applications on each individual server that they buy. There are also many companies that simply have too much legacy technology to use the cloud effectively. For example, Credit Suisse has 7,000 software applications running on its systems that have been developed over the past 20 years. Ensuring that all of these applications would work the same way in the cloud would be more trouble than it's worth.

Many other companies share Zynga's concern about cloud reliability and security, and this remains a major barrier to widespread cloud adoption. Amazon's cloud experienced significant outages in April and August 2011 and again on June 14 and 29, 2012. Normally, cloud networks are very reliable, often more so than private networks operated by individual companies. But when a cloud of significant size like Amazon's goes down, it sends ripples across the entire Web.

According to Amazon, a simple network configuration error caused a major multiday service outage in Amazon's East Coast region from April 21–24, 2011. Amazingly, the error was most likely a simple error made by a human being during a routine network adjustment. Sites affected included Reddit, Foursquare, Engine Yard, HootSuite, Quora, Zynga, and many more. On June 14 and June 29, 2012, AWS suffered outages due to power failures in its primary East Coast data center in North Virginia. Many popular Web sites, including Netflix, Heroku, Quora, and Pinterest, as well as Web sites of smaller companies, were knocked offline for hours.

The outages were proof that the vision of a cloud with 100 percent uptime is still far from reality. Experts have conflicting opinions of how serious this is. A June 2012 report issued by the Paris-based International Working Group on Cloud Computing Resiliency estimated that the major cloud computing services were down about 10 hours per year or more, with average availability at 99.9 percent or less. Even this small amount of downtime can lead to large revenue losses for firms that need 24/7 availability. Nevertheless, some large cloud users such as Netflix believe that overall cloud service availability has steadily improved. Neil Hunt, Netflix's chief product officer, believes the cloud is becoming more reliable, and that AWS gives Netflix much larger scale and technical expertise than it would have otherwise. A number of experts recommend that companies for whom an outage would be a major risk consider using another computing service as a backup.

Still, cloud computing has finally gone mainstream, and the major cloud providers have the sales numbers to prove it. Amazon, Microsoft, Google, and other cloud providers will have to continue to work to avoid outages, while other companies must decide whether the cloud is right for them, and if so, how to most effectively use the cloud to enhance their businesses.

Sources: Charles Babcock, "How Game-Maker Zynga Became a Cloud Vendor," *Information Week*, May 14, 2012; Charles Babcock, "Cloud's Thorniest Question: Does It Pay Off?" *Information Week*, June 4, 2012; Zack Whittaker, "Amazon Explains Latest Cloud Outage: Blame the Power," ZDNet, June 18, 2012; Stuart J. Johnston, "Cloud Outage of 13 Providers Reveals Downtime Costs," searchcloud-computing.com, June 22, 2012; Charles Babcock, "4 Companies Getting Real Results from Cloud Computing," *Information Week*, January 15, 2011; Charles Babcock, "Amazon Launches CloudFormation to Simplify App Development," *Information Week*, February 28, 2011; Ashlee Vance, "The Cloud: Battle of the Tech Titans." *Bloomberg Businessweek* (March 3, 2011); Peter Svensson; Steve Lohr, "Amazon's Trouble Raises Cloud Computing Doubts," *The New York Times*, April 22, 2011; Charles Babcock. "Post Mortem: When Amazon's Cloud Turned on Itself," *Information Week*, April 29, 2011; Patrick Thibodeau, "Amazon Cloud Outage Was Triggered by Configuration Error, "*Computerworld*, April 29, 2011; and Charles Babcock, "Zynga's Unusual Cloud Strategy is Key To Success," *Information Week*, July 1, 2011.

CASE STUDY QUESTIONS

1. What business benefits do cloud computing services provide? What problems do they solve?

2. What are the disadvantages of cloud computing?

3. How do the concepts of capacity planning, scalability, and TCO apply to this case? Apply these concepts both to Amazon and to subscribers of its services.

4. What kinds of businesses are most likely to benefit from using cloud computing? Why?

Chapter 6

Foundations of Business Intelligence: Databases and Information Management

BAE SYSTEMS

BAE Systems (BAE) is the United Kingdom's largest manufacturing company and one of the largest commercial aerospace and defence organisations in Europe. Its high-technology, information-driven products and services range from one of the world's most capable multi-role combat fighters, the Eurofighter Typhoon, to the Jetstream family of commercial aircraft, to the provision of information technology and information systems for e-business to develop and implement logistics, IT and e-capability services. With sales, manufacturing and support sites throughout the world, including the U.K., Europe, the United States, and Australia, BAE employs 88,000 people and generates more than U.S. $ 30 billion in annual revenue.

Although BAE has consolidated its competitive position in established markets, and continues to expand into new markets in the Middle East and Asia, its performance in the aircraft part of the business was being impeded by legacy information systems which support the computer-aided design (CAD) and computer-aided manufacturing (CAM) of its aircraft. The distributed nature of BAE's design and manufacturing sites meant that storing and analysing accurate sets of operational data describing the complex components of the various aircraft types to produce aircraft assembly reports for the production lines became increasingly challenging and resource-consuming. Data describing the same aircraft component parts might need resolution, such as in the case of various part naming conventions and codes.

Accessing the data from the many systems was a complex task involving many technical challenges. As the aircraft business of BAE grew so did the likelihood for delays in producing the aircraft assembly reports and other operations data sets necessary for aircraft production management decision making. In the worst case, the production of aircraft on the assembly line would stop until accurate information was available, with consequent schedule and cost implications. BAE's CAD/CAM staff were storing and analysing data sets sourced from 5 major aircraft design and manufacturing sites spread throughout the U.K., each host to thousands of staff involved in the design and manufacturing process, so that assembly reports and other operations data could be produced. Although the data that the legacy systems processed were held principally in computer files, there were numerous occasions when paper drawings with annotations containing component design and manufacturing information were used to reconcile ambiguities and inconsistencies in the assembly reports. When these data ambiguities and inconsistencies occurred, this gave rise to a sense of uncertainty in the assembly reports produced.

What BAE needed was a single repository for CAD/CAM data that would also facilitate the integration of data held in its legacy systems. The company decided to replace its legacy systems with an enterprise-wide knowledge management system which would bring the design and manu-

© Kristoffer Tripplaar/Alamy

facturing data into a single database that could be concurrently accessed by the design and manufacturing engineers. BAE implemented Siemens' Teamcenter product lifecycle management software and Dassault Systemes' CATIA CAD/CAM software. Teamcenter can also be configured to take advantage of recent developments in cloud computing using Microsoft's Azure, IBM's SmartCloud Enterprise+, and Amazon Web Services.

Bringing together Siemens' Teamcenter and Dassault Systemes' CATIA has given BAE Systems powerful integrated data management tools. The Teamcenter database includes tools for component markup and rollup capabilities allowing users to visualise the effect of component design changes and configuration selections in real-time.

The new solution has produced significant cost savings at BAE in terms of its design and manufacturing data management and storage, while boosting performance. With fewer legacy systems and data files to manage, BAE has been able to meet quality, time and cost requirements by being able to produce complete and accurate aircraft component definitions and configurations. BAE's new design and manufacturing database technology has improved speed-to-market by synchronising upstream CAD and downstream CAM component definitions, thereby enabling better cross-discipline coordination. With these savings, the company has been able to spend more resources on improving data management across the entire enterprise.

Sources: "BAE Systems Half-Yearly Report and Presentation 2012" www.baesystems.com, accessed November 8, 2012; "Teamcenter supports aircraft through 50-year cycle: BAE Systems Military Air Solutions" www.plm.automation.siemens.com, accessed November 8, 2012; "CATIA V5 Fact Sheet" www.3ds.com, accessed November 8, 2012.

Case contributed by Robert Manderson, University of Roehampton

The experience of BAE Systems illustrates the importance of data management. Business performance depends on the accuracy and reliability of its data. The company has grown its business, but, both operational CAD/CAM efficiency and production management decision making were impeded by data stored in legacy systems that were difficult to access. How businesses store, organise, and manage their data has a huge impact on organisational effectiveness.

The chapter-opening diagram calls attention to important points raised by this case and this chapter. BAE Systems management decided that the firm needed to improve the management of its data. Pieces of data about design components, manufactured components, and their final assembly had been stored in many large legacy systems that made it extremely difficult for the data to be retrieved, correctly unified so that it could be used in the production line assembly of aircraft components. The data were often redundant and inconsistent, limiting their usefulness. Management was unable to obtain an enterprise-view of the company.

In the past, BAE Systems had used manual paper processes to reconcile its inconsistent and redundant data and to assemble data for management reporting. This solution was extremely time-consuming and costly and prevented the company's information technology department from performing higher-value work. A more appropriate solution was to install new hardware and software to create an enterprise-wide repository for business information that would support a more streamlined set of business applications. The new software included enterprise software that was integrated with an up-to-date database management system that could supply data for enterprise-wide reporting. The company had to reorganise its data into a standard company-wide format, eliminate redundancies, and establish rules, responsibilities, and procedures for updating and using the data.

A state-of-the-art database management system suite of software helps BAE Systems boost efficiency by making it easier to locate and assemble data for management reporting and for processing day-to-day CAD/CAM transactions for final aircraft component assembly. The data are more accurate and reliable, and costs for managing and storing the data have been considerably reduced.

Here are some questions to think about: What kinds of data management problems did BAE Systems experience in its legacy database environment? What work had to be done before the company could effectively take advantage of the new data management technology?

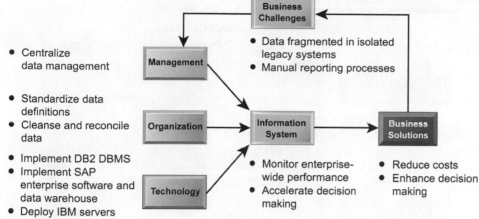

6.1 ORGANIZING DATA IN A TRADITIONAL FILE ENVIRONMENT

An effective information system provides users with accurate, timely, and relevant information. Accurate information is free of errors. Information is timely when it is available to decision makers when it is needed. Information is relevant when it is useful and appropriate for the types of work and decisions that require it.

You might be surprised to learn that many businesses don't have timely, accurate, or relevant information because the data in their information systems have been poorly organized and maintained. That's why data management is so essential. To understand the problem, let's look at how information systems arrange data in computer files and traditional methods of file management.

FILE ORGANIZATION TERMS AND CONCEPTS

A computer system organizes data in a hierarchy that starts with bits and bytes and progresses to fields, records, files, and databases (see Figure 6.1). A **bit** represents the smallest unit of data a computer can handle. A group of bits, called a **byte**, represents a single character, which can be a letter, a number, or another symbol. A grouping of characters into a word, a group of words, or a complete number (such as a person's name or age) is called a **field**. A group of related fields, such as the student's name, the course taken, the date, and the grade, comprises a **record**; a group of records of the same type is called a **file**.

For example, the records in Figure 6.1 could constitute a student course file. A group of related files makes up a database. The student course file illustrated in Figure 6.1 could be grouped with files on students' personal histories and financial backgrounds to create a student database.

A record describes an entity. An **entity** is a person, place, thing, or event on which we store and maintain information. Each characteristic or quality describing a particular entity is called an **attribute**. For example, Student_ID, Course, Date, and Grade are attributes of the entity COURSE. The specific values that these attributes can have are found in the fields of the record describing the entity COURSE.

FIGURE 6.1   THE DATA HIERARCHY

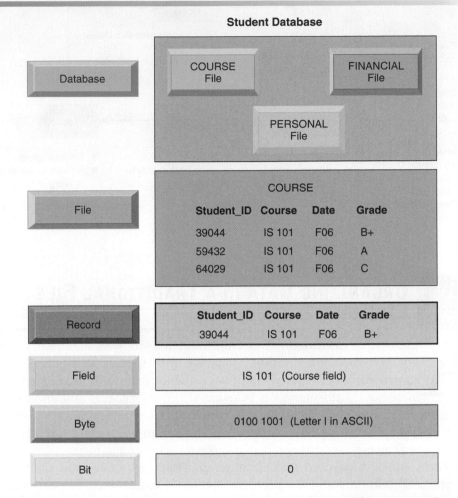

A computer system organizes data in a hierarchy that starts with the bit, which represents either a 0 or a 1. Bits can be grouped to form a byte to represent one character, number, or symbol. Bytes can be grouped to form a field, and related fields can be grouped to form a record. Related records can be collected to form a file, and related files can be organized into a database.

PROBLEMS WITH THE TRADITIONAL FILE ENVIRONMENT

In most organizations, systems tended to grow independently without a company-wide plan. Accounting, finance, manufacturing, human resources, and sales and marketing all developed their own systems and data files. Figure 6.2 illustrates the traditional approach to information processing.

Each application, of course, required its own files and its own computer program to operate. For example, the human resources functional area might have a personnel master file, a payroll file, a medical insurance file, a pension file, a mailing list file, and so forth until tens, perhaps hundreds, of files and programs existed. In the company as a whole, this process led to multiple master files created, maintained, and operated by separate divisions or departments. As this process goes on for 5 or 10 years, the organization is saddled with hundreds of programs and applications that are very difficult to maintain and manage. The resulting problems are data redundancy and inconsistency,

FIGURE 6.2   TRADITIONAL FILE PROCESSING

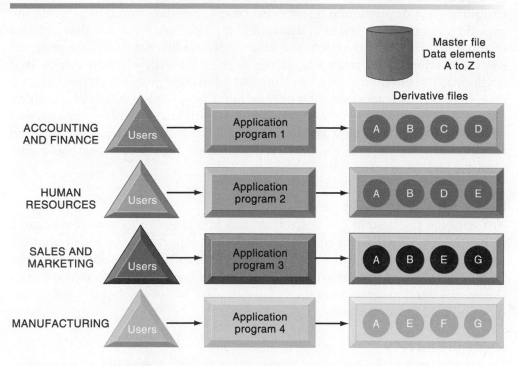

The use of a traditional approach to file processing encourages each functional area in a corporation to develop specialized applications. Each application requires a unique data file that is likely to be a subset of the master file. These subsets of the master file lead to data redundancy and inconsistency, processing inflexibility, and wasted storage resources.

program-data dependence, inflexibility, poor data security, and an inability to share data among applications.

Data Redundancy and Inconsistency

Data redundancy is the presence of duplicate data in multiple data files so that the same data are stored in more than one place or location. Data redundancy occurs when different groups in an organization independently collect the same piece of data and store it independently of each other. Data redundancy wastes storage resources and also leads to **data inconsistency**, where the same attribute may have different values. For example, in instances of the entity COURSE illustrated in Figure 6.1, the Date may be updated in some systems but not in others. The same attribute, Student_ID, may also have different names in different systems throughout the organization. Some systems might use Student_ID and others might use ID, for example.

Additional confusion might result from using different coding systems to represent values for an attribute. For instance, the sales, inventory, and manufacturing systems of a clothing retailer might use different codes to represent clothing size. One system might represent clothing size as "extra large," whereas another might use the code "XL" for the same purpose. The resulting confusion would make it difficult for companies to create customer relationship management, supply chain management, or enterprise systems that integrate data from different sources.

Program-Data Dependence

Program-data dependence refers to the coupling of data stored in files and the specific programs required to update and maintain those files such that changes in programs require changes to the data. Every traditional computer program has to describe the location and nature of the data with which it works. In a traditional file environment, any change in a software program could require a change in the data accessed by that program. One program might be modified from a five-digit to a nine-digit zip code. If the original data file were changed from five-digit to nine-digit zip codes, then other programs that required the five-digit zip code would no longer work properly. Such changes could cost millions of dollars to implement properly.

Lack of Flexibility

A traditional file system can deliver routine scheduled reports after extensive programming efforts, but it cannot deliver ad hoc reports or respond to unanticipated information requirements in a timely fashion. The information required by ad hoc requests is somewhere in the system but may be too expensive to retrieve. Several programmers might have to work for weeks to put together the required data items in a new file.

Poor Security

Because there is little control or management of data, access to and dissemination of information may be out of control. Management may have no way of knowing who is accessing or even making changes to the organization's data.

Lack of Data Sharing and Availability

Because pieces of information in different files and different parts of the organization cannot be related to one another, it is virtually impossible for information to be shared or accessed in a timely manner. Information cannot flow freely across different functional areas or different parts of the organization. If users find different values of the same piece of information in two different systems, they may not want to use these systems because they cannot trust the accuracy of their data.

6.2   THE DATABASE APPROACH TO DATA MANAGEMENT

Database technology cuts through many of the problems of traditional file organization. A more rigorous definition of a **database** is a collection of data organized to serve many applications efficiently by centralizing the data and controlling redundant data. Rather than storing data in separate files for each application, data appears to users as being stored in only one location. A single database services multiple applications. For example, instead of a corporation storing employee data in separate information systems and separate files for personnel, payroll, and benefits, the corporation could create a single common human resources database.

DATABASE MANAGEMENT SYSTEMS

A **database management system (DBMS)** is software that permits an organization to centralize data, manage them efficiently, and provide access to the stored data by application programs. The DBMS acts as an interface between application programs and the physical data files. When the application program calls for a data item, such as gross pay, the DBMS finds this item in the database and presents it to the application program. Using traditional data files, the programmer would have to specify the size and format of each data element used in the program and then tell the computer where they were located.

The DBMS relieves the programmer or end user from the task of understanding where and how the data are actually stored by separating the logical and physical views of the data. The *logical view* presents data as they would be perceived by end users or business specialists, whereas the *physical view* shows how data are actually organized and structured on physical storage media.

The database management software makes the physical database available for different logical views required by users. For example, for the human resources database illustrated in Figure 6.3, a benefits specialist might require a view consisting of the employee's name, social security number, and health insurance coverage. A payroll department member might need data such as the employee's name, social security number, gross pay, and net pay. The data for all these views are stored in a single database, where they can be more easily managed by the organization.

How a DBMS Solves the Problems of the Traditional File Environment

A DBMS reduces data redundancy and inconsistency by minimizing isolated files in which the same data are repeated. The DBMS may not enable the organization to eliminate data redundancy entirely, but it can help control redundancy. Even if the organization maintains some redundant data, using a DBMS eliminates data inconsistency because the DBMS can help the organization ensure that every occurrence of redundant data has the same values. The DBMS uncouples programs and data, enabling data to stand

FIGURE 6.3   HUMAN RESOURCES DATABASE WITH MULTIPLE VIEWS

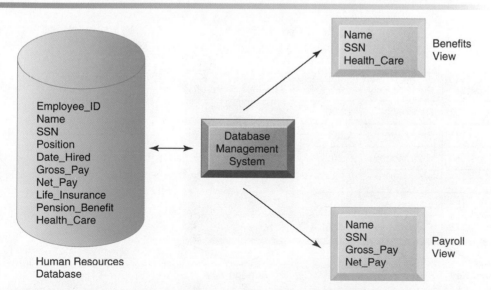

A single human resources database provides many different views of data, depending on the information requirements of the user. Illustrated here are two possible views, one of interest to a benefits specialist and one of interest to a member of the company's payroll department.

on their own. Access and availability of information will be increased and program development and maintenance costs reduced because users and programmers can perform ad hoc queries of data in the database. The DBMS enables the organization to centrally manage data, their use, and security.

Relational DBMS

Contemporary DBMS use different database models to keep track of entities, attributes, and relationships. The most popular type of DBMS today for PCs as well as for larger computers and mainframes is the **relational DBMS**. Relational databases represent data as two-dimensional tables (called relations). Tables may be referred to as files. Each table contains data on an entity and its attributes. Microsoft Access is a relational DBMS for desktop systems, whereas DB2, Oracle Database, and Microsoft SQL Server are relational DBMS for large mainframes and midrange computers. MySQL is a popular open source DBMS, and Oracle Database Lite is a DBMS for mobile computing devices.

Let's look at how a relational database organizes data about suppliers and parts (see Figure 6.4). The database has a separate table for the entity SUPPLIER and a table for the entity PART. Each table consists of a grid of columns and

FIGURE 6.4   RELATIONAL DATABASE TABLES

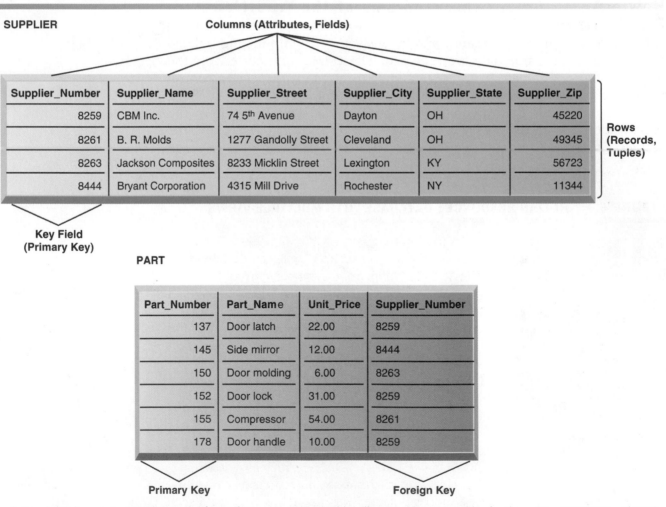

A relational database organizes data in the form of two-dimensional tables. Illustrated here are tables for the entities SUPPLIER and PART showing how they represent each entity and its attributes. Supplier_Number is a primary key for the SUPPLIER table and a foreign key for the PART table.

rows of data. Each individual element of data for each entity is stored as a separate field, and each field represents an attribute for that entity. Fields in a relational database are also called columns. For the entity SUPPLIER, the supplier identification number, name, street, city, state, and zip code are stored as separate fields within the SUPPLIER table and each field represents an attribute for the entity SUPPLIER.

The actual information about a single supplier that resides in a table is called a row. Rows are commonly referred to as records, or in very technical terms, as **tuples**. Data for the entity PART have their own separate table.

The field for Supplier_Number in the SUPPLIER table uniquely identifies each record so that the record can be retrieved, updated, or sorted. It is called a **key field**. Each table in a relational database has one field that is designated as its **primary key**. This key field is the unique identifier for all the information in any row of the table and this primary key cannot be duplicated. Supplier_Number is the primary key for the SUPPLIER table and Part_Number is the primary key for the PART table. Note that Supplier_Number appears in both the SUPPLIER and PART tables. In the SUPPLIER table, Supplier_Number is the primary key. When the field Supplier_Number appears in the PART table, it is called a **foreign key** and is essentially a lookup field to look up data about the supplier of a specific part.

Operations of a Relational DBMS

Relational database tables can be combined easily to deliver data required by users, provided that any two tables share a common data element. Suppose we wanted to find in this database the names of suppliers who could provide us with part number 137 or part number 150. We would need information from two tables: the SUPPLIER table and the PART table. Note that these two files have a shared data element: Supplier_Number.

In a relational database, three basic operations, as shown in Figure 6.5, are used to develop useful sets of data: select, join, and project. The *select* operation creates a subset consisting of all records in the file that meet stated criteria. Select creates, in other words, a subset of rows that meet certain criteria. In our example, we want to select records (rows) from the PART table where the Part_Number equals 137 or 150. The *join* operation combines relational tables to provide the user with more information than is available in individual tables. In our example, we want to join the now-shortened PART table (only parts 137 or 150 will be presented) and the SUPPLIER table into a single new table.

The *project* operation creates a subset consisting of columns in a table, permitting the user to create new tables that contain only the information required. In our example, we want to extract from the new table only the following columns: Part_Number, Part_Name, Supplier_Number, and Supplier_Name.

Non-Relational Databases and Databases in the Cloud

For over 30 years, relational database technology has been the gold standard. Cloud computing, unprecedented data volumes, massive workloads for Web services, and the need to store new types of data require database alternatives to the traditional relational model of organizing data in the form of tables, columns, and rows. Companies are turning to "*NoSQL*" non-relational database technologies for this purpose. **Non-relational database management systems** use a more flexible data model and are designed for managing large data sets across many distributed machines and for easily scaling up or down. They are useful for accelerating simple queries against large volumes of structured and

FIGURE 6.5 THE THREE BASIC OPERATIONS OF A RELATIONAL DBMS

PART

Part_Number	Part_Name	Unit_Price	Supplier_Number
137	Door latch	22.00	8259
145	Side mirror	12.00	8444
150	Door molding	6.00	8263
152	Door lock	31.00	8259
155	Compressor	54.00	8261
178	Door handle	10.00	8259

Select Part_Number = 137 or 150

SUPPLIER

Supplier_Number	Supplier_Name	Supplier_Street	Supplier_City	Supplier_State	Supplier_Zip
8259	CBM Inc.	74 5th Avenue	Dayton	OH	45220
8261	B. R. Molds	1277 Gandolly Street	Cleveland	OH	49345
8263	Jackson Components	8233 Micklin Street	Lexington	KY	56723
8444	Bryant Corporation	4315 Mill Drive	Rochester	NY	11344

Join by Supplier_Number

Part_Number	Part_Name	Supplier_Number	Supplier_Name
137	Door latch	8259	CBM Inc.
150	Door molding	8263	Jackson Components

Project selected columns

The select, join, and project operations enable data from two different tables to be combined and only selected attributes to be displayed.

unstructured data, including Web, social media, graphics, and other forms of data that are difficult to analyze with traditional SQL-based tools.

There are several different kinds of NoSQL databases, each with its own technical features and behavior. Oracle NoSQL Database is one example, as is Amazon's SimpleDB, one of the Amazon Web Services that run in the cloud. SimpleDB provides a simple Web services interface to create and store multiple data sets, query data easily, and return the results. There is no need to pre-define a formal database structure or change that definition if new data are added later.

Amazon and other cloud computing vendors provide relational database services as well. Amazon Relational Database Service (Amazon RDS) offers MySQL, SQL Server, or Oracle Database as database engines. Pricing is based on usage. Oracle has its own Database Cloud Service using its relational Oracle Database 11g, and Microsoft SQL Azure Database is a cloud-based relational database service based on Microsoft's SQL Server DBMS. Cloud-based data management services have special appeal for Web-focused start-ups or small to medium-sized businesses seeking database capabilities at a lower price than in-house database products.

TicketDirect, which sells tickets to concerts, sporting events, theater performances, and movies in Australia and New Zealand, adopted the SQL Azure Database cloud platform in order to improve management of peak system loads during major ticket sales. It migrated its data to the SQL Azure database. By moving to a cloud solution, TicketDirect is able to scale its computing resources in response to real-time demand while keeping costs low.

In addition to public cloud-based data management services, companies now have the option of using databases in private clouds. For example, Sabre Holdings, the world's largest software as a service (SaaS) provider for the aviation industry, has a private database cloud that supports more than 100 projects and 700 users. A consolidated database spanning a pool of standardized servers running Oracle Database 11g provides database services for multiple applications. Workload management tools ensure sufficient resources are available to meet application needs even when the workload changes. The shared hardware and software platform reduces the number of servers, DBMS, and storage devices needed for these projects, which consist of custom airline travel applications along with rail, hotel, and other travel industry applications (Baum, 2011).

Private clouds consolidate servers, storage, operating systems, databases, and mixed workloads onto a shared hardware and software infrastructure. Deploying databases on a consolidated private cloud enables IT departments to improve quality of service levels and reduce capital and operating costs. The higher the consolidation density achieved, the greater the return on investment.

CAPABILITIES OF DATABASE MANAGEMENT SYSTEMS

A DBMS includes capabilities and tools for organizing, managing, and accessing the data in the database. The most important are its data definition language, data dictionary, and data manipulation language.

DBMS have a **data definition** capability to specify the structure of the content of the database. It would be used to create database tables and to define the characteristics of the fields in each table. This information about the database would be documented in a data dictionary. A **data dictionary** is an automated or manual file that stores definitions of data elements and their characteristics.

Microsoft Access has a rudimentary data dictionary capability that displays information about the name, description, size, type, format, and other properties of each field in a table (see Figure 6.6). Data dictionaries for large corporate databases may capture additional information, such as usage, ownership (who in the organization is responsible for maintaining the data), authorization, security, and the individuals, business functions, programs, and reports that use each data element.

Querying and Reporting

DBMS includes tools for accessing and manipulating information in databases. Most DBMS have a specialized language called a **data manipulation language** that is used to add, change, delete, and retrieve the data in the database. This language contains commands that permit end users and programming specialists to extract data from the database to satisfy information requests and develop applications. The most prominent data manipulation language today is **Structured Query Language**, or **SQL**. Figure 6.7 illustrates the SQL query that would produce the new resultant table in Figure 6.5. You can find out more about how to perform SQL queries in our Learning Tracks for this chapter.

Users of DBMS for large and midrange computers, such as DB2, Oracle, or SQL Server, would employ SQL to retrieve information they needed from the database. Microsoft Access also uses SQL, but it provides its own set of user-friendly tools for querying databases and for organizing data from databases into more polished reports.

In Microsoft Access, you will find features that enable users to create queries by identifying the tables and fields they want and the results, and then selecting the rows from the database that meet particular criteria. These actions in turn are translated into SQL commands. Figure 6.8 illustrates how the same query as the SQL query to select parts and suppliers would be constructed using the Microsoft query-building tools.

FIGURE 6.6   ACCESS DATA DICTIONARY FEATURES

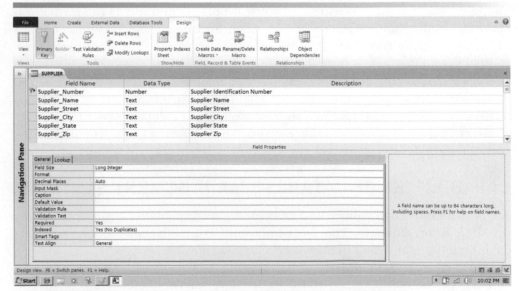

Microsoft Access has a rudimentary data dictionary capability that displays information about the size, format, and other characteristics of each field in a database. Displayed here is the information maintained in the SUPPLIER table. The small key icon to the left of Supplier_Number indicates that it is a key field.

FIGURE 6.7   EXAMPLE OF AN SQL QUERY

```
SELECT PART.Part_Number, PART.Part_Name, SUPPLIER.Supplier_Number,
SUPPLIER.Supplier_Name
FROM PART, SUPPLIER
WHERE PART.Supplier_Number = SUPPLIER.Supplier_Number AND
Part_Number = 137 OR Part_Number = 150;
```

Illustrated here are the SQL statements for a query to select suppliers for parts 137 or 150.
They produce a list with the same results as Figure 6.5.

Microsoft Access and other DBMS include capabilities for report generation so that the data of interest can be displayed in a more structured and polished format than would be possible just by querying. Crystal Reports is a popular report generator for large corporate DBMS, although it can also be used with Access. Access also has capabilities for developing desktop system applications. These include tools for creating data entry screens, reports, and developing the logic for processing transactions.

DESIGNING DATABASES

To create a database, you must understand the relationships among the data, the type of data that will be maintained in the database, how the data will be used, and how the organization will need to change to manage data from a company-wide perspective. The database requires both a conceptual design and a physical design. The conceptual, or logical, design of a database is an abstract model of the database from a business perspective, whereas the physical design shows how the database is actually arranged on direct-access storage devices.

FIGURE 6.8   AN ACCESS QUERY

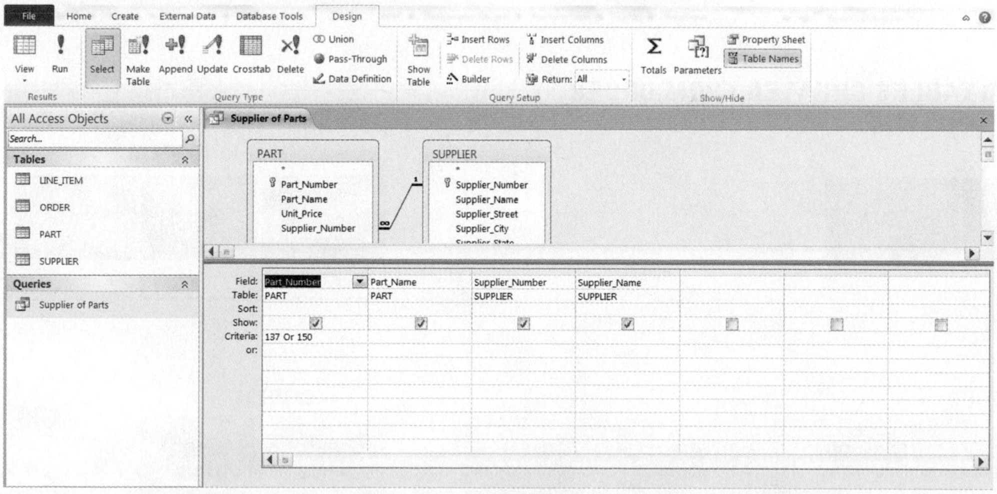

Illustrated here is how the query in Figure 6.7 would be constructed using Microsoft Access query-building tools. It shows the tables, fields, and selection criteria used for the query.

FIGURE 6.9 AN UNNORMALIZED RELATION FOR ORDER

ORDER (Before Normalization)

| Order_ Number | Order_ Date | Part_ Number | Part_ Name | Unit_ Price | Part_ Quantity | Supplier_ Number | Supplier_ Name | Supplier_ Street | Supplier_ City | Supplier_ State | Supplier_ Zip |

An unnormalized relation contains repeating groups. For example, there can be many parts and suppliers for each order. There is only a one-to-one correspondence between Order_Number and Order_Date.

Normalization and Entity-Relationship Diagrams

The conceptual database design describes how the data elements in the database are to be grouped. The design process identifies relationships among data elements and the most efficient way of grouping data elements together to meet business information requirements. The process also identifies redundant data elements and the groupings of data elements required for specific application programs. Groups of data are organized, refined, and streamlined until an overall logical view of the relationships among all the data in the database emerges.

To use a relational database model effectively, complex groupings of data must be streamlined to minimize redundant data elements and awkward many-to-many relationships. The process of creating small, stable, yet flexible and adaptive data structures from complex groups of data is called **normalization**. Figures 6.9 and 6.10 illustrate this process.

In the particular business modeled here, an order can have more than one part but each part is provided by only one supplier. If we build a relation called ORDER with all the fields included here, we would have to repeat the name and address of the supplier for every part on the order, even though the order is for parts from a single supplier. This relationship contains what are called repeating data groups because there can be many parts on a single order to a given supplier. A more efficient way to arrange the data is to break down ORDER into smaller relations, each of which describes a single entity. If we go step by step and normalize the relation ORDER, we emerge with the relations illustrated in Figure 6.10. You can find out more about normalization,

FIGURE 6.10 NORMALIZED TABLES CREATED FROM ORDER

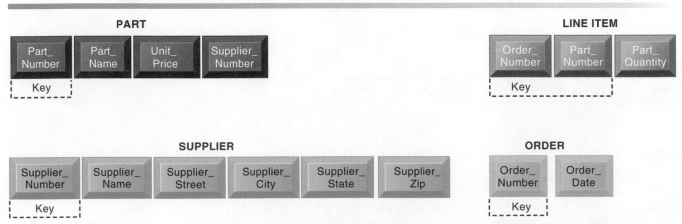

PART

| Part_ Number | Part_ Name | Unit_ Price | Supplier_ Number |

Key

LINE ITEM

| Order_ Number | Part_ Number | Part_ Quantity |

Key

SUPPLIER

| Supplier_ Number | Supplier_ Name | Supplier_ Street | Supplier_ City | Supplier_ State | Supplier_ Zip |

Key

ORDER

| Order_ Number | Order_ Date |

Key

After normalization, the original relation ORDER has been broken down into four smaller relations. The relation ORDER is left with only two attributes and the relation LINE_ITEM has a combined, or concatenated, key consisting of Order_Number and Part_Number.

entity-relationship diagramming, and database design in the Learning Tracks for this chapter.

Relational database systems try to enforce **referential integrity** rules to ensure that relationships between coupled tables remain consistent. When one table has a foreign key that points to another table, you may not add a record to the table with the foreign key unless there is a corresponding record in the linked table. In the database we examined earlier in this chapter, the foreign key Supplier_Number links the PART table to the SUPPLIER table. We may not add a new record to the PART table for a part with Supplier_Number 8266 unless there is a corresponding record in the SUPPLIER table for Supplier_Number 8266. We must also delete the corresponding record in the PART table if we delete the record in the SUPPLIER table for Supplier_Number 8266. In other words, we shouldn't have parts from nonexistent suppliers!

Database designers document their data model with an **entity-relationship diagram**, illustrated in Figure 6.11. This diagram illustrates the relationship between the entities SUPPLIER, PART, LINE_ITEM, and ORDER. The boxes represent entities. The lines connecting the boxes represent relationships. A line connecting two entities that ends in two short marks designates a one-to-one relationship. A line connecting two entities that ends with a crow's foot topped by a short mark indicates a one-to-many relationship. Figure 6.11 shows that one ORDER can contain many LINE_ITEMs. (A PART can be ordered many times and appear many times as a line item in a single order.) Each PART can have only one SUPPLIER, but many PARTs can be provided by the same SUPPLIER.

It can't be emphasized enough: If the business doesn't get its data model right, the system won't be able to serve the business well. The company's systems will not be as effective as they could be because they'll have to work with data that may be inaccurate, incomplete, or difficult to retrieve. Understanding the organization's data and how they should be represented in a database is perhaps the most important lesson you can learn from this course.

For example, Famous Footwear, a shoe store chain with more than 800 locations in 49 states, could not achieve its goal of having "the right style of shoe in the right store for sale at the right price" because its database was not properly designed for rapidly adjusting store inventory. The company had an Oracle relational database running on a midrange computer, but the database was designed primarily for producing standard reports for management rather than for reacting to marketplace changes. Management could not obtain precise data on specific items in inventory in each of its stores. The company had to work around this problem by building a new database where the sales and inventory data could be better organized for analysis and inventory management.

FIGURE 6.11 AN ENTITY-RELATIONSHIP DIAGRAM

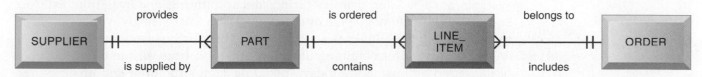

This diagram shows the relationships between the entities SUPPLIER, PART, LINE_ITEM, and ORDER that might be used to model the database in Figure 6.10.

6.3 USING DATABASES TO IMPROVE BUSINESS PERFORMANCE AND DECISION MAKING

Businesses use their databases to keep track of basic transactions, such as paying suppliers, processing orders, keeping track of customers, and paying employees. But they also need databases to provide information that will help the company run the business more efficiently, and help managers and employees make better decisions. If a company wants to know which product is the most popular or who is its most profitable customer, the answer lies in the data.

THE CHALLENGE OF BIG DATA

Up until about five years ago, most data collected by organizations consisted of transaction data that could easily fit into rows and columns of relational database management systems. Since then, there has been an explosion of data from Web traffic, e-mail messages, and social media content (tweets, status messages), as well as machine-generated data from sensors (used in smart meters, manufacturing sensors, and electrical meters) or from electronic trading systems. These data may be unstructured or semi-structured and thus not suitable for relational database products that organize data in the form of columns and rows. We now use the term **big data** to describe these datasets with volumes so huge that they are beyond the ability of typical DBMS to capture, store, and analyze.

Big data doesn't refer to any specific quantity, but usually refers to data in the petabyte and exabyte range—in other words, billions to trillions of records, all from different sources. Big data are produced in much larger quantities and much more rapidly than traditional data. For example, a single jet engine is capable of generating 10 terabytes of data in just 30 minutes, and there are more than 25,000 airline flights each day. Even though "tweets" are limited to 140 characters each, Twitter generates over 8 terabytes of data daily. According to the International Data Center (IDC) technology research firm, data are more than doubling every two years, so the amount of data available to organizations is skyrocketing.

Businesses are interested in big data because they can reveal more patterns and interesting anomalies than smaller data sets, with the potential to provide new insights into customer behavior, weather patterns, financial market activity, or other phenomena. However, to derive business value from these data, organizations need new technologies and tools capable of managing and analyzing non-traditional data along with their traditional enterprise data.

BUSINESS INTELLIGENCE INFRASTRUCTURE

Suppose you wanted concise, reliable information about current operations, trends, and changes across the entire company. If you worked in a large company, the data you need might have to be pieced together from separate systems, such as sales, manufacturing, and accounting, and even from external sources, such as demographic or competitor data. Increasingly, you might need to use big data. A contemporary infrastructure for business intelligence has an array of tools for obtaining useful information from all the different types of data used by businesses today, including semi-structured and unstructured big data in vast quantities. These capabilities include data warehouses and data marts, Hadoop, in-memory computing, and analytical platforms.

Data Warehouses and Data Marts

The traditional tool for analyzing corporate data for the past two decades has been the data warehouse. A **data warehouse** is a database that stores current and historical data of potential interest to decision makers throughout the company. The data originate in many core operational transaction systems, such as systems for sales, customer accounts, and manufacturing, and may include data from Web site transactions. The data warehouse extracts current and historical data from multiple operational systems inside the organization. These data are combined with data from external sources and transformed by correcting inaccurate and incomplete data and restructuring the data for management reporting and analysis before being loaded into the data warehouse.

The data warehouse makes the data available for anyone to access as needed, but it cannot be altered. A data warehouse system also provides a range of ad hoc and standardized query tools, analytical tools, and graphical reporting facilities .

Companies often build enterprise-wide data warehouses, where a central data warehouse serves the entire organization, or they create smaller, decentralized warehouses called data marts. A **data mart** is a subset of a data warehouse in which a summarized or highly focused portion of the organization's data is placed in a separate database for a specific population of users. For example, a company might develop marketing and sales data marts to deal with customer information. Bookseller Barnes & Noble used to maintain a series of data marts—one for point-of-sale data in retail stores, another for college bookstore sales, and a third for online sales.

Hadoop

Relational DBMS and data warehouse products are not well-suited for organizing and analyzing big data or data that do not easily fit into columns and rows used in their data models. For handling unstructured and semi-structured data in vast quantities, as well as structured data, organizations are using **Hadoop**. Hadoop is an open source software framework managed by the Apache Software Foundation that enables distributed parallel processing of huge amounts of data across inexpensive computers. It breaks a big data problem down into sub-problems, distributes them among up to thousands of inexpensive computer processing nodes, and then combines the result into a smaller data set that is easier to analyze. You've probably used Hadoop to find the best airfare on the Internet, get directions to a restaurant, do a search on Google, or connect with a friend on Facebook.

Hadoop consists of several key services: the Hadoop Distributed File System (HDFS) for data storage and MapReduce for high-performance parallel data processing. HDFS links together the file systems on the numerous nodes in a Hadoop cluster to turn them into one big file system. Hadoop's MapReduce was inspired by Google's MapReduce system for breaking down processing of huge datasets and assigning work to the various nodes in a cluster. HBase, Hadoop's non-relational database, provides rapid access to the data stored on HDFS and a transactional platform for running high-scale real-time applications.

Hadoop can process large quantities of any kind of data, including structured transactional data, loosely structured data such as Facebook and Twitter feeds, complex data such as Web server log files, and unstructured audio and video data. Hadoop runs on a cluster of inexpensive servers, and processors can be added or removed as needed. Companies use Hadoop for analyzing very large volumes of data as well as for a staging area for unstructured and semi-structured data before they are loaded into a data warehouse. Facebook stores much of its data on its massive Hadoop cluster, which holds an estimated 100 petabytes, about 10,000 times more information than the Library of Congress. Yahoo uses Hadoop to track user behavior so it can modify its home page to fit their interests. Life sciences research firm NextBio uses Hadoop and HBase to process data for pharmaceutical companies conducting genomic research. Top database vendors such as IBM, Hewlett-Packard, Oracle, and Microsoft have their own Hadoop software distributions. Other vendors offer tools for moving data into and out of Hadoop or for analyzing data within Hadoop.

In-Memory Computing

Another way of facilitating big data analysis is to use **in-memory computing**, which relies primarily on a computer's main memory (RAM) for data storage. (Conventional DBMS use disk storage systems.) Users access data stored in system primary memory, thereby eliminating bottlenecks from retrieving and reading data in a traditional, disk-based database and dramatically shortening query response times. In-memory processing makes it possible for very large sets of data, amounting to the size of a data mart or small data warehouse, to reside entirely in memory. Complex business calculations that used to take hours or days are able to be completed within seconds, and this can even be accomplished on handheld devices.

The previous chapter describes some of the advances in contemporary computer hardware technology that make in-memory processing possible, such as powerful high-speed processors, multicore processing, and falling computer memory prices. These technologies help companies optimize the use of memory and accelerate processing performance while lowering costs.

Leading commercial products for in-memory computing include SAP's High Performance Analytics Appliance (HANA) and Oracle Exalytics. Each provides a set of integrated software components, including in-memory database software and specialized analytics software, that run on hardware optimized for in-memory computing work.

Centrica, a gas and electric utility, uses HANA to quickly capture and analyze the vast amounts of data generated by smart meters. The company is able to analyze usage every 15 minutes, giving it a much clearer picture of usage by neighborhood, home size, type of business served, or building type. HANA also helps Centrica show its customers their energy usage patterns in real-time using online and mobile tools.

Analytic Platforms

Commercial database vendors have developed specialized high-speed **analytic platforms** using both relational and non-relational technology that are optimized for analyzing large datasets. These analytic platforms, such as IBM Netezza and Oracle Exadata, feature preconfigured hardware-software systems that are specifically designed for query processing and analytics. For example, IBM Netezza features tightly integrated database, server, and storage components that handle complex analytic queries 10 to 100 times faster than traditional systems. Analytic platforms also include in-memory systems and NoSQL non-relational database management systems.

Figure 6.12 illustrates a contemporary business intelligence infrastructure using the technologies we have just described. Current and historical data are extracted from multiple operational systems along with Web data, machine-generated data, unstructured audio/visual data, and data from external sources

FIGURE 6.12 COMPONENTS OF A DATA WAREHOUSE

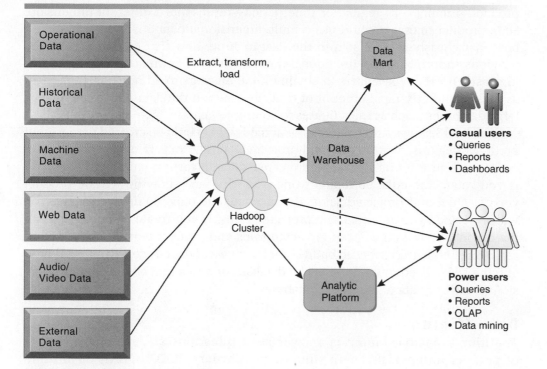

A contemporary business intelligence infrastructure features capabilities and tools to manage and analyze large quantities and different types of data from multiple sources. Easy-to-use query and reporting tools for casual business users and more sophisticated analytical toolsets for power users are included.

that's been restructured and reorganized for reporting and analysis. Hadoop clusters pre-process big data for use in the data warehouse, data marts, or an analytic platform, or for direct querying by power users. Outputs include reports and dashboards as well as query results. Chapter 12 discusses the various types of BI users and BI reporting in greater detail.

ANALYTICAL TOOLS: RELATIONSHIPS, PATTERNS, TRENDS

Once data have been captured and organized using the business intelligence technologies we have just described, they are available for further analysis using software for database querying and reporting, multidimensional data analysis (OLAP), and data mining. This section will introduce you to these tools, with more detail about business intelligence analytics and applications in Chapter 12.

Online Analytical Processing (OLAP)

Suppose your company sells four different products—nuts, bolts, washers, and screws—in the East, West, and Central regions. If you wanted to ask a fairly straightforward question, such as how many washers sold during the past quarter, you could easily find the answer by querying your sales database. But what if you wanted to know how many washers sold in each of your sales regions and compare actual results with projected sales?

To obtain the answer, you would need **online analytical processing (OLAP)**. OLAP supports multidimensional data analysis, enabling users to view the same data in different ways using multiple dimensions. Each aspect of information—product, pricing, cost, region, or time period—represents a different dimension. So, a product manager could use a multidimensional data analysis tool to learn how many washers were sold in the East in June, how that compares with the previous month and the previous June, and how it compares with the sales forecast. OLAP enables users to obtain online answers to ad hoc questions such as these in a fairly rapid amount of time, even when the data are stored in very large databases, such as sales figures for multiple years.

Figure 6.13 shows a multidimensional model that could be created to represent products, regions, actual sales, and projected sales. A matrix of actual sales can be stacked on top of a matrix of projected sales to form a cube with six faces. If you rotate the cube 90 degrees one way, the face showing will be product versus actual and projected sales. If you rotate the cube 90 degrees again, you will see region versus actual and projected sales. If you rotate 180 degrees from the original view, you will see projected sales and product versus region. Cubes can be nested within cubes to build complex views of data. A company would use either a specialized multidimensional database or a tool that creates multidimensional views of data in relational databases.

Data Mining

Traditional database queries answer such questions as, "How many units of product number 403 were shipped in February 2013?" OLAP, or multidimensional analysis, supports much more complex requests for information, such as, "Compare sales of product 403 relative to plan by quarter and sales region for the past two years." With OLAP and query-oriented data analysis, users need to have a good idea about the information for which they are looking.

Data mining is more discovery-driven. Data mining provides insights into corporate data that cannot be obtained with OLAP by finding hidden patterns and relationships in large databases and inferring rules from them to predict future behavior. The patterns and rules are used to guide decision making and forecast

FIGURE 6.13   MULTIDIMENSIONAL DATA MODEL

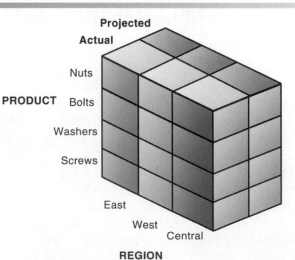

This view shows product versus region. If you rotate the cube 90 degrees, the face that will show is product versus actual and projected sales. If you rotate the cube 90 degrees again, you will see region versus actual and projected sales. Other views are possible.

the effect of those decisions. The types of information obtainable from data mining include associations, sequences, classifications, clusters, and forecasts.

- *Associations* are occurrences linked to a single event. For instance, a study of supermarket purchasing patterns might reveal that, when corn chips are purchased, a cola drink is purchased 65 percent of the time, but when there is a promotion, cola is purchased 85 percent of the time. This information helps managers make better decisions because they have learned the profitability of a promotion.

- In *sequences*, events are linked over time. We might find, for example, that if a house is purchased, a new refrigerator will be purchased within two weeks 65 percent of the time, and an oven will be bought within one month of the home purchase 45 percent of the time.

- *Classification* recognizes patterns that describe the group to which an item belongs by examining existing items that have been classified and by inferring a set of rules. For example, businesses such as credit card or telephone companies worry about the loss of steady customers. Classification helps discover the characteristics of customers who are likely to leave and can provide a model to help managers predict who those customers are so that the managers can devise special campaigns to retain such customers.

- *Clustering* works in a manner similar to classification when no groups have yet been defined. A data mining tool can discover different groupings within data, such as finding affinity groups for bank cards or partitioning a database into groups of customers based on demographics and types of personal investments.

- Although these applications involve predictions, *forecasting* uses predictions in a different way. It uses a series of existing values to forecast what other values will be. For example, forecasting might find patterns in data to help managers estimate the future value of continuous variables, such as sales figures.

These systems perform high-level analyses of patterns or trends, but they can also drill down to provide more detail when needed. There are data mining applications for all the functional areas of business, and for government and scientific work. One popular use for data mining is to provide detailed analyses of patterns in customer data for one-to-one marketing campaigns or for identifying profitable customers.

Caesars Entertainment, formerly known as Harrah's Entertainment, is the largest gaming company in the world. It continually analyzes data about its customers gathered when people play its slot machines or use its casinos and hotels. The corporate marketing department uses this information to build a detailed gambling profile, based on a particular customer's ongoing value to the company. For instance, data mining lets Caesars know the favorite gaming experience of a regular customer at one of its riverboat casinos, along with that person's preferences for room accommodations, restaurants, and entertainment. This information guides management decisions about how to cultivate the most profitable customers, encourage those customers to spend more, and attract more customers with high revenue-generating potential. Business intelligence improved Caesars's profits so much that it became the centerpiece of the firm's business strategy.

Text Mining and Web Mining

However, unstructured data, most in the form of text files, is believed to account for over 80 percent of useful organizational information and is one of the major sources of big data that firms want to analyze. E-mail, memos, call center transcripts, survey responses, legal cases, patent descriptions, and service reports are all valuable for finding patterns and trends that will help employees make better business decisions. **Text mining** tools are now available to help businesses analyze these data. These tools are able to extract key elements from unstructured big data sets, discover patterns and relationships, and summarize the information.

Businesses might turn to text mining to analyze transcripts of calls to customer service centers to identify major service and repair issues or to measure customer sentiment about their company. **Sentiment analysis** software is able to mine text comments in an e-mail message, blog, social media conversation, or survey form to detect favorable and unfavorable opinions about specific subjects.

For example, the discount broker Charles Schwab uses Attensity Analyze software to analyze hundreds of thousands of its customer interactions each month. The software analyzes Schwab's customer service notes, e-mails, survey responses, and online discussions to discover signs of dissatisfaction that might cause a customer to stop using the company's services. Attensity is able to automatically identify the various "voices" customers use to express their feedback (such as a positive, negative, or conditional voice) to pinpoint a person's intent to buy, intent to leave, or reaction to a specific product or marketing message. Schwab uses this information to take corrective actions such as stepping up direct broker communication with the customer and trying to quickly resolve the problems that are making the customer unhappy.

The Web is another rich source of unstructured big data for revealing patterns, trends, and insights into customer behavior. The discovery and analysis of useful patterns and information from the World Wide Web is called **Web mining**. Businesses might turn to Web mining to help them understand customer behavior, evaluate the effectiveness of a particular Web site, or quantify the success of a marketing campaign. For instance, marketers use the Google Trends and Google Insights for Search services, which track the popularity of various words and phrases used in Google search queries, to learn what people are interested in and what they are interested in buying.

Web mining looks for patterns in data through content mining, structure mining, and usage mining. Web content mining is the process of extracting knowledge from the content of Web pages, which may include text, image, audio, and video data. Web structure mining examines data related to the structure of a particular Web site. For example, links pointing to a document indicate the popularity of the document, while links coming out of a document indicate the richness or perhaps the variety of topics covered in the document. Web usage mining examines user interaction data recorded by a Web server whenever requests for a Web site's resources are received. The usage data records the user's behavior when the user browses or makes transactions on the Web site and collects the data in a server log. Analyzing such data can help companies determine the value of particular customers, cross marketing strategies across products, and the effectiveness of promotional campaigns.

The Interactive Session on Technology describes organizations' experiences as they use the analytical tools and business intelligence technologies we have described to grapple with "big data" challenges.

INTERACTIVE SESSION: TECHNOLOGY

BIG DATA, BIG REWARDS

Today's companies are dealing with an avalanche of data from social media, search, and sensors as well as from traditional sources. In 2012, the amount of digital information generated is expected to reach 988 exabytes, which is the equivalent to a stack of books from the sun to the planet Pluto and back. Making sense of "big data" has become one of the primary challenges for corporations of all shapes and sizes, but it also represents new opportunities. How are companies currently taking advantage of big data opportunities?

The British Library had to adapt to handle big data. Every year visitors to the British Library Web site perform over 6 billion searches, and the library is also responsible for preserving British Web sites that no longer exist but need to be preserved for historical purposes, such as the Web sites for past politicians. Traditional data management methods proved inadequate to archive millions of these Web pages, and legacy analytics tools couldn't extract useful knowledge from such quantities of data. So the British Library partnered with IBM to implement a big data solution to these challenges. IBM BigSheets is an insight engine that helps extract, annotate, and visually analyze vast amounts of unstructured Web data, delivering the results via a Web browser. For example, users can see search results in a pie chart. IBM BigSheets is built atop the Hadoop framework, so it can process large amounts of data quickly and efficiently.

State and federal law enforcement agencies are analyzing big data to discover hidden patterns in criminal activity such as correlations between time, opportunity, and organizations, or non-obvious relationships (see Chapter 4) between individuals and criminal organizations that would be difficult to uncover in smaller data sets. Criminals and criminal organizations are increasingly using the Internet to coordinate and perpetrate their crimes. New tools allow agencies to analyze data from a wide array of sources and apply analytics to predict future crime patterns. This means that law enforcement can become more proactive in its efforts to fight crime and stop it before it occurs.

In New York City, the Real Time Crime Center data warehouse contains millions of data points on city crime and criminals. IBM and the New York City Police Department (NYPD) worked together to create the warehouse, which contains data on over 120 million criminal complaints, 31 million national crime records, and 33 billion public records. The system's search capabilities allow the NYPD to quickly obtain data from any of these data sources. Information on criminals, such as a suspect's photo with details of past offenses or addresses with maps, can be visualized in seconds on a video wall or instantly relayed to officers at a crime scene.

Other organizations are using the data to go green, or, in the case of Vestas, to go even greener. Headquartered in Denmark, Vestas is the world's largest wind energy company, with over 43,000 wind turbines across 66 countries. Location data are important to Vestas so that it can accurately place its turbines for optimal wind power generation. Areas without enough wind will not generate the necessary power, but areas with too much wind may damage the turbines. Vestas relies on location-based data to determine the best spots to install their turbines.

To gather data on prospective turbine locations, Vestas's wind library combines data from global weather systems along with data from existing turbines. The company's previous wind library provided information in a grid pattern, with each grid measuring 27 x 27 kilometers (17 x 17 miles). Vestas engineers were able to bring the resolution down to about 10 x 10 meters (32 x 32 feet) to establish the exact wind flow pattern at a particular location. To further increase the accuracy of its turbine placement models, Vestas needed to shrink the grid area even more, and this required 10 times as much data as the previous system and a more powerful data management platform.

The company implemented a solution consisting of IBM InfoSphere BigInsights software running on a high-performance IBM System x iDataPlex server. (InfoSphere BigInsights is a set of software tools for big data analysis and visualization, and is powered by Apache Hadoop.) Using these technologies, Vestas increased the size of its wind library and is able manage and analyze location and weather data with models that are much more powerful and precise.

Vestas's wind library currently stores 2.8 petabytes of data and includes approximately 178 parameters, such as barometric pressure, humidity, wind direction, temperature, wind velocity, and other company historical data. Vestas plans to add global deforestation metrics, satellite images, geospatial data, and data on phases of the moon and tides.

The company can now reduce the resolution of its wind data grids by nearly 90 percent, down to a 3 x 3 kilometer area (about 1.8 x 1.8 miles). This capability enables Vestas to forecast optimal turbine placement in 15 minutes instead of three weeks, saving a month of development time for a turbine site and enabling Vestas customers to achieve a return on investment much more quickly.

Companies are also using big data solutions to analyze consumer sentiment. For example, car-rental giant Hertz gathers data from Web surveys, e-mails, text messages, Web site traffic patterns, and data generated at all of Hertz's 8,300 locations in 146 countries. The company now stores all of that data centrally instead of within each branch, reducing time spent processing data and improving company response time to customer feedback and changes in sentiment. For example, by analyzing data generated from multiple sources, Hertz was able to determine that delays were occurring for returns in Philadelphia during specific times of the day. After

investigating this anomaly, the company was able to quickly adjust staffing levels at its Philadelphia office during those peak times, ensuring a manager was present to resolve any issues. This enhanced Hertz's performance and increased customer satisfaction.

There are limits to using big data. Swimming in numbers doesn't necessarily mean that the right information is being collected or that people will make smarter decisions. Last year, a McKinsey Global Institute report cautioned there is a shortage of specialists who can make sense of all the information being generated. Nevertheless, the trend towards big data shows no sign of slowing down; in fact, it's much more likely that big data is only going to get bigger.

Sources: Samuel Greengard," Big Data Unlocks Business Value," Baseline, January 2012; Paul S. Barth, "Managing Big Data: What Every CIO Needs to Know," *CIO Insight*, January 12, 2012; IBM Corporation, "Vestas: Turning Climate into Capital with Big Data," 2011; IBM Corporation, "Extending and enhancing law enforcement capabilities," "How Big Data Is Giving Hertz a Big Advantage," and "British Library and J Start Team Up to Archive the Web," 2010.

CASE STUDY QUESTIONS

1. Describe the kinds of big data collected by the organizations described in this case.

2. List and describe the business intelligence technologies described in this case.

3. Why did the companies described in this case need to maintain and analyze big data? What business benefits did they obtain?

4. Identify three decisions that were improved by using big data.

5. What kinds of organizations are most likely to need big data management and analytical tools? Why?

DATABASES AND THE WEB

Have you ever tried to use the Web to place an order or view a product catalog? If so, you were probably using a Web site linked to an internal corporate database. Many companies now use the Web to make some of the information in their internal databases available to customers and business partners.

Suppose, for example, a customer with a Web browser wants to search an online retailer's database for pricing information. Figure 6.14 illustrates how that customer might access the retailer's internal database over the Web. The user accesses the retailer's Web site over the Internet using Web browser software on his or her client PC. The user's Web browser software requests data from the organization's database, using HTML commands to communicate with the Web server.

Because many back-end databases cannot interpret commands written in HTML, the Web server passes these requests for data to software that translates HTML commands into SQL so the commands can be processed by the DBMS working with the database. In a client/server environment, the

FIGURE 6.14 LINKING INTERNAL DATABASES TO THE WEB

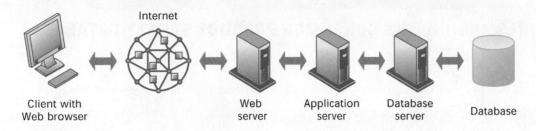

Users access an organization's internal database through the Web using their desktop PCs and Web browser software.

DBMS resides on a dedicated computer called a **database server**. The DBMS receives the SQL requests and provides the required data. Middleware transfers information from the organization's internal database back to the Web server for delivery in the form of a Web page to the user.

Figure 6.14 shows that the middleware working between the Web server and the DBMS is an application server running on its own dedicated computer (see Chapter 5). The application server software handles all application operations, including transaction processing and data access, between browser-based computers and a company's back-end business applications or databases. The application server takes requests from the Web server, runs the business logic to process transactions based on those requests, and provides connectivity to the organization's back-end systems or databases. Alternatively, the software for handling these operations could be a custom program or a CGI script. A CGI script is a compact program using the *Common Gateway Interface (CGI)* specification for processing data on a Web server.

There are a number of advantages to using the Web to access an organization's internal databases. First, Web browser software is much easier to use than proprietary query tools. Second, the Web interface requires few or no changes to the internal database. It costs much less to add a Web interface in front of a legacy system than to redesign and rebuild the system to improve user access.

Accessing corporate databases through the Web is creating new efficiencies, opportunities, and business models. ThomasNet.com provides an up-to-date online directory of more than 650,000 suppliers of industrial products, such as chemicals, metals, plastics, rubber, and automotive equipment. Formerly called Thomas Register, the company used to send out huge paper catalogs with this information. Now it provides this information to users online via its Web site and has become a smaller, leaner company.

Other companies have created entirely new businesses based on access to large databases through the Web. One is the social networking service Facebook, which helps users stay connected with each other and meet new people. Facebook features "profiles" with information on more than 950 million active users with information about themselves, including interests, friends, photos, and groups with which they are affiliated. Facebook maintains a massive database to house and manage all of this content.

There are also many Web-enabled databases in the public sector to help consumers and citizens access helpful information. The Interactive Session on Organizations describes one of these databases, which has generated controversy over its methods for providing consumer product safety data.

INTERACTIVE SESSION: ORGANIZATIONS

CONTROVERSY WHIRLS AROUND THE CONSUMER PRODUCT SAFETY DATABASE

Michele Witte was one of dozens of parents who lost their children because of the defective design of drop-side cribs. In 1997, Witte's 10-month-old son Tyler perished when the drop-side rail on his crib came loose, partially detached, and then trapped his neck between the rail and the headboard. The cribs are now banned. Witte wishes that a public information resource for consumer complaints had been available prior to the death of her child. Reading other parents' horror stories might have dissuaded her from purchasing a drop-side crib.

In March 2011, the U.S. Consumer Product Safety Commission (CPSC) stood poised to meet the needs of parents like Witte by launching an online database, located at www.saferproducts.gov. The database will provide the public with access to the full repository of product safety complaints that it has received. Users can submit these complaints online directly into the database. Visitors to the database will be able to search for products, read other complaints, and view safety warnings issued by the CPSC. Complaints in the database will include a description of product, the harm or risk from the product, the name of the manufacturer, contact information, and an affirmation that the submitter is telling the truth. The submitter's name will not appear in the database but could be provided to manufacturers if the submitter agreed.

Consumer advocates such as the Consumer Federation of America are praising the database as a revolutionary resource that will drastically improve the way consumers buy products. However, manufacturing companies and many members of Congress are in opposition. They argue that because any user can submit a complaint, the database will be filled with inaccurate and misleading information—"fictitious slams" against products. It will also be open to abuse from customers with an axe to grind, or trial lawyers seeking to tarnish a product or manufacturer's reputation for personal gain.

The database represents an increase in visibility and authority for the CPSC, which was formed in 1972 by the Consumer Product Safety Act. The role of the CPSC is to regulate thousands of different types of products, with special focus on those that are not regulated by other areas of the government already, like food, firearms, and automobiles. (The CPSC database does not include safety problems with these products.)

The CPSC collects reports on defective products from consumers, health care providers, death certificates, media accounts, and other sources. It uses that information to make decisions on product recalls and bans, but until recently, very little of that information was accessible to the public. Federal law formerly required the approval of manufacturers to publicize that information, and manufacturers weren't eager to release information about their faulty products. Not only that, but the CPSC had to negotiate directly with manufacturers to determine the terms of product recalls. Because this process usually takes a year or more, consumers continue to buy shoddy and perhaps dangerous products like drop-side cribs in the interim.

Under the new system, complaints filed by consumers will be posted online and be available to the public within 15 days. Companies will be notified within 5 days when complaints are made about their products, and the CPSC will give them 10 days to respond publicly and have their comments published alongside the complaints in the database. Users will have the option for their comments to remain confidential if they prefer. Manufacturers will be able to appeal to the CPSC to eliminate false or misleading complaints, and complaints will be limited to defects that can cause injury, not reliability or product quality.

At a time when the federal budget is under increased scrutiny, programs like the CPSC database have become targets for cost-cutting, and manufacturers have seized an opportunity to stop the database in its tracks. The law gave CPSC new authority to regulate unsafe products but businesses say it is overly burdensome. A House Energy and Commerce subcommittee is considering draft legislation to restrict who can submit reports to the database, to improve how products are identified, and to resolve claims that reports are inaccurate.

Despite strong opposition from manufacturers and others, in March 2011, the site was launched to generally positive reviews. The CPSC provided additional features, like the ability to attach images to comments. Commenters must provide their name, mailing address, telephone number, and e-mail address, which is expected to curtail the types of anonymous comments that manufacturers fear. Even so, keeping the database free of inaccurate reports is likely to require more time and hours than the CPSC staff will be able to provide.

Since the database went live, there have been hundreds of thousands of visits to the site and millions of product searches conducted by visitors, according to the Consumer Product Safety commission. Despite its growing popularity, it may not survive congressional attempts to take away its funding, in response to pressures to reduce the federal budget as well as crit-

icism from the business community. Time will tell whether saferproducts.gov becomes an indispensable consumer resource.

Sources: www.SaferProducts.gov, accessed May 22, 2012; Josh Cable, "Democrats Defend Consumer Product Safety Database," *Industry Week,* July 7, 2011; Don Mays, "My Experience With the CPSC Database," blogs.consumerreports.com, March 16, 2011; Andrew Martin, "Child-Product Makers Seek to Soften New Rules," *The New York Times,* February 21, 2011; Lyndsey Layton, "Consumer Product Safety Commission to Launch Public Database of Complaints," *Washington Post,* January 10, 2011; Jayne O'Donnell, "Product-Safety Database Under Multiple Attacks," *USA Today,* April 12, 2011.

CASE STUDY QUESTIONS

1. What is the value of the CPSC database to consumers, businesses, and the U.S. government?

2. What problems are raised by this database? Why is it so controversial? Why is data quality an issue?

3. Name two entities in the CPSC database and describe some of their attributes.

4. When buying a crib, or other consumer product for your family, would you use this database? Why or why not?

6.4 MANAGING DATA RESOURCES

Setting up a database is only a start. In order to make sure that the data for your business remain accurate, reliable, and readily available to those who need it, your business will need special policies and procedures for data management.

ESTABLISHING AN INFORMATION POLICY

Every business, large and small, needs an information policy. Your firm's data are an important resource, and you don't want people doing whatever they want with them. You need to have rules on how the data are to be organized and maintained, and who is allowed to view the data or change them.

An **information policy** specifies the organization's rules for sharing, disseminating, acquiring, standardizing, classifying, and inventorying information. Information policy lays out specific procedures and accountabilities, identifying which users and organizational units can share information, where information can be distributed, and who is responsible for updating and maintaining the information. For example, a typical information policy would specify that only selected members of the payroll and human resources department would have the right to change and view sensitive employee data, such as an employee's salary or social security number, and that these departments are responsible for making sure that such employee data are accurate.

If you are in a small business, the information policy would be established and implemented by the owners or managers. In a large organization, managing and planning for information as a corporate resource often requires a formal data administration function. **Data administration** is responsible for the specific policies and procedures through which data can be managed as an organizational resource. These responsibilities include developing information policy, planning for data, overseeing logical database design and data dictionary development, and monitoring how information systems specialists and end-user groups use data.

You may hear the term **data governance** used to describe many of these activities. Promoted by IBM, data governance deals with the policies and processes for managing the availability, usability, integrity, and security of the data employed in an enterprise, with special emphasis on promoting privacy, security, data quality, and compliance with government regulations.

A large organization will also have a database design and management group within the corporate information systems division that is responsible for defining and organizing the structure and content of the database, and maintaining the database. In close cooperation with users, the design group establishes the physical database, the logical relations among elements, and the access rules and security procedures. The functions it performs are called **database administration**.

ENSURING DATA QUALITY

A well-designed database and information policy will go a long way toward ensuring that the business has the information it needs. However, additional steps must be taken to ensure that the data in organizational databases are accurate and remain reliable.

What would happen if a customer's telephone number or account balance were incorrect? What would be the impact if the database had the wrong price for the product you sold or your sales system and inventory system showed different prices for the same product? Data that are inaccurate, untimely, or inconsistent with other sources of information lead to incorrect decisions, product recalls, and financial losses. Gartner Inc. reported that more than 25 percent of the critical data in large Fortune 1000 companies' databases is inaccurate or incomplete, including bad product codes and product descriptions, faulty inventory descriptions, erroneous financial data, incorrect supplier information, and incorrect employee data. A Sirius Decisions study on "The Impact of Bad Data on Demand Creation" found that 10 to 25 percent of customer and prospect records contain critical data errors. Correcting these errors at their source and following best practices for promoting data quality increased the productivity of the sales process and generated a 66 percent increase in revenue.

Some of these data quality problems are caused by redundant and inconsistent data produced by multiple systems feeding a data warehouse. For example, the sales ordering system and the inventory management system might both maintain data on the organization's products. However, the sales ordering system might use the term *Item Number* and the inventory system might call the same attribute *Product Number*. The sales, inventory, or manufacturing systems of a clothing retailer might use different codes to represent values for an attribute. One system might represent clothing size as "extra large," whereas the other system might use the code "XL" for the same purpose. During the design process for the warehouse database, data describing entities, such as a customer, product, or order, should be named and defined consistently for all business areas using the database.

Think of all the times you've received several pieces of the same direct mail advertising on the same day. This is very likely the result of having your name maintained multiple times in a database. Your name may have been misspelled or you used your middle initial on one occasion and not on another or the information was initially entered onto a paper form and not scanned properly into the system. Because of these inconsistencies, the database would treat you as different people! We often receive redundant mail addressed to Laudon, Lavdon, Lauden, or Landon.

If a database is properly designed and enterprise-wide data standards established, duplicate or inconsistent data elements should be minimal. Most data quality problems, however, such as misspelled names, transposed numbers, or incorrect or missing codes, stem from errors during data input. The incidence of such errors is rising as companies move their businesses to the Web and allow customers and suppliers to enter data into their Web sites that directly update internal systems.

Before a new database is in place, organizations need to identify and correct their faulty data and establish better routines for editing data once their database is in operation. Analysis of data quality often begins with a **data quality audit**, which is a structured survey of the accuracy and level of completeness of the data in an information system. Data quality audits can be performed by surveying entire data files, surveying samples from data files, or surveying end users for their perceptions of data quality.

Data cleansing, also known as *data scrubbing*, consists of activities for detecting and correcting data in a database that are incorrect, incomplete, improperly formatted, or redundant. Data cleansing not only corrects errors but also enforces consistency among different sets of data that originated in separate information systems. Specialized data-cleansing software is available to automatically survey data files, correct errors in the data, and integrate the data in a consistent company-wide format.

Data quality problems are not just business problems. They also pose serious problems for individuals, affecting their financial condition and even their jobs. For example, inaccurate or outdated data about consumers' credit histories maintained by credit bureaus can prevent creditworthy individuals from obtaining loans or lower their chances of finding or keeping a job.

LEARNING TRACK MODULES

The following Learning Tracks provide content relevant to topics covered in this chapter:

1. Database Design, Normalization, and Entity-Relationship Diagramming
2. Introduction to SQL
3. Hierarchical and Network Data Models

Review Summary

1. *What are the problems of managing data resources in a traditional file environment and how are they solved by a database management system?*

    Traditional file management techniques make it difficult for organizations to keep track of all of the pieces of data they use in a systematic way and to organize these data so that they can be easily accessed. Different functional areas and groups were allowed to develop their own files independently. Over time, this traditional file management environment creates problems such as data redundancy and inconsistency, program-data dependence, inflexibility, poor security, and lack of data sharing and availability. A database management system (DBMS) solves these problems with software that permits centralization of data and data management so that businesses have a single consistent source for all their data needs. Using a DBMS minimizes redundant and inconsistent files.

2. *What are the major capabilities of DBMS and why is a relational DBMS so powerful?*

    The principal capabilities of a DBMS includes a data definition capability, a data dictionary capability, and a data manipulation language. The data definition capability specifies the structure and content of the database. The data dictionary is an automated or manual file that stores information about the data in the database, including names, definitions, formats, and descriptions of data elements. The data manipulation language, such as SQL, is a specialized language for accessing and manipulating the data in the database.

    The relational database has been the primary method for organizing and maintaining data in information systems because it is so flexible and accessible. It organizes data in two-dimensional tables called relations with rows and columns. Each table contains data about an entity and its attributes. Each row represents a record and each column represents an attribute or field. Each table also contains a key field to uniquely identify each record for retrieval or manipulation. Relational database tables can be combined easily to deliver data required by users, provided that any two tables share a common data element. Non-relational databases are becoming popular for managing types of data that can't be handled easily by the relational data model. Both relational and non-relational database products are available as cloud computing services.

3. *What are some important database design principles?*

    Designing a database requires both a logical design and a physical design. The logical design models the database from a business perspective. The organization's data model should reflect its key business processes and decision-making requirements. The process of creating small, stable, flexible, and adaptive data structures from complex groups of data when designing a relational database is termed normalization. A well-designed relational database will not have many-to-many relationships, and all attributes for a specific entity will only apply to that entity. It will try to enforce referential integrity rules to ensure that relationships between coupled tables remain consistent. An entity-relationship diagram graphically depicts the relationship between entities (tables) in a relational database.

4. *What are the principal tools and technologies for accessing information from databases to improve business performance and decision making?*

    Contemporary data management technology has an array of tools for obtaining useful information from all the different types of data used by businesses today, including semi-structured and unstructured big data in vast quantities. These capabilities include data warehouses and data marts, Hadoop, in-memory computing, and analytical platforms. OLAP represents relationships among data as a multidimensional structure, which can be visualized as cubes of data and cubes within cubes of data, enabling more sophisticated data analysis. Data mining analyzes large pools of data, including the contents of data warehouses, to find patterns and rules that can be used to predict future behavior and guide decision making. Text mining tools help businesses analyze large unstructured data sets consisting of text. Web mining tools focus on analysis of useful patterns and information from the World Wide Web, examining the structure of Web sites and activities of Web site users as well as the contents of Web pages. Conventional databases can be linked via middleware to the Web or a Web interface to facilitate user access to an organization's internal data.

5. *Why are information policy, data administration, and data quality assurance essential for managing the firm's data resources?*

   Developing a database environment requires policies and procedures for managing organizational data as well as a good data model and database technology. A formal information policy governs the maintenance, distribution, and use of information in the organization. In large corporations, a formal data administration function is responsible for information policy, as well as for data planning, data dictionary development, and monitoring data usage in the firm.

   Data that are inaccurate, incomplete, or inconsistent create serious operational and financial problems for businesses because they may create inaccuracies in product pricing, customer accounts, and inventory data, and lead to inaccurate decisions about the actions that should be taken by the firm. Firms must take special steps to make sure they have a high level of data quality. These include using enterprise-wide data standards, databases designed to minimize inconsistent and redundant data, data quality audits, and data cleansing software.

Key Terms

Analytic platform, 256

Attribute, 241

Big data, 254

Bit, 241

Byte, 241

Data administration, 265

Data cleansing, 267

Data definition, 249

Data dictionary, 249

Data governance, 266

Data inconsistency, 243

Data manipulation language, 250

Data mart, 255

Data mining, 258

Data quality audit, 267

Data redundancy, 243

Data warehouse, 255

Database, 244

Database administration, 266

Database management system (DBMS), 244

Database server, 263

Entity, 241

Entity-relationship diagram, 253

Field, 241

File, 241

Foreign key, 247

Hadoop, 255

In-memory computing, 256

Information policy, 265

Key field, 247

Non-relational database management systems, 247

Normalization, 252

Online analytical processing (OLAP), 257

Primary key, 247

Program-data dependence, 244

Record, 241

Referential integrity, 253

Relational DBMS, 246

Sentiment analysis, 260

Structured Query Language (SQL), 250

Text mining, 260

Tuple, 247

Web mining, 260

Review Questions

1. What are the problems of managing data resources in a traditional file environment and how are they solved by a database management system?

   - List and describe each of the components in the data hierarchy.

   - Define and explain the significance of entities, attributes, and key fields.

   - List and describe the problems of the traditional file environment.

   - Define a database and a database management system and describe how it solves the problems of a traditional file environment.

2. What are the major capabilities of DBMS and why is a relational DBMS so powerful?

   - Name and briefly describe the capabilities of a DBMS.

   - Define a relational DBMS and explain how it organizes data.

- List and describe the three operations of a relational DBMS.
- Explain why non-relational databases are useful.

3. What are some important database design principles?

- Define and describe normalization and referential integrity and explain how they contribute to a well-designed relational database.
- Define and describe an entity-relationship diagram and explain its role in database design.

4. What are the principal tools and technologies for accessing information from databases to improve business performance and decision making?

- Define big data and describe the technologies for managing and analyzing it.
- List and describe the components of a contemporary business intelligence infrastructure.

- Describe the capabilities of online analytical processing (OLAP).
- Define data mining, describing how it differs from OLAP and the types of information it provides.
- Explain how text mining and Web mining differ from conventional data mining.
- Describe how users can access information from a company's internal databases through the Web.

5. Why are information policy, data administration, and data quality assurance essential for managing the firm's data resources?

- Describe the roles of information policy and data administration in information management.
- Explain why data quality audits and data cleansing are essential.

Discussion Questions

1. It has been said there is no bad data, just bad management. Discuss the implications of this statement.

2. To what extent should end users be involved in the selection of a database management system and database design?

3. What are the consequences of an organization not having an information policy?

Hands-On MIS Projects

The projects in this section give you hands-on experience in analyzing data quality problems, establishing company-wide data standards, creating a database for inventory management, and using the Web to search online databases for overseas business resources.

Management Decision Problems

1. Emerson Process Management, a global supplier of measurement, analytical, and monitoring instruments and services based in Austin, Texas, had a new data warehouse designed for analyzing customer activity to improve service and marketing. However, the data warehouse was full of inaccurate and redundant data. The data in the warehouse came from numerous transaction processing systems in Europe, Asia, and other locations around the world. The team that designed the warehouse had assumed that sales groups in all these areas would enter customer names and addresses the same way. In fact, companies in different countries were using multiple ways of entering quote, billing, shipping, and other data. Assess the potential business impact of these data quality problems. What decisions have to be made and steps taken to reach a solution?

2. Your industrial supply company wants to create a data warehouse where management can obtain a single corporate-wide view of critical sales information to identify bestselling products, key customers, and sales trends. Your sales and product information are stored in several different systems: a divisional sales system running on a Unix server and a corporate sales system running on an IBM mainframe. You would like to create a single standard format that consolidates these data from both systems. In MyMISLab, you can review the proposed format, along with sample files from the two systems that would supply the data for the data warehouse. Then answer the following questions:

- What business problems are created by not having these data in a single standard format?

- How easy would it be to create a database with a single standard format that could store the data from both systems? Identify the problems that would have to be addressed.

- Should the problems be solved by database specialists or general business managers? Explain.

- Who should have the authority to finalize a single company-wide format for this information in the data warehouse?

Achieving Operational Excellence: Building a Relational Database for Inventory Management

Software skills: Database design, querying, and reporting
Business skills: Inventory management

In this exercise, you will use database software to design a database for managing inventory for a small business. Sylvester's Bike Shop, located in San Francisco, California, sells road, mountain, hybrid, leisure, and children's bicycles. Currently, Sylvester's purchases bikes from three suppliers, but plans to add new suppliers in the near future. Using the information found in the tables in MyMISLab, build a simple relational database to manage information about Sylvester's suppliers and products. Once you have built the database, perform the following activities.

- Prepare a report that identifies the five most expensive bicycles. The report should list the bicycles in descending order from most expensive to least expensive, the quantity on hand for each, and the markup percentage for each.

- Prepare a report that lists each supplier, its products, the quantities on hand, and associated reorder levels. The report should be sorted alphabetically by supplier. For each supplier, the products should be sorted alphabetically.

- Prepare a report listing only the bicycles that are low in stock and need to be reordered. The report should provide supplier information for the items identified.

- Write a brief description of how the database could be enhanced to further improve management of the business. What tables or fields should be added? What additional reports would be useful?

Improving Decision Making: Searching Online Databases for Overseas Business Resources

Software skills: Online databases
Business skills: Researching services for overseas operations

This project develops skills in searching Web-enabled databases with information about products and services in faraway locations.

Your company is located in Greensboro, North Carolina, and manufactures office furniture of various types. You are considering opening a facility to manufacture and sell your products in Australia. You would like to contact organizations that offer many services necessary for you to open your Australian office and manufacturing facility, including lawyers, accountants, import-export experts, and telecommunications equipment and support firm. Access the following online databases to locate companies that you would like to meet with during your upcoming trip: Australian Business Register (abr.gov.au), AustraliaTrade Now (australiatradenow.com), and the Nationwide Business Directory of Australia (www.nationwide.com.au). If necessary, use search engines such as Yahoo and Google.

- List the companies you would contact on your trip to determine whether they can help you with these and any other functions you think are vital to establishing your office.
- Rate the databases you used for accuracy of name, completeness, ease of use, and general helpfulness.

Video Cases

Video Cases and Instructional Videos illustrating some of the concepts in this chapter are available. Contact your instructor to access these videos.

Collaboration and Teamwork Project

In MyMISLab, you will find a Collaboration and Teamwork Project dealing with the concepts in this chapter. You will be able to use Google Sites, Google Docs, and other open source collaboration tools to complete the assignment.

Lego: Embracing Change by Combining BI with a Flexible Information System
CASE STUDY

The Lego Group, which is headquartered in Billund, Denmark, is one of the largest toy manufacturers in the world. Lego's main products have been the bricks and figures that children have played with for generations. The Danish company has experienced sustained growth since its founding in 1932, and for most of its history its major manufacturing facilities were located in Denmark.

In 2003, Lego was facing tough competition from imitators and manufacturers of electronic toys. In an effort to reduce costs, the group decided to initiate a gradual restructuring process that continues today. In 2006, the company announced that a large part of its production would be outsourced to the electronics manufacturing service company Flextronics, which has plants in Mexico, Hungary, and the Czech Republic. The decision to outsource production came as a direct consequence of an analysis of Lego's total supply chain. To reduce labor costs, manually intensive processes were outsourced, keeping only the highly skilled workers in Billund. Lego's workforce was gradually reduced from 8,300 employees in 2003 to approximately 4,200 in 2010. Additionally, production had to be relocated to places closer to its natural markets. As a consequence of all these changes, Lego transformed itself from a manufacturing firm to a market-oriented company that is capable of reacting fast to changing global demand.

Lego's restructuring process, coupled with double-digit sales growth in the past few years, has led to the company's expansion abroad and made its workforce more international. These changes presented supply chain and human resources challenges to the company. The supply chain had to be reengineered to simplify production without reducing quality. Improved logistics planning allowed Lego to work more closely with retailers, suppliers, and the new outsourcing companies. At the same time, the human resources (HR) department needed to play a more strategic role inside the company. HR was now responsible for implementing effective policies aimed at retaining and recruiting the most qualified employees from a diversity of cultural backgrounds.

Adapting company operations to these changes required a flexible and robust IT infrastructure with business intelligence capabilities that could help management perform better forecasting and planning. As part of the solution, Lego chose to move to SAP business suite software. SAP AG, a German company that specializes in enterprise software solutions, is one of the leading software companies in the world. SAP's software products include a variety of applications designed to efficiently support all of a company's essential functions and operations. Lego chose to implement SAP's Supply Chain Management (SCM), Product Lifecycle Management (PLM), and Enterprise Resources Planning (ERP) modules.

The SCM module includes essential features such as supply chain monitoring and analysis as well as forecasting, planning, and inventory optimization. The PLM module enables managers to optimize development processes and systems. The ERP module includes, among other applications, the Human Capital Management (HCM) application for personnel administration and development.

SAP's business suite is based on a flexible three-tier client-server architecture that can easily be adapted to the new Service-Oriented Architecture (SOA) available in the latest versions of the software. In the first tier, a client interface—a browser-type graphical user interface (GUI) running on either a laptop, desktop, or mobile device—submits users' requests to the application servers. The applications servers—the second tier in the system—receive and process clients' requests. In turn, these application servers send the processed requests to the database system—the third tier—which consists of one or more relational databases. SAP's business suite supports databases from different vendors, including those offered by Oracle, Microsoft, MySQL, and others. The relational databases contain the tables that store data on Lego's products, daily operations, the supply chain, and thousands of employees. Managers can easily use the SAP query tool to obtain reports from the databases, because it does not require any technical skill. Additionally, the distributed architecture enables authorized personnel to have direct access to the database system from the company's various locations, including those in Europe, North America, and Asia.

SAP's ERP-HCM module includes advanced features such as "Talent Manager" as well those for handling employee administration, reporting, and travel and time management. These features allow Lego's HR personnel to select the best candidates, schedule their training, and create a stimulus plan to retain them. It is also possible to include performance measurements and get real-time insight into HR trends. Using these advanced features, together with tools from other software vendors, Lego's managers are able to track employees' leadership potential, develop their careers, and forecast the recruiting of new employees with certain skills. n.

Sources: "Business 2010: Embracing the Challenge of Change," The Economist Intelligence Unit, February 2005 (http://graphics.eiu.com/files/ad_pdfs/Business%202010_Global_ FINAL. pdf, accessed November 16, 2010); "Lego Creates Model Business Success with SAP and IBM," IBM Global Financing, May 19, 2010 (www-01.ibm.com/software/success/cssdb.nsf/CS/STRD-85KGS6?OpenDocument, October 20, 2010); "Human Resources as an Exponent of Good Governance" (in Danish) (www.sat.com, October 20, 2010); "Lego, The Toy of the Century Had to Reinvent the Supply-Chain to Save the Company," Supply Chain Digest, September 25, 2007 (www.scdigest.com/assets/on_target/07-09-25-7.php?cid=1237, accessed November 16, 2010); G. W. Anderson, T. Rhodes, J. Davis, and J. Dobbins, SAMS Teach Yourself SAP in 24 hours (Indianapolis, IN: SAMS, 2008).

CASE STUDY QUESTIONS

1. Explain the role of the database in SAP's three-tier system.

2. Explain why distributed architectures are flexible.

3. Identify some of the business intelligence features included in SAP's business software suite.

4. What are the main advantages and disadvantages of having multiple databases in a distributed architecture? Explain.

Case contributed by Daniel Ortiz Arroyo, Aalborg University

Chapter 7

Telecommunications, the Internet, and Wireless Technology

LEARNING OBJECTIVES

After reading this chapter, you will be able to answer the following questions:

1. What are the principal components of telecommunications networks and key networking technologies?

2. What are the different types of networks?

3. How do the Internet and Internet technology work and how do they support communication and e-business?

4. What are the principal technologies and standards for wireless networking, communication, and Internet access?

5. Why are radio frequency identification (RFID) and wireless sensor networks valuable for business?

CHAPTER OUTLINE

Interactive Sessions:

The Battle Over Net Neutrality

Monitoring Employees on
   Networks: Unethical or
   Good Business?

RFID AND WIRELESS TECHNOLOGY SPEED UP PRODUCTION AT CONTINENTAL TIRES

Continental AG, headquartered in Hanover, Germany, is a global auto and truck parts manufacturing company, with 164,000 employees in 46 countries. It is also the world's fourth largest tire manufacturer and one of the top five automotive suppliers in the world.

One of the factories for Continental's Tire Division is located in Sarreguemines, France. This facility produces 1,000 different kinds of tires and encompasses nearly 1.5 million square feet. The production process requires large wheeled carts loaded with sheets of rubber or other components to be transported from storage to workstations as tires are being built. Until recently, if a carrier was not in its expected location, a worker had to look for it manually. Manual tracking was time-consuming and inaccurate, and the plant often lost track of tire components altogether.

Missing materials created bottlenecks and production delays at a time when business was growing and the company needed to increase production capacity. Continental found a solution in a new real-time location system based on a Wi-Fi wireless network using radio frequency identification (RFID) tags, AeroScout MobileView software, mobile computers, and Global Data Sciences' material inventory tracking system software.

The Sarreguemines plant mounted AeroScout T2-EB Industrial RFID tags on the sides of 1,100 of its carriers. As the carriers move from one manufacturing or storage station to another, location information about the cart is transmitted to nearby nodes of a Cisco Wi-Fi wireless network. AeroScout's MobileView software picks up the location and represents the carrier as an icon on a map of the facility displayed on computer screens. Fifteen Honeywell Dolphin 6500 and Motorola Solutions MC9190 handheld computers are used to confirm that a carrier has been loaded with components or has arrived at a specific workstation.

Seven of the plant's tuggers, which are small trucks for hauling the carriers around the plant, are equipped with DLOG mobile vehicle-mounted computers. When a tugger driver is looking for a specific component, he or she can use the mobile device to access the MobileView system, pull up a map of the facility, and see an icon indicating where that component's carrier is located. The location tracking system provides a real-time snapshot of all the components used in the factory.

A bar code label is attached to each component and carrier, and the system starts tracking that component as soon as it is placed in a carrier. Plant workers use one of the Motorola or Honeywell handhelds and the MobileView software to scan the bar code labels on both the component and its carrier, which is associated with the ID number transmitted by an RFID tag mounted on the carrier. The scanned bar code data are stored in a material inventory tracking system. The MobileView software tracks the carrier's location as

© Caro / Alamy

it is being transported to a storage area, and also the location where it is placed in storage.

When components are needed for manufacturing, a tugger driver uses the DLOG mobile computer to identify the location of the carrier with those specific components, and then goes to that location. After the carrier has been retrieved and taken to a workstation, its bar code is scanned by an employee at that station using one of the handheld computers. This updates the system to show that the required components have been received.

By enabling tugger drivers to quickly locate components, the new system has increased productivity and ensures that materials are not overlooked or misplaced. Fewer materials are thrown away because they expired and were not used when they were needed. The system is able to send alerts of materials that have been sitting too long in one spot.

When AeroScout and the new material inventory tracking system were implemented in September 2011, Continental made sure all production employees, including truckers, tire builders, and management, received training in the new system functions. The company also provided workers with instruction cards with detailed descriptions of system functions that they could use for reference.

Thanks to the new system, the Sarreguemines tire factory has increased production from 33,000 to 38,000 tires per day. Wastage of tire components has been reduced by 20 percent.

Sources: Claire Swedberg, "Continental Tire Plant Increases Productivity, Reduces Waste," *RFID Journal*, April 25, 2012 and www.conti-online.com, accessed May 2, 2012.

Continental Tires's experience illustrates some of the powerful capabilities and opportunities provided by contemporary networking technology. The company uses wireless networking, radio frequency identification (RFID) technology, mobile computers, and materials inventory management software to automate tracking of components as they move through the production process.

The chapter-opening diagram calls attention to important points raised by this case and this chapter. Continental Tires' production environment extends over a very large area, and requires intensive oversight and coordination to make sure that components are available when and where they are needed in the production process. Tracking components manually was very slow and cumbersome, increasing the possibility that components would be overlooked or lost.

Management decided that wireless technology and RFID tagging provided a solution and arranged for the deployment of a wireless RFID network throughout the entire Sarreguemines production facility. The network made it much easier to track components and to optimize tugger truck movements. Continental Tires had to redesign its production and other work processes and train employees in the new system to take advantage of the new technology.

Here are some questions to think about: How did Continental's real-time location system transform operations? Why was training so important?

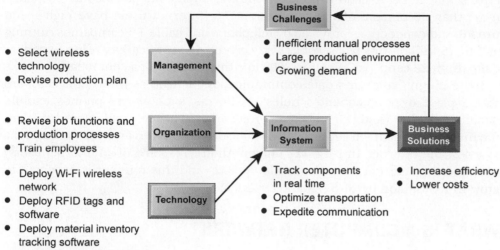

- Select wireless technology
- Revise production plan

- Revise job functions and production processes
- Train employees

- Deploy Wi-Fi wireless network
- Deploy RFID tags and software
- Deploy material inventory tracking software
- Deploy Honeywell, Motorola, and DLOG mobile computers

7.1 TELECOMMUNICATIONS AND NETWORKING IN TODAY'S BUSINESS WORLD

If you run or work in a business, you can't do without networks. You need to communicate rapidly with your customers, suppliers, and employees. Until about 1990, businesses used the postal system or telephone system with voice or fax for communication. Today, however, you and your employees use computers, e-mail and messaging, the Internet, cell phones, and mobile computers connected to wireless networks for this purpose. Networking and the Internet are now nearly synonymous with doing business.

NETWORKING AND COMMUNICATION TRENDS

Firms in the past used two fundamentally different types of networks: telephone networks and computer networks. Telephone networks historically handled voice communication, and computer networks handled data traffic. Telephone networks were built by telephone companies throughout the twentieth century using voice transmission technologies (hardware and software), and these companies almost always operated as regulated monopolies throughout the world. Computer networks were originally built by computer companies seeking to transmit data between computers in different locations.

Thanks to continuing telecommunications deregulation and information technology innovation, telephone and computer networks are converging into a single digital network using shared Internet-based standards and equipment. Telecommunications providers today, such as AT&T and Verizon, offer data transmission, Internet access, cellular telephone service, and television programming as well as voice service. Cable companies, such as Cablevision and Comcast, offer voice service and Internet access. Computer networks have expanded to include Internet telephone and video services. Increasingly, all of these voice, video, and data communications are based on Internet technology.

Both voice and data communication networks have also become more powerful (faster), more portable (smaller and mobile), and less expensive. For instance, the typical Internet connection speed in 2000 was 56 kilobits per second, but today more than 68 percent of the 239 million U.S. Internet users have high-speed **broadband** connections provided by telephone and cable TV companies running at 1 to 15 million bits per second. The cost for this service has fallen exponentially, from 25 cents per kilobit in 2000 to a tiny fraction of a cent today.

Increasingly, voice and data communication, as well as Internet access, are taking place over broadband wireless platforms, such as cell phones, mobile handheld devices, and PCs in wireless networks. In a few years, more than half the Internet users in the United States will use smartphones and mobile netbooks to access the Internet. In 2012, 122 million Americans (50% of all Internet users) accessed the Internet through mobile devices, and this number is expected to grow to 135 million by 2015 (eMarketer, 2012).

WHAT IS A COMPUTER NETWORK?

If you had to connect the computers for two or more employees together in the same office, you would need a computer network. Exactly what is a network? In its simplest form, a network consists of two or more connected computers. Figure 7.1 illustrates the major hardware, software, and transmission components used in a simple network: a client computer and a dedicated server computer, network interfaces, a connection medium, network operating system software, and either a hub or a switch.

Each computer on the network contains a network interface device to link the computer to the network. The connection medium for linking network components can be a telephone wire, coaxial cable, or radio signal in the case of cell phone and wireless local area networks (Wi-Fi networks).

FIGURE 7.1 COMPONENTS OF A SIMPLE COMPUTER NETWORK

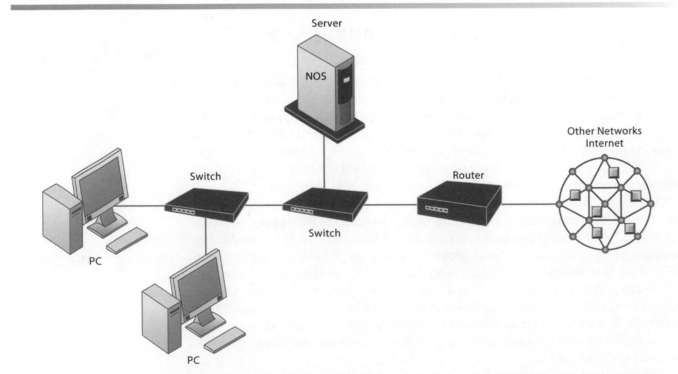

Illustrated here is a very simple computer network, consisting of computers, a network operating system (NOS) residing on a dedicated server computer, cable (wiring) connecting the devices, switches, and a router.

The **network operating system (NOS)** routes and manages communications on the network and coordinates network resources. It can reside on every computer in the network, or it can reside primarily on a dedicated server computer for all the applications on the network. A server computer is a computer on a network that performs important network functions for client computers, such as serving up Web pages, storing data, and storing the network operating system (and hence controlling the network). Server software such as Microsoft Windows Server, Linux, and Novell Open Enterprise Server are the most widely used network operating systems.

Most networks also contain a switch or a hub acting as a connection point between the computers. **Hubs** are very simple devices that connect network components, sending a packet of data to all other connected devices. A **switch** has more intelligence than a hub and can filter and forward data to a specified destination on the network.

What if you want to communicate with another network, such as the Internet? You would need a router. A **router** is a communications processor used to route packets of data through different networks, ensuring that the data sent gets to the correct address.

Network switches and routers have proprietary software built into their hardware for directing the movement of data on the network. This can create network bottlenecks and makes the process of configuring a network more complicated and time-consuming. **Software-defined networking (SDN)** is a new networking approach in which many of these control functions are managed by one central program, which can run on inexpensive commodity servers that are separate from the network devices themselves. This is especially helpful in a cloud computing environment with many different pieces of hardware because it allows a network administrator to manage traffic loads in a flexible and more efficient manner.

Networks in Large Companies

The network we've just described might be suitable for a small business. But what about large companies with many different locations and thousands of employees? As a firm grows, and collects hundreds of small local area networks, these networks can be tied together into a corporate-wide networking infrastructure. The network infrastructure for a large corporation consists of a large number of these small local area networks linked to other local area networks and to firmwide corporate networks. A number of powerful servers support a corporate Web site, a corporate intranet, and perhaps an extranet. Some of these servers link to other large computers supporting back-end systems.

Figure 7.2 provides an illustration of these more complex, larger scale corporate-wide networks. Here you can see that the corporate network infrastructure supports a mobile sales force using cell phones and smartphones, mobile employees linking to the company Web site, internal company networks using mobile wireless local area networks (Wi-Fi networks), and a videoconferencing system to support managers across the world. In addition to these computer networks, the firm's infrastructure usually includes a separate telephone network that handles most voice data. Many firms are dispensing with their traditional telephone networks and using Internet telephones that run on their existing data networks (described later).

As you can see from this figure, a large corporate network infrastructure uses a wide variety of technologies—everything from ordinary telephone service and corporate data networks to Internet service, wireless Internet, and cell phones. One of the major problems facing corporations today is how to integrate all

FIGURE 7.2 CORPORATE NETWORK INFRASTRUCTURE

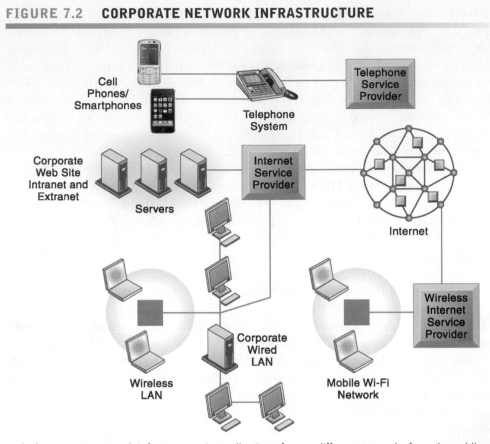

Today's corporate network infrastructure is a collection of many different networks from the public switched telephone network, to the Internet, to corporate local area networks linking workgroups, departments, or office floors.

the different communication networks and channels into a coherent system that enables information to flow from one part of the corporation to another, and from one system to another. As more and more communication networks become digital, and based on Internet technologies, it will become easier to integrate them.

KEY DIGITAL NETWORKING TECHNOLOGIES

Contemporary digital networks and the Internet are based on three key technologies: client/server computing, the use of packet switching, and the development of widely used communications standards (the most important of which is Transmission Control Protocol/Internet Protocol, or TCP/IP) for linking disparate networks and computers.

Client/Server Computing

Client/server computing, introduced in Chapter 5, is a distributed computing model in which some of the processing power is located within small, inexpensive client computers, and resides literally on desktops, laptops, or in handheld devices. These powerful clients are linked to one another through a network that is controlled by a network server computer. The server sets the rules of communication for the network and provides every client with an address so others can find it on the network.

Client/server computing has largely replaced centralized mainframe computing in which nearly all of the processing takes place on a central large mainframe computer. Client/server computing has extended computing to departments, workgroups, factory floors, and other parts of the business that could not be served by a centralized architecture. The Internet is the largest implementation of client/server computing.

Packet Switching

Packet switching is a method of slicing digital messages into parcels called packets, sending the packets along different communication paths as they become available, and then reassembling the packets once they arrive at their destinations (see Figure 7.3). Prior to the development of packet switching, computer networks used leased, dedicated telephone circuits to communicate with other computers in remote locations. In circuit-switched networks, such as the telephone system, a complete point-to-point circuit is assembled, and then communication can proceed. These dedicated circuit-switching techniques were expensive and wasted available communications capacity—the circuit was maintained regardless of whether any data were being sent.

Packet switching makes much more efficient use of the communications capacity of a network. In packet-switched networks, messages are first broken down into small fixed bundles of data called packets. The packets include information for directing the packet to the right address and for checking transmission errors along with the data. The packets are transmitted over various communications channels using routers, each packet traveling independently. Packets of data originating at one source will be routed through many different paths and networks before being reassembled into the original message when they reach their destinations.

FIGURE 7.3   PACKED-SWITCHED NETWORKS AND PACKET COMMUNICATIONS

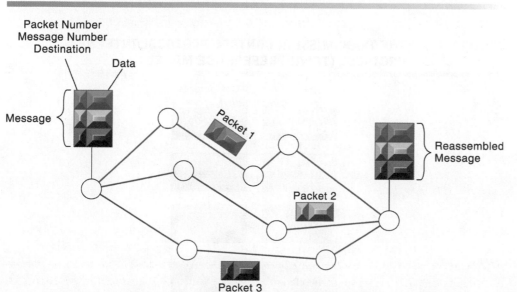

Data are grouped into small packets, which are transmitted independently over various communications channels and reassembled at their final destination.

TCP/IP and Connectivity

In a typical telecommunications network, diverse hardware and software components need to work together to transmit information. Different components in a network communicate with each other only by adhering to a common set of rules called protocols. A **protocol** is a set of rules and procedures governing transmission of information between two points in a network.

In the past, many diverse proprietary and incompatible protocols often forced business firms to purchase computing and communications equipment from a single vendor. But today, corporate networks are increasingly using a single, common, worldwide standard called **Transmission Control Protocol/Internet Protocol (TCP/IP)**. TCP/IP was developed during the early 1970s to support U.S. Department of Defense Advanced Research Projects Agency (DARPA) efforts to help scientists transmit data among different types of computers over long distances.

TCP/IP uses a suite of protocols, the main ones being TCP and IP. TCP refers to the Transmission Control Protocol, which handles the movement of data between computers. TCP establishes a connection between the computers, sequences the transfer of packets, and acknowledges the packets sent. IP refers to the Internet Protocol (IP), which is responsible for the delivery of packets and includes the disassembling and reassembling of packets during transmission. Figure 7.4 illustrates the four-layered Department of Defense reference model for TCP/IP, and the layers are described as follows:

1. *Application layer.* The Application layer enables client application programs to access the other layers and defines the protocols that applications use to exchange data. One of these application protocols is the Hypertext Transfer Protocol (HTTP), which is used to transfer Web page files.

2. *Transport layer.* The Transport layer is responsible for providing the Application layer with communication and packet services. This layer includes TCP and other protocols.

3. *Internet layer.* The Internet layer is responsible for addressing, routing, and packaging data packets called IP datagrams. The Internet Protocol is one of the protocols used in this layer.

FIGURE 7.4   **THE TRANSMISSION CONTROL PROTOCOL/INTERNET PROTOCOL (TCP/IP) REFERENCE MODEL**

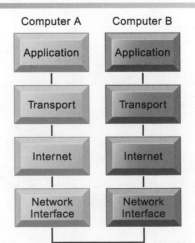

This figure illustrates the four layers of the TCP/IP reference model for communications.

4. *Network Interface layer.* At the bottom of the reference model, the Network Interface layer is responsible for placing packets on and receiving them from the network medium, which could be any networking technology.

Two computers using TCP/IP are able to communicate even if they are based on different hardware and software platforms. Data sent from one computer to the other passes downward through all four layers, starting with the sending computer's Application layer and passing through the Network Interface layer. After the data reach the recipient host computer, they travel up the layers and are reassembled into a format the receiving computer can use. If the receiving computer finds a damaged packet, it asks the sending computer to retransmit it. This process is reversed when the receiving computer responds.

7.2   COMMUNICATIONS NETWORKS

Let's look more closely at alternative networking technologies available to businesses.

SIGNALS: DIGITAL VS. ANALOG

There are two ways to communicate a message in a network: either using an analog signal or a digital signal. An *analog signal* is represented by a continuous waveform that passes through a communications medium and has been used for voice communication. The most common analog devices are the telephone handset, the speaker on your computer, or your iPod earphone, all of which create analog waveforms that your ear can hear.

A *digital signal* is a discrete, binary waveform, rather than a continuous waveform. Digital signals communicate information as strings of two discrete states: one bit and zero bits, which are represented as on-off electrical pulses. Computers use digital signals and require a modem to convert these digital signals into analog signals that can be sent over (or received from) telephone lines, cable lines, or wireless media that use analog signals (see Figure 7.5). **Modem** stands for modulator-demodulator. Cable modems connect your computer to the Internet using a cable network. DSL modems connect your computer to the Internet using a telephone company's landline network. Wireless modems perform the same function as traditional modems, connecting your computer to a wireless network that could be a cell phone network, or a Wi-Fi network. Without modems, computers could not communicate with one another using analog networks (which include the telephone system and cable networks).

FIGURE 7.5   FUNCTIONS OF THE MODEM

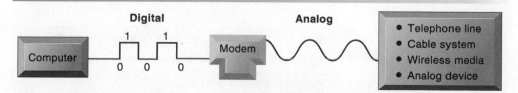

A modem is a device that translates digital signals into analog form (and vice versa) so that computers can transmit data over analog networks such as telephone and cable networks.

TYPES OF NETWORKS

There are many different kinds of networks and ways of classifying them. One way of looking at networks is in terms of their geographic scope (see Table 7.1).

Local Area Networks

If you work in a business that uses networking, you are probably connecting to other employees and groups via a local area network. A **local area network (LAN)** is designed to connect personal computers and other digital devices within a half-mile or 500-meter radius. LANs typically connect a few computers in a small office, all the computers in one building, or all the computers in several buildings in close proximity. LANs also are used to link to long-distance wide area networks (WANs, described later in this section) and other networks around the world using the Internet.

Review Figure 7.1, which could serve as a model for a small LAN that might be used in an office. One computer is a dedicated network file server, providing users with access to shared computing resources in the network, including software programs and data files.

The server determines who gets access to what and in which sequence. The router connects the LAN to other networks, which could be the Internet or another corporate network, so that the LAN can exchange information with networks external to it. The most common LAN operating systems are Windows, Linux, and Novell. Each of these network operating systems supports TCP/IP as their default networking protocol.

Ethernet is the dominant LAN standard at the physical network level, specifying the physical medium to carry signals between computers, access control rules, and a standardized set of bits used to carry data over the system. Originally, Ethernet supported a data transfer rate of 10 megabits per second (Mbps). Newer versions, such as Gigabit Ethernet, support a data transfer rate of 1 gigabit per second (Gbps), respectively, and are used in network backbones.

The LAN illustrated in Figure 7.1 uses a client/server architecture where the network operating system resides primarily on a single file server, and the server provides much of the control and resources for the network. Alternatively, LANs may use a peer-to-peer architecture. A peer-to-peer network treats all processors equally and is used primarily in small networks with 10 or fewer users. The various computers on the network can exchange data by direct access and can share peripheral devices without going through a separate server.

In LANs using the Windows Server family of operating systems, the **peer-to-peer** architecture is called the *workgroup network model*, in which a small group of computers can share resources, such as files, folders, and printers, over the

TABLE 7.1 **TYPES OF NETWORKS**

TYPE	AREA
Local area network (LAN)	Up to 500 meters (half a mile); an office or floor of a building
Campus area network (CAN)	Up to 1,000 meters (a mile); a college campus or corporate facility
Metropolitan area network (MAN)	A city or metropolitan area
Wide area network (WAN)	A transcontinental or global area

network without a dedicated server. The *Windows domain network model*, in contrast, uses a dedicated server to manage the computers in the network.

Larger LANs have many clients and multiple servers, with separate servers for specific services, such as storing and managing files and databases (file servers or database servers), managing printers (print servers), storing and managing e-mail (mail servers), or storing and managing Web pages (Web servers).

Metropolitan and Wide Area Networks

Wide area networks (WANs) span broad geographical distances—entire regions, states, continents, or the entire globe. The most universal and powerful WAN is the Internet. Computers connect to a WAN through public networks, such as the telephone system or private cable systems, or through leased lines or satellites. A **metropolitan area network (MAN)** is a network that spans a metropolitan area, usually a city and its major suburbs. Its geographic scope falls between a WAN and a LAN.

TRANSMISSION MEDIA AND TRANSMISSION SPEED

Networks use different kinds of physical transmission media, including twisted pair wire, coaxial cable, fiber optics, and media for wireless transmission. Each has advantages and limitations. A wide range of speeds is possible for any given medium depending on the software and hardware configuration. Table 7.2 compares these media.

Bandwidth: Transmission Speed

The total amount of digital information that can be transmitted through any telecommunications medium is measured in bits per second (bps). One signal change, or cycle, is required to transmit one or several bits; therefore, the transmission capacity of each type of telecommunications medium is a function of its frequency. The number of cycles per second that can be sent through that medium is measured in **hertz**—one hertz is equal to one cycle of the medium.

TABLE 7.2 PHYSICAL TRANSMISSION MEDIA

TRANSMISSION MEDIUM	DESCRIPTION	SPEED
Twisted pair wire (CAT 5)	Strands of copper wire twisted in pairs for voice and data communications. CAT 5 is the most common 10 Mbps LAN cable. Maximum recommended run of 100 meters.	10 Mbps to 1 Gbps
Coaxial cable	Thickly insulated copper wire, which is capable of high-speed data transmission and less subject to interference than twisted wire. Currently used for cable TV and for networks with longer runs (more than 100 meters).	Up to 1 Gbps
Fiber optic cable	Strands of clear glass fiber, transmitting data as pulses of light generated by lasers. Useful for high-speed transmission of large quantities of data. More expensive than other physical transmission media and harder to install; often used for network backbone.	500 Kbps to 6+Tbps
Wireless transmission media	Based on radio signals of various frequencies and includes both terrestrial and satellite microwave systems and cellular networks. Used for long-distance, wireless communication and Internet access.	Up to 600+ Mbps

The range of frequencies that can be accommodated on a particular telecommunications channel is called its **bandwidth**. The bandwidth is the difference between the highest and lowest frequencies that can be accommodated on a single channel. The greater the range of frequencies, the greater the bandwidth and the greater the channel's transmission capacity.

7.3 THE GLOBAL INTERNET

We all use the Internet, and many of us can't do without it. It's become an indispensable personal and business tool. But what exactly is the Internet? How does it work, and what does Internet technology have to offer for business? Let's look at the most important Internet features.

WHAT IS THE INTERNET?

The Internet has become the world's most extensive, public communication system that now rivals the global telephone system in reach and range. It's also the world's largest implementation of client/server computing and internetworking, linking millions of individual networks all over the world. This global network of networks began in the early 1970s as a U.S. Department of Defense network to link scientists and university professors around the world.

Most homes and small businesses connect to the Internet by subscribing to an Internet service provider. An **Internet service provider (ISP)** is a commercial organization with a permanent connection to the Internet that sells temporary connections to retail subscribers. EarthLink, NetZero, AT&T, and Time Warner are ISPs. Individuals also connect to the Internet through their business firms, universities, or research centers that have designated Internet domains.

There are a variety of services for ISP Internet connections. Connecting via a traditional telephone line and modem, at a speed of 56.6 kilobits per second (Kbps) used to be the most common form of connection worldwide, but it has been largely replaced by broadband connections. Digital subscriber line, cable, satellite Internet connections, and T lines provide these broadband services.

Digital subscriber line (DSL) technologies operate over existing telephone lines to carry voice, data, and video at transmission rates ranging from 385 Kbps all the way up to 40 Mbps, depending on usage patterns and distance. **Cable Internet connections** provided by cable television vendors use digital cable coaxial lines to deliver high-speed Internet access to homes and businesses. They can provide high-speed access to the Internet of up to 50 Mbps, although most providers offer service ranging from 1 Mbps to 6 Mbps. In areas where DSL and cable services are unavailable, it is possible to access the Internet via satellite, although some satellite Internet connections have slower upload speeds than other broadband services.

T1 and T3 are international telephone standards for digital communication. They are leased, dedicated lines suitable for businesses or government agencies requiring high-speed guaranteed service levels. **T1 lines** offer guaranteed delivery at 1.54 Mbps, and T3 lines offer delivery at 45 Mbps. The Internet does not provide similar guaranteed service levels, but simply "best effort."

INTERNET ADDRESSING AND ARCHITECTURE

The Internet is based on the TCP/IP networking protocol suite described earlier in this chapter. Every computer on the Internet is assigned a unique **Internet**

Protocol (IP) address, which currently is a 32-bit number represented by four strings of numbers ranging from 0 to 255 separated by periods. For instance, the IP address of www.microsoft.com is 207.46.250.119.

When a user sends a message to another user on the Internet, the message is first decomposed into packets using the TCP protocol. Each packet contains its destination address. The packets are then sent from the client to the network server and from there on to as many other servers as necessary to arrive at a specific computer with a known address. At the destination address, the packets are reassembled into the original message.

The Domain Name System

Because it would be incredibly difficult for Internet users to remember strings of 12 numbers, the **Domain Name System (DNS)** converts domain names to IP addresses. The **domain name** is the English-like name that corresponds to the unique 32-bit numeric IP address for each computer connected to the Internet. DNS servers maintain a database containing IP addresses mapped to their corresponding domain names. To access a computer on the Internet, users need only specify its domain name.

DNS has a hierarchical structure (see Figure 7.6). At the top of the DNS hierarchy is the root domain. The child domain of the root is called a top-level domain, and the child domain of a top-level domain is called is a second-level domain. Top-level domains are two- and three-character names you arc familiar with from surfing the Web, for example, .com, .edu, .gov, and the various country codes such as .ca for Canada or .it for Italy. Second-level domains have two parts, designating a top-level name and a second-level name—such as buy.com, nyu.edu, or amazon.ca. A host name at the bottom of the hierarchy designates a specific computer on either the Internet or a private network.

FIGURE 7.6   THE DOMAIN NAME SYSTEM

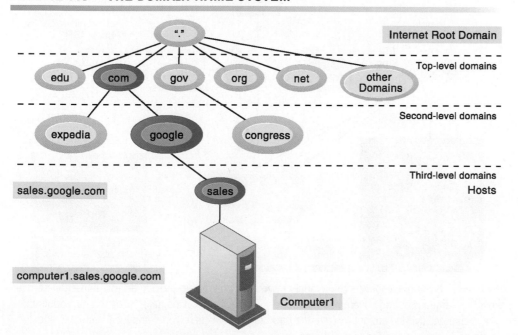

Domain Name System is a hierarchical system with a root domain, top-level domains, second-level domains, and host computers at the third level.

The most common domain extensions currently available and officially approved are shown in the following list. Countries also have domain names such as .uk, .au, and .fr (United Kingdom, Australia, and France, respectively), and there is a new class of "internationalized" top-level domains that use non-English characters (ICANN, 2010). In the future, this list will expand to include many more types of organizations and industries.

.com   Commercial organizations/businesses

.edu   Educational institutions

.gov   U.S. government agencies

.mil   U.S. military

.net   Network computers

.org   Nonprofit organizations and foundations

.biz   Business firms

.info   Information providers

Internet Architecture and Governance

Internet data traffic is carried over transcontinental high-speed backbone networks that generally operate in the range of 45 Mbps to 2.5 Gbps (see Figure 7.7). These trunk lines are typically owned by long-distance telephone companies (called *network service providers*) or by national governments.

FIGURE 7.7   INTERNET NETWORK ARCHITECTURE

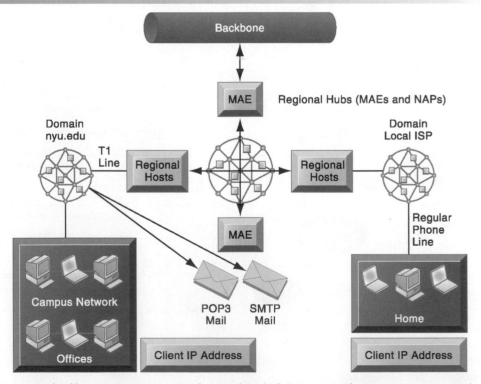

The Internet backbone connects to regional networks, which in turn provide access to Internet service providers, large firms, and government institutions. Network access points (NAPs) and metropolitan area exchanges (MAEs) are hubs where the backbone intersects regional and local networks and where backbone owners connect with one another.

Local connection lines are owned by regional telephone and cable television companies in the United States that connect retail users in homes and businesses to the Internet. The regional networks lease access to ISPs, private companies, and government institutions.

Each organization pays for its own networks and its own local Internet connection services, a part of which is paid to the long-distance trunk line owners. Individual Internet users pay ISPs for using their service, and they generally pay a flat subscription fee, no matter how much or how little they use the Internet. A debate is now raging on whether this arrangement should continue or whether heavy Internet users who download large video and music files should pay more for the bandwidth they consume. The Interactive Session on Organizations explores this topic, by examining the pros and cons of network neutrality.

No one "owns" the Internet, and it has no formal management. However, worldwide Internet policies are established by a number of professional organizations and government bodies, including the Internet Architecture Board (IAB), which helps define the overall structure of the Internet; the Internet Corporation for Assigned Names and Numbers (ICANN), which assigns IP addresses; and the World Wide Web Consortium (W3C), which sets Hypertext Markup Language and other programming standards for the Web.

These organizations influence government agencies, network owners, ISPs, and software developers with the goal of keeping the Internet operating as efficiently as possible. The Internet must also conform to the laws of the sovereign nation-states in which it operates, as well as the technical infrastructures that exist within the nation-states. Although in the early years of the Internet and the Web there was very little legislative or executive interference, this situation is changing as the Internet plays a growing role in the distribution of information and knowledge, including content that some find objectionable.

The Future Internet: IPv6 and Internet2

The Internet was not originally designed to handle the transmission of massive quantities of data and billions of users. Because many corporations and governments have been given large blocks of millions of IP addresses to accommodate current and future workforces, and because of sheer Internet population growth, the world is about to run out of available IP addresses using the old addressing convention. The old addressing system is being replaced by a new version of the IP addressing schema called **IPv6** (Internet Protocol version 6), which contains 128-bit addresses (2 to the power of 128), or more than a quadrillion possible unique addresses. IPv6 is not compatible with the existing Internet addressing system, so the transition to the new standard will take years.

Internet2 is an advanced networking consortium representing over 350 U.S. universities, private businesses, and government agencies working with 66,000 institutions across the United States and international networking partners from more than 50 countries. To connect these communities, Internet2 developed a high-capacity 100 Gbps network that serves as a testbed for leading-edge technologies that may eventually migrate to the public Internet, including telemedicine, distance learning, and other advanced applications not possible with consumer-grade Internet services. The fourth generation of this network is being rolled out to provide 8.8 terabits of capacity.

INTERACTIVE SESSION: ORGANIZATIONS

THE BATTLE OVER NET NEUTRALITY

What kind of Internet user are you? Do you primarily use the Net to do a little e-mail and look up phone numbers? Or are you online all day, watching YouTube videos, downloading music files, or playing online games? If you have a smartphone, do you use it to make calls and check the Web every so often, or do you stream TV shows and movies on a regular basis? If you're a power Internet or smartphone user, you are consuming a great deal of bandwidth, and hundreds of millions of people like you might start to slow the Internet down. YouTube consumed as much bandwidth in 2007 as the entire Internet did in 2000, and AT&T's mobile network will carry more data in the first two months of 2015 than in all of 2010.

If user demand for the Internet overwhelms network capacity, the Internet might not come to a screeching halt, but users would be faced with very sluggish download speeds and slow performance of Netflix, Spotify, YouTube, and other data-heavy services. Heavy use of iPhones in urban areas such as New York and San Francisco has already degraded service on the AT&T wireless network. AT&T reports that 3 percent of its subscriber base accounts for 40 percent of its data traffic.

Some analysts believe that as digital traffic on the Internet grows, even at a rate of 50 percent per year, the technology for handling all this traffic is advancing at an equally rapid pace. But regardless of what happens with Internet infrastructure, costs for Internet providers will continue to increase, and prominent media companies are searching for new revenue streams to meet those costs. One solution is to make Internet users pay for the amount of bandwidth they use. But metering Internet use is not universally accepted, because of an ongoing debate about network neutrality.

Network neutrality is the idea that Internet service providers must allow customers equal access to content and applications, regardless of the source or nature of the content. Presently, the Internet is indeed neutral: all Internet traffic is treated equally on a first-come, first-served basis by Internet backbone owners. However, this arrangement prevents telecommunications and cable companies from charging differentiated prices based on the amount of bandwidth consumed by content being delivered over the Internet. These companies believe that dif-

ferentiated pricing is "the fairest way" to finance necessary investments in their network infrastructures.

Internet service providers point to the upsurge in piracy of copyrighted materials over the Internet. Comcast, the second largest U.S. Internet service provider, reported that illegal file sharing of copyrighted material was consuming 50 percent of its network capacity. In 2008, the company slowed down transmission of BitTorrent files used extensively for piracy and illegal sharing of copyrighted materials, including video. The Federal Communications Commission (FCC) ruled that Comcast had to stop slowing peer-to-peer traffic in the name of network management. Comcast then filed a lawsuit challenging the FCC's authority to enforce network neutrality. In April 2010, a federal appeals court ruled in favor of Comcast that the FCC did not have the authority to regulate how an Internet provider manages its network. This was a considerable blow to net neutrality. In late 2010, Comcast reportedly began charging Level 3 Communications, which helps stream Netflix's movies, an additional fee for continued normal service. Level 3 asked the FCC to investigate the action.

Groups favoring net neutrality are pushing Congress to find ways to regulate the industry to prevent network providers from adopting Comcast-like practices. The strange alliance of net neutrality advocates includes MoveOn.org, the Christian Coalition, the American Library Association, every major consumer group, and a host of bloggers and small businesses, as well as streaming-video services like Netflix.

Net neutrality advocates argue that the risk of censorship increases when network operators can selectively block or slow access to certain content such as Netflix video streams or access to competing low-cost services such as Skype. Proponents of net neutrality also argue that a neutral Internet encourages everyone to innovate without permission from the phone and cable companies or other authorities, and this level playing field has spawned countless new businesses. Allowing unrestricted information flow becomes essential to free markets and democracy as commerce and society increasingly move online.

Network owners believe regulation to enforce net neutrality will impede U.S. competitiveness by stifling innovation, discouraging capital expenditures for new networks, and curbing their networks' ability to cope with the exploding demand for Internet and wireless traffic. U.S. Internet service lags behind many other nations in overall speed, cost, and quality of service, adding credibility to this argument.

And with enough options for Internet access, regulation would not be essential for promoting net neutrality. Dissatisfied consumers could simply switch to providers who enforce net neutrality and allow unlimited Internet use.

In December 2010, the FCC approved measures that would allow the federal government to regulate Internet traffic. Broadband providers would be required to provide information regarding Internet speeds and service to their subscribers, and they could not block access to sites or products that compete against their own products. However, the regulations did not officially safeguard net neutrality, and wireless providers may block applications that use too much bandwidth.

Wireless providers have already moved to develop tiered plans that charge heavy bandwidth users larger service fees, and online content providers have struck exclusive deals with distributors that leave their competitors at a disadvantage. For example, in 2012, Comcast struck a deal with Microsoft to provide streaming video via its Xfinity TV service through the Xbox 360 that does not count against its broadband data cap of 250 gigabytes per month. This gives Comcast's television programming an edge over rival streaming shows, which will consume subscribers' data allotment. Netflix and other competitors are incensed, arguing that this flies in the face of the concept of net neutrality and represents an anti-competitive practice.

In 2011, nearly every broadband provider instituted a cap on data, charging additional fees to users that go over that limit. Many analysts have long argued in favor of these caps, but deals like those between Comcast and Microsoft are likely to draw the ire of the FCC going forward. Currently, the net neutrality laws on the books are riddled with loopholes. For example, they allow broadband providers to allocate portions of their networks for special "managed" services. Still, public sentiment in favor of net neutrality is still strong.

Sources: Eduardo Porter, "Keeping the Internet Neutral," *The New York Times*, May 8, 2012; Matt Peckham, "Netflix CEO Takes Swing at Comcast Xfinity over Net Neutrality," *Time Techland*, April 16, 2012; Greg Bensinger, "AT&T Ends All-You-Can-Eat," *The Wall Street Journal*, March 1, 2012; John Eggerton, "Net Neutrality Rules Signed Off On By OMB," *Broadcasting & Cable*, September 13, 2011; "FCC Approves Net Neutrality But With Concessions," *eWeek*, December 22, 2010; and Brian Stelter, "Comcast Fee Ignites Fight Over Videos on Internet," *The New York Times*, November 30, 2010.

CASE STUDY QUESTIONS

1. What is network neutrality? Why has the Internet operated under net neutrality up to this point in time?

2. Who's in favor of net neutrality? Who's opposed? Why?

3. What would be the impact on individual users, businesses, and government if Internet providers switched to a tiered service model?

4. Are you in favor of legislation enforcing network neutrality? Why or why not?

INTERNET SERVICES AND COMMUNICATION TOOLS

The Internet is based on client/server technology. Individuals using the Internet control what they do through client applications on their computers, such as Web browser software. The data, including e-mail messages and Web pages, are stored on servers. A client uses the Internet to request information from a particular Web server on a distant computer, and the server sends the requested information back to the client over the Internet. Chapters 5 and 6 describe how Web servers work with application servers and database servers to access information from an organization's internal information systems applications and their associated databases. Client platforms today include not only PCs and other computers but also cell phones, small handheld digital devices, and other information appliances.

Internet Services

A client computer connecting to the Internet has access to a variety of services. These services include e-mail, chatting and instant messaging, electronic discussion groups, **Telnet, File Transfer Protocol (FTP)**, and the Web. Table 7.3 provides a brief description of these services.

Each Internet service is implemented by one or more software programs. All of the services may run on a single server computer, or different services may be allocated to different machines. Figure 7.8 illustrates one way that these services can be arranged in a multitiered client/server architecture.

E-mail enables messages to be exchanged from computer to computer, with capabilities for routing messages to multiple recipients, forwarding messages, and attaching text documents or multimedia files to messages. Most e-mail today is sent through the Internet. The cost of e-mail is far lower than equivalent voice, postal, or overnight delivery costs, making the Internet a very inexpensive and rapid communications medium. Most e-mail messages arrive anywhere in the world in a matter of seconds.

Nearly 90 percent of U.S. workplaces have employees communicating interactively using **chat** or instant messaging tools. Chatting enables two or more people who are simultaneously connected to the Internet to hold live, interactive conversations. Chat systems now support voice and video chat as well as written conversations. Many online retail businesses offer chat services on their Web sites to attract visitors, to encourage repeat purchases, and to improve customer service.

Instant messaging is a type of chat service that enables participants to create their own private chat channels. The instant messaging system alerts the user whenever someone on his or her private list is online so that the user can initiate a chat session with other individuals. Instant messaging systems for consumers include Yahoo! Messenger, Google Talk, and Windows Messenger. Companies concerned with security use proprietary communications and messaging systems such as IBM Sametime.

Newsgroups are worldwide discussion groups posted on Internet electronic bulletin boards on which people share information and ideas on a defined topic, such as radiology or rock bands. Anyone can post messages on these bulletin boards for others to read. Many thousands of groups exist that discuss almost all conceivable topics.

Employee use of e-mail, instant messaging, and the Internet is supposed to increase worker productivity, but the accompanying Interactive Session on

TABLE 7.3 MAJOR INTERNET SERVICES

CAPABILITY	FUNCTIONS SUPPORTED
E-mail	Person-to-person messaging; document sharing
Chatting and instant messaging	Interactive conversations
Newsgroups	Discussion groups on electronic bulletin boards
Telnet	Logging on to one computer system and doing work on another
File Transfer Protocol (FTP)	Transferring files from computer to computer
World Wide Web	Retrieving, formatting, and displaying information (including text, audio, graphics, and video) using hypertext links

FIGURE 7.8   CLIENT/SERVER COMPUTING ON THE INTERNET

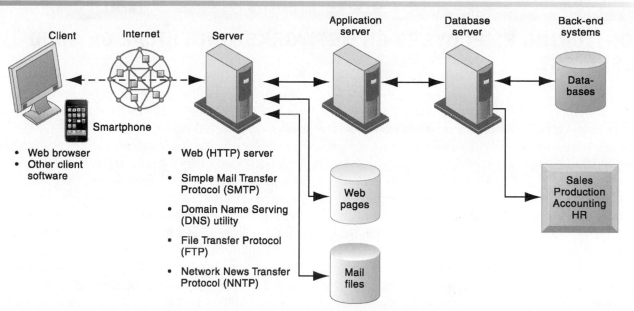

Client computers running Web browser and other software can access an array of services on servers over the Internet. These services may all run on a single server or on multiple specialized servers.

Management shows that this may not always be the case. Many company managers now believe they need to monitor and even regulate their employees' online activity. But is this ethical? Although there are some strong business reasons why companies may need to monitor their employees' e-mail and Web activities, what does this mean for employee privacy?

Voice over IP

The Internet has also become a popular platform for voice transmission and corporate networking. **Voice over IP (VoIP)** technology delivers voice information in digital form using packet switching, avoiding the tolls charged by local and long-distance telephone networks (see Figure 7.9). Calls that

FIGURE 7.9   HOW VOICE OVER IP WORKS

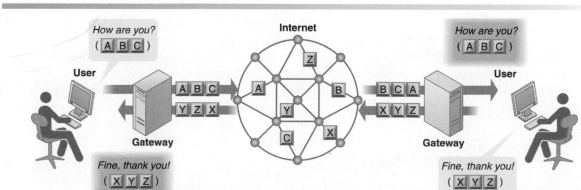

A VoIP phone call digitizes and breaks up a voice message into data packets that may travel along different routes before being reassembled at the final destination. A processor nearest the call's destination, called a gateway, arranges the packets in the proper order and directs them to the telephone number of the receiver or the IP address of the receiving computer.

INTERACTIVE SESSION: MANAGEMENT

MONITORING EMPLOYEES ON NETWORKS: UNETHICAL OR GOOD BUSINESS?

When you were at work, how many minutes (or hours) did you spend on Facebook today? Did you send personal e-mail or visit some sports Web sites? If so, you're not alone. According to a Nucleus Research study, 77 percent of workers with Facebook accounts use them during work hours. A Ponemon Institute study reported that the average employee wastes approximately 30 percent of the workday on non-work-related Web browsing, while other studies report as many as 90 percent of employees receive or send personal e-mail at work.

This behavior creates serious business problems. Checking e-mail, responding to instant messages, or sneaking in a brief YouTube video creates a series of nonstop interruptions that divert employee attention from the job tasks they are supposed to be performing. According to Basex, a New York City business research company, these distractions result in $650 billion in lost productivity each year!

Many companies have begun monitoring employee use of e-mail and the Internet, sometimes without their knowledge. A 2010 study from Proofpoint Plus found that more than one in three large U.S corporations assign staff to read or analyze employee e-mail. Another recent survey from the American Management Association (AMA) and the ePolicy Institute found that two out of three of the small, medium, and large companies surveyed monitored Web use. Instant messaging and text message monitoring are also increasing. Although U.S. companies have the legal right to monitor employee Internet and e-mail activity while they are at work, is such monitoring unethical, or is it simply good business?

Managers worry about the loss of time and employee productivity when employees are focusing on personal rather than company business. Too much time on personal business translates into lost revenue. Some employees may even be billing time they spend pursuing personal interests online to clients, thus overcharging them.

If personal traffic on company networks is too high, it can also clog the company's network so that legitimate business work cannot be performed. Procter & Gamble (P&G) found that on an average day, employees were listening to 4,000 hours of music on Pandora and viewing 50,000 five-minute YouTube videos. These activities involved streaming huge quantities of data, which slowed down P&G's Internet connection.

When employees use e-mail or the Web (including social networks) at employer facilities or with employer equipment, anything they do, including anything illegal, carries the company's name. Therefore, the employer can be traced and held liable. Management in many firms fear that racist, sexually explicit, or other potentially offensive material accessed or traded by their employees could result in adverse publicity and even lawsuits for the firm. Even if the company is found not to be liable, responding to lawsuits could run up huge legal bills. Symantec's 2011 Social Media Protection Flash Poll found that the average litigation cost for companies with social media incidents ran over $650,000.

Companies also fear leakage of confidential information and trade secrets through e-mail or social networks. Another survey conducted by the American Management Association and the ePolicy Institute found that 14 percent of the employees polled admitted they had sent confidential or potentially embarrassing company e-mails to outsiders.

U.S. companies have the legal right to monitor what employees are doing with company equipment during business hours. The question is whether electronic surveillance is an appropriate tool for maintaining an efficient and positive workplace. Some companies try to ban all personal activities on corporate networks—zero tolerance. Others block employee access to specific Web sites or social sites, closely monitor e-mail messages, or limit personal time on the Web.

For example, P&G blocks Netflix and has asked employees to limit their use of Pandora. It still allows some YouTube viewing, and is not blocking access to social networking sites because staff use them for digital marketing campaigns. Ajax Boiler in Santa Ana, California, uses software from SpectorSoft Corporation that records all the Web sites employees visit, time spent at each site, and all e-mails sent. Financial services and investment firm Wedbush Securities monitors the daily e-mails, instant messaging, and social networking activity of its 1,000-plus employees. The firm's e-mail monitoring software flags certain types of messages and keywords within messages for further investigation.

A number of firms have fired employees who have stepped out of bounds. A Proofpoint survey found that one in five large U.S. companies fired an employee for violating e-mail policies in the past year. Among managers who fired employees for Internet misuse, the majority did so because the employees' e-mail contained sensitive, confidential, or embarrassing information.

No solution is problem free, but many consultants believe companies should write corporate policies on employee e-mail, social media, and Web use. The policies should include explicit ground rules that state, by position or level, under what circumstances employees can use company facilities for e-mail, blogging, or Web surfing. The policies should also inform employees whether these activities are monitored and explain why.

IBM now has "social computing guidelines" that cover employee activity on sites such as Facebook and Twitter. The guidelines urge employees not to conceal their identities, to remember that they are personally responsible for what they publish, and to refrain from discussing controversial topics that are not related to their IBM role.

The rules should be tailored to specific business needs and organizational cultures. For example, investment firms will need to allow many of their employees access to other investment sites. A company dependent on widespread information sharing, innovation, and independence could very well find that monitoring creates more problems than it solves.

Sources: Emily Glazer, "P&G Curbs Employees' Internet Use," *The Wall Street Journal*, April 4, 2012; David L. Barron, "Social Media: Frontier for Employee Disputes," *Baseline*, January 19, 2012; Jennifer Lawinski, "Social Media Costs Companies Bigtime," *Baseline*, August 29, 2011; Don Reisinger, "March Madness: The Great Productivity Killer," *CIO Insight*, March 18, 2011; "Seven Employee Monitoring Tips for Small Business," IT BusinessEdge, May 29, 2011; Catey Hill, "Things Your Boss Won't Tell You," *Smart Money*, January 12, 2011.

CASE STUDY QUESTIONS

1. Should managers monitor employee e-mail and Internet usage? Why or why not?

2. Describe an effective e-mail and Web use policy for a company.

3. Should managers inform employees that their Web behavior is being monitored? Or should managers monitor secretly? Why or why not?

would ordinarily be transmitted over public telephone networks travel over the corporate network based on the Internet Protocol, or the public Internet. Voice calls can be made and received with a computer equipped with a microphone and speakers or with a VoIP-enabled telephone.

Cable firms such as Time Warner and Cablevision provide VoIP service bundled with their high-speed Internet and cable offerings. Skype offers free VoIP worldwide using a peer-to-peer network, and Google has its own free VoIP service.

Although there are up-front investments required for an IP phone system, VoIP can reduce communication and network management costs by 20 to 30 percent. For example, VoIP saves Virgin Entertainment Group $700,000 per year in long-distance bills. In addition to lowering long-distance costs and eliminating monthly fees for private lines, an IP network provides a single voice-data infrastructure for both telecommunications and computing services. Companies no longer have to maintain separate networks or provide support services and personnel for each different type of network.

Another advantage of VoIP is its flexibility. Unlike the traditional telephone network, phones can be added or moved to different offices without rewiring or reconfiguring the network. With VoIP, a conference call is arranged by a simple click-and-drag operation on the computer screen to select the names of the conferees. Voice mail and e-mail can be combined into a single directory.

Unified Communications

In the past, each of the firm's networks for wired and wireless data, voice communications, and videoconferencing operated independently of each other and had to be managed separately by the information systems department. Now, however, firms are able to merge disparate communications modes into a single universally accessible service using unified communications technology. **Unified communications** integrates disparate channels for voice communications, data communications, instant messaging, e-mail, and electronic conferencing into a single experience where users can seamlessly switch back and forth between different communication modes. Presence technology shows whether a person is available to receive a call. Companies will need to examine how work flows and business processes will be altered by this technology in order to gauge its value.

CenterPoint Properties, a major Chicago area industrial real estate company, used unified communications technology to create collaborative Web sites for each of its real estate deals. Each Web site provides a single point for accessing structured and unstructured data. Integrated presence technology lets team members e-mail, instant message, call, or videoconference with one click.

Virtual Private Networks

What if you had a marketing group charged with developing new products and services for your firm with members spread across the United States? You would want to be able to e-mail each other and communicate with the home office without any chance that outsiders could intercept the communications. In the past, one answer to this problem was to work with large private networking firms who offered secure, private, dedicated networks to customers. But this was an expensive solution. A much less-expensive solution is to create a virtual private network within the public Internet.

A **virtual private network (VPN)** is a secure, encrypted, private network that has been configured within a public network to take advantage of the economies of scale and management facilities of large networks, such as the Internet (see Figure 7.10). A VPN provides your firm with secure, encrypted communications at a much lower cost than the same capabilities offered by traditional non-Internet providers who use their private networks to secure communications. VPNs also provide a network infrastructure for combining voice and data networks.

Several competing protocols are used to protect data transmitted over the public Internet, including *Point-to-Point Tunneling Protocol (PPTP)*. In a process called tunneling, packets of data are encrypted and wrapped inside IP packets. By adding this wrapper around a network message to hide its content, business firms create a private connection that travels through the public Internet.

THE WEB

About 239 million people of all ages use the Web in the U.S.—three-quarters of the population. The Web is the most popular Internet service. It's a system with universally accepted standards for storing, retrieving, formatting, and displaying information using a client/server architecture. Web pages are formatted using

FIGURE 7.10 **A VIRTUAL PRIVATE NETWORK USING THE INTERNET**

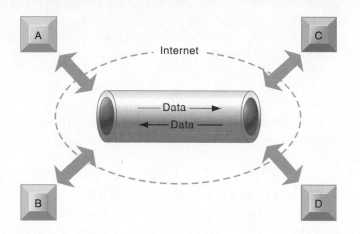

This VPN is a private network of computers linked using a secure "tunnel" connection over the Internet. It protects data transmitted over the public Internet by encoding the data and "wrapping" them within the Internet Protocol (IP). By adding a wrapper around a network message to hide its content, organizations can create a private connection that travels through the public Internet.

hypertext with embedded links that connect documents to one another and that also link pages to other objects, such as sound, video, or animation files. When you click a graphic and a video clip plays, you have clicked a hyperlink. A typical **Web site** is a collection of Web pages linked to a home page.

Hypertext

Web pages are based on a standard Hypertext Markup Language (HTML), which formats documents and incorporates dynamic links to other documents and pictures stored in the same or remote computers (see Chapter 5). Web pages are accessible through the Internet because Web browser software operating your computer can request Web pages stored on an Internet host server using the **Hypertext Transfer Protocol (HTTP)**. HTTP is the communications standard used to transfer pages on the Web. For example, when you type a Web address in your browser, such as http://www.sec.gov, your browser sends an HTTP request to the sec.gov server requesting the home page of sec.gov.

HTTP is the first set of letters at the start of every Web address, followed by the domain name, which specifies the organization's server computer that is storing the document. Most companies have a domain name that is the same as or closely related to their official corporate name. The directory path and document name are two more pieces of information within the Web address that help the browser track down the requested page. Together, the address is called a **uniform resource locator (URL)**. When typed into a browser, a URL tells the browser software exactly where to look for the information. For example, in the URL *http://www.megacorp.com/content/features/082610.html*, *http* names the protocol used to display Web pages, *www.megacorp.com* is the domain name, *content/features* is the directory path that identifies where on the domain Web server the page is stored, and *082610.html* is the document name and the name of the format it is in (it is an HTML page).

Web Servers

A Web server is software for locating and managing stored Web pages. It locates the Web pages requested by a user on the computer where they are stored and delivers the Web pages to the user's computer. Server applications usually run on dedicated computers, although they can all reside on a single computer in small organizations.

The most common Web server in use today is Apache HTTP Server, which controls 65 percent of the market. Apache is an open source product that is free of charge and can be downloaded from the Web. Microsoft Internet Information Services (IIS) is the second most commonly used Web server, with 15 percent market share.

Searching for Information on the Web

No one knows for sure how many Web pages there really are. The surface Web is the part of the Web that search engines visit and about which information is recorded. For instance, Google visited about 400 billion pages in 2012, and this reflects a large portion of the publicly accessible Web page population. But there is a "deep Web" that contains an estimated 1 trillion additional pages, many of them proprietary (such as the pages of the *Wall Street Journal Online*, which cannot be visited without a subscription or access code) or that are stored in protected corporate databases.

Search Engines Obviously, with so many Web pages, finding specific Web pages that can help you or your business, nearly instantly, is an important problem. The question is, how can you find the one or two pages you really want and need out of billions of indexed Web pages? **Search engines** attempt to solve the problem of finding useful information on the Web nearly instantly, and, arguably, they are the "killer app" of the Internet era. Today's search engines can sift through HTML files, files of Microsoft Office applications, PDF files, as well as audio, video, and image files. There are hundreds of different search engines in the world, but the vast majority of search results are supplied by Google, Yahoo!, Baidu, and Microsoft's Bing search engine (see Figure 7.11).

Web search engines started out in the early 1990s as relatively simple software programs that roamed the nascent Web, visiting pages and gathering

FIGURE 7.11 TOP WEB SEARCH ENGINES

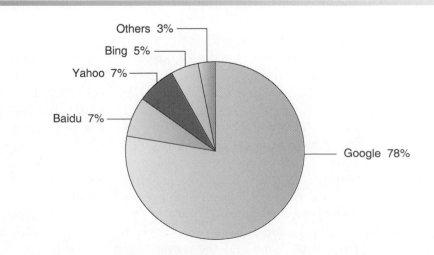

Google is the most popular search engine, handling 78 percent of Web searches.

Sources: Based on data from comScore Inc., September 2012.

information about the content of each page. The first search engines were simple keyword indexes of all the pages they visited, leaving the user with lists of pages that may not have been truly relevant to their search.

In 1994, Stanford University computer science students David Filo and Jerry Yang created a hand-selected list of their favorite Web pages and called it "Yet Another Hierarchical Officious Oracle," or Yahoo. Yahoo was not initially a search engine but rather an edited selection of Web sites organized by categories the editors found useful, but currently relies on Microsoft for search results.

In 1998, Larry Page and Sergey Brin, two other Stanford computer science students, released their first version of Google. This search engine was different: Not only did it index each Web page's words but it also ranked search results based on the relevance of each page. Page patented the idea of a page ranking system (called PageRank System), which essentially measures the popularity of a Web page by calculating the number of sites that link to that page as well as the number of pages which it links to. The premise is that really popular Web pages are more "relevant" to users. Brin contributed a unique Web crawler program that indexed not only keywords on a page but also combinations of words (such as authors and the titles of their articles). These two ideas became the foundation for the Google search engine. Figure 7.12 illustrates how Google works.

Search engine Web sites are so popular that many people use them as their home page, the page where they start surfing the Web (see Chapter 10). Search engines are also the foundation for the fastest growing form of marketing and advertising, search engine marketing.

FIGURE 7.12 HOW GOOGLE WORKS

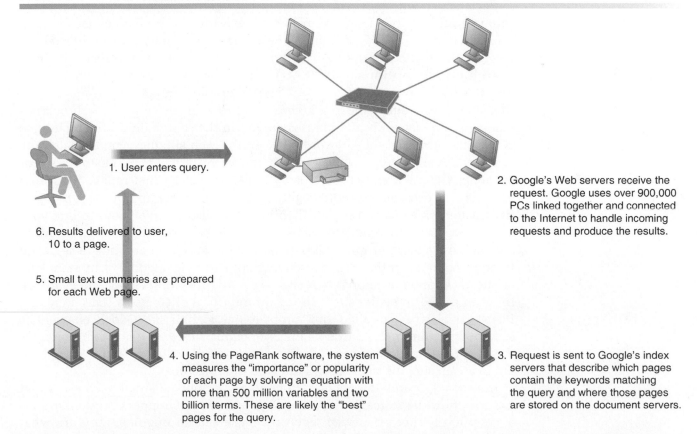

1. User enters query.

2. Google's Web servers receive the request. Google uses over 900,000 PCs linked together and connected to the Internet to handle incoming requests and produce the results.

6. Results delivered to user, 10 to a page.

5. Small text summaries are prepared for each Web page.

4. Using the PageRank software, the system measures the "importance" or popularity of each page by solving an equation with more than 500 million variables and two billion terms. These are likely the "best" pages for the query.

3. Request is sent to Google's index servers that describe which pages contain the keywords matching the query and where those pages are stored on the document servers.

The Google search engine is continuously crawling the Web, indexing the content of each page, calculating its popularity, and storing the pages so that it can respond quickly to user requests to see a page. The entire process takes about one-half second.

Mobile Search With the growth of mobile smartphones and tablet computers, and with about 122 million Americans accessing the Internet via mobile devices, the nature of e-commerce and search is changing. Mobile search now makes up about 20 percent of all searches in 2012, and according to Google will expand rapidly in the next few years. Both Google and Yahoo have developed new search interfaces to make searching and shopping from smartphones more convenient. Amazon, for instance, sold over $1 billion in goods in 2012 through mobile searches of its store (Marin Software, 2012; Miller, 2012; eMarketer, 2011).

Search Engine Marketing Search engines have become major advertising platforms and shopping tools by offering what is now called **search engine marketing**. When users enter a search term at Google, Bing, Yahoo, or any of the other sites serviced by these search engines, they receive two types of listings: sponsored links, for which advertisers have paid to be listed (usually at the top of the search results page), and unsponsored "organic" search results. In addition, advertisers can purchase small text boxes on the side of search results pages. The paid, sponsored advertisements are the fastest growing form of Internet advertising and are powerful new marketing tools that precisely match consumer interests with advertising messages at the right moment. Search engine marketing monetizes the value of the search process. In 2012, search engine marketing generated $19.5 billion in revenue, over half of all online advertising ($37.3 billion). Google will account for over 40% of all online advertising in 2012. About 97% of Google's revenue of $39 billion in 2011 comes from online advertising, and 95% of the ad revenue comes from search engine marketing (Google,2012; eMarketer, 2012).

Because search engine marketing is so effective (it has the highest click-through rate and the highest return on ad investment), companies seek to optimize their Web sites for search engine recognition. The better optimized the page is, the higher a ranking it will achieve in search engine result listings. **Search engine optimization (SEO)** is the process of improving the quality and volume of Web traffic to a Web site by employing a series of techniques that help a Web site achieve a higher ranking with the major search engines when certain keywords and phrases are put in the search field. One technique is to make sure that the keywords used in the Web site description match the keywords likely to be used as search terms by prospective customers. For example, your Web site is more likely to be among the first ranked by search engines if it uses the keyword "lighting" rather than "lamps" if most prospective customers are searching for "lighting." It is also advantageous to link your Web site to as many other Web sites as possible because search engines evaluate such links to determine the popularity of a Web page and how it is linked to other content on the Web. Search engines can be gamed by scammers who create thousands of phony Web site pages and link them altogether, or link them to a single retailer's site in an attempt to fool Google's search engine. Firms can also pay so-called "link farms" to link to their site. Google changed its search algorithm in 2012. Code named "Penguin," the new algorithm examines the quality of links more carefully. The assumption is that the more links there are to a Web site, the more useful the Web site must be.

In general, search engines have been very helpful to small businesses that cannot afford large marketing campaigns. Because shoppers are looking for a specific product or service when they use search engines, they are what marketers call "hot prospects"—people who are looking for information and often intending to buy. Moreover, search engines charge only for click-throughs to a site. Merchants do not have to pay for ads that don't work, only for ads that receive a click. Consumers benefit from search engine marketing because ads for merchants appear only when consumers are looking for a specific product. There are no pop-ups, Flash animations, videos, interstitials, e-mails, or other irrelevant communications to deal with. Thus, search engine marketing saves consumers cognitive energy and reduces search costs (including the cost of transportation needed to physically search for products). In a recent study, the global value of search to both merchants and consumers was estimated to be more than $800 billion, with about 65 percent of the benefit going to consumers in the form of lower search costs and lower prices (McKinsey, 2011).

Social Search One problem with Google and mechanical search engines is that they are so thorough: enter a search for "ultra computers" and in .2 seconds you will receive over 300 million reponses! Search engines are not very discriminating. **Social search** is an effort to provide fewer, more relevant, and trustworthy search results based on a person's network of social contacts. In contrast to the top search engines that use a mathematical algorithm to find pages that satisfy your query, a social search Web site would review your friends' recommendations (and their friends'), their past Web visits, and their use of "Like" buttons.

For instance, Google has developed Google +1 as a social layer on top of its existing search engine. Users can place a +1 next to the Web sites they found helpful, and their friends will be notified automatically. Subsequent searches by their friends would list the +1 sites recommended by friends higher up on the page. Facebook's Like button is a similar social search tool. So far, neither Facebook nor Google has fully implemented a social search engine (Efrati, 2011). One problem with social search is that your close friends may not have intimate knowledge of topics you are exploring, or they may have tastes you don't appreciate. It's also possible your close friends don't have any knowledge about what you are searching for.

Semantic Search   Another way for search engines to become more discriminating and helpful is to make search engines that could understand what it is we are really looking for. Called "semantic search" the goal is to build a search engine that could really understand human language and behavior. For instance, in 2012 Google's search engine began delivering more than millions of links. It started to give users more facts and direct answers, and to provide more relevant links to sites based on the search engines estimation of what the user intended, and even on the user's past search behavior. Google's search engine is trying to understand what people are most likely thinking about when they search for something. Google hopes to use its massive database of objects (people, places, things), and smart software, to provide users a better resulting than just millions of hits. For instance, do a search on "Lake Tahoe" and the search engine will return basic facts about Tahoe (altitude, average temperature, and local fish), a map, and hotel accommodations. (Efrati, 2012).

Although search engines were originally designed to search text documents, the explosion of photos and videos on the Internet created a demand for searching and classifying these visual objects. Facial recognition software can create a digital version of a human face. In 2012 Facebook introduced its facial recognition software and combined it with tagging, to create a new feature called Tag Suggest. The software creates a digital facial print, similar to a finger print. Users can put their own tagged photo on their timeline, and their friend's timelines. Once a person's photo is tagged, Facebook can pick that person out of a group photo, and identify for others who is in the photo. You can also search for people on Facebook using their digital image to find and identify them.

Intelligent Agent Shopping Bots   Chapter 11 describes the capabilities of software agents with built-in intelligence that can gather or filter information and perform other tasks to assist users. **Shopping bots** use intelligent agent software for searching the Internet for shopping information. Shopping bots such as MySimon or Google Product Search can help people interested in making a purchase filter and retrieve information about products of interest, evaluate competing products according to criteria the users have established, and negotiate with vendors for price and delivery terms. Many of these shopping agents search the Web for pricing and availability of products specified by the user and return a list of sites that sell the item along with pricing information and a purchase link.

Web 2.0

Today's Web sites don't just contain static content—they enable people to collaborate, share information, and create new services and content online. These second-generation interactive Internet-based services are referred to as **Web 2.0**. If you have shared photos over the Internet at Flickr or another photo site, pinned a photo on Pinterest, posted a video to YouTube, created a blog, or added an app to your Facebook page, you've used some of these Web 2.0 services.

Web 2.0 has four defining features: interactivity, real-time user control, social participation (sharing), and user-generated content. The technologies and services behind these features include cloud computing, software mashups and apps, blogs, RSS, wikis, and social networks.

Mashups, which we introduced in Chapter 5, are software services that enable users and system developers to mix and match content or software components to create something entirely new. For example, Yahoo's photo storage and sharing site Flickr combines photos with other information about the images provided by users and tools to make it usable within other programming environments. Web 2.0 tools and services have fueled the creation of social networks and other online communities where people can interact with one another in the manner of their choosing.

A **blog**, the popular term for a Weblog, is a personal Web site that typically contains a series of chronological entries (newest to oldest) by its author, and links to related Web pages. The blog may include a *blogroll* (a collection of links to other blogs) and *trackbacks* (a list of entries in other blogs that refer to a post on the first blog). Most blogs allow readers to post comments on the blog entries as well. The act of creating a blog is often referred to as "blogging." Blogs can be hosted by a third-party service such as Blogger.com, TypePad.com, and Xanga.com, and blogging features have been incorporated into social networks such as Facebook and collaboration platforms such as Lotus Notes. WordPress is a leading open source blogging tool and content management system. **Microblogging**, used in Twitter, is a type of blogging that features short posts of 140 characters or less.

Blog pages are usually variations on templates provided by the blogging service or software. Therefore, millions of people without HTML skills of any kind can post their own Web pages and share content with others. The totality of blog-related Web sites is often referred to as the **blogosphere**. Although blogs have become popular personal publishing tools, they also have business uses (see Chapters 2 and 10).

If you're an avid blog reader, you might use RSS to keep up with your favorite blogs without constantly checking them for updates. **RSS**, which stands for

Really Simple Syndication or Rich Site Summary, pulls specified content from Web sites and feeds it automatically to users' computers. RSS reader software gathers material from the Web sites or blogs that you tell it to scan and brings new information from those sites to you. RSS readers are available through Web sites such as Google and Yahoo, and they have been incorporated into the major Web browsers and e-mail programs.

Blogs allow visitors to add comments to the original content, but they do not allow visitors to change the original posted material. **Wikis**, in contrast, are collaborative Web sites where visitors can add, delete, or modify content on the site, including the work of previous authors. Wiki comes from the Hawaiian word for "quick."

Wiki software typically provides a template that defines layout and elements common to all pages, displays user-editable software program code, and then renders the content into an HTML-based page for display in a Web browser. Some wiki software allows only basic text formatting, whereas other tools allow the use of tables, images, or even interactive elements, such as polls or games. Most wikis provide capabilities for monitoring the work of other users and correcting mistakes.

Because wikis make information sharing so easy, they have many business uses. The U.S. Department of Homeland Security's National Cyber Security Center (NCSC) deployed a wiki to facilitate collaboration among federal agencies on cybersecurity. NCSC and other agencies use the wiki for real-time information sharing on threats, attacks, and responses and as a repository for technical and standards information. Pixar Wiki is a collaborative community wiki for publicizing the work of Pixar Animation Studios. The wiki format allows anyone to create or edit an article about a Pixar film.

Social networking sites enable users to build communities of friends and professional colleagues. Members typically create a "profile," a Web page for posting photos, videos, MP3 files, and text, and then share these profiles with others on the service identified as their "friends" or contacts. Social networking sites are highly interactive, offer real-time user control, rely on user-generated content, and are broadly based on social participation and sharing of content and opinions. Leading social networking sites include Facebook, Twitter (with 1 billion and 140 million active users respectively in 2012), and LinkedIn (for professional contacts).

For many, social networking sites are the defining Web 2.0 application, and one that has radically changed how people spend their time online; how people communicate and with whom; how business people stay in touch with customers, suppliers, and employees; how providers of goods and services learn about their customers; and how advertisers reach potential customers. The large social networking sites are also morphing into application development platforms where members can create and sell software applications to other members of the community. Facebook alone has over 1 million developers who created over 550,000 applications for gaming, video sharing, and communicating with friends and family. We talk more about business applications of social networking in Chapters 2 and 10, and you can find social networking discussions in many other chapters of this book. You can also find a more detailed discussion of Web 2.0 in our Learning Tracks.

Web 3.0: The Future Web

Every day, about 120 million Americans enter 600 million queries into search engines (about 17 billion per month). How many of these 600 million queries produce a meaningful result (a useful answer in the first three listings)?

Arguably, fewer than half. Google, Yahoo, Microsoft, and Amazon are all trying to increase the odds of people finding meaningful answers to search engine queries. But with over 400 billion Web pages indexed, the means available for finding the information you really want are quite primitive, based on the words used on the pages, and the relative popularity of the page among people who use those same search terms. In other words, it's hit or miss.

To a large extent, the future of the Web involves developing techniques to make searching the 400 billion public Web pages more productive and meaningful for ordinary people. Web 1.0 solved the problem of obtaining access to information. Web 2.0 solved the problem of sharing that information with others and building new Web experiences. **Web 3.0** is the promise of a future Web where all this digital information, all these contacts, can be woven together into a single meaningful experience.

Sometimes this is referred to as the **Semantic Web**. "Semantic" refers to meaning. Most of the Web's content today is designed for humans to read and for computers to display, not for computer programs to analyze and manipulate. Semantic Search, described above, is a subset of a larger effort to make the Web more intelligent, more human like (W3C, 2012). Search engines can discover when a particular term or keyword appears in a Web document, but they do not really understand its meaning or how it relates to other information on the Web. You can check this out on Google by entering two searches. First, enter "Paris Hilton". Next, enter "Hilton in Paris". Because Google does not understand ordinary English, it has no idea that you are interested in the Hilton Hotel in Paris in the second search. Because it cannot understand the meaning of pages it has indexed, Google's search engine returns the most popular pages for those queries where "Hilton" and "Paris" appear on the pages.

First described in a 2001 *Scientific American* article, the Semantic Web is a collaborative effort led by the World Wide Web Consortium to add a layer of meaning atop the existing Web to reduce the amount of human involvement in searching for and processing Web information (Berners-Lee et al., 2001). For instance, in 2011 the New York Times lanched a semantic application called Longitude which provides a graphical interface to access the Times content. For instance, you can ask for stories about Germany in the last 24 hours, or a city in the United States, to retrieve all recent stories in the Times. (Donaldson, 2012).

Views on the future of the Web vary, but they generally focus on ways to make the Web more "intelligent," with machine-facilitated understanding of information promoting a more intuitive and effective user experience. For instance, let's say you want to set up a party with your tennis buddies at a local restaurant Friday night after work. One problem is that you are already scheduled to go to a movie with another friend. In a Semantic Web 3.0 environment, you would be able to coordinate this change in plans with the schedules of your tennis buddies and the schedule of your movie friend, and make a reservation at the restaurant all with a single set of commands issued as text or voice to your handheld smartphone. Right now, this capability is beyond our grasp.

Work proceeds slowly on making the Web a more intelligent experience, in large part because it is difficult to make machines, including software programs, that are truly intelligent like humans. But there are other views of the future Web. Some see a 3-D Web where you can walk through pages in a 3-D environment. Others point to the idea of a pervasive Web that controls everything from the lights in your living room to your car's rear view mirror, not to mention managing your calendar and appointments. This is referred to as the "Web of things."

Other complementary trends leading toward a future Web 3.0 include more widespread use of cloud computing and software as a service (SaaS) business models, ubiquitous connectivity among mobile platforms and Internet access devices, and the transformation of the Web from a network of separate siloed applications and content into a more seamless and interoperable whole. These more modest visions of the future Web 3.0 are more likely to be realized in the near term.

7.4   THE WIRELESS REVOLUTION

Welcome to the wireless revolution! Cell phones, smartphones, tablets, and wireless-enabled personal computers have morphed into portable media and computing platforms that let you perform many of the computing tasks you used to do at your desk, and a whole lot more. We introduced smartphones in our discussions of the mobile digital platform in Chapters 1 and 5. **Smartphones** such as the iPhone, Android phones, and BlackBerry combine the functionality of a cell phone with that of a mobile laptop computer with Wi-Fi capability. This makes it possible to combine music, video, Internet access, and telephone service in one device. Smartphones are the fastest growing wireless devices with respect to Internet access. A large part of the Internet is becoming a mobile, access-anywhere, broadband service for the delivery of video, music, and Web search.

CELLULAR SYSTEMS

In 2012, an estimated 1.5 billion cell phones will be sold worldwide. In the United States, there are 358 million cell phone subscriptions, and 115 million people have smartphones. About 120 million people access the Web using their phone (eMarketer, 2012). In a few years, smartphones will be the predominant source of searches, not the desktop PC. Digital cellular service uses several competing standards. In Europe and much of the rest of the world outside the United Sates, the standard is Global System for Mobile Communications (GSM). GSM's strength is its international roaming capability. There are GSM cell phone systems in the United States, including T-Mobile and AT&T.

A competing standard in the United States is Code Division Multiple Access (CDMA), which is the system used by Verizon and Sprint. CDMA was developed by the military during World War II. It transmits over several frequencies, occupies the entire spectrum, and randomly assigns users to a range of frequencies over time, making it more efficient than GSM.

Earlier generations of cellular systems were designed primarily for voice and limited data transmission in the form of short text messages. Today wireless carriers offer 3G and 4G networks. **3G networks**, with transmission speeds ranging from 144 Kbps for mobile users in, say, a car, to more than 2 Mbps for stationary users, offer fair transmission speeds for e-mail, browsing the Web, and online shopping, but are too slow for videos. **4G networks,** also called Long Term Evolution (LTE) networks, have much higher speeds: 100 megabits/second download, and 50 megabits upload speed. Equivalent to a home Wi-Fi connection, LTE provides more than enough capacity for watching high definition video on your smartphone. A less well developed high speed network standard is WiMax which uses Wi-Fi standards but with an extended range of nearly 30 miles, enough to cover a metropolitan area, and potentially entire small countries.

WIRELESS COMPUTER NETWORKS AND INTERNET ACCESS

If you have a laptop computer, you might be able to use it to access the Internet as you move from room to room in your home or dorm, or table to table in your university library. An array of technologies provide high-speed wireless access to the Internet for PCs and other wireless handheld devices as well as for cell phones. These new high-speed services have extended Internet access to numerous locations that could not be covered by traditional wired Internet services.

Bluetooth

Bluetooth is the popular name for the 802.15 wireless networking standard, which is useful for creating small **personal area networks (PANs)**. It links up to eight devices within a 10-meter area using low-power, radio-based communication and can transmit up to 722 Kbps in the 2.4-GHz band.

Wireless phones, pagers, computers, printers, and computing devices using Bluetooth communicate with each other and even operate each other without direct user intervention (see Figure 7.13). For example, a person could direct a notebook computer to send a document file wirelessly to a printer. Bluetooth connects wireless keyboards and mice to PCs or cell phones to earpieces without wires. Bluetooth has low-power requirements, making it appropriate for battery-powered handheld computers or cell phones.

Although Bluetooth lends itself to personal networking, it has uses in large corporations. For example, FedEx drivers use Bluetooth to transmit the delivery data captured by their handheld PowerPad computers to cellular transmitters, which forward the data to corporate computers. Drivers no longer need to spend time docking their handheld units

FIGURE 7.13 A BLUETOOTH NETWORK (PAN)

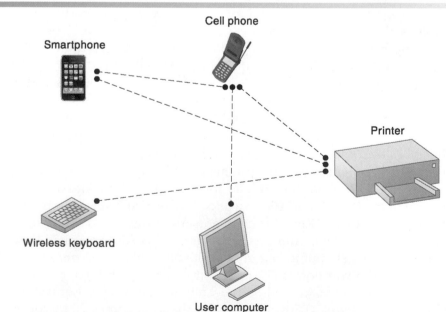

Bluetooth enables a variety of devices, including cell phones, smartphones, wireless keyboards and mice, PCs, and printers, to interact wirelessly with each other within a small 30-foot (10-meter) area. In addition to the links shown, Bluetooth can be used to network similar devices to send data from one PC to another, for example.

physically in the transmitters, and Bluetooth has saved FedEx $20 million per year.

Wi-Fi and Wireless Internet Access

The 802.11 set of standards for wireless LANs and wireless Internet access is also known as **Wi-Fi**. The first of these standards to be widely adopted was 802.11b, which can transmit up to 11 Mbps in the unlicensed 2.4-GHz band and has an effective distance of 30 to 50 meters. The 802.11g standard can transmit up to 54 Mbps in the 2.4-GHz range. 802.11n is capable of transmitting over 100 Mbps. Today's PCs and netbooks have built-in support for Wi-Fi, as do the iPhone, iPad, and other smartphones.

In most Wi-Fi communication, wireless devices communicate with a wired LAN using access points. An access point is a box consisting of a radio receiver/transmitter and antennas that links to a wired network, router, or hub. Mobile access points such as Verizon's Mobile Hotspots use the existing cellular network to create Wi-Fi connections.

Figure 7.14 illustrates an 802.11 wireless LAN that connects a small number of mobile devices to a larger wired LAN and to the Internet. Most wireless devices are client machines. The servers that the mobile client stations need to use are on the wired LAN. The access point controls the wireless stations and acts as a bridge between the main wired LAN and the wireless LAN. (A bridge connects two LANs based on different technologies.) The access point also controls the wireless stations.

FIGURE 7.14 AN 802.11 WIRELESS LAN

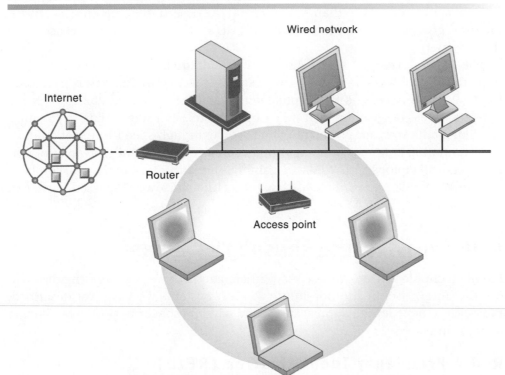

Mobile laptop computers equipped with network interface cards link to the wired LAN by communicating with the access point. The access point uses radio waves to transmit network signals from the wired network to the client adapters, which convert them into data that the mobile device can understand. The client adapter then transmits the data from the mobile device back to the access point, which forwards the data to the wired network.

The most popular use for Wi-Fi today is for high-speed wireless Internet service. In this instance, the access point plugs into an Internet connection, which could come from a cable service or DSL telephone service. Computers within range of the access point use it to link wirelessly to the Internet.

Hotspots typically consist of one or more access points providing wireless Internet access in a public place. Some hotspots are free or do not require any additional software to use; others may require activation and the establishment of a user account by providing a credit card number over the Web.

Businesses of all sizes are using Wi-Fi networks to provide low-cost wireless LANs and Internet access. Wi-Fi hotspots can be found in hotels, airport lounges, libraries, cafes, and college campuses to provide mobile access to the Internet. Dartmouth College is one of many campuses where students now use Wi-Fi for research, course work, and entertainment.

Wi-Fi technology poses several challenges, however. One is Wi-Fi's security features, which make these wireless networks vulnerable to intruders. We provide more detail about Wi-Fi security issues in Chapter 8.

Another drawback of Wi-Fi networks is susceptibility to interference from nearby systems operating in the same spectrum, such as wireless phones, microwave ovens, or other wireless LANs. However, wireless networks based on the 802.11n standard are able to solve this problem by using multiple wireless antennas in tandem to transmit and receive data and technology called *MIMO* (multiple input multiple output) to coordinate multiple simultaneous radio signals.

WiMax

A surprisingly large number of areas in the United States and throughout the world do not have access to Wi-Fi or fixed broadband connectivity. The range of Wi-Fi systems is no more than 300 feet from the base station, making it difficult for rural groups that don't have cable or DSL service to find wireless access to the Internet.

The IEEE developed a new family of standards known as WiMax to deal with these problems. **WiMax**, which stands for Worldwide Interoperability for Microwave Access, is the popular term for IEEE Standard 802.16. It has a wireless access range of up to 31 miles and transmission speed of up to 75 Mbps.

WiMax antennas are powerful enough to beam high-speed Internet connections to rooftop antennas of homes and businesses that are miles away. Cellular handsets and laptops with WiMax capabilities are appearing in the marketplace. Mobile WiMax is one of the 4G network technologies we discussed earlier in this chapter.

RFID AND WIRELESS SENSOR NETWORKS

Mobile technologies are creating new efficiencies and ways of working throughout the enterprise. In addition to the wireless systems we have just described, radio frequency identification systems and wireless sensor networks are having a major impact.

Radio Frequency Identification (RFID)

Radio frequency identification (RFID) systems provide a powerful technology for tracking the movement of goods throughout the supply chain. RFID systems use tiny tags with embedded microchips containing data about an item and its location to transmit radio signals over a short distance to RFID readers. The RFID readers then pass the data over a network to a computer for

FIGURE 7.15 HOW RFID WORKS

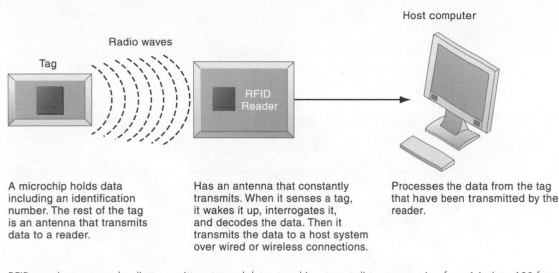

A microchip holds data including an identification number. The rest of the tag is an antenna that transmits data to a reader.

Has an antenna that constantly transmits. When it senses a tag, it wakes it up, interrogates it, and decodes the data. Then it transmits the data to a host system over wired or wireless connections.

Processes the data from the tag that have been transmitted by the reader.

RFID uses low-powered radio transmitters to read data stored in a tag at distances ranging from 1 inch to 100 feet. The reader captures the data from the tag and sends them over a network to a host computer for processing.

processing. Unlike bar codes, RFID tags do not need line-of-sight contact to be read.

The RFID tag is electronically programmed with information that can uniquely identify an item plus other information about the item, such as its location, where and when it was made, or its status during production. Embedded in the tag is a microchip for storing the data. The rest of the tag is an antenna that transmits data to the reader.

The reader unit consists of an antenna and radio transmitter with a decoding capability attached to a stationary or handheld device. The reader emits radio waves in ranges anywhere from 1 inch to 100 feet, depending on its power output, the radio frequency employed, and surrounding environmental conditions. When an RFID tag comes within the range of the reader, the tag is activated and starts sending data. The reader captures these data, decodes them, and sends them back over a wired or wireless network to a host computer for further processing (see Figure 7.15). Both RFID tags and antennas come in a variety of shapes and sizes.

Active RFID tags are powered by an internal battery and typically enable data to be rewritten and modified. Active tags can transmit for hundreds of feet but may cost several dollars per tag. Automated toll-collection systems such as New York's E-ZPass use active RFID tags.

Passive RFID tags do not have their own power source and obtain their operating power from the radio frequency energy transmitted by the RFID reader. They are smaller, lighter, and less expensive than active tags, but only have a range of several feet.

In inventory control and supply chain management, RFID systems capture and manage more detailed information about items in warehouses or in production than bar coding systems. If a large number of items are shipped together, RFID systems track each pallet, lot, or even unit item in the shipment. This technology may help companies such as Walmart improve receiving and storage operations by improving their ability to "see" exactly what stock is stored in warehouses or on retail store shelves. Continental Tires, described

FIGURE 7.16 A WIRELESS SENSOR NETWORK

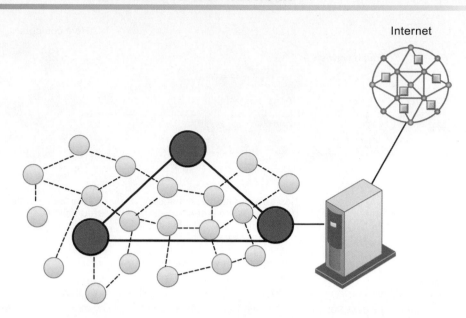

The small circles represent lower-level nodes and the larger circles represent high-end nodes. Lower-level nodes forward data to each other or to higher-level nodes, which transmit data more rapidly and speed up network performance.

in the chapter-opening case, used RFID technology to precisely track the location of tire components as they moved through the production process.

Walmart has installed RFID readers at store receiving docks to record the arrival of pallets and cases of goods shipped with RFID tags. The RFID reader reads the tags a second time just as the cases are brought onto the sales floor from backroom storage areas. Software combines sales data from Walmart's point-of-sale systems and the RFID data regarding the number of cases brought out to the sales floor. The program determines which items will soon be depleted and automatically generates a list of items to pick in the warehouse to replenish store shelves before they run out. This information helps Walmart reduce out-of-stock items, increase sales, and further shrink its costs.

The cost of RFID tags used to be too high for widespread use, but now it starts at around 7 cents per passive tag in the United States. As the price decreases, RFID is starting to become cost-effective for many applications.

In addition to installing RFID readers and tagging systems, companies may need to upgrade their hardware and software to process the massive amounts of data produced by RFID systems—transactions that could add up to tens or hundreds of terabytes.

Software is used to filter, aggregate, and prevent RFID data from overloading business networks and system applications. Applications often need to be redesigned to accept large volumes of frequently generated RFID data and to share those data with other applications. Major enterprise software vendors, including SAP and Oracle PeopleSoft, now offer RFID-ready versions of their supply chain management applications.

Wireless Sensor Networks

If your company wanted state-of-the art technology to monitor building security or detect hazardous substances in the air, it might deploy a wireless sensor network. **Wireless sensor networks (WSNs)** are networks of interconnected wireless devices that are embedded into the physical environment to provide measurements of many points over large spaces. These devices have built-in processing, storage, and radio frequency sensors and antennas. They are linked into an interconnected network that routes the data they capture to a computer for analysis.

These networks range from hundreds to thousands of nodes. Because wireless sensor devices are placed in the field for years at a time without any maintenance or human intervention, they must have very low power requirements and batteries capable of lasting for years.

Figure 7.16 illustrates one type of wireless sensor network, with data from individual nodes flowing across the network to a server with greater processing power. The server acts as a gateway to a network based on Internet technology.

Wireless sensor networks are valuable in areas such as monitoring environmental changes, monitoring traffic or military activity, protecting property, efficiently operating and managing machinery and vehicles, establishing security perimeters, monitoring supply chain management, or detecting chemical, biological, or radiological material.

LEARNING TRACK MODULES

The following Learning Tracks provide content relevant to topics covered in this chapter:

1. LAN Topologies
2. Broadband Network Services and Technologies
3. Cellular System Generations
4. Wireless Applications for Customer Relationship Management, Supply Chain Management, and Healthcare
5. Web 2.0

Review Summary

1. *What are the principal components of telecommunications networks and key networking technologies?*

   A simple network consists of two or more connected computers. Basic network components include computers, network interfaces, a connection medium, network operating system software, and either a hub or a switch. The networking infrastructure for a large company includes the traditional telephone system, mobile cellular communication, wireless local area networks, videoconferencing systems, a corporate Web site, intranets, extranets, and an array of local and wide area networks, including the Internet.

   Contemporary networks have been shaped by the rise of client/server computing, the use of packet switching, and the adoption of Transmission Control Protocol/Internet Protocol (TCP/IP) as a universal communications standard for linking disparate networks and computers, including the Internet. Protocols provide a common set of rules that enable communication among diverse components in a telecommunications network.

2. *What are the different types of networks?*

   The principal physical transmission media are twisted copper telephone wire, coaxial copper cable, fiber-optic cable, and wireless transmission.

   Local area networks (LANs) connect PCs and other digital devices together within a 500-meter radius and are used today for many corporate computing tasks. Wide area networks (WANs) span broad geographical distances, ranging from several miles to continents, and are private networks that are independently managed. Metropolitan area networks (MANs) span a single urban area.

   Digital subscriber line (DSL) technologies, cable Internet connections, and T1 lines are often used for high-capacity Internet connections.

3. *How do the Internet and Internet technology work, and how do they support communication and e-business?*

   The Internet is a worldwide network of networks that uses the client/server model of computing and the TCP/IP network reference model. Every computer on the Internet is assigned a unique numeric IP address. The Domain Name System (DNS) converts IP addresses to more user-friendly domain names. Worldwide Internet policies are established by organizations and government bodies, such as the Internet Architecture Board (IAB) and the World Wide Web Consortium (W3C).

   Major Internet services include e-mail, newsgroups, chatting, instant messaging, Telnet, FTP, and the Web. Web pages are based on Hypertext Markup Language (HTML) and can display text, graphics, video, and audio. Web site directories, search engines, and RSS technology help users locate the information they need on the Web. RSS, blogs, social networking, and wikis are features of Web 2.0.

   Firms are also starting to realize economies by using VoIP technology for voice transmission and by using virtual private networks (VPNs) as low-cost alternatives to private WANs.

4. *What are the principal technologies and standards for wireless networking, communication, and Internet access?*

   Cellular networks are evolving toward high-speed, high-bandwidth, digital packet-switched transmission. Broadband 3G networks are capable of transmitting data at speeds ranging from 144 Kbps to more than 2 Mbps. 4G networks capable of transmission speeds that could reach 1 Gbps are starting to be rolled out.

   Major cellular standards include Code Division Multiple Access (CDMA), which is used primarily in the United States, and Global System for Mobile Communications (GSM), which is the standard in Europe and much of the rest of the world.

   Standards for wireless computer networks include Bluetooth (802.15) for small personal area networks (PANs), Wi-Fi (802.11) for local area networks (LANs), and WiMax (802.16) for metropolitan area networks (MANs).

5. *Why are radio frequency identification (RFID) and wireless sensor networks valuable for business?*

   Radio frequency identification (RFID) systems provide a powerful technology for tracking the movement of goods by using tiny tags with embedded data about an item and its location. RFID readers read the radio signals transmitted by these tags and pass the data over a network to a computer for processing. Wireless sensor networks (WSNs) are networks of interconnected wireless sensing and transmitting devices that are embedded into the physical environment to provide measurements of many points over large spaces.

Key Terms

3G Networks, 307

4G networks, 307

Bandwidth, 288

Blog, 304

Blogosphere, 304

Bluetooth, 308

Broadband, 280

Cable Internet connections, 288

Chat, 294

Digital subscriber line (DSL), 288

Domain name, 289

Domain Name System (DNS), 289

E-mail, 294

File Transfer Protocol (FTP), 294

Hertz, 287

Hotspots, 310

Hubs, 281

Hypertext Transfer Protocol (HTTP), 299

Instant messaging, 294

Internet Protocol (IP) address, 288

Internet service provider (ISP), 288

Internet2, 291

IPv6, 291

Local area network (LAN), 286

Metropolitan area network (MAN), 287

Microblogging, 304

Modem, 285

Network operating system (NOS), 281

Packet switching, 283

Peer-to-peer, 286

Personal area networks (PANs), 308

Protocol, 284

Radio frequency identification (RFID), 310

Router, 281

RSS, 304

Search engines, 300

Search engine marketing, 302

Search engine optimization (SEO), 302

Semantic Web, 306

Shopping bots, 304

Smartphones, 307

Social networking, 305

Social search, 303

Software-defined networking, 281

Switch, 281

T1 lines, 288

Telnet, 294

Transmission Control Protocol/Internet Protocol (TCP/IP), 284

Unified communications, 298

Uniform resource locator (URL), 299

Virtual private network (VPN), 298

Voice over IP (VoIP), 295

Web 2.0, 304

Web 3.0, 306

Web site, 299

Wide area networks (WANs), 287

Wi-Fi, 309

Wiki, 305

WiMax, 310

Wireless sensor networks (WSNs), 313

Review Questions

1. What are the principal components of telecommunications networks and key networking technologies?

   - Describe the features of a simple network and the network infrastructure for a large company.

   - Name and describe the principal technologies and trends that have shaped contemporary telecommunications systems.

2. What are the main telecommunications transmission media and types of networks?

   - Name the different types of physical transmission media and compare them in terms of speed and cost.

   - Define a LAN, and describe its components and the functions of each component.

   - Name and describe the principal network topologies.

3. How do the Internet and Internet technology work, and how do they support communication and e-business?

   - Define the Internet, describe how it works, and explain how it provides business value.

   - Explain how the Domain Name System (DNS) and IP addressing system work.

   - List and describe the principal Internet services.

- Define and describe VoIP and virtual private networks, and explain how they provide value to businesses.
- List and describe alternative ways of locating information on the Web.
- Compare Web 2.0 and Web 3.0.

4. What are the principal technologies and standards for wireless networking, communications, and Internet access?
   - Define Bluetooth, Wi-Fi, WiMax, and 3G and 4G networks.

- Describe the capabilities of each and for which types of applications each is best suited.

5. Why are RFID and wireless sensor networks (WSNs) valuable for business?
   - Define RFID, explain how it works, and describe how it provides value to businesses.
   - Define WSNs, explain how they work, and describe the kinds of applications that use them.

Discussion Questions

1. It has been said that within the next few years, smartphones will become the single most important digital device we own. Discuss the implications of this statement.

2. Should all major retailing and manufacturing companies switch to RFID? Why or why not?

3. Compare Wi-Fi and high-speed cellular systems for accessing the Internet. What are the advantages and disadvantages of each?

Hands-On MIS Projects

The projects in this section give you hands-on experience evaluating and selecting communications technology, using spreadsheet software to improve selection of telecommunications services, and using Web search engines for business research.

Management Decision Problems

1. Your company supplies ceramic floor tiles to Home Depot, Lowe's, and other home improvement stores. You have been asked to start using radio frequency identification tags on each case of tiles you ship to help your customers improve the management of your products and those of other suppliers in their warehouses. Use the Web to identify the cost of hardware, software, and networking components for an RFID system for your company. What factors should be considered? What are the key decisions that have to be made in determining whether your firm should adopt this technology?

2. BestMed Medical Supplies Corporation sells medical and surgical products and equipment from over 700 different manufacturers to hospitals, health clinics, and medical offices. The company employs 500 people at seven different locations in western and midwestern states, including account managers, customer service and support representatives, and warehouse staff. Employees communicate via traditional telephone voice services, e-mail, instant messaging, and cell phones. Management is inquiring about whether the company should adopt a system for unified communications. What factors should be considered? What are the key decisions that have to be made in determining whether to adopt this technology? Use the Web, if necessary, to find out more about unified communications and its costs.

Improving Decision Making: Using Spreadsheet Software to Evaluate Wireless Services

Software skills: Spreadsheet formulas, formatting
Business skills: Analyzing telecommunications services and costs

In this project, you'll use the Web to research alternative wireless services and use spreadsheet software to calculate wireless service costs for a sales force.

You would like to equip your sales force of 35, based in Cincinnati, Ohio, with mobile phones that have capabilities for voice transmission, text messaging, and taking and sending photos. Use the Web to select a wireless service provider that provides nationwide service as well as good service in your home area. Examine the features of the mobile handsets offered by each of these vendors. Assume that each of the 35 salespeople will need to spend three hours per weekday between 8 a.m. and 6 p.m. on mobile voice communication, send 30 text messages per weekday, and send five photos per week. Use your spreadsheet software to determine the wireless service and handset that will offer the best pricing per user over a two-year period. For the purposes of this exercise, you do not need to consider corporate discounts.

Achieving Operational Excellence: Using Web Search Engines for Business Research

Software skills: Web search tools
Business skills: Researching new technologies

This project will help develop your Internet skills in using Web search engines for business research.

Use Google and Bing to obtain information about ethanol as an alternative fuel for motor vehicles. If you wish, try some other search engines as well. Compare the volume and quality of information you find with each search tool. Which tool is the easiest to use? Which produced the best results for your research? Why?

Video Cases

Video Cases and Instructional Videos illustrating some of the concepts in this chapter are available. Contact your instructor to access these videos.

Collaboration and Teamwork Project

In MyMISLab, you will find a Collaboration and Teamwork Project dealing with the concepts in this chapter. You will be able to use Google Sites, Google Docs, and other open source collaboration tools to complete the assignment.

Apple, Google, and Microsoft Battle for your Internet Experience
CASE STUDY

The three Internet titans—Google, Microsoft, and Apple—are in an epic struggle to dominate your Internet experience. They are competing on several fronts: digital content, from music to videos and books for sale in their online stores; physical devices, from Apple's iPhone to Google's Android phones, to Microsoft's Windows 8 phones. And let's not forget they all offer tablets as well. The prize is a projected $400 billion e-commerce marketplace by 2015 where the major access device will be a smartphone or tablet computer. Each firm generates extraordinary amounts of cash based on different business models and is using that cash in hopes of being the top dog on the Internet.

In this triangular fight, at one point or another, each firm has allied with one of their two major foes to team up on the third. Two of the firms—Google and Apple—are determined to prevent Microsoft from expanding its dominance beyond the PC desktop and onto the new mobile platform. So Google and Apple are friends. But when it comes to mobile phones and apps, Google and Apple are enemies: both want to dominate the mobile market. Apple and Microsoft are determined to prevent Google from extending beyond its dominance in search and advertising. So Apple and Microsoft are friends. But when it comes to the mobile marketplace for devices and apps, Apple and Microsoft are enemies. Google and Microsoft are just plain enemies in a variety of battles. Google is trying to weaken Microsoft's PC software dominance, and Microsoft is trying to break into the search advertising market with Bing.

The Internet, along with hardware devices and software applications, is going through a major expansion. Mobile devices with advanced functionality and ubiquitous Internet access are rapidly gaining on traditional desktop computing as the most popular form of computing, changing the basis for competition throughout the industry. Some analysts predict that by 2015, mobile devices will account for the majority of Internet traffic. Today, mobile devices account for approximately 30 percent of the traffic on the Web. These mobile Internet devices are made possible by a growing cloud of computing capacity available to anyone with a smartphone and Internet connectivity. Who needs a desktop PC anymore when you can listen to music and watch videos anytime, anywhere on mobile devices? It's no surprise, then, that today's tech titans are so aggressively battling for control of this brave new mobile world.

Apple, Google, and Microsoft already compete in an assortment of fields. Google has a huge edge in advertising, thanks to its dominance in Internet search. Microsoft's offering, Bing, has about 5 percent of the search market, and about 80 percent belongs to Google. Apple is the leader in mobile software applications, thanks to the popularity of the App Store for its iPhones. Google and Microsoft have less popular app offerings on the Web. Microsoft is still the leader in PC operating systems, but has struggled with many of its other efforts, including smartphone hardware and software, mobile computing, cloud-based software apps, and its Internet portal. Even though Microsoft's Xbox consoles and games are popular, they contribute less than 5 percent of Microsoft's revenue (the rest of its revenue comes from Windows, Office, and network software). While Windows XP, Windows 7, and Windows Vista are still the operating systems for approximately 90 percent of the world's PCs, Google's Android OS and Apple's iOS are the dominant players in the mobile computing market, and all three of these companies now realize that this market will only increase in size and scope going forward.

Apple has several advantages that will serve it well in the battle for mobile supremacy. It's no coincidence that since the Internet exploded in size and popularity, so too did Apple's revenue, which totaled well over $108 billion in 2011, up from $65 billion the previous year despite an ongoing economic downturn. The iMac, iPod, and iPhone have all contributed to the company's enormous success in the Internet era, and the iPad has followed the trend of profitability set by these previous products. Apple has a loyal user base that has steadily grown and is very likely to buy future product and offerings.

Part of the reason for the popularity of the iPhone, and for the optimism surrounding Internet-equipped smartphones in general, has been the success of the App Store. A vibrant selection of applications distinguishes Apple's offerings from its competitors', and gives Apple a measurable head start in this marketplace. Apple already offers approximately 700,000 applications for their devices, and Apple takes a 30 percent cut of all app sales. Applications greatly enrich the experience of using a mobile device, and without them, the predictions for the future of mobile Internet would not be nearly as bright. Whoever creates the most appealing set of devices and applications will derive a significant competitive advantage over rival companies. Right now, that company is Apple.

But the development of smartphones and mobile Internet is still in its infancy. Google has acted swiftly to enter the battle for mobile supremacy while they can still "win." More and more people are likely to switch to mobile computing as their primary method of using the Internet, so it's no surprise that Google is aggressively following the eyeballs. Google is as strong as the size of its advertising network. With the impending shift towards mobile computing looming, it's not certain that they'll be able to maintain their dominant position in search. That's why the dominant online search company began developing its Android operating system, which is used on almost 60 percent of smartphones worldwide. Google offers Android for free to manufacturers of handsets that run the operating system. Via Android, Google hopes to control its own destiny in an increasingly mobile world.

Because Google provides Android at no cost to smartphone manufacturers, competitors have sought to weigh it down with patent claims and other lawsuits. That's part of the reason why Google made its biggest acquisition yet in August 2011, buying Motorola Mobility Holdings for $12.5 billion. The deal gives Google 17,000 patents and another 7,000 more in the pipeline that will help the company defend Android from these patent lawsuits. But buying Motorola's phone business does more than just give Google patents. It also gives Google the ability to make its own cell phones and tablet devices, which would be its most aggressive move against Apple yet.

Analysts were skeptical regarding whether or not Google would even try to enter this marketplace, let alone whether it could succeed in doing so. But in June 2012, Google released its Nexus 7 tablet, developed by Asus, to rave reviews. The sleek 7-inch tablet is priced between $199 and $249, and effectively competes with the iPad and Kindle Fire. Google is entering completely new territory. It has never sold devices before, the profit margins will be much tighter than they are for their search business, and it places Motorola in an awkward position

among the smartphone manufacturers that Google works with. And Google's previous attempts to sell hardware have been unsuccessful: their Nexus One smartphone, released in 2010, was widely considered to be a failure despite impressive technical capabilities.

Google has been particularly aggressive with moves such as the acquisition of Motorola's phone business because it is concerned about Apple's preference for "closed," proprietary standards on its phones. Apple retains the final say over whether or not its users can access various services on the Web, and that includes services provided by Google. Google doesn't want Apple to be able to block it from providing its services on iPhones, or any other smartphone. Apple is reliant on sales of its devices to remain profitable. It has had no problems with this so far, but Google only needs to spread its advertising networks onto these devices to make a profit. In fact, some analysts speculate that Google envisions a future where mobile phones cost a fraction of what they do today, or are even free, requiring only the advertising revenue generated by the devices to turn a profit. Apple would struggle to remain competitive in this environment. Apple has kept the garden closed for a simple reason: you need an Apple device to play there.

Apple's $1.05 billion victory in a patent lawsuit against Samsung on August 24, 2012, could be a blow to Google. Samsung smartphones and tablets were found to have violated a series of Apple patents protecting a number of designs and functions, including the pinch-to-zoom gesture in the user interface. The verdict discourages other handset companies from making devices that use Google's Android operating system, and Android may be forced to make design changes.

In 2012, Apple announced a mapping application to rival Google Maps. Approximately half of Google Maps traffic comes from Apple devices, and that traffic generates valuable location data that helps to improve the service, holding great value for marketers and advertisers. Apple has made several smaller acquisitions in the past two years that have prepared it to compete with Google in this field, and Apple now has its sights set on the valuable location data generated by Google Maps. Apple does not want Google gathering useful data about Apple users on their own devices.

Microsoft hasn't given up trying to establish a cloud and mobile presence. Its Office 2013 productivity suite operates in the cloud as well as on the desktop, giving users the option of saving documents to Microsoft's

SkyDrive cloud storage service. Microsoft launched its Surface tablet computers around the same time as the launch of the Windows 8 operating system.

The struggle between Apple, Google, and Microsoft wouldn't matter much if there wasn't so much potential money at stake. Billions of dollars hang in the balance, and the majority of that money will come from advertising. App sales are another important component, especially for Apple. Apple has the edge in selection and quality of apps, but while sales have been brisk, developers have complained that making money is too difficult. Roughly a quarter of the apps available in the App Store are free, which makes no money for developers or for Apple, but it does bring consumers to the Apple marketplace where they can be sold other apps or entertainment services.

The three-way struggle between Microsoft, Apple, and Google really has no precedent in the history of computing platforms. In early contests, it was typically a single firm that rode the crest of a new technology to become the dominant player. Examples include IBM's dominance of the mainframe market, Digital Equipment's dominance of minicomputers, Microsoft's dominance of operating systems and PC productivity applications, and Cisco's dominance of the Internet router market. In the current struggle, three firms are trying to dominate the customer experience on the Internet. Each firm brings certain strengths and weaknesses to the fray. It's too early to tell if a single firm will "win," or if all three can survive the contest for the consumer Internet experience.

Sources: Nick Wingfield, "Apple Case Muddies the Future of Innovations," *The New York Times*, August 27, 2012; Michael Vizard, "The Path of Least Mobile Computing Resistance", Channel Insider. com, June 6, 2012; Reuters, "Apple Versus Google War Heats Up," June 9, 2012; "Microsoft Counting on Office 2013 to Retain Enterprise App Dominance," *CIO Insight*, July 18, 2012; John Letzing and Amir Efrati, "Google's New Role as Gadget Maker," *The Wall Street Journal*, June 28, 2012; Nick Wingfield, "With Tablet, Microsoft Takes Aim at Hardware Missteps," *The New York Times*, June 24, 2012; Jessica Vascellaro, "Apple and Google Expand Their Battle to Mobile Maps," *The Wall Street Journal*, June 4, 2012; Amir Efrati and Spencer E. Ante, "Google's $12.5 Billion Gamble," *The Wall Street Journal*, August 16, 2011; Evelyn M. Rusli, "Google's Big Bet on the Mobile Future," *The New York Times*, August 15, 2011; Claire Cain Miller, "Google, a Giant in Mobile Search, Seeks New Ways to Make It Pay," *The New York Times*, April 24, 2011; Brad Stone and Miguel Helft, "Apple's Spat with Google Is Getting Personal," *The New York Times*, March 12, 2010; and Peter Burrows, "Apple vs. Google," *BusinessWeek*, January 14, 2010.

CASE STUDY QUESTIONS

1. Compare the business models and areas of strength of Apple, Google, and Microsoft.

2. Why is mobile computing so important to these three firms? Evaluate the mobile platform offerings of each firm.

3. What is the significance of mobile applications, app stores, and closed vs. open app standards to the success or failure of mobile computing?

4. Which company and business model do you think will prevail in this epic struggle? Explain your answer.

5. What difference would it make to a business or to an individual consumer if Apple, Google, or Microsoft dominated the Internet experience? Explain your answer.

Chapter 8

Securing Information Systems

LEARNING OBJECTIVES

After reading this chapter, you will be able to answer the following questions:

1. Why are information systems vulnerable to destruction, error, and abuse?

2. What is the business value of security and control?

3. What are the components of an organizational framework for security and control?

4. What are the most important tools and technologies for safeguarding information resources?

CHAPTER OUTLINE

Interactive Sessions:

Stuxnet and the Changing Face of Cyberwarfare

MWEB Business: Hacked

LinkedIn is one of the most prominent social networking sites on the Web. LinkedIn has over 160 million members, mostly career minded white-collar workers more interested in networking than being social. Users maintain online resumes, establish links with their colleagues and business contacts, and search for experts with answers to their daily business problems. People looking for jobs or to advance their careers take this service very seriously. By any measure, LinkedIn has been one of the top tech success stories in the last decade. The company is now valued at over $12 billion.

In June 2012, however, the company suffered a staggering data breach that exposed the passwords of millions of LinkedIn users. Hackers breached LinkedIn's security and stole 6.5 million user passwords, then posted the passwords publicly on a Russian hacking forum. In the aftermath of the breach, LinkedIn users and security experts alike were stunned that a company whose primary function is to collect and manage customer data had done so little to safeguard it. LinkedIn had woefully inadequate computer security, especially for a highly successful tech company with healthy cash reserves, a strong bottom line, and talented employees.

Security experts criticized LinkedIn for not having a chief security officer whose primary job is to guard against security breaches. But even more surprisingly, LinkedIn was found to have minimal password protection via encryption and did not employ several standard encryption techniques used to protect passwords. Most companies will use a technique known as "salting," which adds a series of random digits to the end of hashed passwords to make them more difficult to crack. Salting can be performed at little to no cost with just a few additional lines of code. Most companies use complicated cryptographic functions to salt passwords, but, incredibly LinkedIn had not salted its users' passwords at all, the security equivalent of leaving one's valuables unattended in a crowded area.

Most companies store hashed passwords on separate, secure Web servers to make it more difficult for hackers to break in. The total cost for a company like LinkedIn to set up robust password, Web server, and application security would be in the low six figures, but the average data breach costs companies $5.5 million, according to a Symantec-sponsored study by the Ponemon Institute. LinkedIn's losses might end up being even higher than that, which makes their near total disregard for data security even more surprising.

Some security experts believe that the lack of liability for companies like LinkedIn is a major reason for their lax security policies. Unlike other industries, where basic consumer protections are overseen and protected, computer security and social network data security are not regulated and are poorly protected by many companies. Additionally, with social networks, people tend not to leave a service because of a data breach. For example, in the wake of the breach, many users wanted to leave LinkedIn, but opted not to because it is the most prominent social network for business networking.

© Rafal Olechowski/Shutterstock

Immediately after the password theft, LinkedIn quickly assured its customers that their data were secure. The company disabled the 6.5 million published passwords and announced that it had begun an initiative to salt passwords to increase security. Nevertheless, LinkedIn now faces a $5 million class-action lawsuit that asserts that LinkedIn failed to follow even the minimal industry-standard practices for data protection, specifically more recent forms of salting hashed passwords.

Security experts noted that LinkedIn's security procedures would have been state of the art several years ago, but that they had done little to keep up with and protect themselves from the surge in data breaches in the last year or two. LinkedIn must not only update their security to today's standards, but must also adopt the mindset that protecting consumer data is an ongoing effort, not a one-time fix.

Sources: LinkedIn Faces $5 Million Lawsuit After Password Breach," *CIO Insight*, June 22, 2012; "LinkedIn Defends Reaction in Wake of Password Theft," *The Wall Street Journal*, June 10, 2012; "Lax Security at LinkedIn Is Laid Bare," *The New York Times*, June 10, 2012; "Why ID Thieves Love Social Media," *Marketwatch*, March 25, 2012.

The problems created by the theft of 6.5 million passwords at LinkedIn illustrate some of the reasons why businesses need to pay special attention to information system security. LinkedIn provides important benefits to both individuals and businesses. But from a security standpoint, LinkedIn did not sufficiently protect its Web site from hackers, who were able to steal sensitive user information.

The chapter-opening diagram calls attention to important points raised by this case and this chapter. Although LinkedIn's management has some security technology and procedures in place, it has not done enough to protect its user data. It failed to use standard password encryption techniques, including "salting," to protect user passwords.

The "social" nature of this site and large number of users make it unusually attractive for criminals and hackers intent on stealing valuable personal and financial information and propagating malicious software. Given LinkedIn's large user base and the social nature of the site, management did not do enough to protect LinkedIn's data. LinkedIn's loyal user base prevented the fallout from the breach from being much greater, and most people decided they needed to stay with the site because it was so valuable for their careers. Nevertheless, the company faces a multimillion-dollar class action suit as well as reputational damage. For all companies the lesson is clear: difficulties of eradicating malicious software or repairing damage caused by identity theft add to operational costs and make both individuals and businesses less effective.

Here are some questions to think about: What management, organization, and technology factors contributed to the LinkedIn data breach? What was the business impact of the data breach?

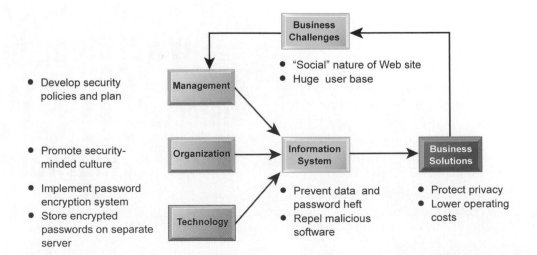

8.1   SYSTEM VULNERABILITY AND ABUSE

Can you imagine what would happen if you tried to link to the Internet without a firewall or antivirus software? Your computer would be disabled in a few seconds, and it might take you many days to recover. If you used the computer to run your business, you might not be able to sell to your customers or place orders with your suppliers while it was down. And you might find that your computer system had been penetrated by outsiders, who perhaps stole or destroyed valuable data, including confidential payment data from your customers. If too much data were destroyed or divulged, your business might never be able to operate!

In short, if you operate a business today, you need to make security and control a top priority. **Security** refers to the policies, procedures, and technical measures used to prevent unauthorized access, alteration, theft, or physical damage to information systems. **Controls** are methods, policies, and organizational procedures that ensure the safety of the organization's assets, the accuracy and reliability of its records, and operational adherence to management standards.

WHY SYSTEMS ARE VULNERABLE

When large amounts of data are stored in electronic form, they are vulnerable to many more kinds of threats than when they existed in manual form. Through communications networks, information systems in different locations are interconnected. The potential for unauthorized access, abuse, or fraud is not limited to a single location but can occur at any access point in the network. Figure 8.1 illustrates the most common threats against contemporary information systems. They can stem from technical, organizational, and environmental factors compounded by poor management decisions. In the multi-tier client/server computing environment illustrated here, vulnerabilities exist at each layer and in the communications between the layers. Users at the client

FIGURE 8.1   CONTEMPORARY SECURITY CHALLENGES AND VULNERABILITIES

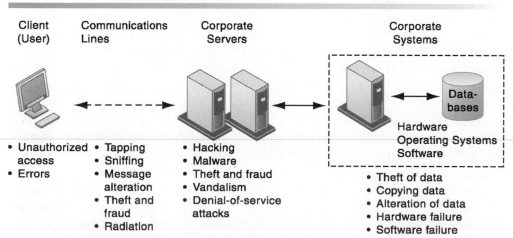

The architecture of a Web-based application typically includes a Web client, a server, and corporate information systems linked to databases. Each of these components presents security challenges and vulnerabilities. Floods, fires, power failures, and other electrical problems can cause disruptions at any point in the network.

layer can cause harm by introducing errors or by accessing systems without authorization. It is possible to access data flowing over networks, steal valuable data during transmission, or alter messages without authorization. Radiation may disrupt a network at various points as well. Intruders can launch denial-of-service attacks or malicious software to disrupt the operation of Web sites. Those capable of penetrating corporate systems can destroy or alter corporate data stored in databases or files.

Systems malfunction if computer hardware breaks down, is not configured properly, or is damaged by improper use or criminal acts. Errors in programming, improper installation, or unauthorized changes cause computer software to fail. Power failures, floods, fires, or other natural disasters can also disrupt computer systems.

Domestic or offshore partnering with another company adds to system vulnerability if valuable information resides on networks and computers outside the organization's control. Without strong safeguards, valuable data could be lost, destroyed, or could fall into the wrong hands, revealing important trade secrets or information that violates personal privacy.

The popularity of handheld mobile devices for business computing adds to these woes. Portability makes cell phones, smartphones, and tablet computers easy to lose or steal. Smartphones share the same security weaknesses as other Internet devices, and are vulnerable to malicious software and penetration from outsiders. Smartphones used by corporate employees often contain sensitive data such as sales figures, customer names, phone numbers, and e-mail addresses. Intruders may be able to access internal corporate systems through these devices.

Internet Vulnerabilities

Large public networks, such as the Internet, are more vulnerable than internal networks because they are virtually open to anyone. The Internet is so huge that when abuses do occur, they can have an enormously widespread impact. When the Internet becomes part of the corporate network, the organization's information systems are even more vulnerable to actions from outsiders.

Computers that are constantly connected to the Internet by cable modems or digital subscriber line (DSL) lines are more open to penetration by outsiders because they use fixed Internet addresses where they can be easily identified. (With dial-up service, a temporary Internet address is assigned for each session.) A fixed Internet address creates a fixed target for hackers.

Telephone service based on Internet technology (see Chapter 7) is more vulnerable than the switched voice network if it does not run over a secure private network. Most Voice over IP (VoIP) traffic over the public Internet is not encrypted, so anyone with a network can listen in on conversations. Hackers can intercept conversations or shut down voice service by flooding servers supporting VoIP with bogus traffic.

Vulnerability has also increased from widespread use of e-mail, instant messaging (IM), and peer-to-peer file-sharing programs. E-mail may contain attachments that serve as springboards for malicious software or unauthorized access to internal corporate systems. Employees may use e-mail messages to transmit valuable trade secrets, financial data, or confidential customer information to unauthorized recipients. Popular IM applications for consumers do not use a secure layer for text messages, so they can be intercepted and read by outsiders during transmission over the public Internet. Instant messaging activity over the Internet can in some cases be used as a back door to an otherwise secure network. Sharing files over peer-to-peer (P2P) networks, such as those for illegal music sharing, may also transmit malicious software or expose information on either individual or corporate computers to outsiders.

Wireless Security Challenges

Is it safe to log onto a wireless network at an airport, library, or other public location? It depends on how vigilant you are. Even the wireless network in your home is vulnerable because radio frequency bands are easy to scan. Both Bluetooth and Wi-Fi networks are susceptible to hacking by eavesdroppers. Local area networks (LANs) using the 802.11 standard can be easily penetrated by outsiders armed with laptops, wireless cards, external antennae, and hacking software. Hackers use these tools to detect unprotected networks, monitor network traffic, and, in some cases, gain access to the Internet or to corporate networks.

Wi-Fi transmission technology was designed to make it easy for stations to find and hear one another. The *service set identifiers (SSIDs)* that identify the access points in a Wi-Fi network are broadcast multiple times and can be picked up fairly easily by intruders' sniffer programs (see Figure 8.2). Wireless networks in many locations do not have basic protections against **war driving**, in which eavesdroppers drive by buildings or park outside and try to intercept wireless network traffic.

An intruder that has associated with an access point by using the correct SSID is capable of accessing other resources on the network. For example, the intruder could use the Windows operating system to determine which other users are connected to the network, access their computer hard drives, and open or copy their files.

FIGURE 8.2   WI-FI SECURITY CHALLENGES

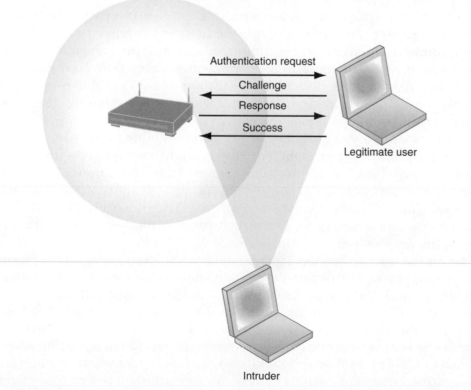

Many Wi-Fi networks can be penetrated easily by intruders using sniffer programs to obtain an address to access the resources of a network without authorization.

Intruders also use the information they have gleaned to set up rogue access points on a different radio channel in physical locations close to users to force a user's radio network interface controller (NIC) to associate with the rogue access point. Once this association occurs, hackers using the rogue access point can capture the names and passwords of unsuspecting users.

MALICIOUS SOFTWARE: VIRUSES, WORMS, TROJAN HORSES, AND SPYWARE

Malicious software programs are referred to as **malware** and include a variety of threats, such as computer viruses, worms, and Trojan horses. A **computer virus** is a rogue software program that attaches itself to other software programs or data files in order to be executed, usually without user knowledge or permission. Most computer viruses deliver a "payload." The payload may be relatively benign, such as instructions to display a message or image, or it may be highly destructive—destroying programs or data, clogging computer memory, reformatting a computer's hard drive, or causing programs to run improperly. Viruses typically spread from computer to computer when humans take an action, such as sending an e-mail attachment or copying an infected file.

Most recent attacks have come from **worms**, which are independent computer programs that copy themselves from one computer to other computers over a network. Unlike viruses, worms can operate on their own without attaching to other computer program files and rely less on human behavior in order to spread from computer to computer. This explains why computer worms spread much more rapidly than computer viruses. Worms destroy data and programs as well as disrupt or even halt the operation of computer networks.

Worms and viruses are often spread over the Internet from files of downloaded software, from files attached to e-mail transmissions, or from compromised e-mail messages, online ads, or instant messaging. Viruses have also invaded computerized information systems from "infected" disks or infected machines. Especially prevalent today are **drive-by downloads**, consisting of malware that comes with a downloaded file that a user intentionally or unintentionally requests.

Hackers can do to a smartphone just about anything they can do to any Internet device: request malicious files without user intervention, delete files, transmit files, install programs running in the background to monitor user actions, and potentially convert the smartphone into a robot in a botnet to send e-mail and text messages to anyone. With smartphones starting to outsell PCs, and smartphones increasingly used as payment devices, they are becoming a major avenue for malware.

Malware targeting mobile devices is not yet as extensive as that targeting larger computers, but nonetheless is spreading using e-mail, text messages, Bluetooth, and file downloads from the Web via Wi-Fi or cellular networks. The security firm McAfee found nearly 13,000 different kinds of malware targeting mobile devices in 2012 compared to less than 2,000 in 2011, with almost all attacks targeting devices using Google's Android operating system. (Graziano, 2012). Mobile device viruses pose serious threats to enterprise computing because so many wireless devices are now linked to corporate information systems.

Blogs, wikis, and social networking sites such as Facebook have emerged as new conduits for malware or spyware. These applications allow users to post software code as part of the permissible content, and such code can be launched automatically as soon as a Web page is viewed. On July 4, 2011, hackers broke into the "Fox News Politics" Twitter account, sending fake messages about President Barack Obama. The hackers changed the account's password, preventing Fox from correcting the messages for hours (Sherr, 2011).

Internet security firm Symantec reported in 2012 that it had detected 403 million new and unique threats from malicious software in 2011, up from 286 million in 2010. Symantec observed that the amount of harmful software in the world passed the amount of beneficial software in 2007, and as many as one of every 10 downloads from the Web includes harmful programs (Drew and Kopytoff, 2011). According to Symantec, 36 percent of malware today is being targeted at small businesses, because it is more difficult for such companies to protect themselves against so many different types of attacks (Symantec, 2012). Table 8.1 describes the characteristics of some of the most harmful worms and viruses that have appeared to date.

A **Trojan horse** is a software program that appears to be benign but then does something other than expected. The Trojan horse is not itself a virus because it does not replicate, but it is often a way for viruses or other malicious code to be introduced into a computer system. The term *Trojan horse* is based on the huge

TABLE 8.1 EXAMPLES OF MALICIOUS CODE

NAME	TYPE	DESCRIPTION
Conficker (aka Downadup, Downup)	Worm	First detected in November 2008 and still prevalent. Uses flaws in Windows software to take over machines and link them into a virtual computer that can be commanded remotely. Had more than 5 million computers worldwide under its control. Difficult to eradicate.
Storm	Worm/ Trojan horse	First identified in January 2007. Spreads via e-mail spam with a fake attachment. Infected up to 10 million computers, causing them to join its zombie network of computers engaged in criminal activity.
Sasser.ftp	Worm	First appeared in May 2004. Spread over the Internet by attacking random IP addresses. Causes computers to continually crash and reboot, and infected computers to search for more victims. Affected millions of computers worldwide, disrupting British Airways flight check-ins, operations of British coast guard stations, Hong Kong hospitals, Taiwan post office branches, and Australia's Westpac Bank. Sasser and its variants caused an estimated $14.8 billion to $18.6 billion in damages worldwide.
MyDoom.A	Worm	First appeared on January 26, 2004. Spreads as an e-mail attachment. Sends e-mail to addresses harvested from infected machines, forging the sender's address. At its peak, this worm lowered global Internet performance by 10 percent and Web page loading times by as much as 50 percent. Was programmed to stop spreading after February 12, 2004.
Sobig.F	Worm	First detected on August 19, 2003. Spreads via e-mail attachments and sends massive amounts of mail with forged sender information. Deactivated itself on September 10, 2003, after infecting more than 1 million PCs and doing $5 to $10 billion in damage.
ILOVEYOU	Virus	First detected on May 3, 2000. Script virus written in Visual Basic script and transmitted as an attachment to e-mail with the subject line ILOVEYOU. Overwrites music, image, and other files with a copy of itself and did an estimated $10 billion to $15 billion in damage.
Melissa	Macro virus/ worm	First appeared in March 1999. Word macro script mailing infected Word file to first 50 entries in user's Microsoft Outlook address book. Infected 15 to 29 percent of all business PCs, causing $300 million to $600 million in damage.

wooden horse used by the Greeks to trick the Trojans into opening the gates to their fortified city during the Trojan War. Once inside the city walls, Greek soldiers hidden in the horse revealed themselves and captured the city.

An example of a modern-day Trojan horse is the MMarketPay.A Trojan for Android phones. This Trojan is hidden in several apps that appear to be legitimate, including travel and weather apps. It places orders for applications and movies automatically without the user's permission, potentially causing users to be hit with unexpectedly high phone bills. MMarketPay.A has been detected in multiple app stores and has spread to more than 100,000 devices.

SQL injection attacks have become a major malware threat. SQL injection attacks take advantage of vulnerabilities in poorly coded Web application software to introduce malicious program code into a company's systems and networks. These vulnerabilities occur when a Web application fails to properly validate or filter data entered by a user on a Web page, which might occur when ordering something online. An attacker uses this input validation error to send a rogue SQL query to the underlying database to access the database, plant malicious code, or access other systems on the network. Large Web applications have hundreds of places for inputting user data, each of which creates an opportunity for an SQL injection attack.

A large number of Web-facing applications are believed to have SQL injection vulnerabilities, and tools are available for hackers to check Web applications for these vulnerabilities. Such tools are able to locate a data entry field on a Web page form, enter data into it, and check the response to see if shows vulnerability to a SQL injection.

Some types of spyware also act as malicious software. These small programs install themselves surreptitiously on computers to monitor user Web surfing activity and serve up advertising. Thousands of forms of spyware have been documented.

Many users find such **spyware** annoying, and some critics worry about its infringement on computer users' privacy. Some forms of spyware are especially nefarious. **Keyloggers** record every keystroke made on a computer to steal serial numbers for software, to launch Internet attacks, to gain access to e-mail accounts, to obtain passwords to protected computer systems, or to pick up personal information such as credit card numbers. For example, the Zeus Trojan stole financial and personal data from online banking and social networking sites by surreptitiously tracking users' keystrokes as they entered data into their computers. Other spyware programs reset Web browser home pages, redirect search requests, or slow performance by taking up too much memory.

HACKERS AND COMPUTER CRIME

A **hacker** is an individual who intends to gain unauthorized access to a computer system. Within the hacking community, the term *cracker* is typically used to denote a hacker with criminal intent, although in the public press, the terms hacker and cracker are used interchangeably. Hackers and crackers gain unauthorized access by finding weaknesses in the security protections employed by Web sites and computer systems, often taking advantage of various features of the Internet that make it an open system and easy to use.

Hacker activities have broadened beyond mere system intrusion to include theft of goods and information, as well as system damage and **cybervandalism**, the intentional disruption, defacement, or even destruction of a Web site or corporate information system. For example, cybervandals have turned many of the MySpace "group" sites, which are dedicated to interests such as home beer brewing or animal welfare, into cyber-graffiti walls, filled with offensive comments and photographs.

Spoofing and Sniffing

Hackers attempting to hide their true identities often spoof, or misrepresent, themselves by using fake e-mail addresses or masquerading as someone else. **Spoofing** also may involve redirecting a Web link to an address different from the intended one, with the site masquerading as the intended destination. For example, if hackers redirect customers to a fake Web site that looks almost exactly like the true site, they can then collect and process orders, effectively stealing business as well as sensitive customer information from the true site. We provide more detail on other forms of spoofing in our discussion of computer crime.

A **sniffer** is a type of eavesdropping program that monitors information traveling over a network. When used legitimately, sniffers help identify potential network trouble spots or criminal activity on networks, but when used for criminal purposes, they can be damaging and very difficult to detect. Sniffers enable hackers to steal proprietary information from anywhere on a network, including e-mail messages, company files, and confidential reports.

Denial-of-Service Attacks

In a **denial-of-service (DoS) attack**, hackers flood a network server or Web server with many thousands of false communications or requests for services to crash the network. The network receives so many queries that it cannot keep up with them and is thus unavailable to service legitimate requests. A **distributed denial-of-service (DDoS)** attack uses numerous computers to inundate and overwhelm the network from numerous launch points.

For example, hours after the U.S. Department of Justice shut down file-sharing site Megaupload on January 19 2012, the Anonymous hacker collective launched extensive retaliatory DDoS attacks against federal and entertainment industry Web sites. Web sites belonging to the FBI, U.S. Department of Justice, U.S. Copyright Office, Universal Music, the Recording Industry Association of America, and the Motion Picture Association of America, were knocked offline for a large part of the day.

Although DoS attacks do not destroy information or access restricted areas of a company's information systems, they often cause a Web site to shut down, making it impossible for legitimate users to access the site. For busy e-commerce sites, these attacks are costly; while the site is shut down, customers cannot make purchases. Especially vulnerable are small and midsize businesses whose networks tend to be less protected than those of large corporations.

Perpetrators of DDoS attacks often use thousands of "zombie" PCs infected with malicious software without their owners' knowledge and organized into a **botnet**. Hackers create these botnets by infecting other people's computers with bot malware that opens a back door through which an attacker can give instructions. The infected computer then becomes a slave, or zombie, serving a master computer belonging to someone else. Once hackers infect enough computers, they can use the amassed resources of the botnet to launch DDos attacks, phishing campaigns, or unsolicited "spam" e-mail.

Ninety percent of the world's spam and 80 percent of the world's malware are delivered via botnets. For example, the Grum botnet, once the world's third-largest botnet, was reportedly responsible for 18% of worldwide spam traffic (amounting to 18 billion spam messages per day) when it was shut down on July 19, 2012. At one point Grum had infected and controlled 560,000–840,000 computers.

Computer Crime

Most hacker activities are criminal offenses, and the vulnerabilities of systems we have just described make them targets for other types of **computer crime** as well. In November, 2010, New York resident George Castro was charged with grand larceny for allegedly stealing nearly $4.5 million from Columbia University over the course of two months. Castro had added a TD Bank account belonging to him as a payee in the Columbia University Medical Center's accounts payable system (El-Ghobashy, 2010). Computer crime is defined by the U.S. Department of Justice as "any violations of criminal law that involve a knowledge of computer technology for their perpetration, investigation, or prosecution." Table 8.2 provides examples of the computer as both a target and an instrument of crime.

No one knows the magnitude of the computer crime problem—how many systems are invaded, how many people engage in the practice, or the total economic damage. According to the Ponemon Institute's Second Annual Cost of Cyber Crime Study sponsored by ArcSight, the median annualized cost of cyber-crime for the organizations in the study was $5.9 million per year (Ponemon Institute, 2011). Many companies are reluctant to report computer crimes because the crimes may involve employees, or the company fears that publicizing its vulnerability will hurt its reputation. The most economically damaging kinds of computer crime are DoS attacks, introducing viruses, theft of services, and disruption of computer systems.

Identity Theft

With the growth of the Internet and electronic commerce, identity theft has become especially troubling. **Identity theft** is a crime in which an imposter obtains key pieces of personal information, such as social security identification numbers, driver's license numbers, or credit card numbers, to impersonate someone else. The information may be used to obtain credit, merchandise, or services in the name of the victim or to provide the thief with false credentials.

TABLE 8.2 EXAMPLES OF COMPUTER CRIME

COMPUTERS AS TARGETS OF CRIME

Breaching the confidentiality of protected computerized data

Accessing a computer system without authority

Knowingly accessing a protected computer to commit fraud

Intentionally accessing a protected computer and causing damage, negligently or deliberately

Knowingly transmitting a program, program code, or command that intentionally causes damage to a protected computer

Threatening to cause damage to a protected computer

COMPUTERS AS INSTRUMENTS OF CRIME

Theft of trade secrets

Unauthorized copying of software or copyrighted intellectual property, such as articles, books, music, and video

Schemes to defraud

Using e-mail for threats or harassment

Intentionally attempting to intercept electronic communication

Illegally accessing stored electronic communications, including e-mail and voice mail

Transmitting or possessing child pornography using a computer

Identify theft has flourished on the Internet, with credit card files a major target of Web site hackers. According to the Identity Fraud Report by Javelin Strategy & Research, identity theft increased by 13 percent in 2011, with the total number of victims increasing to 11.6 million adults. However, the total dollar losses from identity theft have remained steady at about $18 billion (Javelin, 2012). Moreover, e-commerce sites are wonderful sources of customer personal information—name, address, and phone number. Armed with this information, criminals are able to assume new identities and establish new credit for their own purposes.

One increasingly popular tactic is a form of spoofing called **phishing**. Phishing involves setting up fake Web sites or sending e-mail messages that look like those of legitimate businesses to ask users for confidential personal data. The e-mail message instructs recipients to update or confirm records by providing social security numbers, bank and credit card information, and other confidential data either by responding to the e-mail message, by entering the information at a bogus Web site, or by calling a telephone number. EBay, PayPal, Amazon.com, Walmart, and a variety of banks are among the top spoofed companies. In a more targeted form of phishing called *spear phishing*, messages appear to come from a trusted source, such as an individual within the recipient's own company or a friend.

Phishing techniques called evil twins and pharming are harder to detect. **Evil twins** are wireless networks that pretend to offer trustworthy Wi-Fi connections to the Internet, such as those in airport lounges, hotels, or coffee shops. The bogus network looks identical to a legitimate public network. Fraudsters try to capture passwords or credit card numbers of unwitting users who log on to the network.

Pharming redirects users to a bogus Web page, even when the individual types the correct Web page address into his or her browser. This is possible if pharming perpetrators gain access to the Internet address information stored by Internet service providers to speed up Web browsing and the ISP companies have flawed software on their servers that allows the fraudsters to hack in and change those addresses.

According to the Ponemon Institute's seventh annual U.S. Cost of a Data Breach Study, data breach incidents cost U.S. companies $194 per compromised customer record in 2011. The average total per-incident cost in 2011 was $5.5 million (Strom, 2012). Additionally, brand damage can be significant, albeit hard to quantify. Table 8.3 describes the most expensive data breaches that have occurred to date.

The U.S. Congress addressed the threat of computer crime in 1986 with the Computer Fraud and Abuse Act, which makes it illegal to access a computer system without authorization. Most states have similar laws, and nations in Europe have comparable legislation. Congress passed the National Information Infrastructure Protection Act in 1996 to make malware distribution and hacker attacks to disable Web sites federal crimes.

U.S. legislation, such as the Wiretap Act, Wire Fraud Act, Economic Espionage Act, Electronic Communications Privacy Act, E-Mail Threats and Harassment Act, and Child Pornography Act, covers computer crimes involving intercepting electronic communication, using electronic communication to defraud, stealing trade secrets, illegally accessing stored electronic communications, using e-mail for threats or harassment, and transmitting or possessing child pornography. A proposed federal Data Security and Breach Notification Act would mandate organizations that possess personal information to put in place

TABLE 8.3 THE FIVE MOST EXPENSIVE DATA BREACHES

DATA BREACH	DESCRIPTION
U.S. Veterans Affairs Department	In 2006, the names, birth dates, and social security numbers of 17.5 million military veterans and personnel were stolen from a laptop that a Department of Veterans Affairs employee had taken home. The VA spent at least $25 million to run call centers, send out mailings, and pay for a year of a credit-monitoring service for victims.
Heartland Payment Systems	In 2008, criminals led by Miami hacker Albert Gonzales installed spying software on the computer network of Heartland Payment Systems, a payment processor based in Princeton, NJ, and stole the numbers of as many as 100 million credit and debit cards. Gonzales was sentenced in 2010 to 20 years in federal prison, and Heartland paid about $140 million in fines and settlements.
TJX	A 2007 data breach at TJX, the retailer that owns national chains including TJ Maxx and Marshalls, cost at least $250 million. Cyber criminals took more than 45 million credit and debit card numbers, some of which were used later to buy millions of dollars in electronics from Walmart and elsewhere. Albert Gonzales, who played a major role in the Heartland hack, was linked to this cyberattack as well.
Epsilon	In March 2011, hackers stole millions of names and e-mail addresses from the Epsilon e-mail marketing firm, which handles e-mail lists for major retailers and banks like Best Buy, JPMorgan, TiVo, and Walgreens. Costs could range from $100 million to $4 billion, depending on what happens to the stolen data, with most of the costs from losing customers due to a damaged reputation.
Sony	In April 2011, hackers obtained personal information, including credit, debit, and bank account numbers, from over 100 million PlayStation Network users and Sony Online Entertainment users. The breach could cost Sony and credit card issuers up to a total of $2 billion.

"reasonable" security procedures to keep the data secure and to notify anyone affected by a data breach, but it has not been enacted.

Click Fraud

When you click on an ad displayed by a search engine, the advertiser typically pays a fee for each click, which is supposed to direct potential buyers to its products. **Click fraud** occurs when an individual or computer program fraudulently clicks on an online ad without any intention of learning more about the advertiser or making a purchase. Click fraud has become a serious problem at Google and other Web sites that feature pay-per-click online advertising.

Some companies hire third parties (typically from low-wage countries) to fraudulently click on a competitor's ads to weaken them by driving up their marketing costs. Click fraud can also be perpetrated with software programs doing the clicking, and botnets are often used for this purpose. Search engines such as Google attempt to monitor click fraud but have been reluctant to publicize their efforts to deal with the problem.

Global Threats: Cyberterrorism and Cyberwarfare

The cyber criminal activities we have described—launching malware, denial-of-service attacks, and phishing probes—are borderless. China, the United States, South Korea, Russia, and Taiwan are currently the sources of most of the world's malware (King, 2012). The global nature of the Internet makes it possible for cybercriminals to operate—and to do harm—anywhere in the world.

Internet vulnerabilities have also turned individuals and even entire nation states into easy targets for politically-motivated hacking to conduct sabotage and espionage. **Cyberwarfare** is a state-sponsored activity designed to cripple and defeat another state or nation by penetrating its computers or networks for the purposes of causing damage and disruption.

In general, cyberwarfare attacks have become much more widespread, sophisticated, and potentially devastating. There are 250,000 probes trying to find their way into the U.S. Department of Defense networks every hour, and cyberattacks on U.S. federal agencies have increased 150 percent since 2008. Over the years, hackers have stolen plans for missile tracking systems, satellite navigation devices, surveillance drones, and leading-edge jet fighters.

Cyberwarfare poses a serious threat to the infrastructure of modern societies, since their major financial, health, government, and industrial institutions rely on the Internet for daily operations. Cyberwarfare also involves defending against these types of attacks. The Interactive Session on Organizations describes some recent cyberwarfare attacks and their growing sophistication and severity.

INTERNAL THREATS: EMPLOYEES

We tend to think the security threats to a business originate outside the organization. In fact, company insiders pose serious security problems. Employees have access to privileged information, and in the presence of sloppy internal security procedures, they are often able to roam throughout an organization's systems without leaving a trace.

Studies have found that user lack of knowledge is the single greatest cause of network security breaches. Many employees forget their passwords to access computer systems or allow co-workers to use them, which compromises the system. Malicious intruders seeking system access sometimes trick employees into revealing their passwords by pretending to be legitimate members of the company in need of information. This practice is called **social engineering**.

Both end users and information systems specialists are also a major source of errors introduced into information systems. End users introduce errors by entering faulty data or by not following the proper instructions for processing data and using computer equipment. Information systems specialists may create software errors as they design and develop new software or maintain existing programs.

SOFTWARE VULNERABILITY

Software errors pose a constant threat to information systems, causing untold losses in productivity. Growing complexity and size of software programs, coupled with demands for timely delivery to markets, have contributed to an increase in software flaws or vulnerabilities. For example, a software error in an iPad app for paying bills caused Citibank to double the charge for customer payments between July and December 2011. Some customers using their iPads to settle their cable bill or mortgage payment, for example, actually paid twice (Protess, 2012).

A major problem with software is the presence of hidden **bugs** or program code defects. Studies have shown that it is virtually impossible to eliminate all bugs from large programs. The main source of bugs is the complexity of decision-making code. A relatively small program of several hundred lines will contain tens of decisions leading to hundreds or even thousands of different paths. Important programs within most corporations are usually much larger, containing tens of thousands or even millions of lines of code, each with many times the choices and paths of the smaller programs.

Zero defects cannot be achieved in larger programs. Complete testing simply is not possible. Fully testing programs that contain thousands of choices and

INTERACTIVE SESSION: ORGANIZATIONS

STUXNET AND THE CHANGING FACE OF CYBERWARFARE

In July 2010, reports surfaced about a Stuxnet worm that had been targeting Iran's nuclear facilities. In November of that year, Iran's President Mahmoud Ahmadinejad publicly acknowledged that malicious software had infected the Iranian nuclear facilities and disrupted the nuclear program by disabling the facilities' centrifuges. Stuxnet had earned its place in history as the first visible example of industrial cyberwarfare.

To date, Stuxnet is the most sophisticated cyberweapon ever deployed. Stuxnet's mission was to activate only computers that ran Supervisory Control and Data Acquisition (SCADA) software used in Siemens centrifuges to enrich uranium. The Windows-based worm had a "dual warhead." One part was designed to lay dormant for long periods, then speed up Iran's nuclear centrifuges so that they spun wildly out of control. Another secretly recorded what normal operations at the nuclear plant looked like and then played those recordings back to plant operators so it would appear that the centrifuges were operating normally when they were actually tearing themselves apart.

The worm's sophistication indicated the work of highly skilled professionals. Michael Assante, president and CEO at the National Board of Information Security Examiners, views Stuxnet as a weapons delivery system like the B-2 Bomber. The software program code was highly modular, so that it could be easily changed to attack different systems. Stuxnet only became active when it encountered a specific configuration of controllers, running a set of processes limited to centrifuge plants.

Over 60 percent of Stuxet-infected computers are in Iran, and digital security company Kaspersky Labs speculates that the worm was launched with nation-state support (probably from Israel and the United States) with the intention of disabling some or all of Iran's uranium enrichment program. Stuxnet wiped out about one-fifth of Iran's nuclear centrifuges. The damage was irreparable and is believed to have delayed Iran's ability to make nuclear arms by as much as five years. And no one is certain that the Stuxnet attacks are over. Some experts who examined the Stuxnet software code believe it contains the seeds for more versions and attacks.

According to a Tofino Security report, Stuxnet is capable of infecting even well-secured computer systems that follow industry best practices. Companies' need for interonnectivity between control systems make it nearly impossible to defend against a well-constructed, multi-pronged attack such as Stuxnet.

And Stuxnet is not the only cyberweapon currently at work. The Flame virus, released about five years ago, has been infecting computers in Iran, Lebanon, Sudan, Saudi Arabia, Egypt, Syria, and Israel. While researchers are still analyzing the program, the attack's main goal is stealing information and espionage. Flame is able to grab images of users' computer screens, record their instant messaging chats, collect passwords, remotely turn on their microphones to record audio conversations, scan disks for specific files, and monitor their keystrokes and network traffic. The software also records Skype conversations and can turn infected computers into Bluetooth beacons which attempt to download contact information from nearby Bluetooth-enabled devices These data, along with locally stored documents, can be sent to one of several command and control servers that are scattered around the world. The program then awaits further instructions from these servers.

The Duqu worm, discovered in September 2011, also aims to steal information by scanning systems. Duqu infects a very small number of very specific systems around the world, but may use completely different modules for infiltrating those separate systems. One of Duqu's actions is to steal digital certificates used for authentication from attacked computers to help future viruses appear as secure software. It is going largely undetected. Security researchers believe Duqu was created by the same group of programmers behind Stuxnet.

The real worry for security experts and government officials is an act of cyberwarfare against a critical resource, such as the electric grid, financial systems, or communications systems. (In April 2009, cyberspies infiltrated the U.S. electrical grid, using weak points where computers on the grid are connected to the Internet, and left behind software programs whose purpose is unclear, but which presumably could be used to disrupt the system.)

The U.S. has no clear strategy about how the country would respond to that level of cyberattack, and the effects of such an attack would likely be devastating. Mike McConnell, the former director of national intelligence, stated that if even a single large American bank were successfully attacked, it would have an order-of-magnitude greater impact on the global economy than the World Trade Center attacks, and that the ability to threaten the U.S. money supply is the financial equivalent of a nuclear weapon.

Many security experts believe that U.S. cybersecurity is not well-organized. Several different agencies, including the Pentagon and the National Security Agency (NSA), have their sights on being the leading agency in the ongoing efforts to combat cyberwarfare. The first headquarters designed to coordinate government cybersecurity efforts, called Cybercom, was activated in May 2010 in the hope of resolving this organizational tangle. In May 2011 President Barack Obama signed executive orders weaving cyber capabilities into U.S. military strategy, but

these capabilities are still evolving. Will the United States and other nations be ready when the next Stuxnet appears?

Sources: Brian Royer, "Stuxnet, The Nation's Power Grid, And The Law Of Unintended Consequences, *Dark Reading*, March 12, 2012; Thomas Erdbrink, "Iran Confirms Attack by Virus That Collects Information," *The New York Times*, May 29, 2012; Nicole Perlroth, "Virus Infects Computers Across Middle East," *The New York Times*, May 28, 2012; Thom Shanker and Elisabeth Bumiller, "After Suffering Damaging Cyberattack, the Pentagon Takes Defensive Action," *The New York Times*, July 15, 2011; Robert Leos, "Secure Best Practices No Proof Against Stuxnet," CSO, March 3, 2011; Lolita C. Baldor, "Pentagon Gets Cyberwar Guidelines," Associated Press, June 22, 2011; William J. Broad, John Markoff, and David E. Sanger, "Israel Tests on Worm Called Crucial in Iran Nuclear Delay," *The New York Times*, January 15, 2011; George V. Hulme, "SCADA Insecurity" and Michael S. Mimoso, "Cyberspace Has Gone Offensive," *Information Security's Essential Guide to Threat Management* (June 14, 2011); and Sibhan Gorman and Julian A. Barnes, "Cyber Combat: Act of War," *The Wall Street Journal*, May 31, 2011.

CASE STUDY QUESTIONS

1. Is cyberwarfare a serious problem? Why or why not?

2. Assess the management, organization, and technology factors that have created this problem.

3. What makes Stuxnet different from other cyberwarfare attacks? How serious a threat is this technology?

4. What solutions for have been proposed for this problem? Do you think they will be effective? Why or why not?

millions of paths would require thousands of years. Even with rigorous testing, you would not know for sure that a piece of software was dependable until the product proved itself after much operational use.

Flaws in commercial software not only impede performance but also create security vulnerabilities that open networks to intruders. Each year security firms identify thousands of software vulnerabilities in Internet and PC software. For instance, in 2011, Symantec identified 351 browser vulnerabilities: 70 in Chrome, about 50 in Safari and Firefox, and 50 in Internet Explorer. Some of these vulnerabilities were critical (Symantec, 2012).

To correct software flaws once they are identified, the software vendor creates small pieces of software called **patches** to repair the flaws without disturbing the proper operation of the software. An example is Microsoft's Windows 7 Service Pack 1, which features security, performance, and stability updates for Windows 7. It is up to users of the software to track these vulnerabilities, test, and apply all patches. This process is called *patch management*.

Because a company's IT infrastructure is typically laden with multiple business applications, operating system installations, and other system services, maintaining patches on all devices and services used by a company is often time-consuming and costly. Malware is being created so rapidly that companies have very little time to respond between the time a vulnerability and a patch are announced and the time malicious software appears to exploit the vulnerability.

8.2   BUSINESS VALUE OF SECURITY AND CONTROL

Many firms are reluctant to spend heavily on security because it is not directly related to sales revenue. However, protecting information systems is so critical to the operation of the business that it deserves a second look.

Companies have very valuable information assets to protect. Systems often house confidential information about individuals' taxes, financial assets, medical records, and job performance reviews. They also can contain information on corporate operations, including trade secrets, new product development plans, and marketing strategies. Government systems may store information on weapons systems, intelligence operations, and military targets. These information assets have tremendous value, and the repercussions can be devastating if they are lost, destroyed, or placed in the wrong hands. Systems that are unable to function because of security breaches, disasters, or malfunctioning technology can permanently impact a company's financial health. Some experts believe that 40 percent of all businesses will not recover from application or data losses that are not repaired within three days (Focus Research, 2010).

Inadequate security and control may result in serious legal liability. Businesses must protect not only their own information assets but also those of customers, employees, and business partners. Failure to do so may open the firm to costly litigation for data exposure or theft. An organization can be held liable for needless risk and harm created if the organization fails to take appropriate protective action to prevent loss of confidential information, data corruption, or breach of privacy. For example, BJ's Wholesale Club was sued by the U.S. Federal Trade Commission for allowing hackers to access its systems and steal credit and debit card data for fraudulent purchases. Banks that issued the cards with the stolen data sought $13 million from BJ's to compensate them for reimbursing card holders for the fraudulent purchases. A sound security and control framework that protects business information assets can thus produce a high return on investment. Strong security and control also increase employee productivity and lower operational costs.

LEGAL AND REGULATORY REQUIREMENTS FOR ELECTRONIC RECORDS MANAGEMENT

Recent U.S. government regulations are forcing companies to take security and control more seriously by mandating the protection of data from abuse, exposure, and unauthorized access. Firms face new legal obligations for the retention and storage of electronic records as well as for privacy protection.

If you work in the health care industry, your firm will need to comply with the Health Insurance Portability and Accountability Act (HIPAA) of 1996. **HIPAA** outlines medical security and privacy rules and procedures for simplifying the administration of health care billing and automating the transfer of health care data between health care providers, payers, and plans. It requires members of the health care industry to retain patient information for six years and ensure the confidentiality of those records. It specifies privacy, security, and electronic transaction standards for health care providers handling patient information, providing penalties for breaches of medical privacy, disclosure of patient records by e-mail, or unauthorized network access.

If you work in a firm providing financial services, your firm will need to comply with the Financial Services Modernization Act of 1999, better known as the **Gramm-Leach-Bliley Act** after its congressional sponsors. This act requires financial institutions to ensure the security and confidentiality of customer data. Data must be stored on a secure medium, and special security measures must be enforced to protect such data on storage media and during transmittal.

If you work in a publicly traded company, your company will need to comply with the Public Company Accounting Reform and Investor Protection Act of 2002, better known as the **Sarbanes-Oxley Act** after its sponsors Senator Paul Sarbanes of Maryland and Representative Michael Oxley of Ohio. This Act was designed to protect investors after the financial scandals at Enron, WorldCom, and other public companies. It imposes responsibility on companies and their management to safeguard the accuracy and integrity of financial information that is used internally and released externally. One of the Learning Tracks for this chapter discusses Sarbanes-Oxley in detail.

Sarbanes-Oxley is fundamentally about ensuring that internal controls are in place to govern the creation and documentation of information in financial statements. Because information systems are used to generate, store, and transport such data, the legislation requires firms to consider information systems security and other controls required to ensure the integrity, confidentiality, and accuracy of their data. Each system application that deals with critical financial reporting data requires controls to make sure the data are accurate. Controls to secure the corporate network, prevent unauthorized access to systems and data, and ensure data integrity and availability in the event of disaster or other disruption of service are essential as well.

ELECTRONIC EVIDENCE AND COMPUTER FORENSICS

Security, control, and electronic records management have become essential for responding to legal actions. Much of the evidence today for stock fraud, embezzlement, theft of company trade secrets, computer crime, and many civil cases is in digital form. In addition to information from printed or typewritten pages, legal cases today increasingly rely on evidence represented as digital data stored on portable storage devices, CDs, and computer hard disk drives, as well as in e-mail, instant messages, and e-commerce transactions over the Internet. E-mail is currently the most common type of electronic evidence.

In a legal action, a firm is obligated to respond to a discovery request for access to information that may be used as evidence, and the company is required by law to produce those data. The cost of responding to a discovery request can be enormous if the company has trouble assembling the required data or the data have been corrupted or destroyed. Courts now impose severe financial and even criminal penalties for improper destruction of electronic documents.

An effective electronic document retention policy ensures that electronic documents, e-mail, and other records are well organized, accessible, and neither retained too long nor discarded too soon. It also reflects an awareness of how to preserve potential evidence for computer forensics. **Computer forensics** is the scientific collection, examination, authentication, preservation, and analysis of data held on or retrieved from computer storage media in such a way that the information can be used as evidence in a court of law. It deals with the following problems:

- Recovering data from computers while preserving evidential integrity
- Securely storing and handling recovered electronic data
- Finding significant information in a large volume of electronic data
- Presenting the information to a court of law

Electronic evidence may reside on computer storage media in the form of computer files and as *ambient data*, which are not visible to the average user. An example might be a file that has been deleted on a PC hard drive. Data that a computer user may have deleted on computer storage media can be recovered through various techniques. Computer forensics experts try to recover such hidden data for presentation as evidence.

An awareness of computer forensics should be incorporated into a firm's contingency planning process. The CIO, security specialists, information systems staff, and corporate legal counsel should all work together to have a plan in place that can be executed if a legal need arises. You can find out more about computer forensics in the Learning Tracks for this chapter.

8.3 ESTABLISHING A FRAMEWORK FOR SECURITY AND CONTROL

Even with the best security tools, your information systems won't be reliable and secure unless you know how and where to deploy them. You'll need to know where your company is at risk and what controls you must have in place to protect your information systems. You'll also need to develop a security policy and plans for keeping your business running if your information systems aren't operational.

INFORMATION SYSTEMS CONTROLS

Information systems controls are both manual and automated and consist of general and application controls. **General controls** govern the design, security, and use of computer programs and the security of data files in general throughout the organization's information technology infrastructure. On the whole, general controls apply to all computerized applications and consist of a combination of hardware, software, and manual procedures that create an overall control environment.

General controls include software controls, physical hardware controls, computer operations controls, data security controls, controls over implementation of system processes, and administrative controls. Table 8.4 describes the functions of each of these controls.

Application controls are specific controls unique to each computerized application, such as payroll or order processing. They include both automated and manual procedures that ensure that only authorized data are completely and accurately processed by that application. Application controls can be classified as (1) input controls, (2) processing controls, and (3) output controls.

Input controls check data for accuracy and completeness when they enter the system. There are specific input controls for input authorization, data conversion, data editing, and error handling. *Processing controls* establish that data are complete and accurate during updating. *Output controls* ensure that the results of computer processing are accurate, complete, and properly distributed.

TABLE 8.4 GENERAL CONTROLS

TYPE OF GENERAL CONTROL	DESCRIPTION
Software controls	Monitor the use of system software and prevent unauthorized access of software programs, system software, and computer programs.
Hardware controls	Ensure that computer hardware is physically secure, and check for equipment malfunction. Organizations that are critically dependent on their computers also must make provisions for backup or continued operation to maintain constant service.
Computer operations controls	Oversee the work of the computer department to ensure that programmed procedures are consistently and correctly applied to the storage and processing of data. They include controls over the setup of computer processing jobs and backup and recovery procedures for processing that ends abnormally.
Data security controls	Ensure that valuable business data files on either disk or tape are not subject to unauthorized access, change, or destruction while they are in use or in storage.
Implementation controls	Audit the systems development process at various points to ensure that the process is properly controlled and managed.
Administrative controls	Formalize standards, rules, procedures, and control disciplines to ensure that the organization's general and application controls are properly executed and enforced.

You can find more detail about application and general controls in our Learning Tracks.

RISK ASSESSMENT

Before your company commits resources to security and information systems controls, it must know which assets require protection and the extent to which these assets are vulnerable. A risk assessment helps answer these questions and determine the most cost-effective set of controls for protecting assets.

A **risk assessment** determines the level of risk to the firm if a specific activity or process is not properly controlled. Not all risks can be anticipated and measured, but most businesses will be able to acquire some understanding of the risks they face. Business managers working with information systems specialists should try to determine the value of information assets, points of vulnerability, the likely frequency of a problem, and the potential for damage. For example, if an event is likely to occur no more than once a year, with a maximum of a $1,000 loss to the organization, it is not wise to spend $20,000 on the design and maintenance of a control to protect against that event. However, if that same event could occur at least once a day, with a potential loss of more than $300,000 a year, $100,000 spent on a control might be entirely appropriate.

Table 8.5 illustrates sample results of a risk assessment for an online order processing system that processes 30,000 orders per day. The likelihood of each exposure occurring over a one-year period is expressed as a percentage. The next column shows the highest and lowest possible loss that could be expected each time the exposure occurred and an average loss calculated by adding the highest and lowest figures together and dividing by two. The expected annual loss for each exposure can be determined by multiplying the average loss by its probability of occurrence.

This risk assessment shows that the probability of a power failure occurring in a one-year period is 30 percent. Loss of order transactions while power is down could range from $5,000 to $200,000 (averaging $102,500) for each occurrence,

TABLE 8.5 ONLINE ORDER PROCESSING RISK ASSESSMENT

EXPOSURE	PROBABILITY OF OCCURRENCE (%)	LOSS RANGE/ AVERAGE ($)	EXPECTED ANNUAL LOSS ($)
Power failure	30%	$5,000–$200,000 ($102,500)	$30,750
Embezzlement	5%	$1,000–$50,000 ($25,500)	$1,275
User error	98%	$200–$40,000 ($20,100)	$19,698

depending on how long processing is halted. The probability of embezzlement occurring over a yearly period is about 5 percent, with potential losses ranging from $1,000 to $50,000 (and averaging $25,500) for each occurrence. User errors have a 98 percent chance of occurring over a yearly period, with losses ranging from $200 to $40,000 (and averaging $20,100) for each occurrence.

Once the risks have been assessed, system builders will concentrate on the control points with the greatest vulnerability and potential for loss. In this case, controls should focus on ways to minimize the risk of power failures and user errors because anticipated annual losses are highest for these areas.

SECURITY POLICY

Once you've identified the main risks to your systems, your company will need to develop a security policy for protecting the company's assets. A **security policy** consists of statements ranking information risks, identifying acceptable security goals, and identifying the mechanisms for achieving these goals. What are the firm's most important information assets? Who generates and controls this information in the firm? What existing security policies are in place to protect the information? What level of risk is management willing to accept for each of these assets? Is it willing, for instance, to lose customer credit data once every 10 years? Or will it build a security system for credit card data that can withstand the once-in-a-hundred-year disaster? Management must estimate how much it will cost to achieve this level of acceptable risk.

The security policy drives other policies determining acceptable use of the firm's information resources and which members of the company have access to its information assets. An **acceptable use policy (AUP)** defines acceptable uses of the firm's information resources and computing equipment, including desktop and laptop computers, wireless devices, telephones, and the Internet. The policy should clarify company policy regarding privacy, user responsibility, and personal use of company equipment and networks. A good AUP defines unacceptable and acceptable actions for every user and specifies consequences for noncompliance. For example, security policy at Unilever, the giant multinational consumer goods company, requires every employee to use a company-specified device and employ a password or other method of identification when logging onto the corporate network.

Security policy also includes provisions for identity management. **Identity management** consists of business processes and software tools for identifying the valid users of a system and controlling their access to system resources. It includes policies for identifying and authorizing different categories of system users, specifying what systems or portions of systems each user is allowed to access, and the processes and technologies for authenticating users and protecting their identities.

FIGURE 8.3   ACCESS RULES FOR A PERSONNEL SYSTEM

SECURITY PROFILE 1

User: Personnel Dept. Clerk

Location: Division 1

Employee Identification
Codes with This Profile: 00753, 27834, 37665, 44116

Data Field Restrictions	Type of Access
All employee data for Division 1 only	Read and Update
• Medical history data	None
• Salary	None
• Pensionable earnings	None

SECURITY PROFILE 2

User: Divisional Personnel Manager

Location: Division 1

Employee Identification
Codes with This Profile: 27321

Data Field Restrictions	Type of Access
All employee data for Division 1 only	Read Only

These two examples represent two security profiles or data security patterns that might be found in a personnel system. Depending on the security profile, a user would have certain restrictions on access to various systems, locations, or data in an organization.

Figure 8.3 is one example of how an identity management system might capture the access rules for different levels of users in the human resources function. It specifies what portions of a human resource database each user is permitted to access, based on the information required to perform that person's job. The database contains sensitive personal information such as employees' salaries, benefits, and medical histories.

The access rules illustrated here are for two sets of users. One set of users consists of all employees who perform clerical functions, such as inputting employee data into the system. All individuals with this type of profile can update the system but can neither read nor update sensitive fields, such as salary, medical history, or earnings data. Another profile applies to a divisional manager, who cannot update the system but who can read all employee data fields for his or her division, including medical history and salary. We provide more detail on the technologies for user authentication later on in this chapter.

DISASTER RECOVERY PLANNING AND BUSINESS CONTINUITY PLANNING

If you run a business, you need to plan for events, such as power outages, floods, earthquakes, or terrorist attacks that will prevent your information systems and your business from operating. **Disaster recovery planning** devises plans for the restoration of computing and communications services after they have been disrupted. Disaster recovery plans focus primarily on the technical issues involved in keeping systems up and running, such as which files to back up and the maintenance of backup computer systems or disaster recovery services.

For example, MasterCard maintains a duplicate computer center in Kansas City, Missouri, to serve as an emergency backup to its primary computer center in St. Louis. Rather than build their own backup facilities, many firms contract with disaster recovery firms, such as Comdisco Disaster Recovery Services in Rosemont, Illinois, and SunGard Availability Services, headquartered in Wayne, Pennsylvania. These disaster recovery firms provide hot sites housing spare computers at locations around the country where subscribing firms can run their critical applications in an emergency. For example, Champion Technologies, which supplies chemicals used in oil and gas operations, is able to switch its enterprise systems from Houston to a SunGard hot site in Scottsdale, Arizona, in two hours.

Business continuity planning focuses on how the company can restore business operations after a disaster strikes. The business continuity plan identifies critical business processes and determines action plans for handling mission-critical functions if systems go down. For example, Deutsche Bank, which provides investment banking and asset management services in 74 different countries, has a well-developed business continuity plan that it continually updates and refines. It maintains full-time teams in Singapore, Hong Kong, Japan, India, and Australia to coordinate plans addressing loss of facilities, personnel, or critical systems so that the company can continue to operate when a catastrophic event occurs. Deutsche Bank's plan distinguishes between processes critical for business survival and those critical to crisis support and is coordinated with the company's disaster recovery planning for its computer centers.

Business managers and information technology specialists need to work together on both types of plans to determine which systems and business processes are most critical to the company. They must conduct a business impact analysis to identify the firm's most critical systems and the impact a systems outage would have on the business. Management must determine the maximum amount of time the business can survive with its systems down and which parts of the business must be restored first.

THE ROLE OF AUDITING

How does management know that information systems security and controls are effective? To answer this question, organizations must conduct comprehensive and systematic audits. An **MIS audit** examines the firm's overall security environment as well as controls governing individual information systems. The auditor should trace the flow of sample transactions through the system and perform tests, using, if appropriate, automated audit software. The MIS audit may also examine data quality.

Security audits review technologies, procedures, documentation, training, and personnel. A thorough audit will even simulate an attack or disaster to test the response of the technology, information systems staff, and business employees.

The audit lists and ranks all control weaknesses and estimates the probability of their occurrence. It then assesses the financial and organizational impact

FIGURE 8.4 **SAMPLE AUDITOR'S LIST OF CONTROL WEAKNESSES**

Function: Loans Location: Peoria, IL	Prepared by: J. Ericson Date: June 16, 2013		Received by: T. Benson Review date: June 28, 2013	
Nature of Weakness and Impact	**Chance for Error/Abuse**		**Notification to Management**	
	Yes/No	Justification	Report date	Management response
User accounts with missing passwords	Yes	Leaves system open to unauthorized outsiders or attackers	5/10/13	Eliminate accounts without passwords
Network configured to allow some sharing of system files	Yes	Exposes critical system files to hostile parties connected to the network	5/10/13	Ensure only required directories are shared and that they are protected with strong passwords
Software patches can update production programs without final approval from Standards and Controls group	No	All production programs require management approval; Standards and Controls group assigns such cases to a temporary production status		

This chart is a sample page from a list of control weaknesses that an auditor might find in a loan system in a local commercial bank. This form helps auditors record and evaluate control weaknesses and shows the results of discussing those weaknesses with management, as well as any corrective actions taken by management.

of each threat. Figure 8.4 is a sample auditor's listing of control weaknesses for a loan system. It includes a section for notifying management of such weaknesses and for management's response. Management is expected to devise a plan for countering significant weaknesses in controls.

8.4 TECHNOLOGIES AND TOOLS FOR PROTECTING INFORMATION RESOURCES

Businesses have an array of technologies for protecting their information resources. They include tools for managing user identities, preventing unauthorized access to systems and data, ensuring system availability, and ensuring software quality.

IDENTITY MANAGEMENT AND AUTHENTICATION

Midsize and large companies have complex IT infrastructures and many different systems, each with its own set of users. Identity management software automates the process of keeping track of all these users and their system privileges, assigning each user a unique digital identity for accessing each system. It also includes tools for authenticating users, protecting user identities, and controlling access to system resources.

To gain access to a system, a user must be authorized and authenticated. **Authentication** refers to the ability to know that a person is who he or she claims to be. Authentication is often established by using **passwords** known only to authorized users. An end user uses a password to log on to a computer system and may also use passwords for accessing specific systems and files. However, users often forget passwords, share them, or choose poor passwords that are easy to guess, which compromises security. Password systems that are too rigorous hinder employee productivity. When employees must change complex passwords frequently, they often take shortcuts, such as choosing passwords that are easy to guess or keeping their passwords at their workstations in plain view. Passwords can also be "sniffed" if transmitted over a network or stolen through social engineering.

New authentication technologies, such as tokens, smart cards, and biometric authentication, overcome some of these problems. A **token** is a physical device, similar to an identification card, that is designed to prove the identity of a single user. Tokens are small gadgets that typically fit on key rings and display passcodes that change frequently. A **smart card** is a device about the size of a credit card that contains a chip formatted with access permission and other data. (Smart cards are also used in electronic payment systems.) A reader device interprets the data on the smart card and allows or denies access.

Biometric authentication uses systems that read and interpret individual human traits, such as fingerprints, irises, and voices, in order to grant or deny access. Biometric authentication is based on the measurement of a physical or behavioral trait that makes each individual unique. It compares a person's unique characteristics, such as the fingerprints, face, or retinal image, against a stored profile of these characteristics to determine whether there are any differences between these characteristics and the stored profile. If the two profiles match, access is granted. Fingerprint and facial recognition technologies are just beginning to be used for security applications, with many PC laptops equipped with fingerprint identification devices and several models with built-in webcams and face recognition software.

This PC has a biometric fingerprint reader for fast yet secure access to files and networks. New models of PCs are starting to use biometric identification to authenticate users.

© Jochen Tack/Alamy

FIREWALLS, INTRUSION DETECTION SYSTEMS, AND ANTIVIRUS SOFTWARE

Without protection against malware and intruders, connecting to the Internet would be very dangerous. Firewalls, intrusion detection systems, and antivirus software have become essential business tools.

Firewalls

Firewalls prevent unauthorized users from accessing private networks. A firewall is a combination of hardware and software that controls the flow of incoming and outgoing network traffic. It is generally placed between the organization's private internal networks and distrusted external networks, such as the Internet, although firewalls can also be used to protect one part of a company's network from the rest of the network (see Figure 8.5).

The firewall acts like a gatekeeper who examines each user's credentials before access is granted to a network. The firewall identifies names, IP addresses, applications, and other characteristics of incoming traffic. It checks this information against the access rules that have been programmed into the system by the network administrator. The firewall prevents unauthorized communication into and out of the network.

In large organizations, the firewall often resides on a specially designated computer separate from the rest of the network, so no incoming request directly accesses private network resources. There are a number of firewall screening technologies, including static packet filtering, stateful inspection, Network

FIGURE 8.5   A CORPORATE FIREWALL

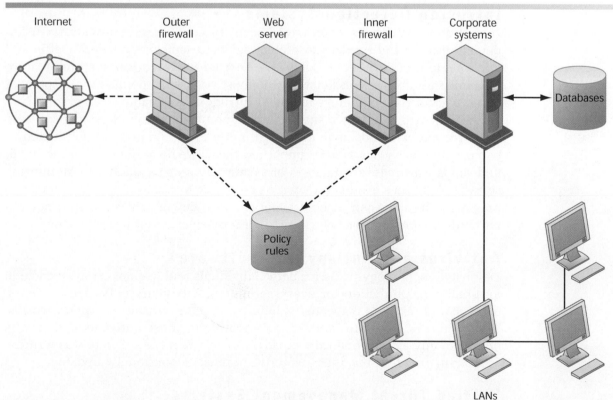

The firewall is placed between the firm's private network and the public Internet or another distrusted network to protect against unauthorized traffic.

Address Translation, and application proxy filtering. They are frequently used in combination to provide firewall protection.

Packet filtering examines selected fields in the headers of data packets flowing back and forth between the trusted network and the Internet, examining individual packets in isolation. This filtering technology can miss many types of attacks. *Stateful inspection* provides additional security by determining whether packets are part of an ongoing dialogue between a sender and a receiver. It sets up state tables to track information over multiple packets. Packets are accepted or rejected based on whether they are part of an approved conversation or whether they are attempting to establish a legitimate connection.

Network Address Translation (NAT) can provide another layer of protection when static packet filtering and stateful inspection are employed. NAT conceals the IP addresses of the organization's internal host computer(s) to prevent sniffer programs outside the firewall from ascertaining them and using that information to penetrate internal systems.

Application proxy filtering examines the application content of packets. A proxy server stops data packets originating outside the organization, inspects them, and passes a proxy to the other side of the firewall. If a user outside the company wants to communicate with a user inside the organization, the outside user first "talks" to the proxy application and the proxy application communicates with the firm's internal computer. Likewise, a computer user inside the organization goes through the proxy to talk with computers on the outside.

To create a good firewall, an administrator must maintain detailed internal rules identifying the people, applications, or addresses that are allowed or rejected. Firewalls can deter, but not completely prevent, network penetration by outsiders and should be viewed as one element in an overall security plan.

Intrusion Detection Systems

In addition to firewalls, commercial security vendors now provide intrusion detection tools and services to protect against suspicious network traffic and attempts to access files and databases. **Intrusion detection systems** feature full-time monitoring tools placed at the most vulnerable points or "hot spots" of corporate networks to detect and deter intruders continually. The system generates an alarm if it finds a suspicious or anomalous event. Scanning software looks for patterns indicative of known methods of computer attacks, such as bad passwords, checks to see if important files have been removed or modified, and sends warnings of vandalism or system administration errors. Monitoring software examines events as they are happening to discover security attacks in progress. The intrusion detection tool can also be customized to shut down a particularly sensitive part of a network if it receives unauthorized traffic.

Antivirus and Antispyware Software

Defensive technology plans for both individuals and businesses must include anti-malware protection for every computer. **Antivirus software** prevents, detects, and removes malware, including computer viruses, computer worms, Trojan horses, spyware, and adware. However, most antivirus software is effective only against malware already known when the software was written. To remain effective, the antivirus software must be continually updated.

Unified Threat Management Systems

To help businesses reduce costs and improve manageability, security vendors have combined into a single appliance various security tools, including firewalls, virtual private networks, intrusion detection systems, and Web content filtering and antispam software. These comprehensive security management products are called **unified threat management (UTM)** systems. Although initially aimed at small and medium-sized businesses, UTM products are available for all sizes of networks. Leading UTM vendors include Crossbeam, Fortinent, and Check Point, and networking vendors such as Cisco Systems and Juniper Networks provide some UTM capabilities in their equipment.

SECURING WIRELESS NETWORKS

The initial security standard developed for Wi-Fi, called Wired Equivalent Privacy (WEP), is not very effective because its encryption keys are relatively easy to crack. WEP provides some margin of security, however, if users remember to enable it. Corporations can further improve Wi-Fi security by using it in conjunction with virtual private network (VPN) technology when accessing internal corporate data.

In June 2004, the Wi-Fi Alliance industry trade group finalized the 802.11i specification (also referred to as Wi-Fi Protected Access 2 or WPA2) that replaces WEP with stronger security standards. Instead of the static encryption keys used in WEP, the new standard uses much longer keys that continually change, making them harder to crack. It also employs an encrypted authentication system with a central authentication server to ensure that only authorized users access the network.

ENCRYPTION AND PUBLIC KEY INFRASTRUCTURE

Many businesses use encryption to protect digital information that they store, physically transfer, or send over the Internet. **Encryption** is the process of transforming plain text or data into cipher text that cannot be read by anyone other than the sender and the intended receiver. Data are encrypted by using a secret numerical code, called an encryption key, that transforms plain data into cipher text. The message must be decrypted by the receiver.

Two methods for encrypting network traffic on the Web are SSL and S-HTTP. **Secure Sockets Layer (SSL)** and its successor Transport Layer Security (TLS) enable client and server computers to manage encryption and decryption activities as they communicate with each other during a secure Web session. **Secure Hypertext Transfer Protocol (S-HTTP)** is another protocol used for encrypting data flowing over the Internet, but it is limited to individual messages, whereas SSL and TLS are designed to establish a secure connection between two computers.

The capability to generate secure sessions is built into Internet client browser software and servers. The client and the server negotiate what key and what level of security to use. Once a secure session is established between the client and the server, all messages in that session are encrypted.

There are two alternative methods of encryption: symmetric key encryption and public key encryption. In symmetric key encryption, the sender and receiver establish a secure Internet session by creating a single encryption key and sending it to the receiver so both the sender and receiver share the same key. The strength of the encryption key is measured by its bit length. Today, a typical key will be 128 bits long (a string of 128 binary digits).

The problem with all symmetric encryption schemes is that the key itself must be shared somehow among the senders and receivers, which exposes the key to outsiders who might just be able to intercept and decrypt the key.

A more secure form of encryption called **public key encryption** uses two keys: one shared (or public) and one totally private as shown in Figure 8.6. The keys are mathematically related so that data encrypted with one key can be decrypted using only the other key. To send and receive messages, communicators first create separate pairs of private and public keys. The public key is kept in a directory and the private key must be kept secret. The sender encrypts a message with the recipient's public key. On receiving the message, the recipient uses his or her private key to decrypt it.

Digital certificates are data files used to establish the identity of users and electronic assets for protection of online transactions (see Figure 8.7). A digital certificate system uses a trusted third party, known as a certificate authority (CA, or certification authority), to validate a user's identity. There are many CAs in the United States and around the world, including Symantec, GoDaddy, and Comodo.

The CA verifies a digital certificate user's identity offline. This information is put into a CA server, which generates an encrypted digital certificate containing owner identification information and a copy of the owner's public key. The certificate authenticates that the public key belongs to the designated owner. The CA makes its own public key available either in print or perhaps on the Internet. The recipient of an encrypted message uses the CA's public key to decode the digital certificate attached to the message, verifies it was issued by the CA, and then obtains the sender's public key and identification information contained in the certificate. Using this information, the recipient can send an encrypted reply. The digital certificate system would enable, for example, a credit card user and a merchant to validate that their digital certificates were issued by an authorized and trusted third party before they exchange data. **Public key infrastructure (PKI)**, the use of public key cryptography working with a CA, is now widely used in e-commerce.

ENSURING SYSTEM AVAILABILITY

As companies increasingly rely on digital networks for revenue and operations, they need to take additional steps to ensure that their systems and applications are always available. Firms such as those in the airline and financial services industries with critical applications requiring online transaction processing have traditionally used fault-tolerant computer systems for many years to ensure 100

FIGURE 8.6   PUBLIC KEY ENCRYPTION

A public key encryption system can be viewed as a series of public and private keys that lock data when they are transmitted and unlock the data when they are received. The sender locates the recipient's public key in a directory and uses it to encrypt a message. The message is sent in encrypted form over the Internet or a private network. When the encrypted message arrives, the recipient uses his or her private key to decrypt the data and read the message.

FIGURE 8.7 DIGITAL CERTIFICATES

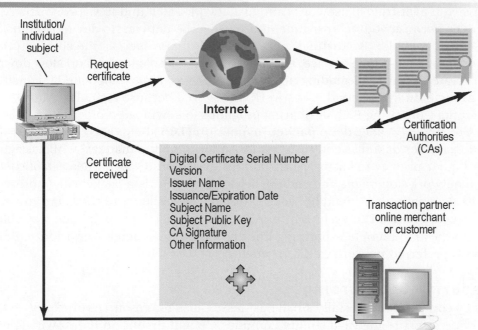

Digital certificates help establish the identity of people or electronic assets. They protect online transactions by providing secure, encrypted, online communication.

percent availability. In **online transaction processing**, transactions entered online are immediately processed by the computer. Multitudinous changes to databases, reporting, and requests for information occur each instant.

Fault-tolerant computer systems contain redundant hardware, software, and power supply components that create an environment that provides continuous, uninterrupted service. Fault-tolerant computers use special software routines or self-checking logic built into their circuitry to detect hardware failures and automatically switch to a backup device. Parts from these computers can be removed and repaired without disruption to the computer system.

Fault tolerance should be distinguished from **high-availability computing**. Both fault tolerance and high-availability computing try to minimize downtime. **Downtime** refers to periods of time in which a system is not operational. However, high-availability computing helps firms recover quickly from a system crash, whereas fault tolerance promises continuous availability and the elimination of recovery time altogether.

High-availability computing environments are a minimum requirement for firms with heavy e-commerce processing or for firms that depend on digital networks for their internal operations. High-availability computing requires backup servers, distribution of processing across multiple servers, high-capacity storage, and good disaster recovery and business continuity plans. The firm's computing platform must be extremely robust with scalable processing power, storage, and bandwidth.

Researchers are exploring ways to make computing systems recover even more rapidly when mishaps occur, an approach called **recovery-oriented computing**. This work includes designing systems that recover quickly, and implementing capabilities and tools to help operators pinpoint the sources of faults in multi-component systems and easily correct their mistakes.

Controlling Network Traffic: Deep Packet Inspection

Have you ever tried to use your campus network and found it was very slow? It may be because your fellow students are using the network to download music or watch YouTube. Bandwith-consuming applications such as file-sharing programs, Internet phone service, and online video are able to clog and slow down corporate networks, degrading performance. For example, Ball State University in Muncie, Indiana, found its network had slowed because a small minority of students were using P2P file-sharing programs to download movies and music.

A technology called **deep packet inspection (DPI)** helps solve this problem. DPI examines data files and sorts out low-priority online material while assigning higher priority to business-critical files. Based on the priorities established by a network's operators, it decides whether a specific data packet can continue to its destination or should be blocked or delayed while more important traffic proceeds. Using a DPI system from Allot Communications, Ball State was able to cap the amount of file-sharing traffic and assign it a much lower priority. Ball State's preferred network traffic speeded up.

Security Outsourcing

Many companies, especially small businesses, lack the resources or expertise to provide a secure high-availability computing environment on their own. They can outsource many security functions to **managed security service providers (MSSPs)** that monitor network activity and perform vulnerability testing and intrusion detection. SecureWorks, BT Managed Security Solutions Group, and Symantec are leading providers of MSSP services.

SECURITY ISSUES FOR CLOUD COMPUTING AND THE MOBILE DIGITAL PLATFORM

Although cloud computing and the emerging mobile digital platform have the potential to deliver powerful benefits, they pose new challenges to system security and reliability. We now describe some of these challenges and how they should be addressed.

Security in the Cloud

When processing takes place in the cloud, accountability and responsibility for protection of sensitive data still reside with the company owning that data. Understanding how the cloud computing provider organizes its services and manages the data is critical. The Interactive Session on Technology describes how even sophisticated Web-based firms can experience security breakdowns.

Cloud computing is highly distributed. Cloud applications reside in large remote data centers and server farms that supply business services and data management for multiple corporate clients. To save money and keep costs low, cloud computing providers often distribute work to data centers around the globe where work can be accomplished most efficiently. When you use the cloud, you may not know precisely where your data are being hosted.

The dispersed nature of cloud computing makes it difficult to track unauthorized activity. Virtually all cloud providers use encryption, such as Secure Sockets Layer, to secure the data they handle while the data are being transmitted. But if the data are stored on devices that also store other companies' data, it's important to ensure these stored data are encrypted as well.

Companies expect their systems to be running 24/7, but cloud providers haven't always been able to provide this level of service. On several occasions over the past few years, the cloud services of Amazon.com and Salesforce.com experienced outages that disrupted business operations for millions of users (see the Chapter 5 ending case study).

Cloud users need to confirm that regardless of where their data are stored, they are protected at a level that meets their corporate requirements. They should stipulate that the cloud provider store and process data in specific jurisdictions according to the privacy rules of those jurisdictions. Cloud clients should find how the cloud provider segregates their corporate data from those of other companies and ask for proof that encryption mechanisms are sound. It's also important to know how the cloud provider will respond if a disaster strikes, whether the provider will be able to completely restore your data, and how long this should take. Cloud users should also ask whether cloud providers will submit to external audits and security certifications. These kinds of controls can be written into the service level agreement (SLA) before signing with a cloud provider.

Securing Mobile Platforms

If mobile devices are performing many of the functions of computers, they need to be secured like desktops and laptops against malware, theft, accidental loss, unauthorized access, and hacking attempts.

Mobile devices accessing corporate systems and data require special protection. Companies should make sure that their corporate security policy includes mobile devices, with additional details on how mobile devices should be supported, protected, and used. They will need mobile device management tools to authorize all devices in use; to maintain accurate inventory records on all mobile devices, users, and applications; to control updates to applications; and to lock down or erase lost or stolen devices so they can't be compromised. Firms should develop guidelines stipulating approved mobile platforms and software applications as well as the required software and procedures for remote access of corporate systems.

Companies should encrypt communication whenever possible. All mobile device users should be required to use the password feature found in every smartphone. Mobile security products are available from Kaspersky, Lookout, and DroidSecurity.

Some companies insist that employees use only company-issued smartphones. BlackBerry devices are considered the most secure because they run within their own secure system. But, increasingly, companies are allowing employees to use their own smartphones, including iPhones and Android phones, for work, to make employees more available and productive (see the Chapter 5 discussion of BYOD). Protective software products, such as the tools from Good Technology, are now available for segregating corporate data housed within personally owned mobile devices from the device's personal content.

ENSURING SOFTWARE QUALITY

In addition to implementing effective security and controls, organizations can improve system quality and reliability by employing software metrics and rigorous software testing. Software metrics are objective assessments of the system in the form of quantified measurements. Ongoing use of metrics allows the information systems department and end users to jointly measure the performance of the system and identify problems as they occur. Examples

INTERACTIVE SESSION: TECHNOLOGY

MWEB BUSINESS: HACKED

MWEB, launched in 1997, became South Africa's leading ISP in 1998. It has established itself as a company that provides a cutting-edge network and service infrastructure and outstanding customer service. Currently, MWEB's customer base of 320,000 includes home users; small, medium, and large business customers; and corporate clients. MWEB won the ISP of the Year award at the MyBroadband Conference in Johannesburg in 2010. The award was based on the performance of its various broadband services as well as on customer satisfaction.

Its business division, MWEB Business, was founded in January 1998. MWEB Business prides itself as being a business partner that is perfectly positioned to leverage the power of Web-based technologies in all areas of an organization. MWEB Business helps companies:

- Manage business data in ways that add real value and insight to their operations
- Integrate existing systems with the Internet so as to close the gap between technology, strategy, and the organization's bottom line
- Develop, manage, and maintain solutions that include all aspects of Internet connectivity, Web site development and hosting, broadband and wireless applications, e-commerce, and consultancy services
- Manage internal information among employees, as well as among business partners and suppliers

MWEB has moved forward in publicizing its plans for the South African Internet market. According to MWEB CEO Rudi Jansen, the company needs to improve the quality of their network, which is not only an MWEB problem, but also a Telkom network problem. Despite having a less-than-ideal network infrastructure, MWEB uses AVG Internet Security to offer its customers the best possible security while online. AVG Internet Security offers MWEB customers the following features:

- Identity protection for safe banking and shopping
- LinkScanner for safe surfing and searching
- WebShield for safe social networking, chatting, and downloading
- Antiphishing and antispam for a safe uncluttered inbox

- High-speed antivirus/antispyware software with automatic updates
- An enhanced firewall

In addition, MWEB automatically protects customers against junk email and viruses that are sent via email. Its virus filter ensures that only virus-free email is delivered to clients' inboxes by automatically cleaning e-mails from recognized malware sources. MWEB advises its customers to keep their ADSL connections safe from bandwidth theft and account abuse by blocking unsolicited incoming connections to network ports commonly used by hackers.

Despite the multitude of security services offered by MWEB, a number of MWEB Business subscribers' account details were compromised when their logon and password details were published on the Internet by hackers. Initial reports indicated that as many as 2,390 users of MWEB's business digital subscriber lines were affected. The company disclosed the security breach on October 25, 2010. It appears that hackers gained access to the Internet Solutions' self-service management system that MWEB Business uses to provide and manage business accounts that have not yet been migrated to the MWEB network.

Historically, MWEB Business was a reseller of Internet Solutions' Uncapped & Fixed IP ADSL services, which were provisioned and managed by MWEB using a Web-based management interface provided by Internet Solutions. All new Business ADSL services provided after April 2010, as well as the bulk of legacy services already migrated, used MWEB's internal authentication systems, which were completely unaffected by this incident.

MWEB responded quickly to the hacking incident. According to Jansen, about 1,000 clients on the Internet Solutions network needed to be migrated from the old server which was attacked by hackers. Although the network was quickly secured, most customers had recently been moved to MWEB's IPC network. MWEB would also be contacting these customers to reset their passwords, as an added security measure. Jansen was quick to note that no personal information was lost and that none of MWEB's clients suffered any losses as their usernames and passwords had been recreated and changed. He further added that MWEB successfully repels 5,000 attacks a day.

Andre Joubert, general manager of MWEB Business, emphasized that only ADSL authentication usernames and passwords had been compromised. The integrity of the personal or private data related to the accounts remained intact, as did the access credentials for each customer's bundled onsite router. Joubert did acknowledge the seriousness of the hack, apologizing for any inconvenience the breach may have caused to MWEB's customers. As soon as the breach was identified, MWEB took immediate action to evaluate the extent of the breach and to limit any damage. In MWEB's defense, Jansen said that MWEB constantly advises its customers to be vigilant regarding their online data and security. In addition, MWEB was working closely with Internet Solutions to investigate the nature and source of the breach to ensure that it does not happen again.

Sources: "2010 MyBroadband Awards: The Winners and Losers," MyBroadband, October 19, 2010 (http://mybroadband.co.za/news/ broadband/15951-2010-MyBroadband-Awards-The-winners-andlosers. html, accessed November 17, 2010); "About MWEB," MWEB (www.mweb.co.za/productspricing/MWEBBusiness/AboutMWEBB usiness.aspx, accessed November 17, 2010); "Hackers Target MWEB," NewsTime, October 25, 2010 (www.newstime.co.za/ ScienceandTech/Hackers_Target_M-Web/13618/, accessed November 17, 2010); "MWEB Business Tackles 'ADSL Hacking' Incident," MyBroadband, October 25, 2010 (http://mybroadband.co.za/news/adsl/16077-MWEB-Businesstackles- ADSL-hacking-incident.html, accessed November 17, 2010); "MWEB Business Takes Action in 'Hacking' Incident," Moneyweb, October 25, 2010 (www.moneyweb.co.za/mw/view/mw/en/ page295027?oid = 5 12545&sn = 2009 + Detail&pid = 287226, accessed November 17, 2010); "MWeb hacked, users' details exposed," TechCentral, October 26, 2010 (www.techcentral.co.za/mwebhacked- users-details-exposed/18366/, accessed November 17, 2010).

Case contributed by Upasana Singh, University of KwaZulu-Natal

CASE STUDY QUESTIONS

1. What technology issues led to the security breach at MWEB?

2. What is the possible business impact of this security breach for both MWEB and its customers?

3. If you were an MWEB customer, would you consider MWEB's response to the security breach to be acceptable? Why or why not?

4. What should MWEB do in the future to avoid similar incidents?

of software metrics include the number of transactions that can be processed in a specified unit of time, online response time, the number of payroll checks printed per hour, and the number of known bugs per hundred lines of program code. For metrics to be successful, they must be carefully designed, formal, objective, and used consistently.

Early, regular, and thorough testing will contribute significantly to system quality. Many view testing as a way to prove the correctness of work they have done. In fact, we know that all sizable software is riddled with errors, and we must test to uncover these errors.

Good testing begins before a software program is even written by using a *walkthrough*—a review of a specification or design document by a small group of people carefully selected based on the skills needed for the particular objectives being tested. Once developers start writing software programs, coding walkthroughs also can be used to review program code. However, code must be tested by computer runs. When errors are discovered, the source is found and eliminated through a process called *debugging*. You can find out more about the various stages of testing required to put an information system into operation in Chapter 11. Our Learning Tracks also contain descriptions of methodologies for developing software programs that also contribute to software quality.

LEARNING TRACK MODULES

The following Learning Tracks provide content relevant to topics covered in this chapter:

1. The Booming Job Market in IT Security
2. The Sarbanes-Oxley Act
3. Computer Forensics
4. General and Application Controls for Information Systems
5. Management Challenges of Security and Control
6. Software Vulnerability and Reliability

Review Summary

1. *Why are information systems vulnerable to destruction, error, and abuse?*

   Digital data are vulnerable to destruction, misuse, error, fraud, and hardware or software failures. The Internet is designed to be an open system and makes internal corporate systems more vulnerable to actions from outsiders. Hackers can unleash denial-of-service (DoS) attacks or penetrate corporate networks, causing serious system disruptions. Wi-Fi networks can easily be penetrated by intruders using sniffer programs to obtain an address to access the resources of the network. Computer viruses and worms can disable systems and Web sites. The dispersed nature of cloud computing makes it difficult to track unauthorized activity or to apply controls from afar. Software presents problems because software bugs may be impossible to eliminate and because software vulnerabilities can be exploited by hackers and malicious software. End users often introduce errors.

2. *What is the business value of security and control?*

   Lack of sound security and control can cause firms relying on computer systems for their core business functions to lose sales and productivity. Information assets, such as confidential employee records, trade secrets, or business plans, lose much of their value if they are revealed to outsiders or if they expose the firm to legal liability. New laws, such as HIPAA, the Sarbanes-Oxley Act, and the Gramm-Leach-Bliley Act, require companies to practice stringent electronic records management and adhere to strict standards for security, privacy, and control. Legal actions requiring electronic evidence and computer forensics also require firms to pay more attention to security and electronic records management.

3. *What are the components of an organizational framework for security and control?*

   Firms need to establish a good set of both general and application controls for their information systems. A risk assessment evaluates information assets, identifies control points and control weaknesses, and determines the most cost-effective set of controls. Firms must also develop a coherent corporate security policy and plans for continuing business operations in the event of disaster or disruption. The security policy includes policies for acceptable use and identity management. Comprehensive and systematic MIS auditing helps organizations determine the effectiveness of security and controls for their information systems.

4. *What are the most important tools and technologies for safeguarding information resources?*

   Firewalls prevent unauthorized users from accessing a private network when it is linked to the Internet. Intrusion detection systems monitor private networks from suspicious network traffic and attempts to access corporate systems. Passwords, tokens, smart cards, and biometric authentication are used to authenticate system users. Antivirus software checks computer systems for infections by viruses and worms and often eliminates the malicious software, while antispyware software combats intrusive and harmful spyware programs. Encryption, the coding and scrambling of messages, is a widely used technology for securing electronic transmissions over unprotected networks. Digital certificates combined with public key encryption provide further protection of electronic transactions by authenticating a user's identity. Companies can use fault-tolerant computer systems or create high-availability computing environments to make sure that their information systems are always available. Use of software metrics and rigorous software testing help improve software quality and reliability.

Key Terms

Acceptable use policy (AUP), 342

Antivirus software, 348

Application controls, 340

Authentication, 346

Biometric authentication, 346

Botnet, 331

Bugs, 335

Business continuity planning, 344

Click fraud, 334

Computer crime, 332

Computer forensics, 339

Computer virus, 328

Controls, 325

Cybervandalism, 330

Cyberwarfare, 334

Deep packet inspection (DPI), 352

Denial-of-service (DoS) attack, 331

Digital certificates, 350

Disaster recovery planning, 344

Distributed denial-of-service (DDoS) attack, 331

Downtime, 351

Drive-by download, 328

Encryption, 349

Evil twin, 333

Fault-tolerant computer systems, 351

Firewall, 347

General controls, 340

Gramm-Leach-Bliley Act, 339

Hacker, 330

High-availability computing, 351

HIPAA, 338

Identity management, 342

Identity theft, 332

Intrusion detection systems, 348

Keyloggers, 330

Malware, 328

Managed security service providers (MSSPs), 352

MIS audit, 344

Online transaction processing, 351

Password, 346

Patches, 337

Pharming, 333

Phishing, 333

Public key encryption, 350

Public key infrastructure (PKI), 350

Recovery-oriented computing, 351

Risk assessment, 341

Sarbanes-Oxley Act, 339

Secure Hypertext Transfer Protocol (S-HTTP), 349

Secure Sockets Layer (SSL), 349

Security, 325

Security policy, 342

Smart card, 346

Sniffer, 331

Social engineering, 335

Spoofing, 331

Spyware, 330

SQL injection attack, 330

Token, 346

Trojan horse, 329

Unified threat management (UTM), 349

War driving, 327

Worms, 328

Review Questions

1. Why are information systems vulnerable to destruction, error, and abuse?

   • List and describe the most common threats against contemporary information systems.

   • Define malware and distinguish among a virus, a worm, and a Trojan horse.

   • Define a hacker and explain how hackers create security problems and damage systems.

   • Define computer crime. Provide two examples of crime in which computers are targets and two examples in which computers are used as instruments of crime.

   • Define identity theft and phishing and explain why identity theft is such a big problem today.

   • Describe the security and system reliability problems created by employees.

   • Explain how software defects affect system reliability and security.

2. What is the business value of security and control?

   • Explain how security and control provide value for businesses.

   • Describe the relationship between security and control and recent U.S. government regulatory requirements and computer forensics.

3. What are the components of an organizational framework for security and control?

   • Define general controls and describe each type of general control.

   • Define application controls and describe each type of application control.

- Describe the function of risk assessment and explain how it is conducted for information systems.
- Define and describe the following: security policy, acceptable use policy, and identity management.
- Explain how MIS auditing promotes security and control.

4. What are the most important tools and technologies for safeguarding information resources?

- Name and describe three authentication methods.
- Describe the roles of firewalls, intrusion detection systems, and antivirus software in promoting security.

- Explain how encryption protects information.
- Describe the role of encryption and digital certificates in a public key infrastructure.
- Distinguish between fault tolerance and high-availability computing, and between disaster recovery planning and business continuity planning.
- Identify and describe the security problems posed by cloud computing.
- Describe measures for improving software quality and reliability.

Discussion Questions

1. Security isn't simply a technology issue, it's a business issue. Discuss.

2. If you were developing a business continuity plan for your company, where would you start? What aspects of the business would the plan address?

3. Suppose your business had an e-commerce Web site where it sold goods and accepted credit card payments. Discuss the major security threats to this Web site and their potential impact. What can be done to minimize these threats?

Hands-On MIS Projects

The projects in this section give you hands-on experience analyzing security vulnerabilities, using spreadsheet software for risk analysis, and using Web tools to research security outsourcing services.

Management Decision Problems

1. K2 Network operates online game sites used by about 16 million people in over 100 countries. Players are allowed to enter a game for free, but must buy digital "assets" from K2, such as swords to fight dragons, if they want to be deeply involved. The games can accommodate millions of players at once and are played simultaneously by people all over the world. Prepare a security analysis for this Internet-based business. What kinds of threats should it anticipate? What would be their impact on the business? What steps can it take to prevent damage to its Web sites and continuing operations?

2. A survey of your firm's IT infastructure has identified a number of security vulnerabilities. Review the data on these vulnerabilities, which can be found in a table in MyMISLab. Use the table to answer the following questions:

- Calculate the total number of vulnerabilities for each platform. What is the potential impact of the security problems for each computing platform on the organization?

- If you only have one information systems specialist in charge of security, which platforms should you address first in trying to eliminate these vulnerabilities? Second? Third? Last? Why?

- Identify the types of control problems illustrated by these vulnerabilities and explain the measures that should be taken to solve them.

- What does your firm risk by ignoring the security vulnerabilities identified?

Improving Decision Making: Using Spreadsheet Software to Perform a Security Risk Assessment

Software skills: Spreadsheet formulas and charts
Business skills: Risk assessment

This project uses spreadsheet software to calculate anticipated annual losses from various security threats identified for a small company.

Mercer Paints is a paint manufacturing company located in Alabama that uses a network to link its business operations. A security risk assessment requested by management identified a number of potential exposures. These exposures, their associated probabilities, and average losses are summarized in a table, which can be found in MyMISLab. Use the table to answer the following questions:

- In addition to the potential exposures listed, identify at least three other potential threats to Mercer Paints, assign probabilities, and estimate a loss range.

- Use spreadsheet software and the risk assessment data to calculate the expected annual loss for each exposure.

- Present your findings in the form of a chart. Which control points have the greatest vulnerability? What recommendations would you make to Mercer Paints? Prepare a written report that summarizes your findings and recommendations.

Improving Decision Making: Evaluating Security Outsourcing Services

Software skills: Web browser and presentation software
Business skills: Evaluating business outsourcing services

This project will help develop your Internet skills in using the Web to research and evaluate security outsourcing services.

You have been asked to help your company's management decide whether to outsource security or keep the security function within the firm. Search the Web to find information to help you decide whether to outsource security and to locate security outsourcing services.

- Present a brief summary of the arguments for and against outsourcing computer security for your company.
- Select two firms that offer computer security outsourcing services, and compare them and their services.
- Prepare an electronic presentation for management summarizing your findings. Your presentation should make the case on whether or not your company should outsource computer security. If you believe your company should outsource, the presentation should identify which security outsourcing service you selected and justify your decision.

Video Cases

Video Cases and Instructional Videos illustrating some of the concepts in this chapter are available. Contact your instructor to access these videos.

Collaboration and Teamwork Project

In MyMISLab you will find a Collaboration and Teamwork Project dealing with the concepts in this chapter. You will be able to use Google Sites, Google Docs, and other open source collaboration tools to complete the assignment.

Information Security Threats and Policies in Europe
CASE STUDY

The IT sector is one of the key drivers of the European economy. It has been estimated that 60 percent of Europeans use the Internet regularly. Additionally, 87 percent own or have access to mobile phones. In 2009, the European broadband market was the largest in the world. These facts demonstrate the importance of ensuring the security and safe operation of the Internet for the well-being of the European economy. The safety and security of the Internet have been threatened in recent years, as Internet-based cyber attacks have become increasingly sophisticated.

In 2007, Estonia suffered a massive cyber attack that affected the government, the banking system, media, and other services. The attack was performed using a variety of techniques, ranging from simple individual ping commands and message flooding to more sophisticated distributed denial of service (DDoS) attacks. Hackers coordinated the attack by using a large number of compromised servers organized in a botnet distributed around the world. A botnet is a network of autonomous malicious software agents that are under the control of a bot commander. The network is created by installing malware that exploits the vulnerabilities of Web servers, operating systems, or applications to take control of the infected computers. Once a computer is infected it becomes part of a network of thousands of "zombies," machines that are commanded to carry out the attack.

The cyber attack on Estonia started in late April 2007 and lasted for almost 3 weeks. During this period, vital parts of the Estonian Internet network had to be closed from access from outside the country, causing millions of dollars in economic losses.

At around the same time, Arsys, an important Spanish domain registration company, was also targeted by international hackers. Arsys reported that hackers had stolen codes that were then used to insert links to external servers containing malicious codes in the Web pages of some of its clients.

In 2009, an estimated 10 million computers were infected with the Conflicker worm worldwide. France, the UK, and Germany were among the European countries that suffered the most infections. The French navy had to ground all military planes when it was discovered that its computer network was infected. In the UK, the worm infected computers in the Ministry of Defense, the city of Manchester's city council and police IT network, some hospitals in the city of Sheffield, and other government offices across the country. Computers in the network of the German army were also reported as infected. Once installed on a computer, Conflicker is able to download and install other malware from controlled Web sites, thus infected computers could be under full control of the hackers.

More recently, a sophisticated malware threat targeting industrial systems was detected in Germany, Norway, China, Iran, India, Indonesia, and other countries. The malware, known as Stuxnet, infected Windows PCs running the Supervisory Control and Data Acquisition (SCADA) control system from the German company Siemens. Stuxnet was propagated via USB devices. Experts estimated that up to 1,000 machines were infected on a daily basis at the peak of the infection. The malware, hidden in shortcuts to executable programs (files with extension .lnk), was executed automatically when the content of an infected USB drive was displayed. Employing this same technique, the worm was capable of installing other malware. Initially, security experts disclosed that Stuxnet was designed to steal industrial secrets from SIMATIC WinCC, a visualization and control software system from Siemens. However, data gathered later by other experts indicates that the worm was actually looking for some specific Programmable Logic Controllers (PLC) devices used in a specific industrial plant, a fact that points to the possibility that the malware was part of a well-planned act of sabotage. Even though none of the sites infected with Stuxnet suffered physical damage, the significance that such a sophisticated threat represents to the industrial resources in Europe and other parts of the world cannot be underestimated.

As of 2001, EU member states had independent groups of experts that were responsible for responding to incidents in information security. These groups lacked coordination and did not exchange much information. To overcome this, in 2004 the European Commission established the European Network and Information Security Agency (ENISA) with the goal of coordinating efforts to prevent and respond more effectively to potentially more harmful security threats. ENISA's main objectives are to secure

Europe's information infrastructure, promote security standards, and educate the general public about security issues.

ENISA organized the first pan-European Critical Information Infrastructure Protection (CIIP) exercise, which took place in November 2010. This exercise tested the efficiency of procedures and communication links between member states in case an incident were to occur that would affect the normal operation of the Internet. ENISA acts as a facilitator and information broker for the Computer Emergency Response Teams (CERT), working with the public and private sectors of most EU member states.

The European Commission has recently launched the Digital Agenda for Europe. The goal of this initiative is to define the key role that information and communication technologies will play in 2020. The initiative calls for a single, open European digital market. Another goal is that broadband speeds of 30Mbps be available to all European citizens by 2020. In terms of security, the initiative is considering the implementation of measures to protect privacy and the establishment of a well-functioning network of CERT to prevent cybercrime and respond effectively to cyber attacks.

Sources: "Digital Agenda for Europe," European Commission, August 2010 (http://ec.europa.eu/information_society/ digitalagenda/ index_en.htm, accessed October 20, 2010); "The Cyber Raiders Hitting Estonia," BBC News, May 17, 2007 (http://news.bbc.co.uk/2/hi/europe/6665195.stm, accessed November 17, 2010); Robert McMillan, "Estonia Ready for the Next Cyberattack," Computerworld, April 7, 2010 (www.computerworld. com/s/article/9174923/Estonia_readies_for_the_next_cyber attack, accessed November 17, 2010); "Another Cyber Attack Hits Europe," Internet Business Law Services, June 18, 2007 (www.ibls.com/internet_law_news_portal_view.aspx?id=1782&s= latestnews, accessed November 17, 2010); "New Cyber Attack Hits Norway," Views and News from Norway, August 30, 2010 (www.newsinenglish.no/2010/08/30/new-cyber-attacks-hit-norway, accessed November 17, 2010); Gregg Keiser, "Is Stuxnet the 'Best' Malware Ever?" Computerworld, September 16, 2010; Robert McMillan, "Was Stuxnet Built to Attack Iran's Nuclear Program," Computerworld, September 21 2010 (www.computerworld.com/s/article/9186920/Was_Stuxnet_built_t o attack Iran s nuclear program , accessed November 17, 2010); Ellen Messmer, "Downadup/Conflicker Worm. When Will the Next Shoe Fall?" Network World, January 23 2009 (www.networkworld.com/news/2009/012309-downadup-conflicker-worm.html?hpg1=bn, accessed November 17, 2010); Erik Larkin, "Protecting Against the Rampant Conflicker Worm," PCWorld, January 16, 2009; "War in the Fifth Domain," The Economist, July 1, 2010 (www.economist.com/node/16478792, accessed November 17, 2010).

CASE STUDY QUESTIONS

1. What is a botnet?
2. Describe some of the main points of the Digital Agenda for Europe.
3. Explain how a cyber attack can be carried out.
4. Describe some of the weaknesses exploited by malware.

Case contributed by Daniel Ortiz-Arroyo, Aalborg University

Key System Applications for the Digital Age

Part Three examines the core information system applications businesses are using today to improve operational excellence and decision making. These applications include enterprise systems; systems for supply chain management, customer relationship management, and knowledge management; e-commerce applications; and business-intelligence systems. This part answers questions such as: How can enterprise applications improve business performance? How do firms use e-commerce to extend the reach of their businesses? How can systems improve decision making and help companies make better use of their knowledge assets?

Chapter 9

Achieving Operational Excellence and Customer Intimacy: Enterprise Applications

Interactive Sessions:

DP World Takes Port
   Management To The Next
   Level with RFID

Customer Relationship
   Management Heads to the
   Cloud

TECHNOLOGY HELPS NVIDIA ANTICIPATE THE FUTURE

In 1999, NVIDIA made history when it invented the graphics processing unit (GPU). Today, Nvidia's chips can be found in a broad range of products, including video game consoles, smartphones, tablets, auto infotainment systems, and supercomputers. Headquartered in Santa Clara, California, the company has 7,000 employees across 20 countries, and earned $3.5 billion in revenue in 2011.

Because so many Nvidia chips are made for the consumer electronics industry, one of the company's toughest challenges is to accurately forecast customer demand and to adjust its inventory levels accordingly. Consumer trends can be fickle and subject to sudden shifts one way or the other. If, for example, the demand for a video game console drops unexpectedly, Nvidia might be stuck with thousands of excess chips for those systems, which represents a significant loss for the company.

Nvidia's chips are created long before they are sold to customers, requiring production planners to make estimates of how much material the company will need and how much production time to schedule at Nvidia's foundries, which are located primarily in Asia. When Nvidia's customers estimated how many Nvidia chips they would need, Nvidia's planners made their own independent estimates. Using these estimates, Nvidia would buy enough material (primarily silicon wafers) in advance and schedule enough capacity at the company's foundries (which are primarily in Asia) to meet what it thought would be the right level of demand.

Business units would meet with Nvidia's finance unit to discuss the number of chips to be produced, based on high-level estimates. Nvidia's chip operations group, which was responsible for the actual production, never received the forecasts and could only see existing inventory. Nvidia's production department used spreadsheets to create rough inventory forecasts, but those spreadsheets did not allow planners to drill down, sort data by product, compare different types of inventory, or view data by business segment, and the data for these spreadsheets had to be gathered from a number of systems.

Management received a wake-up call when Nvidia switched its old manufacturing process to a 40 nanometer process. The company was forced to carry inventory created by the old manufacturing process as well as for customers who were not ready to change. Management discovered that the current system lacked the ability to handle the complexity of two separate sets of inventory and was unable to balance supply and demand for its new products and its existing products, as well as predict how long it would take for its customers to transition to the 40 nanometer method. Nvidia wound up with way too much inventory, and when it started cutting back, its suppliers were caught off guard.

To address these problems, Nvidia set up a supply chain steering committee to review its supply chain processes. The steering committee recommended that Nvidia replace its spreadsheet-based inventory forecasting system with something more current. SAP software proved to be the logical choice. Most of Nvidia's data were already located within its SAP advanced planning and optimization (APO) system. Nvidia built a customized interface on top of its APO system for its new inventory forecasting solution using SAP BusinessObjects Web Intelligence. SAP BusinessObjects Web Intelligence is a tool for analyzing business data and creating ad hoc reports, with access to company data via an easy-to-use Web-based interface.

Another part of the solution was to use SAP BusinessObjects Dashboards to create state-of-the-art supply and demand dashboards where executives could easily access high-level inventory data. Using these dashboards, Nvidia executives are able to drill down into details at the product level and to perform forward- and backward-looking calculations, with or without inventory reserves. The information is presented in user-friendly charts and tables.

These solutions allow Nvidia to forecast inventory levels for the next four quarters based on anticipated demand, as well as to view six months' worth of current inventory. The error rate has been reduced to 3 percent or less compared to a 5 percent error rate in the company's old spreadsheet-based forecasts. With a $500 million tied up in inventory, the company saves $25 million by being able to reduce its forecasting errors.

Not only has the new system improved accuracy, the dashboards have also helped to reduce the amount of time required for Nvidia executives and planners to build and approve a forecast. The old manual system required 140 hours to prepare a quarterly forecast; the new system has reduced that to only 30 hours. Best of all, all of Nvidia's inventory data are located centrally and are accessible to all of the company's different business divisions. Nvidia now has a consistent method of forecasting, instead of multiple models, and managers clearly are able to make better decisions.

Sources: David Hannon, "Inventory Forecasting at Nvidia," SAP *InsiderPROFILES*, April–June 2012; www.nvidia.com, accessed July 20, 2012; andwww.mysap.com, accessed July 20, 2012.

Nvidia's problems with inventory forecasting illustrate the critical role of supply chain management systems in business. Nvidia's business performance was impeded because it could not balance supply and demand for its products. Costs were unnecessarily high because the company was unable to accurately determine the exact amount of each of its chips needed to fulfill orders and hold just that amount in inventory. Production plans were based on "best guesses." Sometimes this left the company holding too much inventory it couldn't sell or not enough to fulfill customer orders.

The chapter-opening diagram calls attention to important points raised by this case and this chapter. Nvidia supplies the consumer electronics industry, where customer tastes change rapidly and demand is very volatile. The company has a fairly long production lead time required to fulfill orders. Nvidia used a spreadsheet-based planning system that was heavily manual and unable to forecast precisely.

Nvidia's management realized it needed better forecasting tools and appointed a supply chain steering committee to recommend a solution. The company was able to create a much more accurate inventory forecasting system by using SAP BusinessObjects Web Intelligence and BusinessObjects Dashboards to analyze data that had already been captured in its SAP Advanced Planning and Optimization (APO) system. These tools have made it much easier for Nvidia's management to access and analyze production data for forecasting and inventory planning, greatly improving both decision making and operational efficiency.

Here are some questions to think about: How did Nvidia's inability to forecast demand affect its suppliers and customers? How is Nvidia's business affected by having a global supply chain?

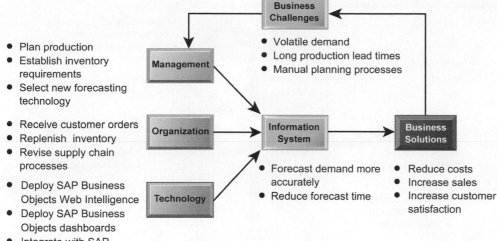

- Plan production
- Establish inventory requirements
- Select new forecasting technology

- Receive customer orders
- Replenish inventory
- Revise supply chain processes

- Deploy SAP Business Objects Web Intelligence
- Deploy SAP Business Objects dashboards
- Integrate with SAP APO

Business Challenges
- Volatile demand
- Long production lead times
- Manual planning processes

Management

Organization

Technology

Information System

Business Solutions

- Forecast demand more accurately
- Reduce forecast time

- Reduce costs
- Increase sales
- Increase customer satisfaction

A round the globe, companies are increasingly becoming more connected, both internally and with other companies. If you run a business, you'll want to be able to react instantaneously when a customer places a large order or when a shipment from a supplier is delayed. You may also want to know the impact of these events on every part of the business and how the business is performing at any point in time, especially if you're running a large company. Enterprise systems provide the integration to make this possible. Let's look at how they work and what they can do for the firm.

WHAT ARE ENTERPRISE SYSTEMS?

Imagine that you had to run a business based on information from tens or even hundreds of different databases and systems, none of which could speak to one another? Imagine your company had 10 different major product lines, each produced in separate factories, and each with separate and incompatible sets of systems controlling production, warehousing, and distribution.

At the very least, your decision making would often be based on manual hard-copy reports, often out of date, and it would be difficult to really understand what is happening in the business as a whole. Sales personnel might not be able to tell at the time they place an order whether the ordered items are in inventory, and manufacturing could not easily use sales data to plan for new production. You now have a good idea of why firms need a special enterprise system to integrate information.

Chapter 2 introduced enterprise systems, also known as enterprise resource planning (ERP) systems, which are based on a suite of integrated software modules and a common central database. The database collects data from many different divisions and departments in a firm, and from a large number of key business processes in manufacturing and production, finance and account-ing, sales and marketing, and human resources, making the data available for applications that support nearly all of an organization's internal business

FIGURE 9.1 **HOW ENTERPRISE SYSTEMS WORK**

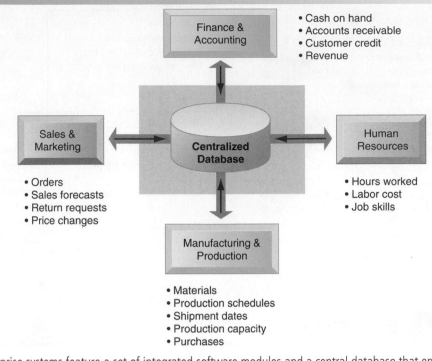

Enterprise systems feature a set of integrated software modules and a central database that enables data to be shared by many different business processes and functional areas throughout the enterprise.

activities. When new information is entered by one process, the information is made immediately available to other business processes (see Figure 9.1).

If a sales representative places an order for tire rims, for example, the system verifies the customer's credit limit, schedules the shipment, identifies the best shipping route, and reserves the necessary items from inventory. If inventory stock were insufficient to fill the order, the system schedules the manufacture of more rims, ordering the needed materials and components from suppliers. Sales and production forecasts are immediately updated. General ledger and corporate cash levels are automatically updated with the revenue and cost information from the order. Users could tap into the system and find out where that particular order was at any minute. Management could obtain information at any point in time about how the business was operating. The system could also generate enterprise-wide data for management analyses of product cost and profitability.

ENTERPRISE SOFTWARE

Enterprise software is built around thousands of predefined business processes that reflect best practices. Table 9.1 describes some of the major business processes supported by enterprise software.

Companies implementing this software would have to first select the functions of the system they wished to use and then map their business processes to the predefined business processes in the software. (One of our Learning Tracks shows how SAP enterprise software handles the procurement process for a new piece of equipment.) A firm would use configuration tables provided by the software manufacturer to tailor a particular aspect of

TABLE 9.1 BUSINESS PROCESSES SUPPORTED BY ENTERPRISE SYSTEMS

Financial and accounting processes, including general ledger, accounts payable, accounts receivable, fixed assets, cash management and forecasting, product-cost accounting, cost-center accounting, asset accounting, tax accounting, credit management, and financial reporting

Human resources processes, including personnel administration, time accounting, payroll, personnel planning and development, benefits accounting, applicant tracking, time management, compensation, workforce planning, performance management, and travel expense reporting

Manufacturing and production processes, including procurement, inventory management, purchasing, shipping, production planning, production scheduling, material requirements planning, quality control, distribution, transportation execution, and plant and equipment maintenance

Sales and marketing processes, including order processing, quotations, contracts, product configuration, pricing, billing, credit checking, incentive and commission management, and sales planning

the system to the way it does business. For example, the firm could use these tables to select whether it wants to track revenue by product line, geographical unit, or distribution channel.

If the enterprise software does not support the way the organization does business, companies can rewrite some of the software to support the way their business processes work. However, enterprise software is unusually complex, and extensive customization may degrade system performance, compromising the information and process integration that are the main benefits of the system. If companies want to reap the maximum benefits from enterprise software, they must change the way they work to conform to the business processes defined by the software.

To implement a new enterprise system, Tasty Baking Company identified its existing business processes and then translated them into the business processes built into the SAP ERP software it had selected. To ensure it obtained the maximum benefits from the enterprise software, Tasty Baking Company deliberately planned for customizing less than 5 percent of the system and made very few changes to the SAP software itself. It used as many tools and features that were already built into the SAP software as it could. SAP has more than 3,000 configuration tables for its enterprise software.

Leading enterprise software vendors include SAP, Oracle, IBM, Infor Global Solutions, and Microsoft. There are versions of enterprise software packages designed for small and medium-sized businesses and on-demand versions, including software services running in the cloud (see Section 9.4).

BUSINESS VALUE OF ENTERPRISE SYSTEMS

Enterprise systems provide value both by increasing operational efficiency and by providing firmwide information to help managers make better decisions. Large companies with many operating units in different locations have used enterprise systems to enforce standard practices and data so that everyone does business the same way worldwide.

Coca-Cola, for instance, implemented a SAP enterprise system to standardize and coordinate important business processes in 200 countries. Lack of standard, company-wide business processes prevented the company from leveraging its worldwide buying power to obtain lower prices for raw materials and from reacting rapidly to market changes.

Enterprise systems help firms respond rapidly to customer requests for information or products. Because the system integrates order, manufacturing, and delivery data, manufacturing is better informed about producing only what customers have ordered, procuring exactly the right amount of components or raw materials to fill actual orders, staging production, and minimizing the time that components or finished products are in inventory.

Alcoa, the world's leading producer of aluminum and aluminum products with operations spanning 31 countries and over 200 locations, had initially been organized around lines of business, each of which had its own set of information systems. Many of these systems were redundant and inefficient. Alcoa's costs for executing requisition-to-pay and financial processes were much higher and its cycle times were longer than those of other companies in its industry. (Cycle time refers to the total elapsed time from the beginning to the end of a process.) The company could not operate as a single worldwide entity.

After implementing enterprise software from Oracle, Alcoa eliminated many redundant processes and systems. The enterprise system helped Alcoa reduce requisition-to-pay cycle time by verifying receipt of goods and automatically generating receipts for payment. Alcoa's accounts payable transaction processing dropped 89 percent. Alcoa was able to centralize financial and procurement activities, which helped the company reduce nearly 20 percent of its worldwide costs.

Enterprise systems provide much valuable information for improving management decision making. Corporate headquarters has access to up-to-the-minute data on sales, inventory, and production, and uses this information to create more accurate sales and production forecasts. Enterprise software includes analytical tools for using data captured by the system to evaluate overall organizational performance. Enterprise system data have common standardized definitions and formats that are accepted by the entire organization. Performance figures mean the same thing across the company. Enterprise systems allow senior management to easily find out at any moment how a particular organizational unit is performing, determine which products are most or least profitable, and calculate costs for the company as a whole.

For example, Alcoa's enterprise system includes functionality for global human resources management that shows correlations between investment in employee training and quality, measures the company-wide costs of delivering services to employees, and measures the effectiveness of employee recruitment, compensation, and training.

9.2 SUPPLY CHAIN MANAGEMENT SYSTEMS

If you manage a small firm that makes a few products or sells a few services, chances are you will have a small number of suppliers. You could coordinate your supplier orders and deliveries using a telephone and fax machine. But if you manage a firm that produces more complex products and services, then you will have hundreds of suppliers, and your suppliers will each have their own set of suppliers. Suddenly, you are in a situation where you will need to coordinate the activities of hundreds or even thousands of other firms in order to produce your products and services. Supply chain management (SCM) systems, which we introduced in Chapter 2, are an answer to the problems of supply chain complexity and scale.

THE SUPPLY CHAIN

A firm's **supply chain** is a network of organizations and business processes for procuring raw materials, transforming these materials into intermediate and finished products, and distributing the finished products to customers. It links suppliers, manufacturing plants, distribution centers, retail outlets, and customers to supply goods and services from source through consumption. Materials, information, and payments flow through the supply chain in both directions.

Goods start out as raw materials and, as they move through the supply chain, are transformed into intermediate products (also referred to as components or parts), and finally, into finished products. The finished products are shipped to distribution centers and from there to retailers and customers. Returned items flow in the reverse direction from the buyer back to the seller.

Let's look at the supply chain for Nike sneakers as an example. Nike designs, markets, and sells sneakers, socks, athletic clothing, and accessories throughout the world. Its primary suppliers are contract manufacturers with factories in China, Thailand, Indonesia, Brazil, and other countries. These companies fashion Nike's finished products.

Nike's contract suppliers do not manufacture sneakers from scratch. They obtain components for the sneakers—the laces, eyelets, uppers, and soles—from other suppliers and then assemble them into finished sneakers. These suppliers in turn have their own suppliers. For example, the suppliers of soles have suppliers for synthetic rubber, suppliers for chemicals used to melt the rubber for molding, and suppliers for the molds into which to pour the rubber. Suppliers of laces have suppliers for their thread, for dyes, and for the plastic lace tips.

Figure 9.2 provides a simplified illustration of Nike's supply chain for sneakers; it shows the flow of information and materials among suppliers, Nike, Nike's distributors, retailers, and customers. Nike's contract manufacturers are

FIGURE 9.2 NIKE'S SUPPLY CHAIN

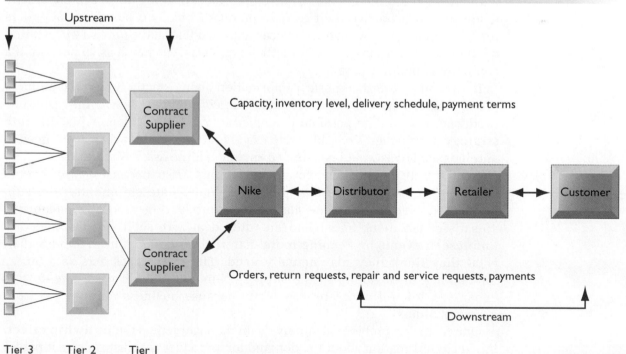

This figure illustrates the major entities in Nike's supply chain and the flow of information upstream and downstream to coordinate the activities involved in buying, making, and moving a product. Shown here is a simplified supply chain, with the upstream portion focusing only on the suppliers for sneakers and sneaker soles.

its primary suppliers. The suppliers of soles, eyelets, uppers, and laces are the secondary (Tier 2) suppliers. Suppliers to these suppliers are the tertiary (Tier 3) suppliers.

The *upstream* portion of the supply chain includes the company's suppliers, the suppliers' suppliers, and the processes for managing relationships with them. The *downstream* portion consists of the organizations and processes for distributing and delivering products to the final customers. Companies doing manufacturing, such as Nike's contract suppliers of sneakers, also manage their own *internal supply chain* processes for transforming materials, components, and services furnished by their suppliers into finished products or intermediate products (components or parts) for their customers and for managing materials and inventory.

The supply chain illustrated in Figure 9.2 has been simplified. It only shows two contract manufacturers for sneakers and only the upstream supply chain for sneaker soles. Nike has hundreds of contract manufacturers turning out finished sneakers, socks, and athletic clothing, each with its own set of suppliers. The upstream portion of Nike's supply chain would actually comprise thousands of entities. Nike also has numerous distributors and many thousands of retail stores where its shoes are sold, so the downstream portion of its supply chain is also large and complex.

INFORMATION SYSTEMS AND SUPPLY CHAIN MANAGEMENT

Inefficiencies in the supply chain, such as parts shortages, underutilized plant capacity, excessive finished goods inventory, or high transportation costs, are caused by inaccurate or untimely information. For example, manufacturers may keep too many parts in inventory because they do not know exactly when they will receive their next shipments from their suppliers. Suppliers may order too few raw materials because they do not have precise information on demand. These supply chain inefficiencies waste as much as 25 percent of a company's operating costs.

If a manufacturer had perfect information about exactly how many units of product customers wanted, when they wanted them, and when they could be produced, it would be possible to implement a highly efficient **just-in-time strategy**. Components would arrive exactly at the moment they were needed and finished goods would be shipped as they left the assembly line.

In a supply chain, however, uncertainties arise because many events cannot be foreseen—uncertain product demand, late shipments from suppliers, defective parts or raw materials, or production process breakdowns. To satisfy customers, manufacturers often deal with such uncertainties and unforeseen events by keeping more material or products in inventory than what they think they may actually need. The *safety stock* acts as a buffer for the lack of flexibility in the supply chain. Although excess inventory is expensive, low fill rates are also costly because business may be lost from canceled orders.

One recurring problem in supply chain management is the **bullwhip effect**, in which information about the demand for a product gets distorted as it passes from one entity to the next across the supply chain. A slight rise in demand for an item might cause different members in the supply chain—distributors, manufacturers, suppliers, secondary suppliers (suppliers' suppliers), and tertiary suppliers (suppliers' suppliers' suppliers)—to stockpile inventory so each has enough "just in case." These changes ripple throughout the supply chain, magnifying what started out as a small change from planned orders, creating excess inventory, production, warehousing, and shipping costs (see Figure 9.3).

For example, Procter & Gamble (P&G) found it had excessively high inventories of its Pampers disposable diapers at various points along its supply chain because of such distorted information. Although customer purchases in stores were fairly stable, orders from distributors would spike when P&G offered aggressive price promotions. Pampers and Pampers' components accumulated in warehouses along the supply chain to meet demand that did not actually exist. To eliminate this problem, P&G revised its marketing, sales, and supply chain processes and used more accurate demand forecasting.

The bullwhip is tamed by reducing uncertainties about demand and supply when all members of the supply chain have accurate and up-to-date information. If all supply chain members share dynamic information about inventory levels, schedules, forecasts, and shipments, they have more precise knowledge about how to adjust their sourcing, manufacturing, and distribution plans. Supply chain management systems provide the kind of information that helps members of the supply chain make better purchasing and scheduling decisions.

FIGURE 9.3 THE BULLWHIP EFFECT

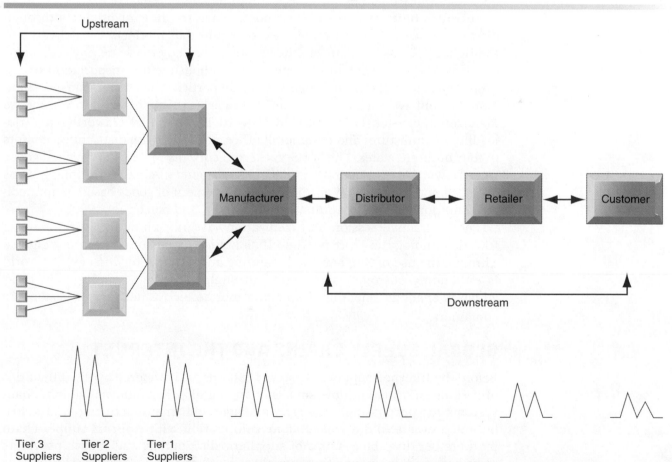

Inaccurate information can cause minor fluctuations in demand for a product to be amplified as one moves further back in the supply chain. Minor fluctuations in retail sales for a product can create excess inventory for distributors, manufacturers, and suppliers.

SUPPLY CHAIN MANAGEMENT SOFTWARE

Supply chain software is classified as either software to help businesses plan their supply chains (supply chain planning) or software to help them execute the supply chain steps (supply chain execution). **Supply chain planning systems** enable the firm to model its existing supply chain, generate demand forecasts for products, and develop optimal sourcing and manufacturing plans. Such systems help companies make better decisions such as determining how much of a specific product to manufacture in a given time period; establishing inventory levels for raw materials, intermediate products, and finished goods; determining where to store finished goods; and identifying the transportation mode to use for product delivery.

For example, if a large customer places a larger order than usual or changes that order on short notice, it can have a widespread impact throughout the supply chain. Additional raw materials or a different mix of raw materials may need to be ordered from suppliers. Manufacturing may have to change job scheduling. A transportation carrier may have to reschedule deliveries. Supply chain planning software makes the necessary adjustments to production and distribution plans. Information about changes is shared among the relevant supply chain members so that their work can be coordinated. One of the most important—and complex—supply chain planning functions is **demand planning**, which determines how much product a business needs to make to satisfy all of its customers' demands. JDA Software, SAP, and Oracle all offer supply chain management solutions.

Supply chain execution systems manage the flow of products through distribution centers and warehouses to ensure that products are delivered to the right locations in the most efficient manner. They track the physical status of goods, the management of materials, warehouse and transportation operations, and financial information involving all parties. The Oracle Transportation Management system used by Land O'Lakes is an example, as is the Warehouse Management System (WMS) used by Haworth Incorporated. Haworth is a world-leading manufacturer and designer of office furniture, with distribution centers in four different states. The WMS tracks and controls the flow of finished goods from Haworth's distribution centers to its customers. Acting on shipping plans for customer orders, the WMS directs the movement of goods based on immediate conditions for space, equipment, inventory, and personnel.

The Interactive Session on organizations describes how DP World is using RFID technology to increase the efficiency of its customers' supply chains. Through the use of RFID-enabled scanning and tracking technology, DP World is enhancing customer satisfaction through optimized supply chain flow, which is enabling smoother, faster, and more effective delivery of customers' containers.

GLOBAL SUPPLY CHAINS AND THE INTERNET

Before the Internet, supply chain coordination was hampered by the difficulties of making information flow smoothly among disparate internal supply chain systems for purchasing, materials management, manufacturing, and distribution. It was also difficult to share information with external supply chain partners because the systems of suppliers, distributors, or logistics providers were based on incompatible technology platforms and standards. Enterprise and supply chain management systems enhanced with Internet technology supply some of this integration.

INTERACTIVE SESSION: ORGANIZATIONS

DP WORLD TAKES PORT MANAGEMENT TO THE NEXT LEVEL WITH RFID

DP (Dubai Ports) World has reason to be proud of its accomplishment of becoming one of the leading terminal operators in the world. Today, DP World has 60 terminals across 6 continents, and 11 new terminals are under development. The firm employs an international professional team of more than 30,000 people to serve customers in some of the most dynamic economies in the world.

DP World has adopted a customer-centric approach to enhancing its customers' supply chains by providing quality, innovative services to effectively manage container, bulk, and other terminal cargo. The firm invests heavily in terminal infrastructures, technologies, and people to best serve its customers.

Like other global port and terminal operators, DP World helps shippers around the world address the often complex and costly challenges of managing the supply chain. One of the typical problems encountered in container terminal operations is traffic congestion at port entry points. This congestion is often due to delays introduced by lengthy procedures and paper-based logistics. In response, DP World has introduced many IT-based solutions to enhance terminal capacity utilization. These solutions include the electronic custom release of cargo, Electronic Data Interchange (EDI) reporting, two-way digital radio communications, and the "e-token" advanced booking system.

DP World management wanted to take things a step further and decided to make the loading and unloading of containers operate on "just in time" principles to improve container turnaround. It found that Radio Frequency Identification (RFID) technology was an effective way of increasing the efficiency of truck movements through port access gates. Today, DP World uses RFID-enabled automatic gate systems at the port terminals it operates in Dubai and Australia. According to Mohammed Al Muallem, managing director of DP World UAE, the introduction of an automated gate system would not only eliminate traffic congestion but would also help to eliminate a number of lengthy procedures, increasing productivity at the ports, and improving customer satisfaction. This will in turn, increase the turnaround of shipping goods.

Prior to the RFID deployment, DP World spent several months performing proof-of-concept trials involving several competing RFID suppliers. Because of the rugged environmental conditions at the ports, DP World required that 99.5 percent of all tags be read successfully, which was a key challenge for many vendors. After extensive testing and evaluation, DP World selected Identec Solutions, a global leader in active wireless tracking solutions, as its RFID supplier.

How does the RFID tracking system work? Trucks that visit a port terminal are equipped with active RFID tags supplied by Identec Solutions that are fixed on the rear chassis. As a truck moves towards the gate, its unique tag ID number is read by an RFID reader, which is integrated with an automated gate system. At the gate, an optical character recognition (OCR) system determines if the truck is loaded with a container, identifies the ID number of the truck's container, and reads the truck license plate number as a backup identification. The system uses the supplied information to automatically issue a ticket to the driver that specifies the lane the truck should proceed to in order to load or unload the container. The system can also automatically determine if the truck is on time, which is essential information for the efficient pickup and drop off of containers. As the truck leaves the gate, the RFID tag is read once again, and the driver receives a receipt for the completed transaction.

RFID has enabled DP World to increase the productivity of container handoffs, speed the entry and exit of trucks through terminal gates, and increase fuel efficiency. Victoria Rose, regional office project coordinator at DP World Sydney maintained that RFID would improve gate efficiency through improved truck management, reducing queues and congestion around gates, and removing the number of trucks from public roads by streamlining procedures.

Identec's RFID-based solution has also enabled DP World to improve customer satisfaction by enhancing the efficiency of customers' supply chains through smoother, faster, and more effective delivery of their containers at terminal gates. The elimination of lengthy paper transactions and manual inspections at gates and the reduction in manual data input errors demonstrate DP World's customer-centric approach to delivering a superior level of service. The technology also allows transport companies to save time, increase revenues, and reduce costs.

DP World's use of RFID has also helped it to tighten security by providing better accuracy on inbound and outbound truck movements through the terminals. For instance, the system can automatically check whether a truck has a booking and whether it is authorized to enter the port.

As a next step, DP World will consider expanding its use of RFID-enabled scanning and tracking technology to further optimize supply chain flow. In the future, Rose hopes DP World will focus on

investigating its use within the yard, and how data captured can be used.

Sources: Dave Friedlos, "RFID Boosts DP World's Productivity in Australia," RFID Journal, July 27, 2009 (www.rfidjournal.com/article/view/5086, accessed October 20, 2010); Rhea Wessel, "DP World Ramps Up Its Dubai Deployment," RFID Journal, August 13, 2009 (www.rfidjournal.com/article/view/5130, accessed October 20, 2010); "DP World UAE Implements Automated Gate System at Jebel Ali Port," The Zone, May-June 2008 (www.jafza.ae/mediafiles/2008/10/23/20081023_Issue-11.pdf, accessed October 20, 2010), p. 11; DP World (www.dpworld.com, accessed October 20, 2010); Identec Solutions (www.identecsolutions.com, accessed October 20, 2010).

Case contributed by Faouzi Kamoun, The University of Dubai

CASE STUDY QUESTIONS

1. How did Identec Solutions' RFID-based technology help DP World increase the efficiency and effectiveness of its customers' supply chains?

2. Describe two improvements that resulted from implementing the Identec RFID-based solution.

3. How does the concept of supply chain execution relate to this interactive session?

4. What managerial, organizational, and technological challenges might DP World have faced in the early stages of the RFID project's deployment?

A manager uses a Web interface to tap into suppliers' systems to determine whether inventory and production capabilities match demand for the firm's products. Business partners use Web-based supply chain management tools to collaborate online on forecasts. Sales representatives access suppliers' production schedules and logistics information to monitor customers' order status.

Global Supply Chain Issues

More and more companies are entering international markets, outsourcing manufacturing operations, and obtaining supplies from other countries as well as selling abroad. Their supply chains extend across multiple countries and regions. There are additional complexities and challenges to managing a global supply chain.

Global supply chains typically span greater geographic distances and time differences than domestic supply chains and have participants from a number of different countries. Performance standards may vary from region to region or from nation to nation. Supply chain management may need to reflect foreign government regulations and cultural differences.

The Internet helps companies manage many aspects of their global supply chains, including sourcing, transportation, communications, and international finance. Today's apparel industry, for example, relies heavily on outsourcing to contract manufacturers in China and other low-wage countries. Apparel companies are starting to use the Web to manage their global supply chain and production issues. (Review the discussion of Li & Fung in Chapter 3.)

In addition to contract manufacturing, globalization has encouraged outsourcing warehouse management, transportation management, and related operations to third-party logistics providers, such as UPS Supply Chain Solutions and Schneider Logistics Services. These logistics services offer Web-based software to give their customers a better view of their global supply chains. Customers are able to check a secure Web site to monitor inventory and shipments, helping them run their global supply chains more efficiently.

Demand-Driven Supply Chains: From Push to Pull Manufacturing and Efficient Customer Response

In addition to reducing costs, supply chain management systems facilitate efficient customer response, enabling the workings of the business to be driven more by customer demand. (We introduced efficient customer response systems in Chapter 3.)

Earlier supply chain management systems were driven by a push-based model (also known as build-to-stock). In a **push-based model**, production master schedules are based on forecasts or best guesses of demand for products, and products are "pushed" to customers. With new flows of information made possible by Web-based tools, supply chain management more easily follows a pull-based model. In a **pull-based model**, also known as a demand-driven or build-to-order model, actual customer orders or purchases trigger events in the supply chain. Transactions to produce and deliver only what customers have ordered move up the supply chain from retailers to distributors to manufacturers and eventually to suppliers. Only products to fulfill these orders move back down the supply chain to the retailer. Manufacturers use only actual order demand information to drive their production schedules and the procurement of components or raw materials, as illustrated in Figure 9.4. Walmart's continuous replenishment system described in Chapter 3 is an example of the pull-based model.

The Internet and Internet technology make it possible to move from sequential supply chains, where information and materials flow sequentially from company to company, to concurrent supply chains, where information flows in many directions simultaneously among members of a supply chain network. Complex supply networks of manufacturers, logistics suppliers, outsourced manufacturers, retailers, and distributors are able to adjust immediately to changes in schedules or orders. Ultimately, the Internet could create a "digital logistics nervous system" throughout the supply chain (see Figure 9.5).

BUSINESS VALUE OF SUPPLY CHAIN MANAGEMENT SYSTEMS

You have just seen how supply chain management systems enable firms to streamline both their internal and external supply chain processes and provide management with more accurate information about what to produce, store, and move. By implementing a networked and integrated supply chain management system, companies match supply to demand, reduce inventory

FIGURE 9.4   PUSH- VERSUS PULL-BASED SUPPLY CHAIN MODELS

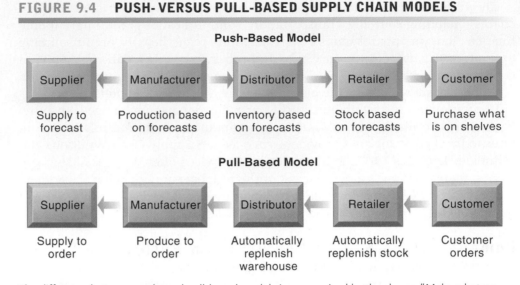

The difference between push- and pull-based models is summarized by the slogan "Make what we sell, not sell what we make."

levels, improve delivery service, speed product time to market, and use assets more effectively.

Total supply chain costs represent the majority of operating expenses for many businesses and in some industries approach 75 percent of the total operating budget. Reducing supply chain costs has a major impact on firm profitability.

FIGURE 9.5   THE EMERGING INTERNET-DRIVEN SUPPLY CHAIN

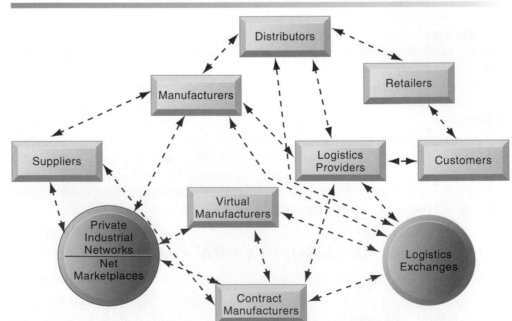

The emerging Internet-driven supply chain operates like a digital logistics nervous system. It provides multidirectional communication among firms, networks of firms, and e-marketplaces so that entire networks of supply chain partners can immediately adjust inventories, orders, and capacities.

In addition to reducing costs, supply chain management systems help increase sales. If a product is not available when a customer wants it, customers often try to purchase it from someone else. More precise control of the supply chain enhances the firm's ability to have the right product available for customer purchases at the right time.

9.3 CUSTOMER RELATIONSHIP MANAGEMENT SYSTEMS

You've probably heard phrases such as "the customer is always right" or "the customer comes first." Today these words ring truer than ever. Because competitive advantage based on an innovative new product or service is often very short lived, companies are realizing that their most enduring competitive strength may be their relationships with their customers. Some say that the basis of competition has switched from who sells the most products and services to who "owns" the customer, and that customer relationships represent a firm's most valuable asset.

WHAT IS CUSTOMER RELATIONSHIP MANAGEMENT?

What kinds of information would you need to build and nurture strong, long-lasting relationships with customers? You'd want to know exactly who your customers are, how to contact them, whether they are costly to service and sell to, what kinds of products and services they are interested in, and how much money they spend on your company. If you could, you'd want to make sure you knew each of your customers well, as if you were running a small-town store. And you'd want to make your good customers feel special.

In a small business operating in a neighborhood, it is possible for business owners and managers to really know their customers on a personal, face-to-face basis. But in a large business operating on a metropolitan, regional, national, or even global basis, it is impossible to "know your customer" in this intimate way. In these kinds of businesses there are too many customers and too many different ways that customers interact with the firm (over the Web, the phone, e-mail, blogs, and in person). It becomes especially difficult to integrate information from all theses sources and to deal with the large numbers of customers.

A large business's processes for sales, service, and marketing tend to be highly compartmentalized, and these departments do not share much essential customer information. Some information on a specific customer might be stored and organized in terms of that person's account with the company. Other pieces of information about the same customer might be organized by products that were purchased. There is no way to consolidate all of this information to provide a unified view of a customer across the company.

This is where customer relationship management systems help. Customer relationship management (CRM) systems, which we introduced in Chapter 2, capture and integrate customer data from all over the organization, consolidate the data, analyze the data, and then distribute the results to various systems and customer touch points across the enterprise. A **touch point** (also known as a contact point) is a method of interaction with the customer, such as telephone, e-mail, customer service desk, conventional mail, Facebook, Twitter, Web site, wireless device, or retail store. Well-designed CRM systems provide a

FIGURE 9.6 **CUSTOMER RELATIONSHIP MANAGEMENT (CRM)**

CRM systems examine customers from a multifaceted perspective. These systems use a set of integrated applications to address all aspects of the customer relationship, including customer service, sales, and marketing.

single enterprise view of customers that is useful for improving both sales and customer service (see Figure 9.6.)

Good CRM systems provide data and analytical tools for answering questions such as these: What is the value of a particular customer to the firm over his or her lifetime? Who are our most loyal customers? It can cost six times more to sell to a new customer than to an existing customer. Who are our most profitable customers? What do these profitable customers want to buy? Firms use the answers to these questions to acquire new customers, provide better service and support to existing customers, customize their offerings more precisely to customer preferences, and provide ongoing value to retain profitable customers.

CUSTOMER RELATIONSHIP MANAGEMENT SOFTWARE

Commercial CRM software packages range from niche tools that perform limited functions, such as personalizing Web sites for specific customers, to large-scale enterprise applications that capture myriad interactions with customers, analyze them with sophisticated reporting tools, and link to other major enterprise applications, such as supply chain management and enterprise systems. The more comprehensive CRM packages contain modules for **partner relationship management (PRM)** and **employee relationship management (ERM)**.

PRM uses many of the same data, tools, and systems as customer relationship management to enhance collaboration between a company and its selling partners. If a company does not sell directly to customers but rather works through distributors or retailers, PRM helps these channels sell to customers directly. It provides a company and its selling partners with the ability to trade information and distribute leads and data about customers, integrating lead generation, pricing, promotions, order configurations, and availability. It also provides a firm with tools to assess its partners' performances so it can make sure its best partners receive the support they need to close more business.

ERM software deals with employee issues that are closely related to CRM, such as setting objectives, employee performance management, performance-based compensation, and employee training. Major CRM application software vendors include Oracle, SAP, Salesforce.com, and Microsoft Dynamics CRM.

Customer relationship management systems typically provide software and online tools for sales, customer service, and marketing. We briefly describe some of these capabilities.

Sales Force Automation (SFA)

Sales force automation modules in CRM systems help sales staff increase their productivity by focusing sales efforts on the most profitable customers, those who are good candidates for sales and services. CRM systems provide sales prospect and contact information, product information, product configuration capabilities, and sales quote generation capabilities. Such software can assemble information about a particular customer's past purchases to help the salesperson make personalized recommendations. CRM software enables sales, marketing, and delivery departments to easily share customer and prospect information. It increases each salesperson's efficiency in reducing the cost per sale as well as the cost of acquiring new customers and retaining old ones. CRM software also has capabilities for sales forecasting, territory management, and team selling.

Customer Service

Customer service modules in CRM systems provide information and tools to increase the efficiency of call centers, help desks, and customer support staff. They have capabilities for assigning and managing customer service requests.

One such capability is an appointment or advice telephone line: When a customer calls a standard phone number, the system routes the call to the correct service person, who inputs information about that customer into the system only once. Once the customer's data are in the system, any service representative can handle the customer relationship. Improved access to consistent and accurate customer information helps call centers handle more calls per day and decrease the duration of each call. Thus, call centers and customer service groups achieve greater productivity, reduced transaction time, and higher quality of service at lower cost. The customer is happier because he or she spends less time on the phone restating his or her problem to customer service representatives.

CRM systems may also include Web-based self-service capabilities: The company Web site can be set up to provide inquiring customers personalized support information as well as the option to contact customer service staff by phone for additional assistance.

Marketing

CRM systems support direct-marketing campaigns by providing capabilities for capturing prospect and customer data, for providing product and service information, for qualifying leads for targeted marketing, and for scheduling and tracking direct-marketing mailings or e-mail (see Figure 9.7). Marketing modules also include tools for analyzing marketing and customer data, identifying profitable and unprofitable customers, designing products and services to satisfy specific customer needs and interests, and identifying opportunities for cross-selling.

FIGURE 9.7   HOW CRM SYSTEMS SUPPORT MARKETING

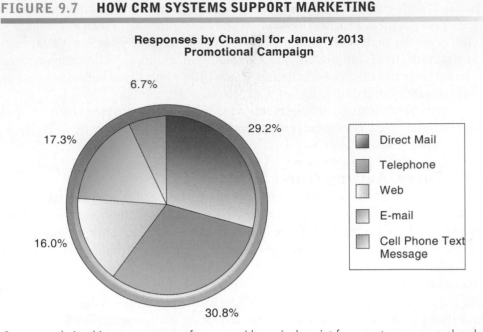

Customer relationship management software provides a single point for users to manage and evaluate marketing campaigns across multiple channels, including e-mail, direct mail, telephone, the Web, and wireless messages.

Cross-selling is the marketing of complementary products to customers. (For example, in financial services, a customer with a checking account might be sold a money market account or a home improvement loan.) CRM tools also help firms manage and execute marketing campaigns at all stages, from planning to determining the rate of success for each campaign.

Figure 9.8 illustrates the most important capabilities for sales, service, and marketing processes that would be found in major CRM software products. Like enterprise software, this software is business-process driven, incorporating hundreds of business processes thought to represent best practices in each of these areas. To achieve maximum benefit, companies need to revise and model their business processes to conform to the best-practice business processes in the CRM software.

Figure 9.9 illustrates how a best practice for increasing customer loyalty through customer service might be modeled by CRM software. Directly servicing customers provides firms with opportunities to increase customer retention by singling out profitable long-term customers for preferential treatment. CRM software can assign each customer a score based on that person's value and loyalty to the company and provide that information to help call centers route each customer's service request to agents who can best handle that customer's needs. The system would automatically provide the service agent with a detailed profile of that customer that includes his or her score for value and loyalty. The service agent would use this information to present special offers or additional service to the customer to encourage the customer to keep transacting business with the company. You will find more information on other best-practice business processes in CRM systems in our Learning Tracks.

FIGURE 9.8   **CRM SOFTWARE CAPABILITIES**

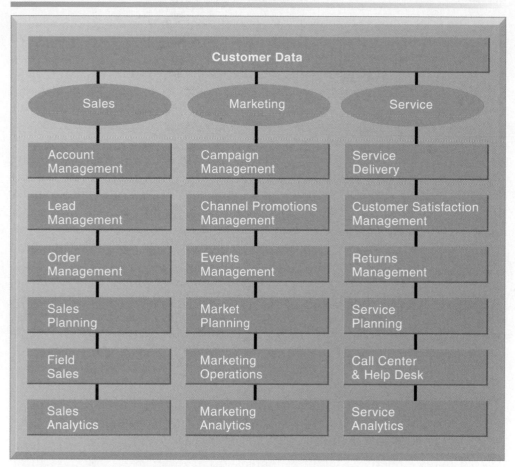

Customer Data		
Sales	**Marketing**	**Service**
Account Management	Campaign Management	Service Delivery
Lead Management	Channel Promotions Management	Customer Satisfaction Management
Order Management	Events Management	Returns Management
Sales Planning	Market Planning	Service Planning
Field Sales	Marketing Operations	Call Center & Help Desk
Sales Analytics	Marketing Analytics	Service Analytics

The major CRM software products support business processes in sales, service, and marketing, integrating customer information from many different sources. Included are support for both the operational and analytical aspects of CRM.

FIGURE 9.9   **CUSTOMER LOYALTY MANAGEMENT PROCESS MAP**

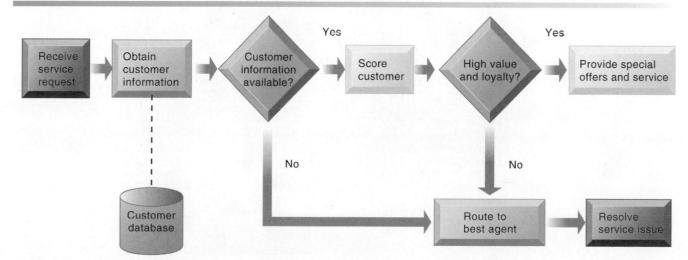

This process map shows how a best practice for promoting customer loyalty through customer service would be modeled by customer relationship management software. The CRM software helps firms identify high-value customers for preferential treatment.

OPERATIONAL AND ANALYTICAL CRM

All of the applications we have just described support either the operational or analytical aspects of customer relationship management. **Operational CRM** includes customer-facing applications, such as tools for sales force automation, call center and customer service support, and marketing automation. **Analytical CRM** includes applications that analyze customer data generated by operational CRM applications to provide information for improving business performance.

Analytical CRM applications are based on data from operational CRM systems, customer touch points, and other sources that have been organized in data warehouses or analytic platforms for use in online analytical processing (OLAP), data mining, and other data analysis techniques (see Chapter 6). Customer data collected by the organization might be combined with data from other sources, such as customer lists for direct-marketing campaigns purchased from other companies or demographic data. Such data are analyzed to identify buying patterns, to create segments for targeted marketing, and to pinpoint profitable and unprofitable customers (see Figure 9.10).

Another important output of analytical CRM is the customer's lifetime value to the firm. **Customer lifetime value (CLTV)** is based on the relationship between the revenue produced by a specific customer, the expenses incurred in acquiring and servicing that customer, and the expected life of the relationship between the customer and the company.

BUSINESS VALUE OF CUSTOMER RELATIONSHIP MANAGEMENT SYSTEMS

Companies with effective customer relationship management systems realize many benefits, including increased customer satisfaction, reduced direct-marketing costs, more effective marketing, and lower costs for customer

FIGURE 9.10 ANALYTICAL CRM

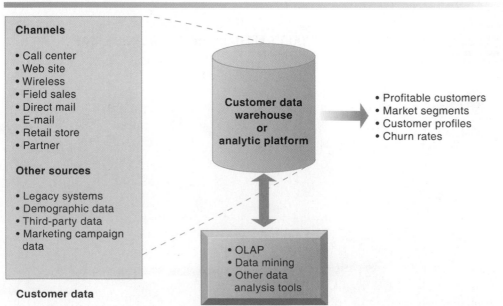

Analytical CRM uses a customer data warehouse or analytic platform and tools to analyze customer data collected from the firm's customer touch points and from other sources.

acquisition and retention. Information from CRM systems increases sales revenue by identifying the most profitable customers and segments for focused marketing and cross-selling.

Customer churn is reduced as sales, service, and marketing better respond to customer needs. The **churn rate** measures the number of customers who stop using or purchasing products or services from a company. It is an important indicator of the growth or decline of a firm's customer base.

9.4 ENTERPRISE APPLICATIONS: NEW OPPORTUNITIES AND CHALLENGES

Many firms have implemented enterprise systems and systems for supply chain and customer relationship management because they are such powerful instruments for achieving operational excellence and enhancing decision making. But precisely because they are so powerful in changing the way the organization works, they are challenging to implement. Let's briefly examine some of these challenges, as well as new ways of obtaining value from these systems.

ENTERPRISE APPLICATION CHALLENGES

Promises of dramatic reductions in inventory costs, order-to-delivery time, as well as more efficient customer response and higher product and customer profitability make enterprise systems and systems for supply chain management and customer relationship management very alluring. But to obtain this value, you must clearly understand how your business has to change to use these systems effectively.

Enterprise applications involve complex pieces of software that are very expensive to purchase and implement. It might take a large Fortune 500 company several years to complete a large-scale implementation of an enterprise system or a system for SCM or CRM. The total cost for an average large system implementation based on SAP or Oracle software, including software, database tools, consulting fees, personnel costs, training, and perhaps hardware costs, runs over $12 million. The implementation cost of an enterprise system for a mid-sized company based on software from a "Tier II" vendor such as Epicor or Lawson averages $3.5 million. Changes in project scope and additional customization work add to implementation delays and costs (Kanaracus, 2012; Wailgum, 2009).

Enterprise applications require not only deep-seated technological changes but also fundamental changes in the way the business operates. Companies must make sweeping changes to their business processes to work with the software. Employees must accept new job functions and responsibilities. They must learn how to perform a new set of work activities and understand how the information they enter into the system can affect other parts of the company. This requires new organizational learning.

Supply chain management systems require multiple organizations to share information and business processes. Each participant in the system may have to change some of its processes and the way it uses information to create a system that best serves the supply chain as a whole.

Some firms experienced enormous operating problems and losses when they first implemented enterprise applications because they didn't understand how much organizational change was required. For example, Kmart had trouble getting products to store shelves when it first implemented i2 Technologies supply chain management software. The i2 software did not work well with Kmart's promotion-driven business model, which created sharp downward spikes in demand for products. Overstock.com's order tracking system went down for a full week when the company replaced a homegrown system with an Oracle enterprise system. The company rushed to implement the software, and did not properly synchronize the Oracle software's process for recording customer refunds with its accounts receivable system. These problems contributed to a third-quarter loss of $14.5 million that year.

Enterprise applications also introduce "switching costs." Once you adopt an enterprise application from a single vendor, such as SAP, Oracle, or others, it is very costly to switch vendors, and your firm becomes dependent on the vendor to upgrade its product and maintain your installation.

Enterprise applications are based on organization-wide definitions of data. You'll need to understand exactly how your business uses its data and how the data would be organized in a customer relationship management, supply chain management, or enterprise system. CRM systems typically require some data cleansing work.

Enterprise software vendors are addressing these problems by offering pared-down versions of their software and "fast-start" programs for small and medium-sized businesses and best-practice guidelines for larger companies. The Interactive Session on Technology describes how on-demand and cloud-based tools deal with this problem as well.

Companies adopting enterprise applications can also save time and money by keeping customizations to a minimum. For example, Kennametal, a $2 billion metal-cutting tools company in Pennsylvania, had spent $10 million over 13 years maintaining an ERP system with over 6,400 customizations. The company is now replacing it with a "plain vanilla," non-customized version of SAP enterprise software and changing its business processes to conform to the software (Johnson, 2010).

NEXT-GENERATION ENTERPRISE APPLICATIONS

Today, enterprise application vendors are delivering more value by becoming more flexible, Web-enabled, and capable of integration with other systems. Stand-alone enterprise systems, customer relationship management systems, and supply chain management systems are becoming a thing of the past. The major enterprise software vendors have created what they call *enterprise solutions, enterprise suites*, or e-business suites to make their customer relationship management, supply chain management, and enterprise systems work closely with each other, and link to systems of customers and suppliers. SAP Business Suite, Oracle e-Business Suite, and Microsoft Dynamics suite (aimed at mid-sized companies) are examples, and they now utilize Web services and service-oriented architecture (SOA) (see Chapter 5).

SAP's next-generation enterprise applications incorporate SOA standards and are able to link SAP's own applications and Web services developed by independent software vendors. Oracle also has included SOA and business process management capabilities in its Fusion middleware products. Businesses can use these tools to create platforms for new or improved business processes that integrate information from multiple applications.

Next-generation enterprise applications also include open source and on-demand solutions, as well as more functionality available on mobile platforms. Open source products such as Compiere, Apache Open for Business (OFBiz), and Openbravo lack the functionality and support provided by commercial enterprise application software, but are attractive to companies such as small manufacturers because there are no software licensing charges and fees are based on usage. For small and medium-sized businesses in select countries, SAP now offers cloud-based versions of its Business One OnDemand and Business ByDesign enterprise software solutions. Software as a service (SaaS) and cloud-based versions of enterprise systems are starting to be offered by smaller vendors such as NetSuite and Plex Online. The Interactive Session on Technology describes some of the cloud-based systems for CRM. Over time, more companies will be choosing to run all or part of their enterprise applications in the cloud on an as-needed basis.

Social CRM and Business Intelligence

CRM software vendors are enhancing their products to take advantage of social networking technologies. These social enhancements help firms identify new ideas more rapidly, improve team productivity, and deepen interactions with customers. For example, Salesforce IdeaExchange enables subscribers to harness the "wisdom of crowds" by allowing their customers to submit and discuss new ideas. Dell Computer deployed this technology to encourage its customers to suggest and vote on new concepts and feature changes in Dell products. Chapter 2 described Salesforce Chatter, which enables users to create Facebook-like profiles and receive real-time news feeds about co-workers, projects, and customers. Users can also form groups and post messages on each other's profiles to collaborate on projects.

Employees who interact with customers via social networking sites such as Facebook and Twitter are often able to provide customer service functions much faster and at lower cost than by using telephone conversations or e-mail. Customers who are active social media users increasingly want—and expect—businesses to respond to their questions and complaints through this channel.

Social CRM tools enable a business to connect customer conversations and relationships from social networking sites to CRM processes. The leading CRM vendors now offer such tools to link data from social networks into their CRM software. Salesforce.com and Oracle CRM products are incorporating technology to monitor, track, and analyze social media activity in Facebook, LinkedIn, Twitter, YouTube, and other sites.

Salesforce recently acquired social media monitoring company Radian6, which helps companies such as Dell, GE, Kodak, and UPS monitor, analyze, and engage in hundreds of millions of social media conversations. Salesforce has added these capabilities to its software line. Oracle has enhanced its CRM products with Buzzient, which provides tools for integrating social media with enterprise applications. The Buzzient platform automatically collects information from a huge number of online sources in real time and analyzes the content based on users' specifications. Buzzient supplies this information to CRM systems to help companies uncover sales leads and identify customer support issues.

Business Intelligence in Enterprise Applications Enterprise application vendors have added business intelligence features to help managers obtain more meaningful information from the massive amounts of data generated by these systems. Included are tools for flexible reporting, ad hoc analysis, interactive dashboards, what-if scenario analysis, and data visualization (see the Chapter 12 Interactive Session on Management). Rather than requiring users to leave an application and launch separate reporting and analytics tools, the vendors are starting to embed analytics within the context of the application itself. They are also offering complementary stand-alone analytics products, such as SAP Business Objects and Oracle Business Intelligence Enterprise Edition.

INTERACTIVE SESSION: TECHNOLOGY

CUSTOMER RELATIONSHIP MANAGEMENT HEADS TO THE CLOUD

Salesforce.com is the most successful enterprise-scale software as a service (SaaS) and the undisputed global leader in cloud-based customer relationship management (CRM) systems. Users can access Salesforce applications anywhere through an Internet-enabled mobile device or a connected computer. Subscriptions start as low as $15 per user per month for the pared-down Group version for small sales and marketing teams, with monthly subscriptions for large enterprises ranging from $65–$250 per user.

Salesforce has over 100,000 customers. Small businesses find the on-demand model especially appealing because there are no large up-front hardware and software investments or lengthy implementations on corporate computer systems. Fireclay Tile, a 37-employee environmentally friendly sustainable tile manufacturer, adopted Salesforce and realized multiple benefits. Salesforce's e-mail and Web-to-lead capabilities helped the company quadruple new sales leads. (Web-to-lead automatically adds leads collected from the Web to the company's master database). A task feature automatically generates specific tasks based on the type of lead (architect, contractor, dealer, or homeowner) and the stage in the sales process. The system automates customer service functions including order confirmations, follow-up customer satisfaction surveys, and shipping notifications

Salesforce's social tools enable Fireclay to compete successfully against large flooring manufacturers and other custom tile producers by providing superior customer service. The company uses Salesforce.com to maintain customer profiles, so its sales, service, and production teams have complete customer views as soon as leads come in from the Web. Fireclay's internal social network based on Salesforce Chatter helps employees track orders and work closely together to meet customer needs. Customer satisfaction has increased 90 percent.

But Salesforce.com also appeals to large companies. Dr. Pepper Snapple Group adopted Salesforce CRM to replace an outmoded Excel application that required extensive manual data input to compile reports on more than 50 beverage brands and to track sales performance against objectives in real time. The system now tracks field activities for more than 10,000 accounts, with automated reports and dashboards monitoring key performance indicators, sales calls, and sales volume. The Wall Street Journal, Pitney Bowes, Kimberly-Clark, and Starbucks are among Salesforce's other large corporate CRM users.

Not to be outdone, established on-premise enterprise software companies such as Oracle have moved into cloud software services. Pricing starts at $70 per month per user. Oracle's CRM on Demand system has many capabilities, including embedded tools for forecasting and analytics and interactive dashboards. Subscribers are able to use these tools to answer questions such as "How efficient is your sales effort?" or "How much are your customers spending?"

GRT Hotels & Resorts, a leading hotel group in South India with 10 hotels, used Oracle CRM on Demand to create a centralized CRM system for all of its properties. The system makes it possible for all the hotels in the group to share customer data, such as room and rate preferences, and to create unified marketing programs that eliminate unnecessary price competition between the company's hotels. GRT believes that by making customer behavior data available for forecasting sales and by creating more targeted marketing campaigns, the CRM system has increased productivity about 25 percent. Managers are able to monitor the number of customer calls that employees answer each month regarding bookings and general hotel information to identify underperformers. GRT management believes that using a hosted CRM service with a monthly fee costs 65 percent less than if it had purchased and maintained its own CRM software. Moreover, Oracle's centralized, secure Web-based CRM application ensures that confidential data, such as promotion plans, cannot be removed by GRT employees when they leave the organization.

While traditional enterprise software vendors like Oracle are using their market-leading position to penetrate the cloud-based application market, newcomers such as SugarCRM have found success, even among larger companies. Thomas Cook France, a subsidiary of the worldwide Thomas Cook Group Travel plc, is an example. Thomas Cook France has 1,700 employees and is the second largest travel company in France, providing leisure travel programs for groups of 15 travelers. The company is able to distinguish itself among competitors and Internet travel services by providing an outstanding customer experience. Thomas Cook France had been using pen and paper to track most of its calls and other customer interactions, so its customer data were fragmented and redundant, and could not be used by management to analyze agent productivity and revenue opportunities.

SugarCRM monthly subscriptions range from $30–$100 per user. Thomas Cook France found SugarCRM to be a user-friendly yet scalable system that could be customized, deployed quickly, and managed without a large internal information systems staff. With the help of Synolia consultants, Thomas Cook had its SugarCRM system up and running within 15 days. Cook's agents are able to manage leads with integration and importation into their system. The system allows for team and role-based access and the ability to attach documents to contacts. In addition, Thomas Cook France is using the CRM software for high-level outbound e-mail marketing efforts, FAQ modules, and dashboards that drive immediate business activities and also analyze high-level business issues.

Not all companies experience gains of that magnitude, and cloud computing does have drawbacks. Many companies are concerned about maintaining control of their data and security. Although cloud computing companies are prepared to handle these issues, availability assurances and service level agreements are not always available. Companies that manage their CRM apps with a cloud infrastructure have no guarantees that their data will be available at all times, or even that the provider will still exist in the future, although CRM vendors have taken great pains to address these issues.

Sources: "Salesforce.com Inc. 10-K Report," March 9, 2012; Ziff Davis," SMB On Demand CRM Comparison Guide, January 2012; "Fireclay Heats Up Its Small Business as a Social Enterprise," www.salesforce.com, accessed July 17, 2012; "GRT Hotels & Resorts Increases Productivity by 25%, Improves Customer Service and Resource Allocation with Centralized CRM System," www.oracle.com, May 1, 2012; www.sugarcrm.com, accessed July 17, 2012; and "Thomas Cook Begins a Successful CRM Voyage with SugarCRM and Synolia," SugarCRM, 2010.

CASE STUDY QUESTIONS

1. What types of companies are most likely to adopt cloud-based CRM software services? Why? What companies might not be well-suited for this type of software?

2. What are the advantages and disadvantages of using cloud-based enterprise applications?

3. What management, organization, and technology issues should be addressed in deciding whether to use a conventional CRM system versus a cloud-based version?

The major enterprise application vendors also offer portions of their products that work on mobile handhelds. You can find out more about this topic in our Chapter 7 Learning Track on Wireless Applications for Customer Relationship Management, Supply Chain Management, and Healthcare.

LEARNING TRACK MODULES

The following Learning Tracks provide content relevant to topics covered in this chapter.

1. SAP Business Process Map

2. Business Processes in Supply Chain Management and Supply Chain Metrics

3. Best-Practice Business Processes in CRM Software

Review Summary

1. **How do enterprise systems help businesses achieve operational excellence?**

   Enterprise software is based on a suite of integrated software modules and a common central database. The database collects data from and feeds the data into numerous applications that can support nearly all of an organization's internal business activities. When new information is entered by one process, the information is made available immediately to other business processes.

   Enterprise systems support organizational centralization by enforcing uniform data standards and business processes throughout the company and a single unified technology platform. The firmwide data generated by enterprise systems helps managers evaluate organizational performance.

2. **How do supply chain management systems coordinate planning, production, and logistics with suppliers?**

   Supply chain management (SCM) systems automate the flow of information among members of the supply chain so they can use it to make better decisions about when and how much to purchase, produce, or ship. More accurate information from supply chain management systems reduces uncertainty and the impact of the bullwhip effect.

   Supply chain management software includes software for supply chain planning and for supply chain execution. Internet technology facilitates the management of global supply chains by providing the connectivity for organizations in different countries to share supply chain information. Improved communication among supply chain members also facilitates efficient customer response and movement toward a demand-driven model.

3. **How do customer relationship management systems help firms achieve customer intimacy?**

   Customer relationship management (CRM) systems integrate and automate customer-facing processes in sales, marketing, and customer service, providing an enterprise-wide view of customers. Companies can use this customer knowledge when they interact with customers to provide them with better service or to sell new products and services. These systems also identify profitable or nonprofitable customers or opportunities to reduce the churn rate.

   The major customer relationship management software packages provide capabilities for both operational CRM and analytical CRM. They often include modules for managing relationships with selling partners (partner relationship management) and for employee relationship management.

4. **What are the challenges posed by enterprise applications?**

   Enterprise applications are difficult to implement. They require extensive organizational change, large new software investments, and careful assessment of how these systems will enhance organizational performance. Enterprise applications cannot provide value if they are implemented atop flawed processes or if firms do not know how to use these systems to measure performance improvements. Employees require training to prepare for new procedures and roles. Attention to data management is essential.

5. **How are enterprise applications taking advantage of new technologies?**

   Enterprise applications are now more flexible, Web-enabled, and capable of integration with other systems, using Web services and service-oriented architecture (SOA). They also have open source and on-demand versions and are able to run in cloud infrastructures or on mobile platforms. CRM software has added social networking capabilities to enhance internal collaboration, deepen interactions with customers, and utilize data from social networking sites. Open source, mobile, and cloud versions of some of these products are becoming available.

Key Terms

Analytical CRM, 386
Bullwhip effect, 374
Churn rate, 387
Cross-selling, 384
Customer lifetime value (CLTV), 386
Demand planning, 376
Employee relationship management (ERM), 382
Enterprise software, 370
Just-in-time strategy, 374

Operational CRM, 386
Partner relationship management (PRM), 382
Pull-based model, 379
Push-based model, 379
Social CRM, 389
Supply chain, 372
Supply chain execution systems, 376
Supply chain planning systems, 376
Touch point, 381

Review Questions

1. How do enterprise systems help businesses achieve operational excellence?
   - Define an enterprise system and explain how enterprise software works.
   - Describe how enterprise systems provide value for a business.
2. How do supply chain management systems coordinate planning, production, and logistics with suppliers?
   - Define a supply chain and identify each of its components.
   - Explain how supply chain management systems help reduce the bullwhip effect and how they provide value for a business.
   - Define and compare supply chain planning systems and supply chain execution systems.
   - Describe the challenges of global supply chains and how Internet technology can help companies manage them better.
   - Distinguish between a push-based and a pull-based model of supply chain management and explain how contemporary supply chain management systems facilitate a pull-based model.
3. How do customer relationship management systems help firms achieve customer intimacy?

   - Define customer relationship management and explain why customer relationships are so important today.
   - Describe how partner relationship management (PRM) and employee relationship management (ERM) are related to customer relationship management (CRM).
   - Describe the tools and capabilities of customer relationship management software for sales, marketing, and customer service.
   - Distinguish between operational and analytical CRM.
4. What are the challenges posed by enterprise applications?
   - List and describe the challenges posed by enterprise applications.
   - Explain how these challenges can be addressed.
5. How are enterprise applications taking advantage of new technologies?
   - How are enterprise applications taking advantage of SOA, Web services, open source software, and wireless technology?
   - Define social CRM and explain how customer relationship management systems are using social networking.

Discussion Questions

1. Supply chain management is less about managing the physical movement of goods and more about managing information. Discuss the implications of this statement.
2. If a company wants to implement an enterprise application, it had better do its homework. Discuss the implications of this statement.

3. Which enterprise application should a business install first: ERP, SCM, or CRM? Explain your answer.

Hands-On MIS Projects

The projects in this section give you hands-on experience analyzing business process integration, suggesting supply chain management and customer relationship management applications, using database software to manage customer service requests, and evaluating supply chain management business services.

Management Decision Problems

1. Toronto-based Mercedes-Benz Canada, with a network of 55 dealers, did not know enough about its customers. Dealers provided customer data to the company on an ad hoc basis. Mercedes did not force dealers to report this information. There was no real incentive for dealers to share information with the company. How could CRM and PRM systems help solve this problem?

2. Office Depot sells a wide range of office supply products and services in the United States and internationally. The company tries to offer a wider range of office supplies at lower cost than other retailers by using just-in-time replenishment and tight inventory control systems. It uses information from a demand forecasting system and point-of-sale data to replenish its inventory in its 1,600 retail stores. Explain how these systems help Office Depot minimize costs and any other benefits they provide. Identify and describe other supply chain management applications that would be especially helpful to Office Depot.

Improving Decision Making: Using Database Software to Manage Customer Service Requests

Software skills: Database design; querying and reporting
Business skills: Customer service analysis

In this exercise, you'll use database software to develop an application that tracks customer service requests and analyzes customer data to identify customers meriting priority treatment.

Prime Service is a large service company that provides maintenance and repair services for close to 1,200 commercial businesses in New York, New Jersey, and Connecticut. Its customers include businesses of all sizes. Customers with service needs call into its customer service department with requests for repairing heating ducts, broken windows, leaky roofs, broken water pipes, and other problems. The company assigns each request a number and writes down the service request number, identification number of the customer account, the date of the request, the type of equipment requiring repair, and a brief description of the problem. The service requests are handled on a first-come-first-served basis. After the service work has been completed, Prime calculates the cost of the work, enters the price on the service request form, and bills the client. This arrangement treats the most important and profitable clients—those with accounts of more than $70,000—no differently from its clients with small accounts. Managment would like to find a way to provide its best customers with better service. Management would also like to know which types of service problems occur most frequently so that it can make sure it has adequate resources to address them.

Prime Service has a small database with client account information, which can be found in MyMISLab. Use database software to design a solution that would enable Prime's customer service representatives to identify the most important customers so that they could receive priority service. Your solution will require more than one table. Populate your database with at least 10 service requests. Create several reports that would be of interest to management, such as a list of the highest—and lowest— priority accounts and a report showing the most frequently occurring service problems. Create a report listing service calls that customer service representatives should respond to first on a specific date.

Achieving Operational Excellence: Evaluating Supply Chain Management Services

Software skills: Web browser and presentation software
Business skills: Evaluating supply chain management services

In addition to carrying goods from one place to another, some trucking companies provide supply chain management services and help their customers manage their information. In this project, you'll use the Web to research and evaluate two of these business services. Investigate the Web sites of two companies, UPS Logistics and Schneider Logistics, to see how these companies' services can be used for supply chain management. Then respond to the following questions:

- What supply chain processes can each of these companies support for their clients?
- How can customers use the Web sites of each company to help them with supply chain management?
- Compare the supply chain management services provided by these companies. Which company would you select to help your firm manage its supply chain? Why?

Video Cases

Video Cases and Instructional Videos illustrating some of the concepts in this chapter are available. Contact your instructor to access these videos.

Collaboration and Teamwork Project

In MyMISLab, you will find a Collaboration and Teamwork Project dealing with the concepts in this chapter. You will be able to use Google Sites, Google Docs, and other open source collaboration tools to complete the assignment.

Summit Electric Lights Up with a New ERP System
CASE STUDY

Summit Electric Supply is one of the top wholesale distributors of industrial electrical equipment and supplies in the United States, with 500 employees and nearly $358 million in sales in 2011. Summit operates in four states and has a global export division based in Houston, a marine division based in New Orleans, and a sales office in Dubai.

Summit distributes products that include motor controls, wire and cable, cords, lighting, conduit and fittings, wiring devices, support systems and fasteners, outlet boxes and enclosures, and transformers and power protection equipment. The company obtains finished goods from manufacturers and then sells them to electrical contractors working on projects ranging from small construction jobs to sophisticated industrial projects. As a distributor, Summit Electric Supply is a "middle man" on the supply chain, and must be able to rapidly handle a high volume of transactions and swift inventory turnover.

Since its founding in 1977 in Albuquerque, New Mexico, Summit has grown very quickly. Unfortunately, its homegrown legacy information systems built in the 1980s could not keep up with the business. One legacy system was for sales entries and purchase orders and another was for back-end reporting. Integration between the two systems was done manually in batches. The systems could only handle a fixed number of locations and limited the range of numbers that could be used on documents. This meant that Summit's information systems department had to use the same range of document numbers over again every few months. Once the company found it could no longer process its nightly inventory and financial updates in the amount of time that was available, the systems had reached their breaking point. A new solution was in order.

Summit started looking for a new enterprise resource planning (ERP) system. This would prove to be challenging, because the company's legacy systems were so old that the business had built many of its processes around them. A new system would require changes to business processes and the way people worked.

Summit also found that most of the available ERP software on the market had been designed for manufacturing or retailing businesses, and did not address some of the unique processes and priorities of the distribution industry. Summit needed a system that could handle a very large number of SKUs (stock-keeping units, which are numbers or codes for identifying each unique product or item for sale) and transactions, very short lead times for order processing, inventory distributed in various models, products sold in one quantity that could be sold in another, and no-touch inventory. Summit handles some products that are shipped directly from the manufacturer to the customer's job site.

Scalability and inventory visibility were Summit's top requirements. The company needed a system that would handle orders and inventory as it continued its rapid pace of growth. In the distribution business, the lead times for fulfilling an order can be only minutes: a Summit customer might call to place an order while driving to pick up the order, so the company has to know immediately what product is available at what location.

After extensively reviewing ERP vendors, Summit selected ERP software from SAP because of its functionality in sales and distribution, materials management, and financials, and its knowledge of the distribution business. Summit visited other electrical distributors using SAP, including some of its competitors, to make sure the software would work in its line of business. Summit was able to go live with its new ERP system across 19 locations in January 2007.

Nevertheless, Summit still had to customize its SAP software to meet its unique business requirements. Most SAP delivery and material scheduling functions were designed for overnight processing, because many industries have longer lead times for order fulfillment. Waiting for overnight inventory updates would significantly delay Summit's sales. Summit found it could solve this problem by running smaller, more frequent updates for just the material received during the day, rather than running big inventory updates less often. This provided more timely and accurate snapshots of what was actually available in inventory so that orders could be rapidly processed.

Wire and cable are one of Summit's most popular product categories. Summit buys these products by the reel in lengths up to 5,000 feet and then cuts them into various lengths to sell to customers. This makes it difficult to determine how much of this type of inventory has been sold and when it is time to replenish. To address this issue, Summit used a batch management solution in SAP's ERP materials management software that treats a wire reel as a batch rather than as a single product. Every time a customer buys a length of wire, the length can be entered into the system to track how much of the batch was sold. Summit is able to use this capability to find which other customers bought wire from the same reel and trace the wire back to the manufacturer.

To accommodate large customers with long-term job sites, Summit sets up temporary warehouses on-site to supply these customers with its electrical products. Summit still owns the inventory, but it's dedicated to these customers and can't be treated as standard inventory in the ERP system. SAP's ERP software didn't support that way of doing business. Summit used some of the standard functionality in the SAP software to change how it allocated materials into temporary storage locations by creating a parent-child warehouse relationship. If, for instance, Summit's Houston office has several temporary on-site warehouses, the warehouses are managed as subparts of its main warehouse. That prevents someone from selling the consigned inventory in the warehouse.

Summit's old legacy systems used separate systems for orders and financials, so the data could not be easily combined for business intelligence reporting and analysis. To solve this problem, Summit implemented SAP's NetWeaver BW data warehouse and business intelligence solution to make better use of the data in its ERP system. These tools have helped the company evaluate the profitability of its sales channels, using what-if scenarios. For instance, Summit is now able to analyze profitability by sales person, manufacturer, customer, or branch. Business intelligence findings have encouraged Summit to focus more attention to areas such as sales order quotations and to supplier performance and delivery times. Management has much greater visibility into how the organization is operating and is able to make better decisions.

Summit's SAP software also produced a significant return on investment (ROI) from automating sales tax processing and chargebacks. In the distribution industry, chargebacks occur when a supplier sells a product at a higher wholesale price to the distributor than the price the distributor has set with a retail customer. A chargeback agreement allows the distributor to bill the manufacturer an additional contracted amount in order to make some profit on the deal.

Processing chargebacks requires a very close comparison of sales to contracts, and a distributor can have hundreds or thousands of different chargeback contracts. The distributor must not only be able to identify chargeback deals but also provide the manufacturer with sufficient documentation of the specific chargeback contract that is being invoked. Chargeback management is a large part of any wholesale distributor's profit model, and Summit was losing revenue opportunities because its chargeback process was flawed.

In the past, Summit's outdated legacy system was not able to handle the volume and complexity of the company's chargeback agreements, and reporting capabilities were limited. Processing chargebacks required a great deal of manual work. Summit employees had to pore through customer invoices for specific manufacturers to identify which chargebacks Summit could claim. They would then input the data they had found manually into a Microsoft Excel spreadsheet. Gathering and reviewing invoices sometimes took an entire month, and each month the paper copies of the invoices to give to Summit's vendors consumed an entire case of paper. By the time Summit's vendors responded to the chargeback invoices, the invoices were two or three months old. This cumbersome process inevitably missed some chargebacks for which Summit was eligible, resulting in lost revenue opportunities.

As part of its ERP solution, Summit implemented the SAP Paybacks and Chargebacks application, which was developed specifically for the distribution industry. At the end of each business day, this application automatically reviews Summit's billing activity for that day and compares it to all chargeback agreements loaded in the SAP system. (Summit's system automatically keeps track of 35 vendors with whom it has more than 6,600 chargeback agreements.) Where there is a match, a chargeback can be claimed, and the application creates a separate chargeback document outside of the customer invoice. Depending on the type of vendor, the application consolidates identified chargebacks by vendor daily or monthly, and automatically submits the information to the vendor along with the chargeback document. The vendor can then approve the chargeback or make changes, which are reconciled against individual chargeback documents.

The new system processes chargebacks much more quickly and also makes it possible for Summit to review them more frequently. Where vendors are exchanging data with Summit electronically, Summit is able to make a chargeback claim and obtain vendor approval the same day. By fully automating the chargeback process, the company has increased its chargeback claims by 118 percent over its legacy systems, thereby boosting chargeback revenue as a percentage of sales. Summit is now able to see which vendors, customers, and products are producing the most chargeback revenue.

A key lesson from Summit's ERP implementation was not to force the new system to look like the legacy system. Not only is such customization expensive to set up and maintain, it can perpetuate outdated ways of doing business. According to Summit's CIO David Wascom, "We've done a lot to maintain flexibility (for our users), but still run within a standard SAP business flow."

Sources: "Summit Electric Supply Energizes Its ERP 6.0 Upgrade with Panaya," www.panayainc.com, accessed July 14, 2012; www.summit.com, accessed July 14, 2012; David Hannon, "Bringing More Revenue to the Table," SAP InsiderPROFILES, April–June 2011 and "Finding the Right ERP Fit," SAP InsiderPROFILES,

January–March 2011; "Summit Electric Supply Drives Business Transformation Through SAP and ASUG," SAPInsider (October–December 2010), and Neetin Datar, "Summit Electric Improves Chargebacks," SAP.info, June 18, 2009.

CASE STUDY QUESTIONS

1. Which business processes are the most important at Summit Electric Supply? Why?

2. What problems did Summit have with its old systems? What was the business impact of those problems?

3. How did Summit's ERP system improve operational efficiency and decision making? Give several examples.

4. Describe two ways in which Summit's customers benefit from the new ERP system.

5. Diagram Summit's old and new process for handling chargebacks.

Chapter 10

E-commerce: Digital Markets, Digital Goods

LEARNING OBJECTIVES

After reading this chapter, you will be able to answer the following questions:

1. What are the unique features of e-commerce, digital markets, and digital goods?

2. What are the principal e-commerce business and revenue models?

3. How has e-commerce transformed marketing?

4. How has e-commerce affected business-to-business transactions?

5. What is the role of m-commerce in business, and what are the most important m-commerce applications?

6. What issues must be addressed when building an e-commerce presence?

Interactive Sessions:

Location-Based Marketing and Advertising

Social Commerce Creates New Customer Relationships

CHAPTER OUTLINE

GROUPON'S BUSINESS MODEL: SOCIAL AND LOCAL

Groupon is a business that offers subscribers daily deals from local merchants. The catch: a group of people (usually at least 25) has to purchase the discounted coupon (a "Groupon"). If you really want to go to that Italian restaurant in your area with a 50 percent discount coupon, you will need to message your friends to pay for the coupon as well. As soon as the minimum number of coupons is sold, the offer is open to everyone.

Here's how it works: Most Groupon deals give the customer 50 percent off the retail price of a product or service offered by a local merchant. For example, a $50 hair styling is offered at $25. The Groupon offer is e-mailed to thousands of potential customers within driving distance of the retailer. If enough people use their PCs or smartphones to sign up and buy the Groupon, the deal is on, and the customer receives a Groupon by e-mail. Groupon takes a 50 percent cut of the revenue ($12.50), leaving the merchant with $12.50. In other words, the merchant takes a haircut of 75 percent! Instead of generating $50 in revenue for hair styling, the merchant receives only $12.50.

Who wins here? The customer gets a hairstyling for half price. Groupon gets a hefty percentage of the Groupon's face value. The merchant receives many (sometimes too many) customers. Although merchants may lose money on these single offers, they are hoping to generate repeat purchases, loyal customers, and a larger customer base. Moreover, the deals are short term, often good for only a day. The hope: lose money on a single day, make money on all the other days when regular prices are in effect. It's a customer acquisition cost.

Founded in 2008 by Andrew Mason, Groupon rocketed to prominence in less than three years, going public in June 2011. By that time, Groupon had more than 83 million customers, operated in 43 countries, and had sold over 70 million Groupons. Nevertheless, Groupon, like many social network sites, has been struggling to show a profit. In 2011, it lost $254 million on $1.6 billion in revenue. Its biggest expense is customer acquisition. Groupon clearly believes that new customers are worth it: Groupon spent $768 million in marketing in 2011.

The question is whether Groupon's business model can work in the long run. Critics point out that Groupon's revenue per customer has been falling, the conversion rate of customers into subscribers is slowing down, the tens of millions of e-mails Groupon uses to inform users of deals are poorly targeted, there are increasingly fewer Groupons sold per customer, and the revenue per Groupon is falling.

The solution, according to the company, is scale: get big really quick, and develop the brand so that competitors will never be able to find an audience. With enough customers and fast enough growth, Groupon may still turn out to be profitable. Groupon embarked on an acquisition spree in the first part of 2012, purchasing companies such as Uptake, Hyperpublic, Adku, and FeeFighters, which it believes will help its position in the small and medium-sized business market.

© Web Pix / Alamy

No one knows if this business strategy will work. Many merchants report that the Groupon deals are not creating a larger group of repeat customers. Instead, only the most price-sensitive customers show up at the door, and then never return when prices go back to normal levels. Competitors are springing up everywhere around the globe, including Google Offers and AmazonLocal.

Groupon may overcome some of the hurdles it faces by virtue of its brand and scale. But investors will want a return, and Groupon's biggest challenge will be showing a profit of any kind in the next few years.

Sources: Alistair Bart, "Groupon's New Operations Czar Grasps Shaky Helm," Reuters, August 22, 2012; Shayndi Rice and Shira Ovide, "Groupon Investors Give Up," *The Wall Street Journal*, August 20, 2012; Stephanie Clifford and Claire Cain Miller, "Ready to Ditch the Deal," *The New York Times*, August 17, 2012; Chunka Moi, "Google Offers a Two-Pronged Attack on Groupon's Business Model," *Forbes*, June 29, 2011; Jenna Wortham, "Loopt Flips Daily Deal Model Upside Down With U-Deal," *The New York Times*, June 23, 2011; Don Dodge, "How Does Groupon Work? Is Its Business Model Sustainable?" Dondodge.wordpad.com, June 11, 2011; Michel de la Merced, "Is Groupon's Business Model Sustainable?" *The New York Times*, June 8, 2011; and Utpal M. Dholakia, "How Effective are Groupon Promotions for Businesses?" Rice University, March 12, 2011.

Groupon combines two of the major new trends in e-commerce: localization and social networks. Selling goods and services on the Internet is increasingly based on social networking—friends recommending friends, as is the case with Groupon, and companies targeting individuals and their friends who are members of social networking communities such as Facebook and Twitter. E-commece is also becoming increasingly localized, as companies armed with detailed knowledge of customer locations target special offers of location-based goods and services. There are mobile apps for Groupon as well as for many other companies that are increasingly pitching and selling over mobile platforms, and e-commerce is becoming more mobile as well.

The chapter-opening diagram calls attention to important points raised by this case and this chapter. The business challenge facing Groupon is how to create a profitable business that can take advantage of Internet technology and social networking tools in the face of powerful competitors. Groupon's management decided to base its business model on localization and social technology. The business earns revenue by asking people to recruit their friends and acquaintances to sign up for discount coupons to create a "critical mass" of potential customers for a local product or service. Participating merchants sign up with the expectation of attracting large numbers of new customers. But Groupon has serious competition, participating merchants do not always reap benefits, and it is unclear whether the business model is solid and profitable.

Here are some questions to think about: How does Groupon take advantage of social networking and location technology? Do you think this business model is viable? Why or why not?

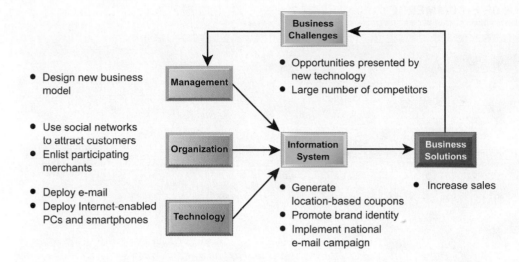

10.1   E-COMMERCE AND THE INTERNET

Bought an iTunes track lately, streamed a Netflix movie to your home TV, purchased a book at Amazon, or a diamond at Blue Nile? If so you've engaged in e-commerce. In 2012, an estimated 184 million Americans went shopping online, and 150 million purchased something online as did millions of others worldwide. And although most purchases still take place through traditional channels, e-commerce continues to grow rapidly and to transform the way many companies do business. In 2012, e-commerce consumer sales of goods, services, and content will reach $363 billion, about 9 percent of all retail sales, and it is growing at 15 percent annually (compared to 3.5 percent for traditional retailers) (eMarketer, 2012a). In just the past two years, e-commerce has expanded from the desktop and home computer to mobile devices, from an isolated activity to a new social commerce, and from a Fortune 1000 commerce with a national audience to local merchants and consumers whose location is known to mobile devices. The key words for understanding this new e-commerce in 2013 are "social, mobile, local."

E-COMMERCE TODAY

E-commerce refers to the use of the Internet and the Web to transact business. More formally, e-commerce is about digitally enabled commercial transactions between and among organizations and individuals. For the most part, this means transactions that occur over the Internet and the Web. Commercial transactions involve the exchange of value (e.g., money) across organizational or individual boundaries in return for products and services.

E-commerce began in 1995 when one of the first Internet portals, Netscape. com, accepted the first ads from major corporations and popularized the idea that the Web could be used as a new medium for advertising and sales. No one envisioned at the time what would turn out to be an exponential growth curve for e-commerce retail sales, which doubled and tripled in the early years. E-commerce grew at double-digit rates until the recession of 2008–2009 when growth slowed to

FIGURE 10.1 THE GROWTH OF E-COMMERCE

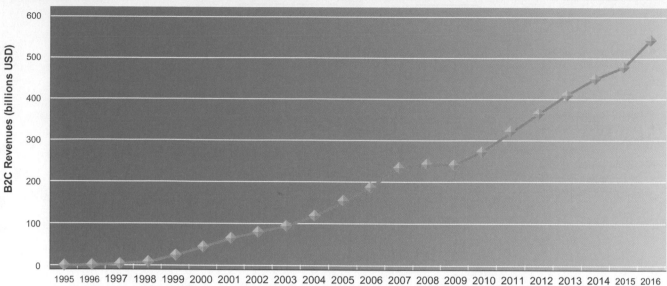

Retail e-commerce revenues grew 15–25 percent per year until the recession of 2008–2009, when they slowed measurably. In 2012, e-commerce revenues are growing again at an estimated 15 percent annually.

a crawl. In 2009, e-commerce revenues were flat (Figure 10.1), not bad considering that traditional retail sales were shrinking by 5 percent annually. In fact, e-commerce during the recession was the only stable segment in retail. Some online retailers forged ahead at a record pace: Amazon's 2009 revenues were up 25 percent over 2008 sales. Despite the continuing slow growth in 2012, the number of online buyers increased by 5 percent to 150 million, and the number of online retail transactions was up 7 percent. Amazon's sales grew to $48 billion in 2011, up an incredible 41 percent from 2010!

Mirroring the history of many technological innovations, such as the telephone, radio, and television, the very rapid growth in e-commerce in the early years created a market bubble in e-commerce stocks. Like all bubbles, the "dot-com" bubble burst (in March 2001). A large number of e-commerce companies failed during this process. Yet for many others, such as Amazon, eBay, Expedia, and Google, the results have been more positive: soaring revenues, fine-tuned business models that produce profits, and rising stock prices. By 2006, e-commerce revenues returned to solid growth, and have continued to be the fastest growing form of retail trade in the United States, Europe, and Asia.

- Online consumer sales grew to an estimated $362 billion in 2012, an increase of more than 15 percent over 2010 (including travel services and digital downloads), with 150 million people purchasing online and an additional 34 million shopping and gathering information but not purchasing (eMarketer, 2012a).

- The number of individuals of all ages online in the United States expanded to 239 million in 2012, up from 147 million in 2004. In the world, over 2.3 billion people are now connected to the Internet. Growth in the overall Internet population has spurred growth in e-commerce (eMarketer, 2012b).

- Approximately 82.5 million households have broadband access to the Internet in 2012, representing about 69 percent of all households (96 percent of all Internet households have broadband).

- About 122 million Americans now access the Internet using a smartphone such as an iPhone, Droid, or BlackBerry. Mobile e-commerce has begun a rapid growth based on apps, ring tones, downloaded entertainment, and location-based services. Mobile commerce will add up to about $11.7 billion in 2012 (roughly double 2010's revenue). Amazon sold an estimated $1.5 billion in retail goods to mobile users in 2011. In a few years, mobile phones will be the most common Internet access device. Currently half of all mobile phone users access the Internet using their phones.

- On an average day, an estimated 158 million adult U.S. Internet users go online. About 114 million send e-mail, 114 million use a search engine, and 87 million get news. Around 93 million use a social network, 46 million do online banking, 54 million watch an online video, and 33 million look for information on Wikipedia (Pew Internet & American Life Project, 2012).

- B2B e-commerce-use of the Internet for business-to-business commerce and collaboration among business partners expanded to more than $4.1 trillion.

The e-commerce revolution is still unfolding. Individuals and businesses will increasingly use the Internet to conduct commerce as more products and services come online and households switch to broadband telecommunications. More industries will be transformed by e-commerce, including travel reservations, music and entertainment, news, software, education, and finance. Table 10.1 highlights these new e-commerce developments.

WHY E-COMMERCE IS DIFFERENT

Why has e-commerce grown so rapidly? The answer lies in the unique nature of the Internet and the Web. Simply put, the Internet and e-commerce technologies are much more rich and powerful than previous technology revolutions like radio, television, and the telephone. Table 10.2 describes the unique features of the Internet and Web as a commercial medium. Let's explore each of these unique features in more detail.

Ubiquity

In traditional commerce, a marketplace is a physical place, such as a retail store, that you visit to transact business. E-commerce is ubiquitous, meaning that is it available just about everywhere, at all times. It makes it possible to shop from your desktop, at home, at work, or even from your car, using smartphones. The result is called a **marketspace**—a marketplace extended beyond traditional boundaries and removed from a temporal and geographic location.

From a consumer point of view, ubiquity reduces **transaction costs**—the costs of participating in a market. To transact business, it is no longer necessary that you spend time or money traveling to a market, and much less mental effort is required to make a purchase.

Global Reach

E-commerce technology permits commercial transactions to cross cultural and national boundaries far more conveniently and cost effectively than is true in traditional commerce. As a result, the potential market size for e-commerce merchants is roughly equal to the size of the world's online population (estimated to be more than 2 billion).

In contrast, most traditional commerce is local or regional—it involves local merchants or national merchants with local outlets. Television, radio stations

TABLE 10.1 THE GROWTH OF E-COMMERCE

BUSINESS TRANSFORMATION

- E-commerce remains the fastest growing form of commerce when compared to physical retail stores, services, and entertainment.

- Social, mobile, and local commerce have become the fastest growing forms of e-commerce.

- The first wave of e-commerce transformed the business world of books, music, and air travel. In the second wave, nine new industries are facing a similar transformation scenario: marketing and advertising, telecommunications, movies, television, jewelry and luxury goods, real estate, online travel, bill payments, and software.

- The breadth of e-commerce offerings grows, especially in the services economy of social networking, travel, information clearinghouses, entertainment, retail apparel, appliances, and home furnishings.

- The online demographics of shoppers broaden to match that of ordinary shoppers.

- Pure e-commerce business models are refined further to achieve higher levels of profitability, whereas traditional retail brands, such as Sears, JCPenney, L.L.Bean, and Walmart, use e-commerce to retain their dominant retail positions.

- Small businesses and entrepreneurs continue to flood the e-commerce marketplace, often riding on the infrastructures created by industry giants, such as Amazon, Apple, and Google, and increasingly taking advantage of cloud-based computing resources.

- Mobile e-commerce begins to take off in the United States with location-based services and entertainment downloads including e-books, movies, and television shows.

TECHNOLOGY FOUNDATIONS

- Wireless Internet connections (Wi-Fi, WiMax, and 3G/4G smartphones) grow rapidly.

- Powerful smartphones, tablet computers, and mobile devices support music, Web surfing, and entertainment as well as voice communication. Podcasting and streaming take off as mediums for distribution of video, radio, and user-generated content.

- The Internet broadband foundation becomes stronger in households and businesses as transmission prices fall. More than 82 million households had broadband cable or DSL access to the Internet in 2012, about 69 percent of all households in the United States (eMarketer, 2012a).

- Social networking software and sites such as Facebook, MySpace, Twitter, LinkedIn, and thousands of others become a major new platform for e-commerce, marketing, and advertising. Facebook hits 1 billion users worldwide, and 160 million in the United States (comScore, 2012).

- New Internet-based models of computing, such as smartphone apps, cloud computing, software as a service (SaaS), and Web 2.0 software greatly reduce the cost of e-commerce Web sites.

NEW BUSINESS MODELS EMERGE

- More than half the Internet user population have joined an online social network, contribute to social bookmarking sites, create blogs, and share photos. Together these sites create a massive online audience as large as television that is attractive to marketers. In 2012, social networking accounts for an estimated 20 percent of online time.

- The traditional advertising industry is disrupted as online advertising grows twice as fast as TV and print advertising; Google, Yahoo, and Facebook display nearly 1 trillion ads a year.

- Newspapers and other traditional media adopt online, interactive models but are losing advertising revenues to the online players despite gaining online readers. The New York Times adopts a paywall for its online edition and succeeds in capturing 500,000 subscribers.

- Online entertainment business models offering television, movies, music, sports, and e-books surge, with cooperation among the major copyright owners in Hollywood and New York and with Internet distributors like Apple, Amazon, Google, YouTube, and Facebook.

TABLE 10.2 EIGHT UNIQUE FEATURES OF E-COMMERCE TECHNOLOGY

E-COMMERCE TECHNOLOGY DIMENSION	BUSINESS SIGNIFICANCE
Ubiquity. Internet/Web technology is available everywhere: at work, at home, and elsewhere via desktop and mobile devices. Mobile devices extend service to local areas and merchants.	The marketplace is extended beyond traditional boundaries and is removed from a temporal and geographic location. "Marketspace" anytime, is created; shopping can take place anywhere. Customer convenience is enhanced, and shopping costs are reduced.
Global reach. The technology reaches across national boundaries, around the earth.	Commerce is enabled across cultural and national boundaries seamlessly and without modification. The marketspace includes, potentially, billions of consumers and millions of businesses worldwide.
Universal Standards. There is one set of technology standards, namely Internet standards.	With one set of technical standards across the globe, disparate computer systems can easily communicate with each other.
Richness. Video, audio, and text messages are possible.	Video, audio, and text marketing messages are integrated into a single marketing message and consumer experience.
Interactivity. The technology works through interaction with the user.	Consumers are engaged in a dialog that dynamically adjusts the experience to the individual, and makes the consumer a co-participant in the process of delivering goods to the market.
Information Density. The technology reduces information costs and raises quality.	Information processing, storage, and communication costs drop dramatically, whereas currency, accuracy, and timeliness improve greatly. Information becomes plentiful, cheap, and more accurate.
Personalization/Customization. The technology allows personalized messages to be delivered to individuals as well as groups.	Personalization of marketing messages and customization of products and services are based on individual characteristics.
Social Technology. The technology supports content generation and social networking.	New Internet social and business models enable user content creation and distribution, and support social networks.

and newspapers, for instance, are primarily local and regional institutions with limited, but powerful, national networks that can attract a national audience but not easily cross national boundaries to a global audience.

Universal Standards

One strikingly unusual feature of e-commerce technologies is that the technical standards of the Internet and, therefore, the technical standards for conducting e-commerce are universal standards. They are shared by all nations around the world and enable any computer to link with any other computer regardless of the technology platform each is using. In contrast, most traditional commerce technologies differ from one nation to the next. For instance, television and radio standards differ around the world, as does cell telephone technology.

The universal technical standards of the Internet and e-commerce greatly lower **market entry costs**—the cost merchants must pay simply to bring their goods to market. At the same time, for consumers, universal standards reduce **search costs**—the effort required to find suitable products.

Richness

Information **richness** refers to the complexity and content of a message. Traditional markets, national sales forces, and small retail stores have great richness: They are able to provide personal, face-to-face service using aural and visual cues when making a sale. The richness of traditional markets makes them powerful selling or commercial environments. Prior to the development of the Web, there was a trade-off between richness and reach: The larger the audience reached, the less rich the message. The Web makes it possible to deliver rich messages with text, audio, and video simultaneously to large numbers of people.

Interactivity

Unlike any of the commercial technologies of the twentieth century, with the possible exception of the telephone, e-commerce technologies are interactive, meaning they allow for two-way communication between merchant and consumer. Television, for instance, cannot ask viewers any questions or enter into conversations with them, and it cannot request that customer information be entered into a form. In contrast, all of these activities are possible on an e-commerce Web site. Interactivity allows an online merchant to engage a consumer in ways similar to a face-to-face experience but on a massive, global scale.

Information Density

The Internet and the Web vastly increase **information density**—the total amount and quality of information available to all market participants, consumers, and merchants alike. E-commerce technologies reduce information collection, storage, processing, and communication costs while greatly increasing the currency, accuracy, and timeliness of information.

Information density in e-commerce markets make prices and costs more transparent. **Price transparency** refers to the ease with which consumers can find out the variety of prices in a market; **cost transparency** refers to the ability of consumers to discover the actual costs merchants pay for products.

There are advantages for merchants as well. Online merchants can discover much more about consumers than in the past. This allows merchants to segment the market into groups that are willing to pay different prices and permits the merchants to engage in **price discrimination**—selling the same goods, or nearly the same goods, to different targeted groups at different prices. For instance, an online merchant can discover a consumer's avid interest in expensive, exotic vacations and then pitch high-end vacation plans to that consumer at a premium price, knowing this person is willing to pay extra for such a vacation. At the same time, the online merchant can pitch the same vacation plan at a lower price to a more price-sensitive consumer. Information density also helps merchants differentiate their products in terms of cost, brand, and quality.

Personalization/Customization

E-commerce technologies permit **personalization**: Merchants can target their marketing messages to specific individuals by adjusting the message to a person's clickstream behavior, name, interests, and past purchases. The technology also permits **customization**—changing the delivered product or service based on a user's preferences or prior behavior. Given the interactive nature of e-commerce technology, much information about the consumer can be gathered in the marketplace at the moment of purchase. With the increase in information density, a great deal of information about the consumer's past purchases and behavior can be stored and used by online merchants.

The result is a level of personalization and customization unthinkable with traditional commerce technologies. For instance, you may be able to shape what you see on television by selecting a channel, but you cannot change the content of the channel you have chosen. In contrast, the *Wall Street Journal Online* allows you to select the type of news stories you want to see first and gives you the opportunity to be alerted when certain events happen.

Social Technology: User Content Generation and Social Networking

In contrast to previous technologies, the Internet and e-commerce technologies have evolved to be much more social by allowing users to create and share with their personal friends (and a larger worldwide community) content in the form of text, videos, music, or photos. Using these forms of communication, users are able to create new social networks and strengthen existing ones.

All previous mass media in modern history, including the printing press, use a broadcast model (one-to-many) where content is created in a central location by experts (professional writers, editors, directors, and producers) and audiences are concentrated in huge numbers to consume a standardized product. The new Internet and e-commerce empower users to create and distribute content on a large scale, and permit users to program their own content consumption. The Internet provides a unique many-to-many model of mass communications.

KEY CONCEPTS IN E-COMMERCE: DIGITAL MARKETS AND DIGITAL GOODS IN A GLOBAL MARKETPLACE

The location, timing, and revenue models of business are based in some part on the cost and distribution of information. The Internet has created a digital marketplace where millions of people all over the world are able to exchange massive amounts of information directly, instantly, and for free. As a result, the Internet has changed the way companies conduct business and increased their global reach.

The Internet reduces information asymmetry. An **information asymmetry** exists when one party in a transaction has more information that is important for the transaction than the other party. That information helps determine their relative bargaining power. In digital markets, consumers and suppliers can "see" the prices being charged for goods, and in that sense digital markets are said to be more "transparent" than traditional markets.

For example, before auto retailing sites appeared on the Web, there was a significant information asymmetry between auto dealers and customers. Only the auto dealers knew the manufacturers' prices, and it was difficult for consumers to shop around for the best price. Auto dealers' profit margins depended on this asymmetry of information. Today's consumers have access to a legion of Web sites providing competitive pricing information, and three-fourths of U.S. auto buyers use the Internet to shop around for the best deal. Thus, the Web has reduced the information asymmetry surrounding an auto purchase. The Internet has also helped businesses seeking to purchase from other businesses reduce information asymmetries and locate better prices and terms.

Digital markets are very flexible and efficient because they operate with reduced search and transaction costs, lower **menu costs** (merchants' costs of changing prices), greater price discrimination, and the ability to change prices dynamically based on market conditions. In **dynamic pricing**, the price of a product varies depending on the demand characteristics of the customer or the supply situation of the seller. For instance, online retailers from Amazon to Walmart change prices on many products based on time of day, demand for the product, and users' prior visits to their sites.

These new digital markets may either reduce or increase switching costs, depending on the nature of the product or service being sold, and they may cause some extra delay in gratification. Unlike a physical market, you can't immediately consume a product such as clothing purchased over the Web (although immediate consumption is possible with digital music downloads and other digital products.)

Digital markets provide many opportunities to sell directly to the consumer, bypassing intermediaries, such as distributors or retail outlets. Eliminating intermediaries in the distribution channel can significantly lower purchase transaction costs. To pay for all the steps in a traditional distribution channel, a product may have to be priced as high as 135 percent of its original cost to manufacture.

Figure 10.2 illustrates how much savings result from eliminating each of these layers in the distribution process. By selling directly to consumers or reducing the number of intermediaries, companies are able to raise profits while charging lower prices. The removal of organizations or business process layers responsible for intermediary steps in a value chain is called **disintermediation**.

Disintermediation is affecting the market for services. Airlines and hotels operating their own reservation sites online earn more per ticket because they have eliminated travel agents as intermediaries. Table 10.3 summarizes the differences between digital markets and traditional markets.

FIGURE 10.2 THE BENEFITS OF DISINTERMEDIATION TO THE CONSUMER

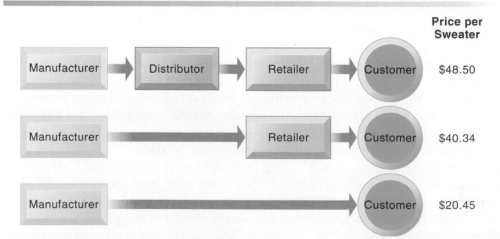

The typical distribution channel has several intermediary layers, each of which adds to the final cost of a product, such as a sweater. Removing layers lowers the final cost to the consumer.

TABLE 10.3 DIGITAL MARKETS COMPARED TO TRADITIONAL MARKETS

	DIGITAL MARKETS	TRADITIONAL MARKETS
Information asymmetry	Asymmetry reduced	Asymmetry high
Search costs	Low	High
Transaction costs	Low (sometimes virtually nothing)	High (time, travel)
Delayed gratification	High (or lower in the case of a digital good)	Lower: purchase now
Menu costs	Low	High
Dynamic pricing	Low cost, instant	High cost, delayed
Price discrimination	Low cost, instant	High cost, delayed
Market segmentation	Low cost, moderate precision	High cost, less precision
Switching costs	Higher/lower (depending on product characteristics)	High
Network effects	Strong	Weaker
Disintermediation	More possible/likely	Less possible/unlikely

Digital Goods

The Internet digital marketplace has greatly expanded sales of digital goods. **Digital goods** are goods that can be delivered over a digital network. Music tracks, video, Hollywood movies, software, newspapers, magazines, and books can all be expressed, stored, delivered, and sold as purely digital products. Today, all these products are delivered as digital streams or downloads, while their physical counterparts decline in sales.

In general, for digital goods, the marginal cost of producing another unit is about zero (it costs nothing to make a copy of a music file). However, the cost of producing the original first unit is relatively high—in fact, it is nearly the total cost of the product because there are few other costs of inventory and distribution. Costs of delivery over the Internet are very low, marketing costs often remain the same, and pricing can be highly variable. (On the Internet, the merchant can change prices as often as desired because of low menu costs.)

The impact of the Internet on the market for these kinds of digital goods is nothing short of revolutionary, and we see the results around us every day. Businesses dependent on physical products for sales—such as bookstores, music stores, book publishers, music labels, and film studios—face the possibility of declining sales and even destruction of their businesses. Newspapers and magazines subscriptions to hard copies are declining, while online readership and subscriptions are expanding.

Total record label industry revenues have fallen from $14 billion in 1999, to $5.4 billion estimated in 2012, a drop of 61 percent, due almost entirely to the decline in CD album sales, and the growth of digital music services (both legal and illegal music piracy). On the plus side, the Apple iTunes Store has sold 16 billion songs for 99 cents each since opening in 2001, providing the industry with a digital distribution model that has restored some of the revenues lost to digital music channels. Since iTunes, illegal downloading has been cut in half, and legitimate online music sales are estimated to be approximately $4 billion in 2012. As cloud streaming services expand, illegal downloading will decline further. In that sense, Apple, along with other Internet distributors, saved the record labels from extinction. In 2012, digital music sales accounted for over 50 percent of all music revenues for the first time. Yet the music labels make only about 32 cents from a single track download or from a streamed track.

Hollywood has not been similarly disrupted by digital distribution platforms, in part because it is more difficult to download high-quality, pirated copies of full-length movies. To avoid the fate of the music industry, Hollywood has struck lucrative distribution deals with Netflix, Google, Amazon, and Apple. Nevertheless, these arrangements are not enough to compensate entirely for the loss in DVD sales, which fell 50 percent from 2006 to 2012, although this is changing rapidly as the online distributors like Netflix are forced to pay billions for high-quality Hollywood content. In 2012, for the first time, consumers will view more and pay more for Web-based movie downloads, rentals, and streams than for DVDs or related physical products. As with television, the demand for feature-length Hollywood movies appears to be expanding in part because of the growth of smartphones and tablets. In addition, the surprising resurgence of music videos, led by the Web site VEVO, is attracting millions of younger viewers on smartphones and tablets. Online movies began a growth spurt in 2010 as broadband services spread throughout the country. In 2011, movie viewing doubled in a single year. In 2012, about 60 million Internet users are expected to view movies, about one-third of the adult Internet audience. Online movie viewing is growing faster than all video viewing (which includes TV shows). While this rapid growth will not continue forever, there is little doubt that the Internet is becoming a movie distribution channel that rivals cable television. Table 10.4 describes digital goods and how they differ from traditional physical goods.

10.2 E-COMMERCE: BUSINESS AND TECHNOLOGY

E-commerce has grown from a few advertisements on early Web portals in 1995 to over 9 percent of all retail sales in 2012 (an estimated $362 billion), surpassing the mail order catalog business. E-commerce is a fascinating combination of business models and new information technologies. Let's start with a basic understanding of the types of e-commerce, and then describe e-commerce

TABLE 10.4 HOW THE INTERNET CHANGES THE MARKETS FOR DIGITAL GOODS

	DIGITAL GOODS	TRADITIONAL GOODS
Marginal cost/unit	Zero	Greater than zero , high
Cost of production	High (most of the cost)	Variable
Copying cost	Approximately zero	Greater than zero, high
Distributed delivery cost	Low	High
Inventory cost	Low	High
Marketing cost	Variable	Variable
Pricing	More variable (bundling, random pricing games)	Fixed, based on unit costs

business and revenue models. We'll also cover new technologies that help companies reach over 184 million online consumers in the United States, and an estimated 2 billion more worldwide.

TYPES OF E-COMMERCE

There are many ways to classify electronic commerce transactions—one is by looking at the nature of the participants. The three major electronic commerce categories are business-to-consumer (B2C) e-commerce, business-to-business (B2B) e-commerce, and consumer-to-consumer (C2C) e-commerce.

- **Business-to-consumer (B2C)** electronic commerce involves retailing products and services to individual shoppers. BarnesandNoble.com, which sells books, software, and music to individual consumers, is an example of B2C e-commerce.
- **Business-to-business (B2B)** electronic commerce involves sales of goods and services among businesses. ChemConnect's Web site for buying and selling chemicals and plastics is an example of B2B e-commerce.
- **Consumer-to-consumer (C2C)** electronic commerce involves consumers selling directly to consumers. For example, eBay, the giant Web auction site, enables people to sell their goods to other consumers by auctioning their merchandise off to the highest bidder, or for a fixed price. Craigslist is the most widely used platform used by consumers to buy from and sell directly to others.

Another way of classifying electronic commerce transactions is in terms of the platforms used by participants in a transaction. Until recently, most e-commerce transactions took place using a personal computer connected to the Internet over wired networks. Several wireless mobile alternatives have emerged: smartphones, tablet computers like iPads, and dedicated e-readers like the Kindle using cellular networks, and smartphones and small tablet computers using Wi-Fi wireless networks. The use of handheld wireless devices for purchasing goods and services from any location is termed **mobile commerce** or **m-commerce**. Both business-to-business and business-to-consumer e-commerce transactions can take place using m-commerce technology, which we discuss in detail in Section 10.3.

E-COMMERCE BUSINESS MODELS

Changes in the economics of information described earlier have created the conditions for entirely new business models to appear, while destroying older business models. Table 10.5 describes some of the most important Internet business models that have emerged. All, in one way or another, use the Internet to add extra value to existing products and services or to provide the foundation for new products and services.

Portal

Portals are gateways to the Web, and are often defined as those sites which users set as their home page. Some definitions of a portal include search engines like Google and Bing even if few make these sites their home page. Portals such as Yahoo, Facebook, MSN, and AOL offer powerful Web search tools as well as an integrated package of content and services, such as news, e-mail, instant messaging, maps, calendars, shopping, music downloads, video streaming, and more, all in one place. Initially, portals were primarily "gateways" to

TABLE 10.5 INTERNET BUSINESS MODELS

CATEGORY	DESCRIPTION	EXAMPLES
E-tailer	Sells physical products directly to consumers or to individual businesses.	Amazon RedEnvelope.com
Transaction broker	Saves users money and time by processing online sales transactions and generating a fee each time a transaction occurs.	ETrade.com Expedia
Market creator	Provides a digital environment where buyers and sellers can meet, search for products, display products, and establish prices for those products. Can serve consumers or B2B e-commerce, generating revenue from transaction fees.	eBay Priceline.com
Content provider	Creates revenue by providing digital content, such as news, music, photos, or video, over the Web. The customer may pay to access the content, or revenue may be generated by selling advertising space.	WSJ.com GettyImages.com iTunes.com Games.com
Community provider	Provides an online meeting place where people with similar interests can communicate and find useful information.	Facebook Google+ iVillage, Twitter
Portal	Provides initial point of entry to the Web along with specialized content and other services.	Yahoo Bing Google
Service provider	Provides Web 2.0 applications such as photo sharing, video sharing, and user-generated content as services. Provides other services such as online data storage and backup.	Google Apps Photobucket.com Dropbox

the Internet. Today, however, the portal business model provides a destination site where users start their Web searching and linger to read news, find entertainment, meet other people, and be exposed to advertising. Portals generate revenue primarily by attracting very large audiences, charging advertisers for ad placement, collecting referral fees for steering customers to other sites, and charging for premium services. In 2012, portals (not including Google or Bing) generated an estimated $8.5 billion in revenues. Although there are hundreds of portal/search engine sites, the top four portals (Yahoo, Facebook, MSN, and AOL) gather more than 95 percent of the Internet portal traffic because of their superior brand recognition (eMarketer, 2012).

E-tailer

Online retail stores, often called **e-tailers**, come in all sizes, from giant Amazon with 2011 revenues of more than $48 billion, to tiny local stores that have Web sites. An e-tailer is similar to the typical bricks-and-mortar storefront, except that customers only need to connect to the Internet to check their inventory and place an order. Altogether, online retail will generate about $224 billion in revenues for 2012. The value proposition of e-tailers is to provide convenient, low-cost shopping 24/7, offering large selections and consumer choice. Some e-tailers, such as Walmart.com or Staples.com, referred to as "bricks-and-clicks," are subsidiaries or divisions of existing physical stores and carry the same products. Others, however, operate only in the virtual world, without any ties to physical locations. Amazon, BlueNile.com, and Drugstore.com are examples of this type of e-tailer. Several other variations of e-tailers—such as online versions of direct mail catalogs, online malls, and manufacturer-direct online sales—also exist.

Content Provider

While e-commerce began as a retail product channel, it has increasingly turned into a global content channel. "Content" is defined broadly to include all forms of intellectual property. **Intellectual property** refers to all forms of human expression that can be put into a tangible medium such as text, CDs, or DVDs, or stored on any digital (or other) media, including the Web. Content providers distribute information content, such as digital video, music, photos, text, and artwork, over the Web. The value proposition of online content providers is that consumers can find a wide range of content online, conveniently, and purchase this content inexpensively, to be played, or viewed, on multiple computer devices or smartphones.

Providers do not have to be the creators of the content (although sometimes they are, like Disney.com), and are more likely to be Internet-based distributors of content produced and created by others. For example, Apple sells music tracks at its iTunes Store, but it does not create or commission new music.

The phenomenal popularity of the iTunes Store, and Apple's Internet-connected devices like the iPhone, iPod, and iPad, have enabled new forms of digital content delivery from podcasting to mobile streaming. **Podcasting** is a method of publishing audio or video broadcasts via the Internet, allowing subscribing users to download audio or video files onto their personal computers or portable music players. **Streaming** is a publishing method for music and video files that flows a continuous stream of content to a user's device without being stored locally on the device.

Estimates vary, but total download, streaming, and subscription media revenues for 2012 are estimated at $19 billion annually. They are the fastest growing segment within e-commerce, growing at an estimated 20 percent annual rate.

Transaction Broker

Sites that process transactions for consumers normally handled in person, by phone, or by mail are transaction brokers. The largest industries using this model are financial services and travel services. The online transaction broker's primary value propositions are savings of money and time, as well as providing an extraordinary inventory of financial products and travel packages, in a single location. Online stock brokers and travel booking services charge fees that are considerably less than traditional versions of these services.

Market Creator

Market creators build a digital environment in which buyers and sellers can meet, display products, search for products, and establish prices. The value proposition of online market creators is that they provide a platform where sellers can easily display their wares and where purchasers can buy directly from sellers. Online auction markets like eBay and Priceline are good examples of the market creator business model. Another example is Amazon's Merchants platform (and similar programs at eBay) where merchants are allowed to set up stores on Amazon's Web site and sell goods at fixed prices to consumers. This is reminiscent of open air markets where the market creator operates a facility (a town square) where merchants and consumers meet. Online market creators will generate about $18 billion in revenues for 2012.

Service Provider

While e-tailers sell products online, service providers offer services online. There's been an explosion in online services. Web 2.0 applications, photo sharing, and online sites for data backup and storage all use a service provider business model. Software is no longer a physical product with a CD in a box, but increasingly software as a service (SaaS) that you subscribe to online rather than purchase from a retailer, or an app that you download. Google has led the way in developing online software service applications such as Google Apps, Google Sites, Gmail, and online data storage services.

Community Provider

Community providers are sites that create a digital online environment where people with similar interests can transact (buy and sell goods); share interests, photos, videos; communicate with like-minded people; receive interest-related information; and even play out fantasies by adopting online personalities called avatars. The social networking sites Facebook, Google +, Tumblr, LinkedIn, and Twitter; online communities such as iVillage; and hundreds of other smaller, niche sites such as Doostang and Sportsvite all offer users community-building tools and services. Social networking sites have been the fastest growing Web sites in recent years, often doubling their audience size in a year. However, they are struggling to achieve profitability.

E-COMMERCE REVENUE MODELS

A firm's **revenue model** describes how the firm will earn revenue, generate profits, and produce a superior return on investment. Although there are many different e-commerce revenue models that have been developed, most companies rely on one, or some combination, of the following six revenue models: advertising, sales, subscription, free/freemium, transaction fee, and affiliate.

Advertising Revenue Model

In the **advertising revenue model**, a Web site generates revenue by attracting a large audience of visitors who can then be exposed to advertisements. The advertising model is the most widely used revenue model in e-commerce, and arguably, without advertising revenues, the Web would be a vastly different experience from what it is now. Content on the Web—everything from news to videos and opinions—is "free" to visitors because advertisers pay the production and distribution costs in return for the right to expose visitors to ads. Companies will spend an estimated $166 billion on online advertising in 2012, and an estimated $39.5 billion of that amount on online advertising (in the form of a paid message on a Web site, paid search listing, video, app, game, or other online medium, such as instant messaging). In the last five years, advertisers have increased online spending and cut outlays on traditional channels such as radio and newspapers. In 2012, online advertising will grow at 15 percent and constitute about 30 percent of all advertising in the United States. Television advertising has also expanded along with online advertising revenues.

INTERACTIVE SESSION: ORGANIZATIONS

LOCATION-BASED MARKETING AND ADVERTISING

In October 2010, the UK-based cell phone carrier O2 launched the country's first large-scale, location-based service for delivering targeted marketing to mobile devices. The concept of targeted marketing is considered to be a vital part of any business. O2 Media, the mobile marketing division of the company, already uses customer data to provide personalized marketing to companies. For example, an iPhone application ("app") for a theme park that was targeted at families with children had great success, with approximately 30 percent of those targeted eventually downloading the app. The traditional targets for marketing are age, gender, interests, and so on. Location-based marketing can go further by targeting marketing at the right individuals at the right time, when they are in the right location to make a purchase.

Here's how O2's system works. O2 customers opt into the system by providing their age, gender, and interests. When customers are near an outlet that matches their profile, they receive an SMS message for discounts or other special offers. As of O2's launch, it was limited to providing discounts to Starbucks coffee shops and outlets supplying L'Oréal hair products, but O2 Media was confident that other partners will come on board.

The service is based on a technology called "geo-fencing," which is provided to O2 by a California based company called Placecast. In 2009, Placecast conducted a trial, under the name of ShopAlerts, involving three different types of retailers— American Eagle Outfitters (clothing for young adults), North Face (outdoor equipment and apparel), and Sonic (fast-food outlet). Although there may be some overlap between potential customers at these three retailers, plenty of people will fit one category but not the other two. Targeted marketing reduces the likelihood of relevant marketing messages being lost in "junk mail"; that is, customers get SMS messages that they know are probably relevant. According to research carried out by Placecast on ShopAlerts users, most customers opened the alerts immediately, and 65 percent made a purchase as a result of receiving the SMS message (interestingly, not always a purchase mentioned in the message).

O2 had to resolve several issues with this type of marketing.

- Opt in and opt out. Customers must be able to opt out of the system at any time and must be required to opt in at the start.

- Age. The O2 scheme is not available to customers younger than age 16.
- Data sharing. The targeted marketing is based on information supplied by the customer. This data must not be shared with other customers.
- Frequency. Because the SMS is triggered by the customer moving into the geo-fenced area, there is a danger that the customer will be bombarded with messages as he or she walks up and down the street. The Placecast American trial capped messages at one per every 48 hours and three per week. The O2 scheme limits the frequency of messages to one per day.
- Devices. The O2 scheme works on any mobile phone. It is not necessary to download an app (i.e., a smartphone is not required), and it does not affect the device's battery life.

As you might expect, O2 and its partners were enthusiastic about the venture. According to Shaun Gregory, managing director of O2 Media, the market potential is huge and this is a modern and efficient way to reach a mass audience in one go. Hal Kimber, head of CRM for L'Oréal, noted that the opportunity was very exciting and L'Oréal would learn a great deal which it could implement in future initiatives.

The use of text alerts for marketing does need to consider the potential customer and their use of texting. A survey conducted in October 2010 by comScore, a marketing research company that studies online behavior, found huge differences in mobile behavior in different parts of the world. The survey included cell phone users in Japan, the United States, and Europe. The researchers found that in the European sample more than 80 percent of people sent SMS messages to one another; in the United States the figure was 66.8 percent. In Japan, however, the figure was much lower—40.1 percent. Of course the lack of enthusiasm for sending messages does not necessarily reflect an unwillingness to receive marketing texts.

It appears that in Japan the emphasis is less on the opt-in approach of Placecast and more on location- based mobile advertising, a more sophisticated way of changing the advertising that a user receives when using an application. For example, someone using an iPhone or Android app typically also sees banner advertisements. AdLocal (now part of Yahoo! Japan) has the largest share of Japan's location-based advertising market (valued at US $1 billion!), and such technology can make sure that the advertising that the user receives is based not necessarily on who they are but where they are. Advertisers create their own advertisements using a wizard and then specify the desired locations and dates to display them (for special promotions, discounts, etc.). It seems that the success of this type of intelligent marketing is likely to spread to the United States and Europe.

Sources: "O2 Launches UK's First Location-Based Mobile Marketing," O2 news release, October 15, 2010; Katheryn Koegel, "Consumer Insights on Location-based Mobile Marketing," January 2010; "comScore Releases First Comparative Report on Mobile Usage in Japan, United States, and Europe," comScore press release, October 7, 2010; Farukh Shaikh, "Yahoo Japan Scoops Up Location-Based Mobile Ad Firm Cirius Technologies," eBrands, August 17, 2010 (http://news. ebrandz.com/yahoo/2010/3515-yahoo-japan-scoops-uplocation-based-mobile-ad-firm-cirius-technologies-.html, accessed October 25, 2010).

Case contributed by Andy Jones, Staffordshire University

CASE STUDY QUESTIONS

1. Two different approaches to capturing consumer interest are described in this case. How do the Placecast and AdLocal approaches differ?

2. Do you think that targeted advertising is better than a blanket approach? What is the difference for the advertiser? For the consumer?

3. The information from the comScore survey did not differentiate between age groups, only country. Do you think there are differences in behavior among different age groups that would make location-based marketing better for one group than another?

4. Think of businesses in your area that might benefit from joining the O2 scheme. What could they offer?

Web sites with the largest viewership or that attract a highly specialized, differentiated viewership and are able to retain user attention ("stickiness") are able to charge higher advertising rates. Yahoo, for instance, derives nearly all its revenue from display ads (banner ads) and to a lesser extent search engine text ads. Ninety-five percent of Google's revenue derives from advertising, including selling keywords (AdWord), selling ad spaces (AdSense), and selling display ad spaces to advertisers (DoubleClick). Facebook will display one-third of the trillion display ads shown on all sites in 2012. Facebook's users spend an average of over 8 hours a week on the site, far longer than any of the other portal sites.

Sales Revenue Model

In the **sales revenue model**, companies derive revenue by selling goods, information, or services to customers. Companies such as Amazon (which sells books, music, and other products), LLBean.com, and Gap.com, all have sales revenue models. Content providers make money by charging for downloads of entire files such as music tracks (iTunes Store) or books or for downloading music and/or video streams (Hulu.com TV shows). Apple has pioneered and strengthened the acceptance of micropayments. **Micropayment systems** provide content providers with a cost-effective method for processing high volumes of very small monetary transactions (anywhere from $.25 to $5.00 per transaction). The largest micropayment system on the Web is Apple's iTunes Store, which has more than 250 million credit customers who frequently purchase individual music tracks for 99 cents. MyMISlab has a Learning Track with more detail on micropayment and other e-commerce payment systems.

Subscription Revenue Model

In the **subscription revenue model**, a Web site offering content or services charges a subscription fee for access to some or all of its offerings on an ongoing basis. Content providers often use this revenue model. For instance, the online version of *Consumer Reports* provides access to premium content, such as detailed ratings, reviews, and recommendations, only to subscribers, who have a choice of paying a $5.95 monthly subscription fee or a $26.00 annual fee. Netflix is one of the most successful subscriber sites with more that 25 million subscribers in September 2012. The Wall Street Journal has the largest online subscription newspaper with more than 1 million online subscribers. To be successful, the subscription model requires that the content be perceived as having high added value, differentiated, and not readily available elsewhere nor easily replicated. Companies successfully offering content or services online on a subscription basis include Match.com and eHarmony (dating services), Ancestry.com and Genealogy.com (genealogy research), Microsoft's Xboxlive.com (video games), and Pandora.com (music).

Free/Freemium Revenue Model

In the **free/freemium revenue model**, firms offer basic services or content for free, while charging a premium for advanced or special features. For example, Google offers free applications but charges for premium services. Pandora, the subscription radio service, offers a free service with limited play time and advertising, and a premium service with unlimited play. The Flickr photo-sharing service offers free basic services for sharing photos with friends and family, and also sells a $24.95 "premium" package that provides users unlimited storage, high-definition video storage and playback, and freedom from display advertising. The idea is to attract very large audiences with free services, and then to convert some of this audience to pay a subscription for premium services. One problem with this model is converting people from being "free loaders" into paying customers. "Free" can be a powerful model for losing money.

Transaction Fee Revenue Model

In the **transaction fee revenue model**, a company receives a fee for enabling or executing a transaction. For example, eBay provides an online auction marketplace and receives a small transaction fee from a seller if the seller is successful in selling an item. E*Trade, an online stockbroker, receives transaction fees each time it executes a stock transaction on behalf of a customer. The transaction revenue model enjoys wide acceptance in part because the true cost of using the platform is not immediately apparent to the user.

Affiliate Revenue Model

In the **affiliate revenue model**, Web sites (called "affiliate Web sites") send visitors to other Web sites in return for a referral fee or percentage of the revenue from any resulting sales. For example, MyPoints makes money by connecting companies to potential customers by offering special deals to its members. When members take advantage of an offer and make a purchase, they earn "points" they can redeem for free products and services, and MyPoints receives a referral fee. Community feedback sites such as Epinions and Yelp receive much of their revenue from steering potential customers to Web sites where they make a purchase. Amazon uses affiliates who steer business to the Amazon Web site by placing the Amazon logo on their blogs. Personal blogs often contain display ads as a part of affiliate programs. Some bloggers are paid directly by manufacturers, or receive free products, for speaking highly of products and providing links to sales channels.

SOCIAL NETWORKING AND THE WISDOM OF CROWDS

One of the fastest growing areas of e-commerce revenues are Web 2.0 online services, which we described in Chapter 7. The most popular Web 2.0 service is social networking, online meeting places where people can meet their friends and their friends' friends. Every day over 93 million Internet users in the United States visit a social networking site like Facebook, Google+, Tumblr, MySpace, LinkedIn, and hundreds of others.

Social networking sites link people through their mutual business or personal connections, enabling them to mine their friends (and their friends' friends) for sales leads, job-hunting tips, or new friends. Google+, MySpace, Facebook, and Friendster appeal to people who are primarily interested in extending their friendships, while LinkedIn focuses on job networking for professionals.

At **social shopping** sites like Pinterest, Kaboodle, ThisNext, and Stylehive, you can swap shopping ideas with friends. Facebook offers the Like button and Google the +1 button to let your friends know you admire something, and in some cases, purchase something online. Online communities are also ideal venues to employ viral marketing techniques. Online viral marketing is like traditional word-of-mouth marketing except that the word can spread across an online community at the speed of light, and go much further geographically than a small network of friends.

The Wisdom of Crowds

Creating sites where thousands, even millions, of people can interact offers business firms new ways to market and advertise, to discover who likes (or hates) their products. In a phenomenon called "the **wisdom of crowds**," some argue that large numbers of people can make better decisions about a wide range of topics or products than a single person or even a small committee of experts (Surowiecki, 2004).

Obviously this is not always the case, but it can happen in interesting ways. In marketing, the wisdom of crowds concept suggests that firms should consult with thousands of their customers first as a way of establishing a relationship with them; and second, to better understand how their products and services are used and appreciated (or rejected). Actively soliciting the comments of your customers builds trust and sends the message to your customers that you care what they are thinking, and that you need their advice.

Beyond merely soliciting advice, firms can be actively helped in solving some business problems using what is called **crowdsourcing**. For instance, in 2006, Netflix announced a contest in which it offered to pay $1 million to the person or team who comes up with a method for improving by 10 percent Netflix's prediction of what movies customers would like as measured against their actual choices. By 2009, Netflix received 44,014 entries from 5,169 teams in 186 countries. The winning team improved a key part of Netflix's business: a recommender system that recommends to its customers what new movies to order based on their personal past movie choices and the choices of millions of other customers who are like them (Howe, 2008; Resnick and Varian, 1997). In 2012, BMW launched a crowdsourcing project to enlist the aid of customers in designing an urban vehicle for 2025. Kickstarter.com is arguably one of the most famous e-commerce crowd funding sites where visitors invest in start-up companies.

Firms can also use the wisdom of crowds in the form of prediction markets. **Prediction markets** are established as peer-to-peer betting markets where participants make bets on specific outcomes of, say, quarterly sales of a new product, designs for new products, or political elections. The world's largest commercial prediction market is Betfair, founded in 2000, where you bet for or against specific outcomes on football games, horse races, and whether or not the Dow Jones will go up or down in a single day. Iowa Electronic Markets (IEM) is an academic market focused on elections. You can place bets on the outcome of local and national elections. In the United States, the largest prediction market is Intrade.com where users can buy or sell shares in predictions.

E-COMMERCE MARKETING

While e-commerce and the Internet have changed entire industries and enabled new business models, no industry has been more affected than marketing and marketing communications. The Internet provides marketers with new ways of identifying and communicating with millions of potential customers at costs far lower than traditional media, including search engine marketing, data mining, recommender systems, and targeted e-mail. The Internet enables **long tail marketing**. Before the Internet, reaching a large audience was very expensive, and marketers had to focus on attracting the largest number of consumers with popular hit products, whether music, Hollywood movies, books, or cars. In contrast, the Internet allows marketers to inexpensively find potential customers for products where demand is very low. For instance, the Internet makes it possible to sell independent music profitably to very small audiences. There's always some demand for almost any product. Put a string of such long tail sales together and you have a profitable business.

The Internet also provides new ways—often instantaneous and spontaneous—to gather information from customers, adjust product offerings, and increase customer value. Table 10.6 describes the leading marketing and advertising formats used in e-commerce.

Many e-commerce marketing firms use behavioral targeting techniques to increase the effectiveness of banner, rich media, and video ads. **Behavioral targeting** refers to tracking the clickstreams (history of clicking behavior) of individuals on thousands of Web sites for the purpose of understanding their interests and intentions, and exposing them to advertisements that are uniquely suited to their behavior. Proponents believe this more precise understanding of the customer leads to more efficient marketing (the firm pays for ads only to those shoppers who are most interested in their products) and larger sales and revenues. Unfortunately, behavioral targeting of millions of Web users also

TABLE 10.6 ONLINE MARKETING AND ADVERTISING FORMATS (BILLIONS)

MARKETING FORMAT	2012 REVENUE	DESCRIPTION
Search engine	$17.6	Text ads targeted at precisely what the customer is looking for at the moment of shopping and purchasing. Sales oriented.
Display ads	$8.7	Banner ads (pop-ups and leave-behinds) with interactive features; increasingly behaviorally targeted to individual Web activity. Brand development and sales. Includes blog display ads.
Video	$2.9	Fastest growing format, engaging and entertaining; behaviorally targeted, interactive. Branding and sales.
Classified	$2.6	Job, real estate, and services ads; interactive, rich media, and personalized to user searches. Sales and branding.
Rich media	$1.8	Animations, games, and puzzles. Interactive, targeted, and entertaining. Branding orientation.
Lead generation	$1.7	Marketing firms that gather sales and marketing leads online, and then sell them to online marketers for a variety of campaign types. Sales or branding orientation.
Sponsorships	$1.61	Online games, puzzles, contests, and coupon sites sponsored by firms to promote products. Sales orientation.
E-mail	$.22	Effective, targeted marketing tool with interactive and rich media potential. Sales oriented.

leads to the invasion of personal privacy without user consent. When consumers lose trust in their Web experience, they tend not to purchase anything.

Behavioral targeting takes place at two levels: at individual Web sites and on various advertising networks that track users across thousands of Web sites. All Web sites collect data on visitor browser activity and store it in a database. They have tools to record the site that users visited prior to coming to the Web site, where these users go when they leave that site, the type of operating system they use, browser information, and even some location data. They also record the specific pages visited on the particular site, the time spent on each page of the site, the types of pages visited, and what the visitors purchased (see Figure 10.3). Firms analyze this information about customer interests and behavior to develop precise profiles of existing and potential customers. In addition, most major Web sites have hundreds of tracking programs on their home pages, which track your clickstream behavior across the Web by following you from site to site and re-target ads to you by showing you the same ads on different sites. The leading online advertising networks are Google's DoubleClick, Yahoo's RightMedia, and AOL's Ad Network. Ad networks represent publishers who have space to sell, and advertisers who want to market online. The lubricant of this trade is information on millions of Web shoppers, which helps advertisers target their ads to precisely the groups and individuals they desire.

This information enables firms to understand how well their Web site is working, create unique personalized Web pages that display content or ads for products or services of special interest to each user, improve the customer's experience, and create additional value through a better understanding of the shopper (see Figure 10.4). By using personalization technology to modify the Web pages presented to each customer, marketers achieve some of the

FIGURE 10.3 **WEB SITE VISITOR TRACKING**

The shopper clicks on the home page. The store can tell that the shopper arrived from the Yahoo! portal at 2:30 PM (which might help determine staffing for customer service centers) and how long she lingered on the home page (which might indicate trouble navigating the site). Tracking beacons load cookies on the shopper's browser to follow her across the Web.

The shopper clicks on blouses, clicks to select a woman's white blouse, then clicks to view the same item in pink. The shopper clicks to select this item in a size 10 in pink and clicks to place it in her shopping cart. This information can help the store determine which sizes and colors are most popular. If the visitor moves to a different site, ads for pink blouses will appear from the same or different vendor.

From the shopping cart page, the shopper clicks to close the browser to leave the Web site without purchasing the blouse. This action could indicate the shopper changed her mind or that she had a problem with the Web site's checkout and payment process. Such behavior might signal that the Web site was not well designed.

E-commerce Web sites and advertising platforms like Google's DoubleClick have tools to track a shopper's every step through an online store and then across the Web as shoppers move from site to site. Close examination of customer behavior at a Web site selling women's clothing shows what the store might learn at each step and what actions it could take to increase sales.

FIGURE 10.4 **WEB SITE PERSONALIZATION**

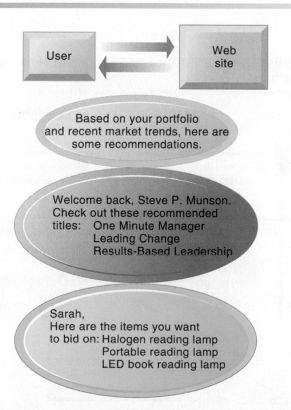

Firms can create unique personalized Web pages that display content or ads for products or services of special interest to individual users, improving the customer experience and creating additional value.

benefits of using individual salespeople at dramatically lower costs. For instance, General Motors will show a Chevrolet banner ad to women emphasizing safety and utility, while men will receive different ads emphasizing power and ruggedness.

What if you are a large national advertising company with many different clients trying to reach millions of consumers? What if you were a large global manufacturer trying to reach potential consumers for your products? With millions of Web sites, working with each one would be impractical. Advertising networks solve this problem by creating a network of several thousand of the most popular Web sites visited by millions of people, tracking the behavior of these users across the entire network, building profiles of each user, and then selling these profiles to advertisers. Popular Web sites download dozens of Web tracking cookies, bugs, and beacons, which report user online behavior to remote servers without the users' knowledge. Looking for young, single consumers, with college degrees, living in the Northeast, in the 18–34 age range who are interested purchasing a European car? Not a problem. Advertising networks can identify and deliver hundreds of thousands of people who fit this profile and expose them to ads for European cars as they move from one Web site to another. Estimates vary, but behaviorally targeted ads are generally 10 times more likely to produce a consumer response than a randomly chosen banner or video ad (see Figure 10.5). So-called advertising exchanges use this same technology to auction access to people with very specific profiles to advertisers in a few milliseconds. In 2012, about 20 percent of online display ads are targeted, and the rest depend on the context of the pages shoppers visit, the estimated demographics of visitors, or so-called "blast and scatter" advertising, which is placed randomly on any available page with minimal targeting, such as time of day or season.

FIGURE 10.5 HOW AN ADVERTISING NETWORK SUCH AS DOUBLECLICK WORKS

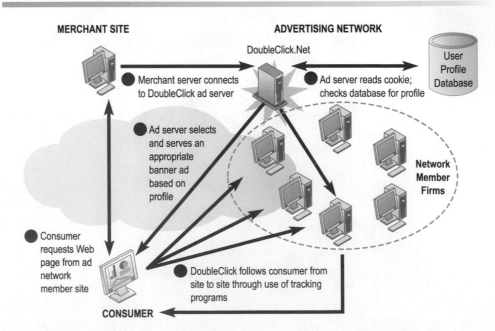

Advertising networks and their use of tracking programs have become controversial among privacy advocates because of their ability to track individual consumers across the Internet.

Social E-commerce and Social Network Marketing

Social e-commerce is commerce based on the idea of the digital **social graph**. The digital social graph is a mapping of all significant online social relationships. The social graph is synonymous with the idea of a "social network" used to describe offline relationships. You can map your own social graph (network) by drawing lines from yourself to the 10 closest people you know. If they know one another, draw lines between these people. If you are ambitious, ask these 10 friends to list and draw in the names of the 10 people closest to them. What emerges from this exercise is a preliminary map of your social network. Now imagine if everyone on the Internet did the same, and posted the results to a very large database with a Web site. Ultimately, you would end up with Facebook or a site like it. The collection of all these personal social networks is called "the social graph."

According to small world theory, you are only six links away from any other person on earth. If you entered your personal address book, say 100 names, on to a list and sent it to your friends, and they in turn entered 50 new names of their friends, and so on, six times, the social network created would encompass 31 billion people! The social graph is therefore a collection of millions of personal social graphs (and all the people in them). So it's a small world indeed, and we are all more closely linked than we ever thought.

Ultimately, you will find that you are directly connected to many friends and relatives, and indirectly connected to an even larger universe of indirect friends and relatives (your distant second and third cousins, and their friends). Theoretically, it takes six links for any one person to find another person anywhere on earth.

If you understand the inter-connectedness of people, you will see just how important this concept is to e-commerce: The products and services you buy will influence the decisions of your friends, and their decisions will in turn influence you. If you are a marketer trying to build and strengthen a brand, the implication is clear: Take advantage of the fact that people are enmeshed in social networks, share interests and values, and communicate and influence one another. As a marketer, your target audience is not a million isolated people watching a TV show, but the social network of people who watch the show, and the viewers' personal networks. Table 10.7 describes four features of social commerce that are driving its growth.

In 2012 and 2013, one of the fastest growing media for branding and marketing is social media. Expenditures for social media marketing are much smaller than television, magazines, and even newspapers, but this will change in the future. Social networks in the offline world are collections of people who voluntarily communicate with one another over an extended period of time. Online social networks, such as Facebook, MySpace, LinkedIn, Twitter, Tumblr, and Google +, along with tens of other sites with social components, are Web sites that enable users to communicate with one another, form group and individual relationships, and share interests, values, and ideas. Individuals establish online profiles with text and photos, creating an online profile of how they want others to see them, and then invite their friends to link to their profile. The network grows by word of mouth and through e-mail links. One of the most ubiquitous graphical elements on Web sites in 2012 is Facebook's Like button, which allows users to tell their friends they like a product, service, or content. Facebook processes around 50 million Likes a day, or 1.5 billion a year.

While Facebook, with 150 million U.S. monthly visitors, receives most of the public attention given to social networking, the other top four social sites are growing very rapidly with the exception of MySpace. LinkedIn has grown 58 percent in 2012 to reach 40 million monthly visitors; Twitter grew 13 percent

TABLE 10.7 FEATURES OF SOCIAL COMMERCE

SOCIAL COMMERCE FEATURE	DESCRIPTION
Social sign-on	Web sites allow users to sign into their sites through their social network pages on Facebook or another social site. This allows Web sites to receive valuable social profile information from Facebook and use it in their own marketing efforts.
Collaborative shopping	Creating an environment where consumers can share their shopping experiences with one another by viewing products, chatting, or texting. Friends can chat online about brands, products, and services.
Network notification	Creating an environment where consumers can share their approval (or disapproval) of products, services, or content, or share their geo-location, perhaps a restaurant or club, with friends. Facebook's ubiquitous Like button is an example. Twitter tweets and followers are another example.
Social search (recommendations)	Enabling an environment where consumers can ask their friends for advice on purchases of products, services, and content. While Google can help you find things, social search can help you evaluate the quality of things by listening to the evaluations of your friends, or their friends. For instance, Amazon's social recommender system can use your Facebook social profile to recommend products.

in 2012 to reach 37 million; and the social blogging site Tumblr reached 27 million people a month, growing 166 percent that year. MySpace, in contrast, has been shrinking but nevertheless attracted 28 million visitors a month in 2012. According to ComScore, about 20 percent of the total time spent online in the United States was spent on social network sites, up from around 8 percent in 2007 (ComScore, 2012). The fastest growing smartphone applications are social network apps: about 30 percent of smartphone users use their phones to visit social sites. Half of all visits to Facebook in 2012 come from smartphones.

Marketers cannot ignore these huge audiences which rival television and radio in size. In 2012, 72 percent of the U.S. Fortune 500 companies had a Twitter account, 66 percent had a Facebook account, 62 percent had a YouTube account, and 28 percent had a corporate blog. Marketers will spend over $3 billion on social network marketing in 2012 (twice the level of 2010), about 9 percent of all online marketing (eMarketer Inc., 2012).

Marketing via social media is still in its early stages, and companies are experimenting in hopes of finding a winning formula. Social interactions and customer sentiment are not always easy to manage, presenting new challenges for companies eager to protect their brands. The Interactive Session on Management provides specific examples of companies' social marketing efforts using Facebook and Twitter.

B2B E-COMMERCE: NEW EFFICIENCIES AND RELATIONSHIPS

The trade between business firms (business-to-business commerce or B2B) represents a huge marketplace. The total amount of B2B trade in the United States in 2012 is estimated to be about $16 trillion, with B2B e-commerce (online

INTERACTIVE SESSION: MANAGEMENT

SOCIAL COMMERCE CREATES NEW CUSTOMER RELATIONSHIPS

To most people, Facebook and Twitter are ways to keep in touch with friends and to let them know what they are doing. For companies of all shapes and sizes, however, Facebook and Twitter have become powerful tools for engaging customers. Location-based businesses like gourmet food trucks can tweet their current location to loyal followers and fans. Appointment-based businesses can easily tweet or post cancellations and unexpected openings. Larger companies run sweepstakes and promotions. And companies of all sizes have an opportunity to shape the perception of their brands and to solidify relationships with their customers.

Companies are rolling out ads that capitalize on the social media features of Facebook to achieve greater visibility. For example, many Facebook ads feature the ability to 'Like' a brand, send a virtual gift, answer a poll question, or instantly stream information to your news feed. Twitter has developed many new offerings to interested advertisers, like 'Promoted Tweets' and 'Promoted Trends'. These features give advertisers the ability to have their tweets displayed more prominently when Twitter users search for certain keywords.

Levi's was one of the first national brands to use Facebook and Twitter to allow consumers to socialize and share their purchases with friends. The Levi's Facebook page has posted 500,000 Like messages posted by friends sharing their favorite jeans. Within the first week of its share campaign, Levis received 4,000 Likes. The company began using Twitter in 2010 by creating a "Levi's Guy," 23-year-old USC graduate Gareth, to interest customers. He has over 6,000 followers and is responsible for responding to queries and engaging in conversations about the Levi's brand on Twitter. In 2011, the company created a personalized Friends Store where shoppers can see what their friends Liked and bought.

The all-purpose electronics retailer Best Buy has 4.6 million fans on Facebook and 200,000 followers on Twitter. Best Buy uses a dedicated team of Twitter responders, called the "Twelp Force," to answer user questions and respond to complaints. Because Best Buy has so many social media followers who are generating feedback on social networks and related sites, the company uses text mining to gather these data and convert them to useful information. Best Buy has a central analytical platform that can ana-

lyze any kind of unstructured data it supplies. The company uses that information to gauge the success of promotions, which products are hot and which are duds, and the impact of advertising campaigns.

Wrigleyville Sports is a small business with three retail stores and e-commerce sites selling sports-related clothing and novelties like a panini maker that puts the Chicago Cubs logo on your sandwich. The company has been building a Facebook following for over three years. Facebook page posts use much of the same content as its e-mail campaigns, but the company's Twitter campaigns have to be condensed to 140 characters. Some Wrigleyville promotions use all of these channels while others are more social-specific. For example, in 2011, the company ran a Mother's Day contest on its Facebook page exhorting visitors to post a picture of Mom demonstrating why she's the biggest Chicago Cubs fan. Wrigleyville tracks purchases related to its promotions with its NetSuite customer relationship management system and is able to tell which promotions yield the most profitable new customers. Wrigleyville knows which customers responded, how much they spent, and what they purchased, so it can measure conversion rates, the value of keyword buys, and the ultimate return on campaigns.

Many companies are running online ads that focus less on pitching their products than on promoting their Facebook pages and Twitter accounts. The ads feature menu tabs and allow users to click within the ad to see a brand's Twitter messages or Facebook Wall posts in real time, or to watch a brand's video content from YouTube—all within the Web page where the ad appears. Incorporating live content from Facebook and Twitter makes online ads appear less "static" and more current than other content.

For example, a recent online ad for the Mrs. Meyers cleaning brand stating "Clean should smell better" instructed users to "hover to expand." When a cursor was placed over the ad, it exposed an area that displayed Facebook Wall posts, Twitter postings about Mrs. Meyers, or a company video, all without leaving the Web page being visited. Consumers spent an average of 30 seconds interacting with the ad, compared to 11 seconds for other types of online ads, according to Google. Consumers were also more likely to click on a "Learn More" button to go to Mrs. Meyers' own Web site, with 35 of every 1,000 users clicking through, compared with an average of just one in 1,000 for traditional online ads.

Even if the Facebook or Twitter postings in ads show brands apologizing about missteps or customer complaints, advertisers may still benefit. Today, the more honest and human companies appear, the more likely consumers are to like them and stick with them. For example, JCD Repair, a six-year-old iPhone, iPad, and Android repair business based in Chicago, found that encouraging customers to post reviews of its service on Facebook, Yelp, and Google+ Local helped generate more business. Although the vast majority of the reviews are overwhelmingly positive, Matt McCormick, JCD's owner, believes that even the bad reviews can be useful. A bad review here and there not only helps you look more credible, it can also give you very valuable feedback on what you're doing wrong, McCormick believes. It also gives you a chance to set the situation right with the customer. If you deal with problems swiftly and set things right, people are impressed.

Still, the results can be unpredictable, and not always beneficial, as Starbucks learned. Starbucks runs contests on Twitter regularly and uses the service to spread free product samples. In 2009, Starbucks launched a social media contest that was essentially a scavenger hunt for advertising posters. Users who found the posters and posted photos of them on Twitter would win a prize. The campaign backfired. At the urging of anti-Starbucks protesters, users flooded Starbucks' Twitter feed with pictures of employees and protesters holding signs criticizing Starbucks' labor practices.

Sources: Melinda F. Emerson, "Even Bad Reviews on the Web Can Help Your Business," *The New York Times*, July 17, 2012; Doug Henschen, "How to Get from CRM to Social," *InformationWeek*, February 22, 2012; Betsy Sigman, "Social Media Helps Build Strong Brands," Baseline, March 9, 2012; Andrew Adam Newman, "Brands Now Direct Their Followers to Social Media," *The New York Times*, August 3, 2011; Geoffrey A. Fowler, "Are You Talking to Me?" *The Wall Street Journal*, April 25, 2011; "In a Few Words, Growth," *The Wall Street Journal*, June 6, 2011; "Starbucks and Twitter: Hash Tag Hell," Viva Visibility, vivavisibilityblog.com/hash-tag-hell/; and "Anti-Starbucks Filmmakers Hijack the Coffee Company's Own Twitter Marketing Campaign," bloggasm.com, May 21, 2009.

CASE STUDY QUESTIONS

1. Assess the management, organization, and technology issues for using social media to engage with customers.

2. What are the advantages and disadvantages of using social media for advertising, brand building, market research, and customer service?

3. Give some examples of management decisions that were facilitated by using social media to interact with customers.

4. Should all companies use Facebook and Twitter for customer service and advertising? Why or why not? What kinds of companies are best suited to use these platforms?

B2B) contributing about $4.1 trillion of that amount (U.S. Census Bureau, 2012; authors' estimates). By 2016, B2B e-commerce should grow to about $5.6 trillion in the United States. The process of conducting trade among business firms is complex and requires significant human intervention, and therefore, it consumes significant resources. Some firms estimate that each corporate purchase order for support products costs them, on average, at least $100 in administrative overhead. Administrative overhead includes processing paper, approving purchase decisions, spending time using the telephone and fax machines to search for products and arrange for purchases, arranging for shipping, and receiving the goods. Across the economy, this adds up to trillions of dollars annually being spent for procurement processes that could potentially be automated. If even just a portion of inter-firm trade were automated, and parts of the entire procurement process assisted by the Internet, literally trillions of dollars might be released for more productive uses, consumer prices potentially would fall, productivity would increase, and the economic wealth of the nation would expand. This is the promise of B2B e-commerce. The challenge of B2B e-commerce is changing existing patterns and systems of procurement, and designing and implementing new Internet-based B2B solutions.

Business-to-business e-commerce refers to the commercial transactions that occur among business firms. Increasingly, these transactions are flowing through a variety of different Internet-enabled mechanisms. About 80 percent of online B2B e-commerce is still based on proprietary systems for **electronic data interchange (EDI)**. Electronic data interchange enables the computer-to-computer exchange between two organizations of standard transactions such as invoices, bills of lading, shipment schedules, or purchase orders. Transactions are automatically transmitted from one information system to another through a network, eliminating the printing and handling of paper at one end and the inputting of data at the other. Each major industry in the United States and much of the rest of the world has EDI standards that define the structure and information fields of electronic documents for that industry.

EDI originally automated the exchange of documents such as purchase orders, invoices, and shipping notices. Although many companies still use EDI for document automation, firms engaged in just-in-time inventory replenishment and continuous production use EDI as a system for continuous replenishment. Suppliers have online access to selected parts of the purchasing firm's production and delivery schedules and automatically ship materials and goods to meet prespecified targets without intervention by firm purchasing agents (see Figure 10.6).

Although many organizations still use private networks for EDI, they are increasingly Web-enabled because Internet technology provides a much more flexible and low-cost platform for linking to other firms. Businesses are able to extend digital technology to a wider range of activities and broaden their circle of trading partners.

Take procurement, for example. Procurement involves not only purchasing goods and materials but also sourcing, negotiating with suppliers, paying for goods, and making delivery arrangements. Businesses can now use the Internet to locate the lowest-cost supplier, search online catalogs of supplier products, negotiate with suppliers, place orders, make payments, and arrange transportation. They are not limited to partners linked by traditional EDI networks.

The Internet and Web technology enable businesses to create new electronic storefronts for selling to other businesses with multimedia graphic displays and interactive features similar to those for B2C commerce. Alternatively, businesses can use Internet technology to create extranets or electronic marketplaces for linking to other businesses for purchase and sale transactions.

FIGURE 10.6 ELECTRONIC DATA INTERCHANGE (EDI)

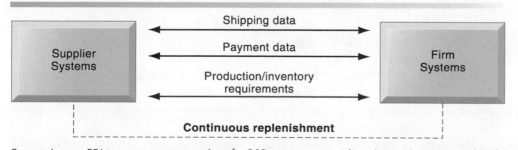

Companies use EDI to automate transactions for B2B e-commerce and continuous inventory replenishment. Suppliers can automatically send data about shipments to purchasing firms. The purchasing firms can use EDI to provide production and inventory requirements and payment data to suppliers.

FIGURE 10.7 A PRIVATE INDUSTRIAL NETWORK

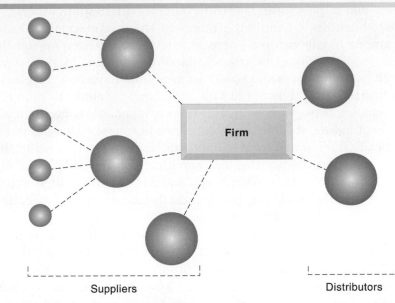

Suppliers   Distributors

A private industrial network, also known as a private exchange, links a firm to its suppliers, distributors, and other key business partners for efficient supply chain management and other collaborative commerce activities.

Private industrial networks typically consist of a large firm using a secure Web site to link to its suppliers and other key business partners (see Figure 10.7). The network is owned by the buyer, and it permits the firm and designated suppliers, distributors, and other business partners to share product design and development, marketing, production scheduling, inventory management, and unstructured communication, including graphics and e-mail. Another term for a private industrial network is a **private exchange**.

An example is VW Group Supply, which links the Volkswagen Group and its suppliers. VW Group Supply handles 90 percent of all global purchasing for Volkswagen, including all automotive and parts components.

Net marketplaces, which are sometimes called e-hubs, provide a single, digital marketplace based on Internet technology for many different buyers and sellers (see Figure 10.8). They are industry owned or operate as independent intermediaries between buyers and sellers. Net marketplaces generate revenue from purchase and sale transactions and other services provided to clients. Participants in Net marketplaces can establish prices through online negotiations, auctions, or requests for quotations, or they can use fixed prices.

There are many different types of Net marketplaces and ways of classifying them. Some Net marketplaces sell direct goods and some sell indirect goods. **Direct goods** are goods used in a production process, such as sheet steel for auto body production. **Indirect goods** are all other goods not directly involved in the production process, such as office supplies or products for maintenance and repair. Some Net marketplaces support contractual purchasing based on long-term relationships with designated suppliers, and others support short-term spot purchasing, where goods are purchased based on immediate needs, often from many different suppliers.

Some Net marketplaces serve vertical markets for specific industries, such as automobiles, telecommunications, or machine tools, whereas others serve horizontal markets for goods and services that can be found in many different industries, such as office equipment or transportation.

FIGURE 10.8 A NET MARKETPLACE

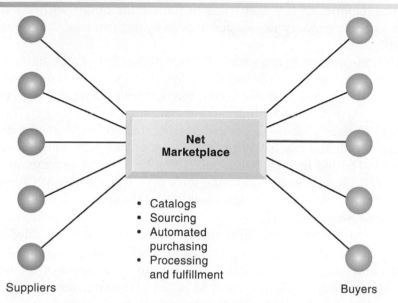

Suppliers

Buyers

Net marketplaces are online marketplaces where multiple buyers can purchase from multiple sellers.

Exostar is an example of an industry-owned Net marketplace, focusing on long-term contract purchasing relationships and on providing common networks and computing platforms for reducing supply chain inefficiencies. This aerospace and defense industry-sponsored Net marketplace was founded jointly by BAE Systems, Boeing, Lockheed Martin, Raytheon, and Rolls-Royce plc to connect these companies to their suppliers and facilitate collaboration. More than 70,000 trading partners in the commercial, military, and government sectors use Exostar's sourcing, e-procurement, and collaboration tools for both direct and indirect goods.

Exchanges are independently owned third-party Net marketplaces that connect thousands of suppliers and buyers for spot purchasing. Many exchanges provide vertical markets for a single industry, such as food, electronics, or industrial equipment, and they primarily deal with direct inputs. For example, Go2Paper enables a spot market for paper, board, and kraft among buyers and sellers in the paper industries from over 75 countries.

Exchanges proliferated during the early years of e-commerce but many have failed. Suppliers were reluctant to participate because the exchanges encouraged competitive bidding that drove prices down and did not offer any long-term relationships with buyers or services to make lowering prices worthwhile. Many essential direct purchases are not conducted on a spot basis because they require contracts and consideration of issues such as delivery timing, customization, and quality of products.

10.3 THE MOBILE DIGITAL PLATFORM AND MOBILE E-COMMERCE

Walk down the street in any major metropolitan area and count how many people are pecking away at their iPhones or BlackBerrys. Ride the trains, fly the planes, and you'll see your fellow travelers reading an online newspaper, watching a video on their phone, or reading a novel on their Kindle. In five years, the majority of Internet users in the United States will rely on mobile devices as their primary device for accessing the Internet. M-commerce has taken off.

In 2012, m-commerce represented about 10 percent of all e-commerce, with about $30 billion in annual revenues generated by retail goods and services, apps, advertising, music, videos, ring tones, applications, movies, television, and location-based services like local restaurant locators and traffic updates. However, m-commerce is the fastest growing form of e-commerce, with some areas expanding at a rate of 50 percent or more per year, and is estimated to grow to $150 billion in 2016 (see Figure 10.9). In 2012, there were an estimated 4 billion cell phone users worldwide, with over 855 million in China and 242 million in the United States (eMarketer, 2012 (M-commerce sales); eMarketer, 2012 (mobile phone users)).

The main areas of growth in mobile e-commerce are retail sales at the top Mobile 400 companies, including Amazon and eBay (about $18.8 billion); sales of Apple and Android apps (about $8.7 billion); and sales of digital content music, TV shows and movies (about $3 billion) (Internet Retailer, 2012). These estimates do not include mobile advertising or location-based services.

M-commerce applications have taken off for services that are time-critical, that appeal to people on the move, or that accomplish a task more efficiently than other methods. The following sections describe some examples.

LOCATION-BASED SERVICES AND APPLICATIONS

Location-based services include geosocial services, geoadvertising, and geo-information services. Seventy-four percent of smartphone owners use location-based services. What ties these activities together and is the foundation for mobile commerce is global positioning system (GPS) enabled map services

FIGURE 10.9 CONSOLIDATED MOBILE COMMERCE REVENUES

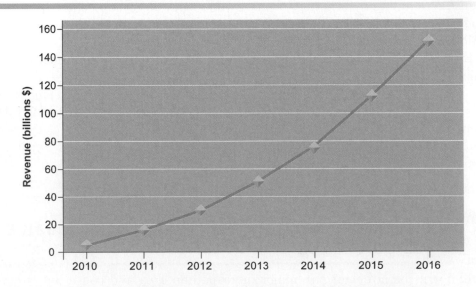

Mobile e-commerce is the fastest growing type of B2C e-commerce although it represents only a small part of all e-commerce in 2012.

available on smartphones. A **geosocial service** can tell you where your friends are meeting. **Geoadvertising services** can tell you where to find the nearest Italian restaurant, and **geoinformation services** can tell you the price of a house you are looking at, or about special exhibits at a museum you are passing.

Wikitude.me is an example of a geoinformation service. Wikitude.me provides a special kind of browser for smartphones equipped with a built-in GPS and compass that can identify your precise location and where the phone is pointed. Using information from over 800,000 points of interest available on Wikipedia, plus thousands of other local sites, the browser overlays information about points of interest you are viewing, and displays that information on your smartphone screen, superimposed on a map or photograph that you just snapped. For example, users can point their smartphone cameras towards mountains from a tour bus and see the names and heights of the mountains displayed on the screen. Wikitude.me also allows users to geo-tag the world around them, and then submit the tags to Wikitude in order to share content with other users.

Foursquare, Gowalla (now owned by Facebook), Loopt, and new offerings by Facebook and Google are examples of geosocial services. Geosocial services help you find friends, or be found by your friends, by "checking in" to the service, announcing your presence in a restaurant or other place. Your friends are instantly notified. About 20 percent of smartphone owners use geosocial services. The popularity of specialized sites like Foursquare has waned as Facebook and Google+ have moved into geosocial services and turned them into extensions of their larger social networks.

Loopt has 5 million users in 2012. The service doesn't sell information to advertisers, but does post ads based on user location. Loopt's target is to deal with advertisers at the walking level (within 200 to 250 meters). Foursquare provides a similar location-based social networking service to 22 million registered users, who may connect with friends and update their location. Points are awarded for checking in at designated venues. Users choose to have their check-ins posted on their accounts on Twitter, Facebook, or both. Users also earn badges by checking in at locations with certain tags, for check-in frequency, or for the time of check-in. More than 500,000 local merchants worldwide use the merchant platform for marketing.

Connecting people to local merchants in the form of geoadvertising is the economic foundation for mobile commerce. Mobile advertising in 2012 will reach $2.6 billion in 2012. Geoadvertising sends ads to users based on their GPS locations. Smartphones report their locations back to Google and Apple. Merchants buy access to these consumers when they come within range of a merchant. For instance, Kiehl Stores, a cosmetics retailer, sent special offers and announcements to customers who came within 100 yards of their store (eMarketer, 2012).

OTHER MOBILE COMMERCE SERVICES

Banks and credit card companies are rolling out services that let customers manage their accounts from their mobile devices. JPMorgan Chase and Bank of America customers can use their cell phones to check account balances, transfer funds, and pay bills. An estimated 134 million people bank online at least once a month.

Although the mobile advertising market is currently small ($2.6 billion), it is rapidly growing (up 44 percent from last year and expected to grow to over $12 billion by 2016), as more and more companies seek ways to exploit new databases of location-specific information (eMarketer, 2012). The largest providers of mobile display advertising are Apple's iAd platform and Google's AdMob platform (both with a 21 percent market share) followed by Millenial Media. Facebook is a distant fourth but moving rapidly to catch up. Alcatel-Lucent offers a new service to be managed by Placecast that will identify cell phone users within a specified distance of an advertiser's nearest outlet and notify them about the outlet's address and phone number, perhaps including a link to a coupon or other promotion. Placecast's clients include Hyatt, FedEx, and Avis Rent A Car.

Yahoo displays ads on its mobile home page for companies such as Pepsi, Procter & Gamble, Hilton, Nissan, and Intel. Google is displaying ads linked to cell phone searches by users of the mobile version of its search engine, while Microsoft offers banner and text advertising on its MSN Mobile portal in the United States. Ads are embedded in games, videos, and other mobile applications.

Shopkick is a mobile application that enables retailers such as Best Buy, Sports Authority, and Macy's to offer coupons to people when they walk into their stores. The Shopkick app automatically recognizes when the user has entered a partner retail store and offers a new virtual currency called "kickbucks," which can be redeemed for Facebook credits, iTunes Gift Cards, travel vouchers, DVDs, or immediate cash-back rewards at any of the partner stores.

Fifty-five percent of online retailers now have m-commerce Web sites—simplified versions of their Web sites that make it possible for shoppers to use cell phones to place orders. Clothing retailers Lilly Pulitzer and Armani Exchange, Home Depot, Amazon, Walmart, and 1–800 Flowers are among those companies with apps for m-commerce sales.

Games and Entertainment

Smartphones and tablets have developed into portable entertainment platforms. Smartphones like the iPhone and Android-based devices offer downloadable and streaming digital games, movies, TV shows, music, and ring tones.

Users of broadband services from the major wireless vendors can stream on-demand video clips, news clips, and weather reports. MobiTV, offered by Verizon Wireless, AT&T Wireless, and other mobile carriers, features live TV programs, including MSNBC and Fox Sports. Film companies are starting to produce short films explicitly designed to play on mobile phones. User-generated content is also appearing in mobile form. Facebook, MySpace, YouTube, and other social networking sites have versions for mobile devices. In 2012, the top 10 most popular apps on Facebook are games, led by *Words with Friends*, *FarmVille*, and *CityVille*, each with over 5 million daily users.

10.4 BUILDING AN E-COMMERCE PRESENCE

Building a successful e-commerce presence requires a keen understanding of business, technology, and social issues, as well as a systematic approach. In 2012, an e-commerce presence is not just a corporate Web site, but may also include a social network site on Facebook, a Twitter company feed, and smartphone apps where customers can access your services. Developing and coordinating all these different customer venues can be difficult. A complete treatment of the topic is beyond the scope of this text, and students should consult books devoted to just this topic (Laudon and Traver, 2013). The two most important management challenges in building a successful e-commerce presence are (1) developing a clear understanding of your business objectives and (2) knowing how to choose the right technology to achieve those objectives.

PIECES OF THE SITE-BUILDING PUZZLE

Let's assume you are a manager for a medium-sized, industrial parts firm of around 10,000 employees worldwide, operating in eight countries in Europe, Asia, and North America. Senior management has given you a budget of $1 million to build an e-commerce site within one year. The purpose of this site will be to sell and service the firm's 20,000 customers, who are mostly small machine and metal fabricating shops around the world. Where do you start?

First, you must be aware of the main areas where you will need to make decisions. On the organizational and human resources fronts, you will have to bring together a team of individuals who possess the skill sets needed to build and manage a successful e-commerce site. This team will make the key decisions about technology, site design, and social and information policies that will be applied at your site. The entire site development effort must be closely managed if you hope to avoid the disasters that have occurred at some firms.

You will also need to make decisions about your site's hardware, software, and telecommunications infrastructure. The demands of your customers should drive your choices of technology. Your customers will want technology that enables them to find what they want easily, view the product, purchase the product, and then receive the product from your warehouses quickly. You will also have to carefully consider your site's design. Once you have identified the key decision areas, you will need to think about a plan for the project.

BUSINESS OBJECTIVES, SYSTEM FUNCTIONALITY, AND INFORMATION REQUIREMENTS

You need to answer this question when planning your Web site: "What do we want the e-commerce site to do for our business?" The key lesson to be learned here is to let the business decisions drive the technology, not the reverse. This will ensure that your technology platform is aligned with your business. We will assume that you have identified a business strategy and chosen a business model to achieve your strategic objectives. But how do you translate your strategies, business models, and ideas into a working e-commerce site?

Your planning should identify the specific business objectives for your site, and then you must develop a list of system functionalities and information requirements. Business objectives are simply capabilities you want your site to have. System functionalities are types of information systems capabilities you will need to achieve your business objectives. The information requirements for a system are the information elements that the system must produce in order to achieve the business objectives.

Table 10.8 describes some basic business objectives, system functionalities, and information requirements for a typical e-commerce site. The objectives must be translated into a description of system functionalities and ultimately into a set of precise information requirements. The specific information requirements for a system typically are defined in much greater detail than Table 10.8

TABLE 10.8 SYSTEM ANALYSIS: BUSINESS OBJECTIVES, SYSTEM FUNCTIONALITY, AND INFORMATION REQUIREMENTS FOR A TYPICAL E-COMMERCE SITE

BUSINESS OBJECTIVE	SYSTEM FUNCTIONALITY	INFORMATION REQUIREMENTS
Display goods	Digital catalog	Dynamic text and graphics catalog
Provide product information (content)	Product database	Product description, stocking numbers, inventory levels
Personalize/customize product	Customer on-site tracking	Site log for every customer visit; data mining capability to identify common customer paths and appropriate responses
Execute a transaction payment	Shopping cart/payment system	Secure credit card clearing; multiple options
Accumulate customer information	Customer database	Name, address, phone, and e-mail for all customers; online customer registration
Provide after-sale customer support	Sales database and customer relationship management system (CRM)	Customer ID, product, date, payment, shipment date
Coordinate marketing/advertising	Ad server, e-mail server, e-mail, campaign manager, ad banner manager	Site behavior log of prospects and customers linked to e-mail and banner ad campaigns
Understand marketing effectiveness	Site tracking and reporting system	Number of unique visitors, pages visited, products purchased, identified by marketing campaign
Provide production and supplier links	Inventory management system	Product and inventory levels, supplier ID and contact, order quantity data by product

indicates. The business objectives of an e-commerce site are similar to those of a physical retail store, but they must be provided entirely in digital form, 24 hours a day, 7 days a week.

BUILDING THE WEB SITE: IN-HOUSE VERSUS OUTSOURCING

There are many choices for building and maintaining Web sites. Much depends on how much money you are willing to spend. Choices range from outsourcing the entire Web site development to an external vendor to building everything yourself (in-house). You also have a second decision to make: will you host (operate) the site on your firm's own servers or will you outsource the hosting to a Web host provider? There are some vendors who will design, build, and host your site, while others will either build or host (but not both). Figure 10.10 illustrates the alternatives.

The Building Decision

If you elect to build your own site, there are a range of options. Unless you are fairly skilled, you should use a pre-built template to create the Web site. For example, Yahoo! Merchant Solutions, Amazon Stores, and eBay all provide

FIGURE 10.10 CHOICES IN BUILDING AND HOSTING WEB SITES

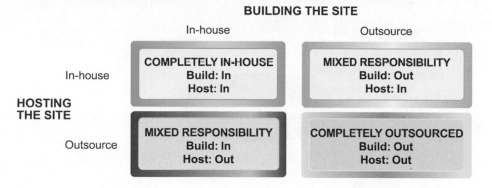

You have a number of alternatives to consider when building and hosting an e-commerce site.

templates that merely require you to input text, graphics, and other data, as well as provide the infrastructure to run the Web site once it has been created. This is the least costly and simplest solution, but you will be limited to the "look and feel" and functionality provided by the template and infrastructure.

If you have some experience with computers, you might decide to build the site yourself. There is a broad variety of tools, ranging from those that help you build everything truly "from scratch," such as Adobe Dreamweaver, Adobe InDesign, and Microsoft Expression, to top-of-the-line prepackaged site-building tools that can create sophisticated sites customized to your needs.

The decision to build a Web site on your own has a number of risks. Given the complexity of features such as shopping carts, credit card authentication and processing, inventory management, and order processing, development costs are high, as are the risks of doing a poor job. You will be reinventing what other specialized firms have already built, and your staff may face a long, difficult learning curve, delaying your entry to market. Your efforts could fail. On the positive side, you may able to build a site that does exactly what you want, and develop the in-house knowledge to revise the site rapidly if necessitated by a changing business environment.

If you choose more expensive site-building packages, you will be purchasing state-of-the-art software that is well tested. You could get to market sooner. However, to make a sound decision, you will have to evaluate many different software packages and this can take a long time. You may have to modify the packages to fit your business needs and perhaps hire additional outside consultants to do the modifications. Costs rise rapidly as modifications mount. A $4,000 package can easily become a $40,000 to $60,000 development project simply because of all the code changes required.

The Hosting Decision

Now let's look at the hosting decision. Most businesses choose to outsource hosting and pay a company to host their Web site, which means that the hosting company is responsible for ensuring the site is "live" or accessible, 24 hours a day. By agreeing to a monthly fee, the business need not concern itself with technical aspects of setting up and maintaining a Web server, telecommunications links, or specialized staffing. With a **co-location agreement**, your firm purchases or leases a Web server (and has total control over its operation) but

FIGURE 10.11 COMPONENTS OF A WEB SITE BUDGET

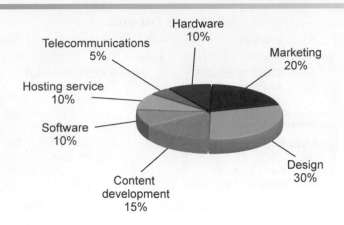

locates the server in a vendor's physical facility. The vendor maintains the facility, communications lines, and the machinery. In the age of cloud computing, it is much less expensive to host your Web site in virtualized computing facilities. In this case, you do not purchase the server, but rent the capabilities of a cloud computing center such as Rackspace (a popular hosting site). There is an extraordinary range of prices for cloud hosting, ranging from $4.95 a month to several hundred thousands of dollars per month depending on the size of the Web site, bandwidth, storage, and support requirements. Very large providers (such as IBM, HP, and Oracle) achieve large economies of scale by establishing huge "server farms" located strategically around the country and the globe. What this means is that the cost of pure hosting has fallen as fast as the fall in server prices, dropping about 50 percent every year.

Web Site Budgets

Simple Web sites can be built and hosted with a first-year cost of $5,000 or less. The Web sites of large firms with high levels of interactivity and linkage to corporate systems cost several million dollars a year to create and operate. For instance, Bluefly, which sells discounted women's and men's designer clothes online, invested over $5.3 million in connection with the redevelopment of its Web site. In 2011, Bluefly had online sales of $88 million, and is growing revenues at 10 percent a year. Its e-commerce technology budget is over $8 million a year, roughly 10 percent of its total revenues (Bluefly, Inc., 2011).

Figure 10.11 provides some idea of the relative size of various Web site cost components. In general, the cost of hardware, software, and telecommunications for building and operating a Web site has fallen dramatically (by over 50 percent) since 2000, making it possible for very small entrepreneurs to create fairly sophisticated sites. At the same time, the costs of system maintenance and content creation have risen to make up more than half of typical Web site budgets. Providing content and smooth 24/7 operations are both labor-intensive.

LEARNING TRACK MODULES

The following Learning Tracks provide content relevant to topics covered in this chapter:

1. E-commerce Challenges: The Story of Online Groceries
2. Build an E-commerce Business Plan
3. Hot New Careers in E-commerce
4. E-commerce Payment Systems

Review Summary

1. *What are the unique features of e-commerce, digital markets, and digital goods?*

    E-commerce involves digitally enabled commercial transactions between and among organizations and individuals. Unique features of e-commerce technology include ubiquity, global reach, universal technology standards, richness, interactivity, information density, capabilities for personalization and customization, and social technology.

    Digital markets are said to be more "transparent" than traditional markets, with reduced information asymmetry, search costs, transaction costs, and menu costs, along with the ability to change prices dynamically based on market conditions. Digital goods, such as music, video, software, and books, can be delivered over a digital network. Once a digital product has been produced, the cost of delivering that product digitally is extremely low.

2. *What are the principal e-commerce business and revenue models?*

    E-commerce business models are e-tailers, transaction brokers, market creators, content providers, community providers, service providers, and portals. The principal e-commerce revenue models are advertising, sales, subscription, free/freemium, transaction fee, and affiliate.

3. *How has e-commerce transformed marketing?*

    The Internet provides marketers with new ways of identifying and communicating with millions of potential customers at costs far lower than traditional media. Crowdsourcing utilizing the "wisdom of crowds" helps companies learn from customers in order to improve product offerings and increase customer value. Behavioral targeting techniques increase the effectiveness of banner, rich media, and video ads. Social commerce uses social networks and social network sites to improve targeting of products and services.

4. *How has e-commerce affected business-to-business transactions?*

    B2B e-commerce generates efficiencies by enabling companies to locate suppliers, solicit bids, place orders, and track shipments in transit electronically. Net marketplaces provide a single, digital marketplace for many buyers and sellers. Private industrial networks link a firm with its suppliers and other strategic business partners to develop highly efficient and responsive supply chains.

5. *What is the role of m-commerce in business, and what are the most important m-commerce applications?*

    M-commerce is especially well-suited for location-based applications, such as finding local hotels and restaurants, monitoring local traffic and weather, and providing personalized location-based marketing. Mobile phones and handhelds are being used for mobile bill payment, banking, securities trading, transportation schedule updates, and downloads of digital content, such as music, games, and video clips. M-commerce requires wireless portals and special digital payment systems that can handle micropayments. The GPS capabilities of smartphones make possible geoadvertising, geosocial, and geoinformation services.

6. *What issues must be addressed when building an e-commerce presence?*

Building a successful e-commerce site requires a clear understanding of the business objectives to be achieved by the site and selection of the right technology to achieve those objectives. E-commerce sites can be built and hosted in-house or partially or fully outsourced to external service providers.

Key Terms

Advertising revenue model, 416
Affiliate revenue model, 420
Behavioral targeting, 421
Business-to-business (B2B), 413
Business-to-consumer (B2C), 413
Co-location, 437
Community providers, 416
Consumer-to-consumer (C2C), 413
Cost transparency, 408
Crowdsourcing, 420
Customization, 409
Digital goods, 411
Direct goods, 430
Disintermediation, 410
Dynamic pricing, 410
Electronic data interchange (EDI), 429
E-tailer, 414
Exchanges, 431
Free/freemium revenue model, 419
Geoadvertising, 433
Geoinformation services, 433
Geosocial services, 433
Indirect goods, 430
Information asymmetry, 409
Information density, 408
Intellectual property, 415
Location-based services, 432

Long tail marketing, 421
Market creator, 415
Market entry costs, 408
Marketspace, 405
Menu costs, 410
Micropayment systems, 419
Mobile commerce (m-commerce), 413
Net marketplaces, 430
Personalization, 408
Podcasting, 415
Prediction market, 421
Price discrimination, 408
Price transparency, 408
Private exchange, 430
Private industrial networks, 430
Revenue model, 416
Richness, 408
Sales revenue model, 418
Search costs, 408
Social graph, 425
Social shopping, 420
Streaming, 415
Subscription revenue model, 419
Transaction costs, 405
Transaction fee revenue model, 419
Wisdom of crowds, 420

Review Questions

1. What are the unique features of e-commerce, digital markets, and digital goods?

   - Name and describe four business trends and three technology trends shaping e-commerce today.
   - List and describe the eight unique features of e-commerce.
   - Define a digital market and digital goods and describe their distinguishing features.

2. What are the principal e-commerce business and revenue models?

   - Name and describe the principal e-commerce business models.

   - Name and describe the e-commerce revenue models.

3. How has e-commerce transformed marketing?

   - Explain how social networking and the "wisdom of crowds" help companies improve their marketing.
   - Define behavioral targeting and explain how it works at individual Web sites and on advertising networks.
   - Define the social graph and explain how it is used in e-commerce marketing.

4. How has e-commerce affected business-to-business transactions?

- Explain how Internet technology supports business-to-business electronic commerce.
- Define and describe Net marketplaces and explain how they differ from private industrial networks (private exchanges).

5. What is the role of m-commerce in business, and what are the most important m-commerce applications?

- List and describe important types of m-commerce services and applications.

6. What issues must be addressed when building an e-commerce presence?

- List and describe each of the factors that go into the building of an e-commerce Web site.
- List and describe four business objectives, four system functionalities, and four information requirements of a typical e-commerce Web site.
- List and describe each of the options for building and hosting e-commerce Web sites.

Discussion Questions

1. How does the Internet change consumer and supplier relationships?

2. The Internet may not make corporations obsolete, but the corporations will have to change their business models. Do you agree? Why or why not?

3. How have social technologies changed e-commerce?

Hands-On MIS Projects

The projects in this section give you hands-on experience developing e-commerce strategies for businesses, using spreadsheet software to research the profitability of an e-commerce company, and using Web tools to research and evaluate e-commerce hosting services.

Management Decision Problems

1. Columbiana is a small, independent island in the Caribbean that has many historical buildings, forts, and other sites, along with rain forests and striking mountains. A few first-class hotels and several dozen less-expensive accommodations can be found along its beautiful white sand beaches. The major airlines have regular flights to Columbiana, as do several small airlines. Columbiana's government wants to increase tourism and develop new markets for the country's tropical agricultural products. How can a Web presence help? What Internet business model would be appropriate? What functions should the Web site perform?

2. Explore the Web sites of the following companies: Blue Nile, J.Crew, Lowe's, and Priceline. Determine which of these Web sites would benefit most from adding a company-sponsored blog to the Web site. List the business benefits of the blog. Specify the intended audience for the blog. Decide who in the company should author the blog, and select some topics for the blog.

Improving Decision Making: Using Spreadsheet Software to Analyze a Dot-Com Business

Software skills: Spreadsheet downloading, formatting, and formulas
Business skills: Financial statement analysis

Pick one e-commerce company on the Internet, for example, Ashford, Buy.com, Yahoo, or Priceline. Study the Web pages that describe the company and explain its purpose and structure. Use the Web to find articles that comment on the company. Then visit the Securities and Exchange Commission's Web site at www. sec.gov to access the company's 10-K (annual report) form showing income statements and balance sheets. Select only the sections of the 10-K form containing the desired portions of financial statements that you need to examine, and download them into your spreadsheet. (MyMISLab provides more detailed instructions on how to download this 10-K data into a spreadsheet.) Create simplified spreadsheets of the company's balance sheets and income statements for the past three years.

- Is the company a dot-com success, borderline business, or failure? What information provides the basis of your decision? Why? When answering these questions, pay special attention to the company's three-year trends in revenues, costs of sales, gross margins, operating expenses, and net margins.
- Prepare an overhead presentation (with a minimum of five slides), including appropriate spreadsheets or charts, and present your work to your professor and classmates.

Achieving Operational Excellence: Evaluating E-Commerce Hosting Services

Software skills: Web browser software
Business skills: Evaluating e-commerce hosting services

This project will help develop your Internet skills in commercial services for hosting an e-commerce site for a small start-up company.

You would like to set up a Web site to sell towels, linens, pottery, and tableware from Portugal and are examining services for hosting small business Internet storefronts. Your Web site should be able to take secure credit card payments and to calculate shipping costs and taxes. Initially, you would like to display photos and descriptions of 40 different products. Visit Yahoo! Small Business, GoDaddy, and Comcast Business Class and compare the range of e-commerce hosting services they offer to small businesses, their capabilities, and costs. Also examine the tools they provide for creating an e-commerce site. Compare these services and decide which you would use if you were actually establishing a Web store. Write a brief report indicating your choice and explaining the strengths and weaknesses of each.

Video Cases

Video Cases and Instructional Videos illustrating some of the concepts in this chapter are available. Contact your instructor to access these videos.

Collaboration and Teamwork Project

In MyMISLab, you will find a Collaboration and Teamwork Project dealing with the concepts in this chapter. You will be able to use Google Sites, Google Docs, and other open source collaboration tools to complete the assignment.

To Pay or Not to Pay: Zagat's Dilemma
CASE STUDY

Founded by Tim and Nina Zagat, the Zagat Survey has collected and published ratings of restaurants by diners since 1979. Zagat publishes surveys for restaurants, hotels, and nightlife in 70 major cities. Zagat has come a long way from its roots in the early 1980s, when the food-loving Zagats started compiling lists of their favorite restaurants for personal use and to share with their closest friends. But with the rise of the Internet, e-commerce, and mobile technology, Zagat has struggled to find a business model that stayed true to the company's origins.

To generate their first survey, the Zagats polled 200 people, and increased that number over time. Executives, tourists, and New York foodies alike found the list to be indispensable. Spurred by this success, the Zagats decided to publish their survey themselves. The few booksellers that took a risk in stocking the book were rewarded with sales so robust that the Zagat Surveys became best sellers.

The pair also published similar lists for other major cities, including Chicago, San Francisco, and Washington, D.C. In addition to print books, Zagat opened a unit that creates custom guides for corporate clients, like the ones at Citibank. For a long time, this business model was sufficient to ensure that Zagat Survey was successful and profitable.

When the dot-com bubble came along, venture capitalists were attracted to Zagat for its brand recognition—the Zagat name is instantly recognizable to food-lovers, travelers, and restaurateurs alike. Zagat was one of the first companies to popularize user-generated content, collecting restaurant reviews from its readers, aggregating those reviews, and computing ratings. In addition to numeric rating scores, the survey also includes a short descriptive paragraph that incorporates selected quotations from several reviewers' comments about each restaurant or service. Venture capitalists saw that Zagat had a golden opportunity to migrate its content from offline to online, Web, and mobile.

Of the many decisions the Zagats faced in bringing their content to the Web, perhaps the most important- was how much to charge for various types of content. They ultimately decided to place all of their content behind a pay wall, relying on the Zagat brand to entice customers to purchase full online access. One of the most prominent members of the Zagat investment group was Nathan Myhrvold, formerly the chief technology officer at Microsoft. Myhrvold supported the Zagats' decision to use a pay wall for their content and maintained that putting all of their content online for free would have undermined their book sales.

Although Myhrvold and the Zagats themselves favored the pay wall, other Zagat investors argued that placing content online for free allowed companies like Yelp to get its results on the first page of Google search results, which is critical for maintaining the strength of a brand in today's advertising environment. By not taking this approach, Zagat left itself open to be surpassed by Yelp, Groupon, Google Places, and other similar services offering free content supported by advertising from local businesses. Sure enough, these companies soon began attracting numbers of online visitors that dwarfed Zagat's.

In 2008, the Zagats tried to sell their company. They failed to do so, partially due to Yelp's growing popularity. Prospective buyers were more intrigued by Yelp's much larger online audience and growth potential. The Zagats' failure to sell the company in 2008 highlighted their failure to effectively go digital. Food blogs and similar sites abound on the Web nowadays, but Zagat was in a unique position to get there first and establish itself as a market leader, and it failed to do so.

For much of 2011, Zagat continued to lag behind Yelp and other free review sites in the battle for eyeballs. Yelp drew much greater traffic than Zagat.com. From January to April 2012, Zagat.com had only 310,000 visitors, while Yelp had 31 million. The Zagat Web site claimed it has more users, but the disparity was still significant.

Zagat saw its fortunes change in September 2011, when Google paid $151 million to buy the company. Although the Zagats had sought $200 million in 2008, the deal was considered by analysts to be generous. Google was seeking to establish itself in the local search marketspace, and after failing to purchase Yelp for $500 million in 2009, Zagat was next on their shopping list. In fact, after the Yelp deal fell through, Google and Yelp have become heated rivals, and Yelp has alleged that Google is rigging its search results to favor its own services over those of its competitors.

In the year following the acquisition, Google and Zagat worked together to allow Zagat reviews to appear alongside Google searches on various platforms. Google wanted to use Zagat's customer generated guide format and apply it to any place that can be searched for: restaurants, retail outlets, nightlife, hotels, resorts, spas, golf courses, and more. A growing percentage of Google searches are for information on nearby locations—20 percent of all searches, and 40 percent of that subset are made using mobile phones.

In May 2012, Google formally announced the inclusion of Zagat guides and online reviews in its new service, Google+ Local. With this service, Google hopes to more effectively compete with Yelp in local search. Because Google values eyeballs over all else, the company opted to remove the pay wall from Zagat content for the first time. Zagat had been charging $25 per year or $5 per month for access to its online reviews. Zagat will still charge $10 a year to use its iPhone app, and after a free six-month trial, it will charge $25 annually to see reviews on devices running Android. Still, normal Google searches on the Web will feature Zagat content for free, and Google is considering dropping the other subscription fees for mobile devices.

Google hopes to combine Zagat reviews with its mapping technology to better compete with Yelp. Trying out both services highlights some of the differences between them. Zagat.com's home page is streamlined, with a minimal number of search boxes and links immediately available. Restaurant reviews are organized by several major "hub" cities as well as popular lists of the top restaurants of a certain type. Clicking on a restaurant shows visitors a portion of the data Zagat maintains on that restaurant. For example, the site now shows the percentage of users that "like" the restaurant, and several featured reviews. Many more reviews of the restaurant are available if the user wants to keep scrolling.

Yelp's front page is much busier and less streamlined than Zagat's, but has a great deal more content available immediately. The front page has lists of the most popular restaurants, retail outlets, bars and clubs, and many other categories, all free to the user. Looking for a dentist in New York City? Yelp has reviews of doctors and dentists that include videos put together by the practices to give visitors more information. Like Zagat.com, Yelp's reviews are organized into a similar list of larger cities, but reviews exist for almost any location you can think of, including less prominent cities and towns. Google is also working towards the goal of ubiquity.

Yelp's strategy is to sell local advertisements wherever businesses exist and to provide free content funded by these sales. Yelp has also relied more on individual reviewers. Instead of distilling reviews into one coherent whole, as Zagat's does, Yelp allows its reviewers to post full, unaltered reviews, which allows top reviewers to gain followings and even receive invitations to special events. The drawback of this approach is that many reviews are far longer than necessary and individual reviews may contain distortions or false claims designed to damage reputations. Zagat reviews give a clearer and more concise impression of a restaurant than most Yelp reviews, and they are aggregated and given a score.

Investors believe that Yelp is on "a different trajectory" because of its unique business model. Zagat sold content to consumers and corporations; Yelp sells advertising to local businesses. Many analysts believe there is much more potential for growth with Yelp's business model than with Zagat's old model because it is a useful advertising vehicle for small businesses everywhere, not just major cities. Zagat may also have hurt itself with its slow response to the emergence of the mobile digital platform.

Most analysts agree that Zagat could have avoided this state of affairs by making a more aggressive effort to go digital. The choice to use a pay wall may be the biggest culprit. But did it necessarily hurt Zagat's bottom line? The company has always been profitable, according to Tim and Nina Zagat. Other successful Web sites have used a pay wall. Zagat book revenue is still strong—the New York survey is still on the New York nonfiction best-seller list, and its corporate custom guide unit is very profitable. Despite their acquisition by Google, the Zagats plan to continue to publish their physical books. Nevertheless, it's also possible that going with a pay wall before establishing a loyal online audience may not be the right time to make the move towards a paid model.

So far, the pairing of Google and Zagat has been successful, and will allow the two companies to better compete with Yelp in local search. But Google also hopes that incorporating Zagat's user-generated content model into Google+ will help its fledgling social network to better compete with Facebook by providing uniquely valuable services to its users. Google envisions Google+ users searching for "pizza", and being given a map with the closest pizzerias marked with Zagat reviews, some of which may be written by their friends on the network. For Google, acquiring Zagat was just one of a myriad of acquisitions they made in 2011; but from Zagat's perspective, its acquisition represents another phase in a long e-commerce journey, and illustrates the difficulty of developing just the right business model for your company.

Sources: Glenn Collins, "Google to Use Zag to Refine Local Search," *The New York Times*, May 30, 2012; Michael Liedtke, "Google's Giving Away Free Zag Ratings in Search Results," Associated Press, May 31, 2012; Samantha Murphy, "Google Plus Local Unlocks the Power of Zag, Mashable.com, May 30, 2012; Tim Carmody, "Google Buys Zagat to Reinvent Mobile Search Engine," *Wired*, September 10, 2011; Adam Clark Estes, "Google Buying Zagat Makes Instant Sense," *Atlantic Wire*, September 8, 2011; Leena Rao, "Zagat.com Relaunches With More Free Content, Including Maps, Lists, Third-Party Reviews," TechCrunch.com, February 21, 2011; Erik Berte, "As Online Competition Grows, Zagat.com Relaunches With More Free Features," FoxBusiness.com, February 21, 2011; Ben Parr, "Yelp's Growth is Accelerating, Despite Increased Competition From Groupon & Google," Mashable.com, February 17, 2011; "ZAGAT for Android Features Foodspotting Photos, Foursquare Tips and In-App Review Capabilities," PR Newswire, February 7, 2011; and Ron Lieber, "Zagat Survey Aims to Regain Its Online Balance," *The New York Times*, November 13, 2010.

CASE STUDY QUESTIONS

1. Evaluate Zagat using the competitive forces and value chain models.

2. Compare Zagat's and Yelp's e-commerce business models. How have those models affected each company's Web strategy?

3. Why was Zagat's content well suited for the Web and for the mobile digital platform?

4. Do you think Zagat's decision to use a pay wall for its Web site was a mistake? Why or why not?

5. Will Zagat's acquisition by Google make it more competitive? Explain your answer.

Chapter 11

Managing Knowledge

LEARNING OBJECTIVES

After reading this chapter, you will be able to answer the following questions:

1. What is the role of knowledge management and knowledge management programs in business?

2. What types of systems are used for enterprise-wide knowledge management and how do they provide value for businesses?

3. What are the major types of knowledge work systems and how do they provide value for firms?

4. What are the business benefits of using intelligent techniques for knowledge management?

CHAPTER OUTLINE

Interactive Sessions:

Firewire Surfboards Lights Up
    with CAD

Albassami's Job is Not Feasible
    Without IT

DESIGNING DRUGS VIRTUALLY

Pharmaceutical companies and medical researchers are constantly trying to find new drugs that will provide better treatments for cancer and other serious illnesses. Until recently, this process was largely a matter of trial and error.

Disease-fighting drugs typically work by attacking a disease-causing protein that is harmfully interacting with other molecules in the body. The drug is able to stop these interactions by connecting to the protein, and either restoring healthy interactions or compensating for the unhealthy ones.

A drug connecting to a protein has been likened to a key fitting into a lock. In the traditional drug discovery process, drug makers would be looking for the "keys" while ignoring the "locks." They sifted through natural substances found in soil, dyes and industrial chemicals, and failed compounds from previous drug research efforts. They would test their samples for their impact on diseased cells. Once in a great while, as in the case of penicillin, one worked, but for the overwhelming majority of efforts, this was not the case.

Drug development companies tried to speed up the process by creating huge libraries of potential compounds and using robots to quickly review hundreds of thousands of samples to see if any worked. Machines would create thousands of chemicals per day by mixing and matching common building blocks. Then robots would drop bits of each chemical into tiny vials containing samples of a bodily substance involved in a disease, such as the protein that triggers cholesterol production. A "hit" occurred when the substance and the chemical produced a desired reaction. Way too much depended on chance. When researchers did come upon a new treatment that worked, they often had no idea for many years why. They did not understand the "key" or the "lock." Very few effective medications were discovered this way.

Joshua Boger, a former Merck & Company scientist, decided to try a different approach called structure-based design. In 1989, he formed a company called Vertex Pharmaceuticals, which would focus on figuring out what a "lock" looked like so it could fashion the right disease-fighting "key."

It would not be easy to determine the shape of a "lock." Proteins escape when X-rays try to capture their images, so scientists must first crystallize the proteins and try to deduce their shape by examining the patterns left by the X-rays deflecting around them. This work requires powerful computers analyzing thousands of interference patterns.

Next, researchers must find a custom molecule to fit that particular "lock." The molecule must be able to bind to the target, be synthesized and manufactured in large quantities, and be metabolized by the body at just the right rate. Powerful computers help evaluate the structures and properties of molecules that are most likely to bind to that target and rapidly search large database libraries of chemical structures in order to identify the most promising candidates.

The discovery of the drug called Xalkori, a treatment for a rare and resistant form of lung cancer, is one example of how

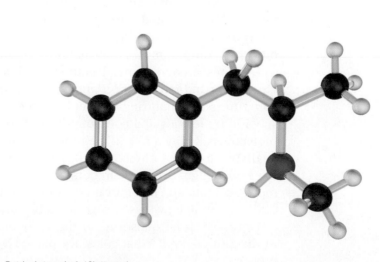

© style-photography.de / Shutterstock

structure-based design helped. Reseachers led by Dr. Jean Cui at the biotech firm Sugen were trying to block a protein called c-Met that was found to play an important role in the growth of cancer tumors. The researchers identified a naturally occurring molecule that connected to c-Met, but the molecule at that stage lacked properties, such as avoiding rapid metabolism in the body, that would make it a workable drug. Other researchers using structure-based design crystallized the c-Met protein with one of the potential drug molecules linked to it, subjected this arrangement to X-rays, and used computer analysis to deduce the structure of the protein and how the prototype drug molecule "key" fit into its "lock."

Dr. Cui was able to use this information to develop an entirely new molecule that could both bind to c-Met and that had properties suitable for a drug. Colleagues used Cui's sketch of what she thought the drug design should look like to model compounds virtually on a computer and make them in test tubes for further study. By February 2003, animal tests showed that the molecule could arrest tumor growth. After Sugen and its parent company Pharmacia were acquired by Pfizer, researchers further refined the molecule to make Xalkori ready for testing in humans. Xalkori was approved by the FDA in the summer of 2011.

In addition to treating lung cancer, Xalkori is being used in conjunction with an Alzheimer's disease treatment developed by Eli Lilly & Co., an antibiotic made by GlaxoSmithKline PLC that is in clinical trials, and a Sanofi SA blood thinner that is in the final stages of development. Vertex's hepatitis C therapy, called Incivek, was FDA-approved in May 2011, and its drug for treating cystic fibrosis, called Ivacaftor, was approved in January 2012.

Sources: Jonathan D. Rockoff, "Drug Discovery Gets an Upgrade," *The Wall Street Journal*, April 16, 2012; www.vrtx.com, accessed July 1, 2012; and Matthew Herperi, "Pfizer Wins Approval For Xalkori, Lung Cancer Drug That Heralds Age Of Expensive, Personalized Medicines," *Forbes*, August 26, 2011.

The experience of the medical researchers engaged in drug discovery described in this case shows how business performance can benefit by using technology to facilitate the acquisition and application of knowledge. Facilitating access to knowledge, improving the quality and currency of knowledge, and using that knowledge to improve business processes are vital to success and survival in all areas of business as well as in medical research.

The chapter-opening diagram calls attention to important points raised by this case and this chapter. Phamaceutical companies trying to develop new drugs are very challenged because the drug discovery process is so painstaking and complicated. Earlier methods were not very accurate or effective and depended too much on trial and error. This is beginning to change, thanks to the development of new processes for visualizing and designing new drugs and the use of powerful computers and information technology.

Drug researchers using structure-based design benefit from a new process of visualizing and modeling promising compounds at the molecular level. Powerful computers for analyzing molecular structure, databases organizing data about specific molecules and compounds, and software for visualizing and modeling molecules all play a role in creating new knowledge and making that knowledge available to researchers. Thanks to better systems for capturing and creating knowledge, drug researchers and pharmaceutical companies have a much more accurate and efficient process for developing effective medications and for understanding how these drugs actually work.

Here are some questions to think about: Why are computers so important in drug discovery? What roles are played by computers in the drug discovery process?

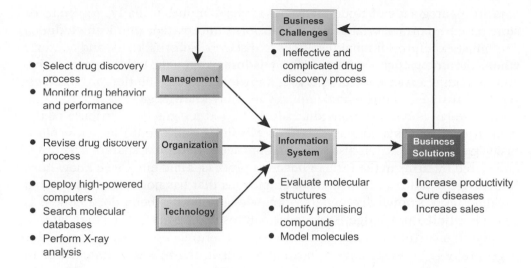

11.1 THE KNOWLEDGE MANAGEMENT LANDSCAPE

Knowledge management and collaboration systems are among the fastest growing areas of corporate and government software investment. The past decade has shown an explosive growth in research on knowledge and knowledge management in the economics, management, and information systems fields.

Knowledge management and collaboration are closely related. Knowledge that cannot be communicated and shared with others is nearly useless. Knowledge becomes useful and actionable when shared throughout the firm. We have already described the major tools for collaboration and social business in Chapter 2. In this chapter, we will focus on knowledge management systems, and be mindful that communicating and sharing knowledge are becoming increasingly important.

We live in an information economy in which the major source of wealth and prosperity is the production and distribution of information and knowledge. An estimated 37 percent of the U.S. labor force consists of knowledge and information workers, the largest single segment of the labor force. About 45 percent of the gross domestic product (GDP) of the United States is generated by the knowledge and information sectors (U.S. Department of Commerce, 2012).

Knowledge management has become an important theme at many large business firms as managers realize that much of their firm's value depends on the firm's ability to create and manage knowledge. Studies have found that a substantial part of a firm's stock market value is related to its intangible assets, of which knowledge is one important component, along with brands, reputations, and unique business processes. Well-executed knowledge-based projects have been known to produce extraordinary returns on investment, although the impacts of knowledge-based investments are difficult to measure (Gu and Lev, 2001).

IMPORTANT DIMENSIONS OF KNOWLEDGE

There is an important distinction between data, information, knowledge, and wisdom. Chapter 1 defines **data** as a flow of events or transactions captured by an organization's systems that, by itself, is useful for transacting but little else. To turn data into useful *information*, a firm must expend resources to organize data into categories of understanding, such as monthly, daily, regional, or store-based reports of total sales. To transform information into **knowledge**, a firm must expend additional resources to discover patterns, rules, and contexts where the knowledge works. Finally, **wisdom** is thought to be the collective and individual experience of applying knowledge to the solution of problems. Wisdom involves where, when, and how to apply knowledge.

Knowledge is both an individual attribute and a collective attribute of the firm. Knowledge is a cognitive, even a physiological, event that takes place inside people's heads. It is also stored in libraries and records, shared in lectures, and stored by firms in the form of business processes and employee know-how. Knowledge residing in the minds of employees that has not been documented is called **tacit knowledge**, whereas knowledge that has been documented is called **explicit knowledge**. Knowledge can reside in e-mail, voice mail, graphics, and unstructured documents as well as structured documents. Knowledge is generally believed to have a location, either in the minds of humans or in specific business processes. Knowledge is "sticky" and not universally applicable or easily moved. Finally, knowledge is thought to be situational and contextual. For example, you must know when to perform a procedure as well as how to perform it. Table 11.1 reviews these dimensions of knowledge.

We can see that knowledge is a different kind of firm asset from, say, buildings and financial assets; that knowledge is a complex phenomenon; and that there are many aspects to the process of managing knowledge. We can also recognize that knowledge-based core competencies of firms—the two or three things that an organization does best—are key organizational assets. Knowing how to do things effectively and efficiently in ways that other organizations cannot duplicate is a primary source of profit and competitive advantage that cannot be purchased easily by competitors in the marketplace.

TABLE 11.1 IMPORTANT DIMENSIONS OF KNOWLEDGE

KNOWLEDGE IS A FIRM ASSET

Knowledge is an intangible asset.

The transformation of data into useful information and knowledge requires organizational resources.

Knowledge is not subject to the law of diminishing returns as are physical assets, but instead experiences network effects as its value increases as more people share it.

KNOWLEDGE HAS DIFFERENT FORMS

Knowledge can be either tacit or explicit (codified).

Knowledge involves know-how, craft, and skill.

Knowledge involves knowing how to follow procedures.

Knowledge involves knowing why, not simply when, things happen (causality).

KNOWLEDGE HAS A LOCATION

Knowledge is a cognitive event involving mental models and maps of individuals.

There is both a social and an individual basis of knowledge.

Knowledge is "sticky" (hard to move), situated (enmeshed in a firm's culture), and contextual (works only in certain situations).

KNOWLEDGE IS SITUATIONAL

Knowledge is conditional; knowing when to apply a procedure is just as important as knowing the procedure (conditional).

Knowledge is related to context; you must know how to use a certain tool and under what circumstances.

For instance, having a unique build-to-order production system constitutes a form of knowledge and perhaps a unique asset that other firms cannot copy easily. With knowledge, firms become more efficient and effective in their use of scarce resources. Without knowledge, firms become less efficient and less effective in their use of resources and ultimately fail.

Organizational Learning and Knowledge Management

Like humans, organizations create and gather knowledge using a variety of organizational learning mechanisms. Through collection of data, careful measurement of planned activities, trial and error (experiment), and feedback from customers and the environment in general, organizations gain experience. Organizations that learn adjust their behavior to reflect that learning by creating new business processes and by changing patterns of management decision making. This process of change is called **organizational learning**. Arguably, organizations that can sense and respond to their environments rapidly will survive longer than organizations that have poor learning mechanisms.

THE KNOWLEDGE MANAGEMENT VALUE CHAIN

Knowledge management refers to the set of business processes developed in an organization to create, store, transfer, and apply knowledge. Knowledge management increases the ability of the organization to learn from its environment and to incorporate knowledge into its business processes. Figure 11.1 illustrates the five value-adding steps in the knowledge management value chain. Each stage in the value chain adds value to raw data and information as they are transformed into usable knowledge.

In Figure 11.1, information systems activities are separated from related management and organizational activities, with information systems activities on

FIGURE 11.1 THE KNOWLEDGE MANAGEMENT VALUE CHAIN

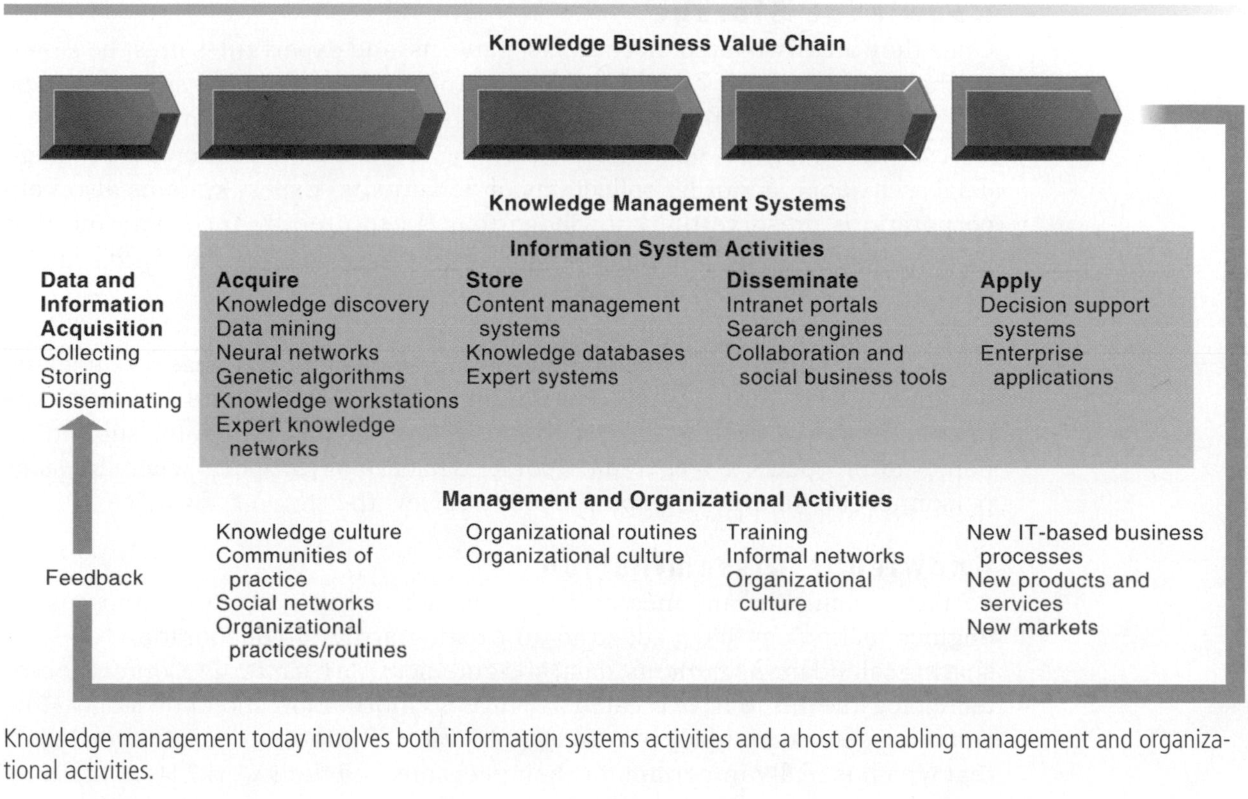

Knowledge management today involves both information systems activities and a host of enabling management and organizational activities.

the top of the graphic and organizational and management activities below. One apt slogan of the knowledge management field is, "Effective knowledge management is 80 percent managerial and organizational, and 20 percent technology."

In Chapter 1, we define *organizational and management capital* as the set of business processes, culture, and behavior required to obtain value from investments in information systems. In the case of knowledge management, as with other information systems investments, supportive values, structures, and behavior patterns must be built to maximize the return on investment in knowledge management projects. In Figure 11.1, the management and organizational activities in the lower half of the diagram represent the investment in organizational capital required to obtain substantial returns on the information technology (IT) investments and systems shown in the top half of the diagram.

Knowledge Acquisition

Organizations acquire knowledge in a number of ways, depending on the type of knowledge they seek. The first knowledge management systems sought to build corporate repositories of documents, reports, presentations, and best practices. These efforts have been extended to include unstructured documents (such as e-mail). In other cases, organizations acquire knowledge by developing online expert networks so that employees can "find the expert" in the company who is personally knowledgeable.

In still other cases, firms must create new knowledge by discovering patterns in corporate data or by using knowledge workstations where engineers can discover new knowledge. These various efforts are described throughout this chapter. A coherent and organized knowledge system also requires systematic data from the firm's transaction processing systems that track sales, payments, inventory, customers, and other vital data, as well as data from external sources such as news feeds, industry reports, legal opinions, scientific research, and government statistics.

Knowledge Storage

Once they are discovered, documents, patterns, and expert rules must be stored so they can be retrieved and used by employees. Knowledge storage generally involves the creation of a database. Document management systems that digitize, index, and tag documents according to a coherent framework are large databases adept at storing collections of documents. Expert systems also help corporations preserve the knowledge that is acquired by incorporating that knowledge into organizational processes and culture. Each of these is discussed later in this chapter and in the following chapter.

Management must support the development of planned knowledge storage systems, encourage the development of corporate-wide schemas for indexing documents, and reward employees for taking the time to update and store documents properly. For instance, it would reward the sales force for submitting names of prospects to a shared corporate database of prospects where all sales personnel can identify each prospect and review the stored knowledge.

Knowledge Dissemination

Portals, e-mail, instant messaging, wikis, social business tools, and search engines technology have added to an existing array of collaboration tools for sharing calendars, documents, data, and graphics (see Chapter 2). Contemporary technology seems to have created a deluge of information and knowledge. How can managers and employees discover, in a sea of information and knowledge, that which is really important for their decisions and their work? Here, training programs, informal networks, and shared management experience communicated through a supportive culture help managers focus their attention on the important knowledge and information.

Knowledge Application

Regardless of what type of knowledge management system is involved, knowledge that is not shared and applied to the practical problems facing firms and managers does not add business value. To provide a return on investment, organizational knowledge must become a systematic part of management decision making and become situated in systems for decision support (described in Chapter 12). Ultimately, new knowledge must be built into a firm's business processes and key application systems, including enterprise applications for managing key internal business processes and relationships with customers and suppliers. Management supports this process by creating—based on new knowledge—new business practices, new products and services, and new markets for the firm.

Building Organizational and Management Capital: Collaboration, Communities of Practice, and Office Environments

In addition to the activities we have just described, managers can help by developing new organizational roles and responsibilities for the acquisition of knowledge, including the creation of chief knowledge officer executive positions, dedicated staff positions (knowledge managers), and communities of practice. **Communities of practice (COPs)** are informal social networks of professionals and employees within and outside the firm who have similar work-related activities and interests. The activities of these communities include self-education and group education, conferences, online newsletters, and day-to-day sharing of experiences and techniques to solve specific work problems. Many organizations, such as IBM, the U.S. Federal Highway Administration, and the World Bank have encouraged the development of thousands of online communities of practice. These communities of practice depend greatly on software environments that enable collaboration and communication.

COPs can make it easier for people to reuse knowledge by pointing community members to useful documents, creating document repositories, and filtering information for newcomers. COPs members act as facilitators, encouraging contributions and discussion. COPs can also reduce the learning curve for new employees by providing contacts with subject matter experts and access to a community's established methods and tools. Finally, COPs can act as a spawning ground for new ideas, techniques, and decision-making behavior.

TYPES OF KNOWLEDGE MANAGEMENT SYSTEMS

There are essentially three major types of knowledge management systems: enterprise-wide knowledge management systems, knowledge work systems, and intelligent techniques. Figure 11.2 shows the knowledge management system applications for each of these major categories.

Enterprise-wide knowledge management systems are general-purpose firmwide efforts to collect, store, distribute, and apply digital content and knowledge. These systems include capabilities for searching for information, storing both structured and unstructured data, and locating employee expertise within the firm. They also include supporting technologies such as portals,

FIGURE 11.2 **MAJOR TYPES OF KNOWLEDGE MANAGEMENT SYSTEMS**

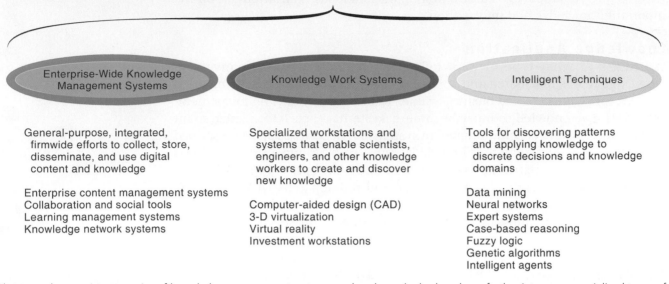

Enterprise-Wide Knowledge Management Systems	Knowledge Work Systems	Intelligent Techniques
General-purpose, integrated, firmwide efforts to collect, store, disseminate, and use digital content and knowledge	Specialized workstations and systems that enable scientists, engineers, and other knowledge workers to create and discover new knowledge	Tools for discovering patterns and applying knowledge to discrete decisions and knowledge domains
Enterprise content management systems Collaboration and social tools Learning management systems Knowledge network systems	Computer-aided design (CAD) 3-D virtualization Virtual reality Investment workstations	Data mining Neural networks Expert systems Case-based reasoning Fuzzy logic Genetic algorithms Intelligent agents

There are three major categories of knowledge management systems, and each can be broken down further into more specialized types of knowledge management systems.

search engines, collaboration and social business tools, and learning management systems.

The development of powerful networked workstations and software for assisting engineers and scientists in the discovery of new knowledge has led to the creation of knowledge work systems such as computer-aided design (CAD), visualization, simulation, and virtual reality systems. **Knowledge work systems (KWS)** are specialized systems built for engineers, scientists, and other knowledge workers charged with discovering and creating new knowledge for a company. We discuss knowledge work applications in detail in Section 11.3.

Knowledge management also includes a diverse group of **intelligent techniques**, such as data mining, expert systems, neural networks, fuzzy logic, genetic algorithms, and intelligent agents. These techniques have different objectives, from a focus on discovering knowledge (data mining and neural networks), to distilling knowledge in the form of rules for a computer program (expert systems and fuzzy logic), to discovering optimal solutions for problems (genetic algorithms). Section 11.4 provides more detail about these intelligent techniques.

11.2 ENTERPRISE-WIDE KNOWLEDGE MANAGEMENT SYSTEMS

Firms must deal with at least three kinds of knowledge. Some knowledge exists within the firm in the form of structured text documents (reports and presentations). Decision makers also need knowledge that is semistructured, such as e-mail, voice mail, chat room exchanges, videos, digital pictures, brochures, or bulletin board postings. In still other cases, there is no formal or digital information of any kind, and the knowledge resides in the heads of employees. Much of this knowledge is tacit knowledge that is rarely written down.

Enterprise-wide knowledge management systems deal with all three types of knowledge.

ENTERPRISE CONTENT MANAGEMENT SYSTEMS

Businesses today need to organize and manage both structured and semistructured knowledge assets. **Structured knowledge** is explicit knowledge that exists in formal documents, as well as in formal rules that organizations derive by observing experts and their decision-making behaviors. But, according to experts, at least 80 percent of an organization's business content is semistructured or unstructured—information in folders, messages, memos, proposals, e-mails, graphics, electronic slide presentations, and even videos created in different formats and stored in many locations.

Enterprise content management systems help organizations manage both types of information. They have capabilities for knowledge capture, storage, retrieval, distribution, and preservation to help firms improve their business processes and decisions. Such systems include corporate repositories of documents, reports, presentations, and best practices, as well as capabilities for collecting and organizing semistructured knowledge such as e-mail (see Figure 11.3). Major enterprise content management systems also enable users to access external sources of information, such as news feeds and research, and to communicate via e-mail, chat/instant messaging, discussion groups, and videoconferencing. They are starting to incorporate blogs, wikis, and other enterprise social networking tools. Open Text Corporation, EMC (Documentum), IBM, and Oracle Corporation are leading vendors of enterprise content management software.

Barrick Gold, headquartered in Toronto, is the world's leading gold producer, and it uses Open Text tools for enterprise content management and for supporting communities of practice. The company has 26 operating mines and 20,000 employees worldwide, who were creating and storing information in many different locations. Barrick needed a way to centralize this organizational

FIGURE 11.3 AN ENTERPRISE CONTENT MANAGEMENT SYSTEM

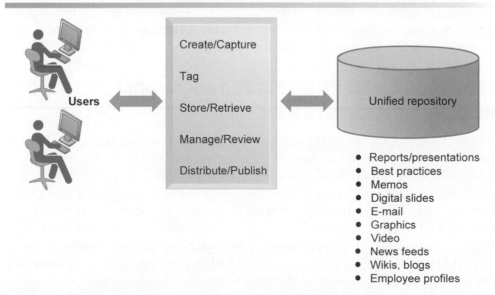

An enterprise content management system has capabilities for classifying, organizing, and managing structured and semistructured knowledge and making it available throughout the enterprise.

expertise, make it easier to access critical company information, and ensure that best practices are documented and shared. Barrick's Knowledge Center is a central repository for documents about policies, procedures, standards, guidelines, new ideas, and best practices, and has capabilities to identify the latest version of each document. Administrators know who is accessing the site and which documents they are using. The content management system includes social networking tools, such as wikis, blogs, and forums, to help communities of practice share their knowledge (Open Text, 2012).

A key problem in managing knowledge is the creation of an appropriate classification scheme, or **taxonomy**, to organize information into meaningful categories so that it can be easily accessed. Once the categories for classifying knowledge have been created, each knowledge object needs to be "tagged," or classified, so that it can be easily retrieved. Enterprise content management systems have capabilities for tagging, interfacing with corporate databases and content repositories, and creating enterprise knowledge portals that provide a single point of access to information resources.

Firms in publishing, advertising, broadcasting, and entertainment have special needs for storing and managing unstructured digital data such as photographs, graphic images, video, and audio content. For example, Coca-Cola must keep track of all the images of the Coca-Cola brand that have been created in the past at all of the company's worldwide offices, to prevent both redundant work and variation from a standard brand image. **Digital asset management systems** help companies classify, store, and distribute these digital objects.

KNOWLEDGE NETWORK SYSTEMS

Knowledge network systems, address the problem that arises when the appropriate knowledge is not in the form of a digital document but instead resides in the memory of individual experts in the firm. Knowledge network systems provide an online directory of corporate experts and their profiles, with details about their job experience, projects, publications, and educational degrees. Search tools make it easy for employees to find the appropriate expert in a company. Knowledge network systems such as Hivemine's AskMe include repositories of expert-generated content. Some knowledge networking capabilities are included in the leading enterprise content management, social networking, and collaboration software products.

COLLABORATION AND SOCIAL TOOLS AND LEARNING MANAGEMENT SYSTEMS

Chapters 2 and 7 have already discussed the importance of collaboration and social tools for information sharing within the firm. For knowledge resources outside the firm, **social bookmarking** makes it easier to search for and share information by allowing users to save their bookmarks to Web pages on a public Web site and tag these bookmarks with keywords. These tags can be used to organize and search for text and images. Lists of tags can be shared with other people to help them find information of interest. The user-created taxonomies created for shared bookmarks are called **folksonomies**. Delicious, Slashdot, and Pinterest are popular social bookmarking sites.

Suppose, for example, that you're on a corporate team researching wind power. If you did a Web search and found relevant Web pages on wind power, you'd click on a bookmarking button on a social bookmarking site and create a tag identifying each Web document you found to link it to wind power. By clicking on the "tags" button at the social networking site, you'd be able to see a list of all the tags you created and select the documents you need.

Companies need ways to keep track of and manage employee learning and to integrate it more fully into their knowledge management and other corporate systems. A **learning management system (LMS)** provides tools for the management, delivery, tracking, and assessment of various types of employee learning and training.

Contemporary LMS support multiple modes of learning, including CD-ROM, downloadable videos, Web-based classes, live instruction in classes or online, and group learning in online forums and chat sessions. The LMS consolidates mixed-media training, automates the selection and administration of courses, assembles and delivers learning content, and measures learning effectiveness.

CVM Solutions, LLC (CVM) uses Digitec's Knowledge Direct learning management system to provide training about how to manage suppliers for clients such as Procter & Gamble, Colgate-Palmolive, and Delta Airlines. Knowledge Direct provides a portal for accessing course content online, along with hands-free administration features such as student registration and assessment tools, built-in Help and Contact Support, automatic e-mail triggers to remind users of courses or deadlines, automatic e-mail acknowledgement of course completions, and Web-based reporting for courses accessed. Knowledge Direct also provides a company-branded login for each client firm and enables CVM to create and assign a company administrator who has access to the student reporting tool for that company.

11.3 KNOWLEDGE WORK SYSTEMS

The enterprise-wide knowledge systems we have just described provide a wide range of capabilities that can be used by many if not all the workers and groups in an organization. Firms also have specialized systems for knowledge workers to help them create new knowledge and to ensure that this knowledge is properly integrated into the business.

KNOWLEDGE WORKERS AND KNOWLEDGE WORK

Knowledge workers, which we introduced in Chapter 1, include researchers, designers, architects, scientists, and engineers who primarily create knowledge and information for the organization. Knowledge workers usually have high levels of education and memberships in professional organizations and are often asked to exercise independent judgment as a routine aspect of their work. For example, knowledge workers create new products or find ways of improving existing ones. Knowledge workers perform three key roles that are critical to the organization and to the managers who work within the organization:

- Keeping the organization current in knowledge as it develops in the external world—in technology, science, social thought, and the arts
- Serving as internal consultants regarding the areas of their knowledge, the changes taking place, and opportunities

- Acting as change agents, evaluating, initiating, and promoting change projects

REQUIREMENTS OF KNOWLEDGE WORK SYSTEMS

Most knowledge workers rely on office systems, such as word processors, voice mail, e-mail, videoconferencing, and scheduling systems, which are designed to increase worker productivity in the office. However, knowledge workers also require highly specialized knowledge work systems with powerful graphics, analytical tools, and communications and document management capabilities.

These systems require sufficient computing power to handle the sophisticated graphics or complex calculations necessary for such knowledge workers as scientific researchers, product designers, and financial analysts. Because knowledge workers are so focused on knowledge in the external world, these systems also must give the worker quick and easy access to external databases. They typically feature user-friendly interfaces that enable users to perform needed tasks without having to spend a great deal of time learning how to use the system. Knowledge workers are highly paid—wasting a knowledge worker's time is simply too expensive. Figure 11.4 summarizes the requirements of knowledge work systems.

Knowledge workstations often are designed and optimized for the specific tasks to be performed; so, for example, a design engineer requires a different workstation setup than a financial analyst. Design engineers need graphics with enough power to handle three-dimensional (3-D) CAD systems. However, financial analysts are more interested in access to a myriad number of external databases and large databases for efficiently storing and accessing massive amounts of financial data.

FIGURE 11.4   REQUIREMENTS OF KNOWLEDGE WORK SYSTEMS

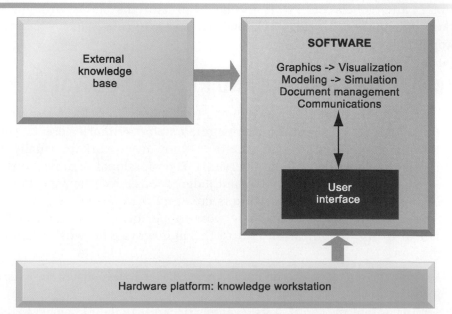

Knowledge work systems require strong links to external knowledge bases in addition to specialized hardware and software.

EXAMPLES OF KNOWLEDGE WORK SYSTEMS

Major knowledge work applications include CAD systems, virtual reality systems for simulation and modeling, and financial workstations. **Computer-aided design (CAD)** automates the creation and revision of designs, using computers and sophisticated graphics software. Using a more traditional physical design methodology, each design modification requires a mold to be made and a prototype to be tested physically. That process must be repeated many times, which is a very expensive and time-consuming process. Using a CAD workstation, the designer need only make a physical prototype toward the end of the design process because the design can be easily tested and changed on the computer. The ability of CAD software to provide design specifications for the tooling and manufacturing processes also saves a great deal of time and money while producing a manufacturing process with far fewer problems. The Interactive Session on Technology illustrates some of these benefits, and shows how they can be a source of competitive advantage.

CAD systems are able to supply data for **3-D printing**, also know known as additive manufacturing, which uses machines to make solid objects, layer by layer, from specifications in a digital file. 3-D printing is currently being used for producing prototypes and small items, such as jewelry and hip implants, as well as aircraft parts. In the future, it may be used for custom-fabricating parts for autos and military equipment.

Virtual reality systems have visualization, rendering, and simulation capabilities that go far beyond those of conventional CAD systems. They use interactive graphics software to create computer-generated simulations that are so close to reality that users almost believe they are participating in a real-world situation. In many virtual reality systems, the user dons special clothing, headgear, and equipment, depending on the application. The clothing contains sensors that record the user's movements and immediately transmit

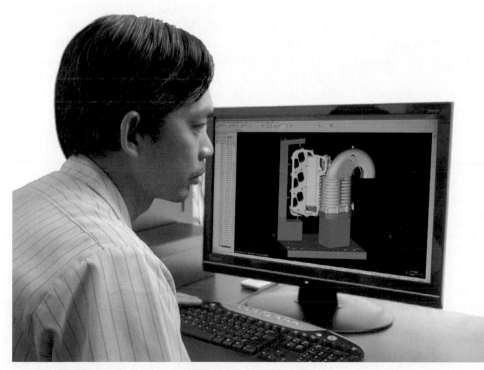

CAD systems improve the quality and precision of product design by performing much of the design and testing work on the computer.

INTERACTIVE SESSION: TECHNOLOGY

FIREWIRE SURFBOARDS LIGHTS UP WITH CAD

Nev Hyman had been building surfboards in Australia for 35 years. In 2005, he teamed up with Mark Price and a group of longtime surfing friends in Carlsbad, California, to form Firewire Surfboards. This company thrives on innovation and was responsible for the first major change in surfboard composition and assembly methods in 40 years. Rather than polyurethane resin and polyurethane foam, Firewire's boards were composed of expanded polystyrene (EPS) foam and epoxy resins. Hyman and Price believed that this composition for the surfboard core, along with aerospace composites for the deck skin and balsa wood rails (the outside edge),created a more flexible and maneuverable product that would attract top surfers and set Firewire apart from its competitors.

Firewire is competing in a crowded field that includes Isle Surfboards, Surftech, Aviso Surf, Board works Surf, Channel Island, and Lost Enterprises. Firewire is alone in the reintroduction of balsa wood to the board rails for added flex response time and the ability to maintain speed during precarious maneuvers. Firewire believes it can compete successfully because its surfboards are far lighter, stronger, and more flexible than those of its competitors. An additional selling point is the reduced environmental impact: Firewire's materials emit only 2 percent of the harmful compounds of traditional boards and recycling excess expanded polystyrene (EPS) foam has earned Firewire international awards and acclaim.

But that isn't enough. To make sure it stays ahead of the competition, Firewire decided to start making custom surfboards instead of just the usual off-the-rack sizes. For the everyday surfer, the durability and flexibility of Firewire's materials was a key selling point. However, custom boards made to surfer specifications are critical in the elite surfboard market, and the ability to claim top-level competitive surfers as customers drives the broader surfboard market as well.

Traditionally, skilled craftsman, called shapers, designed and built surfboards by hand, but Firewire started doing some of this work using computer-aided designs (CAD) sent to cutting facilities. The company's computer-aided manufacturing process returned to the shaper a board that was 85 to 90 percent complete, leaving the artisan to complete the customization and the lamination process.

According to Price, who became Firewire's CEO, there are 29 time-consuming and labor-intensive steps in the surfboard manufacturing process. Initially, the multifaceted manufacturing process made it impossible to offer personalized CAD to the average consumer. Customized boards could only be produced for elite competitive customers. There was no way to offer customization to a wider market without overburdening Firewire's CAD system. Moreover, most custom boards had to be ordered by filling out a piece of paper with various dimensions for the requested changes. There was no way to see a visual representation of these adjustments or assess their impact on the board's volume, which directly affects buoyancy, paddling ability, and performance.

Firewire needed a system that would allow customers to experiment with established designs, feed the CAD process, and integrate it with its computer numerical control (CNC) manufacturing process. Enter ShapeLogic Design-to-Order Live! For NX, which provides an online customization system with a Web-based user interface and advanced 3-D CAD tools.

Firewire started working with the ShapeLogic NX software in 2009 to develop its own Firewire Surfboards' Custom Board Design (CBD) system, which allows users to easily manipulate board dimensions of established models within design parameters. Any registered customer can choose a standard Firewire model and use drag-and-drop tools to adjust the board's length, midpoint width, nose width, tail width, and thickness, as long as these changes don't degrade the board's design integrity. CBD generates a precise three-dimensional model of the stock model used as the base design along with a 3-D portable document format (PDF) file of the customized board. The PDF file documents the board's dimensions and volume. A customer can manipulate the model from all angles and compare the customized board to the standard board to fully understand the design before placing an order. When the customer uses the system to order a custom board, CBD generates a precise solid CAD model of the board that is transmitted directly to the Firewire factory for driving the CNC machines that manufacture the board.

This combination of technologies results in a board that is 97 percent complete, minimizing the manufacturing time, finishing process, and thus, costs to the consumer. In contrast to the earlier CAD assisted, 10 to 15 percent hand-finished boards, once a surfer has designed the board of his or her dreams, it can be remade to those exact specifications time and again. Neither the ideal handmade board nor a shaper-finished board can be replicated with this degree of precision.

An additional benefit of Firewire's online design system is the social networking engendered by the sharing of customers' unique design files. Before placing an order, customers can show their modifications to fellow surfers and ask for opinions and advice. After placing an order and using the product, they can report their experiences and (hopefully)

tout their design or suggest improvements to other customers. Interactive communication such as this drives customers to the Firewire site, creating a marketing buzz that boosts sales.

Sources: "Case Study: NX CAD technology drives custom surfboard design," http://www.plm.automation.siemens.com/en_us, accessed June 14, 2012; "Firewire Surfboards by Nev Hyman," www.allaboutsurfboards.com, accessed June 14, 2012; "Firewire Partners with NanoTune 'Board Tuning Technology,'" www.surfnewsdaily.com, February 22, 2012; William Atkinson, "How Firewire Surfboards Refined Its 3D Order Customization," www.cioinsight. com, November 21, 2011; "Firewire Surfboards Custom Board Design Blends Replicability of Machine Made Boards With Uniqueness of Custom Boards," http://surfingnewsdaily.com, October 12, 2011; and "Firewire Surfboards Garner Recognition for Technological Advances," www.surfermag.com, July 22, 2010.

CASE STUDY QUESTIONS

1. Analyze Firewire using the value chain and competitive forces models.

2. What strategies is Firewire using to differentiate its product, reach its customers, and persuade them to buy its products?

3. What is the role of CAD in Firewire's business model?

4. How did the integration of online custom board design software (CBD), CAD, and computer numerical control (CNC) improve Firewire's operations?

that information back to the computer. For instance, to walk through a virtual reality simulation of a house, you would need garb that monitors the movement of your feet, hands, and head. You also would need goggles containing video screens and sometimes audio attachments and feeling gloves so that you can be immersed in the computer feedback.

At NYU Langone Medical Center in New York City, students wearing 3-D glasses are able to "dissect" a virtual cadaver projected on a screen. With the help of a computer, they can move through the virtual body, scrutinizing layers of muscles or watching a close-up of a pumping heart along with bright red arteries and deep blue veins. The virtual human body was created by BioDigital Systems, a New York City medical visualization firm. The virtual cadaver being used at Langone is a beta version that BioDigital plans to develop into a searchable, customizable map of the human body for medical educators and physicians. NYU medical school has no current plans to phase out dissection, but the 3-D virtual cadaver is a valuable complementary teaching tool (Singer, 2012).

Ford Motor Company has been using virtual reality to help design its vehicles. In one example of Ford's Immersive Virtual Environment, a designer was presented with a car seat, steering wheel, and blank dashboard. Wearing virtual reality glasses and gloves with sensors, the designer was able to "sit" in the seat surrounded by the vehicle's 3-D design to experience how a proposed interior would look and feel. The designer would be able to identify blind spots or see if knobs were in an awkward place. Ford's designers could also use this technology to see the impact of a design on manufacturing. For example, is a bolt that assembly line workers need to tighten too hard to reach (Murphy, 2012)?

Augmented reality (AR) is a related technology for enhancing visualization. AR provides a live direct or indirect view of a physical real-world environment whose elements are augmented by virtual computer-generated imagery. The user is grounded in the real physical world, and the virtual images are merged with the real view to create the augmented display. The digital technology provides additional information to enhance the perception of reality, making the surrounding real world of the user more interactive and meaningful. The yellow first-down markers shown on televised football games are examples of augmented reality as are medical procedures like image-guided surgery, where data acquired from computerized tomography (CT) and magnetic resonance imaging (MRI) scans or from ultrasound imaging are superimposed on the patient in the operating room. Other industries where AR has caught on include military training, engineering design, robotics, and consumer design.

Virtual reality applications developed for the Web use a standard called **Virtual Reality Modeling Language (VRML)**. VRML is a set of specifications for interactive, 3-D modeling on the World Wide Web that can organize multiple media types, including animation, images, and audio to put users in a simulated real-world environment. VRML is platform independent, operates over a desktop computer, and requires little bandwidth.

DuPont, the Wilmington, Delaware, chemical company, created a VRML application called HyperPlant, which enables users to access 3-D data over the Internet using Web browser software. Engineers can go through 3-D models as if they were physically walking through a plant, viewing objects at eye level. This level of detail reduces the number of mistakes they make during construction of oil rigs, oil plants, and other structures.

The financial industry is using specialized **investment workstations** such as Bloomberg Terminals to leverage the knowledge and time of its brokers, traders, and portfolio managers. Firms such as Merrill Lynch and UBS Financial Services have installed investment workstations that integrate a wide range of data from both internal and external sources, including contact management data, real-time and historical market data, and research reports. Previously, financial professionals had to spend considerable time accessing data from separate systems and piecing together the information they needed. By providing one-stop information faster and with fewer errors, the workstations streamline the entire investment process from stock selection to updating client records. Table 11.2 summarizes the major types of knowledge work systems.

TABLE 11.2 EXAMPLES OF KNOWLEDGE WORK SYSTEMS

KNOWLEDGE WORK SYSTEM	FUNCTION IN ORGANIZATION
CAD/CAM (computer-aided manufacturing)	Provides engineers, designers, and factory managers with precise control over industrial design and manufacturing
Virtual reality systems	Provide drug designers, architects, engineers, and medical workers with precise, photorealistic simulations of objects
Investment workstations	High-end PCs used in the financial sector to analyze trading situations instantaneously and facilitate portfolio management

11.4   INTELLIGENT TECHNIQUES

Artificial intelligence and database technology provide a number of intelligent techniques that organizations can use to capture individual and collective knowledge and to extend their knowledge base. Expert systems, case-based reasoning, and fuzzy logic are used for capturing tacit knowledge. Neural networks and data mining are used for **knowledge discovery**. They can discover underlying patterns, categories, and behaviors in large data sets that could not be discovered by managers alone or simply through experience. Genetic algorithms are used for generating solutions to problems that are too large and complex for human beings to analyze on their own. Intelligent agents can automate routine tasks to help firms search for and filter information for use in electronic commerce, supply chain management, and other activities.

Data mining, which we introduced in Chapter 6, helps organizations capture undiscovered knowledge residing in large databases, providing managers with new insight for improving business performance. It has become an important tool for management decision making, and we provide a detailed discussion of data mining for management decision support in Chapter 12.

The other intelligent techniques discussed in this section are based on **artificial intelligence (AI)** technology, which consists of computer-based systems (both hardware and software) that attempt to emulate human behavior. Such systems would be able to learn languages, accomplish physical tasks, use a perceptual apparatus, and emulate human expertise and decision making. Although AI applications do not exhibit the breadth, complexity, originality, and generality of human intelligence, they play an important role in contemporary knowledge management.

CAPTURING KNOWLEDGE: EXPERT SYSTEMS

Expert systems are an intelligent technique for capturing tacit knowledge in a very specific and limited domain of human expertise. These systems capture the knowledge of skilled employees in the form of a set of rules in a software system that can be used by others in the organization. The set of rules in the expert system adds to the memory, or stored learning, of the firm.

Expert systems lack the breadth of knowledge and the understanding of fundamental principles of a human expert. They typically perform very limited tasks that can be performed by professionals in a few minutes or hours, such as diagnosing a malfunctioning machine or determining whether to grant credit for a loan. Problems that cannot be solved by human experts in the same short period of time are far too difficult for an expert system. However, by capturing human expertise in limited areas, expert systems can provide benefits, helping organizations make high-quality decisions with fewer people. Today, expert systems are widely used in business in discrete, highly structured decision-making situations.

How Expert Systems Work

Human knowledge must be modeled or represented in a way that a computer can process. Expert systems model human knowledge as a set of rules that collectively are called the **knowledge base**. Expert systems have from 200 to many thousands of these rules, depending on the complexity of the problem. These rules are much more interconnected and nested than in a traditional software program (see Figure 11.5).

FIGURE 11.5 RULES IN AN EXPERT SYSTEM

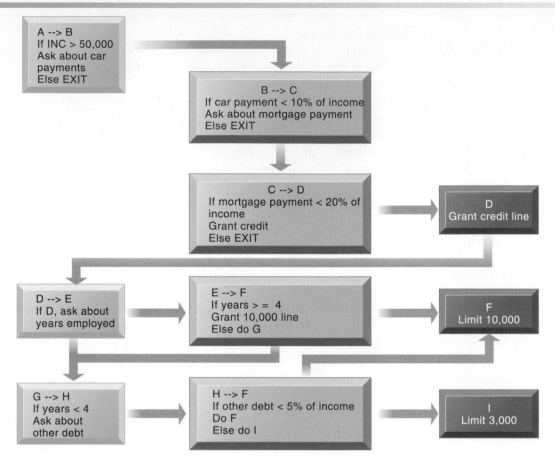

An expert system contains a number of rules to be followed. The rules are interconnected; the number of outcomes is known in advance and is limited; there are multiple paths to the same outcome; and the system can consider multiple rules at a single time. The rules illustrated are for simple credit-granting expert systems.

FIGURE 11.6 INFERENCE ENGINES IN EXPERT SYSTEMS

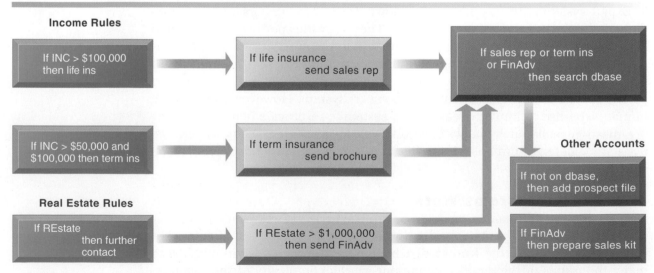

An inference engine works by searching through the rules and "firing" those rules that are triggered by facts gathered and entered by the user. Basically, a collection of rules is similar to a series of nested IF statements in a traditional software program; however, the magnitude of the statements and degree of nesting are much greater in an expert system.

The strategy used to search through the knowledge base is called the **inference engine**. Two strategies are commonly used: forward chaining and backward chaining (see Figure 11.6).

In **forward chaining,** the inference engine begins with the information entered by the user and searches the rule base to arrive at a conclusion. The strategy is to fire, or carry out, the action of the rule when a condition is true. In Figure 11.6, beginning on the left, if the user enters a client's name with income greater than $100,000, the engine will fire all rules in sequence from left to right. If the user then enters information indicating that the same client owns real estate, another pass of the rule base will occur and more rules will fire. Processing continues until no more rules can be fired.

In **backward chaining,** the strategy for searching the rule base starts with a hypothesis and proceeds by asking the user questions about selected facts until the hypothesis is either confirmed or disproved. In our example, in Figure 11.6, ask the question, "Should we add this person to the prospect database?" Begin on the right of the diagram and work toward the left. You can see that the person should be added to the database if a sales representative is sent, term insurance is granted, or a financial adviser visits the client.

Examples of Successful Expert Systems

Expert systems provide businesses with an array of benefits including improved decisions, reduced errors, reduced costs, reduced training time, and higher levels of quality and service. Con-Way Transportation built an expert system called Line-haul to automate and optimize planning of overnight shipment routes for its nationwide freight-trucking business. The expert system captures the business rules that dispatchers follow when assigning drivers, trucks, and trailers to transport 50,000 shipments of heavy freight each night across 25 states and Canada and when plotting their routes. Line-haul runs on a Sun computer platform and uses data on daily customer shipment requests, available drivers, trucks, trailer space, and weight stored in an Oracle database. The expert system uses thousands of rules and 100,000 lines of program code written in C++ to crunch the numbers and create optimum routing plans for 95 percent of daily freight shipments. Con-Way dispatchers tweak the routing plan provided by the expert system and relay final routing specifications to field personnel responsible for packing the trailers for their nighttime runs. Con-Way recouped its $3 million investment in the system within two years by reducing the number of drivers, packing more freight per trailer, and reducing damage from rehandling. The system also reduces dispatchers' arduous nightly tasks.

Although expert systems lack the robust and general intelligence of human beings, they can provide benefits to organizations if their limitations are well understood. Only certain classes of problems can be solved using expert systems. Virtually all successful expert systems deal with problems of classification in limited domains of knowledge where there are relatively few alternative outcomes and these possible outcomes are all known in advance. Expert systems are much less useful for dealing with unstructured problems typically encountered by managers.

Many expert systems require large, lengthy, and expensive development efforts. Hiring or training more experts may be less expensive than building an expert system. Typically, the environment in which an expert system operates is continually changing so that the expert system must also continually change.

Some expert systems, especially large ones, are so complex that in a few years the maintenance costs equal the development costs.

ORGANIZATIONAL INTELLIGENCE: CASE-BASED REASONING

Expert systems primarily capture the tacit knowledge of individual experts, but organizations also have collective knowledge and expertise that they have built up over the years. This organizational knowledge can be captured and stored using case-based reasoning. In **case-based reasoning (CBR)**, descriptions of past experiences of human specialists, represented as cases, are stored in a database for later retrieval when the user encounters a new case with similar parameters. The system searches for stored cases with problem characteristics similar to the new one, finds the closest fit, and applies the solutions of the old case to the new case. Successful solutions are tagged to the new case and both are stored together with the other cases in the knowledge base. Unsuccessful solutions also are appended to the case database along with explanations as to why the solutions did not work (see Figure 11.7).

Expert systems work by applying a set of IF-THEN-ELSE rules extracted from human experts. Case-based reasoning, in contrast, represents knowledge as a

FIGURE 11.7 HOW CASE-BASED REASONING WORKS

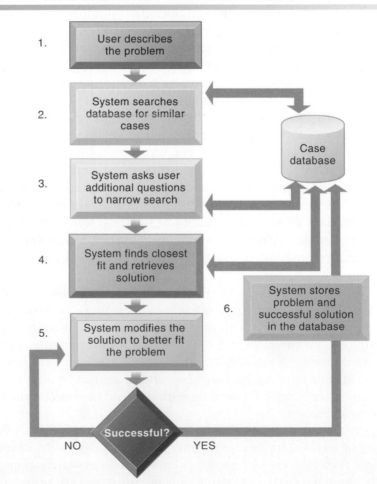

Case-based reasoning represents knowledge as a database of past cases and their solutions. The system uses a six-step process to generate solutions to new problems encountered by the user.

series of cases, and this knowledge base is continuously expanded and refined by users. You'll find case-based reasoning in diagnostic systems in medicine or customer support where users can retrieve past cases whose characteristics are similar to the new case. The system suggests a solution or diagnosis based on the best-matching retrieved case.

FUZZY LOGIC SYSTEMS

Most people do not think in terms of traditional IF-THEN rules or precise numbers. Humans tend to categorize things imprecisely using rules for making decisions that may have many shades of meaning. For example, a man or a woman can be *strong* or *intelligent*. A company can be *large*, *medium*, or *small* in size. Temperature can be *hot*, *cold*, *cool*, or *warm*. These categories represent a range of values.

Fuzzy logic is a rule-based technology that can represent such imprecision by creating rules that use approximate or subjective values. It can describe a particular phenomenon or process linguistically and then represent that description in a small number of flexible rules. Organizations can use fuzzy logic to create software systems that capture tacit knowledge where there is linguistic ambiguity.

Let's look at the way fuzzy logic would represent various temperatures in a computer application to control room temperature automatically. The terms (known as *membership functions*) are imprecisely defined so that, for example, in Figure 11.8, cool is between 45 degrees and 70 degrees, although the temperature is most clearly cool between about 60 degrees and 67 degrees. Note that *cool* is overlapped by *cold* or *norm*. To control the room environment using this logic, the programmer would develop similarly imprecise definitions for humidity and other factors, such as outdoor wind and temperature. The rules might include one that says: "If the temperature is *cool* or *cold* and the humidity is low while the outdoor wind is high and the outdoor temperature is low, raise the heat and humidity in the room."

FIGURE 11.8 FUZZY LOGIC FOR TEMPERATURE CONTROL

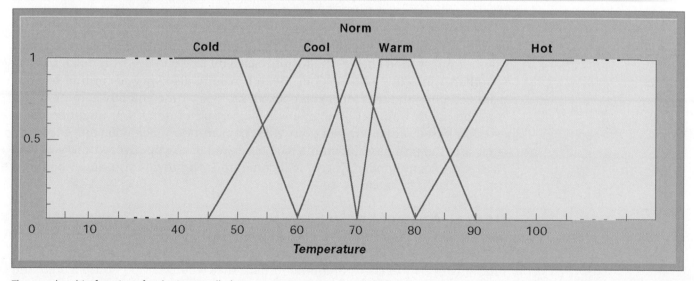

The membership functions for the input called temperature are in the logic of the thermostat to control the room temperature. Membership functions help translate linguistic expressions such as *warm* into numbers that the computer can manipulate.

The computer would combine the membership function readings in a weighted manner and, using all the rules, raise and lower the temperature and humidity.

Fuzzy logic provides solutions to problems requiring expertise that is difficult to represent in the form of crisp IF-THEN rules. In Japan, Sendai's subway system uses fuzzy logic controls to accelerate so smoothly that standing passengers need not hold on. Mitsubishi Heavy Industries in Tokyo has been able to reduce the power consumption of its air conditioners by 20 percent by implementing control programs in fuzzy logic. The autofocus device in cameras is only possible because of fuzzy logic. In these instances, fuzzy logic allows incremental changes in inputs to produce smooth changes in outputs instead of discontinuous ones, making it useful for consumer electronics and engineering applications.

Management also has found fuzzy logic useful for decision making and organizational control. A Wall Street firm created a system that selects companies for potential acquisition, using the language stock traders understand. A fuzzy logic system has been developed to detect possible fraud in medical claims submitted by health care providers anywhere in the United States.

MACHINE LEARNING

Machine learning is the study of how computer programs can improve their performance without explicit programming. Why does this constitute learning? A machine that learns is a machine that, like a human being, can recognize patterns in data, and change its behavior based on its recognition of patterns, experience, or prior learnings (a database). For instance, a car-driving robot should be able to recognize the presence of other cars and objects (people), and change its behavior accordingly (stop, go, slow down, speed up, or turn). The idea of a self-taught, self-correcting, computer program is not new, and has been a part of the artificial intelligence field at least since the 1970s. Up until the 1990s, however, machine learning was not very capable of producing useful devices or solving interesting, business problems.

Machine learning has expanded greatly in the last ten years because of the growth in computing power available to scientists and firms and its falling cost, along with advances in the design of algorithms, databases, and robots. The Internet and the big data (see Chapter 6) made available on the Internet have proved to be very useful testing and proving grounds for machine learning.

We use machine learning everyday but don't recognize it. Every Google search is resolved using algorithms that rank the billions of Web pages based on your query, and change the results based on any changes you make in your search, all in a few milliseconds. Search results also vary according to your prior searches and the items you clicked on. Every time you buy something on Amazon, its recommender engine will suggest other items you might be interested in based on patterns in your prior consumption, behavior on other Web sites, and the purchases of others who are "similar" to you. Every time you visit Netflix, a recommender system will come up with movies you might be interested in based on a similar set of factors.

Neural Networks

Neural networks are used for solving complex, poorly understood problems for which large amounts of data have been collected. They find patterns and relationships in massive amounts of data that would be too complicated and difficult for a human being to analyze. Neural networks discover this knowledge by using hardware and software that parallel the processing patterns of

INTERACTIVE SESSION: ORGANIZATIONS

ALBASSAMI'S JOB IS NOT FEASIBLE WITHOUT IT

If you live in a country with a diverse geography and a climate characterized as being harsh, with a dry desert and great temperature extremes like the Kingdom of Saudi Arabia (area: 2.1 million square kilometers), and you need to move from one city to another, where the distance could be some thousand kilometers, you have two choices: to drive, or to fly and ship your car via a car transport carrier. Many people in the Kingdom prefer the second option. This has created a market for car transportation in the Kingdom that is the largest in the Middle East. Albassami was established to respond to these market needs. The Albassami International Group is considered one of the leading land transporters in the Middle East.

The estimated size of the car transportation market, both inside the Kingdom and with neighboring countries, is about 2 billion Saudi riyals and is increasing considerably annually. There are more than a million cars transported inside and outside the Kingdom. Albassami International Group owns the largest fleet of carriers in the Middle East.

At present, the group is operating all over the Kingdom and extends throughout the Gulf Cooperation Council (GCC) countries, Syria, Lebanon, and Jordan. Throughout these years the company has focused on how to maintain business leadership in order to achieve safe and fast transportation.

Every day there are more than 1,000 shipping contracts, including 2,000 to 2,500 bills of lading daily between the main branches. With the introduction of its new division of Express transportation in 2003, the group owns and allocates 170 heavy duty, medium, and light vehicles of various types for its door-to-door courier services, which operate all over the Kingdom, covering more than 45 locations. It was therefore impossible to properly handle and control the endless number of daily work options and orders related to these operations at a perfect level of service without a robust computerized system. The system needed the facility to serve specific sectors in the organization, in addition to providing information throughout the group.

The system is based on clustered Dell servers running Windows 2003 and connected to over 270 Windows XP clients. The database management system, used as the backbone of the system, is Sybase Adaptive server, whereas clients use SQL Anywhere.

There is replication between the server at head quarters and the client's branches. Throughout the replication, branches' data is sent to the server and aggregated to create the most updated database version, and then sent back to the branches. This means every branch has the most recent version of the client list, trucks' availability, and new shipping contracts so that any customer is able to deal with any branch at any time.

The business process starts when the customer goes to a branch to ship his car to a destination within shipping areas, and the branch then creates a shipping agreement. As the database is sent from the branch to HQ every 30 minutes, an aggregated version of the database of all branches is available at HQ and thereafter sent back to all branches. The recipient branch will create a receipt entry on the system upon arrival of the truck and then an SMS message is created and sent to the customer, who will then go to the destination branch to receive the car.

The shipping information system used at Albassami maintains all the sender information such as the sent car, the truck number, the sender and receiving branches, and it also sends an SMS message to the client acknowledging the arrival of the car. The system also records the client's data, and holds maintenance information. Linking the data of vehicle maintenance centers with the transportation service helps to enhance company performance and achieve better customer service. The system also enables standard reports to be provided to top management and head sectors about the productivity of each branch, resulting in accurate identification of needs for different regions and thus proper budget allocation. In addition, the system allowed a better audit on all drivers' behavior by using the output of the vehicles' tracking information. Proper performance monitoring resulted in adequate employees' appraisals and consequently loyal staff!

All business processes are facilitated by the shipping system, and the knowledge extracted from the central database has enabled the management team to make sound investment and operational decisions and therefore helped the business maintain its success and leadership in the Kingdom.

Sources: Michael Fitzgerald, "Predicting Where You'll Go and What You'll Like," The New York Times, June 22, 2008; Erick Schonfeld, "Location-Tracking Startup Sense Networks Emerges from Stealth to Answer the Question: Where Is Everybody?" TechCrunch.com, June 9, 2008; "Macrosense," sensenetworks.com, accessed July 2008; Caroline McCarthy, "Meet Sense Networks, the Latest Player in the Hot 'Geo' Market," news.cnet.com, June 9, 2008.

Case contributed by Dr Ahmed Elragal, German University in Cairo

CASE STUDY QUESTIONS

1. What systems are described here? What valuable information do they provide?

2. What value did the IT/IS investments add to Albassami?

3. How did implementing the Shipping Information System address the business needs and information requirements of Albassami?

the biological or human brain. Neural networks "learn" patterns from large quantities of data by sifting through data, searching for relationships, building models, and correcting over and over again the model's own mistakes.

A neural network has a large number of sensing and processing nodes that continuously interact with each other. Figure 11.9 represents one type of neural network comprising an input layer, an output layer, and a hidden processing layer. Humans "train" the network by feeding it a set of training data for which the inputs produce a known set of outputs or conclusions. This helps the computer learn the correct solution by example. As the computer is fed more data, each case is compared with the known outcome. If it differs, a correction is calculated and applied to the nodes in the hidden processing layer. These steps are repeated until a condition, such as corrections being less than a certain amount, is reached. The neural network in Figure 11.9 has learned how to identify a fraudulent credit card

FIGURE 11.9 **HOW A NEURAL NETWORK WORKS**

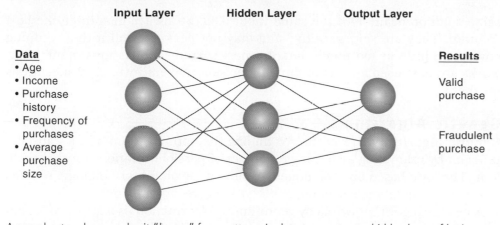

A neural network uses rules it "learns" from patterns in data to construct a hidden layer of logic. The hidden layer then processes inputs, classifying them based on the experience of the model. In this example, the neural network has been trained to distinguish between valid and fraudulent credit card purchases.

purchase. Also, self-organizing neural networks can be trained by exposing them to large amounts of data and allowing them to discover the patterns and relationships in the data.

A Google research team headed by Stanford University computer scientist Andrew Y. Ng and Google fellow Jeff Dean recently created a neural network with more than one billion connections that could identify cats. The network used an array of 16,000 processors and was fed random thumbnails of images, each extracted from a collection of 10 million YouTube videos. The neural network taught itself to recognize cats, without human help in identifying specific features during the learning process. Google believes this neural network has promising applications in image search, speech recognition, and machine language translation (Markoff, 2012).

Whereas expert systems seek to emulate or model a human expert's way of solving problems, neural network builders claim that they do not program solutions and do not aim to solve specific problems. Instead, neural network designers seek to put intelligence into the hardware in the form of a generalized capability to learn. In contrast, the expert system is highly specific to a given problem and cannot be retrained easily.

Neural network applications in medicine, science, and business address problems in pattern classification, prediction, financial analysis, and control and optimization. In medicine, neural network applications are used for screening patients for coronary artery disease, for diagnosing patients with epilepsy and Alzheimer's disease, and for performing pattern recognition of pathology images. The financial industry uses neural networks to discern patterns in vast pools of data that might help predict the performance of equities, corporate bond ratings, or corporate bankruptcies. Visa International uses a neural network to help detect credit card fraud by monitoring all Visa transactions for sudden changes in the buying patterns of cardholders.

There are many puzzling aspects of neural networks. Unlike expert systems, which typically provide explanations for their solutions, neural networks cannot always explain why they arrived at a particular solution. Moreover, they cannot always guarantee a completely certain solution, arrive at the same solution again with the same input data, or always guarantee the best solution. They are very sensitive and may not perform well if their training covers too little or too much data. In most current applications, neural networks are best used as aids to human decision makers instead of substitutes for them.

Genetic Algorithms

Genetic algorithms are useful for finding the optimal solution for a specific problem by examining a very large number of possible solutions for that problem. They are based on techniques inspired by evolutionary biology, such as inheritance, mutation, selection, and crossover (recombination).

A genetic algorithm works by representing information as a string of 0s and 1s. The genetic algorithm searches a population of randomly generated strings of binary digits to identify the right string representing the best possible solution for the problem. As solutions alter and combine, the worst ones are discarded and the better ones survive to go on to produce even better solutions.

In Figure 11.10, each string corresponds to one of the variables in the problem. One applies a test for fitness, ranking the strings in the population according to their level of desirability as possible solutions. After the initial population is evaluated for fitness, the algorithm then produces the next generation of strings, consisting of strings that survived the fitness test plus offspring strings produced from mating pairs of strings, and tests their fitness. The process continues until a solution is reached.

Genetic algorithms are used to solve problems that are very dynamic and complex, involving hundreds or thousands of variables or formulas. The problem must be one where the range of possible solutions can be represented genetically and criteria can be established for evaluating fitness. Genetic algorithms expedite the solution because they are able to evaluate many solution alternatives quickly to find the best one. For example, General

FIGURE 11.10 THE COMPONENTS OF A GENETIC ALGORITHM

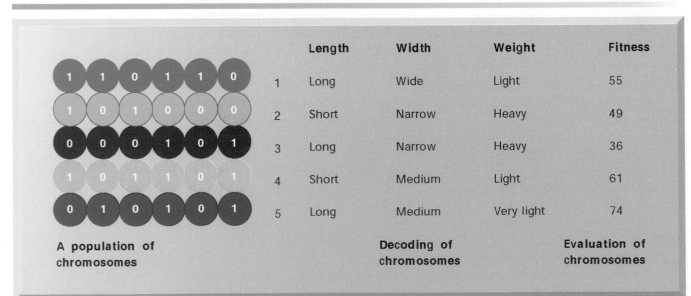

	Length	Width	Weight	Fitness
1	Long	Wide	Light	55
2	Short	Narrow	Heavy	49
3	Long	Narrow	Heavy	36
4	Short	Medium	Light	61
5	Long	Medium	Very light	74

A population of chromosomes — **Decoding of chromosomes** — **Evaluation of chromosomes**

This example illustrates an initial population of "chromosomes," each representing a different solution. The genetic algorithm uses an iterative process to refine the initial solutions so that the better ones, those with the higher fitness, are more likely to emerge as the best solution.

Electric engineers used genetic algorithms to help optimize the design for jet turbine aircraft engines, where each design change required changes in up to 100 variables. The supply chain management software from i2 Technologies uses genetic algorithms to optimize production-scheduling models incorporating hundreds of thousands of details about customer orders, material and resource availability, manufacturing and distribution capability, and delivery dates.

INTELLIGENT AGENTS

Intelligent agent technology helps businesses navigate through large amounts of data to locate and act on information that is considered important. **Intelligent agents** are software programs that work without direct human intervention to carry out specific tasks for an individual user, business process, or software application. The agent uses a built-in or learned knowledge base to accomplish tasks or make decisions on the user's behalf, such as deleting junk e-mail, scheduling appointments, or traveling over interconnected networks to find the cheapest airfare to California.

There are many intelligent agent applications today in operating systems, application software, e-mail systems, mobile computing software, and network tools. For example, the wizards found in Microsoft Office software tools have built-in capabilities to show users how to accomplish various tasks, such as formatting documents or creating graphs, and to anticipate when users need assistance. Chapter 10 describes how intelligent agent shopping bots can help consumers find products they want and assist them in comparing prices and other features.

Although some intelligent agents are programmed to follow a simple set of rules, others are capable of learning from experience and adjusting their behavior. Siri, an application on Apple's iOS operating system for the iPhone and iPad, is an example. Siri is an intelligent personal assistant that uses voice recognition technology to answer questions, make recommendations, and perform actions. The software adapts to the user's individual preferences over time and personalizes results, performing tasks such as finding nearby restaurants, purchasing movie tickets, getting directions, scheduling appointments, and sending messages. Siri understands natural speech, and it asks the user questions if it needs more information to complete a task. Siri does not process speech input locally on the users's device. Instead, it sends commands through a remote server, so users have to be connected to Wi-Fi or a 3G signal.

Many complex phenomena can be modeled as systems of autonomous agents that follow relatively simple rules for interaction. **Agent-based modeling** applications have been developed to model the behavior of consumers, stock markets, and supply chains and to predict the spread of epidemics.

Procter & Gamble (P&G) used agent-based modeling to improve coordination among different members of its supply chain in response to changing business conditions (see Figure 11.11). It modeled a complex supply chain as a group of semiautonomous "agents" representing individual supply chain components, such as trucks, production facilities, distributors, and retail stores. The behavior of each agent is programmed to follow rules that mimic actual behavior, such as "order an item when it is out of stock." Simulations using the agents enable the company to perform what-if analyses on inventory levels, in-store stockouts, and transportation costs.

FIGURE 11.11 **INTELLIGENT AGENTS IN P&G'S SUPPLY CHAIN NETWORK**

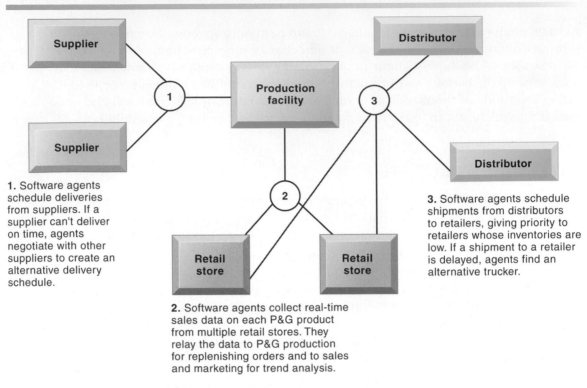

1. Software agents schedule deliveries from suppliers. If a supplier can't deliver on time, agents negotiate with other suppliers to create an alternative delivery schedule.

2. Software agents collect real-time sales data on each P&G product from multiple retail stores. They relay the data to P&G production for replenishing orders and to sales and marketing for trend analysis.

3. Software agents schedule shipments from distributors to retailers, giving priority to retailers whose inventories are low. If a shipment to a retailer is delayed, agents find an alternative trucker.

Intelligent agents are helping P&G shorten the replenishment cycles for products such as a box of Tide.

Using intelligent agent models, P&G discovered that trucks should often be dispatched before being fully loaded. Although transportation costs would be higher using partially loaded trucks, the simulation showed that retail store stockouts would occur less often, thus reducing the amount of lost sales, which would more than make up for the higher distribution costs. Agent-based modeling has saved P&G $300 million annually on an investment of less than 1 percent of that amount.

HYBRID AI SYSTEMS

Genetic algorithms, fuzzy logic, neural networks, and expert systems can be integrated into a single application to take advantage of the best features of these technologies. Such systems are called **hybrid AI systems**. Hybrid applications in business are growing. In Japan, Hitachi, Mitsubishi, Ricoh, Sanyo, and others are starting to incorporate hybrid AI in products such as home appliances, factory machinery, and office equipment. Matsushita has developed a "neurofuzzy" washing machine that combines fuzzy logic with neural networks. Nikko Securities has been working on a neurofuzzy system to forecast convertible-bond ratings.

LEARNING TRACK MODULE

The following Learning Track provides content relevant to topics covered in this chapter:

1. Challenges of Knowledge Management Systems

Review Summary

1. *What is the role of knowledge management and knowledge management programs in business?*

    Knowledge management is a set of processes to create, store, transfer, and apply knowledge in the organization. Much of a firm's value depends on its ability to create and manage knowledge. Knowledge management promotes organizational learning by increasing the ability of the organization to learn from its environment and to incorporate knowledge into its business processes. There are three major types of knowledge management systems: enterprise-wide knowledge management systems, knowledge work systems, and intelligent techniques.

2. *What types of systems are used for enterprise-wide knowledge management and how do they provide value for businesses?*

    Enterprise-wide knowledge management systems are firmwide efforts to collect, store, distribute, and apply digital content and knowledge. Enterprise content management systems provide databases and tools for organizing and storing structured documents and tools for organizing and storing semistructured knowledge, such as e-mail or rich media. Knowledge network systems provide directories and tools for locating firm employees with special expertise who are important sources of tacit knowledge. Often these systems include group collaboration tools (including wikis and social bookmarking), portals to simplify information access, search tools, and tools for classifying information based on a taxonomy that is appropriate for the organization. Enterprise-wide knowledge management systems can provide considerable value if they are well designed and enable employees to locate, share, and use knowledge more efficiently.

3. *What are the major types of knowledge work systems and how do they provide value for firms?*

    Knowledge work systems (KWS) support the creation of new knowledge and its integration into the organization. KWS require easy access to an external knowledge base; powerful computer hardware that can support software with intensive graphics, analysis, document management, and communications capabilities; and a user-friendly interface. Computer-aided design (CAD) systems, augmented reality applications, and virtual reality systems, which create interactive simulations that behave like the real world, require graphics and powerful modeling capabilities. KWS for financial professionals provide access to external databases and the ability to analyze massive amounts of financial data very quickly.

4. *What are the business benefits of using intelligent techniques for knowledge management?*

    Artificial intelligence lacks the flexibility, breadth, and generality of human intelligence, but it can be used to capture, codify, and extend organizational knowledge. Expert systems capture tacit knowledge from a limited domain of human expertise and express that knowledge in the form of rules. Expert systems are most useful for problems of classification or diagnosis. Case-based reasoning represents organizational knowledge as a database of cases that can be continually expanded and refined.

    Fuzzy logic is a software technology for expressing knowledge in the form of rules that use approximate or subjective values. Fuzzy logic has been used for controlling physical devices and is starting to be used for limited decision-making applications.

    Machine learning refers to the ability of computer programs to automatically learn and improve with experience. Neural networks consist of hardware and software that attempt to mimic the thought processes of the human brain. Neural networks are notable for their ability to learn without programming and to recognize patterns that cannot be easily described by humans. They are being used in science, medicine, and business to discriminate patterns in massive amounts of data.

    Genetic algorithms develop solutions to particular problems using genetically based processes such as fitness, crossover, and mutation. Genetic algorithms are beginning to be applied to problems involving optimization, product design, and monitoring industrial systems where many alternatives or variables must be evaluated to generate an optimal solution.

    Intelligent agents are software programs with built-in or learned knowledge bases that carry out specific tasks for an individual user, business process, or software application. Intelligent agents can be programmed to navigate through large amounts of data to locate useful information and in some cases act on that information on behalf of the user.

Key Terms

3-D printing, 459
Agent-based modeling, 473
Artificial intelligence (AI), 463
Augmented reality (AR), 462
Backward chaining, 465
Case-based reasoning (CBR), 466
Communities of practice (COPs), 453
Computer-aided design (CAD), 459
Data, 449
Digital asset management systems, 456
Enterprise content management systems, 455
Enterprise-wide knowledge management systems, 453
Expert systems, 463
Explicit knowledge, 450
Folksonomies, 456
Forward chaining, 465
Fuzzy logic, 467
Genetic algorithms, 472
Hybrid AI systems, 474
Inference engine, 465

Intelligent agents, 473
Intelligent techniques, 454
Investment workstations, 462
Knowledge, 450
Knowledge base, 463
Knowledge discovery, 463
Knowledge management, 451
Knowledge network systems, 456
Knowledge work systems (KWS), 454
Learning management system (LMS), 457
Machine learning, 468
Neural networks, 468
Organizational learning, 451
Social bookmarking, 456
Structured knowledge, 455
Tacit knowledge, 450
Taxonomy, 456
Virtual Reality Modeling Language (VRML), 462
Virtual reality systems, 459
Wisdom, 450

Review Questions

1. What is the role of knowledge management and knowledge management programs in business?
   - Define knowledge management and explain its value to businesses.
   - Describe the important dimensions of knowledge.
   - Distinguish between data, knowledge, and wisdom and between tacit knowledge and explicit knowledge.
   - Describe the stages in the knowledge management value chain.

2. What types of systems are used for enterprise-wide knowledge management and how do they provide value for businesses?
   - Define and describe the various types of enterprise-wide knowledge management systems and explain how they provide value for businesses.
   - Describe the role of the following in facilitating knowledge management: portals, wikis, social bookmarking, and learning management systems.

3. What are the major types of knowledge work systems and how do they provide value for firms?
   - Define knowledge work systems and describe the generic requirements of knowledge work systems.
   - Describe how the following systems support knowledge work: CAD, virtual reality, augmented reality, and investment workstations.

4. What are the business benefits of using intelligent techniques for knowledge management?
   - Define an expert system, describe how it works, and explain its value to business.
   - Define case-based reasoning and explain how it differs from an expert system.
   - Define machine learning and give some examples.
   - Define a neural network, and describe how it works and how it benefits businesses.
   - Define and describe fuzzy logic, genetic algorithms, and intelligent agents. Explain how each works and the kinds of problems for which each is suited.

Discussion Questions

1. Knowledge management is a business process, not a technology. Discuss.

2. Describe various ways that knowledge management systems could help firms with sales and marketing or with manufacturing and production.

3. Your company wants to do more with knowledge management. Describe the steps it should take to develop a knowledge management program and select knowledge management applications.

Hands-On MIS Projects

The projects in this section give you hands-on experience designing a knowledge portal, identifying opportunities for knowledge management, creating a simple expert system, and using intelligent agents to research products for sale on the Web.

Management Decision Problems

1. U.S. Pharma Corporation is headquartered in New Jersey but has research sites in Germany, France, the United Kingdom, Switzerland, and Australia. Research and development of new pharmaceuticals is key to ongoing profits, and U.S. Pharma researches and tests thousands of possible drugs. The company's researchers need to share information with others within and outside the company, including the U.S. Food and Drug Administration, the World Health Organization, and the International Federation of Pharmaceutical Manufacturers & Associations. Also critical is access to health information sites, such as the U.S. National Library of Medicine and to industry conferences and professional journals. Design a knowledge portal for U.S. Pharma's researchers. Include in your design specifications relevant internal systems and databases, external sources of information, and internal and external communication and collaboration tools. Design a home page for your portal.

2. Canadian Tire is one of Canada's largest companies, with 57,000 employees and 1,200 stores and gas bars (gas stations) across Canada selling sports, leisure, home products, apparel; and financial services as well as automotive and petroleum products. The retail outlets are independently owned and operated. Canadian Tire was using daily mailings and thick product catalogs to inform its dealers about new products, merchandise setups, best practices, product ordering, and problem resolution and it is looking for a better way to provide employees with human resources and administrative documents. Describe the problems created by this way of doing business and how knowledge management systems might help.

Improving Decision Making: Building a Simple Expert System for Retirement Planning

Software skills: Spreadsheet formulas and IF function or expert system tool
Business skills: Benefits eligibility determination

Expert systems typically use a large number of rules. This project has been simplified to reduce the number of rules, but it will give you experience working with a series of rules to develop an application.

When employees at your company retire, they are given cash bonuses. These cash bonuses are based on the length of employment and the retiree's age. To receive a bonus, an employee must be at least 50 years of age and have worked for the company for more than five years. The following table summarizes the criteria for determining bonuses.

LENGTH OF EMPLOYMENT	BONUS
<5 years	No bonus
5–10 years	20 percent of current annual salary
11–15 years	30 percent of current annual salary
16–20 years	40 percent of current annual salary
20–25 years	50 percent of current annual salary
26 or more years	100 percent of current annual salary

Using the information provided, build a simple expert system. Find a demonstration copy of an expert system software tool on the Web that you can download. Alternatively, use your spreadsheet software to build the expert system. (If you are using spreadsheet software, we suggest using the IF function so you can see how rules are created.)

Improving Decision Making: Using Intelligent Agents for Comparison Shopping

Software skills: Web browser and shopping bot software
Business skills: Product evaluation and selection

This project will give you experience using shopping bots to search online for products, find product information, and find the best prices and vendors. Select a digital camera you might want to purchase, such as the Canon PowerShot S100 or the Olympus Tough TG-820. Visit MySimon (www.mysimon.com), BizRate.com (www.bizrate.com), and Google Product Search to do price comparisons for you. Evaluate these shopping sites in terms of their ease of use, number of offerings, speed in obtaining information, thoroughness of information offered about the product and seller, and price selection. Which site or sites would you use and why? Which camera would you select and why? How helpful were these sites for making your decision?

Video Cases

Video Cases and Instructional Videos illustrating some of the concepts in this chapter are available. Contact your instructor to access these videos.

Collaboration and Teamwork Project

In MyMISLab, you will find a Collaboration and Teamwork Project dealing with the concepts in this chapter. You will be able to use Google Sites, Google Docs, and other open source collaboration tools to complete the assignment.

Knowledge Management and Collaboration at Tata Consulting Services
CASE STUDY

Tata Consultancy Services (TCS) is an IT-services, business-solutions and out-sourcing organization that offers a portfolio of IT and IT-enabled services to clients all over the globe in horizontal, vertical, and geographical domains. A part of the Tata Group, India's largest industrial conglomerate, TCS has over 108,000 IT consultants in 47 countries.

The concept of knowledge management (KM) was introduced in TCS in 1995 and a dedicated KM team called "Corporate Groupware" was formed in 1998. This group launched the KM-pilot in mid-1999, which was implemented subsequently by a team comprising the steering committee, corporate GroupWare implanters, branch champions, application owners and the infrastructure group.

At that time, KM in TCS covered nearly every function, from quality assurance to HR management. While its 50 offices in India were linked through dedicated communication lines, overseas offices were connected through the Net and the Lotus Notes Domino Servers. The employees could access the knowledge repository that resided on the corporate and branch servers through the intranet, with a browser front-end or a Notes client. The knowledge repository, also called KBases contained a wide range of information about processes, line of business, line of technology, and projects.

Though the formal KM efforts started in TCS in the late 1990s, the informal, closely knit communities of practices (CoPs) had existed at TCS since the 1980s, when it had around a thousand employees. The earliest "group" was based on the migration of technologies. Later, teams were formed for mainframe, Unix, and databases. The groups, consisting of one or two experts in their respective fields, began formal documentation practices with the members writing down the best practices. Recollecting the group practices in the initial days, K. Ananth Krishnan, a technology consultant at that time, recounted that in the mid-eighties, problems and solutions were documented and there were over 1,500 case studies for mainframe. Similarly, for quality area, 40 case studies were reviewed as early as 1993.

The next step was to create Process Asset Libraries (PALs) which contained information related to technology, processes, and case studies for project leaders, which were made available to all development centers through the intranet.

Then Ultimatix, a web-based electronic knowledge management (EKM) portal, which made the knowledge globally available, was developed. The PAL library and KBases, which were hosted on the intranet, were merged with Ultimatix, which had sub-portals for a quality management system, software productivity improvement, training materials, and tools information. There were EKM administrators for each practice and subject group with defined responsibilities, such as editing the documents and approving them for publication. Commenting on the success of CoP, Krishnan maintained that between January 2003 and June 2003, CoP members had exchanged around 10,000 document transactions relating to the industry practices and 21,000 service practices via Ultimatix. The telecom CoP alone had 6,000 transactions, excluding the intranet-based community activities.

To encourage employee conversations, TCS took considerable care in the architecture of its development centers, located across the country. Reflecting on the new design of one of its development centers in Sholinganallur, Chennai, CFO S. Mahalingam commented that the center is made up of modules, each dedicated to one particular technology or a client or an industry practice. These structures lead to garden terraces, where employees gather during their break for informal conversations and brainstorm the solutions to many problems.

TCS also launched a number of training programs such as the Initial Learning Program, targeted at new employees, the Continuous Learning Program for experienced employees, and the Leadership Development Program for employees with more than five years' experience. The integrated competency and learning management systems (iCALMS) that was deployed globally across all TCS offices promoted a culture of learning and growth in the organization. Equipped with data about competency definitions, role definitions, and online/classroom learning objectives it helped the consultants to enhance their skills in a customized manner. To gain cross-industry experience, TCS regularly rotated people across various functions and within other Tata Group companies. Employees were also encouraged to join outside bodies like the IEEE, and go in for certifications.

Knowmax, a knowledge management system, developed using Microsoft sharepoint portal server in 2007, gave TCS consultants access to nearly 40 years of experience and best practices, arranged by type of engagement, the technology in use, and customer requirements. It supported more than 60 knowledge assets and was accessible via Ultimatix to all TCS associates. Any associate could contribute to the K-Bank and Knowledge Officers were made responsible for maintaining the quality of content.

To maintain the work-life balance of its employees, TCS initiated Propel sessions which brought together employees with similar interests to conduct various activities such as reading books. Later, held every quarter through conferences and camps, this initiative also spurred knowledge transfer among the employees. The knowledge sharing at the project level was done through LiveMeeting application, where all the project meetings were recorded and stored in the project repository. Team members who missed the meeting, or any new members in the team, could listen to the recorded sessions and this enabled them to catch up with the rest of the team. Furthermore, Knowledge Transition sessions conducted weekly by the "Subject Matter Expert" helped the team to learn from the experience of the experts. "Tip of the Day" mail, comprising either technical, or conceptual, or human skills tips were also shared within the organization, almost daily.

Though Ultimatix, launched in 2002, digitized the entire organization from end to end and improved the business processes' efficiency, it still couldn't tap the knowledge of employees effectively. To improve collaboration among employees, Project Infinity was launched in 2007; this involved a number of technologies including IBM's Sametime, QuickPlace, Lotus Domino Collaboration tools, Avaya VOIP telephony, and Polycom IP videoconferencing.

As a result of adopting Infinity, collaboration of overseas and local offices improved as instant messaging (IM) got rid of cultural and pronunciation differences that could occur on the phone. Furthermore, corporate communications were able to run a 24-hour internal news broadcast to all TCS offices in the world. In addition, travel and telecommunications costs were reduced by 40 percent and 6 percent respectively.

Other than these channels, the company also used the JustAsk system (embedded into the KM), Blog platform, IdeaStorm, TIP, and My Site. Blogging had caught on rapidly since 2006 when it was first introduced. Almost 40,000-50,000 TCS staff blogged on the intranet. While the JustAsk system allowed employees to post questions that others could answer, Idea Storm was a once-a-year event, where two to three topics were posted by the corporate team on which ideas were invited by everyone. TIP, an open portal for product innovation and potential new ideas was launched to promote the sharing of ideas. MySite, embedded into the KM portal, allowed each associate to have a personal page like Facebook or Orkut.

Sources: Sankaranarayanan G., "Building Communities, the TCS way," expressitpeople.com, September 2003; Kavita Kaur, "Give and Take," india-today.com, January 2000; Sunil Shah, "Network Wonder: Collaborative Tools Help TCS Grow," cio.com, July 2007; Shivani Shinde, "TCS Sees Synergy in Gen X Tools," rediff.com, July 2008.

CASE STUDY QUESTIONS

1. Analyze the knowledge management efforts at TCS using the knowledge management value chain model. Which tools or activities were used for managing tacit knowledge and which ones are used for explicit knowledge?

2. Describe the growth of knowledge management systems at TCS. How have these systems helped TCS in its business?

3. Describe the collaboration tools used at TCS? What benefits did TCS reap from these tools?

4. How did Web 2.0 tools help TCS to manage knowledge and collaboration among its employees?

5. How do you think KM tools have changed some key operational processes at TCS, such as bidding for new projects, project development and implementation, customer service, and so on?

Case contributed by Neerja Sethi and Vijay Sethi, Nanyang Technological University

Chapter 12

Enhancing Decision Making

LEARNING OBJECTIVES

After reading this chapter, you will be able to answer the following questions:

1. What are the different types of decisions and how does the decision-making process work?

2. How do information systems support the activities of managers and management decision making?

3. How do business intelligence and business analytics support decision making?

4. How do different decision-making constituencies in an organization use business intelligence?

5. What is the role of information systems in helping people working in a group make decisions more efficiently?

CHAPTER OUTLINE

Interactive Sessions:

Analytics Help the Cincinnati Zoo Know Its Customers

Colgate-Palmolive Keeps Managers Smiling with Executive Dashboards

MONEYBALL: DATA-DRIVEN BASEBALL

On September 23, 2011, the film *Moneyball* opened in theaters across the United States, starring Brad Pitt as Billy Beane, the iconoclastic general manager of the Oakland Athletics. The film was based on the bestselling book by Michael Lewis that described how Beane led the underdog A's, with one of the tiniest budgets in Major League baseball, to win 103 games in 2002. Under Beane's watch, the A's made the playoffs five times in the next eight seasons.

At the opening of the 2002 baseball season, the wealthiest team was the New York Yankees, with a payroll of $126 million; the Oakland A's and Tampa Bay Devil Rays, each with payrolls of about $41 million, were the poorest. These disparities meant that only the wealthiest teams could afford the best players. A poor team, such as the A's, could only afford what the "better" teams rejected, and thus was almost certain to fail. That is, until Billy Beane and Moneyball entered the picture.

How did Beane do it? He took a close look at the data. Conventional baseball wisdom maintained that big-name highly athletic hitters and skillful young pitchers were the main ingredients for winning. Beane and his assistant general manager Paul DePodesta used advanced statistical analysis of player and team data to prove that wrong. The prevailing metrics for predicting wins, losses, and player performance, such as batting averages, runs batted in, and stolen bases, were vestiges of the early years of baseball and the statistics that were available at that time. Baseball talent scouts used these metrics, as well as their gut intuition, to size up talent for their teams.

Beane and DePodesta found that a different set of metrics, namely, the percentage of time a hitter was on base or forced opposing pitchers to throw a high number of pitches, was more predictive of a team's chances of winning a game. So Beane sought out affordable players who met these criteria (including those who drew lots of "walks") and had been overlooked or rejected by the well-funded teams. He didn't care if a player was overweight or seemed past his prime-he only focused on the numbers. Beane was able to field a consistently winning team by using advanced analytics to gain insights into each player's value and contribution to team success that other richer teams had overlooked.

Beane and his data-driven approach to baseball had a seismic impact on the game. After observing the A's phenomenal success in 2002, the Boston Red Sox used the talents of baseball statistician Bill James and adopted Beane's strategy, only with more money. Two years later, they won the World Series.

Although many experts continue to believe that traditional methods of player evaluation, along with gut instinct, money, and luck, are still the key ingredients for winning teams, the major league teams acknowledge that statistical analysis has a place in baseball. To some degree, most major league teams have embraced sabermetrics, the application of statistical analysis to baseball records to evaluate the performance of individual players. The New York Yankees, New York Mets, San Diego Padres, St. Louis Cardinals, Boston Red Sox, Washington Nationals, Arizona Diamondbacks,

© ZUMA Press, Inc. / Alamy

Cleveland Indians, and Toronto Blue Jays have all hired full-time sabermetric analysts.

Since all the major league teams use sabermetrics in one way or another to guide their decisions, the A's no longer have the competitive edge they once enjoyed when they were the only ones with this knowledge. Even though Beane hasn't taken the A's to the playoffs since 2006, he remains a highly sought after speaker on the corporate management lecture circuit. It's easy to see why. Moneyball isn't just about baseball—it's about learning how to use data as a competitive weapon, especially in environments where resources are scarce and innovation is essential.

Sources: Don Peppers, "Baseball, Business, and Big Data," FastCompany.com, April 24, 2012; Matthew Futterman, "Baseball after Moneyball," *The Wall Street Journal*, September 22, 2011; Adam Sternberge, "Billy Beane of 'Moneyball' Has Given Up on His Own Hollywood Ending," *The New York Times*, September 21, 2011; and Michael Lewis, *Moneyball: The Art of Winning an Unfair Game*, 2003.

Baseball has been, according to the subtitle of Moneyball, an "unfair game." Given the huge disparities in MLB team budgets, wealthier teams definitely have the advantage in recruiting the best players. But by using advanced analytics to guide decisions about what players to recruit and cultivate, Billy Beane was able to turn the underdog Oakland Athletics into a winning team. Baseball is a business and this opening case has important lessons for other businesses as well: You can be more efficient and competitive if, like Moneyball, you know how to use data to drive your decisions.

The chapter-opening diagram calls attention to important points raised by this case and this chapter. Managers at major league baseball teams were hamstrung by earlier models of decision making that used the wrong metrics to predict team performance. Teams with low budgets such as the Oakland A's were stuck in a rut because they could not afford the most highly skilled players, and the advantage went to the teams with the biggest budgets. Beane and Paul DePodesta ran sophisticated statistical analyses of player and game data to devise a better set of metrics for predicting performance. Of course, an individual player's skill is still very important, but Beane showed that a team composed of less skilled players could still win if it focused on players with high on-base percentages and pitchers with large numbers of ground-outs. Beane was able forge a team that delivered a first-rate performance much more cost effectively that competitors because he paid attention to the data.

Here are some questions to think about: Some have said Moneyball isn't really about baseball. What are the implications of this statement? What can businesses learn from Moneyball? What if all businesses were run like Moneyball?

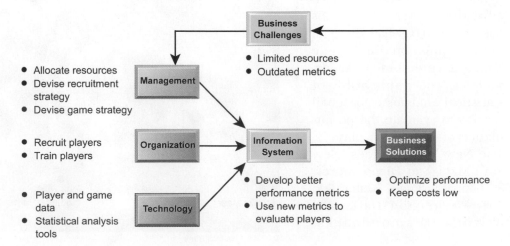

12.1 DECISION MAKING AND INFORMATION SYSTEMS

Decision making in businesses used to be limited to management. Today, lower-level employees are responsible for some of these decisions, as information systems make information available to lower levels of the business. But what do we mean by better decision making? How does decision making take place in businesses and other organizations? Let's take a closer look.

BUSINESS VALUE OF IMPROVED DECISION MAKING

What does it mean to the business to make better decisions? What is the monetary value of improved decision making? Table 12.1 attempts to measure the monetary value of improved decision making for a small U.S. manufacturing firm with $280 million in annual revenue and 140 employees. The firm has identified a number of key decisions where new system investments might improve the quality of decision making. The table provides selected estimates of annual value (in the form of cost savings or increased revenue) from improved decision making in selected areas of the business.

We can see from Table 12.1 that decisions are made at all levels of the firm and that some of these decisions are common, routine, and numerous. Although the value of improving any single decision may be small, improving hundreds of thousands of "small" decisions adds up to a large annual value for the business.

TYPES OF DECISIONS

Chapters 1 and 2 showed that there are different levels in an organization. Each of these levels has different information requirements for decision support and responsibility for different types of decisions (see Figure 12.1). Decisions are classified as structured, semistructured, and unstructured.

TABLE 12.1 BUSINESS VALUE OF ENHANCED DECISION MAKING

EXAMPLE DECISION	DECISION MAKER	NUMBER OF ANNUAL DECISIONS	ESTIMATED VALUE TO FIRM OF A SINGLE IMPROVED DECISION	ANNUAL VALUE
Allocate support to most valuable customers	Accounts manager	12	$100,000	$1,200,000
Predict call center daily demand	Call center management	4	150,000	600,000
Decide parts inventory levels daily	Inventory manager	365	5,000	1,825,000
Identify competitive bids from major suppliers	Senior management	1	2,000,000	2,000,000
Schedule production to fill orders	Manufacturing manager	150	10,000	1,500,000
Allocate labor to complete a job	Production floor manager	100	4,000	400,000

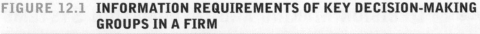

FIGURE 12.1 **INFORMATION REQUIREMENTS OF KEY DECISION-MAKING GROUPS IN A FIRM**

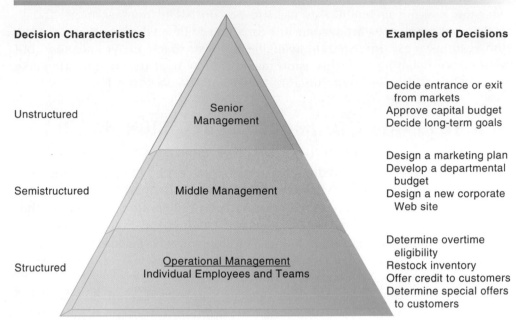

Senior managers, middle managers, operational managers, and employees have different types of decisions and information requirements.

Unstructured decisions are those in which the decision maker must provide judgment, evaluation, and insight to solve the problem. Each of these decisions is novel, important, and nonroutine, and there is no well-understood or agreed-on procedure for making them.

Structured decisions, by contrast, are repetitive and routine, and they involve a definite procedure for handling them so that they do not have to be treated each time as if they were new. Many decisions have elements of both types of decisions and are **semistructured**, where only part of the problem has a clear-cut answer provided by an accepted procedure. In general, structured decisions are more prevalent at lower organizational levels, whereas unstructured problems are more common at higher levels of the firm.

Senior executives face many unstructured decision situations, such as establishing the firm's 5- or 10-year goals or deciding new markets to enter. Answering the question "Should we enter a new market?" would require access to news, government reports, and industry views as well as high-level summaries of firm performance. However, the answer would also require senior managers to use their own best judgment and poll other managers for their opinions.

Middle management faces more structured decision scenarios but their decisions may include unstructured components. A typical middle-level management decision might be "Why is the reported order fulfillment report showing a decline over the past six months at a distribution center in Minneapolis?" This middle manager will obtain a report from the firm's enterprise system or distribution management system on order activity and operational efficiency at the Minneapolis distribution center. This is the structured part of the decision. But before arriving at an answer, this middle manager will have to interview employees and gather more unstructured information from external sources about local economic conditions or sales trends.

Operational management and rank-and-file employees tend to make more structured decisions. For example, a supervisor on an assembly line has to decide whether an hourly paid worker is entitled to overtime pay. If the employee worked more than eight hours on a particular day, the supervisor would routinely grant overtime pay for any time beyond eight hours that was clocked on that day.

A sales account representative often has to make decisions about extending credit to customers by consulting the firm's customer database that contains credit information. If the customer met the firm's prespecified criteria for granting credit, the account representative would grant that customer credit to make a purchase. In both instances, the decisions are highly structured and are routinely made thousands of times each day in most large firms. The answer has been preprogrammed into the firm's payroll and accounts receivable systems.

THE DECISION-MAKING PROCESS

Making a decision is a multistep process. Simon (1960) described four different stages in decision making: intelligence, design, choice, and implementation (see Figure 12.2).

FIGURE 12.2 **STAGES IN DECISION MAKING**

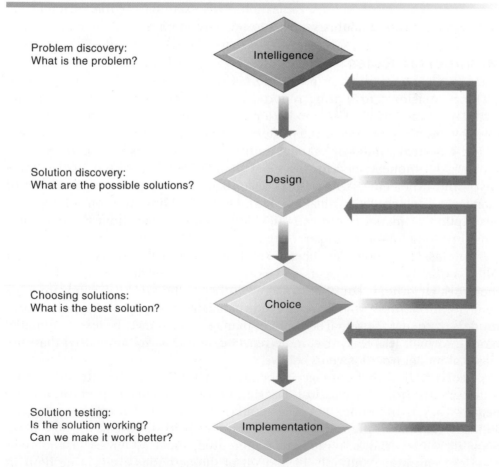

The decision-making process is broken down into four stages.

Intelligence consists of discovering, identifying, and understanding the problems occurring in the organization—why a problem exists, where, and what effects it is having on the firm.

Design involves identifying and exploring various solutions to the problem.

Choice consists of choosing among solution alternatives.

Implementation involves making the chosen alternative work and continuing to monitor how well the solution is working.

What happens if the solution you have chosen doesn't work? Figure 12.2 shows that you can return to an earlier stage in the decision-making process and repeat it if necessary. For instance, in the face of declining sales, a sales management team may decide to pay the sales force a higher commission for making more sales to spur on the sales effort. If this does not produce sales increases, managers would need to investigate whether the problem stems from poor product design, inadequate customer support, or a host of other causes that call for a different solution.

MANAGERS AND DECISION MAKING IN THE REAL WORLD

The premise of this book and this chapter is that systems to support decision making produce better decision making by managers and employees, above average returns on investment for the firm, and ultimately higher profitability. However, information systems cannot improve all the different kinds of decisions taking place in an organization. Let's examine the role of managers and decision making in organizations to see why this is so.

Managerial Roles

Managers play key roles in organizations. Their responsibilities range from making decisions, to writing reports, to attending meetings, to arranging birthday parties. We are able to better understand managerial functions and roles by examining classical and contemporary models of managerial behavior.

The **classical model of management**, which describes what managers do, was largely unquestioned for the more than 70 years since the 1920s. Henri Fayol and other early writers first described the five classical functions of managers as planning, organizing, coordinating, deciding, and controlling. This description of management activities dominated management thought for a long time, and it is still popular today.

The classical model describes formal managerial functions but does not address exactly what managers do when they plan, decide things, and control the work of others. For this, we must turn to the work of contemporary behavioral scientists who have studied managers in daily action. **Behavioral models** state that the actual behavior of managers appears to be less systematic, more informal, less reflective, more reactive, and less well organized than the classical model would have us believe.

Observers find that managerial behavior actually has five attributes that differ greatly from the classical description. First, managers perform a great deal of work at an unrelenting pace—studies have found that managers engage in more than 600 different activities each day, with no break in their pace. Second, managerial activities are fragmented; most activities last for less than nine minutes, and only 10 percent of the activities exceed one hour in duration. Third, managers prefer current, specific, and ad hoc information (printed information often will be too old). Fourth, they prefer oral forms of communication to written forms because oral media provide greater flexibility, require less effort, and bring a faster response. Fifth, managers give high priority to maintaining a diverse and complex web of contacts that act as an informal information system and helps them execute their personal agendas and short- and long-term goals.

Analyzing managers' day-to-day behavior, Henry Mintzberg found that it could be classified into 10 managerial roles. **Managerial roles** are expectations of the activities that managers should perform in an organization. Mintzberg found that these managerial roles fell into three categories: interpersonal, informational, and decisional.

Interpersonal Roles. Managers act as figureheads for the organization when they represent their companies to the outside world and perform symbolic duties, such as giving out employee awards, in their **interpersonal role**. Managers act as leaders, attempting to motivate, counsel, and support subordinates. Managers also act as liaisons between various organizational levels; within each of these levels, they serve as liaisons among the members of the management team. Managers provide time and favors, which they expect to be returned.

Informational Roles. In their **informational role,** managers act as the nerve centers of their organizations, receiving the most concrete, up-to-date information and redistributing it to those who need to be aware of it. Managers are therefore information disseminators and spokespersons for their organizations.

Decisional Roles. Managers make decisions. In their **decisional role**, they act as entrepreneurs by initiating new kinds of activities; they handle disturbances arising in the organization; they allocate resources to staff members who need them; and they negotiate conflicts and mediate between conflicting groups.

Table 12.2, based on Mintzberg's role classifications, is one look at where systems can and cannot help managers. The table shows that information systems are now capable of supporting most, but not all, areas of managerial life.

TABLE 12.2 MANAGERIAL ROLES AND SUPPORTING INFORMATION SYSTEMS

ROLE	BEHAVIOR	SUPPORT SYSTEMS
Interpersonal Roles		
Figurehead		Telepresence systems
Leader	Interpersonal	Telepresence, social networks, Twitter
Liaison		Smartphones, social networks
Informational Roles		
Nerve center		Management information systems, executive support system
Disseminator	Information	E-mail, social networks
Spokesperson	processing	Webinars, telepresence
Decisional Roles		
Entrepreneur	Decision	None exist
Disturbance handler	making	None exist
Resource allocator		Business intelligence, decision-support system
Negotiator		None exist

Sources: Kenneth C. Laudon and Jane P. Laudon; and Mintzberg, 1971.

Real-World Decision Making

We now see that information systems are not helpful for all managerial roles. And in those managerial roles where information systems might improve decisions, investments in information technology do not always produce positive results. There are three main reasons: information quality, management filters, and organizational culture (see Chapter 3).

Information Quality. High-quality decisions require high-quality information. Table 12.3 describes information quality dimensions that affect the quality of decisions.

If the output of information systems does not meet these quality criteria, decision-making will suffer. Chapter 6 has shown that corporate databases and files have varying levels of inaccuracy and incompleteness, which in turn will degrade the quality of decision making.

Management Filters. Even with timely, accurate information, some managers make bad decisions. Managers (like all human beings) absorb information through a series of filters to make sense of the world around them. Managers have selective attention, focus on certain kinds of problems and solutions, and have a variety of biases that reject information that does not conform to their prior conceptions.

For instance, Wall Street firms such as Bear Stearns and Lehman Brothers imploded in 2008 because they underestimated the risk of their investments in complex mortgage securities, many of which were based on subprime loans that were more likely to default. The computer models they and other financial institutions used to manage risk were based on overly optimistic assumptions and overly simplistic data about what might go wrong. Management wanted to make sure that their firms' capital was not all tied up as a cushion against defaults from risky investments, preventing them from investing it to generate profits. So the designers of these risk management systems were encouraged to measure risks in a way that minimzed their importance. Some trading desks also oversimplified the information maintained about the mortgage securities to make them appear as simple bonds with higher ratings than were warranted by their underlying components.

Organizational Inertia and Politics. Organizations are bureaucracies with limited capabilities and competencies for acting decisively. When environments change and businesses need to adopt new business models to

TABLE 12.3 INFORMATION QUALITY DIMENSIONS

QUALITY DIMENSION	DESCRIPTION
Accuracy	Do the data represent reality?
Integrity	Are the structure of data and relationships among the entities and attributes consistent?
Consistency	Are data elements consistently defined?
Completeness	Are all the necessary data present?
Validity	Do data values fall within defined ranges?
Timeliness	Area data available when needed?
Accessibility	Are the data accessible, comprehensible, and usable?

survive, strong forces within organizations resist making decisions calling for major change. Decisions taken by a firm often represent a balancing of the firm's various interest groups rather than the best solution to the problem.

Studies of business restructuring find that firms tend to ignore poor performance until threatened by outside takeovers, and they systematically blame poor performance on external forces beyond their control such as economic conditions (the economy), foreign competition, and rising prices, rather than blaming senior or middle management for poor business judgment.

HIGH-VELOCITY AUTOMATED DECISION MAKING

Today, many decisions made by organizations are not made by managers, or any humans. For instance, when you enter a query into Google's search engine, Google has to decide which URLs to display in about half a second on average (500 milliseconds). Google indexes over 50 billion Web pages, although it does not search the entire index for every query it receives. The same is true of other search engines. The New York Stock Exchange spent over $450 million in 2010–2011 to build a trading platform that executes incoming orders in less than 50 milliseconds. High frequency traders at electronic stock exchanges execute their trades in under 30 milliseconds.

The class of decisions that are highly structured and automated is growing rapidly. What makes this kind of automated high-speed decision making possible are computer algorithms that precisely define the steps to be followed to produce a decision, very large databases, very high-speed processors, and software optimized to the task. In these situations, humans (including managers) are eliminated from the decision chain because they are too slow.

This also means organizations in these areas are making decisions faster than what managers can monitor or control. Inability to control automated decisions was a major factor in the "Flash Crash" experienced by U.S. stock markets on May 6, 2010, when the Dow Jones Industrial Average fell over 600 points in a matter of minutes before rebounding later that day. The stock market was overwhelmed by a huge wave of sell orders triggered primarily by high-speed computerized trading programs within a few seconds, causing shares of some companies like Procter & Gamble to sell for pennies. The past few years have seen a series of similar breakdowns in computerized trading systems, including one on August 1, 2012 when a software error caused Knight Capital to enter millions of faulty trades in less than an hour. The trading glitch created wild surges and plunges in nearly 150 stocks and left Knight with $440 million in losses.

How does the Simon framework of intelligence-design-choice-implementation work in high-velocity decision environments? Essentially, the intelligence, design, choice, and implementation parts of the decision-making process are captured by the software's algorithms. The humans who wrote the software have already identified the problem, designed a method for finding a solution, defined a range of acceptable solutions, and implemented the solution. Obviously, with humans out of the loop, great care needs to be taken to ensure the proper operation of these systems lest they do significant harm to organizations and humans. And even then additional safeguards are wise to observe the behavior of these systems, regulate their performance, and if necessary, turn them off.

12.2 BUSINESS INTELLIGENCE IN THE ENTERPRISE

Chapter 2 introduced you to the different types of systems used for supporting management decision making. At the foundation of all of these decision support systems are a business intelligence and business analytics infrastructure that supplies the data and the analytic tools for supporting decision making. In this section, we want to answer the following questions:

- What are business intelligence (BI) and business analytics (BA)
- Who makes business intelligence and business analytics hardware and software?
- Who are the users of business intelligence?
- What kinds of analytical tools come with a BI/BA suite?
- How do managers use these tools?
- What are some examples of firms who have used these tools?
- What management strategies are used for developing BI/BA capabilities?

WHAT IS BUSINESS INTELLIGENCE?

When we think of humans as intelligent beings we often refer to their ability to take in data from their environment, understand the meaning and significance of the information, and then act appropriately. Can the same be said of business firms? The answer appears to be a qualified "yes." All organizations, including business firms, do indeed take in information from their environments, attempt to understand the meaning of the information, and then attempt to act on the information. Just like human beings, some business firms do this well, and others poorly.

"Business intelligence (BI)" is a term used by hardware and software vendors and information technology consultants to describe the infrastructure for warehousing, integrating, reporting, and analyzing data that comes from the business environment, including big data. The foundation infrastructure collects, stores, cleans, and makes relevant information available to managers. Think databases, data warehouses, data marts, Hadoop, and analytic platforms, which we described in Chapter 6. "Business analytics (BA)" is also a vendor-defined term that focuses more on tools and techniques for analyzing and understanding data. Think online analytical processing (OLAP), statistics, models, and data mining, which we also introduced in Chapter 6.

So, stripped to its essentials, business intelligence and analytics are about integrating all the information streams produced by a firm into a single, coherent enterprise-wide set of data, and then, using modeling, statistical analysis tools (like normal distributions, correlation and regression analysis, Chi square analysis, forecasting, and cluster analysis), and data mining tools (pattern discovery and machine learning), to make sense out of all these data so managers can make better decisions and better plans, or at least know quickly when their firms are failing to meet planned targets.

One company that uses business intelligence is Hallmark Cards. The company uses SAS Analytics software to improve its understanding of buying patterns that could lead to increased sales at more than 3,000 Hallmark Gold Crown stores in the United Sates. Hallmark wanted to strengthen its relationship with frequent buyers. Using data mining and predictive modeling, the company determined how to market to various consumer segments during holidays and special occasions as well as adjust promotions on the fly. Hallmark is able to determine which customer segments are most influenced by direct mail, which should be approached through e-mail, and what specific messages to send each group. Business intelligence has helped boost Hallmark sales to its loyalty program members by 5 to 10 percent. Another organization that has benefited from business intelligence is the Cincinnati Zoo, as described in the Interactive Session on Organizations.

Business Intelligence Vendors

It is important to remember that business intelligence and analytics are products defined by technology vendors and consulting firms. They consist of hardware and software suites sold primarily by large system vendors to very large Fortune 500 firms. The largest five providers of these products are Oracle, SAP, IBM, Microsoft, and SAS (see Table 12.4). Microsoft's products are aimed at small to medium-sized firms, and they are based on desktop tools familiar to employees (such as Excel spreadsheet software), Microsoft SharePoint collaboration tools, and Microsoft SQL Server database software. According to the International Data Corporation, the global business intelligence and analytics market was $35.1 billion in 2012 and is expected to reach $50.7 billion by 2016 (Kern, 2012). This makes business intelligence and business analytics one of the fastest growing and largest segments in the U.S. software market.

THE BUSINESS INTELLIGENCE ENVIRONMENT

Figure 12.3 (on page 495) gives an overview of a business intelligence environment, highlighting the kinds of hardware, software, and management capabilities that the major vendors offer and that firms develop over time. There are six elements in this business intelligence environment:

- **Data from the business environment:** Businesses must deal with both structured and unstructured data from many different sources, including big data. The data need to be integrated and organized so that they can be analyzed and used by human decision makers.

- **Business intelligence infrastructure:** The underlying foundation of business intelligence is a powerful database system that captures all the relevant data to operate the business. The data may be stored in transactional databases or combined and integrated into an enterprise-data warehouse or series of interrelated data marts.

TABLE 12.4 MARKET LEADERS AND SHARE FOR THE TOP BUSINESS INTELLIGENCE VENDORS

VENDOR	MARKET SHARE	BUSINESS INTELLIGENCE SOFTWARE
Oracle	19.3%	Oracle Business Intelligence Foundation Suite
SAP	14.5%	SAP BusinessObjects BI
IBM	13.8%	IBM Cognos
Microsoft	7.4%	Microsoft Excel, PowerPivot, SQL Server 2012 Business Intelligence
SAS Institute	7.1%	SAS Enterprise Business Intelligence

INTERACTIVE SESSION: ORGANIZATIONS

ANALYTICS HELP THE CINCINNATI ZOO KNOW ITS CUSTOMERS

Founded in 1873, the Cincinnati Zoo & Botanical Garden is one of the world's top-rated zoological institutions, and the second oldest zoo in the United States. It is also one of the nation's most popular attractions, a Top 10 Zagat-rated Zoo, and a *Parents Magazine* Top Zoo for Children. The Zoo's 71-acre site is home to more than 500 animal and 3,000 plant species. About 1.3 million people visit this zoo each year.

Although the Zoo is a nonprofit organization partially subsidized by Hamilton County, more than two-thirds of its $26 million annual budget is paid from fundraising efforts, and the remainder comes from admission fees, food, and gifts. To increase revenue and improve performance, the Zoo's senior management team embarked on a comprehensive review of its operations. The review found that management had limited knowledge and understanding of what was actually happening in the Zoo on a day-to-day basis, other than how many people visited every day and the Zoo's total revenue.

Who is coming to the Zoo? How often do they come? What do they do and what do they buy? Management had no idea. Each of the Zoo's four income streams—admissions, membership, retail, and food service—had different point-of-sale platforms, and the food service business, which brings in $4 million a year, still relied on manual cash registers. Management had to sift through paper receipts just to understand daily sales totals.

The Zoo had compiled a spreadsheet that collected visitors' zip codes, hoping to use the data for geographic and demographic analysis. If the data could be combined with insight into visitor activity at the Zoo—what attractions they visited, what they ate and drank, and what they bought at the gift shops —the information would be extremely valuable for marketing.

To achieve this, however, the Zoo needed to change its information systems to focus more on an alytics and data management. The Zoo replaced its four legacy point-of-sale systems with a single platform—Galaxy POS from Gateway Ticketing Systems. It then enlisted IBM and BrightStar Partners (a consulting firm partnering with IBM) to build a centralized data warehouse and implement IBM Cognos Business Intelligence to provide real-time analytics and reporting.

Like all outdoor attractions, the Zoo's business is highly weather-dependent. On rainy days, attendance falls off sharply, often leaving the Zoo overstaffed and overstocked. If the weather is unusually hot, sales of certain items such as ice cream and bottled water are likely to rise, and the Zoo may run out of these items.

The Zoo now feeds weather forecast data from the U.S. National Oceanic and Atmospheric Administration (NOAA) Web site into its business intelligence system. By comparing current forecasts to historic attendance and sales data during similar weather conditions, the Zoo is able to make more accurate decisions about labor scheduling and inventory planning.

As visitors scan their membership cards at the Zoo's entrance, exit, attractions, restaurants, and stores, or use the Zoo's Loyalty Rewards card, the Zoo's system captures these data and analyzes them to determine usage and spending patterns down to the individual customer level. This information helps the Zoo segment visitors based on their spending and visitation behaviors and use this information to target marketing and promotions specifically for each customer segment.

One customer segment the Zoo identified consisted of people who spent nothing other than the price of admissions during their visit. If each of these people spent $20 on their next visit to the Zoo, the Zoo would take in an extra $260,000, which is almost 1 percent of its entire budget. The Zoo used its customer information to devise a direct mail marketing campaign in which this type of visitor would be offered a discount for some of the Zoo's restaurants and gift shops. Loyal customers are also rewarded with targeted marketing and recognition programs.

Instead of sending a special offer to its entire mailing list, the Zoo is able to tailor campaigns more precisely to smaller groups of people, increasing its chances of identifying the people who were most likely to respond to its mailings. More targeted marketing helped the Zoo cut $40,000 from its annual marketing budget.

Management had observed that food sales tend to trail off significantly after 3 p.m. each day, and started closing some of the Zoo's food outlets at that time. But more detailed data analysis showed that a big spike in soft-serve ice cream sales occurs during the last hour before the Zoo closes. As a result, the Zoo's soft-serve ice cream outlets are open for the entire day.

The Zoo's Beer Hut concession features six different brands, which are typically rotated based on sales volume and the seasons. With IBM analytics, management can now instantly identify which beer is selling best, on what day, and at what time to make sure inventory meets demand. Previously, it took 7 to 14 days to get this information, which required hiring part-time staff to sift through register tapes.

The Zoo's ability to make better decisions about operations has led to dramatic improvements

in sales. Six months after deploying its business intelligence solution, the Zoo achieved a 30.7 percent increase in food sales and a 5.9 percent increase in retail sales compared to the same period a year earlier.

Sources: Justin Kern, "Analytics: Coming to a Zoo, Museum, or Park Near You," *Information Management*, August 28, 2012; IBM Corporation, "Cincinnati Zoo Improves Customer Experience and Enhances Performance," 2011; Nucleus Research, "IBM ROI Case Study: Cincinnati Zoo," July 2011; and www.cincinnatizoo.org, accessed May 26, 2012.

CASE STUDY QUESTIONS

1. What management, organization, and technology factors were behind the Cincinnati Zoo losing opportunities to increase revenue?

2. Why was replacing legacy point-of-sale systems and implementing a data warehouse essential to an information system solution?

3. How did the Cincinnati Zoo benefit from business intelligence? How did it enhance operational performance and decision making? What role was played by predictive analytics?

4. Visit the IBM Cognos Web site and describe the business intelligence tools that would be the most useful for the Cincinnati Zoo.

- **Business analytics toolset:** A set of software tools are used to analyze data and produce reports, respond to questions posed by managers, and track the progress of the business using key indicators of performance.

FIGURE 12.3 **BUSINESS INTELLIGENCE AND ANALYTICS FOR DECISION SUPPORT**

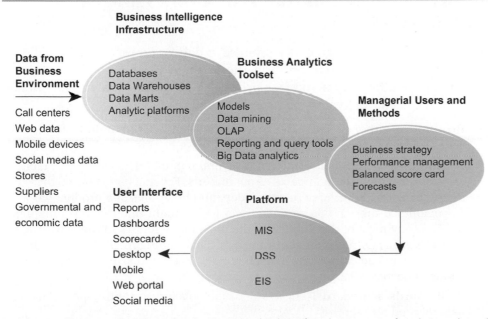

Business intelligence and analytics requires a strong database foundation, a set of analytic tools, and an involved management team that can ask intelligent questions and analyze data.

- **Managerial users and methods:** Business intelligence hardware and software are only as intelligent as the human beings who use them. Managers impose order on the analysis of data using a variety of managerial methods that define strategic business goals and specify how progress will be measured. These include business performance management and balanced scorecard approaches focusing on key performance indicators and industry strategic analyses focusing on changes in the general business environment, with special attention to competitors. Without strong senior management oversight, business analytics can produce a great deal of information, reports, and online screens that focus on the wrong matters and divert attention from the real issues. You need to remember that, so far, only humans can ask intelligent questions.

- **Delivery platform—MIS, DSS, ESS:** The results from business intelligence and analytics are delivered to managers and employees in a variety of ways, depending on what they need to know to perform their jobs. MIS, DSS, and ESS, which we introduced in Chapter 2, deliver information and knowledge to different people and levels in the firm—operational employees, middle managers, and senior executives. In the past, these systems could not share data and operated as independent systems. Today, one suite of hardware and software tools in the form of a business intelligence and analytics package is able to integrate all this information and bring it to managers' desktop or mobile platforms.

- **User interface:** Business people are no longer tied to their desks and desktops. They often learn quicker from a visual representation of data than from a dry report with columns and rows of information. Today's business analytics software suites emphasize visual techniques such as dashboards and scorecards. They also are able to deliver reports on BlackBerrys, iPhones, and other mobile handhelds as well as on the firm's Web portal. BA software is adding capabilities to post information on Twitter, Facebook, or internal social media to support decision making in an online group setting rather than in a face-to-face meeting.

BUSINESS INTELLIGENCE AND ANALYTICS CAPABILITIES

Business intelligence and analytics promise to deliver correct, nearly real-time information to decision makers, and the analytic tools help them quickly understand the information and take action. There are six analytic functionalities that BI systems deliver to achieve these ends:

- **Production reports:** These are predefined reports based on industry-specific requirements (see Table 12.5).
- **Parameterized reports:** Users enter several parameters as in a pivot table to filter data and isolate impacts of parameters. For instance, you might want to enter region and time of day to understand how sales of a product vary by region and time. If you were Starbucks, you might find that customers in the East buy most of their coffee in the morning, whereas in the Northwest customers buy coffee throughout the day. This finding might lead to different marketing and ad campaigns in each region. (See the discussion of pivot tables in Section 12.3.)
- **Dashboards/scorecards:** These are visual tools for presenting performance data defined by users.
- **Ad hoc query/search/report creation:** These allow users to create their own reports based on queries and searches.

- **Drill down:** This is the ability to move from a high-level summary to a more detailed view.
- **Forecasts, scenarios, models:** These include the ability to perform linear forecasting, what-if scenario analysis, and analyze data using standard statistical tools.

Who Uses Business Intelligence and Business Analytics?

In previous chapters, we have described the different information constituencies in business firms—from senior managers to middle managers, analysts, and operational employees. This also holds true for BI and BA systems (see Figure 12.4). Over 80 percent of the audience for BI consists of casual users who rely largely on production reports. Senior executives tend to use BI to monitor firm activities using visual interfaces like dashboards and scorecards. Middle managers and analysts are much more likely to be immersed in the data and software, entering queries and slicing and dicing the data along different dimensions. Operational employees will, along with customers and suppliers, be looking mostly at prepackaged reports.

Production Reports

The most widely used output of a BI suite of tools are pre-packaged production reports. Table 12.5 illustrates some common predefined reports from Oracle's BI suite of tools.

Predictive Analytics

An important capability of business intelligence analytics is the ability to model future events and behaviors, such as the probability that a customer will respond to an offer to purchase a product. **Predictive analytics** use statistical analysis, data mining techniques, historical data, and assumptions about future conditions to predict future trends and behavior patterns. Variables that can be measured to predict future behavior are identified. For example, an insurance company might use variables such as age, gender, and driving record as

FIGURE 12.4 BUSINESS INTELLIGENCE USERS

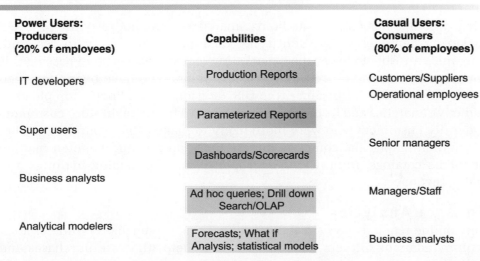

Casual users are consumers of BI output, while intense power users are the producers of reports, new analyses, models, and forecasts.

TABLE 12.5 EXAMPLES OF BUSINESS INTELLIGENCE PREDEFINED PRODUCTION REPORTS

BUSINESS FUNCTIONAL AREA	PRODUCTION REPORTS
Sales	Forecast sales; sales team performance; cross selling; sales cycle times
Service/Call Center	Customer satisfaction; service cost; resolution rates; churn rates
Marketing	Campaign effectiveness; loyalty and attrition; market basket analysis
Procurement and Support	Direct and indirect spending; off-contract purchases; supplier performance
Supply Chain	Backlog; fulfillment status; order cycle time; bill of materials analysis
Financials	General ledger; accounts receivable and payable; cash flow; profitability
Human Resources	Employee productivity; compensation; workforce demographics; retention

predictors of driving safety when issuing auto insurance policies. A collection of such predictors is combined into a predictive model for forecasting future probabilities with an acceptable level of reliability.

FedEx has been using predictive analytics to develop models that predict how customers will respond to price changes and new services, which customers are most at risk of switching to competitors, and how much revenue will be generated by new storefront or drop-box locations. The accuracy rate of FedEx's predictive analytics system ranges from 65 to 90 percent.

Predictive analytics are being incorporated into numerous business intelligence applications for sales, marketing, finance, fraud detection, and health care. One of the most well-known applications is credit scoring, which is used throughout the financial services industry. When you apply for a new credit card, scoring models process your credit history, loan application, and purchase data to determine your likelihood of making future credit payments on time. Telecommunications companies use predictive analytics to identify which customers are most profitable, which are most likely to leave, and which new services and plans will be most likely to retain customers. Health care insurers have been analyzing data for years to identify which patients are most likely to generate high costs.

Many companies employ predictive analytics to predict response to direct marketing campaigns. By identifying customers less likely to respond, companies are able to lower their marketing and sales costs by bypassing this group and focusing their resources on customers who have been identified as more promising. For instance, the U.S. division of The Body Shop plc used predictive analytics and its database of catalog, Web, and retail store customers to identify customers who were more likely to make catalog purchases. That information helped the company build a more precise and targeted mailing list for its catalogs, improving the response rate for catalog mailings and catalog revenues.

Big Data Analytics

Many online retailers have capabilities for making personalized online product recommendations to their Web site visitors to help stimulate purchases and guide their decisions about what merchandise to stock. However, most of these product recommendations are based on the behaviors of similar groups of customers, such as those with incomes under $50,000 or whose ages are between 18–25. Now some are starting to analyze the tremendous quantities of online and in-store customer data they collect along with social media data to make these recommendations more individualized.

Major online companies such as Walmart, Netflix, and eBay are analyzing big data from their customer transactions and social media streams to create real-time personalized shopping experiences. These efforts are translating into higher customer spending and customer retention rates.

EBay uses Hunch.com, which it acquired in 2011, to deliver customized recommendations to individual users based on their specific set of tastes. Hunch has built a massive database that includes data from customer purchases, social networks, and signals from around the Web. Hunch is able to analyze the data to create a "taste graph" that maps users with their predicted affinity for products, services, Web sites, and other people, and use this information to create customized recommendations.

The Hunch "taste graph" includes predictions on about 500 million people, 200 million objects (such as videos, gadgets, or books), and 30 billion connections between people and objects. To generate accurate predictions in near real-time, Hunch transformed each person's tastes into a more manageable "taste fingerprint" extracted from the larger taste graph.

Hunch.com's prediction technology is helping eBay develop recommendations of items that might not be immediately obvious for users to purchase from its online marketplace. For example, for a coin collector purchasing on eBay, Hunch might recommend microscopes that are especially useful for coin analysis. Hunch could also become an important tool for eBay sellers if its customer profiles help them make better decisions about which items to offer, the content they use to describe their inventory, and perhaps even the advertising they use to promote their eBay listings (Grau, 2012).

Data Visualization, Visual Analytics, and Geographic Information Systems

By presenting data in visual form, **data visualization** and visual analytics tools help users see patterns and relationships in large amounts of data that would be difficult to discern if the data were presented as traditional lists of text or numbers. Data are presented in the form of rich graphs, charts, dashboards, and maps. People become more engaged when they can filter information that is presented visually and develop insights on their own.

Geographic information systems (GIS) are a special category of tools for helping decision makers visualize problems requiring knowledge about the geographic distribution of people or other resources. GIS software ties location data to points, lines, and areas on a map. Some GIS have modeling capabilities for changing the data and automatically revising business scenarios. GIS might be used to help state and local governments calculate response times to natural disasters and other emergencies or to help banks identify the best location for installing new branches or ATM terminals.

For example, Columbia, South Carolina-based First Citizens Bank uses GIS software from MapInfo to determine which markets to focus on for retaining customers and which to focus on for acquiring new customers. MapInfo also lets the bank drill down into details at the individual branch level and individualize goals for each branch. Each branch is able to see whether the greatest revenue opportunities are from mining its database of existing customers or from finding new customers.

The U.S. National Marine Fisheries Service (NMFS) created a GIS for identifying critical habitat for steelhead trout on the U.S. West Coast. Red areas show critical habitat. Pink-shaded areas indicate places where the steelhead trout are endangered, and dotted-yellow areas indicate places where the species is threatened.

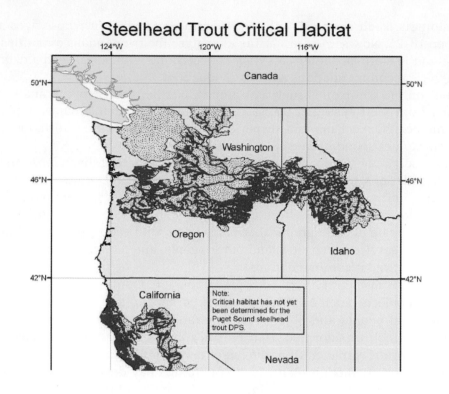

Steelhead Trout Critical Habitat

Note:
Critical habitat has not yet been determined for the Puget Sound steelhead trout DPS.

MANAGEMENT STRATEGIES FOR DEVELOPING BI AND BA CAPABILITIES

There are two different strategies for adopting BI and BA capabilities for the organization: one-stop integrated solutions versus multiple best-of-breed vendor solutions. The hardware firms (IBM, HP, and now Oracle, which owns Sun Microsystems) want to sell your firm integrated hardware/software solutions that tend to run only on their hardware (the totally integrated solution). It's called "one-stop shopping." The software firms (SAP, SAS, and Microsoft) encourage firms to adopt the "best of breed" software and that runs on any machine they want. In this strategy, you adopt the best database and data warehouse solution, and select the best business intelligence and analytics package from whatever vendor you believe is best.

The first solution carries the risk that a single vendor provides your firm's total hardware and software solution, making your firm dependent on its pricing power. It also offers the advantage of dealing with a single vendor who can deliver on a global scale. The second solution offers greater flexibility and independence, but with the risk of potential difficulties integrating the software to the hardware platform, as well as to other software. Vendors always claim their software is "compatible" with other software, but the reality is that it can be very difficult to integrate software from different vendors. Microsoft in particular emphasizes building on its desktop interface and operating system (Windows), which are familiar to many users, and developing server applications that run on Microsoft local area networks. But data from hardware and software produced by different vendors will have to flow seamlessly into Microsoft workstations to make this strategy work. This may not be adequate for Fortune 500 firms needing a global networking solution.

Regardless of which strategy your firm adopts, all BI and BA systems lock the firm into a set of vendors and switching is very costly. Once you train thousands of employees across the world on using a particular set of tools, it is extremely difficult to switch. When you adopt these systems, you are in essence taking in a new partner.

The marketplace is very competitive and given to hyperbole. One BI vendor claims "[Our tools] bring together a portfolio of services, software, hardware and partner technologies to create business intelligence solutions. By connecting intelligence across your company, you gain a competitive advantage for creating new business opportunities." As a manager, you will have to critically evaluate such claims, understand exactly how these systems could improve your business, and determine whether the expenditures are worth the benefits.

12.3 BUSINESS INTELLIGENCE CONSTITUENCIES

There are many different constituencies that make up a modern business firm. Earlier in this text and in this chapter we identified three levels of management: lower supervisory (operational) management, middle management, and senior management (vice president and above, including executive or "C level" management, e.g. chief executive officer, chief financial officers, and chief operational officer.) Each of these management groups has different responsibilities and different needs for information and business intelligence, with decisions becoming less structured among higher levels of management (review Figure 12.1).

DECISION SUPPORT FOR OPERATIONAL AND MIDDLE MANAGEMENT

Operational and middle management are generally charged with monitoring the performance of key aspects of the business, ranging from the down-time of machines on a factory floor, to the daily or even hourly sales at franchise food stores, to the daily traffic at a company's Web site. Most of the decisions they make are fairly structured. Management information systems (MIS) are typically used by middle managers to support this type of decision making, and their primary output is a set of routine production reports based on data extracted and summarized from the firm's underlying transaction processing systems (TPS). Increasingly, middle managers receive these reports online on the company portal, and are able to interactively query the data to find out why events are happening. To save even more analysis time, managers turn to exception reports, which highlight only exceptional conditions, such as when the sales quotas for a specific territory fall below an anticipated level or employees have exceeded their spending limits in a dental care plan. Table 12.6 provides some examples of MIS applications.

Support for Semistructured Decisions

Some managers are "super users" and keen business analysts who want to create their own reports, and use more sophisticated analytics and models to find patterns in data, to model alternative business scenarios, or to test specific hypotheses. Decision-support systems (DSS) are the BI delivery platform for this category of users, with the ability to support semistructured decision making.

TABLE 12.6 EXAMPLES OF MIS APPLICATIONS

COMPANY	MIS APPLICATION
California Pizza Kitchen	Inventory Express application "remembers" each restaurant's ordering patterns and compares the amount of ingredients used per menu item to predefined portion measurements established by management. The system identifies restaurants with out-of-line portions and notifies their managers so that corrective actions will be taken.
PharMark	Extranet MIS identifies patients with drug-use patterns that place them at risk for adverse outcomes.
Black & Veatch	Intranet MIS tracks construction costs for various projects across the United States.
Taco Bell	Total Automation of Company Operations (TACO) system provides information on food, labor, and period-to-date costs for each restaurant.

DSS rely more heavily on modeling than MIS, using mathematical or analytical models to perform what-if or other kinds of analysis. "What-if" analysis, working forward from known or assumed conditions, allows the user to vary certain values to test results to predict outcomes if changes occur in those values. What happens if we raise product prices by 5 percent or increase the advertising budget by $1 million? **Sensitivity analysis** models ask what-if questions repeatedly to predict a range of outcomes when one or more variables are changed multiple times (see Figure 12.5). Backward sensitivity analysis helps decision makers with goal seeking: If I want to sell 1 million product units next year, how much must I reduce the price of the product?

Chapter 6 described multidimensional data analysis and OLAP as one of the key business intelligence technologies. Spreadsheets have a similar feature for multidimensional analysis called a **pivot table**, which manager "super users" and analysts employ to identify and understand patterns in business information that may be useful for semistructured decision making.

Figure 12.6 illustrates a Microsoft Excel 2010 pivot table that examines a large list of order transactions for a company selling online management training videos and books. It shows the relationship between two dimensions: the sales region and the source of contact (Web banner ad or e-mail) for each customer order. It answers the question: does the source of the customer make a difference in addition to region? The pivot table in this figure shows that most customers come from the West and that banner advertising produces most of the customers in all the regions.

One of the Hands-On MIS projects for this chapter asks you to use a pivot table to find answers to a number of other questions using the same list of transactions for the online training company as we used in this discussion. The complete Excel file for these transactions is available in MyMISLab. We have also added a Learning Track on creating pivot tables using Excel.

In the past, much of this modeling was done with spreadsheets and small stand-alone databases. Today these capabilities are incorporated into large enterprise BI systems where they are able to analyze data from large corporate databases. BI analytics include tools for intensive modeling, some of which we described earlier. Such capabilities help Progressive Insurance identify the best customers for its products. Using widely available insurance industry data,

FIGURE 12.5 **SENSITIVITY ANALYSIS**

		Variable Cost per Unit				
Total fixed costs	19000					
Variable cost per unit	3					
Average sales price	17					
Contribution margin	**14**					
Break-even point	1357					
			2	3	4	5	6
Sales	1357		2	3	4	5	6
Price	14	1583	1727	1900	2111	2375
	15	1462	1583	1727	1900	2111
	16	1357	1462	1583	1727	1900
	17	1267	1357	1462	1583	1727
	18	1188	1267	1357	1462	1583

This table displays the results of a sensitivity analysis of the effect of changing the sales price of a necktie and the cost per unit on the product's break-even point. It answers the question, "What happens to the break-even point if the sales price and the cost to make each unit increase or decrease?"

Progressive defines small groups of customers, or "cells," such as motorcycle riders aged 30 or above with college educations, credit scores over a certain level, and no accidents. For each "cell," Progressive performs a regression analysis to identify factors most closely correlated with the insurance losses that are typical for this group. It then sets prices for each cell, and uses simulation software to test whether this pricing arrangement will enable the company to make a profit. These analytic techniques, make it possible for Progressive to profitably insure customers in traditionally high-risk categories that other insurers would have rejected.

FIGURE 12.6 **A PIVOT TABLE THAT EXAMINES CUSTOMER REGIONAL DISTRIBUTION AND ADVERTISING SOURCE**

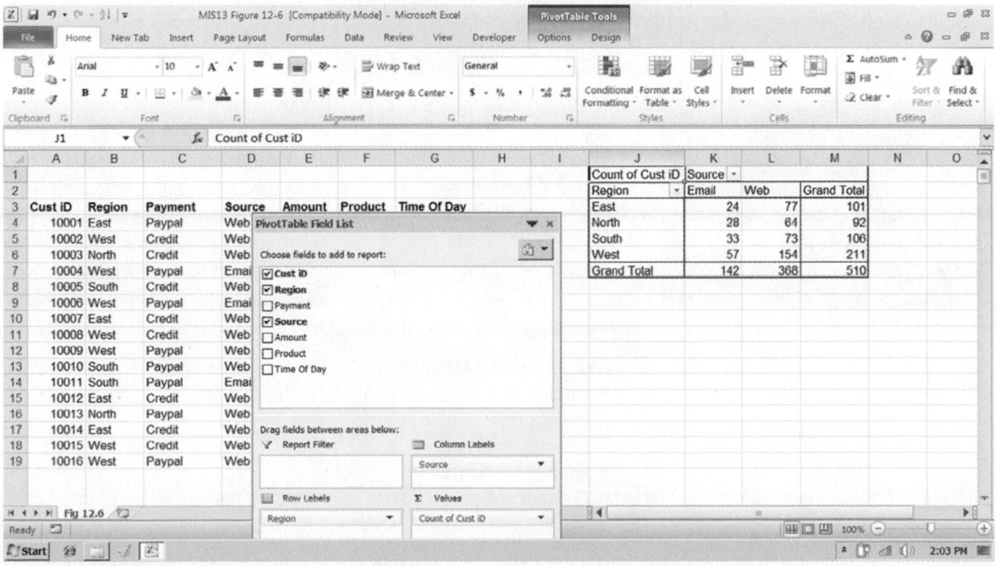

In this pivot table, we are able to examine where an online training company's customers come from in terms of region and advertising source.

DECISION SUPPORT FOR SENIOR MANAGEMENT: BALANCED SCORECARD AND ENTERPRISE PERFORMANCE MANAGEMENT METHODS

The purpose of executive support systems (ESS), introduced in Chapter 2, is to help C-level executive managers focus on the really important performance information that affect the overall profitability and success of the firm. There are two parts to developing ESS. First, you will need a methodology for understanding exactly what is "the really important performance information" for a specific firm that executives need, and second, you will need to develop systems capable of delivering this information to the right people in a timely fashion.

Currently, the leading methodology for understanding the really important information needed by a firm's executives is called the **balanced scorecard method** (Kaplan and Norton, 2004; Kaplan and Norton, 1992). The balanced score card is a framework for operationalizing a firm's strategic plan by focusing on measurable outcomes on four dimensions of firm performance: financial, business process, customer, and learning and growth (Figure 12.7).

Performance on each dimension is measured using **key performance indicators (KPIs)**, which are the measures proposed by senior management for understanding how well the firm is performing along any given dimension. For instance, one key indicator of how well an online retail firm is meeting its customer performance objectives is the average length of time required to deliver a package to a consumer. If your firm is a bank, one KPI of business process performance is the length of time required to perform a basic function like creating a new customer account.

FIGURE 12.7 THE BALANCED SCORECARD FRAMEWORK

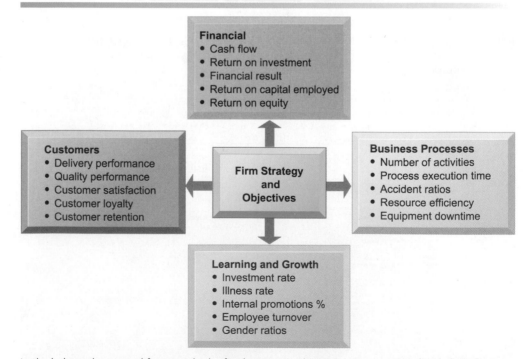

In the balanced scorecard framework, the firm's strategic objectives are operationalized along four dimensions: financial, business process, customer, and learning and growth. Each dimension is measured using several KPIs.

The balanced scorecard framework is thought to be "balanced" because it causes managers to focus on more than just financial performance. In this view, financial performance is past history—the result of past actions—and managers should focus on the things they are able to influence today, such as business process efficiency, customer satisfaction, and employee training. Once a scorecard is developed by consultants and senior executives, the next step is automating a flow of information to executives and other managers for each of the key performance indicators. There are literally hundreds of consulting and software firms that offer these capabilities, which are described below. Once these systems are implemented, they are often referred to as ESS.

Another closely related popular management methodology is **business performance management (BPM)**. Originally defined by an industry group in 2004 (led by the same companies that sell enterprise and database systems like Oracle, SAP, and IBM), BPM attempts to systematically translate a firm's strategies (e.g., differentiation, low-cost producer, market share growth, and scope of operation) into operational targets. Once the strategies and targets are identified, a set of KPIs are developed that measure progress towards the targets. The firm's performance is then measured with information drawn from the firm's enterprise database systems. BPM uses the same ideas as balanced scorecard but with a stronger strategy flavor (BPM Working Group, 2004).

Corporate data for contemporary ESS are supplied by the firm's existing enterprise applications (enterprise resource planning, supply chain management, and customer relationship management). ESS also provide access to news services, financial market databases, economic information, and whatever other external data senior executives require. ESS also have significant **drill-down** capabilities if managers need more detailed views of data.

Well-designed ESS help senior executives monitor organizational performance, track activities of competitors, recognize changing market conditions, and identify problems and opportunities. Employees lower down in the corporate hierarchy also use these systems to monitor and measure business performance in their areas of responsibility. For these and other business intelligence systems to be truly useful, the information must be "actionable"—it must be readily available and also easy to use when making decisions. If users have difficulty identifying critical metrics within the reports they receive, employee productivity and business performance will suffer. The Interactive Session on Management shows how Colgate-Palmolive addressed this problem and helped its managers make more data-driven, actionable decisions.

GROUP DECISION-SUPPORT SYSTEMS (GDSS)

The DSS we have just described focus primarily on individual decision making. However, so much work is accomplished in groups within firms that a special category of systems called **group decision-support systems (GDSS)** has been developed to support group and organizational decision making.

A GDSS is an interactive computer-based system for facilitating the solution of unstructured problems by a set of decision makers working together as a group in the same location or in different locations. Collaboration systems and Web-based tools for videoconferencing and electronic meetings described earlier in this text support some group decision processes, but their focus is primarily on communication. GDSS, however, provide tools and technologies geared explicitly toward group decision making.

GDSS-guided meetings take place in conference rooms with special hardware and software tools to facilitate group decision making. The hardware includes

INTERACTIVE SESSION: MANAGEMENT

COLGATE-PALMOLIVE KEEPS MANAGERS SMILING WITH EXECUTIVE DASHBOARDS

Colgate-Palmolive Company is the second largest consumer products company in the world whose products are marketed in over 200 countries and territories. The company had 38,600 employees worldwide and $16.734 billion in annual revenue in 2011. Colgate has been keeping people smiling and clean around the world, with more than three-quarters of its sales in recent years coming from outside the United States. Colgate's brands in oral products, soap, and pet food, are global names, including Colgate, Palmolive, Mennen, Softsoap, Irish Spring, Protex, Sorriso, Kolynos, Elmex, Tom's of Maine, Ajax, Axion, Fabuloso, Soupline, and Suavitel, as well as Hill's Science Diet and Hill's Prescription Diet.

The secret to continued growth and stability for the past two decades has been Colgate's ability to move its brands off shore to Latin America, Europe and Asia. In the past, Colgate divided the world into geographic regions: Latin American, Europe, Asia, and North America. Each region had its own information systems. As long as the regions did not need to share resources or information this patchwork system worked, more or less. This all changed as global operations became more integrated and senior management needed to oversee and coordinate these operations more closely.

Colgate had been a global SAP user since the early 1990s, but it was running five separate ERP systems to serve its different geographic regions. Over a period of time, disparities in the data developed between different geographic regions and between the data used at the corporate level and the data used by an individual region or business unit. The data were constantly changing. For example, every time a sales report was run, it showed different numbers for orders and shipments. Colgate wanted more usable data to drive business decisions and all of its managers and business units worldwide to use the same version of the data.

Colgate chose to solve this problem by creating a single global data repository using SAP NetWeaver Business Warehouse, SAP's analytical, reporting and data warehousing solution. Colgate's regional ERP systems feed their data to the warehouse, where the data are standardized and formatted for enterprise-wide reporting and analysis. This eliminates differences in data across the enterprise.

One of the outputs of the warehouse for senior managers is a daily HTML table showing a series of financial and operational metrics for the day compared to the previous month and quarter. The data the executives see is exactly the same as what their peers in all Colgate regions and business units see.

However, the data were not being used by enough employees in their decision making to have an impact on business benefits. Colgate's power users had no trouble using the reporting and analytical tools provided by the warehouse, and they were satisfied with the matrix reports from the system. Colgate's senior managers and other casual users, on the other hand, did not feel comfortable running ad hoc reports or drilling down into the layers of data to answer questions the data brought to light. They did not have much time to spend developing reports, and the standard reports produced for them by the warehouse lacked navigation and drill down capabilities. Tables had no color coding so users could only interpret the data by scrutinizing the numbers on the table.

Eventually Colgate's senior managers and other casual users began requesting deeper access to the warehouse data in a more timely and user-friendly format. They wanted reports that were easier to run and where the data could be interpreted faster. Senior management requested customizable, real-time dashboards that could be more easily used to drive performance improvement.

Colgate's information systems specialists then implemented SAP NetWeaver BW Accelerator to speed up data loads and improve user perception and adoption and SAP BusinessObjects Web Intelligence to build customized reports. SAP BusinessObjects Web Intelligence provides a powerful, intuitive interface that enables business analysts and non-technical business professionals to ask spontaneous questions about their data. Casual business users can use simple drag-and-drop techniques to access data sources and create interactive reports that drill, slice and format information based on their needs. Tools for cutting edge visualization allow end users to view two- and three-dimensional charts and hone in on specific areas of focus.

Colgate started using SAP's BusinessObjects tools to build user-friendly dashboards, and quickly created dashboard prototypes for management to review. Once management approved the dashboard design, the dashboards were populated with production data. Now Colgate's senior managers are running the dashboards to monitor the business from a high level.

Employee training was essential to the dashboards' success. Members of Colgate's global information systems development team created customized courses for Colgate's 65 business intelligence experts and ran the classroom training. The training identified people that could be used as resources for developing the reporting tools. When word spread about the dashboards' capabilities, Colgate's power users signed up for the classes as well.

For Colgate, better reporting tools that can support different kinds of users have greatly expanded the use of business intelligence throughout the company. Currently about 4000 users interact with Colgate's SAP systems daily but this number is expected to expand to 15,000 to 20,000 users in the future. People who are accustomed to seeing reports stuffed with numbers are finding that they can use the information presented in dashboards to make faster decisions. For example, managers can determine positive or negative financial conditions by simply looking for where dashboard reports use the color green, which reflects improvements in Colgate's financial position. Executives who formerly relied on other people to obtain their custom reports and data are able to access the information on their own. They can see real data from the system much more easily and quickly.

Sources: Paul Ziobro, "Colgate Shows Improved Growth," *Wall Street Journal*, April 26, 2012; Colgate Palmolive Corporation, "SEC Form 10K for the Fiscal Year Ending December 31, 2011," Colgate Palmolive Corporation, February 26, 2012; David Hannon, "Colgate-Palmolive Empowers Senior Leaders with Executive Dashboards," SAP InsiderPROFILES, April–June 2011; www.colgatepalmolive.com, accessed July 22, 2012; and SAP, "Placing Relevant Business Content within Business User Reach," 2011.

CASE STUDY QUESTIONS

1. Describe the different types of business intelligence users at Colgate-Palmolive.

2. Describe the "people" issues that were affecting Colgate's ability to use business intelligence.

3. What management, organization, and technology factors had to be addressed in providing business intelligence capabilities for each type of user?

4. What kind of decisions does Colgate's new business intelligence capability support? Give three examples. What is their potential business impact?

computer and networking equipment, overhead projectors, and display screens. Special electronic meeting software collects, documents, ranks, edits, and stores the ideas offered in a decision-making meeting. The more elaborate GDSS use a professional facilitator and support staff. The facilitator selects the software tools and helps organize and run the meeting.

A sophisticated GDSS provides each attendee with a dedicated desktop computer under that person's individual control. No one will be able to see what individuals do on their computers until those participants are ready to share information. Their input is transmitted over a network to a central server that stores information generated by the meeting and makes it available to all on the meeting network. Data can also be projected on a large screen in the meeting room.

GDSS make it possible to increase meeting size while at the same time increasing productivity because individuals contribute simultaneously rather than one at a time. A GDSS promotes a collaborative atmosphere by guaranteeing contributors' anonymity so that attendees focus on evaluating the ideas themselves without fear of personally being criticized or of having their ideas rejected based on the contributor. GDSS software tools follow structured methods for organizing and evaluating ideas and for preserving the results of meetings, enabling nonattendees to locate needed information after the meeting. GDSS effectiveness depends on the nature of the problem and the group and on how well a meeting is planned and conducted.

LEARNING TRACK MODULE

The following Learning Track provides content relevant to topics covered in this chapter:

1. Building and Using Pivot Tables

Review Summary

1. *What are the different types of decisions and how does the decision-making process work?*

   The different levels in an organization (strategic, management, operational) have different decision-making requirements. Decisions can be structured, semistructured, or unstructured, with structured decisions clustering at the operational level of the organization and unstructured decisions at the strategic level. Decision making can be performed by individuals or groups and includes employees as well as operational, middle, and senior managers. There are four stages in decision making: intelligence, design, choice, and implementation. Systems to support decision making do not always produce better manager and employee decisions that improve firm performance because of problems with information quality, management filters, and organizational culture.

2. *How do information systems support the activities of managers and management decision making?*

   Early classical models of managerial activities stress the functions of planning, organizing, coordinating, deciding, and controlling. Contemporary research looking at the actual behavior of managers has found that managers' real activities are highly fragmented, variegated, and brief in duration and that managers shy away from making grand, sweeping policy decisions.

   Information technology provides new tools for managers to carry out both their traditional and newer roles, enabling them to monitor, plan, and forecast with more precision and speed than ever before and to respond more rapidly to the changing business environment. Information systems have been most helpful to managers by providing support for their roles in disseminating information, providing liaisons between organizational levels, and allocating resources. However, information systems are less successful at supporting unstructured decisions. Where information systems are useful, information quality, management filters, and organizational culture can degrade decision making.

3. *How do business intelligence and business analytics support decision making?*

   Business intelligence and analytics promise to deliver correct, nearly real-time information to decision makers, and the analytic tools help them quickly understand the information and take action. A business intelligence environment consists of data from the business environment, the BI infrastructure, a BA toolset, managerial users and methods, a BI delivery platform (MIS, DSS, or ESS), and the user interface. There are six analytic functionalities that BI systems deliver to achieve these ends: predefined production reports, parameterized reports, dashboards and scorecards, ad hoc queries and searches, the ability to drill down to detailed views of data, and the ability to model scenarios and create forecasts.

4. *How do different decision-making constituencies in an organization use business intelligence?*

   Operational and middle management are generally charged with monitoring the performance of their firm. Most of the decisions they make are fairly structured. Management information systems (MIS) producing routine production reports are typically used to support this type of decision making.

For making unstructured decisions, middle managers and analysts will use decision-support systems (DSS) with powerful analytics and modeling tools, including spreadsheets and pivot tables. Senior executives making unstructured decisions use dashboards and visual interfaces displaying key performance information affecting the overall profitability, success, and strategy of the firm. The balanced scorecard and business performance management are two methodologies used in designing executive support systems (ESS).

5. *What is the role of information systems in helping people working in a group make decisions more efficiently?*
    Group decision-support systems (GDSS) help people working together in a group arrive at decisions more efficiently. GDSS feature special conference room facilities where participants contribute their ideas using networked computers and software tools for organizing ideas, gathering information, making and setting priorities, and documenting meeting sessions.

Key Terms

Balanced scorecard method, 504
Behavioral models, 488
Business performance management
   (BPM), 505
Choice, 488
Classical model of management, 488
Data visualization, 499
Decisional role, 489
Design, 488
Drill-down, 505
Geographic information systems (GIS), 499
Group decision-support systems (GDSS), 505

Implementation, 488
Informational role, 489
Intelligence, 488
Interpersonal role, 489
Key performance indicators (KPIs), 504
Managerial roles, 489
Pivot table, 502
Predictive analytics, 497
Semistructured decisions, 486
Sensitivity analysis, 502
Structured decisions, 486
Unstructured decisions, 486

Review Questions

1. What are the different types of decisions and how does the decision-making process work?
   - List and describe the different levels of decision making and decision-making constituencies in organizations. Explain how their decision-making requirements differ.
   - Distinguish between an unstructured, semistructured, and structured decision.
   - List and describe the stages in decision making.

2. How do information systems support the activities of managers and management decision making?
   - Compare the descriptions of managerial behavior in the classical and behavioral models.
   - Identify the specific managerial roles that can be supported by information systems.

3. How do business intelligence and business analytics support decision making?
   - Define and describe business intelligence and business analytics.
   - List and describe the elements of a business intelligence environment.

   - List and describe the analytic functionalities provided by BI systems.
   - Compare two different management strategies for developing BI and BA capabilities.

4. How do different decision-making constituencies in an organization use business intelligence?
   - List each of the major decision-making constituencies in an organization and describe the types of decisions each makes.
   - Describe how MIS, DSS, or ESS provide decision support for each of these groups.
   - Define and describe the balanced scorecard method and business performance management.

5. What is the role of information systems in helping people working in a group make decisions more efficiently?
   - Define a group decision-support system (GDSS) and explain how it differs from a DSS.
   - Explain how a GDSS works and how it provides value for a business.

Discussion Questions

1. As a manager or user of information systems, what would you need to know to participate in the design and use of a DSS or an ESS? Why?

2. If businesses used DSS, GDSS, and ESS more widely, would managers and employees make better decisions? Why or why not?

3. How much can business intelligence and business analytics help companies refine their business strategy? Explain your answer.

Hands-On MIS Projects

The projects in this section give you hands-on experience identifying opportunities for DSS, using a spreadsheet pivot table to analyze sales data, and online retirement planning tools for financial planning.

Management Decision Problems

1. Dealerships for Subaru and other automobile manufacturers keep records of the mileage of cars they sell and service. Mileage data are used to remind customers of when they need to schedule service appointments, but they are used for other purposes as well. What kinds of decisions does this piece of data support at the local level and at the corporate level? What would happen if this piece of data were erroneous, for example, showing mileage of 130,000 instead of 30,000? How would it affect decisionmaking? Assess its business impact.

2. Applebee's is the largest casual dining chain in the world, with over 1800 locations throughout the U.S. and also in 20 other countries. The menu features beef, chicken, and pork items, as well as burgers, pasta, and seafood. Applebee's CEO wants to make the restaurant more profitable by developing menus that are tastier and contain more items that customers want and are willing to pay for despite rising costs for gasoline and agricultural products. How might business intelligence help management implement this strategy? What pieces of data would Applebee's need to collect? What kinds of reports would be useful to help management make decisions on how to improve menus and profitability?

Improving Decision Making: Using Pivot Tables to Analyze Sales Data

Software skills: Pivot tables
Business skills: Analyzing sales data

This project gives you an opportunity to learn how to use Excel's PivotTable feature to analyze a database or data list. Use the data file for Online Management Training Inc. described earlier in the chapter. This is a list of the sales transactions at OMT for one day. You can find this spreadsheet file at MyMISLab. Use Excel's PivotTable to help you answer the following questions:

- Where are the average purchases higher? The answer might tell managers where to focus marketing and sales resources, or pitch different messages to different regions.
- What form of payment is the most common? The answer could be used to emphasize in advertising the most preferred means of payment.
- Are there any times of day when purchases are most common? Do people buy are products while at work (likely during the day) or at home (likely in the evening)?
- What's the relationship between region, type of product purchased, and average sales price?

We provide instructions on how to use Excel PivotTables in our Learning Tracks.

Improving Decision Making: Using a Web-Based DSS for Retirement Planning

Software skills: Internet-based software
Business skills: Financial planning

This project will help develop your skills in using Web-based DSS for financial planning.

The Web sites for CNN Money and Kiplinger feature Web-based DSS for financial planning and decision making. Select either site to plan for retirement. Use your chosen site to determine how much you need to save to have enough income for your retirement. Assume that you are 50 years old and plan to retire in 16 years. You have one dependant and $100,000 in savings. Your current annual income is $85,000. Your goal is to be able to generate an annual retirement income of $60,000, including Social Security benefit payments.

Use the Web site you have selected to determine how much money you need to save to help you achieve your retirement goal. To calculate your estimated Social Security benefit, use the Quick Calculator at the Social Security Administration Web site

Critique the site—its ease of use, its clarity, the value of any conclusions reached, and the extent to which the site helps investors understand their financial needs and the financial markets.

Video Cases

Video Cases and Instructional Videos illustrating some of the concepts in this chapter are available. Contact your instructor to access these videos.

Collaboration and Teamwork Project

In MyMISLab, you will find a Collaboration and Teamwork Project dealing with the concepts in this chapter. You will be able to use Google Sites, Google Docs, and other open source collaboration tools to complete the assignment.

Zynga Wins with Business Intelligence
CASE STUDY

The world's fastest growing gaming company doesn't boast top-of-the-line graphics, heart-pounding action, or masterful storytelling. It doesn't make games for the Playstation, Xbox, or Wii. The company in question is Zynga, and if you have a Facebook account, odds are you're already well aware of its most popular games. Zynga's explosive growth illustrates the potential of social gaming and the ability of social networks to provide critical data about a company's customers.

Founded in 2007 by Mark Pincus and a group of other entrepreneurs, Zynga is the leading developer of social network games, such as *CityVille*, *Texas HoldEm Poker*, and *FarmVille*. These games, along with Zynga's *Empires & Allies* game, are the four most frequently used applications on Facebook. Zynga's games have over 290 million monthly active users and 65 million daily players whose gaming keystrokes and clicks generate 3 terabytes of data every day. Since its inception, Zynga has put a priority on data analytics to guide the management of its games and the business decisions of the company.

The company relies heavily on its data to improve user retention and to increase collaboration among its gamers. In the words of Ken Rudin, chief of data analytics at Zynga, to be useful, data must be "actionable"—it has to be information that allows Zynga to make noticeable improvements to its games. Generating and storing game data is only half of the battle. Zynga also uses two analytics teams—a reporting team and analytics team—to work with the data and make concrete recommendations for business improvements based on that data.

There are three key metrics that drive the economics of social gaming: churn rates, the viral coefficient, and revenue per user. Churn, which we discuss in Chapter 9, is the loss rate of game players. Social gaming can have an extraordinarily high churn rate, about 50 percent per month on average. That means that half the new players signing up for a game today will be gone in a month.

The viral coefficient is a measure of the effectiveness of existing game players for drawing new players, an important capability for social network platforms. For example, if 100 Farmville users are likely to cause 5 of their friends to sign up in a given month, that would result in a viral coefficient of 1.05.

Expected revenue per user is an estimate of the lifetime revenue that a game player will generate, based on an estimate of monthly revenue per user and the churn rate. For instance, if the average monthly revenue is $5 per user and the churn rate is 50 percent, the expected revenue can be estimated as $5 the first month + $2.50 the second month + $1.25 the third month, and so forth, or approximately $20.

The first wave of social gaming applications on Facebook tried to increase the viral coefficient with Wall postings advertising in-game actions by players. This approach created too much "Wall spam," or game-related postings that made it difficult for social network users to identify posts by friends. Facebook and other social networking platforms then demanded that gaming firms reduce their Wall spam.

As a result, Zynga turned to social graph analysis. For social games, the "social graph," or relationships between friends, is somewhat different from that of the social networking platform itself. For example, in Zynga's *Mafia Wars* game, players might have two types of friends—those who actively play the game and a more passive group that signed on to help expand a friend's Mafia organization and then leave the game or play very infrequently. Players don't always interact the same way with these two groups, with gifts and offers of help more frequent within the active group. Guiding game players to communicate appropriately with these different types of relationships helps increase revenue and virality while reducing churn. A social gaming company such as Zynga will thus try to improve the player experience to make every aspect of the game more profitable.

Technology from Vertica Systems, an analytic database management company, helps solve this problem. Vertica's Massively Parallel Processing (MPP) architecture enables customers to deploy its analytics platform using industry standard hardware or cloud solutions as building blocks called "nodes." Users can build clusters consisting of 1, 10, or 100 or more nodes, putting thousands of processors, terabytes of computer memory, and petabytes of disk storage to work as a single parallel cluster.

A small start-up company can deploy Vertica on a single node, adding new nodes as needed.

Vertica's data warehouse is columnar, which means that data are stored in columns instead of rows. This allows Zynga's data to be more tightly compressed, at a rate of 10 to 1 (10 terabytes of data become 1 terabyte of compressed data). Vertica's data warehouse is able to work with this compressed data, which improves performance by reducing processor demands, memory, and disk input/output at processing time. Traditional database management systems can't work with compressed data. As a result, Zynga achieves rates of performance that are 50 to 100 times faster than the data warehouses used by other companies.

Vertica software is also able to manipulate the database for social graph analysis, transposing all of an individual user's interactions with other users into a single row, and it can do this quickly. Relational database platforms are unable to cope with the massive volume of data created by all the connections in a social graph.

Zynga's social graph-related data are streamed in real time to a dedicated Vertica cluster where the graph is generated daily. Every night, the models resulting from this graph are fed back into its games for use the next day. Zynga runs as many as 130 experiments to tweak and adjust its games each day and then observe how players react. Within minutes after releasing a new feature, Zynta is able to find out whether millions of players liked it or not. On the basis of this new knowledge, Zynga may make as many as 100 daily updates to its products.

With this business intelligence solution, Zynga has been able to improve the targeting of items such as gifts to effectively increase the level of interaction between active players while minimizing spam to passive players. Zynga is now in a position to identify groups of users with similar behavior or common paths for even more precise targeting of game-related promotions and activities.

Zynga's revenue rose from $121 million in 2009 to $1.14 billion in 2011. Clearly, Zynga's methods are working. Traditional game-makers like Activision Blizzard and Electronic Arts are noting Zynga's growth and success and have moved towards a similar business model. For example, Electronic Arts launched a free Facebook version of the classic game *The Sims*. The game now has 40 million active monthly players and was Facebook's fastest growing app for much of 2011.

Zynga's business model is to offer free games geared towards a larger, more casual gaming audience, and to generate revenue by selling virtual goods in game. The idea of virtual goods has been around for years, most notably in Second Life and other virtual worlds, where users can buy apparel and accessories for their avatars. But Zynga's attention to detail and ability to glean important information from countless terabytes of data generated by its users on a daily basis has set it apart.

For example, product managers in Zynga's *FishVille* Facebook game discovered that players bought a certain type of fish in game, the translucent anglerfish, more frequently than the rest. Zynga began offering fish similar to the anglerfish for about $3 apiece, and *FishVille* players responded by buying many more fish than usual. Analytics have also shown that Zynga's gamers tend to buy more in-game goods when they are offered as limited edition items. Zynga sells advertising, both in and around its games, but the vast majority of its revenue comes from its virtual goods sales.

Zynga also benefits from using Facebook as its gaming platform. When users install a Zynga application, they allow Zynga access to all of their profile information, including their names, genders, and lists of friends. Zynga then uses that information to determine what types of users are most likely to behave in certain ways. Zynga particularly hopes to determine which types of users are most likely to become "whales," or big spenders that buy hundreds of dollars of virtual goods each month. Though only 5 percent of Zynga's active users contribute to corporate revenue, that subset of users is so dedicated that they account for nearly all of the company's earnings.

Zynga's games make heavy use of Facebook's social features. For example, in *CityVille*, users must find friends to fill fictional posts at their "City Hall" to successfully complete the structure. All of Zynga's games have features like this, but Facebook hasn't always fully supported all of Zynga's efforts. Zynga's Facebook apps were formerly able to send messages directly to Facebook members, but they disabled the feature after complaints that it was a form of spam. Still, if your friends use Zynga's Facebook apps, chances are you've seen advertisements encouraging you to play as well in your News Feed.

Zynga's success has disrupted the video game industry. Traditional video game companies begin with an idea for a game that they hope players will buy and enjoy, and then make the game. Zynga begins with a game, but then studies data to determine how its players play, what types of players are most active, and what virtual goods players buy.

Then, Zynga uses the data to get players to play longer, tell more friends, and buy even more goods.

Not everybody is thrilled with Zynga's data-driven approach to making games. Many game industry veterans believe Zynga's games are overly simplistic and have many of the same game elements. The company has also been the target of several lawsuits alleging that Zynga copied other companies' games. Even developers within Zynga have sometimes bristled at the company's prioritization of data analysis over creativity in game design. Some question Zynga's ability to prosper over the long term, saying it would be difficult for the company to create new games to replace old ones whose novelty is fading. In 2011–2012, the average amount of revenue from Zynga's core users dropped 10 percent even though its overall number of users expanded. Zynga's business model also assumes Facebook will continue to operate in the same manner and that customers will continue to expect the same quality of games. That may not always be the case.

In other words, Zynga's games lack artistry. But Zynga readily admits that its target audience is the segment of gamers that prefer casual games, and its goal is to make games that nearly anyone can play. Gamers that want a game requiring high levels of skill or sophisticated graphics can get their fix elsewhere. Zynga is using the measurability of Facebook activity to guide its game management, and this is helping the company create a finely tailored user experience that hasn't been seen before in gaming.

To reduce its reliance on Facebook, Zynga introduced its own independent gaming platform called Project Z in March 2012. The new platform enables customers to play some of Zynga's popular titles from its Web site rather than by accessing them through Facebook. A service called Zynga With Friends will match up players who do not know one another and might not have Facebook profiles or might be playing the game on a mobile application.

That same month Zynga announced it had purchased OMGPop Inc., the maker of the popular *Draw Something* mobile game, which asks players to make sketches illustrating words and have others guess what they drew. Zynga's management hopes that *Draw Something* will be part of a larger plan to build a mobile gaming network based on a portfolio of mobile, casual, and social games across a variety of social networks and platfoms. DreamWorks Animation will work with Zynga to place additional advertising within the game, creating another new source of revenue.

Will these efforts be enough to sustain Zynga's competitive advantage? Will Zynga's business model hold up as more of the Internet goes mobile? It's still too early to tell, but you can bet that Zynga will be poring over the data to find out.

Sources: David Streitfeld and Jenna Wortham, "The News Isn't Good for Zynga, Maker of FarmVille," *The New York Times*, July 25, 2012; Jenna Wortham, "Zynga's Plan to Get Its Groove Back: More Games and Social Upgrades," *The New York Times*, June 26, 2012; Lance Ulanoff, "Zynga Wants to Be a Mobile Gaming Network," *Mashable*, May 30, 2012; Ian Sherr, "Game Changer for Zynga: No Facebook," *The Wall Street Journal*, March 1, 2012 and "Zynga Defends Acquisition," *The Wall Street Journal*, May 24, 2012; David Streitfeld, "Zynga Seeks to Match Up Players for Online Games," *The New York Times*, March 1, 2012; Nick Wingfield, "Virtual Products, Real Profits," *The Wall Street Journal*, September 9, 2011; "The Impact of Social Graphing Analysis on the Bottom Line: How Zynga Performs Graph Analysis with the Vertica Analytics Platform," www.vertica.com, accessed June 2, 2012; and Jacquelyn Gavron, "Vertica: The Analytics Behind all the Zynga Games," *ReadWrite Enterprise*, July 18, 2011.

CASE STUDY QUESTIONS

1. It has been said that Zynga is "an analytics company masquerading as a games company." Discuss the implications of this statement.

2. What role does business intelligence play in Zynga's business model?

3. Give examples of three kinds of decisions supported by business intelligence at Zynga.

4. How much of a competitive advantage does business intelligence provide for Zynga? Explain.

5. What problems can business intelligence solve for Zynga? What problems can't it solve?

Building and Managing Systems

Part Four focuses on building and managing systems in organizations. This part answers questions such as: What activities are required to build a new information system? What alternative approaches are available for building system solutions? How should information systems projects be managed to ensure that new systems provide genuine business benefits and work successfully in the organization? What issues must be addressed when building and managing global systems?

Chapter 13

Building Information Systems

Interactive Sessions:

Burton Snowboards Speeds Ahead with Nimble Business Processes

What Does It Take to Go Mobile?

NEW SYSTEMS AND BUSINESS PROCESSES PUT MONEYGRAM "ON THE MONEY"

I f you use PayPal, you may not have heard of MoneyGram, but millions of people around the globe use this service to send money anywhere within minutes. Dallas-headquartered MoneyGram is one of the world's largest money transfer businesses in the world, with 256,000 partner agents ranging from Walmart to tobacco shops in Paris where customers can send and receive money. In 2011, MoneyGram generated $1.3 billion in revenue.

For a global money transfer company, it's essential to be able to move money between two points around the world within minutes. MoneyGram uses an automated financial management system to make this happen. The system handles hundreds of thousands of money transfer transactions each day and ensures that all of the retail stores, banks, and other MoneyGram agents receive proper financial settlement and commissions for each money transfer.

Despite many years of double-digit growth, MoneyGram's operations were not working well. The company was saddled with outdated systems that required the use of spreadsheets and time-consuming manual processes to calculate payments and close the books each month. Those systems were adequate for a long time, but eventually their complexity and lack of scalability constrained MoneyGram's ability to address market demands, add new products, and serve the sales team. Moreover, lack of a central data storehouse made it difficult to create reports, analyze market opportunities, and spot bottlenecks in the system.

Senior management decided to examine MoneyGram's business processes and legacy systems, some of which were redundant. It assembled the company's top business and technology managers, including the company's chief financial officer, controller, treasurer, and its executive vice president of operations and technology. They concluded that in addition to updating technology, MoneyGram needed to change some of its key business processes.

Culturally, MoneyGram's managers made changes in staff responsibilities to make employees more aware of the company's business processes and ways to improve them. Employees were instructed to understand each step in the business processes they were part of, instead of their own individual job functions. The company used numerous Webinars and other tools to show employees how business processes were being altered.

To that end, MoneyGram created a subset of managers called global process owners or GPOs. Each GPO is responsible for the performance of an individual process, such as cash management, customer onboarding, or credit processing. GPOs were asked to define the current state of their processes, how processes impacted each other, and how they felt they could be improved. They also defined how the success of their process could be measured, and were tasked with gathering performance data to gauge that improvement.

MoneyGram still uses GPOs in its operations., along with subprocess owners (SPOs), who are responsible for handling

© Alistair Laming / Alamy

day-to-day activities and problems. This new process orientation has moved MoneyGram from the old siloed departments to cross-functional work groups that collaborate closely with a long-range view of what's best for the business.

For the technology to support its new global processes, MoneyGram selected Oracle's E-Business Suite with the Oracle Incentive Compensation module. Oracle E-Business Suite consists of enterprise resource planning (ERP), customer relationship management (CRM), and supply chain management (SCM) applications using Oracle's relational database management system. Oracle Incentive Compensation module automates the process of designing, administering, and analyzing variable compensation programs. Management believed the Oracle software was capable of handling the customization work required to integrate with the processes used by the company's back-office and proprietary agents and to handle other unique business requirements. The Oracle system included capabilities for creating, viewing, and managing customer information online.

MoneyGram started implementing Oracle E-Business Suite in September 2012. The new software and business processes streamlined most of MoneyGram's back-office operations, making it easier to process more customer transactions and settlements with agents and billers and to update the company's General Ledger. New partners can be added at a much faster rate.

Commissions are critical for driving profitability in MoneyGram's existing and new products. MoneyGram must track a large number of different plans for calculating the commissions of its partner agents throughout the world. Its legacy system was unable to automate many of the commission plans, so MoneyGram had to use spreadsheets and manual processes to manage several hundred commission plans. MoneyGram built a flexible commission model using Oracle Incentive Compensation that has been able to automate more than 90 percent of its nonstandard commission plans.

In the past, new regional innovations took months to plan, but the Oracle implementation has cut that time by approximately 40 percent. New product introductions will integrate seamlessly with MoneyGram's back-end processes so that new transactions are recorded and accounted for correctly. The new Oracle system allows MoneyGram to configure the processes simply by adjusting currently existing parameters instead of developing new software. MoneyGram is less likely to go to market with a product that has to be initially run on manual processes.

Having an enterprise-wide repository of data located centrally allows MoneyGram employees to better serve customers and agents conducting the money transfers. Centralized data are up-to-date and easily available. Reports used to take 40 hours and three employees to create but now take 80 percent less time. Those workers can spend more time analyzing reports and less time putting them together.

The cost savings of consolidating more than 40 MoneyGram legacy IT systems into one enterprise-wide implementation of Oracle E-business Suite amount to millions of dollars. The company can now handle more transactions without having to hire additional staff. The company estimates that the Oracle software will pay for itself within one year.

Sources: Alan Joch, "On the Money" and "MoneyGram Exploits the Flexibility of Oracle Incentive Compensation," *Profit Magazine*, February 2012; MoneyGram, "MoneyGram, Advance America Renew Contract at Over 2,400 Stores Across USA," August 6, 2012; and www.moneygram.com, accessed August 26, 2012.

The experience of MoneyGram illustrates some of the steps required to design and build new information systems. Building the new financial management system entailed analyzing the organization's problems with existing information systems, assessing information requirements, selecting appropriate technology, and redesigning business processes and jobs. Management had to oversee the systems-building effort and evaluate benefits and costs. The new information system represented a process of planned organizational change.

The chapter-opening case calls attention to important points raised by this case and this chapter. MoneyGram's global operations were hampered by outdated information systems and inefficient manual processes, which raised costs and limited the company's ability to add new products and compensation plans for new partner agents so that it could continue to expand globally.

Management decided to replace 40 outdated legacy systems with an enterprise-wide software suite that could create a single source of centralized data for the company, and support global operations, new financial products, and the back-office accounting of compensation and payment transfers with much less manual effort. The solution entailed not just the application of new technology but changes to corporate culture, business processes, and job functions. Employee education and training were essential. Thanks to the new system, MoneyGram is in a much stronger position to expand globally, add new partner agents, and support new financial products and payment plans.

Here are some questions to think about: What are the advantages and challenges of using an enterprise-wide software suite such as Oracle E-Business Suite in a global company such as MoneyGram? How much did the new system change the way MoneyGram ran its business?

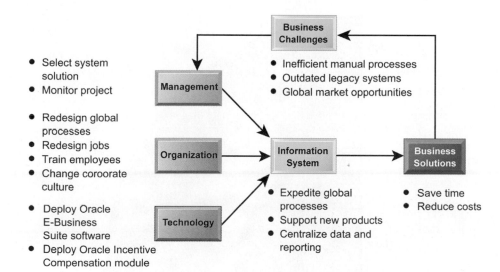

13.1   SYSTEMS AS PLANNED ORGANIZATIONAL CHANGE

Building a new information system is one kind of planned organizational change. The introduction of a new information system involves much more than new hardware and software. It also includes changes in jobs, skills, management, and organization. When we design a new information system, we are redesigning the organization. System builders must understand how a system will affect specific business processes and the organization as a whole.

SYSTEMS DEVELOPMENT AND ORGANIZATIONAL CHANGE

Information technology can promote various degrees of organizational change, ranging from incremental to far-reaching. Figure 13.1 shows four kinds of structural organizational change that are enabled by information technology: (1) automation, (2) rationalization, (3) business process redesign, and (4) paradigm shifts. Each carries different risks and rewards.

The most common form of IT-enabled organizational change is **automation**. The first applications of information technology involved assisting employees with performing their tasks more efficiently and effectively. Calculating paychecks and payroll registers, giving bank tellers instant access to customer deposit records, and developing a nationwide reservation network for airline ticket agents are all examples of early automation.

FIGURE 13.1   ORGANIZATIONAL CHANGE CARRIES RISKS AND REWARDS

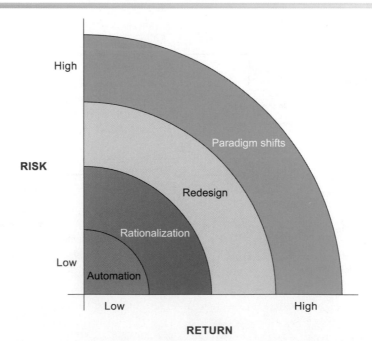

The most common forms of organizational change are automation and rationalization. These relatively slow-moving and slow-changing strategies present modest returns but little risk. Faster and more comprehensive change—such as redesign and paradigm shifts—carries high rewards but offers substantial chances of failure.

A deeper form of organizational change—one that follows quickly from early automation—is **rationalization of procedures**. Automation frequently reveals new bottlenecks in production and makes the existing arrangement of procedures and structures painfully cumbersome. Rationalization of procedures is the streamlining of standard operating procedures. For example, MoneyGram's system for handling global money transfers is effective not only because it uses computer technology but also because the company simplified its business processes for back-office operations. Fewer manual steps are required.

Rationalization of procedures is often found in programs for making a series of continuous quality improvements in products, services, and operations, such as total quality management (TQM) and six sigma. **Total quality management (TQM)** makes achieving quality an end in itself and the responsibility of all people and functions within an organization. TQM derives from concepts developed by American quality experts such as W. Edwards Deming and Joseph Juran, but it was popularized by the Japanese. **Six sigma** is a specific measure of quality, representing 3.4 defects per million opportunities. Most companies cannot achieve this level of quality, but use six sigma as a goal for driving ongoing quality improvement programs.

A more powerful type of organizational change is **business process redesign**, in which business processes are analyzed, simplified, and redesigned. Business process redesign reorganizes workflows, combining steps to cut waste and eliminate repetitive, paper-intensive tasks. (Sometimes the new design eliminates jobs as well.) It is much more ambitious than rationalization of procedures, requiring a new vision of how the process is to be organized.

A widely cited example of business process redesign is Ford Motor Company's invoiceless processing, which reduced headcount in Ford's North American Accounts Payable organization of 500 people by 75 percent. Accounts payable clerks used to spend most of their time resolving discrepancies between purchase orders, receiving documents, and invoices. Ford redesigned its accounts payable process so that the purchasing department enters a purchase order into an online database that can be checked by the receiving department when the ordered items arrive. If the received goods match the purchase order, the system automatically generates a check for accounts payable to send to the vendor. There is no need for vendors to send invoices.

Rationalizing procedures and redesigning business processes are limited to specific parts of a business. New information systems can ultimately affect the design of the entire organization by transforming how the organization carries out its business or even the nature of the business. For instance, the long-haul trucking and transportation firm Schneider National used new information systems to change its business model. Schneider created a new business managing logistics for other companies. This more radical form of business change is called a **paradigm shift**. A paradigm shift involves rethinking the nature of the business and the nature of the organization.

Paradigm shifts and reengineering often fail because extensive organizational change is so difficult to orchestrate (see Chapter 14). Why, then, do so many corporations contemplate such radical change? Because the rewards are equally high (see Figure 13.1). In many instances, firms seeking paradigm shifts and pursuing reengineering strategies achieve stunning, order-of-magnitude increases in their returns on investment (or productivity). Some of these success stories, and some failure stories, are included throughout this book.

BUSINESS PROCESS REDESIGN

Like MoneyGram, described in the chapter-opening case, many businesses today are trying to use information technology to improve their business processes. Some of these systems entail incremental process change, but others require more far-reaching redesign of business processes. To deal with these changes, organizations are turning to business process management. **Business process management** provides a variety of tools and methodologies to analyze existing processes, design new processes, and optimize those processes. BPM is never concluded because process improvement requires continual change. Companies practicing business process management go through the following steps:

1. **Identify processes for change:** One of the most important strategic decisions that a firm can make is not deciding how to use computers to improve business processes, but understanding what business processes need improvement. When systems are used to strengthen the wrong business model or business processes, the business can become more efficient at doing what it should not do. As a result, the firm becomes vulnerable to competitors who may have discovered the right business model. Considerable time and cost may also be spent improving business processes that have little impact on overall firm performance and revenue. Managers need to determine what business processes are the most important and how improving these processes will help business performance.

2. **Analyze existing processes:** Existing business processes should be modeled and documented, noting inputs, outputs, resources, and the sequence of activities. The process design team identifies redundant steps, paper-intensive tasks, bottlenecks, and other inefficiencies.

Figure 13.2 illustrates the "as-is" process for purchasing a book from a physical bookstore. Consider what happens when a customer visits a physical bookstore and searches its shelves for a book. If he or she finds the book, that

FIGURE 13.2 AS-IS BUSINESS PROCESS FOR PURCHASING A BOOK FROM A PHYSICAL BOOKSTORE

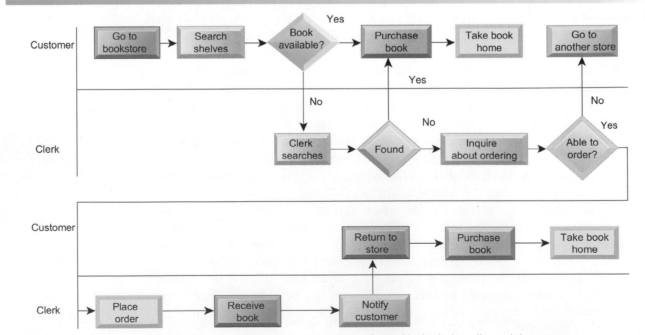

Purchasing a book from a physical bookstore requires many steps to be performed by both the seller and the customer.

person takes it to the checkout counter and pays for it via credit card, cash, or check. If the customer is unable to locate the book, he or she must ask a bookstore clerk to search the shelves or check the bookstore's inventory records to see if it is in stock. If the clerk finds the book, the customer purchases it and leaves. If the book is not available locally, the clerk inquires about ordering it for the customer, from the bookstore's warehouse or from the book's distributor or publisher. Once the ordered book arrives at the bookstore, a bookstore employee telephones the customer with this information. The customer would have to go to the bookstore again to pick up the book and pay for it. If the bookstore is unable to order the book for the customer, the customer would have to try another bookstore. You can see that this process has many steps and might require the customer to make multiple trips to the bookstore.

3. **Design the new process:** Once the existing process is mapped and measured in terms of time and cost, the process design team will try to improve the process by designing a new one. A new streamlined "to-be" process will be documented and modeled for comparison with the old process.

Figure 13.3 illustrates how the book-purchasing process can be redesigned by taking advantage of the Internet. The customer accesses an online bookstore over the Internet from his or her computer. He or she searches the bookstore's online catalog for the book he or she wants. If the book is available, the customer orders the book online, supplying credit card and shipping address information, and the book is delivered to the customer's home. If the online bookstore does not carry the book, the customer selects another online bookstore and searches for the book again. This process has far fewer steps than that for purchasing the book in a physical bookstore, requires much less effort on the part of the customer, and requires less sales staff for customer service. The new process is therefore much more efficient and time-saving.

The new process design needs to be justified by showing how much it reduces time and cost or enhances customer service and value. Management first measures the time and cost of the existing process as a baseline. In our example, the time required for purchasing a book from a physical bookstore might range from 15 minutes (if the customer immediately finds what he or she wants) to 30 minutes if the book is in stock but has to be located by sales staff. If the book has to be ordered from another source, the process might

FIGURE 13.3 REDESIGNED PROCESS FOR PURCHASING A BOOK ONLINE

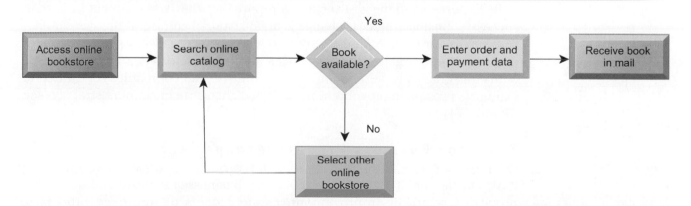

Using Internet technology makes it possible to redesign the process for purchasing a book so that it requires fewer steps and consumes fewer resources.

take one or two weeks and another trip to the bookstore for the customer. If the customer lives far away from the bookstore, the time to travel to the bookstore would have to be factored in. The bookstore will have to pay the costs for maintaining a physical store and keeping the book in stock, for sales staff on site, and for shipment costs if the book has to be obtained from another location.

The new process for purchasing a book online might only take several minutes, although the customer might have to wait several days or a week to receive the book in the mail and will have to pay a shipping charge. But the customer saves time and money by not having to travel to the bookstore or make additional visits to pick up the book. Booksellers' costs are lower because they do not have to pay for a physical store location or for local inventory.

4. **Implement the new process:** Once the new process has been thoroughly modeled and analyzed, it must be translated into a new set of procedures and work rules. New information systems or enhancements to existing systems may have to be implemented to support the redesigned process. The new process and supporting systems are rolled out into the business organization. As the business starts using this process, problems are uncovered and addressed. Employees working with the process may recommend improvements.

5. **Continuous measurement:** Once a process has been implemented and optimized, it needs to be continually measured. Why? Processes may deteriorate over time as employees fall back on old methods, or they may lose their effectiveness if the business experiences other changes.

Although many business process improvements are incremental and ongoing, there are occasions when more radical change must take place. Our example of a physical bookstore redesigning the book-purchasing process so that it can be carried out online is an example of this type of radical, far-reaching change. When properly implemented, business process redesign produces dramatic gains in productivity and efficiency, and may even change the way the business is run. In some instances, it drives a "paradigm shift" that transforms the nature of the business itself.

This actually happened in book retailing when Amazon challenged traditional physical bookstores with its online retail model. By radically rethinking the way a book can be purchased and sold, Amazon and other online bookstores have achieved remarkable efficiencies, cost reductions, and a whole new way of doing business.

BPM poses challenges. Executives report that the largest single barrier to successful business process change is organizational culture. Employees do not like unfamiliar routines and often try to resist change. This is especially true of projects where organizational changes are very ambitious and far-reaching. Managing change is neither simple nor intuitive, and companies committed to extensive process improvement need a good change management strategy (see Chapter 14).

Tools for Business Process Management

Over 100 software firms provide tools for various aspects of BPM, including IBM, Oracle, and TIBCO. These tools help businesses identify and document processes requiring improvement, create models of improved processes, capture and enforce business rules for performing processes, and integrate existing systems to support new or redesigned processes. BPM software tools also provide analytics for verifying that process performance has been improved and for measuring the impact of process changes on key business performance indicators.

Some BPM tools document and monitor business processes to help firms identify inefficiencies, using software to connect with each of the systems a company uses for a particular process to identify trouble spots. Canadian mutual fund company AIC used Sajus BPM monitoring software to check inconsistencies in its process for updating accounts after each client transaction. Sajus specializes in goal-based process management, which focuses on finding the causes of organizational problems through process monitoring before applying tools to address those problems.

Another category of tools automate some parts of a business process and enforce business rules so that employees perform that process more consistently and efficiently.

For example, American National Insurance Company (ANCO), which offers life insurance, medical insurance, property casualty insurance, and investment services, used Pega BPM workflow software to streamline customer service processes across four business groups. The software built rules to guide customer service representatives through a single view of a customer's information that was maintained in multiple systems. By eliminating the need to juggle multiple applications simultaneously to handle customer and agent requests, the improved process increased customer service representative workload capacity by 192 percent.

A third category of tools helps businesses integrate their existing systems to support process improvements. They automatically manage processes across the business, extract data from various sources and databases, and generate transactions in multiple related systems. For example, the Star Alliance of 15 airlines, including United and Lufthansa, used BPM to create common processes shared by all of its members by integrating their existing systems. One project created a new service for frequent fliers on member airlines by consolidating 90 separate business processes across nine airlines and 27 legacy systems. The BPM software documented how each airline processed frequent flier information to help airline managers model a new business process that showed how to share data among the various systems.

The Interactive Session on Organizations provides an example of a company that benefited competitively from business process management. As with any company that rapidly expands from a small business to a global brand, Burton Snowboards found that some of its business processes had become outdated. Burton has made serious efforts to improve these processes and turn their weaknesses into strengths.

13.2 OVERVIEW OF SYSTEMS DEVELOPMENT

New information systems are an outgrowth of a process of organizational problem solving. A new information system is built as a solution to some type of problem or set of problems the organization perceives it is facing. The problem may be one in which managers and employees realize that the organization is not performing as well as expected, or that the organization should take advantage of new opportunities to perform more successfully.

The activities that go into producing an information system solution to an organizational problem or opportunity are called **systems development**.

INTERACTIVE SESSION: ORGANIZATIONS

BURTON SNOWBOARDS SPEEDS AHEAD WITH NIMBLE BUSINESS PROCESSES

When we hear "snowboarding", we tend to think of snow-covered slopes, acrobatic jumps, and high-flying entertainment. We don't usually think of improving business process efficiency. But snowboarding is business for Burton Snowboards, an industry pioneer and market leader. Founded in 1977 by Jake Burton Carpenter and headquartered in Burlington, Vermont, Burton designs, manufactures, and markets equipment, clothing, and related accessories for snowboarders. Today, Burton is a global enterprise that serves customers in 27 countries and has offices in Japan, Austria, and throughout the United States.

At its peak, Burton controlled over 40 percent of the U.S. snowboarding market, and it remains the market leader amidst a growing number of competitors. Now, as Burton continues to expand into a global company, it has a new set of problems: improving its systems for inventory, supply chain, purchasing, and customer service.

Stocking and managing inventory is a difficult problem for Burton, whose inventory changes dramatically depend on product line updates and the time of the year. Burton takes feedback from its customers very seriously, and will move quickly to meet their needs. For instance, if a rider tests a jacket and recommends repositioning a zipper, Burton's production line must be able to make this modification quickly and easily. Being dynamic and adaptable is a competitive necessity.

Burton has implemented and currently maintains SAP enterprise software, an Oracle database, a SUSE Linux enterprise server, and commodity hardware. That's a long way from a lone woodworking shop in Vermont. Before making these upgrades, Burton's information systems were a hodgepodge of inconsistently implemented and underutilized software. The company had to manually allocate product to customers and orders. In 1997, Burton first deployed SAP to begin upgrading its IT landscape, and the company has continued to use SAP since that time. But Burton needed to do more with its systems.

Two of Burton's IT goals, established by CIO Kevin Ubert, are to "strengthen the foundation," and keep their systems "simple, standard, (and) supportable." The foundation Ubert referred to is SAP Enterprise Resource Planning (ERP) software. Rather than buying new software to solve IT problems, Burton decided that it would explore basic functionalities of SAP ERP software that it had not used yet. Often, Burton could resolve problems this way without adding new layers of complexity to its IT infrastructure, and the company gained proficiency with SAP enterprise software in the process. Burton aims for a standard, traditional version of software whenever possible, realizing that with more bells and whistles comes increased maintenance costs and steeper learning curves to understanding the software.

SAP analysts helped Burton identify the top five transactions that were the most critical to its business operations and that needed optimization from a systems standpoint. Burton had to identify unnecessarily complicated processes, backlogs, and design gaps in the flow of its business processes. For example, the available-to-promise process was taking hours to complete. (Available to promise, in response to customer order inquiries, reports on available quantities of a requested product and delivery due dates.) Burton wanted to speed up this process so that its dealers and retail customers would have more precise information about the availability of products not currently in stock. Completing this process now takes 20 minutes.

Other processes in need of improvement included the order-to-cash process (receiving and processing customer sales, including order entry, fulfillment, distribution, and payment); the handling of overdue purchase orders in the procure-to-pay process, which consists of all the steps from purchasing goods from a supplier to paying the supplier; and the electronic data interchange (EDI) inventory feed extract transaction. Burton has an assortment of warehouses that pass inventory data to one another automatically using EDI systems. Thousands of items are moving from warehouse to warehouse and thousands of transactions occur each day at each warehouse. Burton found that the process of reporting inventory was inefficient, and both suppliers and customers could not easily determine up-to-date information on which items were in stock at which warehouse.

SAP and Burton worked together to improve communication between warehouses and supply chain efficiency.

A management dashboard developed with the help of SAP shows how smoothly a critical process is running at a certain point in time. Information from the dashboard helps Burton's key users discover inconsistencies, gaps, or other areas that they should be monitoring more closely.

All of these process improvements proved especially valuable during what Burton calls its "reorder" season. Burton's dealers place orders to stock their stores well before winter sets in. As consumers start buying the merchandise, the dealers reorder with Burton to replenish their stock or to buy new products. Now they are able to see more timely product availability data, and receive orders more rapidly.

Sources: Lauren Bonneau, "How Burton Snowboards Remains as Nimble as Its Riders," SAP InsiderPROFILES, April–June 2011; "The Burton Corporation Company Profile," Yahoo! Finance, accessed August 27, 2012; and www.burton.com, accessed August 27, 2012.

CASE STUDY QUESTIONS

1. Analyze Burton using the value chain and competitive forces models.

2. Why are the business processes described in this case such an important source of competitive advantage for Burton?

3. Explain exactly how these process improvements enhance Burton's operational performance and decision making.

Systems development is a structured kind of problem solved with distinct activities. These activities consist of systems analysis, systems design, programming, testing, conversion, and production and maintenance.

Figure 13.4 illustrates the systems development process. The systems development activities depicted usually take place in sequential order. But some of the activities may need to be repeated or some may take place simultaneously, depending on the approach to system building that is being employed (see Section 13.4).

FIGURE 13.4 THE SYSTEMS DEVELOPMENT PROCESS

Building a system can be broken down into six core activities.

SYSTEMS ANALYSIS

Systems analysis is the analysis of a problem that a firm tries to solve with an information system. It consists of defining the problem, identifying its causes, specifying the solution, and identifying the information requirements that must be met by a system solution.

The systems analyst creates a road map of the existing organization and systems, identifying the primary owners and users of data along with existing hardware and software. The systems analyst then details the problems of existing systems. By examining documents, work papers, and procedures, observing system operations, and interviewing key users of the systems, the analyst can identify the problem areas and objectives a solution would achieve. Often, the solution requires building a new information system or improving an existing one.

The systems analysis also includes a **feasibility study** to determine whether that solution is feasible, or achievable, from a financial, technical, and organizational standpoint. The feasibility study determines whether the proposed system is expected to be a good investment, whether the technology needed for the system is available and can be handled by the firm's information systems specialists, and whether the organization can handle the changes introduced by the system.

Normally, the systems analysis process identifies several alternative solutions that the organization can pursue and assess the feasibility of each. A written systems proposal report describes the costs and benefits, and the advantages and disadvantages, of each alternative. It is up to management to determine which mix of costs, benefits, technical features, and organizational impacts represents the most desirable alternative.

Establishing Information Requirements

Perhaps the most challenging task of the systems analyst is to define the specific information requirements that must be met by the chosen system solution. At the most basic level, the **information requirements** of a new system involve identifying who needs what information, where, when, and how. Requirements analysis carefully defines the objectives of the new or modified system and develops a detailed description of the functions that the new system must perform. Faulty requirements analysis is a leading cause of systems failure and high systems development costs (see Chapter 14). A system designed around the wrong set of requirements will either have to be discarded because of poor performance or will need to undergo major modifications. Section 13.3 describes alternative approaches to eliciting requirements that help minimize this problem.

Some problems do not require an information system solution but instead need an adjustment in management, additional training, or refinement of existing organizational procedures. If the problem is information related, systems analysis still may be required to diagnose the problem and arrive at the proper solution.

SYSTEMS DESIGN

Systems analysis describes what a system should do to meet information requirements, and **systems design** shows how the system will fulfill this objective. The design of an information system is the overall plan or model for that system. Like the blueprint of a building or house, it consists of all the specifications that give the system its form and structure.

The systems designer details the system specifications that will deliver the functions identified during systems analysis. These specifications should address all of the managerial, organizational, and technological components of the system solution. Table 13.1 lists the types of specifications that would be produced during systems design.

Like houses or buildings, information systems may have many possible designs. Each design represents a unique blend of all technical and organizational components. What makes one design superior to others is the ease and efficiency with which it fulfills user requirements within a specific set of technical, organizational, financial, and time constraints.

The Role of End Users

User information requirements drive the entire system-building effort. Users must have sufficient control over the design process to ensure that the system reflects their business priorities and information needs, not the biases of the technical staff. Working on design increases users' understanding and acceptance of the system. As we describe in Chapter 14, insufficient user involvement in the design effort is a major cause of system failure. However, some systems require more user participation in design than others, and Section 13.3 shows how alternative systems development methods address the user participation issue.

COMPLETING THE SYSTEMS DEVELOPMENT PROCESS

The remaining steps in the systems development process translate the solution specifications established during systems analysis and design into a fully operational information system. These concluding steps consist of programming, testing, conversion, production, and maintenance.

TABLE 13.1 DESIGN SPECIFICATIONS

OUTPUT	PROCESSING	DOCUMENTATION
Medium	Computations	Operations documentation
Content	Program modules	Systems documentation
Timing	Required reports	User documentation
INPUT	Timing of outputs	CONVERSION
Origins	MANUAL PROCEDURES	Transfer files
Flow	What activities	Initiate new procedures
Data entry	Who performs them	Select testing method
USER INTERFACE	When	Cut over to new system
Simplicity	How	TRAINING
Efficiency	Where	Select training techniques
Logic	CONTROLS	Develop training modules
Feedback	Input controls (characters, limit,	Identify training facilities
Errors	reasonableness)	ORGANIZATIONAL CHANGES
DATABASE DESIGN	Processing controls (consistency, record counts)	Task redesign
Logical data model	Output controls (totals, samples of output)	Job design
Volume and speed requirements	Procedural controls (passwords, special forms)	Process design
File organization and design	SECURITY	Organization structure design
Record specifications	Access controls	Reporting relationships
	Catastrophe plans	
	Audit trails	

Programming

During the **programming** stage, system specifications that were prepared during the design stage are translated into software program code. Today, many organizations no longer do their own programming for new systems. Instead, they purchase the software that meets the requirements for a new system from external sources such as software packages from a commercial software vendor, software services from an application service provider, or outsourcing firms that develop custom application software for their clients (see Section 13.3).

Testing

Exhaustive and thorough **testing** must be conducted to ascertain whether the system produces the right results. Testing answers the question, "Will the system produce the desired results under known conditions?" As Chapter 5 noted, some companies are starting to use cloud-computing services for this work.

The amount of time needed to answer this question has been traditionally underrated in systems project planning (see Chapter 14). Testing is time-consuming: Test data must be carefully prepared, results reviewed, and corrections made in the system. In some instances, parts of the system may have to be redesigned. The risks resulting from glossing over this step are enormous.

Testing an information system can be broken down into three types of activities: unit testing, system testing, and acceptance testing. **Unit testing**, or program testing, consists of testing each program separately in the system. It is widely believed that the purpose of such testing is to guarantee that programs are error-free, but this goal is realistically impossible. Testing should be viewed instead as a means of locating errors in programs, focusing on finding all the ways to make a program fail. Once they are pinpointed, problems can be corrected.

System testing tests the functioning of the information system as a whole. It tries to determine whether discrete modules will function together as planned and whether discrepancies exist between the way the system actually works and the way it was conceived. Among the areas examined are performance time, capacity for file storage and handling peak loads, recovery and restart capabilities, and manual procedures.

Acceptance testing provides the final certification that the system is ready to be used in a production setting. Systems tests are evaluated by users and reviewed by management. When all parties are satisfied that the new system meets their standards, the system is formally accepted for installation.

The systems development team works with users to devise a systematic test plan. The **test plan** includes all of the preparations for the series of tests we have just described.

Figure 13.5 shows an example of a test plan. The general condition being tested is a record change. The documentation consists of a series of test plan screens maintained on a database (perhaps a PC database) that is ideally suited to this kind of application.

Conversion is the process of changing from the old system to the new system. Four main conversion strategies can be employed: the parallel strategy, the direct cutover strategy, the pilot study strategy, and the phased approach strategy.

In a **parallel strategy,** both the old system and its potential replacement are run together for a time until everyone is assured that the new one functions correctly. This is the safest conversion approach because, in the event of errors or processing disruptions, the old system can still be used as a backup. However, this approach is very expensive, and additional staff or resources may be required to run the extra system.

FIGURE 13.5 **A SAMPLE TEST PLAN TO TEST A RECORD CHANGE**

Procedure	Address and Maintenance "Record Change Series"		Test Series 2		
	Prepared By:		Date:	Version:	
Test Ref.	Condition Tested	Special Requirements	Expected Results	Output On	Next Screen
2.0	Change records				
2.1	Change existing record	Key field	Not allowed		
2.2	Change nonexistent record	Other fields	"Invalid key" message		
2.3	Change deleted record	Deleted record must be available	"Deleted" message		
2.4	Make second record	Change 2.1 above	OK if valid	Transaction file	V45
2.5	Insert record		OK if valid	Transaction file	V45
2.6	Abort during change	Abort 2.5	No change	Transaction file	V45

When developing a test plan, it is imperative to include the various conditions to be tested, the requirements for each condition tested, and the expected results. Test plans require input from both end users and information systems specialists.

The **direct cutover strategy** replaces the old system entirely with the new system on an appointed day. It is a very risky approach that can potentially be more costly than running two systems in parallel if serious problems with the new system are found. There is no other system to fall back on. Dislocations, disruptions, and the cost of corrections may be enormous.

The **pilot study strategy** introduces the new system to only a limited area of the organization, such as a single department or operating unit. When this pilot version is complete and working smoothly, it is installed throughout the rest of the organization, either simultaneously or in stages.

The **phased approach strategy** introduces the new system in stages, either by functions or by organizational units. If, for example, the system is introduced by function, a new payroll system might begin with hourly workers who are paid weekly, followed six months later by adding salaried employees (who are paid monthly) to the system. If the system is introduced by organizational unit, corporate headquarters might be converted first, followed by outlying operating units four months later.

Moving from an old system to a new one requires that end users be trained to use the new system. Detailed **documentation** showing how the system works from both a technical and end-user standpoint is finalized during conversion time for use in training and everyday operations. Lack of proper training and documentation contributes to system failure, so this portion of the systems development process is very important.

Production and Maintenance

After the new system is installed and conversion is complete, the system is said to be in **production**. During this stage, the system will be reviewed by both users and technical specialists to determine how well it has met its original objectives and to decide whether any revisions or modifications are in order. In some instances, a formal **postimplementation audit** document is prepared. After the system has been fine-tuned, it must be maintained while it is in production to correct errors, meet requirements, or improve processing efficiency. Changes in hardware, software, documentation, or procedures to a production system to correct errors, meet new requirements, or improve processing efficiency are termed **maintenance**.

Approximately 20 percent of the time devoted to maintenance is used for debugging or correcting emergency production problems. Another 20 percent is concerned with changes in data, files, reports, hardware, or system software. But 60 percent of all maintenance work consists of making user enhancements, improving documentation, and recoding system components for greater processing efficiency. The amount of work in the third category of maintenance problems could be reduced significantly through better systems analysis and design practices. Table 13.2 summarizes the systems development activities.

MODELING AND DESIGNING SYSTEMS: STRUCTURED AND OBJECT-ORIENTED METHODOLOGIES

There are alternative methodologies for modeling and designing systems. Structured methodologies and object-oriented development are the most prominent.

Structured Methodologies

Structured methodologies have been used to document, analyze, and design information systems since the 1970s. **Structured** refers to the fact that the techniques are step by step, with each step building on the previous one. Structured methodologies are top-down, progressing from the highest, most abstract level to the lowest level of detail—from the general to the specific.

Structured development methods are process-oriented, focusing primarily on modeling the processes, or actions that capture, store, manipulate, and distribute data as the data flow through a system. These methods separate data

TABLE 13.2 SYSTEMS DEVELOPMENT

CORE ACTIVITY	DESCRIPTION
Systems analysis	Identify problem(s) Specify solutions Establish information requirements
Systems design	Create design specifications
Programming	Translate design specifications into program code
Testing	Perform unit testing Perform systems testing Perform acceptance testing
Conversion	Plan conversion Prepare documentation Train users and technical staff
Production and maintenance	Operate the system Evaluate the system Modify the system

from processes. A separate programming procedure must be written every time someone wants to take an action on a particular piece of data. The procedures act on data that the program passes to them.

The primary tool for representing a system's component processes and the flow of data between them is the **data flow diagram (DFD)**. The data flow diagram offers a logical graphic model of information flow, partitioning a system into modules that show manageable levels of detail. It rigorously specifies the processes or transformations that occur within each module and the interfaces that exist between them.

Figure 13.6 shows a simple data flow diagram for a mail-in university course registration system. The rounded boxes represent processes, which portray the transformation of data. The square box represents an external entity, which is an originator or receiver of information located outside the boundaries of the system being modeled. The open rectangles represent data stores, which are either manual or automated inventories of data. The arrows represent data flows, which show the movement between processes, external entities, and data stores. They contain packets of data with the name or content of each data flow listed beside the arrow.

This data flow diagram shows that students submit registration forms with their name, identification number, and the numbers of the courses they wish to take. In process 1.0, the system verifies that each course selected is still open by referencing the university's course file. The file distinguishes courses that are open from those that have been canceled or filled. Process 1.0 then determines which of the student's selections can be accepted or rejected. Process 2.0 enrolls the student in the courses for which he or she has been accepted. It updates the university's course file with the student's name and identification number and recalculates the class size. If maximum enrollment has been reached, the course number is flagged as closed. Process 2.0 also updates the

FIGURE 13.6 DATA FLOW DIAGRAM FOR MAIL-IN UNIVERSITY REGISTRATION SYSTEM

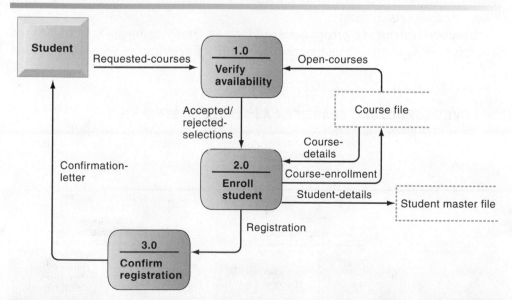

The system has three processes: Verify availability (1.0), Enroll student (2.0), and Confirm registration (3.0). The name and content of each of the data flows appear adjacent to each arrow. There is one external entity in this system: the student. There are two data stores: the student master file and the course file.

university's student master file with information about new students or changes in address. Process 3.0 then sends each student applicant a confirmation-of-registration letter listing the courses for which he or she is registered and noting the course selections that could not be fulfilled.

The diagrams can be used to depict higher-level processes as well as lower-level details. Through leveled data flow diagrams, a complex process can be broken down into successive levels of detail. An entire system can be divided into subsystems with a high-level data flow diagram. Each subsystem, in turn, can be divided into additional subsystems with second-level data flow diagrams, and the lower-level subsystems can be broken down again until the lowest level of detail has been reached.

Another tool for structured analysis is a data dictionary, which contains information about individual pieces of data and data groupings within a system (see Chapter 6). The data dictionary defines the contents of data flows and data stores so that systems builders understand exactly what pieces of data they contain. **Process specifications** describe the transformation occurring within the lowest level of the data flow diagrams. They express the logic for each process.

In structured methodology, software design is modeled using hierarchical structure charts. The **structure chart** is a top-down chart, showing each level of design, its relationship to other levels, and its place in the overall design structure. The design first considers the main function of a program or system, then breaks this function into subfunctions, and decomposes each subfunction until the lowest level of detail has been reached. Figure 13.7 shows a high-level structure chart for a payroll system. If a design has too many levels to fit onto one structure chart, it can be broken down further on more detailed structure charts. A structure chart may document one program, one system (a set of programs), or part of one program.

Object-Oriented Development

Structured methods are useful for modeling processes, but do not handle the modeling of data well. They also treat data and processes as logically separate entities, whereas in the real world such separation seems unnatural. Different modeling conventions are used for analysis (the data flow diagram) and for design (the structure chart).

Object-oriented development addresses these issues. Object-oriented development uses the **object** as the basic unit of systems analysis and design.

FIGURE 13.7 HIGH-LEVEL STRUCTURE CHART FOR A PAYROLL SYSTEM

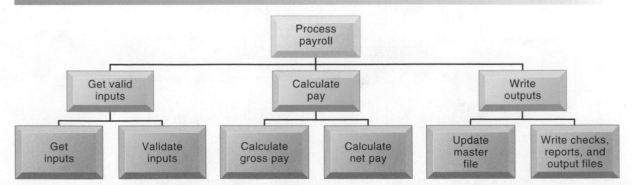

This structure chart shows the highest or most abstract level of design for a payroll system, providing an overview of the entire system.

An object combines data and the specific processes that operate on those data. Data encapsulated in an object can be accessed and modified only by the operations, or methods, associated with that object. Instead of passing data to procedures, programs send a message for an object to perform an operation that is already embedded in it. The system is modeled as a collection of objects and the relationships among them. Because processing logic resides within objects rather than in separate software programs, objects must collaborate with each other to make the system work.

Object-oriented modeling is based on the concepts of *class* and *inheritance*. Objects belonging to a certain class, or general categories of similar objects, have the features of that class. Classes of objects in turn can inherit all the structure and behaviors of a more general class and then add variables and behaviors unique to each object. New classes of objects are created by choosing an existing class and specifying how the new class differs from the existing class, instead of starting from scratch each time.

We can see how class and inheritance work in Figure 13.8, which illustrates the relationships among classes concerning employees and how they are paid. Employee is the common ancestor, or superclass, for the other three classes. Salaried, Hourly, and Temporary are subclasses of Employee. The class name is in the top compartment, the attributes for each class are in the middle portion of each box, and the list of operations is in the bottom portion of each box. The features that are shared by all employees (id, name, address, date hired, position, and pay) are stored in the Employee superclass, whereas each subclass stores features that are specific to that particular type of employee. Specific to hourly employees, for example, are their hourly rates and overtime rates. A solid line from the subclass to the superclass is a generalization path showing that the subclasses Salaried, Hourly, and Temporary have common features that can be generalized into the superclass Employee.

Object-oriented development is more iterative and incremental than traditional structured development. During analysis, systems builders document

FIGURE 13.8 CLASS AND INHERITANCE

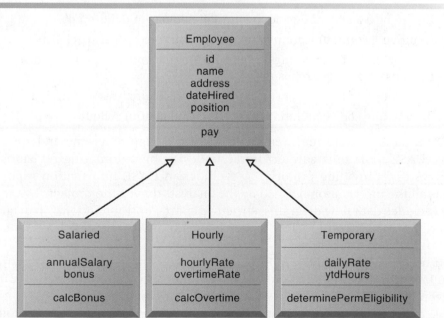

This figure illustrates how classes inherit the common features of their superclass.

the functional requirements of the system, specifying its most important properties and what the proposed system must do. Interactions between the system and its users are analyzed to identify objects, which include both data and processes. The object-oriented design phase describes how the objects will behave and how they will interact with one other. Similar objects are grouped together to form a class, and classes are grouped into hierarchies in which a subclass inherits the attributes and methods from its superclass.

The information system is implemented by translating the design into program code, reusing classes that are already available in a library of reusable software objects, and adding new ones created during the object-oriented design phase. Implementation may also involve the creation of an object-oriented database. The resulting system must be thoroughly tested and evaluated.

Because objects are reusable, object-oriented development could potentially reduce the time and cost of writing software because organizations can reuse software objects that have already been created as building blocks for other applications. New systems can be created by using some existing objects, changing others, and adding a few new objects. Object-oriented frameworks have been developed to provide reusable, semicomplete applications that the organization can further customize into finished applications.

Computer-Aided Software Engineering

Computer-aided software engineering (CASE)—sometimes called *computer-aided systems engineering*—provides software tools to automate the methodologies we have just described to reduce the amount of repetitive work the developer needs to do. CASE tools also facilitate the creation of clear documentation and the coordination of team development efforts. Team members can share their work easily by accessing each other's files to review or modify what has been done. Modest productivity benefits can also be achieved if the tools are used properly.

CASE tools provide automated graphics facilities for producing charts and diagrams, screen and report generators, data dictionaries, extensive reporting facilities, analysis and checking tools, code generators, and documentation generators. In general, CASE tools try to increase productivity and quality by:

- Enforcing a standard development methodology and design discipline
- Improving communication between users and technical specialists
- Organizing and correlating design components and providing rapid access to them using a design repository
- Automating tedious and error-prone portions of analysis and design
- Automating code generation and testing and control rollout

CASE tools contain features for validating design diagrams and specifications. CASE tools thus support iterative design by automating revisions and changes and providing prototyping facilities. A CASE information repository stores all the information defined by the analysts during the project. The repository includes data flow diagrams, structure charts, entity-relationship diagrams, data definitions, process specifications, screen and report formats, notes and comments, and test results.

To be used effectively, CASE tools require organizational discipline. Every member of a development project must adhere to a common set of naming conventions and standards as well as to a development methodology. The best CASE tools enforce common methods and standards, which may discourage their use in situations where organizational discipline is lacking.

13.3 ALTERNATIVE SYSTEMS-BUILDING APPROACHES

Systems differ in terms of their size and technological complexity and in terms of the organizational problems they are meant to solve. A number of systems-building approaches have been developed to deal with these differences. This section describes these alternative methods: the traditional systems life cycle, prototyping, application software packages, end-user development, and outsourcing.

TRADITIONAL SYSTEMS LIFE CYCLE

The **systems life cycle** is the oldest method for building information systems. The life cycle methodology is a phased approach to building a system, dividing systems development into formal stages, as illustrated in Figure 13.9. Systems development specialists have different opinions on how to partition the systems-building stages, but they roughly correspond to the stages of systems development we have just described.

The systems life cycle methodology maintains a formal division of labor between end users and information systems specialists. Technical specialists, such as systems analysts and programmers, are responsible for much of the systems analysis, design, and implementation work; end users are limited to providing information requirements and reviewing the technical staff's work. The life cycle also emphasizes formal specifications and paperwork, so many documents are generated during the course of a systems project.

The systems life cycle is still used for building large complex systems that require a rigorous and formal requirements analysis, predefined specifications, and tight controls over the system-building process. However, the systems life cycle approach can be costly, time-consuming, and

FIGURE 13.9 THE TRADITIONAL SYSTEMS DEVELOPMENT LIFE CYCLE

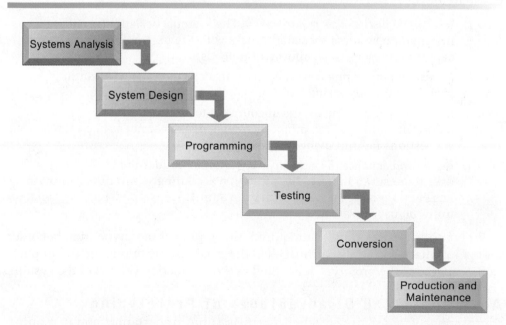

The systems development life cycle partitions systems development into formal stages, with each stage requiring completion before the next stage can begin.

inflexible. Although systems builders can go back and forth among stages in the life cycle, the systems life cycle is predominantly a "waterfall" approach in which tasks in one stage are completed before work for the next stage begins. Activities can be repeated, but volumes of new documents must be generated and steps retraced if requirements and specifications need to be revised. This encourages freezing of specifications relatively early in the development process. The life cycle approach is also not suitable for many small desktop systems, which tend to be less structured and more individualized.

PROTOTYPING

Prototyping consists of building an experimental system rapidly and inexpensively for end users to evaluate. By interacting with the prototype, users can get a better idea of their information requirements. The prototype endorsed by the users can be used as a template to create the final system.

The **prototype** is a working version of an information system or part of the system, but it is meant to be only a preliminary model. Once operational, the prototype will be further refined until it conforms precisely to users' requirements. Once the design has been finalized, the prototype can be converted to a polished production system.

The process of building a preliminary design, trying it out, refining it, and trying again has been called an **iterative** process of systems development because the steps required to build a system can be repeated over and over again. Prototyping is more explicitly iterative than the conventional life cycle, and it actively promotes system design changes. It has been said that prototyping replaces unplanned rework with planned iteration, with each version more accurately reflecting users' requirements.

Steps in Prototyping

Figure 13.10 shows a four-step model of the prototyping process, which consists of the following:

Step 1: *Identify the user's basic requirements.* The systems designer (usually an information systems specialist) works with the user only long enough to capture the user's basic information needs.

Step 2: *Develop an initial prototype.* The systems designer creates a working prototype quickly, using tools for rapidly generating software.

Step 3: *Use the prototype.* The user is encouraged to work with the system to determine how well the prototype meets his or her needs and to make suggestions for improving the prototype.

Step 4: *Revise and enhance the prototype.* The system builder notes all changes the user requests and refines the prototype accordingly. After the prototype has been revised, the cycle returns to Step 3. Steps 3 and 4 are repeated until the user is satisfied.

When no more iterations are required, the approved prototype then becomes an operational prototype that furnishes the final specifications for the application. Sometimes the prototype is adopted as the production version of the system.

Advantages and Disadvantages of Prototyping

Prototyping is most useful when there is some uncertainty about requirements or design solutions and often used for designing an information system's **end-user interface** (the part of the system with which end users interact,

FIGURE 13.10 THE PROTOTYPING PROCESS

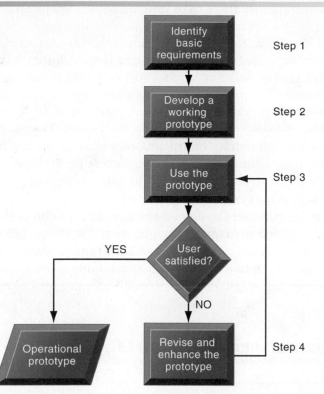

The process of developing a prototype can be broken down into four steps. Because a prototype can be developed quickly and inexpensively, systems builders can go through several iterations, repeating steps 3 and 4, to refine and enhance the prototype before arriving at the final operational one.

such as online display and data entry screens, reports, or Web pages). Because prototyping encourages intense end-user involvement throughout the systems development life cycle, it is more likely to produce systems that fulfill user requirements.

However, rapid prototyping can gloss over essential steps in systems development. If the completed prototype works reasonably well, management may not see the need for reprogramming, redesign, or full documentation and testing to build a polished production system. Some of these hastily constructed systems may not easily accommodate large quantities of data or a large number of users in a production environment.

END-USER DEVELOPMENT

Some types of information systems can be developed by end users with little or no formal assistance from technical specialists. This phenomenon is called **end-user development**. A series of software tools categorized as fourth-generation languages makes this possible. **Fourth-generation languages** are software tools that enable end users to create reports or develop software applications with minimal or no technical assistance. Some of these fourth-generation tools also enhance professional programmers' productivity.

Fourth-generation languages tend to be nonprocedural, or less procedural, than conventional programming languages. Procedural languages require specification of the sequence of steps, or procedures, that tell the computer what to do and how to do it. Nonprocedural languages need only specify what has to be accomplished rather than provide details about how to carry out the task.

Table 13.3 shows that there are seven categories of fourth-generation languages: PC software tools, query languages, report generators, graphics languages, application generators, application software packages, and very high-level programming languages. The table shows the tools ordered in terms of ease of use by nonprogramming end users. End users are most likely to work with PC software tools and query languages. **Query languages** are software tools that provide immediate online answers to requests for information that are not predefined, such as "Who are the highest-performing sales representatives?" Query languages are often tied to data management software and to database management systems (see Chapter 6).

On the whole, end-user-developed systems can be completed more rapidly than those developed through the conventional systems life cycle. Allowing users to specify their own business needs improves requirements gathering and often leads to a higher level of user involvement and satisfaction with the system. However, fourth-generation tools still cannot replace conventional tools

TABLE 13.3 CATEGORIES OF FOURTH-GENERATION LANGUAGES

FOURTH-GENERATION TOOL	DESCRIPTION	EXAMPLE	
PC software tools	General-purpose application software packages for PCs.	Microsoft Excel Microsoft Access	**Oriented toward end users** ↑
Query language	Languages for retrieving data stored in databases or files. Capable of supporting requests for information that are not predefined.	SQL	
Report generator	Extract data from files or databases to create customized reports in a wide range of formats not routinely produced by an information system. Generally provide more control over the way data are formatted, organized, and displayed than query languages.	Crystal Reports	
Graphics language	Retrieve data from files or databases and display them in graphic format. Some graphics software can perform arithmetic or logical operations on data as well.	SAS/GRAPH Systat	
Application generator	Contain preprogrammed modules that can generate entire applications, including Web sites, greatly speeding development. A user can specify what needs to be done, and the application generator will create the appropriate program code for input, validation, update, processing, and reporting.	WebFOCUS QuickBase	
Application software package	Software programs sold or leased by commercial vendors that eliminate the need for custom-written, in-house software.	Oracle PeopleSoft HCM mySAP ERP	
Very high-level programming language	Generate program code with fewer instructions than conventional languages, such as COBOL or FORTRAN. Designed primarily as productivity tools for professional programmers.	APL Nomad2	↓ **Oriented toward IS**

for some business applications because they cannot easily handle the processing of large numbers of transactions or applications with extensive procedural logic and updating requirements.

End-user computing also poses organizational risks because it occurs outside of traditional mechanisms for information systems management and control. When systems are created rapidly, without a formal development methodology, testing and documentation may be inadequate. Control over data can be lost in systems outside the traditional information systems department. To help organizations maximize the benefits of end-user applications development, management should control the development of end-user applications by requiring cost justification of end-user information system projects and by establishing hardware, software, and quality standards for user-developed applications.

APPLICATION SOFTWARE PACKAGES AND OUTSOURCING

Chapter 5 points out that much of today's software is not developed in-house but is purchased from external sources. Firms can rent the software from a software service provider, they can purchase a software package from a commercial vendor, or they can have a custom application developed by an outside outsourcing firm.

Application Software Packages

During the past several decades, many systems have been built on an application software package foundation. Many applications are common to all business organizations—for example, payroll, accounts receivable, general ledger, or inventory control. For such universal functions with standard processes that do not change a great deal over time, a generalized system will fulfill the requirements of many organizations.

If a software package can fulfill most of an organization's requirements, the company does not have to write its own software. The company can save time and money by using the prewritten, predesigned, pretested software programs from the package. Package vendors supply much of the ongoing maintenance and support for the system, including enhancements to keep the system in line with ongoing technical and business developments.

If an organization has unique requirements that the package does not address, many packages include capabilities for customization. **Customization** features allow a software package to be modified to meet an organization's unique requirements without destroying the integrity of the packaged software. If a great deal of customization is required, additional programming and customization work may become so expensive and time-consuming that they negate many of the advantages of software packages.

When a system is developed using an application software package, systems analysis will include a package evaluation effort. The most important evaluation criteria are the functions provided by the package, flexibility, user friendliness, hardware and software resources, database requirements, installation and maintenance efforts, documentation, vendor quality, and cost. The package evaluation process often is based on a **Request for Proposal (RFP)**, which is a detailed list of questions submitted to packaged-software vendors.

When a software package is selected, the organization no longer has total control over the systems design process. Instead of tailoring the systems design specifications directly to user requirements, the design effort will consist of trying to mold user requirements to conform to the features of the package. If the organization's requirements conflict with the way the package works and the package cannot be customized, the organization will have to adapt to the package and change its procedures.

Outsourcing

If a firm does not want to use its internal resources to build or operate information systems, it can outsource the work to an external organization that specializes in providing these services. Cloud computing and software as a service (SaaS) providers, which we described in Chapter 5, are one form of outsourcing. Subscribing companies use the software and computer hardware provided by the service as the technical platform for their systems. In another form of outsourcing, a company could hire an external vendor to design and create the software for its system, but that company would operate the system on its own computers. The outsourcing vendor might be domestic or in another country.

Domestic outsourcing is driven primarily by the fact that outsourcing firms possess skills, resources, and assets that their clients do not have. Installing a new supply chain management system in a very large company might require hiring an additional 30 to 50 people with specific expertise in supply chain management software, licensed from a vendor. Rather than hire permanent new employees, most of whom would need extensive training in the software package, and then release them after the new system is built, it makes more sense, and is often less expensive, to outsource this work for a 12-month period.

In the case of **offshore outsourcing**, the decision tends to be much more cost-driven. A skilled programmer in India or Russia earns about USD $10,000–$20,000 per year, compared to $73,000 per year for a comparable programmer in the United States. The Internet and low-cost communications technology have drastically reduced the expense and difficulty of coordinating the work of global teams in faraway locations. In addition to cost savings, many offshore outsourcing firms offer world-class technology assets and skills. Wage inflation outside the United States has recently eroded some of these advantages, and some jobs have moved back to the United States.

Nevertheless, there is a very strong chance that at some point in your career, you'll be working with offshore outsourcers or global teams. Your firm is most likely to benefit from outsourcing if it takes the time to evaluate all the risks and to make sure outsourcing is appropriate for its particular needs. Any company that outsources its applications must thoroughly understand the project, including its requirements, method of implementation, anticipated benefits, cost components, and metrics for measuring performance.

Many firms underestimate costs for identifying and evaluating vendors of information technology services, for transitioning to a new vendor, for improving internal software development methods to match those of outsourcing vendors, and for monitoring vendors to make sure they are fulfilling their contractual obligations. Companies will need to allocate resources for documenting requirements, sending out RFPs, handling travel expenses, negotiating contracts, and project management. Experts claim it takes from three months to a full year to fully transfer work to an offshore partner and make sure the vendor thoroughly understands your business.

Outsourcing offshore incurs additional costs for coping with cultural differences that drain productivity and dealing with human resources issues, such as terminating or relocating domestic employees. All of these hidden costs undercut some of the anticipated benefits from outsourcing. Firms should be especially cautious when using an outsourcer to develop or to operate applications that give it some type of competitive advantage.

General Motors Corporation (GM) had outsourced 90 percent of its IT services, including its data centers and application development. The company recently decided to bring 90 percent of its IT infrastructure in-house, with only 10 percent managed by outsourcers. Lowering costs is important, but GM's primary reason for cutting back outsourcing is to take back control of its information systems, which it believes were preventing the company from responding quickly to competitive opportunities. Bringing information systems in-house will make it easier for GM to cut its sprawling list of IT applications by at least 40 percent, move to a more standardized platform, complete innovative IT projects more quickly, and get a better grip on customer and production data, which had been housed in too many different systems. The automaker will consolidate 23 data centers worldwide into just two, both in Michigan, and run four software development centers (Murphy, 2012).

Figure 13.11 shows best- and worst-case scenarios for the total cost of an offshore outsourcing project. It shows how much hidden costs affect the total project cost. The best case reflects the lowest estimates for additional costs, and the worst case reflects the highest estimates for these costs. As you can see, hidden costs increase the total cost of an offshore outsourcing project by an extra 15 to 57 percent. Even with these extra costs, many firms will benefit from offshore outsourcing if they manage the work well. Under the worst-case scenario, a firm would still save about 15 percent.

FIGURE 13.11 TOTAL COST OF OFFSHORE OUTSOURCING

TOTAL COST OF OFFSHORE OUTSOURCING				
Cost of outsourcing contract			$10,000,000	
Hidden Costs	Best Case	Additional Cost ($)	Worst Case	Additional Cost ($)
1. Vendor selection	0%	20,000	2%	200,000
2. Transition costs	2%	200,000	3%	300,000
3. Layoffs & retention	3%	300,000	5%	500,000
4. Lost productivity/cultural issues	3%	300,000	27%	2,700,000
5. Improving development processes	1%	100,000	10%	1,000,000
6. Managing the contract	6%	600,000	10%	1,000,000
Total additional costs		1,520,000		5,700,000
	Outstanding Contract ($)	Additional Cost ($)	Total Cost ($)	Additional Cost
Total cost of outsourcing (TCO) best case	10,000,000	1,520,000	11,520,000	15.2%
Total cost of outsourcing (TCO) worst case	10,000,000	5,700,000	15,700,000	57.0%

If a firm spends $10 million on offshore outsourcing contracts, that company will actually spend 15.2 percent in extra costs even under the best-case scenario. In the worst-case scenario, where there is a dramatic drop in productivity along with exceptionally high transition and layoff costs, a firm can expect to pay up to 57 percent in extra costs on top of the $10 million outlay for an offshore contract.

13.4 APPLICATION DEVELOPMENT FOR THE DIGITAL FIRM

In the digital firm environment, organizations need to be able to add, change, and retire their technology capabilities very rapidly to respond to new opportunities, including the need to provide applications for mobile platforms. Companies are starting to use shorter, more informal development processes that provide fast solutions. In addition to using software packages and external service providers, businesses are relying more heavily on fast-cycle techniques such as rapid application development, joint application design, agile development, and reusable standardized software components that can be assembled into a complete set of services for e-commerce and e-business.

RAPID APPLICATION DEVELOPMENT (RAD)

Object-oriented software tools, reusable software, prototyping, and fourth-generation language tools are helping systems builders create working systems much more rapidly than they could using traditional systems-building methods and software tools. The term **rapid application development (RAD)** is used to describe this process of creating workable systems in a very short period of time. RAD can include the use of visual programming and other tools for building graphical user interfaces, iterative prototyping of key system elements, the automation of program code generation, and close teamwork among end users and information systems specialists. Simple systems often can be assembled from prebuilt components. The process does not have to be sequential, and key parts of development can occur simultaneously.

Sometimes a technique called **joint application design (JAD)** is used to accelerate the generation of information requirements and to develop the initial systems design. JAD brings end users and information systems specialists together in an interactive session to discuss the system's design. Properly prepared and facilitated, JAD sessions can significantly speed up the design phase and involve users at an intense level.

Agile development focuses on rapid delivery of working software by breaking a large project into a series of small subprojects that are completed in short periods of time using iteration and continuous feedback. Each mini-project is worked on by a team as if it were a complete project, including planning, requirements analysis, design, coding, testing, and documentation. Improvement or addition of new functionality takes place within the next iteration as developers clarify requirements. This helps to minimize the overall risk, and allows the project to adapt to changes more quickly. Agile methods emphasize face-to-face communication over written documents, encouraging people to collaborate and make decisions quickly and effectively.

COMPONENT-BASED DEVELOPMENT AND WEB SERVICES

We have already described some of the benefits of object-oriented development for building systems that can respond to rapidly changing business environments, including Web applications. To further expedite software creation, groups of objects have been assembled to provide software components for common functions such as a graphical user interface or online ordering capability that can be combined to create large-scale business applications. This approach to software development is called **component-based development**, and it enables a system to be built by assembling and integrating existing software components. Increasingly, these software components are coming from cloud services. Businesses are using component-based development to create their e-commerce applications by combining commercially available components for shopping carts, user authentication, search engines, and catalogs with pieces of software for their own unique business requirements.

Web Services and Service-Oriented Computing

Chapter 5 introduced *Web services* as loosely coupled, reusable software components delivered using Extensible Markup Language (XML) and other open protocols and standards that enable one application to communicate with another with no custom programming required to share data and services. In addition to supporting internal and external integration of systems, Web services can be used as tools for building new information system applications or enhancing existing systems. Because these software services use a universal set of standards, they promise to be less expensive and less difficult to weave together than proprietary components.

Web services can perform certain functions on their own, and they can also engage other Web services to complete more complex transactions, such as checking credit, procurement, or ordering products. By creating software components that can communicate and share data regardless of the operating system, programming language, or client device, Web services can provide significant cost savings in systems building while opening up new opportunities for collaboration with other companies.

MOBILE APPLICATION DEVELOPMENT

Developing applications for mobile platforms is quite different from development for PCs and their much larger screens. The reduced size of mobile devices makes using fingers and multitouch gestures much easier than typing and using keyboards. Mobile apps need to be optimized for the specific tasks they are to perform, they should not try to carry out too many tasks, and they should be designed for usability. The user experience for mobile interaction is fundamentally different from using a desktop or laptop PC. Saving resources—bandwidth, screen space, memory, processing, data entry, and user gestures—is a top priority.

When a full Web site created for the desktop shrinks to the size of a smartphone screen, it is difficult for the user to navigate through the site. The user must continually zoom in and out and scroll to find relevant material. Therefore, companies usually design Web sites specifically for mobile interfaces and create multiple mobile sites to meet the needs of smartphones, tablets, and desktop browsers. This equates to at least three sites with separate content, maintenance, and costs. Currently, Web sites know what device you are using because your browser will send this information to the server when you log on. Based on this information, the server will deliver the appropriate screen.

One solution to the problem of having three different Web sites is to use **responsive Web design**. Responsive Web design enables Web sites to automatically change layouts according to the visitor's screen resolution, whether on a desktop, tablet, or smartphone. This approach uses a mix of flexible grids and layouts, flexible images, and media queries that optimize the design for different viewing contexts. As the user switches from his or her laptop to an iPad, iPhone, or Android handheld, the Web site automatically accommodates the changing resolution and image size. This eliminates the need for separate design and development work for each new device. With responsive design, users across a broad range of devices and browsers will have access to a single source of content, laid out to be easy to read and navigate with a minimum of resizing, panning, and scrolling.

There are three main platforms for mobile apps—iPhone/iPad, Android, and Windows Phone. Each of the platforms for mobile applications has an integrated development environment, such as Apple's iOS SDK (software development kit) for the iPhone/iPad, which provides tools for writing, testing, and deploying applications in the target platform environment. Larger companies or business owners with programming experience use these software development kits to create apps from scratch. App development can also be outsourced to specialized app development firms that charge as much as $20,000 to design and develop an app and additional fees to update the software. A number of firms such as Red Foundry offer app templates for small businesses that cannot afford high-paid programmers. The Interactive Session on Technology describes how some companies have addressed the challenges of mobile development we have just identified.

LEARNING TRACK MODULES

The following Learning Tracks provide content relevant to topics covered in this chapter:

1. Unified Modeling Language (UML)
2. A Primer on Business Process Design and Documentation
3. A Primer on Business Process Management

INTERACTIVE SESSION: TECHNOLOGY

WHAT DOES IT TAKE TO GO MOBILE?

"How should we go mobile?" Almost every company today is asking that question. By 2013, more people will use their mobile phones than PCs to go online, and there will be one mobile device for every person on earth by 2015. The number of Web searches performed on mobile devices has more than quadrupled since 2010. Customers expect, and even demand, to be able to use a mobile device of their choice to obtain information or perform a transaction anywhere and at any time. So if a company wants to stay connected to its customers, it needs some sort of mobile presence.

What do companies do, and where do they start? Developing mobile apps or a mobile Web site has some special challenges. The user experience on a mobile device is fundamentally different from that on a PC. There are special features on mobile devices such as location-based services that that give firms the potential to interact with customers in meaningful new ways. Firms need to be able to take advantage of those features while delivering an experience that is appropriate to a small screen. There are multiple mobile platforms to work with—iPhone, Android, Windows Phone, and possibly BlackBerry, and a firm may need a different version of an application to run on each of these. You can't just port a Web site or desktop application to a smartphone or tablet. It's a different systems development process.

It's important to understand how, why, and where customers use mobile devices and how these mobile experiences change business interactions and behavior. For example, do customers who use an app handle a greater number of transactions on their own and use the phone less? Do they spend more or less time researching products and shopping from a mobile device?

Deckers Outdoor Corporation, the parent company of brands such as UGG Australia, Teva, and Simple Shoes, spent considerable time studying its customers' mobile behavior. It looked at how customers use their mobile devices while shopping and researching brands to find out how consumers would connect with its brand through the mobile channel. When people use mobile devices, how do they research the products? What information do they want about brand? Are they looking for information about product features, product reviews, or retail store locations?

Decker's customer analysis showed that when consumers use mobile devices inside a Deckers store, what is most important is a seamless interaction. The customer wants to be able to look at a product on his or her mobile device and see the same information on that device as that person would obtain in the store, plus some additional information, such as consumer reviews.

A mobile strategy involves much more than selecting mobile devices, operating systems, and applications. It also involves changes to business processes, changing the way people work and the way a firm interacts with its customers. Mobile technology can streamline processes, make them more portable, and enhance them with capabilities such as touch interfaces, location and mapping features, alerts, texting, cameras, and video functionality. The technology can also create less efficient processes or fail to deliver benefits if the mobile application is not properly designed.

USAA, the giant financial services company serving members of the U.S. military and their families, is acutely aware of the need to ensure that mobile technology is aligned with its customer-facing business processes and leads to genuine improvements. The company is using mobile technology to refine its business processes and provide simpler and more powerful ways for customers to interact with the company.

USAA, launched its Web site in 1997 and went mobile ten years later, with about 90 percent of its interactions with customers taking place on these two self-service channels. In 2011, USAA handled 183 million customer contacts through the mobile channel alone, and expects the mobile channel will be its primary point of contact with customers in the next two years. USAA has 100 dedicated mobile developers writing apps for devices using the iPhone, iPad, and Android operating systems, along with apps for the BlackBerry and Windows Phone 7.

USAA developed a smartphone accident report and claims app that enables customers to snap a photo and submit a claim directly from the site of an accident. The app is also able to send geographic information system (GIS) data to a towing service and display nearby car rental locations. Another mobile app supports photo deposits: a customer can capture an image of a check with a smartphone and automatically submit it to the bank. The money is instantly deposited in the customer's account. This system eliminates the labor and expense of processing paper checks, and the time required to mail the check and wait three days for the deposit to clear. In 2011, USAA Federal Savings Bank processed $6.4 billion in deposits through this mobile app.

The mobile app also displays loan and credit card balances, shopping services, homeowners and auto insurance policy information, Home Circle and Auto Circle buying services, retirement products and information, ATM and taxi locators, and a communities feature that lets users see what others are posting about USAA on Twitter, Facebook, and YouTube.

A real estate company may want to display a completely different site to mobile users who are looking for house information after driving by a "For Sale" sign. The realtor may want to optimize the mobile interface to include specific listing and contact information to capture the lead immediately and keep the load time fast. If the mobile site is simply a more user-friendly version of the desktop site, the conversions may not be as high.

Ryland Homes, one of the top U.S. new home builders, has a conventional Web site, but it wanted to be able to engage customers using mobile technol-ogy as well. The company revamped its mobile Web site in March 2011 to increase sales leads by helping potential customers with mobile phones find its loca-tions, look at its products, register with the company, and call directly. Ryland's development team made the site easier to read and capable of fitting on a smartphone or tablet screen without requiring users to pinch and zoom. It used jQuery Mobile software and responsive Web design to create variations of the site that were appropriate for different smartphone or tablet models employed by users. (The jQuery Mobile framework allows developers to design a single Web site or application that will work on all popular smartphone, tablet, and desktop platforms, eliminating the need to write unique apps for each mobile device or operating system.) Ryland focused on features such as location-based driving directions to nearby communities, clickable phone numbers, and brief online registrations to increase the chances of making a sale. The site shows nearby communi-ties in order of distance, based on the location of the mobile device.

Sources: Samuel Greengard, "Mobility Transforms the Customer Relationship," *Baseline*, February 2012; William Atkinson, "How Deckers Used a Mobile Application to Build Customer Traffic," *CIO Insight*, November 9, 2011; "Going Mobile: A Portable Approach to Process Improvement," *Business Agility Insights*, June 2012; Google Inc., "Ryland Homes Opens Doors to Local Sales with Mobile Site for Home-Buyers," 2011.

CASE STUDY QUESTIONS

1. What management, organization, and technology issues need to be addressed when building mobile applications?

2. How does user requirement definition for mobile applications differ from that in traditional systems analysis?

3. Describe the business processes changed by USAA's mobile applications before and after the applications were deployed.

Review Summary

1. *How does building new systems produce organizational change?*

Building a new information system is a form of planned organizational change. Four kinds of technology-enabled change are (a) automation, (b) rationalization of procedures, (c) business process redesign, and (d) paradigm shift, with far-reaching changes carrying the greatest risks and rewards. Many organizations are using business process management to redesign work flows and business processes in the hope of achieving dramatic productivity breakthroughs. Business process manage-ment is also useful for promoting, total quality management (TQM), six sigma, and other initiatives for incremental process improvement.

2. *What are the core activities in the systems development process?*

   The core activities in systems development are systems analysis, systems design, programming, testing, conversion, production, and maintenance. Systems analysis is the study and analysis of problems of existing systems and the identification of requirements for their solutions. Systems design provides the specifications for an information system solution, showing how its technical and organizational components fit together.

3. *What are the principal methodologies for modeling and designing systems?*

   The two principal methodologies for modeling and designing information systems are structured methodologies and object-oriented development. Structured methodologies focus on modeling processes and data separately. The data flow diagram is the principal tool for structured analysis, and the structure chart is the principal tool for representing structured software design. Object-oriented development models a system as a collection of objects that combine processes and data. Object-oriented modeling is based on the concepts of class and inheritance.

4. *What are the alternative methods for building information systems?*

   The oldest method for building systems is the systems life cycle, which requires that information systems be developed in formal stages. The stages must proceed sequentially and have defined outputs; each requires formal approval before the next stage can commence. The systems life cycle is useful for large projects that need formal specifications and tight management control over each stage of systems building, but it is very rigid and costly.

   Prototyping consists of building an experimental system rapidly and inexpensively for end users to interact with and evaluate. Prototyping encourages end-user involvement in systems development and iteration of design until specifications are captured accurately. The rapid creation of prototypes can result in systems that have not been completely tested or documented or that are technically inadequate for a production environment.

   Using a software package reduces the amount of design, programming, testing, installation, and maintenance work required to build a system. Application software packages are helpful if a firm does not have the internal information systems staff or financial resources to custom develop a system. To meet an organization's unique requirements, packages may require extensive modifications that can substantially raise development costs.

   End-user development is the development of information systems by end users, either alone or with minimal assistance from information systems specialists. End-user-developed systems can be created rapidly and informally using fourth-generation software tools. However, end-user development may create information systems that do not necessarily meet quality assurance standards and that are not easily controlled by traditional means.

   Outsourcing consists of using an external vendor to build (or operate) a firm's information systems instead of the organization's internal information systems staff. Outsourcing can save application development costs or enable firms to develop applications without an internal information systems staff. However, firms risk losing control over their information systems and becoming too dependent on external vendors. Outsourcing also entails hidden costs, especially when the work is sent offshore.

5. *What are new approaches for system building in the digital firm era?*

   Companies are turning to rapid application design (RAD), joint application design (JAD), agile development, and reusable software components to accelerate the systems development process. RAD uses object-oriented software, visual programming, prototyping, and fourth-generation tools for very rapid creation of systems. Agile development breaks a large project into a series of small subprojects that are completed in short periods of time using iteration and continuous feedback. Component-based development expedites application development by grouping objects into suites of software components that can be combined to create large-scale business applications. Web services provide a common set of standards that enable organizations to link their systems regardless of their technology platform through standard plug- and-play architecture. Mobile application development must pay attention to simplicity, usability, and the need to optimize tasks for tiny screens.

Key Terms

Acceptance testing, 530	Phased approach strategy, 531
Agile development, 544	Pilot study strategy, 531
Automation, 520	Postimplementation audit, 531
Business process management, 522	Process specifications, 534
Business process redesign, 521	Production, 531
Component-based development, 545	Programming, 530
Computer-aided software engineering (CASE), 536	Prototype, 538
	Prototyping, 538
Conversion, 530	Query languages, 540
Customization, 541	Rapid application development (RAD), 544
Data flow diagram (DFD), 533	Rationalization of procedures, 521
Direct cutover strategy, 531	Request for Proposal (RFP), 541
Documentation, 531	Responsive Web design, 545
End-user development, 539	Six sigma, 521
End-user interface, 538	Structure chart, 534
Feasibility study, 528	Structured, 532
Fourth-generation languages, 539	Systems analysis, 528
Information requirements, 528	Systems design, 528
Iterative, 538	Systems development, 525
Joint application design (JAD), 544	Systems life cycle, 537
Maintenance, 532	System testing, 530
Object, 534	Test plan, 530
Object-oriented development, 534	Testing, 530
Offshore outsourcing, 542	Total quality management (TQM), 521
Paradigm shift, 521	Unit testing, 530
Parallel strategy, 530	

Review Questions

1. How does building new systems produce organizational change?

- Describe each of the four kinds of organizational change that can be promoted with information technology.

- Define business process management and describe the steps required to carry it out.

- Explain how information systems support process changes that promote quality in an organization.

2. What are the core activities in the systems development process?

- Distinguish between systems analysis and systems design. Describe the activities for each.

- Define information requirements and explain why they are difficult to determine correctly.

- Explain why the testing stage of systems development is so important. Name and describe the three stages of testing for an information system.

- Describe the role of programming, conversion, production, and maintenance in systems development.

3. What are the principal methodologies for modeling and designing systems?

- Compare object-oriented and traditional structured approaches for modeling and designing systems.

4. What are the alternative methods for building information systems?

- Define the traditional systems life cycle. Describe each of its steps and its advantages and disadvantages for systems building.

- Define information system prototyping. Describe its benefits and limitations. List and describe the steps in the prototyping process.

- Define an application software package. Explain the advantages and disadvantages of developing information systems based on software packages.

- Define end-user development and describe its advantages and disadvantages. Name some policies and procedures for managing end-user development.

- Describe the advantages and disadvantages of using outsourcing for building information systems.

5. What are new approaches for system building in the digital firm era?

- Define rapid application development (RAD) and agile development and explain how they can speed up system-building.

- Explain how component-based development and Web services help firms build and enhance their information systems.

- Explain the features of mobile application development and responsive Web design.

Discussion Questions

1. Why is selecting a systems development approach an important business decision? Who should participate in the selection process?

2. Some have said that the best way to reduce systems development costs is to use application software packages or fourth-generation tools. Do you agree? Why or why not?

3. Why is is so important to understand how a business process works when trying to develop a new information system?

Hands-On MIS Projects

The projects in this section give you hands-on experience analyzing business processes, designing and building a customer system for auto sales, and analyzing Web site information requirements.

Management Decision Problems

1. For an additional fee, a customer purchasing a Sears Roebuck appliance, such as a washing machine, can purchase a three-year service contract. The contract provides free repair service and parts for the specified appliance using an authorized Sears service provider. When a person with a Sears service contract needs to repair an appliance, such as a washing machine, he or she calls the Sears Repairs & Parts department to schedule an appointment. The department makes the appointment and gives the caller the date and approximate time of the appointment. The repair technician arrives during the designated time framework and diagnoses the problem. If the problem is caused by a faulty part, the technician either replaces the part if he is carrying the part with him or orders the replacement part from Sears. If the part is not in stock at Sears, Sears orders the part and gives the customer an approximate time when the part will arrive. The part is shipped directly to the customer. After the part has arrived, the customer must call Sears to schedule a second appointment for a repair technician to replace the ordered part. This process is very lengthy. It may take two weeks to schedule the first repair visit, another two weeks to order and receive the required part, and another week to schedule a second repair visit after the ordered part has been received.

- Diagram the existing process.

- What is the impact of the existing process on Sears' operational efficiency and customer relationships?

- What changes could be made to make this process more efficient? How could information systems support these changes? Diagram the new improved process.

2. Management at your agricultural chemicals corporation has been dissatisfied with production planning. Production plans are created using best guesses of demand for each product, which are based on how much of each product has been ordered in the past. If a customer places an unexpected order or requests a change to an existing order after it has been placed, there is no way to adjust production plans. The company may have to tell customers it can't fill their orders, or it may run up extra costs maintaining additional inventory to prevent stock-outs.

At the end of each month, orders are totaled and manually keyed into the company's production planning system. Data from the past month's production and inventory systems are manually entered into the firm's order management system. Analysts from the sales department and from the production department analyze the data from their respective systems to determine what the sales targets and production targets should be for the next month. These estimates are usually different. The analysts then get together at a high-level planning meeting to revise the production and sales targets to take into account senior management's goals for market share, revenues, and profits. The outcome of the meeting is a finalized production master schedule.

The entire production planning process takes 17 business days to complete. Nine of these days are required to entire and validate the data. The remaining days are spent developing and reconciling the production and sales targets and finalizing the production master schedule.

- Draw a diagram of the existing production planning process.
- Analyze the problems this process creates for the company.
- How could an enterprise system solve these problems? In what ways could it lower costs? Diagram what the production planning process might look like if the company implemented enterprise software.

Improving Decision Making: Using Database Software to Design a Customer System for Auto Sales

Software skills: Database design, querying, reporting, and forms
Business skills: Sales lead and customer analysis

This project requires you to perform a systems analysis and then design a system solution using database software.

Ace Auto Dealers specializes in selling new vehicles from Subaru in Portland, Oregon. The company advertises in local newspapers and is listed as an authorized dealer on the Subaru Web site and other major Web sites for auto buyers. The company benefits from a good local word-of-mouth reputation and name recognition.

Ace does not believe it has enough information about its customers. It cannot easily determine which prospects have made auto purchases, nor can it identify which customer touch points have produced the greatest number of sales leads or actual sales so it can focus advertising and marketing more on the channels that generate the most revenue. Are purchasers discovering Ace from newspaper ads, from word of mouth, or from the Web?

Prepare a systems analysis report detailing Ace's problem and a system solution that can be implemented using PC database management software. Then use database software to develop a simple system solution. In MyMISLab, you will find more information about Ace and its information requirements to help you develop the solution.

Achieving Operational Excellence: Analyzing Web Site Design and Information Requirements

Software skills: Web browser software
Business skills: Information requirements analysis, Web site design

Visit the Web site of your choice and explore it thoroughly. Prepare a report analyzing the various functions provided by that Web site and its information requirements. Your report should answer these questions: What functions does the Web site perform? What data does it use? What are its inputs, outputs, and processes? What are some of its other design specifications? Does the Web site link to any internal systems or systems of other organizations? What value does this Web site provide the firm?

Video Cases

Video Cases and Instructional Videos illustrating some of the concepts in this chapter are available. Contact your instructor to access these videos.

Collaboration and Teamwork Project

In MyMISLab, you will find a Collaboration and Teamwork Project dealing with the concepts in this chapter. You will be able to use Google Sites, Google Docs, and other open source collaboration tools to complete the assignment.

Honam Petrochemical's Quest for Better Management Reports
CASE STUDY

You may soon hear more about Honam Petrochemical Corporation (HPC). Headquartered in Seoul, South Korea, this company manufactures and sells petrochemical products, including synthetic resins; synthetic industrial materials, including ethylene glycol and ethylene oxide for making polyester; automobile antifreeze solutions; benzene; propylene; and ethylene. HPC has about 1,700 employees, and its 2011 revenues were close to US$7.3 billion. It's a leader in Korea's heavy chemical industry.

HPC's primary market is South Korea, but the company has set its sights on becoming a top-tier chemical company throughout Asia and achieving sales of US$10 billion. Honam plans to do this by strengthening its existing businesses, extending its overseas business, and developing new businesses. Honam has nine affiliate companies in China, Malaysia, Indonesia, Pakistan, and the United Kingdom, and overseas branches in Shanghai, Qingdao, Guangzhou, Hong Kong, Moscow, and New York City.

To manage its far-flung operations, HPC needs reliable reports that are able to accurately measure management performance and provide useful, accurate information for increasing sales and reducing costs. HPC's existing systems provided managers with reports to guide their business decisions, but in many cases the data in the reports were out-of-date and "sanitized." Individual managers were processing and manipulating the data to make their departments "look better" to senior management. The report data were also somewhat stale and presented only on a periodic basis.

Executives at the chemical firm wanted access to the data before they went through manipulation or processing. They didn't want each department's own interpretation of reports. Instead, executives wanted to see current data to get a real view of what was actually happening on the plant floor or in the sales office.

Developing a business intelligence solution specifically for executives requires a good deal of up-front requirements gathering. HPC's executive decision makers did not want to work with last quarter's numbers. They wanted anytime access to the most timely data, but they did not want to be overloaded with unnecessary data so they could focus on the "watch-up indicators" considered crucial to the business. They wanted up-to-the-minute reports that they could see quickly on their desktops. They also wanted access via the Web or their mobile devices. Finally, HPC executives wanted enterprise-wide data that could be accessed and shared easily across various business units and functions to support the company's expansion geographically and by product line.

These requirements drove the technology selection process. HPC's information systems team reviewed a number of different software products and vendors and selected SAP BusinessObjects Dashboards and SAP BusinessObjects Web Intelligence. The company already had seven years' experience running SAP's ERP system, so this vendor seemed like an appropriate choice.

SAP BusinessObjects Dashboards is a drag-and-drop visualization tool designed to create interactive analytics for powerful, personalized dashboards based on SAP's BusinessObjects business intelligence platform. BusinessObjects software tools can be used for performance management, planning, reporting, query and analysis, and enterprise information management, and provide self-service access to data from databases and Excel spreadsheets. SAP BusinessObjects Web Intelligence is an ad hoc query, reporting, and analysis tool that is used to create queries or use existing reports, format retrieved information, and perform analysis to understand trends and root causes.

Once HPC's project team determined the business intelligence tools for the solution, its focus turned to determining which data and reports were required by the company's 200 high-level users of the new system. The information systems team started by asking executives to list existing reports they were already receiving and to assess the usefulness of each. The list was cut to a more manageable size and the executives were asked if there were any additional reports or data from which their organizational groups could benefit. These findings were very useful in determining the right set of reports and dashboards for HPC executives.

Once these user requirements were clarified, the information systems team designed a system that could extract data from a SAP NetWeaver Business Warehouse and present them to executives using the SAP BusinessObjects Dashboards software and SAP Crystal Reports, an application for designing and generating reports from a wide range of data sources. A highly intuitive Web-based user interface was created to make the system very accessible. This interface was so simple and well-designed that users required little training on how to use the system or to access data and reports.

To encourage users to start working with the system, members of the information systems department visited various manufacturing plants where the system was being rolled out and had in-depth discussions with executives about the system's benefits as well as how to use it. Even after the system was up and running, the information systems department continues to run campaigns to ensure that executives are using the system—and using it in the most effective way.

HPC used a phased approach in implementing the new system. Rather than pushing a new system onto executives early in the ERP life cycle, HPC waited until the company was experienced with ERP software and confident in its data quality and its data collection and processing methods. According to HPC CIO Jong Pyo Kim, nothing would sidetrack an executive-level system more quickly than inaccurate or untimely data flowing into an executive's dashboard.

Kim also emphasized the importance of benchmarking before designing and implementing an executive-facing system. Most manufacturing executives will want access to similar data and performance indicators, so benchmarking with other companies in the industry can provide a good look at what data brings the most value.

HPC's system went live in January 2011, and executives started immediately accessing reports and dashboards on a daily, weekly, and monthly basis. The system enabled them to view key performance information such as manufacturing costs by plant, transportation costs, daily production and inventory rates, and global product price trends, and the information can be displayed visually in dashboards and management cockpits. Thirty executives tested mobile devices providing anytime, anywhere access to the new system. Delivery of the information is personalized and differentiated for high-level executives, middle managers, and front-line employees.

It is still too early to assess the long-term business impact of the system, but one benefit was immediate: Executives no longer are limited to sanitized, stale data in an outdated presentation format. Management discussions and decisions are based on timely, consistent, and accurate company-wide data. Because the system reduces the time required to collect, process, and track the data, executive decision making takes place more rapidly. HPC's information systems are now ready for global information-sharing as the company expands.

Sources: Microsoft Corporation, "Case Study: Honam Petrochemical," May 7, 2012; David Hannon, "Searching Beyond Sanitized Data," *SAPInsider* PROFILES, July 2011; David Steier, "Visualizing Success: Analytic User Interfaces that Drive Business," *Information Management*, July/August, 2011; and "Honam Petrochemical Strategy and Financial Highlights from ICIS,"www.icis.com, accessed July 21, 2011.

CASE STUDY QUESTIONS

1. List and describe the information requirements of HPC's new management system. What problems was the new system designed to solve?

2. To what extent were "people" problems affecting management decision making at HPC? What were some of the management, organization, and technology issues that had to be addressed by the new system? How did the system's designers make the system more "people-friendly?"

3. What role did end users play in developing HPC's new system? How did the project team make sure users were involved? What would have happened to the project if they had not done this?

4. What other steps did HPC take to make sure the system was successful?

5. What types of system-building methods and tools did HPC use for building its system?

6. What were the benefits of the new system? How did it change the way Honam ran its business? How successful was this system solution?

Chapter 14

Managing Projects

LEARNING OBJECTIVES

After reading this chapter, you will be able to answer the following questions:

1. What are the objectives of project management and why is it so essential in developing information systems?

2. What methods can be used for selecting and evaluating information systems projects and aligning them with the firm's business goals?

3. How can firms assess the business value of information systems projects?

4. What are the principal risk factors in information systems projects?

5. What strategies are useful for managing project risk and system implementation?

Interactive Sessions:

Austin Energy's Billing System Can't Light Up

Westinghouse Electric Takes on the Risks of a "Big Bang" Project

CHAPTER OUTLINE

14.1 THE IMPORTANCE OF PROJECT MANAGEMENT
Runaway Projects and System Failure
Project Management Objectives

14.2 SELECTING PROJECTS
Management Structure for Information Systems Projects
Linking Systems Projects to the Business Plan
Information Requirements and Key Performance Indicators
Portfolio Analysis
Scoring Models

14.3 ESTABLISHING THE BUSINESS VALUE OF INFORMATION SYSTEMS
Information System Costs and Benefits
Real Options Pricing Models
Limitations of Financial Models

14.4 MANAGING PROJECT RISK
Dimensions of Project Risk
Change Management and the Concept of Implementation
Controlling Risk Factors
Designing for the Organization
Project Management Software Tools

LEARNING TRACK MODULES
Capital Budgeting Methods for Information System Investments
Information Technology Investments and Productivity
Enterprise Analysis (Business Systems Planning) and Critical Success Factors

NU SKIN'S NEW HUMAN RESOURCES SYSTEM PROJECT PUTS PEOPLE FIRST

Nu Skin Enterprises is an American direct-selling and multilevel marketing company which sells more than 200 anti-aging personal care and dietary supplements products through more than 830,000 independent distributors. Since its beginnings in 1984 in Provo, Utah, the company has expanded operations to 52 international markets. Annual revenues have topped 1 billion dollars.

Nu Skin's business model combines direct selling with multilevel marketing. Each distributor markets products directly to potential customers, and can also recruit and train customers to become distributors. Distributors are paid from the retail markup on products they are able to sell personally, as well as a percentage of the sales of distributors they have recruited. To be successful, Nu Skin obviously must pay close attention to how it manages people.

Although Nu Skin has nearly 6,000 employees in 28 different countries, until recently, it did not have a centralized human resources (HR) system to maintain employee data or to provide HR reporting to other parts of the business. Instead, it managed employees manually at the local level or allowed local operating units to use their own systems. In order to obtain employee information at the corporate level, Nu Skin had to contact the region and obtain the data manually. All of this was very time-consuming, and the company really needed more consistent and automated HR processes.

When Nu Skin's management decided to implement a centralized HR system, a cross-functional project team representing human resources and the information systems department conducted a thorough two-year analysis of information needs and searched for the right system. It recommended SAP ERP Human Capital Management (HCM), and started to implement the modules for personnel administration and organizational management.

Members of the project team were selected so that their HR expertise and experience would complement each other. Team members included several SAP business analysts, a programmer analyst, a technical business analyst, an HR information systems analyst, and a team of senior systems engineers. Vice President of Human Resources David Daines and IT Business Integration leaders Amy Camara and Jay Barney supported the team.

External consultants from Symphony Consulting were hired to assist the project team in identifying information requirements from various Nu Skin offices. Consultants were hired on the basis of skills and personality that would enhance the team, as well as the ability to perform on-site training. Nu Skin's users were in so many different geographic locations that it would be impossible for them to train in the new system off-site. The consultants were assigned to train employees on-site during the implementation.

Through every step of the project, the company was careful to put "people" before technology. What kind of people should be on the project team? What consultants should be employed? What are the business and culture requirements that have to be addressed?

The project team visited various Nu Skin sites in each of the company's markets to inquire about the data each

© Yuri Arcurs/Shutterstock

collected, what systems and reports they used with the data, and what they wanted in the future. These face-to-face meetings sensitized the project team to the regional differences in information requirements and corporate culture. The meetings also gave end users a stronger sense of ownership in the project and the belief that the project team was dedicated to making the new system work for their benefit.

The project team used a phased implementation approach for each global region. In 2011, Nu Skin went live with the SAP ERP HCM global functionality. Benefits were immediate. In the past, if the finance department needed a report on the number of full-time employees in a specific market, the Nu Skin HR department had to request the information from the local operating unit, which could take weeks. A report about which employees transferred to another department or left the company had to be manually created by gathering the required data from the various regions and manually sending the report to the different departments. Now all of these reports are automatically generated and distributed by the system.

Sources: "Nu Skin Fights Aging Systems with New HR Software,"SAP Insider Profiles January 2012; "Nu Skin: Invigorating the Customer Interaction Experience," www.sap.com, accessed November 8, 2012; and www.nuskin.com, accessed November 8, 2012.

One of the principal challenges posed by information systems is ensuring they deliver genuine business benefits. There is a very high failure rate among information systems projects because organizations have incorrectly assessed their business value or because firms have failed to manage the organizational change surrounding the introduction of new technology.

Nu Skin's management realized this when it implemented its HR system. The new system involved an enterprise-wide change in HR business processes supported by new software. Nu Skin succeeded in this project because its management clearly understood that attention to organizational "people" issues was essential for success, especially in a multinational company with numerous regional and cultural differences.

The chapter-opening diagram calls attention to important points raised by this case and this chapter. Nu Skin desperately needed to automate its HR processes, which had been entirely manual and made operations highly inefficient. Management wisely selected a project team whose members had both business and technical expertise. The team took great care and time to identify the right software solution and to elicit user information requirements. Staging the system implementation and conducting employee training at each location further contributed to success.

Here are some questions to think about: Why was it important to have representatives from both HR and IT on the project team? What were the risk factors in this project?

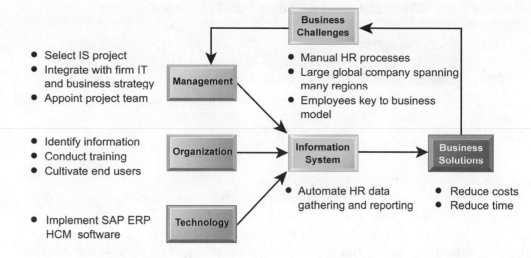

- Select IS project
- Integrate with firm IT and business strategy
- Appoint project team

Management

Business Challenges

- Manual HR processes
- Large global company spanning many regions
- Employees key to business model

- Identify information
- Conduct training
- Cultivate end users

Organization

Information System

Business Solutions

- Implement SAP ERP HCM software

Technology

- Automate HR data gathering and reporting

- Reduce costs
- Reduce time

14.1   THE IMPORTANCE OF PROJECT MANAGEMENT

There is a very high failure rate among information systems projects. In nearly every organization, information systems projects take much more time and money to implement than originally anticipated or the completed system does not work properly. When an information system does not meet expectations or costs too much to develop, companies may not realize any benefit from their information system investment, and the system may not be able to solve the problems for which it was intended. The development of a new system must be carefully managed and orchestrated, and the way a project is executed is likely to be the most important factor influencing its outcome. That's why it's essential to have some knowledge about managing information systems projects and the reasons why they succeed or fail.

RUNAWAY PROJECTS AND SYSTEM FAILURE

How badly are projects managed? On average, private sector projects are underestimated by one-half in terms of budget and time required to deliver the complete system promised in the system plan. Many projects are delivered with missing functionality (promised for delivery in later versions). The Standish Group consultancy, which monitors IT project success rates, found that only 32 percent of all technology investments were completed on time, on budget, and with all features and functions originally specified (McCafferty, 2010). A large global study of 1,471 IT projects reported in *Harvard Business Review* found that the average cost overrun was 27 percent, and that one in six of the projects studied had an average cost overrun of 200 percent and a schedule overrun of almost 70 percent (Flyvbjerg and Budzier, 2011). Between 30 and 40 percent of all software projects are "runaway" projects that far exceed the original schedule and budget projections and fail to perform as originally specified.

As illustrated in Figure 14.1, a systems development project without proper management will most likely suffer these consequences:

- Costs that vastly exceed budgets
- Unexpected time slippage
- Technical performance that is less than expected
- Failure to obtain anticipated benefits

FIGURE 14.1 CONSEQUENCES OF POOR PROJECT MANAGEMENT

Poor Project Management →
Cost overruns
Time slippage
Technical shortfalls impairing performance
Failure to obtain anticipated benefits

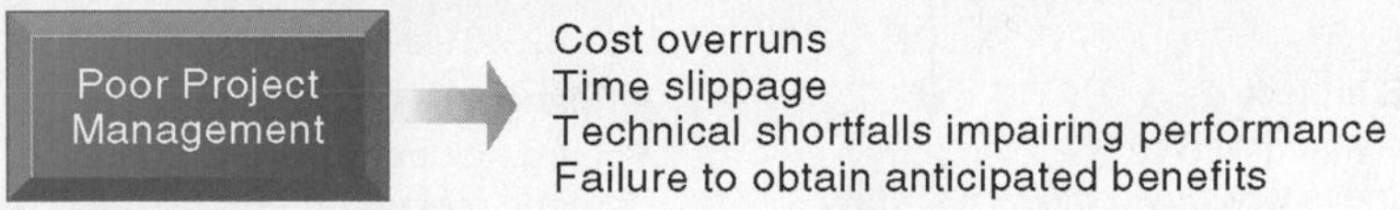

Without proper management, a systems development project takes longer to complete and most often exceeds the allocated budget. The resulting information system most likely is technically inferior and may not be able to demonstrate any benefits to the organization.

The systems produced by failed information projects are often not used in the way they were intended, or they are not used at all. Users often have to develop parallel manual systems to make these systems work.

The actual design of the system may fail to capture essential business requirements or improve organizational performance. Information may not be provided quickly enough to be helpful, it may be in a format that is impossible to digest and use, or it may represent the wrong pieces of data.

The way in which nontechnical business users must interact with the system may be excessively complicated and discouraging. A system may be designed with a poor user interface. The **user interface** is the part of the system with which end users interact. For example, an online input form or data entry screen may be so poorly arranged that no one wants to submit data or request information. System outputs may be displayed in a format that is too difficult to comprehend.

Web sites may discourage visitors from exploring further if the Web pages are cluttered and poorly arranged, if users cannot easily find the information they are seeking, or if it takes too long to access and display the Web page on the user's computer.

Additionally, the data in the system may have a high level of inaccuracy or inconsistency. The information in certain fields may be erroneous or ambiguous, or it may not be organized properly for business purposes. Information required for a specific business function may be inaccessible because the data are incomplete.

The Interactive Session on Management illustrates some of the problems we have just described. As you read this case, try to determine why this project was not successful and the role of project management in the outcome.

PROJECT MANAGEMENT OBJECTIVES

A **project** is a planned series of related activities for achieving a specific business objective. Information systems projects include the development of new information systems, enhancement of existing systems, or upgrade or replacement of the firm's information technology (IT) infrastructure.

Project management refers to the application of knowledge, skills, tools, and techniques to achieve specific targets within specified budget and time constraints. Project management activities include planning the work, assessing risk, estimating resources required to accomplish the work, organizing the work, acquiring human and material resources, assigning tasks, directing activities, controlling project execution, reporting progress, and analyzing the results. As in other areas of business, project management for information systems must deal with five major variables: scope, time, cost, quality, and risk.

INTERACTIVE SESSION: MANAGEMENT

AUSTIN ENERGY'S BILLING SYSTEM CAN'T LIGHT UP

Austin Energy handles electrical, water, and waste disposal for the City of Austin, Texas, and surrounding counties, serving more than 1 million residents. It is a publicly owned company and an arm of city government, and returns its profits to the community each year. The company has provided $1.5 billion in dividends back to Austin since 1976, which help fund city services such as fire, police, emergency medical services, parks, and libraries.

Austin Energy has one of the largest renewable energy programs in the country, but its legacy billing systems did not integrate with smart meters and other newer technologies. It also lacked newer customer assistance options, like the ability to choose the time of the month that a customer prefers to pay bills. To modernize the billing system and to bring its information systems up to date with newer energy conservation methods, Austin Energy contracted with IBM in 2009 to create a centralized billing system and to run the system for five years. Austin agreed to pay IBM $55 million, with $38 million allocated for building and installing the new billing system, and $17 million for operating the system for five years after its completion. The new billing system was slated to handle electricity, water, trash, and recycling. Austin was optimistic that a successful installation would eventually pay for itself in savings.

To date, the project has been a disappointment at best. The system was supposed to go live in early 2011, but is still not fully operational. Software bugs have led to errors in thousands of bills. Over 65,000 customers never received a bill, and another 35,000 have received inaccurate bills. For example, one business that owed Austin Energy $3,000 was instead charged $300,000. Although Austin Energy was able to identify affected accounts and work with customers individually to correct the problems, the company was ill-prepared to handle the outpouring of customer dissatisfaction with the new system, and their customer service department was in danger of being overrun.

According to Austin Energy manager Larry Weiss, "Instability issues . . . continue to have serious and costly impacts on our business and our customers." Persistent system errors prevented the company from billing apartment residents for water, balancing its books, and filing audit reports. Without the ability to bill for utilities properly, the City of Austin was losing revenue.

Officials with Austin Energy put the blame for the project's woes squarely on IBM. Austin Energy's CIO Alan Claypool stated in an interview that "we have yet to reach a stable system (and) we are extremely disappointed and continue to have serious concerns about the quality of service we have received from IBM to date." He noted in a September 2011 message that IBM was repeating mistakes as it tried to implement the system. Two separate errors by IBM cost the project 37 hours of delay, and one of the errors was the same type of error made by the same team in December 2010. "We continue to be gravely disappointed in the delays and seemingly ad hoc methods toward managing this project," Claypool stated.

The company now plans to include provisions in future contracts with IBM that guard against similar mishaps, with a particular focus on system availability, and Austin is withholding $3.8 million in payments currently owed to IBM until the system meets baseline performance benchmarks.

Claypool and other Austin Energy executives have made numerous direct appeals to IBM officials, ranging from the managers of the billing system project all the way up to then IBM CEO Sam Palmisano. Claypool first wrote directly to Marc Lautenbach, the head of IBM's Global Business Services unit in North America, which was responsible for the billing system project. He explained that thousands of customers required one-on-one assistance to access their accounts or correct billing errors. Lautenbach was then replaced as Global Business head by Frank Kern, who wrote back to Austin and described a five-step plan to fix the problems with the billing system.

Kern's plan was to improve communications on business impacts caused by known defects, to ensure that problems with the system are delegated to the correct people, to implement best-practice processes to ensure repeatable success, to work more closely with third-party vendors like Oracle, and to identify gaps outside the project's scope and recommend solutions. Since that time, Kern has retired, and Claypool wrote back to IBM yet again to report that no progress had been made since the five-step plan was first developed for Austin Energy's billing system. Austin Energy officials also objected to IBM's suggestion to add more powerful servers to help fix the problem because that would force the utility to pay more than originally planned on the project.

Despite all of the blunders, Austin Energy continues to hold out hope for a successful and amicable solution to the problem. Austin Energy has a relationship with IBM dating back several years, when the companies contracted together to develop an inventory management system for the city. Though that system also experienced problems, they pale in comparison to the billing system fiasco. Austin Energy also claims that IBM's errors have cost the company $8 million since the project's outset, so switching vendors might simply make matters worse for Austin Energy with so much invested in IBM's project development already. When asked for comment, IBM has only said that it is working with Austin Energy to resolve the billing system issues.

IBM has successfully managed other projects like this one in the past. The IBM billing system consists of Oracle databases running atop IBM's WebSphere middleware and Tivoli management tools. The problems with the system have not stemmed from one root cause. The new billing system is complex, with 73 different interfaces, and getting them all to work seamlessly with one another has been an arduous process. Customers have been unable to access the system's online portal, and Austin Energy employees have described their experience with the system as if they are "alpha testers," meaning they have encountered bugs and issues that should never have made it to a live version.

Roughly one in four Austin customers has had problems with IBM's system. Some customers had their accounts canceled and could only correct the errors after several phone calls. The billing system woes have come at a bad time for Austin Energy, which was preparing to institute its first rate increase in 17 years. In the wake of the public relations disaster brought about by the botched billing system, the company has had to rethink those plans.

As of February 2012, most—but not all—of the billing system errors had been fixed. Claypool remained hopeful that Austin Energy would be able to maintain an amicable relationship with IBM and finish the work successfully. IBM has been responsive, Claypool noted, but Claypool felt its response was too "incremental. . . . We would like to see a faster response." Going forward, Austin Energy's outsourcing contracts will include stronger penalties for vendor nonperformance, including the question of system availability.

Sources: Paul McDougall, "Chronology of an Outsourcing Disaster," *Information Week*, February 23, 2012; "Austin Energy Fixes Billing System Bug," MyFoxAustin.com, February 22, 2012; and www.austinenergy.com, accessed March 22, 2012.

CASE STUDY QUESTIONS

1. Is the Austin Energy project a failure? Explain your answer.

2. Describe the business impact of the faltering Austin Energy project.

3. To what degree was IBM responsible for the problems countered by the Austin Energy billing project? Was Austin Energy at fault for the problems? Explain your answer.

4. What were the specific organizational or technical factors as well as management factors involved in this project failure?

5. Describe the steps Austin Energy and IBM should have taken to better manage this project.

Scope defines what work is or is not included in a project. For example, the scope of a project for a new order processing system might be to include new modules for inputting orders and transmitting them to production and accounting but not any changes to related accounts receivable, manufacturing, distribution, or inventory control systems. Project management defines all the work required to complete a project successfully, and should ensure that the scope of a project does not expand beyond what was originally intended.

Time is the amount of time required to complete the project. Project management typically establishes the amount of time required to complete major components of a project. Each of these components is further broken down into activities and tasks. Project management tries to determine the time required to complete each task and establish a schedule for completing the work.

Cost is based on the time to complete a project multiplied by the cost of human resources required to complete the project. Information systems project costs also include the cost of hardware, software, and work space. Project management develops a budget for the project and monitors ongoing project expenses.

Quality is an indicator of how well the end result of a project satisfies the objectives specified by management. The quality of information systems projects usually boils down to improved organizational performance and decision making. Quality also considers the accuracy and timeliness of information produced by the new system and ease of use.

Risk refers to potential problems that would threaten the success of a project. These potential problems might prevent a project from achieving its objectives by increasing time and cost, lowering the quality of project outputs, or preventing the project from being completed altogether. Section 14.4 describes the most important risk factors for information systems.

14.2 SELECTING PROJECTS

Companies typically are presented with many different projects for solving problems and improving performance. There are far more ideas for systems projects than there are resources. Firms will need to select from this group the projects that promise the greatest benefit to the business. Obviously, the firm's overall business strategy should drive project selection. How should managers choose among all the options?

MANAGEMENT STRUCTURE FOR INFORMATION SYSTEMS PROJECTS

Figure 14.2 shows the elements of a management structure for information systems projects in a large corporation. It helps ensure that the most important projects are given priority.

At the apex of this structure is the corporate strategic planning group and the information system steering committee. The corporate strategic planning group is responsible for developing the firm's strategic plan, which may require the development of new systems. Often, this group will have developed objective measures of firm performance (called "key performance indicators," introduced in Chapter 12) and choose to support IT projects which can make a substantial improvement in one or several key performance indicators. These performance indicators are reviewed and discussed by the firm's board of directors.

The information systems steering committee is the senior management group with responsibility for systems development and operation. It is composed of department heads from both end-user and information systems areas. The steering committee reviews and approves plans for systems in all divisions, seeks to coordinate and integrate systems, and occasionally becomes involved in selecting specific information systems projects. This group also has a keen awareness of the key performance indicators decided on by higher level managers and the board of directors.

FIGURE 14.2 MANAGEMENT CONTROL OF SYSTEMS PROJECTS

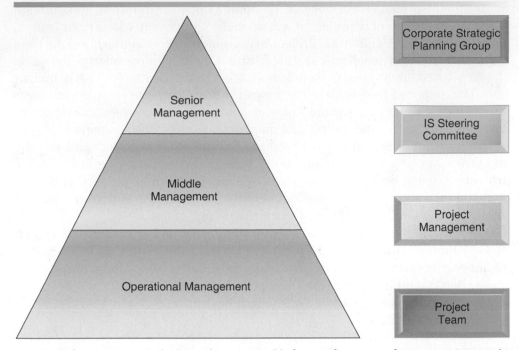

Each level of management in the hierarchy is responsible for specific aspects of systems projects, and this structure helps give priority to the most important systems projects for the organization.

The project team is supervised by a project management group composed of information systems managers and end-user managers responsible for overseeing several specific information systems projects. The project team is directly responsible for the individual systems project. It consists of systems analysts, specialists from the relevant end-user business areas, application programmers, and perhaps database specialists. The mix of skills and the size of the project team depend on the specific nature of the system solution.

LINKING SYSTEMS PROJECTS TO THE BUSINESS PLAN

In order to identify the information systems projects that will deliver the most business value, organizations need to develop an **information systems plan** that supports their overall business plan and in which strategic systems are incorporated into top-level planning. The plan serves as a road map indicating the direction of systems development (the purpose of the plan), the rationale, the current systems/situation, new developments to consider, the management strategy, the implementation plan, and the budget (see Table 14.1).

The plan contains a statement of corporate goals and specifies how information technology will support the attainment of those goals. The report shows how general goals will be achieved by specific systems projects. It identifies specific target dates and milestones that can be used later to evaluate the plan's progress in terms of how many objectives were actually attained in the time frame specified in the plan. The plan indicates the key management decisions concerning hardware acquisition; telecommunications; centralization/decentralization of authority, data, and hardware; and required organizational change. Organizational changes are also usually described, including management

TABLE 14.1 INFORMATION SYSTEMS PLAN

1.   Purpose of the Plan
     Overview of plan contents
     Current business organization and future organization
     Key business processes
     Management strategy

2.   Strategic Business Plan Rationale
     Current situation
     Current business organization
     Changing environments
     Major goals of the business plan
     Firm's strategic plan

3.   Current Systems
     Major systems supporting business functions and processes
     Current infrastructure capabilities
          Hardware
          Software
          Database
          Telecommunications and Internet
     Difficulties meeting business requirements
     Anticipated future demands

4.   New Developments
     New system projects
          Project descriptions
          Business rationale
          Applications' role in strategy
     New infrastructure capabilities required
          Hardware
          Software
          Database
          Telecommunications and Internet

5.   Management Strategy
     Acquisition plans
     Milestones and timing
     Organizational realignment
     Internal reorganization
     Management controls
     Major training initiatives
     Personnel strategy

6.   Implementation Plan
     Anticipated difficulties in implementation
     Progress reports

7.   Budget Requirements
     Requirements
     Potential savings
     Financing
     Acquisition cycle

and employee training requirements, recruiting efforts, changes in business processes, and changes in authority, structure, or management practice.

In order to plan effectively, firms will need to inventory and document all of their information system applications and IT infrastructure components. For projects in which benefits involve improved decision making, managers should try to identify the decision improvements that would provide the greatest additional value to the firm. They should then develop a set of metrics to quantify the value of more timely and precise information on the outcome of the decision. (See Chapter 12 for more detail on this topic.)

INFORMATION REQUIREMENTS AND KEY PERFORMANCE INDICATORS

To develop an effective information systems plan, the organization must have a clear understanding of both its long- and short-term information requirements. A strategic approach to information requirements, strategic analysis, or critical success factors argues that an organization's information requirements are determined by a small number of **key performance indicators (KPIs)** of managers. KPIs are shaped by the industry, the firm, the manager, and the broader environment. For instance, KPIs for an automobile firm might be unit production costs, labor costs, factory productivity, re-work and error rate, customer brand recognition surveys, J.D. Power quality rankings, employee job satisfaction ratings, and health costs. New information systems should focus on providing information that helps the firm meet these goals implied by key performance indicators.

PORTFOLIO ANALYSIS

Once strategic analyses have determined the overall direction of systems development, **portfolio analysis** can be used to evaluate alternative system projects. Portfolio analysis inventories all of the organization's information systems projects and assets, including infrastructure, outsourcing contracts, and licenses. This portfolio of information systems investments can be described as having a certain profile of risk and benefit to the firm (see Figure 14.3) similar to a financial portfolio.

Each information systems project carries its own set of risks and benefits. (Section 14.4 describes the factors that increase the risks of systems projects.) Firms would try to improve the return on their portfolios of IT assets by balancing the risk and return from their systems investments. Although there is no ideal profile for all firms, information-intensive industries (e.g., finance) should have a few high-risk, high-benefit projects to ensure that they stay current with technology. Firms in non-information-intensive industries should focus on high-benefit, low-risk projects.

Most desirable, of course, are systems with high benefit and low risk. These promise early returns and low risks. Second, high-benefit, high-risk systems should be examined; low-benefit, high-risk systems should be totally avoided; and low-benefit, low-risk systems should be reexamined for the possibility of rebuilding and replacing them with more desirable systems having higher benefits. By using portfolio analysis, management can determine the optimal mix of investment risk and reward for their firms, balancing riskier high-reward projects with safer lower-reward ones. Firms where portfolio analysis is aligned with business strategy have been found to have a superior return on their IT

FIGURE 14.3 A SYSTEM PORTFOLIO

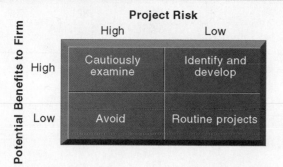

Companies should examine their portfolio of projects in terms of potential benefits and likely risks. Certain kinds of projects should be avoided altogether and others developed rapidly. There is no ideal mix. Companies in different industries have different profiles.

assets, better alignment of IT investments with business objectives, and better organization-wide coordination of IT investments (Jeffrey and Leliveld, 2004).

SCORING MODELS

A **scoring model** is useful for selecting projects where many criteria must be considered. It assigns weights to various features of a system and then calculates the weighted totals. Using Table 14.2, the firm must decide among two alternative enterprise resource planning (ERP) systems. The first column lists the criteria that decision makers will use to evaluate the systems. These criteria are usually the result of lengthy discussions among the decision-making group. Often the most important outcome of a scoring model is not the score but agreement on the criteria used to judge a system.

Table 14.2 shows that this particular company attaches the most importance to capabilities for sales order processing, inventory management, and warehousing. The second column in Table 14.2 lists the weights that decision makers attached to the decision criteria. Columns 3 and 5 show the percentage of requirements for each function that each alternative ERP system can provide. Each vendor's score can be calculated by multiplying the percentage of requirements met for each function by the weight attached to that function. ERP System B has the highest total score.

As with all "objective" techniques, there are many qualitative judgments involved in using the scoring model. This model requires experts who understand the issues and the technology. It is appropriate to cycle through the scoring model several times, changing the criteria and weights, to see how sensitive the outcome is to reasonable changes in criteria. Scoring models are used most commonly to confirm, to rationalize, and to support decisions, rather than as the final arbiters of system selection.

14.3 ESTABLISHING THE BUSINESS VALUE OF INFORMATION SYSTEMS

Even if a system project supports a firm's strategic goals and meets user information requirements, it needs to be a good investment for the firm. The

TABLE 14.2 EXAMPLE OF A SCORING MODEL FOR AN ERP SYSTEM

CRITERIA	WEIGHT	ERP SYSTEM A %	ERP SYSTEM A SCORE	ERP SYSTEM B %	ERP SYSTEM B SCORE
1.0 Order Processing					
1.1 Online order entry	4	67	268	73	292
1.2 Online pricing	4	81	324	87	348
1.3 Inventory check	4	72	288	81	324
1.4 Customer credit check	3	66	198	59	177
1.5 Invoicing	4	73	292	82	328
Total Order Processing			1,370		1,469
2.0 Inventory Management					
2.1 Production forecasting	3	72	216	76	228
2.2 Production planning	4	79	316	81	324
2.3 Inventory control	4	68	272	80	320
2.4 Reports	3	71	213	69	207
Total Inventory Management			1,017		1,079
3.0 Warehousing					
3.1 Receiving	2	71	142	75	150
3.2 Picking/packing	3	77	231	82	246
3.3 Shipping	4	92	368	89	356
Total Warehousing			741		752
Grand Total			3,128		3,300

value of systems from a financial perspective essentially revolves around the issue of return on invested capital. Does a particular information system investment produce sufficient returns to justify its costs?

INFORMATION SYSTEM COSTS AND BENEFITS

Table 14.3 lists some of the more common costs and benefits of systems. **Tangible benefits** can be quantified and assigned a monetary value. **Intangible benefits**, such as more efficient customer service or enhanced decision making, cannot be immediately quantified but may lead to quantifiable gains in the long run. Transaction and clerical systems that displace labor and save space always produce more measurable, tangible benefits than management information systems, decision-support systems, and computer-supported collaborative work systems (see Chapters 2 and 11).

Chapter 5 introduced the concept of total cost of ownership (TCO), which is designed to identify and measure the components of information technology expenditures beyond the initial cost of purchasing and installing hardware and software. However, TCO analysis provides only part of the information needed to evaluate an information technology investment because it does not

TABLE 14.3 COSTS AND BENEFITS OF INFORMATION SYSTEMS

COSTS

Hardware

Telecommunications

Software

Services

Personnel

TANGIBLE BENEFITS (COST SAVINGS)

Increased productivity

Lower operational costs

Reduced workforce

Lower computer expenses

Lower outside vendor costs

Lower clerical and professional costs

Reduced rate of growth in expenses

Reduced facility costs

INTANGIBLE BENEFITS

Improved asset utilization

Improved resource control

Improved organizational planning

Increased organizational flexibility

More timely information

More information

Increased organizational learning

Legal requirements attained

Enhanced employee goodwill

Increased job satisfaction

Improved decision making

Improved operations

Higher client satisfaction

Better corporate image

typically deal with benefits, cost categories such as complexity costs, and "soft" and strategic factors discussed later in this section.

Capital Budgeting for Information Systems

To determine the benefits of a particular project, you'll need to calculate all of its costs and all of its benefits. Obviously, a project where costs exceed benefits should be rejected. But even if the benefits outweigh the costs, additional financial analysis is required to determine whether the project represents a good return on the firm's invested capital. **Capital budgeting** models are one of several techniques used to measure the value of investing in long-term capital investment projects.

Capital budgeting methods rely on measures of cash flows into and out of the firm; capital projects generate those cash flows. The investment cost for information systems projects is an immediate cash outflow caused by expenditures for hardware, software, and labor. In subsequent years, the investment may cause additional cash outflows that will be balanced by cash inflows resulting from the investment. Cash inflows take the form of increased sales of more products (for reasons such as new products, higher quality, or increasing market share) or reduced costs in production and operations. The difference between cash outflows and cash inflows is used for calculating the financial worth of an investment. Once the cash flows have been established, several alternative methods are available for comparing different projects and deciding about the investment.

The principal capital budgeting models for evaluating IT projects are: the payback method, the accounting rate of return on investment (ROI), net present value, and the internal rate of return (IRR). You can find out more about how these capital budgeting models are used to justify information system investments in the Learning Tracks for this chapter.

REAL OPTIONS PRICING MODELS

Some information systems projects are highly uncertain, especially investments in IT infrastructure. Their future revenue streams are unclear and their up-front costs are high. Suppose, for instance, that a firm is considering a $20 million investment to upgrade its IT infrastructure—its hardware, software, data management tools, and networking technology. If this upgraded infrastructure were available, the organization would have the technology capabilities to respond more easily to future problems and opportunities. Although the costs of this investment can be calculated, not all of the benefits of making this investment can be established in advance. But if the firm waits a few years until the revenue potential becomes more obvious, it might be too late to make the infrastructure investment. In such cases, managers might benefit from using real options pricing models to evaluate information technology investments.

Real options pricing models (ROPMs) use the concept of options valuation borrowed from the financial industry. An *option* is essentially the right, but not the obligation, to act at some future date. A typical *call option*, for instance, is a financial option in which a person buys the right (but not the obligation) to purchase an underlying asset (usually a stock) at a fixed price (strike price) on or before a given date.

For instance, let's assume that on April 25, 2012, you could purchase a call option for $17.09 that would give you the right to buy a share of Procter & Gamble (P&G) common stock for $50 per share on a certain date. Options expire over time, and this call option has an expiration date of January 17, 2014. If the price of P&G common stock does not rise above $50 per share by the stock market close on January 17, 2014, you would not exercise the option, and the value of the option would fall to zero on the strike date. If, however, the price of P&G stock rose to, say, $100 per share, you could purchase the stock for the strike price of $50 and retain the profit of $50 per share minus the cost on the option. (Because the option is sold as a 100-share contract, the cost of the contract would be 100 × $17.09 before commissions, or $1,709, and you would be purchasing and obtaining a profit from 100 shares of Procter & Gamble.) The stock option enables the owner to benefit from the upside potential of an opportunity while limiting the downside risk.

ROPMs value information systems projects similar to stock options, where an initial expenditure on technology creates the right, but not the obligation, to obtain the benefits associated with further development and deployment of the technology as long as management has the freedom to cancel, defer, restart, or expand the project. ROPMs give managers the flexibility to stage their IT investment or test the waters with small pilot projects or prototypes to gain more knowledge about the risks of a project before investing in the entire implementation. The disadvantages of this model are primarily in estimating all the key variables affecting option value, including anticipated cash flows from the underlying asset and changes in the cost of implementation. Models for determining option value of information technology platforms are being developed (Fichman, 2004; McGrath and MacMillan, 2000).

LIMITATIONS OF FINANCIAL MODELS

The traditional focus on the financial and technical aspects of an information system tends to overlook the social and organizational dimensions of information systems that may affect the true costs and benefits of the investment. Many companies' information systems investment decisions do not adequately consider costs from organizational disruptions created by a new system, such as the cost to train end users, the impact that users' learning curves for a new system have on productivity, or the time managers need to spend overseeing new system-related changes. Benefits, such as more timely decisions from a new system or enhanced employee learning and expertise, may also be overlooked in a traditional financial analysis (Ryan, Harrison, and Schkade, 2002).

14.4 MANAGING PROJECT RISK

We have already introduced the topic of information system risks and risk assessment in Chapter 8. In this chapter, we describe the specific risks to information systems projects and show what can be done to manage them effectively.

DIMENSIONS OF PROJECT RISK

Systems differ dramatically in their size, scope, level of complexity, and organizational and technical components. Some systems development projects are more likely to create the problems we have described earlier or to suffer delays because they carry a much higher level of risk than others. The level of project risk is influenced by project size, project structure, and the level of technical expertise of the information systems staff and project team.

- *Project size.* The larger the project—as indicated by the dollars spent, the size of the implementation staff, the time allocated for implementation, and the number of organizational units affected—the greater the risk. Very large-scale systems projects have a failure rate that is 50 to 75 percent higher than that for other projects because such projects are complex and difficult to control. The organizational complexity of the system—how many units and groups use it and how much it influences business processes—contribute to the complexity of large-scale systems projects just as much as technical characteristics, such as the number of lines of program code, length of project, and budget. In addition, there are few reliable techniques for estimating the time and cost to develop large-scale information systems.

- *Project structure.* Some projects are more highly structured than others. Their requirements are clear and straightforward so outputs and processes can be easily defined. Users know exactly what they want and what the system should do; there is almost no possibility of the users changing their minds.

Such projects run a much lower risk than those with relatively undefined, fluid, and constantly changing requirements; with outputs that cannot be fixed easily because they are subject to users' changing ideas; or with users who cannot agree on what they want.

- *Experience with technology.* The project risk rises if the project team and the information system staff lack the required technical expertise. If the team is unfamiliar with the hardware, system software, application software, or database management system proposed for the project, it is highly likely that the project will experience technical problems or take more time to complete because of the need to master new skills.

Although the difficulty of the technology is one risk factor in information systems projects, the other factors are primarily organizational, dealing with the complexity of information requirements, the scope of the project, and how many parts of the organization will be affected by a new information system.

CHANGE MANAGEMENT AND THE CONCEPT OF IMPLEMENTATION

The introduction or alteration of an information system has a powerful behavioral and organizational impact. Changes in the way that information is defined, accessed, and used to manage the organization's resources often lead to new distributions of authority and power. This internal organizational change breeds resistance and opposition and can lead to the demise of an otherwise good system.

A very large percentage of information systems projects stumble because the process of organizational change surrounding system building was not properly addressed. Successful system building requires careful **change management**.

The Concept of Implementation

To manage the organizational change surrounding the introduction of a new information system effectively, you must examine the process of implementation. **Implementation** refers to all organizational activities working toward the adoption, management, and routinization of an innovation, such as a new formation system. In the implementation process, the systems analyst is a **change agent**. The analyst not only develops technical solutions but also redefines the configurations, interactions, job activities, and power relationships of various organizational groups. The analyst is the catalyst for the entire change process and is responsible for ensuring that all parties involved accept the changes created by a new system. The change agent communicates with users, mediates between competing interest groups, and ensures that the organizational adjustment to such changes is complete.

The Role of End Users

System implementation generally benefits from high levels of user involvement and management support. User participation in the design and operation of information systems has several positive results. First, if users are heavily involved in systems design, they have more opportunities to mold the system according to their priorities and business requirements, and more opportunities to control the outcome. Second, they are more likely to react positively to the completed system because they have been active participants in the change process. Incorporating user knowledge and expertise leads to better solutions.

The relationship between users and information systems specialists has traditionally been a problem area for information systems implementation efforts. Users and information systems specialists tend to have different backgrounds, interests, and priorities. This is referred to as the **user-designer communications gap**. These differences lead to divergent organizational loyalties, approaches to problem solving, and vocabularies.

Information systems specialists, for example, often have a highly technical, or machine, orientation to problem solving. They look for elegant and sophisticated technical solutions in which hardware and software efficiency is optimized at the expense of ease of use or organizational effectiveness. Users prefer systems that are oriented toward solving business problems or facilitating organizational tasks. Often the orientations of both groups are so at odds that they appear to speak in different tongues.

These differences are illustrated in Table 14.4, which depicts the typical concerns of end users and technical specialists (information systems designers) regarding the development of a new information system. Communication problems between end users and designers are a major reason why user requirements are not properly incorporated into information systems and why users are driven out of the implementation process.

Systems development projects run a very high risk of failure when there is a pronounced gap between users and technical specialists and when these groups continue to pursue different goals. Under such conditions, users are often driven away from the project. Because they cannot comprehend what the technicians are saying, users conclude that the entire project is best left in the hands of the information specialists alone.

Management Support and Commitment

If an information systems project has the backing and commitment of management at various levels, it is more likely to be perceived positively by both users and the technical information services staff. Both groups will believe that their participation in the development process will receive higher-level attention and priority. They will be recognized and rewarded for the time and effort they devote to implementation. Management backing also ensures that a systems project receives sufficient funding and resources to be successful. Furthermore, to be enforced effectively, all the changes in work habits and procedures and any organizational realignments associated with a new system depend on management backing. If a manager considers a new system a priority, the system will more likely be treated that way by his or her subordinates.

TABLE 14.4 THE USER DESIGNER COMMUNICATIONS GAP

USER CONCERNS	DESIGNER CONCERNS
Will the system deliver the information we need for our work?	What demands will this system put on our servers?
Can we access the data on our iPhones, BlackBerrys, tablets, and PCs?	What kind of programming demands will this place on our group?
What new procedures do we need to enter data into the system?	Where will the data be stored? What's the most efficient way to store them?
How will the operation of the system change employees' daily routines?	What technologies should we use to secure the data?

Change Management Challenges for Business Process Reengineering, Enterprise Applications, and Mergers and Acquisitions

Given the challenges of innovation and implementation, it is not surprising to find a very high failure rate among enterprise application and business process reengineering (BPR) projects, which typically require extensive organizational change and which may require replacing old technologies and legacy systems that are deeply rooted in many interrelated business processes. A number of studies have indicated that 70 percent of all business process reengineering projects fail to deliver promised benefits. Likewise, a high percentage of enterprise applications fail to be fully implemented or to meet the goals of their users even after three years of work.

Many enterprise application and reengineering projects have been undermined by poor implementation and change management practices that failed to address employees' concerns about change. Dealing with fear and anxiety throughout the organization, overcoming resistance by key managers, and changing job functions, career paths, and recruitment practices have posed greater threats to reengineering than the difficulties companies faced visualizing and designing breakthrough changes to business processes. All of the enterprise applications require tighter coordination among different functional groups as well as extensive business process change (see Chapter 9).

Projects related to mergers and acquisitions have a similar failure rate. Mergers and acquisitions are deeply affected by the organizational characteristics of the merging companies as well as by their IT infrastructures. Combining the information systems of two different companies usually requires considerable organizational change and complex systems projects to manage. If the integration is not properly managed, firms can emerge with a tangled hodgepodge of inherited legacy systems built by aggregating the systems of one firm after another. Without a successful systems integration, the benefits anticipated from the merger cannot be realized, or, worse, the merged entity cannot execute its business processes effectively.

CONTROLLING RISK FACTORS

Various project management, requirements gathering, and planning methodologies have been developed for specific categories of implementation problems. Strategies have also been devised for ensuring that users play appropriate roles throughout the implementation period and for managing the organizational change process. Not all aspects of the implementation process can be easily controlled or planned. However, anticipating potential implementation problems and applying appropriate corrective strategies can increase the chances for system success.

The first step in managing project risk involves identifying the nature and level of risk confronting the project (Schmidt et al., 2001). Implementers can then handle each project with the tools and risk management approaches geared to its level of risk (Iversen, Mathiassen, and Nielsen, 2004; Barki, Rivard, and Talbot, 2001; McFarlan, 1981).

Managing Technical Complexity

Projects with challenging and complex technology for users to master benefit from **internal integration tools**. The success of such projects depends on how well their technical complexity can be managed. Project leaders need both heavy technical and administrative experience. They must be able to anticipate problems and develop smooth working relationships among a predominantly technical team. The team should be under the leadership of a manager with a strong technical and project management background, and team members should be highly experienced. Team meetings should take place frequently. Essential technical skills or expertise not available internally should be secured from outside the organization.

Formal Planning and Control Tools

Large projects benefit from appropriate use of **formal planning tools** and **formal control tools** for documenting and monitoring project plans. The two most commonly used methods for documenting project plans are Gantt charts and PERT charts. A **Gantt chart** lists project activities and their corresponding start and completion dates. The Gantt chart visually represents the timing and duration of different tasks in a development project as well as their human resource requirements (see Figure 14.4). It shows each task as a horizontal bar whose length is proportional to the time required to complete it.

Although Gantt charts show when project activities begin and end, they don't depict task dependencies, how one task is affected if another is behind schedule, or how tasks should be ordered. That is where **PERT charts** are useful. PERT stands for Program Evaluation and Review Technique, a methodology developed by the U.S. Navy during the 1950s to manage the Polaris submarine missile program. A PERT chart graphically depicts project tasks and their interrelationships. The PERT chart lists the specific activities that make up a project and the activities that must be completed before a specific activity can start, as illustrated in Figure 14.5.

The PERT chart portrays a project as a network diagram consisting of numbered nodes (either circles or rectangles) representing project tasks. Each node is numbered and shows the task, its duration, the starting date, and the completion date. The direction of the arrows on the lines indicates the sequence of tasks and shows which activities must be completed before the commencement of another activity. In Figure 14.5, the tasks in nodes 2, 3, and 4 are not dependent on each other and can be undertaken simultaneously, but each is dependent on completion of the first task. PERT charts for complex projects can be difficult to interpret, and project managers often use both techniques.

These project management techniques can help managers identify bottlenecks and determine the impact that problems will have on project completion times. They can also help systems developers partition projects into smaller, more manageable segments with defined, measurable business results. Standard control techniques can successfully chart the progress of the project against budgets and target dates, so deviations from the plan can be spotted.

Increasing User Involvement and Overcoming User Resistance

Projects with relatively little structure and many undefined requirements must involve users fully at all stages. Users must be mobilized to support one of many possible design options and to remain committed to a single design. **External integration tools** consist of ways to link the work of the implementation team to users at all organizational levels. For instance, users can become active members of the project team, take on leadership roles, and take charge of installation and training. The implementation team can demonstrate its responsiveness to users, promptly answering questions, incorporating user feedback, and showing their willingness to help.

FIGURE 14.4 A GANTT CHART

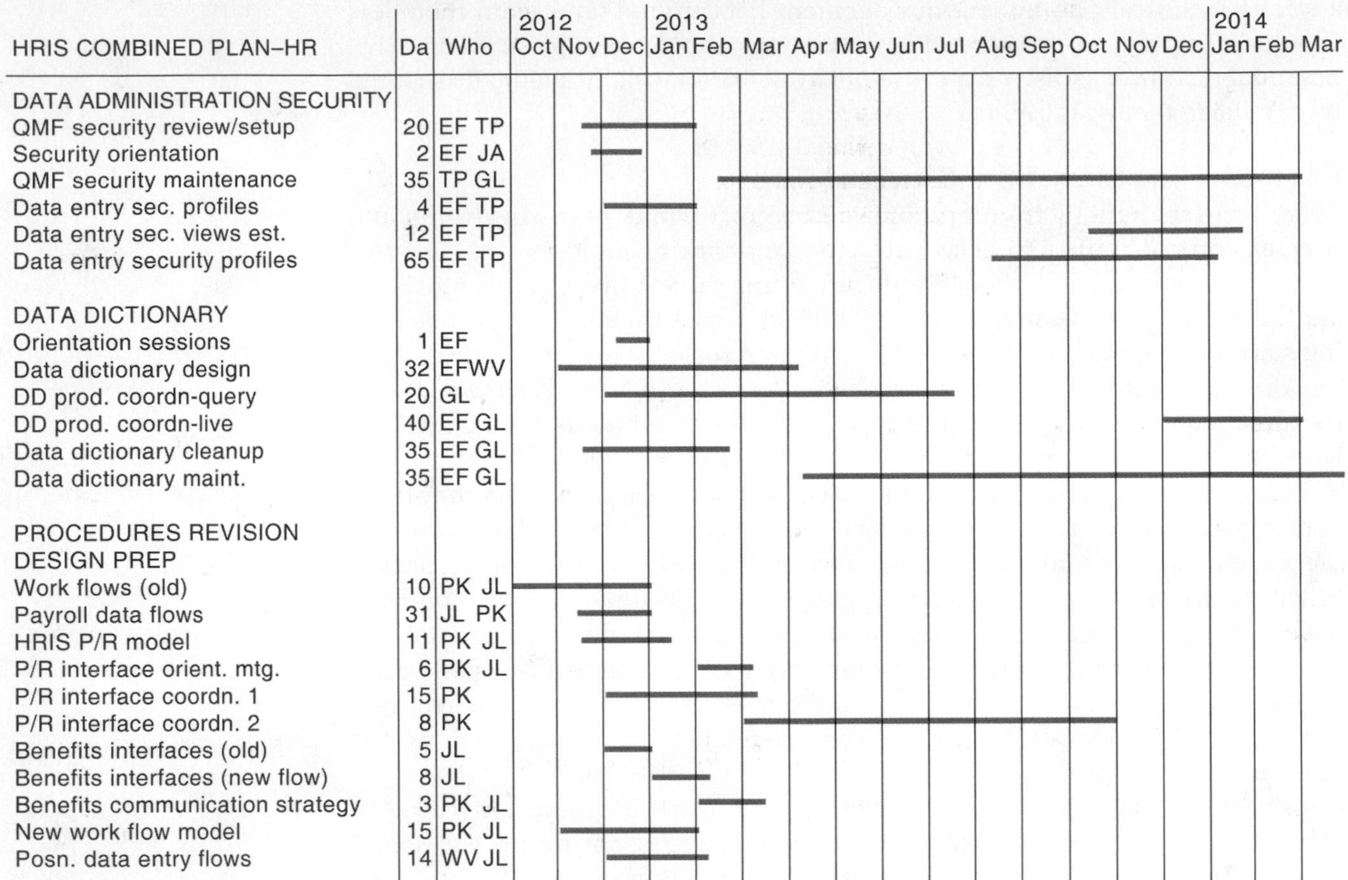

HRIS COMBINED PLAN–HR

Task	Da	Who
DATA ADMINISTRATION SECURITY		
QMF security review/setup	20	EF TP
Security orientation	2	EF JA
QMF security maintenance	35	TP GL
Data entry sec. profiles	4	EF TP
Data entry sec. views est.	12	EF TP
Data entry security profiles	65	EF TP
DATA DICTIONARY		
Orientation sessions	1	EF
Data dictionary design	32	EFWV
DD prod. coordn-query	20	GL
DD prod. coordn-live	40	EF GL
Data dictionary cleanup	35	EF GL
Data dictionary maint.	35	EF GL
PROCEDURES REVISION **DESIGN PREP**		
Work flows (old)	10	PK JL
Payroll data flows	31	JL PK
HRIS P/R model	11	PK JL
P/R interface orient. mtg.	6	PK JL
P/R interface coordn. 1	15	PK
P/R interface coordn. 2	8	PK
Benefits interfaces (old)	5	JL
Benefits interfaces (new flow)	8	JL
Benefits communication strategy	3	PK JL
New work flow model	15	PK JL
Posn. data entry flows	14	WV JL

RESOURCE SUMMARY (person-days per month; year groups: Oct–Dec = 2012, Jan–Dec = 2013, final Jan–Mar = 2014)

Name		Who	Oct	Nov	Dec	Jan	Feb	Mar	Apr	May	Jun	Jul	Aug	Sep	Oct	Nov	Dec	Jan	Feb	Mar
Edith Farrell	5.0	EF	2	21	24	24	23	22	22	27	34	34	29	26	28	19	14			
Woody Vinton	5.0	WV	5	17	20	19	12	10	14	10	2							4	3	
Charles Pierce	5.0	CP		5	11	20	13	9	10	7	6	8	4	4	4	4	4			
Ted Leurs	5.0	TL		12	17	17	19	17	14	12	15	16	2	1	1	1	1			
Toni Cox	5.0	TC	1	11	10	11	11	12	19	19	21	21	21	17	17	12	9			
Patricia Knopp	5.0	PC	7	23	30	34	27	25	15	24	25	16	11	13	17	10	3	3	2	
Jane Lawton	5.0	JL	1	9	16	21	19	21	21	20	17	15	14	12	14	8	5			
David Holloway	5.0	DH	4	4	5	5	5	2	7	5	4	16	2							
Diane O'Neill	5.0	DO	6	14	17	16	13	11	9	4										
Joan Albert	5.0	JA	5	6			7	6	2	1				5	5	1				
Marie Marcus	5.0	MM	15	7	2	1	1													
Don Stevens	5.0	DS	4	4	5	4	5	1												
Casual	5.0	CASL		3	4	3			4	7	9	5	3	2						
Kathy Mendez	5.0	KM		1	5	16	20	19	22	19	20	18	20	11	2					
Anna Borden	5.0	AB						9	10	16	15	11	12	19	10	7	1			
Gail Loring	5.0	GL		3	6	5	9	10	17	18	17	10	13	10	10	7	17			
UNASSIGNED	0.0	X												9	236	225	230	14	13	
Co-op	5.0	CO		6	4				2	3	4	4	2	4	16			216	178	
Casual	5.0	CAUL									3	3	3							
TOTAL DAYS			49	147	176	196	194	174	193	195	190	181	140	125	358	288	284	237	196	12

The Gantt chart in this figure shows the task, person-days, and initials of each responsible person, as well as the start and finish dates for each task. The resource summary provides a good manager with the total person-days for each month and for each person working on the project to manage the project successfully. The project described here is a data administration project.

FIGURE 14.5 A PERT CHART

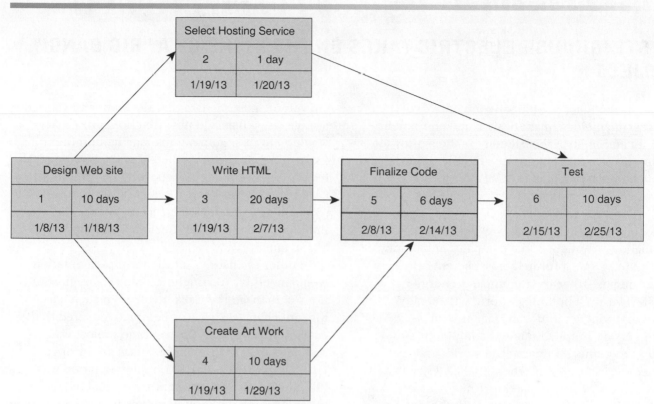

This is a simplified PERT chart for creating a small Web site. It shows the ordering of project tasks and the relationship of a task with preceding and succeeding tasks.

Participation in implementation activities may not be enough to overcome the problem of user resistance to organizational change. Different users may be affected by the system in different ways. Whereas some users may welcome a new system because it brings changes they perceive as beneficial to them, others may resist these changes because they believe the shifts are detrimental to their interests.

If the use of a system is voluntary, users may choose to avoid it; if use is mandatory, resistance will take the form of increased error rates, disruptions, turnover, and even sabotage. Therefore, the implementation strategy must not only encourage user participation and involvement, but it must also address the issue of counterimplementation (Keen, 1981). **Counterimplementation** is a deliberate strategy to thwart the implementation of an information system or an innovation in an organization.

Strategies to overcome user resistance include user participation (to elicit commitment as well as to improve design), user education and training, management edicts and policies, and better incentives for users who cooperate. The new system can be made more user friendly by improving the end-user interface. Users will be more cooperative if organizational problems are solved prior to introducing the new system.

The Interactive Session on Organizations illustrates some of these issues at work. Westinghouse Electric Company launched a sweeping systems modernization program that included re-implementation of its enterprise applications. As you read this case, try to determine how Westinghouse addressed the risks and challenges of this project.

WESTINGHOUSE ELECTRIC TAKES ON THE RISKS OF A "BIG BANG" PROJECT

Westinghouse Electric Company provides fuel, services, technology, plant design, and equipment to utility and industrial customers in the worldwide commercial nuclear electric power industry. A private company created in 1999 after its predecessor was sold and spun off, Westinghouse has 14,500 employees in 17 countries and is headquartered in Cranberry Township, Pennsylvania. Shortly after Westinghouse's creation, the company implemented a full suite of SAP software across the enterprise.

For the past 15 years, the nuclear energy industry was in a holding pattern, with steady business throughout but minimal growth. Westinghouse supplied nuclear equipment and services to plants all around the world, and the business was successful. The initial SAP installation served Westinghouse just fine for nearly an entire decade. From 2010 onward, the nuclear energy industry started to expand. Westinghouse began to experience growth in sales, and its legacy SAP installation was not equipped to handle the increased volume of business.

Westinghouse needed to update its older system to support new processes, configurations, and functionalities that related to the larger amount of business it was conducting. The company estimated that it would increase in size fourfold over the next few years. Westinghouse opted to launch a sweeping new program to update its IT. The program, called Synergy internally, consisted of 40 different projects, and updating the SAP system was one of the largest.

Rather than simply upgrade its existing systems, Westinghouse opted to "re-implement" those systems with much more current SAP technology. Westinghouse did this because its 10-year-old SAP ERP implementation was too outdated. It was easier for the company to simply replace the old SAP ERP systems with a completely new configuration. The division of the Synergy project dedicated to the SAP re-implementation was known as Cornerstone, aptly named because the new system would be the foundation for the company's future growth.

Westinghouse wanted to start with a clean-core SAP environment with a completely new reconfiguration. The company's goals were to convert all existing data that the company wanted to save, as well as add new functionalities that would help the company manage its imminent growth. Westinghouse hoped to add a new general ledger, a new enterprise reporting environment based on SAP NetWeaver Business Warehouse (BW) and SAP BusinessObjects solutions, and new implementations of SAP Customer Relationship Management (CRM).

In order to ensure that the re-implementation went smoothly, Westinghouse took many precautions to manage the risks involved in such a significant change. First, the company ensured that every element of the Cornerstone project was motivated by a particular business driver or goal. For example, the SAP CRM implementation was intended to address the company's goal of aligning three distinct operational regions to present a single face in every customer location, and the SAP ERP Human Capital Management and SAP NetWeaver Portal implementation were intended to support the company's plan to increase global hiring. By associating goals with each element of the project, Westinghouse was able to more precisely control the implementation of the new system.

Once the elements of the new SAP system came into place, Westinghouse had to decide how to actually roll out the new system. It could have used a gradual, phased approach, adding new systems over a three-year period, but the company instead decided on what it called a "big-bang approach." Management decided that the company was growing too fast for a slow approach—it needed the new systems as soon as possible, and hoped to recoup the return on investment sooner rather than later. However, while the phased approach was more expensive, it was also much less risky. To manage the increased risk of the big-bang approach, the company brought in a change management consultant.

The consultant, John Flynn, helped Westinghouse with both the Synergy and Cornerstone projects, but focused on the Cornerstone project. Flynn performed a risk assessment study to identify business areas that were most likely to undergo significant change. He found that the Westinghouse supply chain was one of the areas most likely to endure significant change, since the company's growth would add many new elements to the chain. Therefore, the change management team spent extra time with Westinghouse's supply chain staff members to help them understand the new project and its impact on their day-to-day routines. The project team recruited power users from the supply chain organization and discussed specific project details with business unit leaders. These meetings also helped gain support from supply chain executives who could better understand the link between the information systems project and their business goals, and then articulate this connection to other users.

Next, after mapping the risk associated with each element of the SAP re-implementation, Westinghouse had to finally switch, or cut over, to the new system. To handle that event, Flynn worked with business leaders to recruit coordinators for every site in the organization. Each site coordinator had a list of responsibilities and a checklist to complete prior to the system going live to ensure each site was ready when the switch was flipped. Westinghouse dedicated extra staff to answer employee questions in the problem areas designated by Flynn. The company created

an automatic call distribution system and e-mail system that routed users across all time zones to the employees most able to answer their questions. For example, Westinghouse expected that there would be many questions about passwords, access issues, time entry, and purchase requisition management after the new system went live, so the company provided extra staff to answer those and other frequently asked questions. This "temporary help desk" handled over 2,000 inquiries during the first three weeks of the implementation. The project team also set up a blog where users could share tips and solutions.

The cutover to the new SAP system went smoothly, and the company plans to use many of the techniques that it learned from the implementation in the future. It plans to use the blog as its primary communication method for support solutions and other Synergy projects, and future additions to the SAP suite will be much easier than the sweeping big-bang change.

Sources: David Hannon, "Westinghouse Electric Company Sees Global Standard Processes as the Foundation for Future Business Success," SAP InsiderPROFILES, January–March 2012 and www.westinghousenuclear.com, accessed April 23, 2012.

CASE STUDY QUESTIONS

1. Identify and discuss the risks in Westinghouse Electric's Cornerstone project.

2. Why was change management so important for this project and this company?

3. What management, organization, and technology issues had to be addressed by the Westinghouse project team?

4. Should other companies use a "big-bang" implementation strategy? Why or why not? Explain your answer.

DESIGNING FOR THE ORGANIZATION

Because the purpose of a new system is to improve the organization's performance, information systems projects must explicitly address the ways in which the organization will change when the new system is installed, including installation of intranets, extranets, and Web applications. In addition to procedural changes, transformations in job functions, organizational structure, power relationships, and the work environment should be carefully planned.

Areas where users interface with the system require special attention, with sensitivity to ergonomics issues. **Ergonomics** refers to the interaction of people and machines in the work environment. It considers the design of jobs, health issues, and the end-user interface of information systems. Table 14.5

TABLE 14.5 ORGANIZATIONAL FACTORS IN SYSTEMS PLANNING AND IMPLEMENTATION

Employee participation and involvement
Job design
Standards and performance monitoring
Ergonomics (including equipment, user interfaces, and the work environment)
Employee grievance resolution procedures
Health and safety
Government regulatory compliance

lists the organizational dimensions that must be addressed when planning and implementing information systems.

Although systems analysis and design activities are supposed to include an organizational impact analysis, this area has traditionally been neglected. An **organizational impact analysis** explains how a proposed system will affect organizational structure, attitudes, decision making, and operations. To integrate information systems successfully with the organization, thorough and fully documented organizational impact assessments must be given more attention in the development effort.

Sociotechnical Design

One way of addressing human and organizational issues is to incorporate **sociotechnical design** practices into information systems projects. Designers set forth separate sets of technical and social design solutions. The social design plans explore different workgroup structures, allocation of tasks, and the design of individual jobs. The proposed technical solutions are compared with the proposed social solutions. The solution that best meets both social and technical objectives is selected for the final design. The resulting sociotechnical design is expected to produce an information system that blends technical efficiency with sensitivity to organizational and human needs, leading to higher job satisfaction and productivity.

PROJECT MANAGEMENT SOFTWARE TOOLS

Commercial software tools that automate many aspects of project management facilitate the project management process. Project management software typically features capabilities for defining and ordering tasks, assigning resources to tasks, establishing starting and ending dates to tasks, tracking progress, and facilitating modifications to tasks and resources. Many automate the creation of Gantt and PERT charts.

Some of these tools are large sophisticated programs for managing very large projects, dispersed work groups, and enterprise functions. These high-end tools can manage very large numbers of tasks and activities and complex relationships.

Microsoft Office Project 2010 has become the most widely used project management software today. It is PC-based, with capabilities for producing PERT and Gantt charts and for supporting critical path analysis, resource allocation, project tracking, and status reporting. Project also tracks the way changes in one aspect of a project affect others. Project Professional 2010 provides collaborative project management capabilities when used with Microsoft Office Project Server 2010. Project Server stores project data in a central SQL Server database, enabling authorized users to access and update the data over the Internet. Project Server 2010 is tightly integrated with the Microsoft Windows SharePoint Services collaborative workspace platform. These features help large enterprises manage projects in many different locations. Products such as Easy Projects .NET and Vertabase are also useful for firms that want Web-based project management tools.

Going forward, delivery of project management software as a software service (SaaS) will make this technology accessible to more organizations, especially smaller ones. Open source versions of project management software such as Open Workbench and OpenProj will further reduce the total cost of ownership and attract new users. Thanks to the popularity of social media such as Facebook and Twitter, project management software is also likely to become more flexible, collaborative, and user-friendly.

While project management software helps organizations track individual projects, the resources allocated to them, and their costs, **project portfolio management software** helps organizations manage portfolios of projects and dependencies among them. Project portfolio management software helps managers compare proposals and projects against budgets and resource capacity levels to determine the optimal mix and sequencing of projects that best achieves the organization's strategic goals.

LEARNING TRACK MODULES

The following Learning Tracks provide content relevant to topics covered in this chapter:

1. Capital Budgeting Methods for Information System Investments
2. Information Technology Investments and Productivity
3. Enterprise Analysis (Business Systems Planning) and Critical Success Factors

Review Summary

1. *What are the objectives of project management and why is it so essential in developing information systems?*

   Good project management is essential for ensuring that systems are delivered on time, on budget, and provide genuine business benefits. Project management activities include planning the work, assessing the risk, estimating and acquiring resources required to accomplish the work, organizing the work, directing execution, and analyzing the results. Project management must deal with five major variables: scope, time, cost, quality, and risk.

2. *What methods can be used for selecting and evaluating information systems projects and aligning them with the firm's business goals?*

   Organizations need an information systems plan that describes how information technology supports the attainment of their business goals and documents all their system applications and IT infrastructure components. Large corporations will have a management structure to ensure the most important systems projects receive priority. Key performance indicators, portfolio analysis, and scoring models can be used to identify and evaluate alternative information systems projects.

3. *How can firms assess the business value of information systems projects?*

   To determine whether an information systems project is a good investment, one must calculate its costs and benefits. Tangible benefits are quantifiable, and intangible benefits that cannot be immediately quantified may provide quantifiable benefits in the future. Benefits that exceed costs should be analyzed using capital budgeting methods to make sure a project represents a good return on the firm's invested capital. Real options pricing models, which apply the same techniques for valuing financial options to systems investments, can be useful when considering highly uncertain IT investments.

4. *What are the principal risk factors in information systems projects?*

   The level of risk in a systems development project is determined by (1) project size, (2) project structure, and (3) experience with technology. IS projects are more likely to fail when there is insufficient or improper user participation in the systems development process, lack of management support, and poor management of the implementation process. There is a very high failure rate among projects involving business process reengineering, enterprise applications, and mergers and acquisitions because they require extensive organizational change.

5. *What strategies are useful for managing project risk and system implementation?*

   Implementation refers to the entire process of organizational change surrounding the introduction of a new information system. User support and involvement and management support and control of the implementation process are essential, as are mechanisms for dealing with the level of risk in each new systems project. Project risk factors can be brought under some control by a contingency approach to project management. The risk level of each project determines the appropriate mix of external integration tools, internal integration tools, formal planning tools, and formal control tools to be applied.

Key Terms

Capital budgeting, 569

Change agent, 572

Change management, 572

Counterimplementation, 577

Ergonomics, 579

External integration tools, 575

Formal control tools, 575

Formal planning tools, 575

Gantt chart, 575

Implementation, 572

Information systems plan, 564

Intangible benefits, 568

Internal integration tools, 574

Organizational impact analysis, 580

PERT chart, 575

Portfolio analysis, 566

Project, 560

Project management, 560

Project portfolio management, 581

Real options pricing models (ROPMs), 570

Scope, 562

Scoring model, 567

Sociotechnical design, 580

Tangible benefits, 568

User-designer communications gap, 573

User interface, 560

Review Questions

1. What are the objectives of project management and why is it so essential in developing information systems?

   • Describe information system problems resulting from poor project management.

   • Define project management. List and describe the project management activities and variables addressed by project management.

2. What methods can be used for selecting and evaluating information systems projects and aligning them with the firm's business goals?

   • Name and describe the groups responsible for the management of information systems projects.

   • Describe the purpose of an information systems plan and list the major categories in the plan.

   • Explain how key performance indicators, portfolio analysis, and scoring models can be used to select information systems projects.

3. How can firms assess the business value of information systems projects?

   • List and describe the major costs and benefits of information systems.

   • Distinguish between tangible and intangible benefits.

   • Explain how real options pricing models can help manages evaluate information technology investments.

4. What are the principal risk factors in information systems projects?

   • Identify and describe each of the principal risk factors in information systems projects.

   • Explain why builders of new information systems need to address implementation and change management.

   • Explain why eliciting support of management and end users is so essential for successful implementation of information systems projects.

   • Explain why there is such a high failure rate for implementations involving enterprise applications, business process reengineering, and mergers and acquisitions.

5. What strategies are useful for managing project risk and system implementation?

   • Identify and describe the strategies for controlling project risk.

   • Identify the organizational considerations that should be addressed by project planning and implementation.

   • Explain how project management software tools contribute to successful project management.

Discussion Questions

1. How much does project management impact the success of a new information system?

2. It has been said that most systems fail because systems builders ignore organizational behavior problems. Why might this be so?

3. What is the role of end users in information systems project management?

Hands-On MIS Projects

The projects in this section give you hands-on experience evaluating information systems projects, using spreadsheet software to perform capital budgeting analyses for new information systems investments, and using Web tools to analyze the financing for a new home.

Management Decision Problems

1. The U.S. Census launched an IT project to arm its census takers in the field with high-tech handheld devices that would save taxpayer money by directly beaming population data to headquarters from census takers in the field. Census officials signed a $600 million contract with Harris Corporation in 2006 to build

500,000 devices, but still weren't sure which features they wanted included in the units. Census officials did not specify the testing process to measure the performance of the handheld devices. As the project progressed, 400 change requests to project requirements were added. Two years and hundreds of millions of taxpayer dollars later, the handhelds were far too slow and unreliable to be used for the 2010 U.S. census. What could Census Bureau management and the Harris Corporation have done to prevent this outcome?

2. Caterpillar is the world's leading maker of earth-moving machinery and supplier of agricultural equipment. Caterpillar wants to end its support for its Dealer Business System (DBS), which it licenses to its dealers to help them run their businesses. The software in this system is becoming outdated, and senior management wants to transfer support for the hosted version of the software to Accenture Consultants so it can concentrate on its core business. Caterpillar never required its dealers to use DBS, but the system had become a de facto standard for doing business with the company. The majority of the 50 Cat dealers in North America use some version of DBS, as do about half of the 200 or so Cat dealers in the rest of the world. Before Caterpillar turns the product over to Accenture, what factors and issues should it consider? What questions should it ask? What questions should its dealers ask?

Improving Decision Making: Using Spreadsheet Software for Capital Budgeting for a New CAD System

Software skills: Spreadsheet formulas and functions
Business skills: Capital budgeting

This project provides you with an opportunity to use spreadsheet software to use the capital budgeting models discussed in this chapter to analyze the return on an investment for a new computer-aided design (CAD) system.

Your company would like to invest in a new computer-aided design (CAD) system that requires purchasing hardware, software, and networking technology, as well as expenditures for installation, training, and support. MyMISLab contains tables showing each cost component for the new system as well as annual maintenance costs over a five-year period, along with a Learning Track on capital budgeting models. You believe the new system will reduce the amount of labor required to generate designs and design specifications, thereby increasing your firm's annual cash flow.

- Using the data provided in these tables, create a worksheet that calculates the costs and benefits of the investment over a five-year period and analyzes the investment using the four capital budgeting models presented in this chapter's Learning Track.

- Is this investment worthwhile? Why or why not?

Improving Decision Making: Using Web Tools for Buying and Financing a Home

Software skills: Internet-based software
Business skills: Financial planning

This project will develop your skills using Web-based software for searching for a home and calculating mortgage financing for that home.

You would like to purchase a home in Fort Collins, Colorado. Ideally, it should be a single-family house with at least three bedrooms and one bathroom that costs between $150,000 and $225,000 and finance it with a 30-year fixed rate mortgage. You can afford a down payment that is 20 percent of the value of the house. Before you purchase a house, you would like to find out what homes are available in your price range, find a mortgage, and determine the amount of your monthly payment. Use the Yahoo! Homes site to help you with the following tasks:

- Locate homes in Fort Collins, Colorado, that meet your specifications.

- Find a mortgage for 80 percent of the list price of the home. Compare rates from at least three sites (use search engines to find sites other than Yahoo).

- After selecting a mortgage, calculate your closing costs and the monthly payment.

When you are finished, evaluate the whole process. For example, assess the ease of use of the site and your ability to find information about houses and mortgages, the accuracy of the information you found, and the breadth of choice of homes and mortgages.

Video Cases

Video Cases and Instructional Videos illustrating some of the concepts in this chapter are available. Contact your instructor to access these videos.

Collaboration and Teamwork Project

In MyMISLab, you will find a Collaboration and Teamwork Project dealing with the concepts in this chapter. You will be able to use Google Sites, Google Docs, and other open source collaboration tools to complete the assignment

NYCAPS and CityTime: A Tale of Two New York City IS Projects
CASE STUDY

New York City Mayor Michael Bloomberg made his fortune in information technology, as the owner of Bloomberg L.P., a giant financial news and information services media company. Bloomberg thought he could translate his success in modernizing information technology on Wall Street to modernizing New York City's government, and he launched a series of projects to do just that. Two of those projects proved him dead wrong.

Both the New York City Automated Personnel System (NYCAPS) and the CityTime system for payroll-related employee timekeeping have been fraught with cost overruns, mismanagement, and an overall failure to deliver an information system that has the capabilities sought by New York City government. How could this happen?

Soon after becoming mayor, Bloomberg announced the development of NYCAPS. The NYCAPS project had a budget of $66 million at its outset. The goal of the project was to create a modern, automated system for managing and updating personnel information for New York City's workforce, including employee benefit information. Personnel management was a prime target for a sweeping technological overhaul, since the city was using eight individual citywide systems, 200 systems within individual agencies, and a maze of paperwork for handling employee benefits and job changes. A timely and successful implementation of the NYCAPS project stood to save the city millions of dollars per year in labor and IT costs. To date, the implementation has been anything but timely, and the total expenditures of the project have grown to over $363 million, nearly six times the original budget.

Project monitors from within the administration filed reports that described the chronic mismanagement, cost overruns, and general waste plaguing the project, but the city continued ahead with the project without making any significant changes. One report from as far back as 2003 detailed that "no sense of economy, efficiency, or value is evident in any area of the project." These reports indicated that the primary reason for the project's ballooning costs and myriad delays was lack of strong leadership.

The NYCAPS project was controlled by government officials who did not have the authority or expertise to make important project decisions, and therefore missed many opportunities to lower development costs. Early on, in 2002, NYCAPS's lone functionality was as a Web site where people could apply to take civil service exams. But less than two weeks after the launch of the site, a user found that he could obtain other users' personal information by exploiting a security flaw, and the site was immediately shut down. Officials in charge of the project then vowed to fix the flaw and get the project right.

However, instead of taking charge of more facets of the project, the Bloomberg administration delegated more of the project to Accenture, a prominent consulting firm. Bloomberg has tended to favor outside expertise for improving the workings of government, especially for information technology projects. The city tasked Accenture with both defining the specifications of the system as well as putting it together themselves. Companies and government agencies building a new system rarely do this, since splitting those roles keeps the costs from any one contractor from exploding unchecked.

This is just what happened with Accenture. Accenture consultants charged the city up to $400 an hour, and the company earned $8 million from the city in 2004, then $26 million in 2005, $29 million in 2006, and a whopping $53 million in 2007. Raj Agarwal, the city's appointed project manager, was outspoken in his criticisms of Accenture's billing techniques, claiming that they were billing at rates that reflected many more consultants than were actually on the job, and that the company was using recent college graduates and interns to perform the work, all while billing the city at much higher rates typically used for experienced workers. Agarwal has long since quit his post, and the city has struggled to attract experienced and capable managers from the private sector. The city was eventually able to switch Accenture to fixed-price billing.

Accenture has put the blame on the city for increasing the scope and functionality of the project beyond the original specifications while it was being developed. As time passed and the city grew desperate for a functioning version of the system, the city abandoned development on many of the capabilities that the system was intended to have. Nearly 10 years after the project was launched, the city has a live version of NYCAPS, but thousands of retirees still cannot access the site and thousands more current workers are not included in the system. Even worse, NYCAPS was built to run on the same old legacy systems that used the previous patchwork system, despite the fact that upgrading legacy technology was a major reason for the project's development in the first place.

As bad as the NYCAPS project has become, an earlier, even more ambitious New York City project makes it look tame by comparison. The CityTime payroll system project, first conceived in 1998, has seen its budget grow from approximately $65 million to well over $700 million as of 2012. CityTime was created to automate payroll timekeeping once dependent on pen and paper, and in the process to curb undeserved overtime payments to city workers and improve accountability throughout the government. In an ironic twist, the project has instead been permeated with fraud at every level, and engineers from the main consulting organization, Science Applications International Corporation (SAIC) were charged with fraud.

A June 2011 press release from Manhattan U.S. Attorney Preet Bharara states that "the alleged criminal scheme extended across virtually every level of (CityTime); contractors and subcontractors systematically inflated costs, overbilled for consultants' time, and artificially extended the completion date." Again, the biggest reason for the project's unheard-of budget increases is lack of qualified oversight. The few government employees constantly monitoring the project turned a seemingly blind eye on the ballooning costs incurred by SAIC and the lack of progress in the project. Belief that the software developed for the system could be sold to other governments was perhaps another reason why the city let costs balloon.

Bloomberg's budget director, Mark Page, was reportedly the strongest voice in favor of CityTime. He had hoped to stop the trend of police officers, firefighters, and other aging city workers receiving unnecessary overtime at the end of their careers, presumably to increase their pensions. Page also wanted to limit lawsuits against the city from workers claiming their pay was too low for the hours they had worked. But Page's background was in law, not information systems, making him a poor choice to oversee CityTime. Other government branches, like the city comptroller, left the project mostly to Page. William C. Thompson, the city comptroller from 2002 to 2009, never audited CityTime despite numerous warnings about the project from staffers. Still, an aide for the mayor did suggest that the comptroller's office had raised concerns about the project to

the mayor, but those concerns too were ignored or dismissed by Page.

The lack of adequate government oversight of the CityTime project may have been the biggest reason for the hundreds of millions of dollars in cost overruns incurred since the project's conception in 1998, but the main beneficiary of those overruns has been SAIC. In 2000, work on the project was transferred to SAIC from the first contractor, a subsidiary of MCI. Instead of the usual competitive bidding process for contracts, the city opted simply to pass it off to SAIC, a transfer which is still being reviewed by city investigators. Shortly after SAIC took control of the contract, work on CityTime was switched from fixed-price to hourly billing. This, in turn, inflated costs from $224 million in 2006 to a total of $628 million by 2009. Thanks to the hourly contracts, the city was on the hook for all of the waste incurred by SAIC. The terms of contracts were also constantly changing: another consulting company hired to provide quality assurance for CityTime had its contract amended 11 times, increasing its value to almost $50 million from its original $3.4 million figure.

SAIC delegated most of the work on CityTime to subcontractors, further complicating the chain of command involved in the project. The most prominent of these, Technodyne, received $450 million in funds from the city. When the U.S. Attorney's office released its indictments, Technodyne's owners, Reedy and Padma Allen, fled the country and are believed to be at large in India. Today, over 150,000 city workers use CityTime to keep track of attendance and leave of absence requests, but the cost per user for the project is estimated to be approximately $4,000. The industry standard for projects of this size is between $200 and $1,000 dollars. New York State has developed a much more complicated system to perform similar tasks for only $217 million, which makes CityTime's $720 million price tag look even worse by comparison.

In March 2012, the city received some good news: SAIC agreed to repay $500 million in restitution and penalties back to the city to avoid federal prosecution for various instances of fraud involving the CityTime project. Although the result will lessen the burden of the project on taxpayers, the scandal nevertheless is a black mark for Bloomberg and his goals to modernize city information systems, and there is some doubt about how much of the sum that SAIC will actually be able to pay.

The New York City Council also called a hearing to respond to the budget-crippling cost overruns of both projects. The Bloomberg administration vowed once again to review the way it handles complex, multi-million dollar technology projects. Proposed changes included first looking for commercial software before developing customized software without a real need for it. The city also stated that it would bill contractors as functional benchmarks for projects are achieved instead of hourly, to avoid future partnerships like Accenture and SAIC, and would ensure that multi-million dollar technology projects are overseen by qualified experts, instead of government administrators from other areas with no project management experience.

Sources: "CityTime," *The New York Times*, March 14, 2012; Michael M. Grynbaum, "Contractor Strikes $500 Million Deal in City Payroll Scandal," *The New York Times*, March 14, 2012; David M. Halbfinger, "For Mayor, Waste Mars Another Digital Project," *The New York Times*, September 23, 2011 and "City Hall Admits Mishandling Technology Projects," *The New York Times*, October 31, 2011; Josh Margolin, "277M Overrun a City 'Soar' Point," *The New York Post*, August 11, 2011; Robert Charette, "New York City's $720 Million CityTime Project a Vehicle for Unprecedented Fraud Says US Prosecutor," IEEE Spectrum, June 21, 2011; David W. Chen, Serge F. Kovaleski and John Eligon, "Behind Troubled City Payroll Project, Lax Oversight and One Powerful Insider," *The New York Times*, March 27, 2011.

CASE STUDY QUESTIONS

1. How important were the NYCAPS and CityTime projects for New York City? What were their objectives? What would have been their business benefits?

2. Evaluate the key risk factors in both projects.

3. Classify and describe the problems each project encountered as the NYCAPS and CityTime systems were being implemented. What management, organization, and technology factors were responsible for these problems?

4. What were the similarities and differences in the management of both projects?

5. What was the business impact of these botched implementations? Explain your answer.

6. Describe the steps that should have been taken to prevent negative outcomes in these projects.

Chapter 15

Managing Global Systems

Interactive Sessions:

Hasbro Develops a Global Systems Strategy

CombineNet ASAP Helps Primark Manage Its Global Supply Chain

Chapter 15 is located online at www.pearsonglobaleditions.com/laudon

References

CHAPTER 1

Brynjolfsson, Erik and Lorin M. Hitt. "Beyond Computation: Information Technology, Organizational Transformation, and Business Performance." Journal of Economic Perspectives 14, no. 4 (2000).

Brynjolfsson, Erik. "VII Pillars of IT Productivity." Optimize (May 2005).

Bureau of Economic Analysis. National Income and Product Accounts (2012).

Carr, Nicholas. "IT Doesn't Matter." Harvard Business Review (May 2003).

Davern, Michael J. and Robert J. Kauffman. "Discovering Potential and Realizing Value form Information Technology Investments. " Journal of Management Information Systems 16, no. 4 (Spring 2000).

Dedrick, Jason, Vijay Gurbaxani, and Kenneth L. Kraemer. "Information Technology and Economic Performance: A Critical Review of the Empirical Evidence." Center for Research on Information Technology and Organizations, University of California, Irvine (December 2001).

EMarketer. "Mobile Internet Users Worldwide, by Region and Country, 2010-2016." (April 17, 2012).

Friedman, Thomas. The World is Flat. New York: Picador (2007).

Garretson, Rob. "IT Still Matters." CIO Insight 81 (May 2007).

Hughes, Alan and Michael S. Scott Morton. "The Transforming Power of Complementary Assets." MIT Sloan Management Review 47. No. 4 (Summer 2006).

International Telecommunications Union: "ICT Data and Statistics/Key Global Telecom Indicators for the World Telecommunication Service Sector." (December 2011).

Lamb, Roberta, Steve Sawyer, and Rob Kling. "A Social Informatics Perspective of Socio-Technical Networks." http://lamb.cba.hawaii.edu/pubs (2004).

Laudon, Kenneth C. Computers and Bureaucratic Reform. New York: Wiley (1974).

Lev, Baruch. "Intangibles: Management, Measurement, and Reporting." The Brookings Institution Press (2001).

Lohr, Steve. "Tech's New Wave, Driven by Data." New York Times (September 8, 2012).

Marchand, Donald A. "Extracting the Business Value of IT: IT Is Usage, Not Just Deployment that Counts!"The Copco Institute Journal of Financial Transformation (2004).

Mills, Mark P. and Julio M. Ottino. "The Coming Tech-Led Boom." Wall Street Journal (January 30, 2012).

Nevo, Saggi and Michael R. Wade. "The Formation and Value of IT-Enabled Resources: Antecedents and Consequences of Synergistic Relationships."MIS Quarterly 34, No. 1 (March 2010).

Otim, Samual , Dow, Kevin E. , Grover, Varun and Wong, Jeffrey A. "The Impact of Information Technology Investments on Downside Risk of the Firm: Alternative Measurement of the Business Value of IT." Journal of Management Information Systems 29, No. 1 (Summer 2012).

Pew Internet and American Life Project. "Daily Internet Activities." (January 6, 2012.)

Ross, Jeanne W., and Peter Weill. "Six IT Decisions Your IT People Shouldn't Make." Harvard Business Review (November 2002).

Teece David. Economic Performance and Theory of the Firm: The Selected Papers of David Teece. London: Edward Elgar Publishing (1998).

U.S. Bureau of Labor Statistics. Occupational Outlook Handbook, 2012-2013 Edition. Washington D.C.: Bureau of Labor Statistics (2012).

U.S. Department of Commerce, Bureau of the Census. Statistical Abstract of the United States, 20012. Washington D.C. (2012).

Weill, Peter and Jeanne Ross. IT Savvy: What Top Executives Must Know to Go from Pain to Gain. Boston: Harvard Business School Press (2009).

Whois. "Domain Counts & Internet Statistics" (September 18, 2012). www.whois.sc/internet-statistics/, accessed October 1, 2012.

CHAPTER 2

Aral, Sinan; Erik Brynjolfsson; and Marshall Van Alstyne, "Productivity Effects of Information Diffusion in Networks," MIT Center for Digital Business (July 2007).

Banker, Rajiv D., Nan Hu, Paul A. Pavlou, and Jerry Luftman. "CIO Reporting Structure, Strategic Positioning, and Firm Performance ." MIS Quarterly 35. No. 2 (June 2011).

Bernoff, Josh and Charlene Li."Harnessing the Power of Social Applications." MIT Sloan Management Review (Spring 2008).

Broadbent, Marianne and Ellen Kitzis. The New CIO Leader. Boston, MA: Harvard Business Press (2004).

Bughin, Jacques, Angela Hung Byers, and Michael Chui. " How Social Technologies Are Extending the Organization." McKinsey Quarterly (November 2011).

Bureau of Labor Statistics. "Occupational Outlook Handbook 2012-2013 Edition." Bureau of Labor Statistics (July 2012).

Cash, James I. Jr., Michael J. Earl, and Robert Morison. "Teaming Up to Crack Innovation and Enterprise Integration." Harvard Business Review (November 2008).

Forrester Consulting, "Total Economic Impact of IBM Social Collaboration Tools" (September 2010).

Forrester Research. "Social Business: Delivering Critical Business Value" (April 2012).

Frost & White. "Meetings Around the World II: Charting the Course of Advanced Collaboration." (October 14, 2009).

Guillemette, Manon G. and Guy Pare. "Toward a New Theory of the Contribution of the IT Function in Organizations." MIS Quarterly 36, No. 2 (June 2012).

IBM Corporation. "Magnum Integrates Email and Document Management" (January 13, 2010).

IBM Corporation. "Roland Corporation Boosts Productivity and Creativity Worldwide." (2011).

IBM. "Jamming on Social Business." (2011).

Johnson, Bradfor, James Manyika, and Lareina Yee. "The Next Revolution in Interactions," McKinsey Quarterly No. 4 (2005).

Kiron, David, Doug Palmer, Anh Nguyen Phillips and Nina Kruschwitz . "What Managers Really Think About Social Business." MIT Sloan Management Review 53, No. 4 (Summer 2012).

Kolfschoten, Gwendolyn L. , Niederman, Fred , Briggs, Robert O. and Vreede, Gert-Jan De. "Facilitation Roles and Responsibilities for Sustained Collaboration Support in Organizations." Journal of Management Information Systems 28, No. 4 (Spring 2012).

Li, Charlene. "Making the Business Case for Enterprise Social Networks." Altimeter Group (February 22, 2012).

Malone, Thomas M., Kevin Crowston, Jintae Lee, and Brian Pentland. "Tools for Inventing Organizations: Toward a Handbook of Organizational Processes." Management Science 45, no. 3 (March 1999).

McAfee, Andrew P. "Shattering the Myths About Enterprise 2.0." Harvard Business Review (November 2009).

McKinsey Global Institute. "The Social Economy: Unlocking Value and Productivity Through Social Technologies." McKinsey & Company (July 2012).

Microsoft Corporation. "Construction Firm Speeds Project Completion with Centralized Content Management." (July 7, 2011).

Mossberg, Walter S. "Many Devices, Many Files and Four Ways to Share Them." Wall Street Journal (August 1, 2012).

Nolan, Richard, and F. Warren McFarland. "Information Technology and the Board of Directors." Harvard Business Review (October 1, 2005).

Oracle Corporation. "Alcoa Implements Oracle Solution 20% below Projected Cost, Eliminates 43 Legacy Systems." www.oracle.com, accessed August 21, 2005.

Poltrock, Steven and Mark Handel. "Models of Collaboration as the Foundation for Collaboration Technologies. Journal of Management Information Systems 27, No. 1 (Summer 2010).

Raice, Shayndi. "Social Networking Heads to the Office." Wall Street Journal (April 2, 2012).

Sarker, Saonee, Manju Ahuja , Suprateek Sarker and Sarah Kirkeby. "The Role of Communication and Trust in Global Virtual Teams: A Social Network Perspective." Journal of Management Information Systems 28, No. 1 (Summer 2011).

Saunders, Carol, A. F. Rutkowski, Michiel van Genuchten, Doug Vogel, and Julio Molina Orrego. "Virtual Space and Place: Theory and Test." MIS Quarterly 35, No. 4 (December 2011).

Siebdrat, Frank, Martin Hoegl, and Holger Ernst. "How to Manage Virtual Teams." MIT Sloan Management Review 50, No. 4 (Summer 2009).

Weill, Peter and Jeanne W. Ross. IT Governance. Boston: Harvard Business School Press (2004).

CHAPTER 3

Anderson, Howard. "Why Did Kodak, Motorola, and Nortel Fail?" Information Week (January 12, 2012).

Attewell, Paul, and James Rule. "Computing and Organizations: What We Know and What We Don't Know." Communications of the ACM 27, no. 12 (December 1984).

Bresnahan, Timohy F., Erik Brynjolfsson, and Lorin M. Hitt, "Information Technology, Workplace Organization, and the Demand for Skilled Labor." Quarterly Journal of Economics 117 (February 2002).

Cash, J. I., and Benn R. Konsynski. "IS Redraws Competitive Boundaries." Harvard Business Review (March–April 1985).

Ceccagnoli, Marco, Chris Forman, Peng Huang, and D. J. Wu. "Cocreation of Value in a Platform Ecosystem: The Case of Enterprise Software. MIS Quarterly 36, No. 1 (March 2012).

Champy, James. Outsmart: How to Do What Your Competitors Can't. Upper Saddle River, NJ: FT Press (2008).

Chen, Daniel Q., Martin Mocker, David S. Preston, and Alexander Teubner. "Information Systems Strategy: Reconceptualization, Measurement, and Implications." MIS Quarterly 34, no. 2 (June 2010).

Christensen, Clayton M. The Innovator's Dilemma : The Revolutionary Book That Will Change the Way You Do Business, New York: HarperCollins (2003)

Christensen, Clayton. "The Past and Future of Competitive Advantage." Sloan Management Review 42, no. 2 (Winter 2001).

Clemons, Eric K. "Evaluation of Strategic Investments in Information Technology." Communications of the ACM (January 1991).

Clemons, Eric. "The Power of Patterns and Pattern Recognition When Developing Information-Based Strategy. Journal of Management Information Systems 27, No. 1 (Summer 2010).

Coase, Ronald H. "The Nature of the Firm."(1937) in Putterman, Louis and Randall Kroszner. The Economic Nature of the Firm: A Reader, Cambridge University Press, 1995.

Drucker, Peter. "The Coming of the New Organization." Harvard Business Review (January–February 1988).

Freeman, John, Glenn R. Carroll, and Michael T. Hannan. "The Liability of Newness: Age Dependence in Organizational Death Rates." American Sociological Review 48 (1983).

Gallaugher, John M. and Yu-Ming Wang. "Understanding Network Effects in Software Markets: Evidence from Web Server Pricing." MIS Quarterly 26, no. 4 (December 2002).

Gurbaxani, V., and S. Whang, "The Impact of Information Systems on Organizations and Markets." Communications of the ACM 34, no. 1 (Jan. 1991).

Hitt, Lorin M. "Information Technology and Firm Boundaries: Evidence from Panel Data." Information Systems Research 10, no. 2 (June 1999).

Hitt, Lorin M., and Erik Brynjolfsson. "Information Technology and Internal Firm Organization: An Exploratory Analysis." Journal of Management Information Systems 14, no. 2 (Fall 1997).

Huber, George. "Organizational Learning: The Contributing Processes and Literature." Organization Science, 2 (1991), pp. 88–115.

———. "The Nature and Design of Post-Industrial Organizations." Management Science 30, no. 8 (August 1984).

Iansiti, Marco, and Roy Levien. "Strategy as Ecology." Harvard Business Review (March 2004).

Iyer, Bala and Thomas H. Davenport. "Reverse Engineering Google's Innovation Machine." Harvard Business Review (April 2008).

Jensen, M. C., and W. H. Meckling. "Specific and General Knowledge and Organizational Science." In Contract Economics, edited by L. Wetin and J. Wijkander. Oxford: Basil Blackwell (1992).

Jensen, Michael C., and William H. Meckling. "Theory of the Firm: Managerial Behavior, Agency Costs, and Ownership Structure." Journal of Financial Economics 3 (1976).

Kauffman, Robert J. and Yu-Ming Wang. "The Network Externalities Hypothesis and Competitive Network Growth." Journal of Organizational Computing and Electronic Commerce 12, no. 1 (2002).

Kettinger, William J., Varun Grover, Subashish Guhan, and Albert H. Segors. "Strategic Information Systems Revisited: A Study in Sustainability and Performance." MIS Quarterly 18, no. 1 (March 1994).

King, J. L., V. Gurbaxani, K. L. Kraemer, F. W. McFarlan, K. S. Raman, and C. S. Yap. "Institutional Factors in Information Technology Innovation." Information Systems Research 5, no. 2 (June 1994).

Kling, Rob. "Social Analyses of Computing: Theoretical Perspectives in Recent Empirical Research." Computing Survey 12, no. 1 (March 1980).

Kolb, D. A., and A. L. Frohman. "An Organization Development Approach to Consulting." Sloan Management Review 12, no. 1 (Fall 1970).

Kraemer, Kenneth, John King, Debora Dunkle, and Joe Lane. Managing Information Systems. Los Angeles: Jossey-Bass (1989).

Lamb, Roberta and Rob Kling. "Reconceptualizing Users as Social Actors in Information Systems Research." MIS Quarterly 27, no. 2 (June 2003).

Laudon, Kenneth C. "A General Model of the Relationship Between Information Technology and Organizations." Center for Research on Information Systems, New York University. Working paper, National Science Foundation (1989).

———. "Environmental and Institutional Models of Systems Development." Communications of the ACM 28, no. 7 (July 1985).

———. Dossier Society: Value Choices in the Design of National Information Systems. New York: Columbia University Press (1986).

Laudon, Kenneth C. and Kenneth L. Marr, "Information Technology and Occupational Structure." (April 1995).

Lawrence, Paul, and Jay Lorsch. Organization and Environment. Cambridge, MA: Harvard University Press (1969).

Leavitt, Harold J. "Applying Organizational Change in Industry: Structural, Technological, and Humanistic Approaches." In Handbook of Organizations, edited by James G. March. Chicago: Rand McNally (1965).

Leavitt, Harold J., and Thomas L. Whisler. "Management in the 1980s." Harvard Business Review (November–December 1958).

Ling Xue, Gautam Ray, and Vallabh Sambamurthy. "Efficiency or Innovation: How Do Industry Environments Moderate the Effects of Firms' IT Asset Portfolios ." MIS Quarterly 36, No. 2 (June 2012).

Luftman, Jerry. Competing in the Information Age: Align in the Sand, Oxford University Press , USA; 2 edition (August 6, 2003).

Malone, Thomas W., JoAnne Yates, and Robert I. Benjamin. "Electronic Markets and Electronic Hierarchies." Communications of the ACM (June 1987).

March, James G., and Herbert A. Simon. Organizations. New York: Wiley (1958).

Markus, M. L. "Power, Politics, and MIS Implementation." Communications of the ACM 26, no. 6 (June 1983).

McAfee, Andrew and Erik Brynjolfsson. "Investing in the IT That Makes a Competitive Difference." Harvard Business Review (July/August 2008).

McFarlan, F. Warren. "Information Technology Changes the Way You Compete." Harvard Business Review (May–June 1984).

McLaren, Tim S., Milena M. Head, Yufei Yuan, and Yolande E. Chan. "A Multilevel Model for Measuring Fit Between a Firm's Competitive Strategies and Information Systems Capabilities." MIS Quarterly 35, No. 4 (December 2011).

Mendelson, Haim, and Ravindra R. Pillai. "Clock Speed and Informational Response: Evidence from the Information Technology Industry." Information Systems Research 9, no. 4 (December 1998).

Mintzberg, Henry. "Managerial Work: Analysis from Observation." Management Science 18 (October 1971).

_____. The Structuring of Organizations. Englewood Cliffs, NJ: Prentice Hall (1979).

Orlikowski, Wanda J., and Daniel Robey. "Information Technology and the Structuring of Organizations." Information Systems Research 2, no. 2 (June 1991).

Piccoli, Gabriele, and Blake Ives. "Review: IT-Dependent Strategic Initiatives and Sustained Competitive Advantage: A Review and Synthesis of the Literature." MIS Quarterly 29, no. 4 (December 2005).

Pindyck, Robert S., and Daniel L. Rubinfeld. Microeconomics, 8e. Upper Saddle River, NJ: Prentice Hall (2013).

Porter, Michael E. "The Five Competitive Forces that Shape Strategy." Harvard Business Review (January 2008).

Porter, Michael E. and Scott Stern. "Location Matters." Sloan Management Review 42, no. 4 (Summer 2001).

Porter, Michael. Competitive Advantage. New York: Free Press (1985).

_____. Competitive Strategy. New York: Free Press (1980).

_____ "Strategy and the Internet." Harvard Business Review (March 2001).

Robey, Daniel and Marie-Claude Boudreau. "Accounting for the Contradictory Organizational Consequences of Information Technology: Theoretical Directions and Methodological Implications." Information Systems Research 10, no. 42 (June1999).

Shapiro, Carl, and Hal R. Varian. Information Rules. Boston, MA: Harvard Business School Press (1999).

Shpilberg, David, Steve Berez, Rudy Puryear, and Sachin Shah. "Avoiding the Alignment Trap in Information Technology." MIT Sloan Management Review 49, no. 1 (Fall 2007).

Starbuck, William H. "Organizations as Action Generators." American Sociological Review 48 (1983).

Swanson, E. Burton. "The Manager's Guide to IT Innovation Waves." MIT Sloan Management Review 53, No. 2 (Winter 2012).

Tallon, Paul P. "Value Chain Linkages and the Spillover Effects of Strategic Information Technology Alignment: A Process-Level View." Journal of Management Information Systems 28, No. 3 (Winter 2012).

Tushman, Michael L., and Philip Anderson. "Technological Discontinuities and Organizational Environments." Administrative Science Quarterly 31 (September 1986).

Von Hippel, Eric, Susumu Ogawa, and Jeroen P.J. DeJong. "The Age of the Customer-Innovator." MIT Sloan Management Review 53, No. 1 (Fall 2011).

Weber, Max. The Theory of Social and Economic Organization. Translated by Talcott Parsons. New York: Free Press (1947).

Williamson, Oliver E. The Economic Institutions of Capitalism. New York: Free Press, (1985).

CHAPTER 4

Angst, Corey M. and Ritu Agarwal. "Adoption of Electronic Health Records in the Presence of Privacy Concerns: The Elaboration Likelihood Model and Individual Persuasion." MIS Quarterly 33, No. 2 (June 2009).

Angwin, Julia. "Online Tracking Ramps Up." Wall Street Journal (June 17, 2012).

Austen, Ian. "With Apologies, Officials Say Blackberry Service is Restored." New York Times (October 13, 2011).

Belanger, France and Robert E. Crossler. "Privacy in the Digital Age: A Review of Information Privacy Research in Information Systems." MIS Quarterly 35, No. 4 (December 2011).

Bilski v. Kappos, 561 US, (2010).

Bowen, Jonathan. "The Ethics of Safety-Critical Systems."Communications of the ACM 43, no. 3 (April 2000).

Brown Bag Software vs. Symantec Corp. 960 F2D 1465 (Ninth Circuit, 1992).

Brynjolfsson, Erik and Andrew McAfee. Race Against the Machine. Digital Frontier Press (2011).

Business Software Alliance, "Shadow Market: 2011 BSA Global Software Piracy Study," Ninth edition (May 2012).

Chellappa, Ramnath K. and Shivendu Shivendu. "An Economic Model of Privacy: A Property Rights Approach to Regulatory Choices for Online Personalization." Journal of Management Information Systems 24, no. 3 (Winter 2008).

Computer Security Institute. "CSI Computer Crime and Security Survey 2012." (2012).

Culnan, Mary J. and Cynthia Clark Williams. "How Ethics Can Enhance Organizational Privacy." MIS Quarterly 33, No. 4 (December 2009).

European Parliament. "Directive 2009/136/EC of the European Parliament and of the Council of November 25, 2009." European Parliament (2009).

Fowler, Geoffrey A. "Tech Giants Agree to Deal on Privacy Policies for Apps." Wall Street Journal (February 23, 2012).

Federal Trade Commission. "Protecting Consumer Privacy In an Era of Rapid Change." Washington D.C. (2012).

Hsieh, J.J. Po-An, Arun Rai, and Mark Keil. "Understanding Digital Inequality: Comparing Continued Use Behavioral Models of the Socio-Economically Advantaged and Disadvantaged." MIS Quarterly 32, no. 1 (March 2008).

Laudon, Kenneth C. and Carol Guercio Traver. E-Commerce: Business, Technology, Society 9th Edition. Upper Saddle River, NJ: Prentice-Hall (2013).

Laudon, Kenneth C. Dossier Society: Value Choices in the Design of National Information Systems. New York: Columbia University Press (1986b).

Lee, Dong-Joo, Jae-Hyeon Ahn, and Youngsok Bang. "Managing Consumer Privacy Concerns in Personalization: A Strategic Analysis of Privacy Protection." MIS Quarterly 35, No. 2 (June 2011).

National White Collar Crime Center and the Federal Bureau of Investigation. "Internet Crime Complaint Center 2011 Internet Crime Report. (2012).

Nord, G. Daryl, Tipton F. McCubbins, and Jeretta Horn Nord. "E-Monitoring in the Workplace: Privacy, Legislation, and Surveillance Software. Communications of the ACM 49, No. 8 (August 2006).

Payton, Fay Cobb."Rethinking the Digital Divide." Communications of the ACM 46, no. 6 (June 2003)

Rifkin, Jeremy. "Watch Out for Trickle-Down Technology." The New York Times (March 16, 1993).

Robinson, Francis. "EU Unveils Web-Privacy Rules." Wall Street Journal (January 26, 2012).

Singer, Natasha. "When the Privacy Button Is Already Pressed." New York Times (September 15, 2012).

Smith, H. Jeff, and John Hasnas. "Ethics and Information Systems: The Corporate Domain." MIS Quarterly 23, no. 1 (March 1999).

Smith, H. Jeff. "The Shareholders vs. Stakeholders Debate." MIS Sloan Management Review 44, no. 4 (Summer 2003).

Symantec. "Symantec Intelligence Report: August 2012 Report" (August 2012).

United States Department of Health, Education, and Welfare. Records, Computers, and the Rights of Citizens. Cambridge: MIT Press (1973).

U.S. Senate. "Do-Not-Track Online Act of 2011." Senate 913 (May 9, 2011).

U.S. Sentencing Commission. "Sentencing Commission Toughens Requirements for Corporate Compliance Programs. " (April 13, 2004).

Xu, Heng, Hock-Hai Teo, Bernard C.Y. Tan, and Ritu Agarwal. "The Role of Push-Pull Technology in Privacy Calculus: The Case of Location-Based Services." Journal of Management Information Systems 26, No. 3 (Winter 2010).

CHAPTER 5

Andersson, Henrik, James Kaplan, and Brent Smolinski. "Capturing Value from IT Infrastructure Innovation." McKinsey Quarterly (October 2012).

Babcock, Charles. "Cloud's Thorniest Question: Does It Pay Off?" Information Week (June 4, 2012).

Benlian , Alexander, Marios Koufaris and Thomas Hess. "Service Quality in Software-as-a-Service: Developing the SaaS-Qual Measure and Examining Its Role in Usage Continuance." Journal of Management Information Systems, 28, No. 3 (Winter 2012).

Carr, Nicholas. The Big Switch. New York: Norton (2008).

Choi, Jae, Derek L. Nazareth, and Hemant K. Jain. "Implementing Service-Oriented Architecture in Organizations." Journal of Management Information Systems 26, No. 4 (Spring 2010).

Clark, Don. "HTML5: A Look Behind the Technology Changing the Web." Wall Street Journal (November 11, 2011).

David, Julie Smith, David Schuff, and Robert St. Louis. "Managing Your IT Total Cost of Ownership." Communications of the ACM 45, no. 1 (January 2002).

Fitzgerald, Brian. "The Transformation of Open Source Software." MIS Quarterly 30, No. 3 (September 2006).

Fox, Armando, and David Patterson. "Self-Repairing Computers." Scientific American (May 2003.).

Ganek, A. G., and T. A. Corbi. "The Dawning of the Autonomic Computing Era." IBM Systems Journal 42, no 1, (2003).

Gantz, John and David Reinsal. "Extracting Value from Chaos." IDC (June 2011).

Gartner Inc, "Worldwide IT Outsourcing Services Spending to Hit US $251bn in 2012 ." siliconrepublic.com (August 8, 2012).

Gartner, Inc." Gartner Says Worldwide IT Spending On Pace to Surpass $3.6 Trillion in 2012 ." (July 9, 2012).

Hagel III, John and John Seeley Brown. "Your Next IT Strategy." Harvard Business Review (October, 2001).

Hamblen, Matt. "Consumerization Trends Driving IT Shops Crazy." CIO (May 2, 2012).

Internet World Stats. "World Internet Users and Population Stats." www.inernetworldstats.com, accessed October 14, 2012.

Kauffman, Robert J. and Julianna Tsai. "The Unified Procurement Strategy for Enterprise Software: A Test of the 'Move to the Middle' Hypothesis." Journal of Management Information Systems 26, No. 2 (Fall 2009).

King, John. "Centralized vs. Decentralized Computing: Organizational Considerations and Management Options." Computing Surveys (October 1984).

Kurzweil, Ray. "Exponential Growth an Illusion?: Response to Ilkka Tuomi." KurzweilAI.net, September 23, 2003

Lohr, Steve. "I.B.M. Mainframe Evolves to Serve the Digital World. New York Times (August 28, 2012).

Lyman, Peter and Hal R. Varian. "How Much Information 2003?" University of California at Berkeley School of Information Management and Systems (2003).

Mann, Andi, Kurt Milne and Jeanne Morain. "Calculting the Cost Advantages of a Private Cloud. " Cloud Computing Review 1, No. 1 (June 2011).

Marko, Kurt. "2012 State of the Data Center." Information Week (June 2012).

Markoff, John. "A High-Stakes Search Continues for Silicon's Successor." New York Times (December 5, 2011).

Markoff, John. "New Storage Device Is Very Small, at 12 Atoms." New York Times (January 12, 2012).

McAfee, Andrew. "What Every CEO Needs to Know about the Cloud." Harvard Business Review (November 2011).

McAfee, Andrew. "Will Web Services Really Transform Collaboration?" MIT Sloan Management Review 46, no. 2 (Winter 2005).

McDougall, Paul. "IBM Cements $1 Billion Outsourcing Deal with Cemex." Information Week (July 30, 2012).

Mell, Peter and Tim Grance. "The NIST Definition of Cloud Computing" Version 15. NIST (October 17, 2009).

Moore, Gordon. "Cramming More Components Onto Integrated Circuits," Electronics 38, Number 8 (April 19, 1965).

Mueller, Benjamin, Goetz Viering, Christine Legner, and Gerold Riempp. "Understanding the Economic Potential of Service-Oriented Architecture." Journal of Management Information Systems 26, No. 4 (Spring 2010).

Schuff, David and Robert St. Louis. "Centralization vs. Decentralization of Application Software." Communications of the ACM 44, no. 6 (June 2001).

SeekingAlpha.com (April 24, 2012).

Stango, Victor. "The Economics of Standards Wars." Review of Network Economics 3, Issue 1 (March 2004).

Strom, David. "Shopping Around for Cloud Computing Services." Cloud Computing Review 1, No. 1 (June 2011).

Susarla, Anjana, Anitesh Barua, and Andrew B. Whinston. "A Transaction Cost Perspective of the 'Software as a Service' Business Model. " Journal of Management Information Systems 26, No. 2 (Fall 2009).

Taft, Darryl K. "Application Development: Java Death Debunked: 10 Reasons Why It's Still Hot." eWeek (February 22, 2012).

Tibken, Shara. "Here Come Tablets. Here Come Problems." Wall Street Journal (April 2, 2012).

Tibken, Shara. "Smartphones Challenge Chip Limits." The Wall Street Journal (August 27, 2012).

Weill, Peter, and Marianne Broadbent. Leveraging the New Infrastructure. Cambridge, MA: Harvard Business School Press (1998).

Weitzel, Tim. Economics of Standards in Information Networks. Springer (2004).

"Wintel PCs Down to 50% Share of All Personal Computing," Electronista (January 16, 2012).

CHAPTER 6

Barth, Paul S. "Managing Big Data: What Every CIO Needs to Know." CIO Insight (January 12, 2012).

Barton, Dominic and David Court. "Making Advanced Analytics Work for You." Harvard Business Review (October 2012).

Baum, David. "Flying High with a Private Database Cloud." Oracle Magazine (November/December 2011).

Beath, Cynthia, , Irma Becerra-Fernandez, Jeanne Ross and James Short. "Finding Value in the Information Explosion." MIT Sloan Management Review 53, No. 4 (Summer 2012).

Bughin, Jacques, John Livingston, and Sam Marwaha."Seizing the Potential for Big Data." The McKinsey Quarterly (October 2011).

Cappiello, Cinzia, Chiara Francalanci, and Barbara Pernici. "Time-Related Factors of Data Quality in Multichannel Information Systems." Journal of Management Information Systems 20, no. 3 (Winter 2004).

Clifford, James, Albert Croker, and Alex Tuzhilin. "On Data Representation and Use in a Temporal Relational DBMS." Information Systems Research 7, no. 3 (September 1996).

Davenport, Thomas H. and D.J. Patil. "Data Scientist: The Sexiest Job of the 21st Century." Harvard Business Review (October 2012).

Davenport, Thomas H., Paul Barth, and Randy Bean. "How Big Data Is Different." MIT Sloan Management Review 54, No 1(Fall 2012).

Eckerson, Wayne W. "Data Quality and the Bottom Line." The Data Warehousing Institute (2002).

Eckerson, Wayne. "Big Data Analytics: Profiling the Use of Analytical Platforms in User Organizations." (September 28, 2011).

Gartner Inc. "'Dirty Data' is a Business Problem, not an IT Problem, Says Gartner." Sydney, Australia (March 2, 2007).

Greengard, Samuel. "Big Data Unlocks Business Value." Baseline (January 2012).

Henschen, Doug. "Text Mining for Customer Insight." Information Week (November 30, 2009).

Hoffer, Jeffrey A., Ramesh Venkataraman, and Heikki Toppi. Modern Database Management, 11th ed. Upper Saddle River, NJ: Prentice-Hall (2013).

Jinesh Radadia. "Breaking the Bad Data Bottlenecks." Information Management (May/June 2010).

Kajepeeta, Sreedhar. "How Hadoop Tames Enterprises' Big Data." Information Week (February 2012).

Klau, Rick. "Data Quality and CRM." Line56.com, accessed March 4, 2003.

Kroenke, David M. and David Auer. Database Processing 12e. Upper Saddle River, NJ: Prentice-Hall (2012).

Lee, Yang W., and Diane M. Strong. "Knowing-Why about Data Processes and Data Quality." Journal of Management Information Systems 20, no. 3 (Winter 2004).

Lohr, Steve. "The Age of Big Data." The New York Times (February 11, 2012).

Loveman, Gary. "Diamonds in the Datamine." Harvard Business Review (May 2003).

McAfee, Andrew and Erik Brynjolfsson. "Big Data: The Management Revolution." Harvard Business Review (October 2012).

McKinsey Global Institute. "Big Data: The Next Frontier for Innovation, Competition, and Productivity." McKinsey & Company (2011).

McKnight, William. "Seven Sources of Poor Data Quality." Information Management (April 2009).

Pant, Prashant. "Data Mining and Predictive Analytics." Information Management (January 24, 2012).

Redman, Thomas. Data Driven: Profiting from Your Most Important Business Asset. Boston: Harvard Business Press (2008).

SAP. "SAP HANA Overview." (2011).

CHAPTER 7

Borland, John. "A Smarter Web." Technology Review (March/April 2007).

Cain Miller, Claire. "Seeking to Weed Out Drivel, Google Adjusts Search Engine." The New York Times (February 25, 2011).

comScore. "ComScore Releases August 2012 U.S. Search Engine Rankings." (September 12, 2012).

comScore. "comScore Reports May 2011 U.S. Mobile Subscriber Market Share." comScore, Press Release July 5, 2011.

Donaldson, Sonya. "New York Times Launches Semantic Web Experiment." New York Times (September 3, 2011).

Efrati, Amir. "Google's Search Revamp: A Step Closer to AI." The Wall Street Journal (March 14,2012).

Efrati, Amir. "Google's Search Cleanup Has Big Effect." The Wall Street Journal (February 28, 2011).

eMarketer . "US Mobile Connections, 2010-2016." (April 1, 2012).

eMarketer. "Mobile Internet Users Worldwide, by Region and Country, 2010-2016." (April 17, 2012).

eMarketer. "Mobile Users Expand Their Search Habits." (August 1, 2011).

Fish, Lynn A. and Wayne C. Forrest. "A Worldwide Look at RFID." Supply Chain Management Review (April 1, 2007).

Flynn, Laurie J. "New System to Add Internet Addresses as Numbers Run Out." The New York Times (February 14, 2011).

Google, Inc. "Form 10K for the Fiscal Year 2011." Securities and Exchange Commission, filed February 11, 2012.

Holmes, Sam and Jeffrey A. Trachtenberg. "Web Addresses Enter New Era." The Wall Street Journal (June 21, 2011).

ICANN. "ICANN Policy Update." 10, No. 9 (September 2010).

Lahiri, Atanu, I. "The Disruptive Effect of Open Platforms on Markets for Wireless Services." Journal of Management Information Systems 27, No. 3 (Winter 2011).

Lohr, Steve. "Can Microsoft Make You Bing?" The New York Times (July 30, 2011).

Lohr, Steve. "The Internet Gets Physical." The New York Times (December 17, 2011).

Marin Software, Inc. "The State of Mobile Search Advertising in the US: How the Emergence of Smartphones and Tablets Changes Paid Search." Marin Software Inc. (2012).

Miller, Claire Cain. "Google, a Giant in Mobile Search, Seeks New Ways to Make It Pay," The New York Times (April 24, 2011).

Miller, Miranda. "Mobile to Account for 25% of Paid Search Clicks on Google in 2012." Searchenginewatch.com (March 28, 2012).

Panko, Raymond R. and Julia Panko. Business Data Networks and Telecommunications 8e. Upper Saddle River, NJ: Prentice-Hall (2011).

Shaw, Tony. "Innovation Web 3.0." Baseline (March/April 2011).

Simonite, Tom. "Social Indexing." Technology Review (May/June 2011).

"The Internet of Things." McKinsey Quarterly (March 2010).

The McKinsey&Company. "The Impact of Internet Technologies: Search (July 2011).

Troianovski, Anton. "Optical Delusion? Fiber Booms Again, Despite Bust," The Wall Street Journal, (April 3, 2012).

Worldwide Web Consortium, " Semantic Web." w3.org/standards/semanticweb (October 18, 2012).

Worthen, Ben and Cari Tuna. "Web Running Out of Addresses." The Wall Street Journal (Feb 1, 2011).

Worthen, Ben. "Upgrade Race for Data Centers." The Wall Street Journal (June 25, 2012).

Xiao, Bo and Izak Benbasat. "E-Commerce Product Recommendation Agents: Use, Characteristics, and Impact." MIS Quarterly 31, No. 1 (March 2007).

CHAPTER 8

"Android Malware Spreading for First Time Via Hacked Sites." CIO Insight (May 4, 2012).

Bernstein, Corinne. "The Cost of Data Breaches." Baseline (April 2009)

Boyle, Randy J. and Raymond Panko. Corporate Computer Security 3e. Upper Saddle River, NJ: Prentice Hall (2013).

Bray, Chad. "Global Cyber Scheme Hits Bank Accounts." The Wall Street Journal (October 1, 2010.)

Cavusoglu, Huseyin, Birendra Mishra, and Srinivasan Raghunathan. "A Model for Evaluating IT Security Investments." Communications of the ACM 47, no. 7 (July 2004).

Choe Sang-Hun, "Cyberattacks Hit U.S. and South Korean Web Sites," The New York Times, July 9, 2009.

D'Arcy, John and Anat Hovav. "Deterring Internal Information Systems Use." Communications of the ACM 50, no. 10 (October 2007).

"Devastating Downtime: The Surprising Cost of Human Error and Unforeseen Events." Focus Research (October 2010).

Drew, Christopher and Verne G. Kopytoff. "Deploying New Tools to Stop the Hackers." The New York Times (June 17, 2011).`

El-Ghobashy, Tamer. "Columbia Is Hit with $4.5 Million Bank Fraud." The Wall Street Journal (November 29, 2010).

Fowler, Geoffrey A. "What's a Company's Biggest Security Risk? YOU." The Wall Street Journal (September 26, 2011).

Galbreth, Michael R. and Mikhael Shor. "The Impact of Malicious Agents on the Enterprise Software Industry." MIS Quarterly 34, no. 3 (September 2010).

Giordano, Scott M. "Electronic Evidence and the Law." Information Systems Frontiers 6, No. 2 (June 2004).

Graziano, Dan. "Study Says Malware Attacks Are on the Rise, Mobile Threats Becoming More Serious," BGR.com (September 4, 2012).

Housley, Russ, and William Arbaugh. "Security Problems in 802.11b Networks." Communications of the ACM 46, no. 5 (May 2003).

IBM. "Secure By Design: Building Identity-Based Security into Today's Information Systems." (March 2010).

Ives, Blake, Kenneth R. Walsh, and Helmut Schneider. "The Domino Effect of Password Reuse." Communications of the ACM 47, no.4 (April 2004).

Jagatic Tom, Nathaniel Johnson, Markus Jakobsson, and Filippo Menczer. "Social Phishing." Communications of the ACM 50, no. 10 (October 2007).

Javelin Strategy & Research. "2012 Identity Fraud Survey Report." (2012).

King, Ivory. "The United States, a Top Source and Target of Malware." L'Atelier (August 13, 2012).

McGraw, Gary. "Real-World Software Security." Information Week (August 9, 2010).

Nachenberg, Carey. "A Window into Mobile Device Security." Symantec (2011).

Osterman Research. "The Risks of Social Media and What Can Be Done to Manage Them. Commvault (June 2011).

Ponemon Institute. "Global Study on Mobility Risks." Websense Inc. (February 2012).

Ponemon Institute. "Second Annual Cost of Cyber Crime Study." (August 2011).

Protess, Bill. "Users of Citibank's Bill-Pay App Charged Twice." The New York Times (February 9, 2012).

Pug, Ivan P.L. and Qiu-Hong Wang. "Information Security: Facilitating User Precautions Vis a Vis Enforcement Against Attackers. "Journal of Management Information Systems 26, No. 2 (Fall 2009).

Rashid, Fahmida Y. "Mobile Malware Grew 3000 Percent in 2011: Report." eWeek (February 16,2012).

Rashid, Fahmida. Y. "Anonymous Avenges Megaupload Shutdown With Attacks on FBI, Hollywood Websites. eWeek (January 20, 2012).

Roche, Edward M., and George Van Nostrand. Information Systems, Computer Crime and Criminal Justice. New York: Barraclough Ltd. (2004).

Sadeh, Norman M. "Phish Isn't Spam." Information Week (June 25, 2012).

Schwerha, Joseph J., IV. "Cybercrime: Legal Standards Governing the Collection of Digital Evidence." Information Systems Frontiers 6, no. 2 (June 2004).

Sengupta, Somini. "Logging In with a Touch or a Phrase (Anything But a Password). The New York Times (December 23, 2011).

Sherr, Ian. "Fox Says Hackers Hit Twitter Feed." Wall Street Journal (July 5, 2011).

Spears. Janine L. and Henri Barki. "User Participation in Information Systems Security Risk Management." MIS Quarterly 34, No. 3 (September 2010).

Steinhart, Michael. "A Closer Look at Public Cloud Security." Smartertechnology.com (September 2011).

Strom, David. "Cost of a Data Breach Declines For First Time, According to Ponemon," ReadWriteWeb/Enterprise (March 20, 2012).

Symantec. "Symantec Internet Security Threat Report." (2012).

Symantec. "More Than a Third of Global Cyber Attacks Aimed at Small Businesses, Research Shows. " SupplyChainBrain.com (July 17, 2012).

Temizkan , Orcun, Ram L. Kumar , Sungjune Park and Chandrasekar Subramaniam. "Patch Release Behaviors of Software Vendors in Response to Vulnerabilities: An Empirical Analysis . " Journal of Management Information Systems 28, No. 4 (Spring 2012).

Volonino, Linda and Stephen R. Robinson. Principles and Practice of Information Security. Upper Saddle River, NJ: Pearson Prentice Hall (2004).

Warkentin, Merrill, Xin Luo, and Gary F. Templeton. "A Framework for Spyware Assessement." Communications of the ACM 48, no. 8 (August 2005).

Westerman, George. IT Risk: Turning Business Threats into Competitive Advantage. Harvard Business School Publishing (2007)

Wright, Ryan T. and Kent Marrett."The Influence of Experiental and Dispositional Factors in Phishing: An Empirical Investigation of the Deceived." Journal of Management Information Systems 27, No. 1 (Summer 2010).

CHAPTER 9

Bozarth, Cecil and Robert B. Handfield. Introduction to Operations and Supply Chain Management 3e. Upper Saddle River, NJ: Prentice-Hall (2013).

"Building the Supply Chain of the Future." SupplyChainBrain (March 29, 2012).

Chickowski, Ericka. "5 ERP Disasters Explained."www. Baselinemag.com, accessed October 8, 2009.

D'Avanzo, Robert, Hans von Lewinski, and Luk N. Van Wassenhove. "The Link between Supply Chain and Financial Performance." Supply Chain Management Review (November 1, 2003).

Davenport, Thomas H. Mission Critical: Realizing the Promise of Enterprise Systems. Boston: Harvard Business School Press (2000).

Davenport, Thomas H., Leandro Dalle Mule, and John Lucke. "Know What Your Customers Want Before They Do." Harvard Business Review (December 2011).

Ferrer, Jaume, Johan Karlberg, and Jamie Hintlian."Integration: The Key to Global Success." Supply Chain Management Review (March 1, 2007).

"Future Tech: Where Will ERP Be in 2 Years?" Inside-ERP (2011).

Garber, Randy and Suman Sarkar. "Want a More Flexible Supply Chain?" Supply Chain Management Review (January 1, 2007).

Goodhue, Dale L., Barbara H. Wixom, and Hugh J. Watson. "Realizing Business Benefits through CRM: Hitting the Right Target in the Right Way." MIS Quarterly Executive 1, no. 2 (June 2002).

Henschen, Doug. "SAP Spiffs Up Cloud Suite." Information Week (August 13, 2012).

Hitt, Lorin, D. J. Wu, and Xiaoge Zhou. "Investment in Enterprise Resource Planning: Business Impact and Productivity Measures." Journal of Management Information Systems 19, no. 1 (Summer 2002).

IBM Institute for Business Value. "Customer Analytics Pay Off." IBM Corporation (2011).

Johnson, Maryfran."What's Happening with ERP Today." CIO (January 27, 2010).

Kalakota, Ravi, and Marcia Robinson. E-Business 2.0. Boston: Addison-Wesley (2001).

Kanakamedala, Kishore, Glenn Ramsdell, and Vats Srivatsan. "Getting Supply Chain Software Right." McKinsey Quarterly No. 1 (2003).

Kanaracus, Chris. "ERP Project Overruns 'Distressingly Common': Survey." IDG News Service (July 12, 2012).

Kern, Justin. "Giving SaaS ERP a Second Thought." Information Management (December 19, 2011).

Klein, Richard and Arun Rai. "Interfirm Strategic Information Flows in Logistics Supply Chain Relationships. MIS Quarterly 33, No. 4 (December 2009).

Kopczak, Laura Rock, and M. Eric Johnson. "The Supply-Chain Management Effect." MIT Sloan Management Review 44, no. 3 (Spring 2003).

Laudon, Kenneth C. "The Promise and Potential of Enterprise Systems and Industrial Networks." Working paper, The Concours Group. Copyright Kenneth C. Laudon (1999).

Lee, Hau, L., V. Padmanabhan, and Seugin Whang. "The Bullwhip Effect in Supply Chains." Sloan Management Review (Spring 1997).

Lee, Hau. "The Triple-A Supply Chain." Harvard Business Review (October 2004).

Li, Xinxin and Lorin M. Hitt. "Price Effects in Online Product Reviews: An Analytical Model and Empirical Analysis." MIS Quarterly 34, No. 4 (December 2010).

Liang, Huigang, Nilesh Sharaf, Quing Hu, and Yajiong Xue. "Assimilation of Enterprise Systems: The Effect of Institutional Pressures and the Mediating Role of Top Management." MIS Quarterly 31, no. 1 (March 2007).

Maklan, Stan, Simon Knox, and Joe Peppard. "When CRM Fails." MIT Sloan Management Review 52, No. 4 (Summer 2011).

Malhotra, Arvind, Sanjay Gosain, and Omar A. El Sawy. "Absorptive Capacity Configurations in Supply Chains: Gearing for Partner-Enabled Market Knowledge Creation." MIS Quarterly 29, no. 1 (March 2005).

Malik, Yogesh, Alex Niemeyer, and Brian Ruwadi. "Building the Supply Chain of the Future." McKinsey Quarterly (January 2011).

Mehta, Krishna."Best Practices for Developing a Customer Lifetime Value Program." Information Management (July 28, 2011).

Oracle Corporation. "Alcoa Implements Oracle Solution 20% below Projected Cost, Eliminates 43 Legacy Systems." www.oracle. com, accessed August 21, 2005.

Rai, Arun, Paul A. Pavlou, Ghiyoung Im, and Steve Du. "Interfirm IT Capability Profiles and Communications for Cocreating Relational Value: Evidence from the Logistics Industry." MIS Quarterly 36, No. 1 (March 2012).

Rai, Arun, Ravi Patnayakuni, and Nainika Seth. "Firm Performance Impacts of Digitally Enabled Supply Chain Integration Capabilities." MIS Quarterly 30 No. 2 (June 2006).

Ranganathan, C. and Carol V. Brown. "ERP Iinvestments and the Market Value of Firms: Toward an Understanding of Influential ERP Project Variables." Information Systems Research 17, No. 2 (June 2006).

Robey, Daniel, Jeanne W. Ross, and Marie-Claude Boudreau. "Learning to Implement Enterprise Systems: An Exploratory Study of the Dialectics of Change." Journal of Management Information Systems 19, no. 1 (Summer 2002).

Sarker, Supreteek, Saonee Sarker, Arvin Sahaym, and Bjørn-Andersen. "Exploring Value Cocreation in Relationships Between an ERP Vendor and its Partners: A Revelatory Case Study." MIS Quarterly 36, No. 1 (March 2012).

Scott, Judy E., and Iris Vessey. "Managing Risks in Enterprise Systems Implementations." Communications of the ACM 45, no. 4 (April 2002).

Seldon, Peter B., Cheryl Calvert, and Song Yang. "A Multi-Project Model of Key Factors Affecting Organizational Benefits from Enterprise Systems." MIS Quarterly 34, No. 2 (June 2010).

"Social and Mobile CRM Boost Productivity by 26.4 Percent." DestinationCRM (March 8, 2012).

Strong, Diane M. and Olga Volkoff. "Understanding Organization-Enterprise System Fit: A Path to Theorizing the Information Technology Artifact." MIS Quarterly 34, No.4 (December 2010).

Wailgum, Thomas. "Why ERP Is Still So Hard." CIO (September 9, 2009).

"What is Social CRM?" CRM Magazine (April 2012).

Wing, George. "Unlocking the Value of ERP." Baseline (January/February 2010).

Wong, Christina W.Y. , Lai, Kee-hung and Cheng, T.C.E.. "Value of Information Integration to Supply Chain Management: Roles of Internal and External Contingencies." Journal of Management Information Systems 28, No. 3 (Winter 2012).

CHAPTER 10

Bakos, Yannis. "The Emerging Role of Electronic Marketplaces and the Internet." Communications of the ACM 41, no. 8 (August 1998).

Bell, David R., Jeonghye Choi and Leonard Lodish."What Matters Most in Internet Retailing." MIT Sloan Management Review 54, No. 1 (Fall 2012).

Brynjolfsson, Erik,Yu Hu, and Michael D. Smith."Consumer Surplus in the Digital Economy: Estimating the Value of

Increased Product Variety at Online Booksellers." Management Science 49, no. 11 (November 2003).

Clemons, Eric K. "Business Models for Monetizing Internet Applications and Web Sites: Experience, Theory, and Predictions. "Journal of Management Information Systems 26, No. 2 (Fall 2009).

comScore, Inc. " Facebook's U.S. Visitors Decline in May." (June 20, 2012).

comScore Inc., "Top 50 Properties (US)." (September 2012).

eMarketer, Inc. "US Digital Ad Revenues at Major Digital Ad-Selling Companies, 2010-2014." (September 2012).

eMarketer, Inc. "US Digital Ad Spending, by Format, 2012-2016." (September 1, 2012).

eMarketer. "Facebook Advertising: Why the Marketplace Ad Platform Deserves a Second Look." (June 2012).

eMarketer. "Mobile Phone Users Worldwide, by Region and Country, 2010-2016." (April 17, 2012).

eMarketer. "Mobile Phone User Penetration Worldwide, by Region and Country, 2010-2016." (April 17, 2012).

eMarketer, Inc. "US Ad Spending Forecast." (October 2012).

eMarketer. "US Internet Users and Penetration, 2011-2016." (February 13, 2012).

eMarketer. "US Mobile Commerce Forecast." (January 2012).

Evans, Philip and Thomas S. Wurster. Blown to Bits: How the New Economics of Information Transforms Strategy. Boston, MA: Harvard Business School Press (2000).

Fuller, Johann, Hans Muhlbacher, Kurt Matzler, and Gregor Jawecki. "Customer Empowerment Through Internet-Based Co-Creation." Journal of Management Information Systems 26, No. 3 (Winter 2010).

Gast, Arne and Michele Zanini. "The Social Side of Strategy." McKinsey Quarterly (May 2012).

Giamanco, Barbara and Kent Gregoire. "Tweet Me, Friend Me, Make Me Buy." Harvard Business Review (July-August 2012).

Grau, Jeffery. "US Retail E-commerce Forecast: Entering the Age of Omnichannel Retailing." eMarketer. (March 1, 2012).

Hinz, Oliver , Jochen Eckert, and Bernd Skiera. "Drivers of the Long Tail Phenomenon: An Empirical Analysis." Journal of Management Information Systems 27, No. 4 (Spring 2011).

Hinz, Oliver, Il-Horn Hann, and Martin Spann. Price Discrimination in E-Commerce? An Examination of Dynamic Pricing in Name-Your-Own Price Markets." MIS Quarterly 35, No 1 (March 2011).

Howe, Heff. Crowdsourcing: Why the Power of the Crowd Is Driving the Future of Business. New York: Random House (2008).

Internet Retailer. "Mobile Commerce Top 400 2012." (2012).

Jiang, Zhengrui and Sumit Sarkar. "Speed Matters: The Role of Free Software Offer in Software Diffusion." Journal of Management Information Systems 26, No. 3 (Winter 2010).

Kauffman, Robert J. and Bin Wang. "New Buyers' Arrival Under Dynamic Pricing Market Microstructure: The Case of Group-Buying Discounts on the Internet, Journal of Management Information Systems 18, no. 2 (Fall 2001).

Koch, Hope and Ulrike Schultze. " Stuck in the Conflicted Middle: A Role-Theoretic Perspective on B2B E-Marketplaces." MIS Quarterly 35, No. 1 (March 2011).

Kumar, V. and Rohan Mirchandan "Increasing the ROI of Social Media Marketing." MIT Sloan Management Review 54, No. 1 (Fall 2012).

Laudon, Kenneth C. and Carol Guercio Traver. E-Commerce: Business, Technology, Society, 9th edition. Upper Saddle River, NJ: Prentice-Hall (2013).

Leimeister, Jan Marco, Michael Huber, Ulrich Bretschneider, and Helmut Krcmar." Leveraging Crowdsourcing: Activation-Supporting Components for IT-Based Ideas Competition." Journal of Management Information Systems 26, No. 1 (Summer 2009).

Li, Xinxin and Lorin M. Hitt. "Price Effects in Online Product Reviews: An Analytical Model and Empirical Analysis." MIS Quarterly 34, No. 4 (December 2010).

Lin, Mei , Ke, Xuqing and Whinston, Andrew B. "Vertical Differentiation and a Comparison of Online Advertising Models . " Journal of Management Information Systems 29, No. 1 (Summer 2012).

Moe, Wendy W., David A. Schweidel, and Michael Trusov. '"What Influences Customers' Online Comments." MIT Sloan Management Review 53, No. 1 (Fall 2011).

Oestreicher-Singer, Gal and Arun Sundararajan. "Recommendation Networks and the Long Tail of Electronic Commerce." MIS Quarterly 36, No. 1 (March 2012).

Pavlou, Paul A., Huigang Liang, and Yajiong Xue. "Understanding and Mitigating Uncertainty in Online Exchange Relationships: A Principal-Agent Perspective." MIS Quarterly 31, no. 1 (March 2007).

Pew Internet and American Life Project. "Daily Internet Activities." (January 6, 2012.)

Piskorski, Mikolaj Jan."Social Strategies that Work." Harvard Business Review (November 2011).

Resnick, Paul and Hal Varian. "Recommender Systems." Communications of the ACM (March 2007).

Schoder, Detlef and Alex Talalavesky. "The Price Isn't Right." MIT Sloan Management Review (August 22, 2010).

Schultze, Ulrike and Wanda J. Orlikowski. "A Practice Perspective on Technology-Mediated Network Relations: The Use of Internet-Based Self-Serve Technologies." Information Systems Research 15, no. 1 (March 2004).

Silverman, Rachel Emma. "Big Firms Try Crowdsourcing," The Wall Street Journal, January 17, 2012.

Smith, Michael D. and Rahul Telang. "Competing with Free: The Impact of Movie Broadcasts on DVD Sales and Internet Piracy." MIS Quarterly 33, No. 2 (June 2009).

Smith, Michael D. and Rahul Telang. "Why Digital Media Require a Strategic Rethink." Harvard Business Review (October 2012).

Smith, Michael D., Joseph Bailey and Erik Brynjolfsson."Understanding Digital Markets: Review and Assessment" in Erik Brynjolfsson and Brian Kahin, ed. Understanding the Digital Economy. Cambridge, MA: MIT Press (1999).

Surowiecki, James. The Wisdom of Crowds: Why the Many Are Smarter Than the Few and How Collective Wisdom Shapes Business, Economies, Societies and Nations. Boston: Little, Brown (2004).

Wilson, H. James, PJ. Guinan, Salvatore Parise, and Bruce D. Weinberg. "What's Your Social Media Strategy?" Harvard Business Review (July 2011).

"US M-Commerce Sales, 2010-2015" in "Mobile Commerce Forecast: Capitalizing on Consumers' Urgent Needs." eMarketer (January 2012).

Yang, James. "When Freemium Fails." The Wall Street Journal (August 22, 2012).

CHAPTER 11

Alavi, Maryam and Dorothy Leidner. "Knowledge Management and Knowledge Management Systems: Conceptual Foundations and Research Issues," MIS Quarterly 25, No. 1(March 2001).

Alavi, Maryam, Timothy R. Kayworth, and Dorothy E. Leidner. "An Empirical Investigation of the Influence of Organizational Culture on Knowledge Management Practices." Journal of Management Information Systems 22, No.3 (Winter 2006).

Allen, Bradley P. "CASE-Based Reasoning: Business Applications." Communications of the ACM 37, no. 3 (March 1994).

"Apple's Siri Search Apps Could Save Businesses Millions." CIO Insight (June 14, 2012).

Barker, Virginia E., and Dennis E. O'Connor. "Expert Systems for Configuration at Digital: XCON and Beyond." Communications of the ACM (March 1989).

Birkinshaw, Julian and Tony Sheehan. "Managing the Knowledge Life Cycle." MIT Sloan Management Review 44, no. 1 (Fall 2002).

Booth, Corey and Shashi Buluswar. "The Return of Artificial Intelligence," The McKinsey Quarterly No. 2 (2002).

Boutin, Paul. "A New Reality." Technology Review (May/June 2011).

Burtka, Michael. "Generic Algorithms." The Stern Information Systems Review 1, no. 1 (Spring 1993).

Churchland, Paul M., and Patricia Smith Churchland. "Could a Machine Think?" Scientific American (January 1990).

Cross, Rob and Lloyd Baird."Technology is Not Enough: Improving Performance by Building Organizational Memory." Sloan Management Review 41, no. 3 (Spring 2000).

"CVM Solutions ELearning Portal,"www.knowledgedirectweb.com/lms-elearning-case-studies, accessed July 5, 2012.

Davenport, Thomas H., and Lawrence Prusak. Working Knowledge: How Organizations Manage What They Know. Boston, MA: Harvard Business School Press (1997).

Davenport, Thomas H., David W. DeLong, and Michael C. Beers. "Successful Knowledge Management Projects." Sloan Management Review 39, no. 2 (Winter 1998).

Davenport, Thomas H., Laurence Prusak, and Bruce Strong. "Putting Ideas to Work." The Wall Street Journal (March 10, 2008).

Davenport, Thomas H., Robert J. Thomas and Susan Cantrell. "The Mysterious Art and Science of Knowledge-Worker Performance." MIT Sloan Management Review 44, no. 1 (Fall 2002).

Dhar, Vasant, and Roger Stein. Intelligent Decision Support Methods: The Science of Knowledge Work. Upper Saddle River, NJ: Prentice Hall (1997).

Du, Timon C., Eldon Y. Li, and An-pin Chang. "Mobile Agents in Distributed Network Management." Communications of the ACM 46, no.7 (July 2003).

Earl, Michael. "Knowledge Management Strategies: Toward a Taxonomy." Journal of Management Information Systems 18, no. 1 (Summer 2001).

El Najdawi, M. K., and Anthony C. Stylianou. "Expert Support Systems: Integrating AI Technologies." Communications of the ACM 36, no. 12 (December 1993).

Gast, Arne and Michele Banini. "The Social Side of Strategy." McKinsey Quarterly (May 2012).

Gelernter, David. "The Metamorphosis of Information Management." Scientific American (August 1989).

Gordon, Steven R. and Monideepa Tarafdar. "The IT Audit that Boosts Innovation." MIT Sloan Management Review (June 26, 2010).

Grover, Varun and Thomas H. Davenport. "General Perspectives on Knowledge Management: Fostering a Research Agenda." Journal of Management Information Systems 18, no. 1 (Summer 2001).

Gu, Feng and Baruch Lev. "Intangible Assets. Measurements, Drivers, Usefulness." http://pages.stern.nyu.edu/~blev/.

Hagerty, James R. and Kate Linebaugh. "Next 3-D Frontier: Printed Plane Parts." The Wall Street Journal (July 14, 2012).

Holland, John H. "Genetic Algorithms." Scientific American (July 1992).

Housel Tom and Arthur A. Bell. Measuring and Managing Knowledge. New York: McGraw-Hill (2001).

Jarvenpaa, Sirkka L. and D. Sandy Staples. "Exploring Perceptions of Organizational Ownership of Information and Expertise."Journal of Management Information Systems 18, no. 1 (Summer 2001).

Jones, Quentin, Gilad Ravid, and Sheizaf Rafaeli. "Information Overload and the Message Dynamics of Online Interaction Spaces: A Theoretical Model and Empirical Exploration." Information Systems Research 15, no. 2 (June 2004).

King, William R., Peter V. Marks, Jr. and Scott McCoy. "The Most Important Issues in Knowledge Management." Communications of the ACM 45, no.9 (September 2002).

Kuo, R.J., K. Chang, and S.Y.Chien."Integration and Self-Organizing Feature Maps and Genetic-Algorithm-Based Clustering Method for Market Segmentation." Journal of Organizational Computing and Electronic Commerce 14, no. 1 (2004).

Leonard-Barton, Dorothy and Walter Swap. "Deep Smarts." Harvard Business Review (September 1, 2004).

Leonard-Barton, Dorothy, and John J. Sviokla. "Putting Expert Systems to Work." Harvard Business Review (March–April 1988).

Lev, Baruch, and Theodore Sougiannis. "Penetrating the Book-to-Market Black Box: The R&D Effect," Journal of Business Finance and Accounting (April/May 1999).

Lev, Baruch. "Sharpening the Intangibles Edge." Harvard Business Review (June 1, 2004).

Maglio, Paul P. and Christopher S. Campbell. "Attentive Agents." Communications of the ACM 46, no. 3 (March 2003).

Malone, Thomas W., Robert Laubacher, and Chrysanthos Dellarocas. "The Collective Intelligence Genome." MIT Sloan Management Review 51, No. 3 (Spring 2010).

Maltby, Emily. "Affordable 3-D Arrives." The Wall Street Journal (July 29, 2010).

Marion, Tucker, Sebastian Fixson and Marc H. Meyer. "The Problem With Digital Design." MIT Sloan Management Review 53, No. 1 (Summer 2012).

Markoff, John. "How Many Computers to Identify a Cat? 16,000." The New York Times (June 26, 2012).

Markus, M. Lynne, Ann Majchrzak, and Less Gasser." A Design Theory for Systems that Support Emergent Knowledge Processes." MIS Quarterly 26, no. 3 (September 2002).

Markus, M. Lynne. "Toward a Theory of Knowledge Reuse: Types of Knowledge Reuse Situations and Factors in Reuse Success." Journal of Management Information Systems 18, no. 1 (Summer 2001).

McCarthy, John. "Generality in Artificial Intelligence." Communications of the ACM (December 1987).

Moravec, Hans. "Robots, After All." Communications of the ACM 46, no. 10 (October 2003).

Murphy, Chris "4 Ways Ford Is Exploring Next-Gen Car Tech." Information Week (July 27, 2012).

Nidumolu, Sarma R. Mani Subramani and Alan Aldrich. " Situated Learning and the Situated Knowledge Web: Exploring the Ground Beneath Knowledge Management." Journal of Management Information Systems 18, no. 1 (Summer 2001).

Open Text Corporation. "Barrick's Knowledge Centre Promotes Employee Awareness and Education." (2012).

Orlikowski, Wanda J. "Knowing in Practice: Enacting a Collective Capability in Distributed Organizing." Organization Science 13, no. 3 (May-June 2002).

Sadeh, Norman, David W. Hildum, and Dag Kjenstad."Agent-Based E-Supply Chain Decision Support." Journal of Organizational Computing and Electronic Commerce 13, no. 3 & 4 (2003).

Schrage, Michael. "How You Can Be Two Places at Once." The Wall Street Journal (April 2, 2012).

Schultze, Ulrike and Dorothy Leidner."Studying Knowledge Management in Information Systems Research: Discourses and Theoretical Assumptions." MIS Quarterly 26, no. 3 (September 2002).

Singer, Natasha. "The Virtual Anatomy, Ready for Dissection." The New York Times (January 7, 2012).

Spender, J. C. "Organizational Knowledge, Learning and Memory: Three Concepts In Search of a Theory." Journal of Organizational Change Management 9, 1996.

Starbuck, William H. "Learning by Knowledge-Intensive Firms." Journal of Management Studies 29, no. 6 (November 1992).

Trippi, Robert, and Efraim Turban. "The Impact of Parallel and Neural Computing on Managerial Decision Making." Journal of Management Information Systems 6, no. 3 (Winter 1989–1990).

U.S. Department of Commerce, Bureau of the Census. Statistical Abstract of the United States, 2012 Table 616. Washington, D.C. (2012).

Walczak, Stephen."An Emprical Analysis of Data Requirements for Financial Forecasting with Neural Networks." Journal of Management Information Systems 17, no. 4 (Spring 2001).

Weill, Peter, Thomas Malone, and Thomas G. Apel. "The Business Models Investors Prefer." MIT Sloan Management Review 52, No. 4 (Summer 2011).

Yimam-Seid, Dawit and Alfred Kobsa." Expert-Finding Systems for Organizations: Problem and Domain Analysis and the DEMOIR Approach." Journal of Organizational Computing and Electronic Commerce 13, no. 1 (2003)

Zack, Michael H "Rethinking the Knowledge-Based Organization." MIS Sloan Management Review 44, no. 4 (Summer 2003).

Zadeh, Lotfi A. "Fuzzy Logic, Neural Networks, and Soft Computing." Communications of the ACM 37, no. 3 (March 1994).

Zadeh, Lotfi A. "The Calculus of Fuzzy If/Then Rules." AI Expert (March 1992).

Zeying Wan, Deborah Compeau and Nicole Haggerty. "The Effects of Self-Regulated Learning Processes on E-Learning Outcomes in Organizational Settings." Journal of Management Information Systems 29, No. 1 (Summer 2012).

CHAPTER 12

Bazerman, Max H. and Dolly Chugh. "Decisions Without Blinders." Harvard Business Review (January 2006).

BPM Working Group. "Performance Management Industry Leaders Form BPM Standards Group." Working Group to Establish Common Definition for BPM and Deliver Business Performance Management Framework Press Release. Stamford, CT (March 25, 2004)

Clark, Thomas D., Jr., Mary C. Jones, and Curtis P. Armstrong. "The Dynamic Structure of Management Support Systems: Theory Development, Research Focus, and Direction." MIS Quarterly 31, no. 3 (September 2007).

Davenport, Thomas H. and Jeanne G. Harris. Competing on Analytics: The New Science of Winning. Boston: Harvard Business School Press (2007).

Davenport, Thomas H. and Jim Hagemann Snabe. "How Fast and Flexible to You Want Your Information, Really?" MIT Sloan Management Review 52, No. 3 (Spring 2011).

Davenport, Thomas H., Jeanne G. Harris, and Robert Morison. Analytics at Work: Smarter Decisions, Better Results. Boston: Harvard Business Press (2010).

Davenport, Thomas H., Jeanne Harris, and Jeremy Shapiro. "Competing on Talent Analytics." Harvard Business Review (October 2010).

De la Merced, Michael J. and Ben Protess. "A Fast-Paced Stock Exchange Trips Over Itself." The New York Times (March 23, 2012).

Dennis, Alan R., Jay E. Aronson, William G. Henriger, and Edward D. Walker III. "Structuring Time and Task in Electronic Brainstorming." MIS Quarterly 23, no. 1 (March 1999).

Dennis, Alan R., Joey F. George, Len M. Jessup, Jay F. Nunamaker, and Douglas R. Vogel. "Information Technology to Support Electronic Meetings." MIS Quarterly 12, no. 4 (December 1988).

DeSanctis, Geraldine, and R. Brent Gallupe. "A Foundation for the Study of Group Decision Support Systems." Management Science 33, no. 5 (May 1987).

Gallupe, R. Brent, Geraldine DeSanctis, and Gary W. Dickson. "Computer-Based Support for Group Problem-Finding: An Experimental Investigation." MIS Quarterly 12, no. 2 (June 1988).

Gorry, G. Anthony, and Michael S. Scott Morton. "A Framework for Management Information Systems." Sloan Management Review 13, no. 1 (Fall 1971).

Grau, Jeffrey. "How Retailers Are Leveraging 'Big Data' to Personalize Ecommerce."eMarketer (2012).

Hurst, Cameron with Michael S. Hopkins and Leslie Brokaw. "Matchmaking With Math: How Analytics Beats Intuition to Win Customers." MIT Sloan Management Review 52, No. 2 (Winter 2011).

Jensen, Matthew, Paul Benjamin Lowry, Judee K. Burgoon, and Jay Nunamaker. "Technology Dominance in Complex Decisionmaking." Journal of Management Information Systems 27, No. 1 (Summer 2010).

John, K., L. Lang, and J. Netter. "The Voluntary Restructuring of Large Firms in Response to Performance Decline." Journal of Finance 47, No. 3 (1992).

Kaplan, Robert S. and David P. Norton. "The Balanced Scorecard: Measures that Drive Performance", Harvard Business Review (Jan – Feb 1992).

Kaplan, Robert S. and David P. Norton. Strategy Maps: Converting Intangible Assets into Tangible Outcomes. Boston: Harvard Business School Press (2004).

Kern, Justin. "Big Data, Meet Massive Analytics Market Growth." Information Management (July 11, 2012).

Kiron, David and Rebecca Schockley. "Creating Business Value with Analytics." MIT Sloan Management Review 53, No. 1 (Fall 2011).

Kiron, David, Rebecca Shockley, Nina Kruschwitz, Glenn Finch and Dr. Michael Haydock. "Analytics: The Widening Divide." MIT Sloan Management Review (Fall 2011).

Kiron, David, Pamela Kirk, and Renee Boucher Ferguson. "Innovating with Analytics." MIT Sloan Management Review 54, No. 1 (Fall 2012).

Lauricella, Tom and Scott Patterson. "With Knight Wounded, Traders Ask If Speed Kills." Wall Street Journal (August 2, 2012).

LaValle, Steve, Eric Lesser, Rebecca Shockley, Michael S. Hopkins and Nina Kruschwitz. "Big Data, Analytics, and the Path from Insights to Value." MIT Sloan Management Review 52, No. 2 (Winter 2011).

LaValle, Steve, Michael S. Hopkins, Eric Lesser, Rebecca Shockley, and Nina Kruschwitz. "Analytics: The New Path to Value." MIT Sloan Management Review and IBM Institute for Business Value (Fall 2010).

Leidner, Dorothy E., and Joyce Elam. "The Impact of Executive Information Systems on Organizational Design, Intelligence, and Decision Making." Organization Science 6, no. 6 (November–December 1995).

Rockart, John F., and David W. DeLong. Executive Support Systems: The Emergence of Top Management Computer Use. Homewood, IL: Dow-Jones Irwin (1988).

Rockart, John F., and Michael E. Treacy. "The CEO Goes On-Line." Harvard Business Review (January–February 1982).

Schwabe, Gerhard. "Providing for Organizational Memory in Computer-Supported Meetings." Journal of Organizational Computing and Electronic Commerce 9, no. 2 and 3 (1999).

Simon, H. A. The New Science of Management Decision. New York: Harper & Row (1960).

Tibken, Shara. "Numbers, Numbers and More Numbers," The Wall Street Journal, April 16, 2012

Turban, Efraim, Ramesh Sharda, and Dursun Delen. Decision Support and Business Intelligence Systems, 9th ed. Upper Saddle River, NJ: Prentice Hall (2011).

Turban, Efraim, Ramesh Sharda, Dursun Delen, and David King. Business Intelligence, 2nd ed. Upper Saddle River, NJ: Prentice Hall (2011).

CHAPTER 13

Albert, Terri C., Paulo B. Goes, and Alok Gupta. "GIST: A Model for Design and Management of Content and Interactivity of Customer-Centric Web Sites." MIS Quarterly 28, no. 2 (June 2004).

Armstrong, Deborah J. and Bill C. Hardgrove. "Understanding Mindshift Learning: The Transition to Object-Oriented Development." MIS Quarterly 31, no. 3 (September 2007).

Aron, Ravi, Eric K.Clemons, and Sashi Reddi. "Just Right Outsourcing: Understanding and Managing Risk." Journal of Management Information Systems 22, no. 1 (Summer 2005).

Ashrafi, Noushin and Hessam Ashrafi. Object-Oriented Systems Analysis and Design. Upper Saddle River, NY: Prentice-Hall (2009).

Avison, David E. and Guy Fitzgerald."Where Now for Development Methodologies?" Communications of the ACM 41, no. 1 (January 2003).

Baily, Martin N. and Diana Farrell."Exploding the Myths of Offshoring." The McKinsey Quarterly (July 2004).

Barthelemy, Jerome. "The Hidden Costs of IT Outsourcing." Sloan Management Review (Spring 2001).

Broadbent, Marianne, Peter Weill, and Don St. Clair. "The Implications of Information Technology Infrastructure for Business Process Redesign." MIS Quarterly 23, no. 2 (June 1999).

Cha, Hoon S., David E. Pingry, and Matt E. Thatcher. "A Learning Model of Information Technology Outsourcing: Normative Implications. "Journal of Management Information Systems 26, No. 2 (Fall 2009).

Champy, James A.X-Engineering the Corporation: Reinventing Your Business in the Digital Age. New York: Warner Books (2002).

Davidson, Elisabeth J. "Technology Frames and Framing: A Socio-Cognitive Investigation of Requirements Determination. MIS Quarterly 26, no. 4 (December 2002).

DeMarco, Tom. Structured Analysis and System Specification. New York: Yourdon Press (1978).

Den Hengst, Marielle and Gert-Jan DeVreede. "Collaborative Business Engineering: A Decade of Lessons from the Field." Journal of Management Information Systems 20, no. 4 (Spring 2004).

Dibbern, Jess, Jessica Winkler, and Armin Heinzl. "Explaining Variations in Client Extra Costs between Software Projects Offshored to India." MIS Quarterly 32, no. 2 (June 2008).

Dupont, Ben. "Mobile App Development." Information Week (March 2012).

Edberg , Dana T., Polina Ivanova and William Kucchler. "Methodology Mashups: An Exploration of Processes Used to Maintain Software ." Journal of Management Information Systems 28, No. 4 (Spring 2012).

El Sawy, Omar A.Redesigning Enterprise Processes for E-Business. McGraw-Hill (2001).

Erickson, Jonathan. "Dr Dobb's Report: Agile Development." Information Week (April 27, 2009).

Esposito, Dino. "A Whole New Ball Game: Aspects of Mobile Application Development." Information Week (March 12, 2011).

Feeny, David, Mary Lacity, and Leslie P. Willcocks. "Taking the Measure of Outsourcing Providers." MIT Sloan Management Review 46, No. 3 (Spring 2005).

Finneran, Michael. "A New Approach for Mobile," Information Week, August 15, 2011.

Gefen, David and Erran Carmel. "Is the World Really Flat? A Look at Offshoring in an Online Programming Marketplace." MIS Quarterly 32, no. 2 (June 2008).

George, Joey, Dinesh Batra, Joseph S. Valacich, and Jeffrey A. Hoffer. Object Oriented System Analysis and Design, 2nd ed. Upper Saddle River, NJ: Prentice Hall (2007).

Goo, Jahyun, Rajive Kishore, H. R. Rao, and Kichan Nam. The Role of Service Level Agreements in Relational Management of Information Technology Outsourcing: An Empirical Study." MIS Quarterly 33, No. 1 (March 2009).

Grunbacher, Paul, Michael Halling, Stefan Biffl, Hasan Kitapci, and Barry W. Boehm. "Integrating Collaborative Processes and Quality Assurance Techniques: Experiences from Requirements Negotiation." Journal of Management Information Systems 20, no. 4 (Spring 2004).

Hahn, Eugene D., Jonathan P. Doh, and Kraiwinee Bunyaratavej. "The Evolution of Risk in Information Systems Offshoring: The Impact of Home Country Risk, Firm Learning, and Competitive Dynamics. MIS Quarterly 33, No. 3 (September 2009).

Hammer, Michael, and James Champy. Reengineering the Corporation. New York: HarperCollins (1993).

Hammer, Michael."Process Management and the Future of Six Sigma." "Sloan Management Review 43, no.2 (Winter 2002)

Hickey, Ann M., and Alan M. Davis. "A Unified Model of Requirements Elicitation." Journal of Management Information Systems 20, no. 4 (Spring 2004).

Hirscheim, Rudy and Mary Lacity."The Myths and Realities of Information Technology Insourcing." Communications of the ACM 43, no. 2 (February 2000).

Hoffer, Jeffrey, Joey George, and Joseph Valacich. Modern Systems Analysis and Design, 6th ed. Upper Saddle River, NJ: Prentice Hall (2011).

Irwin, Gretchen. "The Role of Similarity in the Reuse of Object-Oriented Analysis Models." Journal of Management Information Systems 19, no. 2 (Fall 2002).

Ivari, Juhani, Rudy Hirscheim, and Heinz K. Klein. "A Dynamic Framework for Classifying Information Systems Development Methodologies and Approaches." Journal of Management Information Systems 17, no. 3 (Winter 2000-2001).

Johnson, Richard A. The Ups and Downs of Object-Oriented Systems Development." Communications of the ACM 43, no.10 (October 2000).

Kendall, Kenneth E., and Julie E. Kendall. Systems Analysis and Design, 8th ed. Upper Saddle River, NJ: Prentice Hall (2011).

Kettinger, William J., and Choong C. Lee. "Understanding the IS-User Divide in IT Innovation." Communications of the ACM 45, no.2 (February 2002).

Kindler, Noah B., Vasantha Krishnakanthan, and Ranjit Tinaikar. "Applying Lean to Application Development and Maintenance." The McKinsey Quarterly (May 2007).

Koh, Christine, Song Ang, and Detmar W. Straub. "IT Outsourcing Success: A Psychological Contract Perspective." Information Systems Research 15 no. 4 (December 2004).

Le Clair, Craig. "Stuck In Cement: When Packaged Apps Create Barriers To Innovation." Forrester Research (January 9, 2012).

Lee, Gwanhoo and Weidong Xia. "Toward Agile: An Integrated Analysis of Quantitative and Qualitative Field Data." MIS Quarterly 34, no. 1 (March 2010).

Lee, Jae Nam, Shaila M. Miranda, and Yong-Mi Kim."IT Outsourcing Strategies: Universalistic, Contingency, and Configurational Explanations of Success." Information Systems Research 15, no. 2 (June 2004).

Levina, Natalia, and Jeanne W. Ross. "From the Vendor's Perspective: Exploring the Value Proposition in Information

Technology Outsourcing." MIS Quarterly 27, no. 3 (September 2003).

Limayem, Moez, Mohamed Khalifa, and Wynne W. Chin. "Case Tools Usage and Impact on System Development Performance." Journal of Organizational Computing and Electronic Commerce 14, no. 3 (2004).

Majchrzak, Ann, Cynthia M. Beath, and Ricardo A. Lim. "Managing Client Dialogues during Information Systems Design to Facilitate Client Learning." MIS Quarterly 29, no. 4 (December 2005).

Mani, Deepa, Anitesh Barua, and Andrew Whinston. "An Empirical Analysis of the Impact of Information Capabilities Design on Business Process Outsourcing Performance." MIS Quarterly 34, no. 1 (March 2010).

McDougall, Paul. "Outsourcing's New Reality: Choice Beats Costs." Information Week (August 29, 2012).

Murphy, Chris. "GM's U-Turn." Information Week (July 9, 2012).

Nelson, H. James, Deborah J. Armstrong, and Kay M. Nelson. Patterns of Transition: The Shift from Traditional to Object-Oriented Development." Journal of Management Information Systems 25, No. 4 (Spring 2009).

Nidumolu, Sarma R. and Mani Subramani."The Matrix of Control: Combining Process and Structure Approaches to Managing Software Development." Journal of Management Information Systems 20, no. 4 (Winter 2004).

Overby, Stephanie, "The Hidden Costs of Offshore Outsourcing," CIO Magazine (Sept.1, 2003).

Pitts, Mitzi G. and Glenn J. Browne."Stopping Behavior of Systems Analysts During Information Requirements Elicitation." Journal of Management Information Systems 21, no. 1 (Summer 2004).

Silva, Leiser and Rudy Hirschheim. "Fighting Against Windmills: Strategic Information Systems and Organizational Deep Structures." MIS Quarterly 31, no. 2 (June 2007).

Sircar, Sumit, Sridhar P. Nerur, and Radhakanta Mahapatra. "Revolution or Evolution? A Comparison of Object-Oriented and Structured Systems Development Methods." MIS Quarterly 25, no. 4 (December 2001).

Swanson, E. Burton and Enrique Dans. "System Life Expectancy and the Maintenance Effort: Exploring their Equilibration." MIS Quarterly 24, no. 2 (June 2000).

Taft, Darryl K. "Will PAAS Solve All Developer Ills? " eWeek (April 4, 2011).

Vitharana, Padmal."Risks and Challenges of Component-Based Software Development." Communications of the ACM 46, no. 8 (August 2003).

Watad, Mahmoud M. and Frank J. DiSanzo. "Case Study: The Synergism of Telecommuting and Office Automation." Sloan Management Review 41, no. 2 (Winter 2000).

Wulf, Volker, and Matthias Jarke. "The Economics of End-User Development." Communications of the ACM 47, no. 9 (September 2004).

Yourdon, Edward, and L. L. Constantine. Structured Design. New York: Yourdon Press (1978).

CHAPTER 14

Aladwani, Adel M. "An Integrated Performance Model of Information Systems Projects." Journal of Management Information Systems 19, no.1 (Summer 2002).

Andres, Howard P. and Robert W. Zmud. "A Contingency Approach to Software Project Coordination." Journal of Management Information Systems 18, no. 3 (Winter 2001-2002).

Appan, Radha and Glenn J. Browne. "The Impact of Analyst-Induced Misinformation on the Requirements Elicitation Process ." MIS Quarterly 36, No 1 (March 2012).

Armstrong, Curtis P. and V. Sambamurthy."Information Technology Assimilation in Firms: The Influence of Senior Leadership and IT Infrastructures." Information Systems Research 10, no. 4 (December 1999).

Banker, Rajiv. "Value Implications of Relative Investments in Information Technology." Department of Information Systems and Center for Digital Economy Research, University of Texas at Dallas, January 23, 2001.

Barki, Henri and Jon Hartwick. "Interpersonal Conflict and Its Management in Information Systems Development. " MIS Quarterly 25, no.2 (June 2001).

Barki, Henri, Suzanne Rivard, and Jean Talbot. "An Integrative Contingency Model of Software Project Risk Management." Journal of Management Information Systems 17, no. 4 (Spring 2001).

Beath, Cynthia Mathis, and Wanda J. Orlikowski. "The Contradictory Structure of Systems Development Methodologies: Deconstructing the IS-User Relationship in Information Engineering." Information Systems Research 5, no. 4 (December 1994).

Benaroch, Michel and Robert J. Kauffman. "Justifying Electronic Banking Network Expansion Using Real Options Analysis." MIS Quarterly 24, no. 2 (June 2000).

Benaroch, Michel, Sandeep Shah, and Mark Jeffrey. "On the Valuation of Multistage Information Technology Investments Embedding Nested Real Options." Journal of Management Information Systems 23, No. 1 (Summer 2006).

Benaroch, Michel. "Managing Information Technology Investment Risk: A Real Options Perspective." Journal of Management Information Systems 19, no. 2 (Fall 2002).

Bhattacherjee, Anol and G. Premkumar. "Understanding Changes In Belief and Attitude Toward Information Technology Usage: A Theoretical Model and Longitudinal Test." MIS Quarterly 28, no. 2 (June 2004).

Bloch, Michael, Sen Blumberg, and Jurgen Laartz. "Delivering Large-Scale IT Projects on Time, on Budget, and on Value." McKinsey Quarterly (October 2012).

Bostrom, R. P., and J. S. Heinen. "MIS Problems and Failures: A Socio-Technical Perspective. Part I: The Causes." MIS Quarterly 1 (September 1977); "Part II: The Application of Socio-Technical Theory." MIS Quarterly 1 (December 1977).

Brewer, Jeffrey and Kevin Dittman. Methods of IT Project Management. Upper Saddle River, NJ: Prentice-Hall (2010).

Brooks, Frederick P. "The Mythical Man-Month." Datamation (December 1974).

Brynjolfsson, Erik, and Lorin M. Hitt. "Information Technology and Organizational Design: Evidence from Micro Data." (January 1998).

Bullen, Christine, and John F. Rockart. "A Primer on Critical Success Factors." Cambridge, MA: Center for Information Systems Research, Sloan School of Management (1981).

Chatterjee, Debabroto, Rajdeep Grewal, and V. Sabamurthy. "Shaping Up for E-Commerce: Institutional Enablers of the Organizational Assimilation of Web Technologies." MIS Quarterly 26, no. 2 (June 2002).

Chickowski, Ericka. "Projects Gone Wrong." Baseline (May 15, 2009).

Clement, Andrew, and Peter Van den Besselaar. "A Retrospective Look at PD Projects." Communications of the ACM 36, no. 4 (June 1993).

Concours Group. "Delivering Large-Scale System Projects." (2000).

Cooper, Randolph B. "Information Technology Development Creativity: A Case Study of Attempted Radical Change." MIS Quarterly 24, no. 2 (June 2000).

De Meyer, Arnoud, Christoph H. Loch and Michael T. Pich." Managing Project Uncertainty: From Variation to Chaos." Sloan Management Review 43, no.2 (Winter 2002).

Delone, William H. and Ephraim R. McLean. "The Delone and McLean Model of Information Systems Success: A Ten-Year Update. Journal of Management Information Systems 19, no. 4 (Spring 2003).

Doll, William J., Xiaodung Deng, T. S. Raghunathan, Gholamreza Torkzadeh, and Weidong Xia. "The Meaning and Measurement of User Satisfaction: A Multigroup Invariance Analysis of End-User Computing Satisfaction Instrument." Journal of Management Information Systems 21, no. 1 (Summer 2004).

Feldman, Jonathan. "Get Your Projects In Line." Information Week (March 8, 2010).

Fichman, Robert G. "Real Options and IT Platforms Adoption: Implications for Theory and Practice." Information Systems Research 15, no. 2 (June 2004).

Flyvbjerg, Bent and Alexander Budzier. "Why Your IT Project May Be Riskier Than You Think." Harvard Business Review (September 2011).

Fuller, Mark, Joe Valacich, and Joey George. Information Systems Project Management: A Process and Team Approach. Upper Saddle River, NJ: Prentice Hall (2008).

Geng, Xianjun, Lihui Lin, and Andrew B. Whinston."Effects of Organizational Learning and Knowledge Transfer on Investment Decisions Under Uncertainty." "Journal of Management Information Systems 26, No. 2 (Fall 2009).

Goff, Stacy A. "The Future of IT Project Management Software." CIO (January 6, 2010).

Gordon, Steven R. and Monideepa Tarafdar. "The IT Audit that Boosts Innovation." MIT Sloan Management Review 51, No. 4 (Summer 2010).

Hitt, Lorin, D.J. Wu, and Xiaoge Zhou. "Investment in Enterprise Resource Planning: Business Impact and Productivity Measures." Journal of Management Information Systems 19, no. 1 (Summer 2002).

Housel, Thomas J., Omar El Sawy, Jianfang Zhong, and Waymond Rodgers. "Measuring the Return on e-Business Initiatives at the Process Level: The Knowledge Value-Added Approach." ICIS (2001).

Iversen, Jakob H., Lars Mathiassen, and Peter Axel Nielsen."Managing Risk in Software Process Improvement: An Action Research Approach." MIS Quarterly 28, no. 3 (September 2004).

Jeffrey, Mark, and Ingmar Leliveld. "Best Practices in IT Portfolio Management." MIT Sloan Management Review 45, no. 3 (Spring 2004).

Jiang, James J., Gary Klein, Debbie Tesch, and Hong-Gee Chen. "Closing the User and Provider Service Quality Gap," Communications of the ACM 46, no.2 (February 2003).

Jun He and William R. King. "The Role of User Participation In Information Systems Development: Implications from a Meta-Analysis." Journal of Management Information Systems 25, no. 1 (Summer 2008).

Keen, Peter W. "Information Systems and Organizational Change." Communications of the ACM 24 (January 1981).

Keil, Mark and Daniel Robey. "Blowing the Whistle on Troubled Software Projects." Communications of the ACM 44, no. 4 (April 2001).

Keil, Mark and Ramiro Montealegre. "Cutting Your Losses: Extricating Your Organization When a Big Project Goes Awry." Sloan Management Review 41, no. 3 (Spring 2000).

Keil, Mark, Joan Mann, and Arun Rai. "Why Software Projects Escalate: An Empirical Analysis and Test of Four Theoretical Models." MIS Quarterly 24, no. 4 (December 2000).

Keil, Mark, Paul E. Cule, Kalle Lyytinen, and Roy C. Schmidt. "A Framework for Identifying Software Project Risks." Communications of the ACM 41, 11 (November 1998).

Kettinger, William J. and Choong C. Lee. "Understanding the IS-User Divide in IT Innovation." Communications of the ACM 45, no.2 (February 2002).

Kim, Hee Woo and Atreyi Kankanhalli. "Investigating User Resistance to Information Systems Implementation: A Status Quo Bias Perspective." MIS Quarterly 33, No. 3 (September 2009).

Klein, Gary, James J. Jiang, and Debbie B. Tesch. "Wanted: Project Teams with a Blend of IS Professional Orientations." Communications of the ACM 45, no. 6 (June 2002).

Kolb, D. A., and A. L. Frohman. "An Organization Development Approach to Consulting." Sloan Management Review 12 (Fall 1970).

Lapointe, Liette, and Suzanne Rivard. "A Multilevel Model of Resistance to Information Technology Implementation." MIS Quarterly 29, no. 3 (September 2005).

Laudon, Kenneth C. "CIOs Beware: Very Large Scale Systems." Center for Research on Information Systems, New York University Stern School of Business, working paper (1989).

Lee, Jong Seok , Keil, Mark and Kasi, Vijay . "The Effect of an Initial Budget and Schedule Goal on Software Project Escalation." Journal of Management Information Systems 29, No. 1 (Summer 2012).

Liang, Huigang, Nilesh Sharaf, Qing Hu, and Yajiong Xue. "Assimilation of Enterprise Systems: The Effect of Institutional Pressures and the Mediating Role of Top Management." MIS Quarterly 31, no 1 (March 2007).

Markus, M. Lynne, and Robert I. Benjamin. "Change Agentry—The Next IS Frontier." MIS Quarterly 20, no. 4 (December 1996).

Markus, M. Lynne, and Robert I. Benjamin. "The Magic Bullet Theory of IT-Enabled Transformation." Sloan Management Review (Winter 1997).

McCafferty, Dennis. "What Dooms IT Projects." Baseline (June 10, 2010).

McFarlan, F. Warren. "Portfolio Approach to Information Systems." Harvard Business Review (September–October 1981).

McGrath, Rita Gunther and Ian C.McMillan. "Assessing Technology Projects Using Real Options Reasoning." Industrial Research Institute (2000)

Mumford, Enid, and Mary Weir. Computer Systems in Work Design: The ETHICS Method. New York: John Wiley (1979).

Murray, Diane and Al Kagan. "Reinventing Program Management." CIO Insight (2nd Quarter 2010).

Nidumolu, Sarma R. and Mani Subramani. "The Matrix of Control: Combining Process and Structure Approaches to Management Software Development." Journal of Management Information Systems 20, no. 3 (Winter 2004).

Pfefferman, Mark. "App Development Strategy Cuts Costs, Ensures Compliance," Baseline (September/October 2011).

Polites, Greta L. and Elena Karahanna. "Shackled to the Status Quo: The Inhibiting Effects of Incumbent System Habit, Switching Costs, and Inertia on New System Acceptance." MIS Quarterly 36, No. 1 (March 2012).

Quan, Jin "Jim", Quing Hu, and Paul J. Hart."Information Technology Investments and Firms' Performance-A Duopoly Perspective." Journal of Management Information Systems 20, no. 3 (Winter 2004).

Rai, Arun, Sandra S. Lang, and Robert B. Welker. "Assessing the Validity of IS Success Models: An Empirical Test and Theoretical Analysis." Information Systems Research 13, no. 1 (March 2002).

Rivard, Suzanne and Liette Lapointe. "Information Technology Implementers' Responses to User Resistance: Nature and Effects." MIS Quarterly 36, No. 3 (September 2012).

Robey, Daniel, Jeanne W. Ross, and Marie-Claude Boudreau. "Learning to Implement Enterprise Systems: An Exploratory Study of the Dialectics of Change." Journal of Management Information Systems 19, no. 1 (Summer 2002).

Ross, Jeanne W. and Cynthia M. Beath." Beyond the Business Case: New Approaches to IT Investment." Sloan Management Review 43, no.2 (Winter 2002).

Ryan, Sherry D., David A. Harrison, and Lawrence L Schkade." Information Technology Investment Decisions: When Do Cost and Benefits in the Social Subsystem Matter?" Journal of Management Information Systems 19, no. 2 (Fall 2002).

Sambamurthy, V., Anandhi Bharadwaj, and Varun Grover. "Shaping Agility Through Digital Options: Reconceptualizing the Role of Information Technology in Contemporary Firms." MIS Quarterly 27, no. 2 (June 2003).

Santhanam, Radhika and Edward Hartono. "Issues in Linking Information Technology Capability to Firm Performance." MIS Quarterly 27, no. 1 (March 2003).

Sauer, Chris, Andrew Gemino, and Blaize Horner Reich. "The Impact of Size and Volatility on IT Project Performance. "Communications of the ACM 50, no. 11 (November 2007).

Schmidt, Roy, Kalle Lyytinen, Mark Keil, and Paul Cule. "Identifying Software Project Risks: An International Delphi Study." Journal of Management Information Systems 17, no. 4 (Spring 2001)

Schwalbe, Kathy. Information Technology Project Management, 7/e. Cengage (2014).

Sharma, Rajeev and Philip Yetton. "The Contingent Effects of Training, Technical Complexity, and Task Interdependence on Successful Information Systems Implementation." MIS Quarterly 31, no. 2 (June 2007).

Smith, H. Jeff, Mark Keil, and Gordon Depledge. "Keeping Mum as the Project Goes Under." Journal of Management Information Systems 18, no. 2 (Fall 2001)

Speier, Cheri and Michael. G. Morris. "The Influence of Query Interface Design on Decision-Making Performance." MIS Quarterly 27, no. 3 (September 2003).

Straub, Detmar W., Arun Rai and Richard Klein. "Measuring Firm Performance at the Network Level: A Nomology of the Business Impact of Digital Supply Networks." Journal of Management Information Systems 21, no 1 (Summer 2004).

Swanson, E. Burton. Information System Implementation. Homewood, IL: Richard D. Irwin (1988).

Tallon, Paul P, Kenneth L. Kraemer, and Vijay Gurbaxani. "Executives' Perceptions of the Business Value of Information Technology: A Process-Oriented Approach." Journal of Management Information Systems 16, no. 4 (Spring 2000).

Taudes, Alfred, Markus Feurstein, and Andreas Mild. "Options Analysis of Software Platform Decisions: A Case Study." MIS Quarterly 24, no. 2 (June 2000).

Thatcher, Matt E. and Jim R. Oliver. "The Impact of Technology Investments on a Firm's Production Efficiency, Product Quality, and Productivity." Journal of Management Information Systems 18, no. 2 (Fall 2001).

Tiwana, Amrit, and Mark Keil. "Control in Internal and Outsourced Software Projects." Journal of Management Information Systems 26, No. 3 (Winter 2010).

Tornatsky, Louis G., J. D. Eveland, M. G. Boylan, W. A. Hetzner, E. C. Johnson, D. Roitman, and J. Schneider. The Process of Technological Innovation: Reviewing the Literature. Washington, DC: National Science Foundation (1983).

Vaidyanathan, Ganesh. Project Management: Process, Technology and Practice. Upper Saddle River, NJ: Prentice Hall (2013).

Venkatesh, Viswanath, Michael G. Morris, Gordon B Davis, and Fred D. Davis." User Acceptance of Information Technology: Toward a Unified View." MIS Quarterly 27, No. 3 (September 2003).

Wang, Eric T.G., Gary Klein, and James J. Jiang. "ERP Misfit: Country of Origin and Organizational Factors." Journal of Management Information Systems 23, No. 1 (Summer 2006).

Westerman, George. "IT is from Venus, Non-IT Is from Mars," The Wall Street Journal (April 2, 2012).

Xia, Weidong, and Gwanhoo Lee. "Complexity of Information Systems Development Projects." Journal of Management Information Systems 22, no. 1 (Summer 2005).

Xue, Yajion, Huigang Liang, and William R. Boulton. "Information Technology Governance in Information Technology Investment Decision Processes: The Impact of Investment Characteristics, External Environment, and Internal Context." MIS Quarterly 32, no. 1 (March 2008).

Yin, Robert K. "Life Histories of Innovations: How New Practices Become Routinized." Public Administration Review (January–February 1981).

Zhu, Kevin and Kenneth L. Kraemer."E-Commerce Metrics for Net-Enhanced Organizations: Assessing the Value of e-Commerce to Firm Performance in the Manufacturing Sector." Information Systems Research 13, no.3 (September 2002).

Zhu, Kevin, Kenneth L. Kraemer, Sean Xu, and Jason Dedrick. "Information Technology Payoff in E-Business Environments: An International Perspective on Value Creation of E-business in the Financial Services Industry." Journal of Management Information Systems 21, no. 1 (Summer 2004).

Zhu, Kevin. "The Complementarity of Information Technology Infrastructure and E-Commerce Capability: A Resource-Based Assessment of Their Business Value." Journal of Management Information Systems 21, no. 1 (Summer 2004).

CHAPTER 15

Krishna, S., Sundeep Sahay, and Geoff Walsham. "Managing Cross-Cultural Issues in Global Software Outsourcing." Communications of the ACM 47, No. 4 (April 2004).

Barboza, David. "Supply Chain for IPhone Highlights Costs in China." The New York Times (July 5, 2010).

Biehl, Markus. "Success Factors For Implementing Global Information Systems." Communications of the ACM 50, No. 1 (January 2007).

Bisson, Peter, Elizabeth Stephenson, and S. Patrick Viguerie. "Global Forces: An Introduction." McKinsey Quarterly (June 2010).

Cox, Butler. Globalization: The IT Challenge. Sunnyvale, CA: Amdahl Executive Institute (1991).

Davison, Robert. "Cultural Complications of ERP." Communications of the ACM 45, no. 7 (July 2002).

Deans, Candace P., and Michael J. Kane. International Dimensions of Information Systems and Technology. Boston, MA: PWS-Kent (1992).

Dewhurst, Martin, Jonathan Harris, and Suzanne Heywood. "The Global Company's Challenge." McKinsey Quarterly (June 2012).

Duhigg, Charles and Keith Bradsher. "How U.S. Lost Out on iPhone Work" New York Times (January 21, 2012).

Ein-Dor, Philip, Seymour E. Goodman, and Peter Wolcott." From Via Maris to Electronic Highway: The Internet in Canaan." Communications of the ACM 43, no. 7 (July 2000).

Farhoomand, Ali, Virpi Kristiina Tuunainen, and Lester W. Yee. "Barrier to Global Electronic Commerce: A Cross-Country Study of Hong Kong and Finland." Journal of Organizational Computing and Electronic Commerce 10, no. 1 (2000).

Ghislanzoni, Giancarlo, Risto Penttinen, an David Turnbull. "The Multilocal Challenge: Managing Cross-Border Functions." The McKinsey Quarterly (March 2008).

Ives, Blake, and Sirkka Jarvenpaa. "Applications of Global Information Technology: Key Issues for Management." MIS Quarterly 15, no. 1 (March 1991).

Ives, Blake, S. L. Jarvenpaa, R. O. Mason, "Global Business Drivers: Aligning Information Technology to Global Business Strategy," IBM Systems Journal Vol 32, No 1, 1993.

King, William R. and Vikram Sethi. "An Empirical Analysis of the Organization of Transnational Information Systems." Journal of Management Information Systems 15, no. 4 (Spring 1999).

Kirsch, Laurie J. "Deploying Common Systems Globally: The Dynamic of Control." Information Systems Research 15, no. 4 (December 2004).

Liang, Huigang, Yajiong Xue, William R. Boulton, and Terry Anthony Byrd. "Why Western Vendors Don't Dominate China's ERP Market." Communications of the ACM 47, no. 7 (July 2004).

Martinsons, Maris G. "ERP In China: One Package Two Profiles," Communications of the ACM 47, no. 7 (July 2004).

Quelch, John A., and Lisa R. Klein. "The Internet and International Marketing." Sloan Management Review (Spring 1996).

Roche, Edward M. Managing Information Technology in Multinational Corporations. New York: Macmillan (1992).

Shore, Barry. "Enterprise Integration Across the Globally Dispersed Service Organization. Communications of the ACM 49, NO. 6 (June 2006).

Soh, Christina, Sia Siew Kien, and Joanne Tay-Yap. "Cultural Fits and Misfits: Is ERP a Universal Solution? "Communications of the ACM 43, no. 3 (April 2000).

Tractinsky, Noam, and Sirkka L. Jarvenpaa. "Information Systems Design Decisions in a Global Versus Domestic Context." MIS Quarterly 19, no. 4 (December 1995).

Watson, Richard T., Gigi G. Kelly, Robert D. Galliers, and James C. Brancheau. "Key Issues in Information Systems Management: An International Perspective." Journal of Management Information Systems 13, no. 4 (Spring 1997).

Glossary

3-D printing Uses machines to make solid objects, layer by layer, from specifications in a digital file. Also known as additive manufacturing.

3G networks Cellular networks based on packet-switched technology with speeds ranging from 144 Kbps for mobile users to over 2 Mbps for stationary users, enabling users to transmit video, graphics, and other rich media, in addition to voice.

4G networks The next evolution in wireless communication is entirely packet switched and capable of providing between 1 Mbps and 1 Gbps speeds; up to ten times faster than 3G networks. Not widely deployed in 2010.

acceptable use policy (AUP) Defines acceptable uses of the firm's information resources and computing equipment, including desktop and laptop computers, wireless devices, telephones, and the Internet, and specifies consequences for noncompliance.

acceptance testing Provides the final certification that the system is ready to be used in a production setting.

accountability The mechanisms for assessing responsibility for decisions made and actions taken.

advertising revenue model Web site generating revenue by attracting a large audience

affiliate revenue model an e-commerce revenue model in which Web sites are paid as "affiliates" for sending their visitors to other sites in return for a referral fee.

agency theory Economic theory that views the firm as a nexus of contracts among self-interested individuals who must be supervised and managed.

agent-based modeling Modeling complex phenomena as systems of autonomous agents that follow relatively simple rules for interaction.

agile development Rapid delivery of working software by breaking a large project into a series of small sub-projects that are completed in short periods of time using iteration and continuous feedback.

analytic platform Preconfigured hardware-software system that is specifically designed high-speed analysis of large datasets.

analytical CRM Customer relationship management applications dealing with the analysis of customer data to provide information for improving business performance.

Android A mobile operating system developed by Android, Inc. (purchased by Google) and later the Open Handset Alliance as a flexible, upgradeable mobile device platform.

antivirus software Software designed to detect, and often eliminate, computer viruses from an information system.

application controls: Specific controls unique to each computerized application that ensure that only authorized data are completely and accurately processed by that application.

application server Software that handles all application operations between browser-based computers and a company's back-end business applications or databases.

apps Small pieces of software that run on the Internet, on your computer, or on your cell phone and are generally delivered over the Internet.

artificial intelligence (AI) The effort to develop computer-based systems that can behave like humans, with the ability to learn languages, accomplish physical tasks, use a perceptual apparatus, and emulate human expertise and decision making.

attribute A piece of information describing a particular entity.

augmented reality A technology for enhancing visualization. Provides a live direct or indirect view of a physical real-world environment whose elements are augmented by virtual computer-generated imagery.

authentication The ability of each party in a transaction to ascertain the identity of the other party.

automation Using the computer to speed up the performance of existing tasks.

autonomic computing Effort to develop systems that can manage themselves without user intervention.

backward chaining A strategy for searching the rule base in an expert system that acts like a problem solver by beginning with a hypothesis and seeking out more information until the hypothesis is either proved or disproved.

balanced scorecard method Framework for operationalizing a firms strategic plan by focusing on measurable financial, business process, customer, and learning and growth outcomes of firm performance.

bandwidth The capacity of a communications channel as measured by the difference between the highest and lowest frequencies that can be transmitted by that channel.

behavioral models Descriptions of management based on behavioral scientists' observations of what managers actually do in their jobs.

behavioral targeting Tracking the click-streams (history of clicking behavior) of individuals across multiple Web sites for the purpose of understanding their interests and intentions, and exposing them to advertisements which are uniquely suited to their interests.

benchmarking Setting strict standards for products, services, or activities and measuring organizational performance against those standards.

best practices The most successful solutions or problem-solving methods that have been developed by a specific organization or industry.

big data Datasets with volumes so huge that they are beyond the ability of typical relational DBMS to capture, store, and analyze. The data are often unstructured or semi-structured.

biometric authentication Technology for authenticating system users that compares a person's unique characteristics such as fingerprints, face, or retinal image, against a stored set profile of these characteristics.

bit A binary digit representing the smallest unit of data in a computer system. It can only have one of two states, representing 0 or 1.

blade server Entire computer that fits on a single, thin card (or blade) and that is plugged into a single chassis to save space, power and complexity.

blog Popular term for Weblog, designating an informal yet structured Web site where individuals can publish stories, opinions, and links to other Web sites of interest.

blogosphere Totality of blog-related Web sites.

Bluetooth Standard for wireless personal area networks that can transmit up to 722 Kbps within a 10-meter area.

botnet   A group of computers that have been infected with bot malware without users' knowledge, enabling a hacker to use the amassed resources of the computers to launch distributed denial-of-service attacks, phishing campaigns or spam.

broadband   High-speed transmission technology. Also designates a single communications medium that can transmit multiple channels of data simultaneously.

bugs   Software program code defects.

bullwhip effect   Distortion of information about the demand for a product as it passes from one entity to the next across the supply chain.

business continuity planning   Planning that focuses on how the company can restore business operations after a disaster strikes.

business driver   A force in the environment to which businesses must respond and that influences the direction of business.

business ecosystem   Loosely coupled but interdependent networks of suppliers, distributors, outsourcing firms, transportation service firms, and technology manufacturers

business functions   Specialized tasks performed in a business organization, including manufacturing and production, sales and marketing, finance and accounting, and human resources.

business intelligence   Applications and technologies to help users make better business decisions.

business model   An abstraction of what an enterprise is and how the enterprise delivers a product or service, showing how the enterprise creates wealth.

business performance management   Attempts to systematically translate a firm's strategies (e.g., differentiation, low-cost producer, market share growth, and scope of operation) into operational targets.

business process management   Business process management (BPM) is an approach to business which aims to continuously improve and manage business processes.

business process redesign   Type of organizational change in which business processes are analyzed, simplified, and redesigned.

business processes   The unique ways in which organizations coordinate and organize work activities, information, and knowledge to produce a product or service.

business-to-business (B2B) electronic commerce   Electronic sales of goods and services among businesses.

business-to-consumer (B2C) electronic commerce   Electronic retailing of products and services directly to individual consumers.

byte   A string of bits, usually eight, used to store one number or character in a computer system.

cable Internet connections   Internet connections that use digital cable lines to deliver high-speed Internet access to homes and businesses.

capital budgeting   The process of analyzing and selecting various proposals for capital expenditures.

carpal tunnel syndrome (CTS)   Type of RSI in which pressure on the median nerve through the wrist's bony carpal tunnel structure produces pain.

case-based reasoning (CBR)   Artificial intelligence technology that represents knowledge as a database of cases and solutions.

cell phone   A device that transmits voice or data, using radio waves to communicate with radio antennas placed within adjacent geographic areas called cells.

change agent   In the context of implementation, the individual acting as the catalyst during the change process to ensure successful organizational adaptation to a new system or innovation.

change management   Managing the impact of organizational change associated with an innovation, such as a new information system.

chat   Live, interactive conversations over a public network.

chief information officer (CIO)   Senior manager in charge of the information systems function in the firm.

chief knowledge officer (CKO)   Senior executive in charge of the organization's knowledge management program.

chief privacy officer (CPO)   Responsible for ensuring the company complies with existing data privacy laws.

chief security officer (CSO)   Heads a formal security function for the organization and is responsible for enforcing the firm's security policy.

choice   Simon's third stage of decision making, when the individual selects among the various solution alternatives.

Chrome OS   Google's lightweight computer operating system for users who do most of their computing on the Internet; runs on computers ranging from netbooks to desktop computers.

churn rate   Measurement of the number of customers who stop using or purchasing products or services from a company. Used as an indicator of the growth or decline of a firm's customer base.

classical model of management   Traditional description of management that focused on its formal functions of planning, organizing, coordinating, deciding, and controlling.

click fraud   Fraudulently clicking on an online ad in pay per click advertising to generate an improper charge per click.

client   The user point-of-entry for the required function in client/server computing. Normally a desktop computer, workstation, or laptop computer.

client/server computing   A model for computing that splits processing between clients and servers on a network, assigning functions to the machine most able to perform the function.

cloud computing   Web-based applications that are stored on remote servers and accessed via the "cloud" of the Internet using a standard Web browser.

collaboration   Working with others to achieve shared and explicit goals.

co-location   a kind of Web site hosting in which firm purchase or rent a physical server computer at a hosting company's location in order to operate a Web site.

community provider   a Web site business model that creates a digital online environment where people with similar interests can transact (buy and sell goods); share interests, photos, videos; communicate with like-minded people; receive interest-related information; and even play out fantasies by adopting online personalities called avatars.

communities of practice (COPs)   Informal social networks of professionals and employees within and outside the firm who have similar work-related activities and interests and share their knowledge.

competitive forces model   Model used to describe the interaction of external influences, specifically threats and opportunities, that affect an organization's strategy and ability to compete.

complementary assets   Additional assets required to derive value from a primary investment.

component-based development   Building large software systems by combining pre-existing software components.

computer abuse   The commission of acts involving a computer that may not be illegal but are considered unethical.

computer crime   The commission of illegal acts through the use of a computer or against a computer system.

computer forensics   The scientific collection, examination, authentication, preservation, and analysis of data held on or retrieved from computer storage media in such a way that the information can be used as evidence in a court of law.

computer hardware   Physical equipment used for input, processing, and output activities in an information system.

computer literacy   Knowledge about information technology, focusing on understanding of how computer-based technologies work.

computer software   Detailed, preprogrammed instructions that control and coordinate the work of computer hardware components in an information system.

computer virus Rogue software program that attaches itself to other software programs or data files in order to be executed, often causing hardware and software malfunctions.

computer vision syndrome (CVS) Eyestrain condition related to computer display screen use; symptoms include headaches, blurred vision, and dry and irritated eyes.

computer-aided design (CAD) Information system that automates the creation and revision of designs using sophisticated graphics software.

computer-aided software engineering (CASE) Automation of step-by-step methodologies for software and systems development to reduce the amounts of repetitive work the developer needs to do.

consumer-to-consumer (C2C) electronic commerce Consumers selling goods and services electronically to other consumers.

consumerization of IT New information technology originating in the consumer market that spreads to business organizations.

controls All of the methods, policies, and procedures that ensure protection of the organization's assets, accuracy and reliability of its records, and operational adherence to management standards.

conversion The process of changing from the old system to the new system.

cookies Tiny file deposited on a computer hard drive when an individual visits certain Web sites. Used to identify the visitor and track visits to the Web site.

cooptation Bringing the opposition into the process of designing and implementing a solution without giving up control of the direction and nature of the change.

copyright A statutory grant that protects creators of intellectual property against copying by others for any purpose for a minimum of 70 years.

core competency Activity at which a firm excels as a world-class leader.

core systems Systems that support functions that are absolutely critical to the organization.

cost transparency the ability of consumers to discover the actual costs merchants pay for products.

counterimplementation A deliberate strategy to thwart the implementation of an information system or an innovation in an organization.

cross-selling Marketing complementary products to customers.

crowdsourcing Using large Internet audiences for advice, market feedback, new ideas and solutions to business problems. Related to the 'wisdom of crowds' theory.

culture The set of fundamental assumptions about what products the organization should produce, how and where it should produce them, and for whom they should be produced.

customer lifetime value (CLTV) Difference between revenues produced by a specific customer and the expenses for acquiring and servicing that customer minus the cost of promotional marketing over the lifetime of the customer relationship, expressed in today's dollars.

customer relationship management (CRM) Business and technology discipline that uses information systems to coordinate all of the business processes surrounding the firm's interactions with its customers in sales, marketing, and service.

customer relationship management systems Information systems that track all the ways in which a company interacts with its customers and analyze these interactions to optimize revenue, profitability, customer satisfaction, and customer retention.

customization The modification of a software package to meet an organization's unique requirements without destroying the package software's integrity.

customization In e-commerce, changing a delivered product or service based on a user's preferences or prior behavior.

cyberlocker Online file-sharing service that allows users to upload files to a secure online storage site from which the files can be synchronized and shared with others.

cybervandalism Intentional disruption, defacement, or destruction of a Web site or corporate information system.

cyberwarfare State-sponsored activity designed to cripple and defeat another state or nation by damaging or disrupting its computers or networks.

data Streams of raw facts representing events occurring in organizations or the physical environment before they have been organized and arranged into a form that people can understand and use.

data administration A special organizational function for managing the organization's data resources, concerned with information policy, data planning, maintenance of data dictionaries, and data quality standards.

data cleansing Activities for detecting and correcting data in a database or file that are incorrect, incomplete, improperly formatted, or redundant. Also known as data scrubbing.

data definition DBMS capability that specifies the structure and content of the database.

data dictionary An automated or manual tool for storing and organizing information about the data maintained in a database.

data element A field.

data flow diagram (DFD) Primary tool for structured analysis that graphically illustrates a system's component process and the flow of data between them.

data governance Policies and processes for managing the availability, usability, integrity, and security of the firm's data.

data inconsistency The presence of different values for same attribute when the same data are stored in multiple locations.

data management technology Software governing the organization of data on physical storage media.

data manipulation language A language associated with a database management system that end users and programmers use to manipulate data in the database.

data mart A small data warehouse containing only a portion of the organization's data for a specified function or population of users.

data mining Analysis of large pools of data to find patterns and rules that can be used to guide decision making and predict future behavior.

data quality audit A survey and/or sample of files to determine accuracy and completeness of data in an information system.

data redundancy The presence of duplicate data in multiple data files.

data visualization Technology for helping users see patterns and relationships in large amounts of data by presenting the data in graphical form.

data warehouse A database, with reporting and query tools, that stores current and historical data extracted from various operational systems and consolidated for management reporting and analysis.

data workers People such as secretaries or bookkeepers who process the organization's paperwork.

database A group of related files.

database (rigorous definition) A collection of data organized to service many applications at the same time by storing and managing data so that they appear to be in one location.

database administration Refers to the more technical and operational aspects of managing data, including physical database design and maintenance.

database management system (DBMS) Special software to create and maintain a database and enable individual business applications to extract the data they need without having to create separate files or data definitions in their computer programs.

database server A computer in a client/server environment that is responsible for running a DBMS to process SQL statements and perform database management tasks.

decisional roles   Mintzberg's classification for managerial roles where managers initiate activities, handle disturbances, allocate resources, and negotiate conflicts.

decision-support systems (DSS)   Information systems at the organization's management level that combine data and sophisticated analytical models or data analysis tools to support semistructured and unstructured decision making.

deep packet inspection (DPI)   Technology for managing network traffic by examining data packets, sorting out low-priority data from higher priority business-critical data, and sending packets in order of priority.

demand planning   Determining how much product a business needs to make to satisfy all its customers' demands.

denial of service (DoS) attack   Flooding a network server or Web server with false communications or requests for services in order to crash the network.

Descartes' rule of change   A principle that states that if an action cannot be taken repeatedly, then it is not right to be taken at any time.

design   Simon's second stage of decision making, when the individual conceives of possible alternative solutions to a problem.

digital asset management systems   Classify, store, and distribute digital objects such as photographs, graphic images, video, and audio content.

digital certificate   An attachment to an electronic message to verify the identity of the sender and to provide the receiver with the means to encode a reply.

digital dashboard   Displays all of a firm's key performance indicators as graphs and charts on a single screen to provide one-page overview of all the critical measurements necessary to make key executive decisions.

digital divide   Large disparities in access to computers and the Internet among different social groups and different locations.

digital firm   Organization where nearly all significant business processes and relationships with customers, suppliers, and employees are digitally enabled, and key corporate assets are managed through digital means.

digital goods   Goods that can be delivered over a digital network.

Digital Millennium Copyright Act (DMCA)   Adjusts copyright laws to the Internet Age by making it illegal to make, distribute, or use devices that circumvent technology-based protections of copy-righted materials.

digital subscriber line (DSL)   A group of technologies providing high-capacity transmission over existing copper telephone lines.

direct cutover   A risky conversion approach where the new system completely replaces the old one on an appointed day.

disaster recovery planning   Planning for the restoration of computing and communications services after they have been disrupted.

disintermediation   The removal of organizations or business process layers responsible for certain intermediary steps in a value chain.

disruptive technologies   Technologies with disruptive impact on industries and businesses, rendering existing products, services and business models obsolete.

distributed denial-of-service (DDoS) attack   Numerous computers inundating and overwhelming a network from numerous launch points.

documentation   Descriptions of how an information system works from either a technical or end-user standpoint.

domain name   English-like name that corresponds to the unique 32-bit numeric Internet Protocol (IP) address for each computer connected to the Internet

Domain Name System (DNS)   A hierarchical system of servers maintaining a database enabling the conversion of domain names to their numeric IP addresses.

domestic exporter   Form of business organization characterized by heavy centralization of corporate activities in the home county of origin.

downtime   Period of time in which an information system is not operational.

drill down   The ability to move from summary data to lower and lower levels of detail.

drive-by download   Malware that comes with a downloaded file a user intentionally or unintentionally requests.

due process   A process in which laws are well-known and understood and there is an ability to appeal to higher authorities to ensure that laws are applied correctly.

dynamic pricing   Pricing of items based on real-time interactions between buyers and sellers that determine what a item is worth at any particular moment.

e-government   Use of the Internet and related technologies to digitally enable government and public sector agencies' relationships with citizens, businesses, and other arms of government.

efficient customer response system   System that directly links consumer behavior back to distribution, production, and supply chains.

electronic business (e-business)   The use of the Internet and digital technology to execute all the business processes in the enterprise. Includes e-commerce as well as processes for the internal management of the firm and for coordination with suppliers and other business partners.

electronic commerce   The process of buying and selling goods and services electronically involving transactions using the Internet, networks, and other digital technologies.

electronic data interchange (EDI)   The direct computer-to-computer exchange between two organizations of standard business transactions, such as orders, shipment instructions, or payments.

e-mail   The computer-to-computer exchange of messages.

employee relationship management (ERM)   Software dealing with employee issues that are closely related to CRM, such as setting objectives, employee performance management, performance-based compensation, and employee training.

encryption   The coding and scrambling of messages to prevent their being read or accessed without authorization.

end-user development   The development of information systems by end users with little or no formal assistance from technical specialists.

end-user interface   The part of an information system through which the end user interacts with the system, such as on-line screens and commands.

end users   Representatives of departments outside the information systems group for whom applications are developed.

enterprise applications   Systems that can coordinate activities, decisions, and knowledge across many different functions, levels, and business units in a firm. Include enterprise systems, supply chain management systems, and knowledge management systems.

enterprise content management systems   Help organizations manage structured and semistructured knowledge, providing corporate repositories of documents, reports, presentations, and best practices and capabilities for collecting and organizing e-mail and graphic objects.

enterprise software   Set of integrated modules for applications such as sales and distribution, financial accounting, investment management, materials management, production planning, plant maintenance, and human resources that allow data to be used by multiple functions and business processes.

enterprise systems   Integrated enterprise-wide information systems that coordinate key internal processes of the firm.

enterprise-wide knowledge management systems General-purpose, firmwide systems that collect, store, distribute, and apply digital content and knowledge.

entity A person, place, thing, or event about which information must be kept.

entity-relationship diagram A methodology for documenting databases illustrating the relationship between various entities in the database.

ergonomics The interaction of people and machines in the work environment, including the design of jobs, health issues, and the end-user interface of information systems.

e-tailer Online retail stores from the giant Amazon to tiny local stores that have Web sites where retail goods are sold.

ethical "no free lunch" rule Assumption that all tangible and intangible objects are owned by someone else, unless there is a specific declaration otherwise, and that the creator wants compensation for this work.

ethics Principles of right and wrong that can be used by individuals acting as free moral agents to make choices to guide their behavior.

evil twins Wireless networks that pretend to be legitimate to entice participants to log on and reveal passwords or credit card numbers.

exchange Third-party Net marketplace that is primarily transaction oriented and that connects many buyers and suppliers for spot purchasing.

executive support systems (ESS) Information systems at the organization's strategic level designed to address unstructured decision making through advanced graphics and communications.

expert system Knowledge-intensive computer program that captures the expertise of a human in limited domains of knowledge.

explicit knowledge Knowledge that has been documented.

Extensible Markup Language (XML) General purpose language that describes the structure of a document and XML can perform presentation, communication, and storage of data, allowing data to be manipulated by the computer.

external integration tools Project management technique that links the work of the implementation team to that of users at all organizational levels.

extranet Private intranet that is accessible to authorized outsiders.

Fair Information Practices (FIP) A set of principles originally set forth in 1973 that governs the collection and use of information about individuals and forms the basis of most U.S. and European privacy laws.

fault-tolerant computer systems Systems that contain extra hardware, software, and power supply components that can back a system up and keep it running to prevent system failure.

feasibility study As part of the systems analysis process, the way to determine whether the solution is achievable, given the organization's resources and constraints.

feedback Output that is returned to the appropriate members of the organization to help them evaluate or correct input.

field A grouping of characters into a word, a group of words, or a complete number, such as a person's name or age.

file transfer protocol (FTP) Tool for retrieving and transferring files from a remote computer.

file A group of records of the same type.

firewall Hardware and software placed between an organization's internal network and an external network to prevent outsiders from invading private networks.

folksonomies User-created taxonomies for classifying and sharing information.

foreign key Field in a database table that enables users find related information in another database table.

formal control tools Project management technique that helps monitor the progress toward completion of a task and fulfillment of goals.

formal planning tools Project management technique that structures and sequences tasks, budgeting time, money, and technical resources required to complete the tasks.

forward chaining A strategy for searching the rule base in an expert system that begins with the information entered by the user and searches the rule base to arrive at a conclusion.

fourth-generation language A programming language that can be employed directly by end users or less-skilled programmers to develop computer applications more rapidly than conventional programming languages.

franchiser Form of business organization in which a product is created, designed, financed, and initially produced in the home country, but for product-specific reasons relies heavily on foreign personnel for further production, marketing, and human resources.

free/fremium revenue model an e-commerce revenue model in which a firm offers basic services or content for free, while charging a premium for advanced or high value features.

fuzzy logic Rule-based AI that tolerates imprecision by using nonspecific terms called membership functions to solve problems.

Gantt chart Visually representats the timing, duration, and resource requirements of project tasks.

general controls Overall control environment governing the design, security, and use of computer programs and the security of data files in general throughout the organization's information technology infrastructure.

genetic algorithms Problem-solving methods that promote the evolution of solutions to specified problems using the model of living organisms adapting to their environment.

geoadvertising Delivering ads to users based on their GPS location.

geographic information system (GIS) System with software that can analyze and display data using digitized maps to enhance planning and decision-making.

geoinformation services Information on local places and things based on the GPS position of the user.

geosocial services Social networking based on the GPS location of users.

global culture The development of common expectations, shared artifacts, and social norms among different cultures and peoples

Golden Rule Putting oneself in the place of others as the object of a decision.

Gramm-Leach-Bliley Act Requires financial institutions to ensure the security and confidentiality of customer data.

green computing Refers to practices and technologies for designing, manufacturing, using, and disposing of computers, servers, and associated devices such as monitors, printers, storage devices, and networking and communications systems to minimize impact on the environment.

grid computing Applying the resources of many computers in a network to a single problem.

group decision-support system (GDSS) An interactive computer-based system to facilitate the solution to unstructured problems by a set of decision makers working together as a group.

hacker A person who gains unauthorized access to a computer network for profit, criminal mischief, or personal pleasure.

Hadoop Open-source software framework that enables distributed parallel processing of huge amounts of data across many inexpensive computers.

hertz Measure of frequency of electrical impulses per second, with 1 Hertz equivalent to 1 cycle per second.

high-availability computing   Tools and technologies ,including backup hardware resources, to enable a system to recover quickly from a crash.

HIPAA   Law outlining rules for medical security, privacy, and the management of health care records.

hotspot   A specific geographic location in which an access point provides public Wi-Fi network service.

HTML (Hypertext Markup Language) Page description language for creating Web pages.

HTML5   Next evolution of HTML, which will make it possible to embed images, video, and audio directly into a document without add-on software.

hubs   Very simple devices that connect network components, sending a packet of data to all other connected devices.

hybrid AI systems   Integration of multiple AI technologies into a single application to take advantage of the best features of these technologies.

hybrid cloud   Computing model where firms use both their own IT infrastructure and also public cloud computing services.

hypertext transfer protocol (HTTP)   The communications standard used to transfer pages on the Web. Defines how messages are formatted and transmitted.

identity management   Business processes and software tools for identifying the valid users of a system and controlling their access to system resources.

identity theft   Theft of key pieces of personal information, such as credit card or Social Security numbers, in order to obtain merchandise and services in the name of the victim or to obtain false credentials.

Immanuel Kant's Categorical Imperative   A principle that states that if an action is not right for everyone to take it is not right for anyone.

implementation   All the organizational activities surrounding the adoption, management, and routinization of an innovation, such as a new information system.

in-memory computing   Technology for very rapid analysis and processing of large quantities of data by storing the data in the computer's main memory rather than in secondary storage.

inference engine   The strategy used to search through the rule base in an expert system; can be forward or backward chaining.

information   Data that have been shaped into a form that is meaningful and useful to human beings.

information asymmetry   Situation where the relative bargaining power of two parties in a transaction is determined by one party in the transaction possessing more information essential to the transaction than the other party.

information density   The total amount and quality of information available to all market participants, consumers, and merchants.

information policy   Formal rules governing the maintenance, distribution, and use of information in an organization.

information requirements   A detailed statement of the information needs that a new system must satisfy; identifies who needs what information, and when, where, and how the information is needed.

information rights   The rights that individuals and organizations have with respect to information that pertains to themselves.

information system   Interrelated components working together to collect, process, store, and disseminate information to support decision making, coordination, control, analysis, and visualization in an organization.

information systems department   The formal organizational unit that is responsible for the information systems function in the organization.

information systems literacy   Broad-based understanding of information systems that includes behavioral knowledge about organizations and individuals using information systems as well as technical knowledge about computers.

information systems managers   Leaders of the various specialists in the information systems department.

information systems plan   A road map indicating the direction of systems development: the rationale, the current situation, the management strategy, the implementation plan, and the budget.

information technology (IT)   All the hardware and software technologies a firm needs to achieve its business objectives.

information technology (IT) infrastructure   Computer hardware, software, data, storage technology, and networks providing a portfolio of shared IT resources for the organization.

informational roles   Mintzberg's classification for managerial roles where managers act as the nerve centers of their organizations, receiving and disseminating critical information.

informed consent   Consent given with knowledge of all the facts needed to make a rational decision.

input   The capture or collection of raw data from within the organization or from its external environment for processing in an information system.

instant messaging   Chat service that allows participants to create their own private chat channels so that a person can be alerted whenever someone on his or her private list is on-line to initiate a chat session with that particular individual.

intangible benefits   Benefits that are not easily quantified; they include more efficient customer service or enhanced decision making.

intellectual property   Intangible property created by individuals or corporations that is subject to protections under trade secret, copyright, and patent law.

intelligence   The first of Simon's four stages of decision making, when the individual collects information to identify problems occurring in the organization.

intelligent agent   Software program that uses a built-in or learned knowledge base to carry out specific, repetitive, and predictable tasks for an individual user, business process, or software application.

intelligent techniques   Technologies that aid human decision makers by capturing individual and collective knowledge, discovering patterns and behaviors in large quantities of data, and generating solutions to problems that are too large and complex for human beings to solve on their own.

internal integration tools   Project management technique that ensures that the implementation team operates as a cohesive unit.

international information systems architecture   The basic information systems required by organizations to coordinate worldwide trade and other activities.

Internet   Global network of networks using universal standards to connect millions of different networks.

Internet Protocol (IP) address   Four-part numeric address indicating a unique computer location on the Internet.

Internet Service Provider (ISP)   A commercial organization with a permanent connection to the Internet that sells temporary connections to subscribers.

Internet2   Research network with new protocols and transmission speeds that provides an infrastructure for supporting high-bandwidth Internet applications.

interorganizational systems   Information systems that automate the flow of information across organizational boundaries and link a company to its customers, distributors, or suppliers.

interpersonal roles   Mintzberg's classification for managerial roles where managers act as figureheads and leaders for the organization.

intranet   An internal network based on Internet and World Wide Web technology and standards.

intrusion detection system   Tools to monitor the most vulnerable points in a network to detect and deter unauthorized intruders.

investment workstation   Powerful desktop computer for financial specialists, which is optimized to access and manipulate massive amounts of financial data.

iOS Operating system for the Apple iPad, iPhone, and iPod Touch.

IPv6 New IP addressing system using 128-bit IP addresses. Stands for Internet Protocol version 6.

IT governance Strategy and policies for using information technology within an organization, specifying the decision rights and accountabilities to ensure that information technology supports the organization's strategies and objectives.

iterative A process of repeating over and over again the steps to build a system.

Java Programming language that can deliver only the software functionality needed for a particular task, such as a small applet downloaded from a network; can run on any computer and operating system.

Joint Application Design (JAD) Process to accelerate the generation of information requirements by having end users and information systems specialists work together in intensive interactive design sessions.

just-in-time Scheduling system for minimizing inventory by having components arrive exactly at the moment they are needed and finished goods shipped as soon as they leave the assembly line.

key field A field in a record that uniquely identifies instances of that record so that it can be retrieved, updated, or sorted.

key performance indicators Measures proposed by senior management for understanding how well the firm is performing along specified dimensions.

keylogger Spyware that records every keystroke made on a computer to steal personal information or passwords or to launch Internet attacks.

knowledge Concepts, experience, and insight that provide a framework for creating, evaluating, and using information.

knowledge base Model of human knowledge that is used by expert systems.

knowledge discovery Identification of novel and valuable patterns in large databases.

knowledge management The set of processes developed in an organization to create, gather, store, maintain, and disseminate the firm's knowledge.

knowledge management systems Systems that support the creation, capture, storage, and dissemination of firm expertise and knowledge.

knowledge network system Online directory for locating corporate experts in well-defined knowledge domains.

knowledge workers People such as engineers or architects who design products or services and create knowledge for the organization.

knowledge work systems Information systems that aid knowledge workers in the creation and integration of new knowledge into the organization.

learning management system (LMS) Tools for the management, delivery, tracking, and assessment of various types of employee learning.

legacy system A system that has been in existence for a long time and that continues to be used to avoid the high cost of replacing or redesigning it.

legitimacy The extent to which one's authority is accepted on grounds of competence, vision, or other qualities. Making judgments and taking actions on the basis of narrow or personal characteristics.

liability The existence of laws that permit individuals to recover the damages done to them by other actors, systems, or organizations.

Linux Reliable and compactly designed operating system that is an offshoot of UNIX and that can run on many different hardware platforms and is available free or at very low cost. Used as alternative to UNIX and Windows NT.

local area network (LAN) A telecommunications network that requires its own dedicated channels and that encompasses a limited distance, usually one building or several buildings in close proximity.

location-based services GPS map services available on smartphones.

long tail marketing Refers to the ability of firms to profitably market goods to very small online audiences, largely because of the lower costs of reaching very small market segments (people who fall into the long tail ends of a Bell curve).

machine learning Study of how computer programs can improve their performance without explicit programming.

mainframe Largest category of computer, used for major business processing.

maintenance Changes in hardware, software, documentation, or procedures to a production system to correct errors, meet new requirements, or improve processing efficiency.

malware Malicious software programs such as computer viruses, worms, and Trojan horses.

managed security service provider (MSSP) Company that provides security management services for subscribing clients.

management information systems (MIS) Specific category of information system providing reports on organizational performance to help middle management monitor and control the business.

managerial roles Expectations of the activities that managers should perform in an organization.

market creator An e-commerce business model in which firms provide a digital online environment where buyers and sellers can meet, search for products, and engage in transactions.

market entry costs The cost merchants must pay to bring their goods to market.

marketspace A marketplace extended beyond traditional boundaries and removed from a temporal and geographic location.

mashups Composite software applications that depend on high-speed networks, universal communication standards, and open-source code.

mass customization The capacity to offer individually tailored products or services using mass production resources..

menu costs Merchants' costs of changing prices.

metric A standard measurement of performance.

metropolitan area network (MAN) Network that spans a metropolitan area, usually a city and its major suburbs. Its geographic scope falls between a WAN and a LAN.

microblogging Blogging featuring very short posts, such as using Twitter.

micropayment Payment for a very small sum of money, often less than $10.

middle management People in the middle of the organizational hierarchy who are responsible for carrying out the plans and goals of senior management.

minicomputer Middle-range computer used in systems for universities, factories, or research laboratories.

MIS audit Identifies all the controls that govern individual information systems and assesses their effectiveness.

mobile commerce (m-commerce) The use of wireless devices, such as cell phones or handheld digital information appliances, to conduct both business-to-consumer and business-to-business e-commerce transactions over the Internet.

modem A device for translating a computer's digital signals into analog form for transmission over ordinary telephone lines, or for translating analog signals back into digital form for reception by a computer.

Moore's Law Assertion that the number of components on a chip doubles each year

multicore processor Integrated circuit to which two or more processors have been attached for enhanced performance, reduced power consumption and more efficient simultaneous processing of multiple tasks.

multinational   Form of business organization that concentrates financial management and control out of a central home base while decentralizing

multitiered (N-tier) client/server architecture   Client/server network which the work of the entire network is balanced over several different levels of servers.

multitouch   Interface that features the use of one or more finger gestures to manipulate lists or objects on a screen without using a mouse or keyboard.

nanotechnology   Technology that builds structures and processes based on the manipulation of individual atoms and molecules.

net marketplace   A single digital marketplace based on Internet technology linking many buyers to many sellers.

network   The linking of two or more computers to share data or resources, such as a printer.

network economics   Model of strategic systems at the industry level based on the concept of a network where adding another participant entails zero marginal costs but can create much larger marginal gains.

network operating system (NOS)   Special software that routes and manages communications on the network and coordinates network resources.

networking and telecommunications technology   Physical devices and software that link various computer hardware components and transfer data from one physical location to another.

neural network   Hardware or software that attempts to emulate the processing patterns of the biological brain.

non-relational database management system   Database management system for working with large quantities of structured and unstructured data that would be difficult to analyze with a relational model.

nonobvious relationship awareness (NORA)   Technology that can find obscure hidden connections between people or other entities by analyzing information from many different sources to correlate relationships.

normalization   The process of creating small stable data structures from complex groups of data when designing a relational database.

object   Software building block that combines data and the procedures acting on the data.

object-oriented development   Approach to systems development that uses the object as the basic unit of systems analysis and design. The system is modeled as a collection o objects and the relationship between them.

offshore outsourcing   Outsourcing systems development work or maintenance of existing systems to external vendors in another country.

on-demand computing   Firms off-loading peak demand for computing power to remote, large-scale data processing centers, investing just enough to handle average processing loads and paying for only as much additional computing power as the market demands. Also called utility computing.

on-line analytical processing (OLAP)   Capability for manipulating and analyzing large volumes of data from multiple perspectives.

online transaction processing   Transaction processing mode in which transactions entered on-line are immediately processed by the computer.

open-source software   Software that provides free access to its program code, allowing users to modify the program code to make improvements or fix errors.

operating system   Software that manages the resources and activities of the computer.

operational CRM   Customer-facing applications, such as sales force automation, call center and customer service support, and marketing automation.

operational management   People who monitor the day-to-day activities of the organization.

opt-in   Model of informed consent permitting prohibiting an organization from collecting any personal information unless the individual specifically takes action to approve information collection and use.

opt-out   Model of informed consent permitting the collection of personal information until the consumer specifically requests that the data not be collected.

organization (behavioral definition)   A collection of rights, privileges, obligations, and responsibilities that are delicately balanced over a period of time through conflict and conflict resolution.

organization (technical definition)   A stable, formal, social structure that takes resources from the environment and processes them to produce outputs.

organizational and management capital   Investments in organization and management such as new business processes, management behavior, organizational culture, or training.

organizational impact analysis   Study of the way a proposed system will affect organizational structure, attitudes, decision making, and operations.

organizational learning   Creation of new standard operating procedures and business processes that reflect organizations' experience.

output   The distribution of processed information to the people who will use it or to the activities for which it will be used.

outsourcing   The practice of contracting computer center operations, telecommunications networks, or applications development to external vendors.

packet switching   Technology that breaks messages into small, fixed bundles of data and routes them in the most economical way through any available communications channel..

paradigm shift   Radical reconceptualization of the nature of the business and the nature of the organization.

parallel strategy   A safe and conservative conversion approach where both the old system and its potential replacement are run together for a time until everyone is assured that the new one functions correctly.

particularism   Making judgments and taking action on the basis of narrow or personal characteristics, in all its forms (religious, nationalistic, ethnic, regionalism, geopolitical position).

partner relationship management (PRM)   Automation of the firm's relationships with its selling partners using customer data and analytical tools to improve coordination and customer sales.

password   Secret word or string of characters for authenticating users so they can access a resource such as a computer system.

patch   Small pieces of software to repair the software flaws without disturbing the proper operation of the software.

patent   A legal document that grants the owner an exclusive monopoly on the ideas behind an invention for 17 years; designed to ensure that inventors of new machines or methods are rewarded for their labor while making widespread use of their inventions.

peer-to-peer   Network architecture that gives equal power to all computers on the network; used primarily in small networks.

personal area network (PAN)   Computer network used for communication among digital devices (including telephones and PDAs) that are close to one person.

personalization   Ability of merchants to target marketing messages to specific individuals by adjusting the message for a person's name, interests, and past purchases.

PERT chart   Network diagram depicting project tasks and their interrelationships.

pharming   Phishing technique that redirects users to a bogus Web page, even when an individual enters the correct Web page address.

phased approach   Introduces the new system in stages either by functions or by organizational units.

phishing   Form of spoofing involving setting up fake Web sites or sending e-mail messages that resemble those of legitimate businesses that ask users for confidential personal data.

pilot study   A strategy to introduce the new system to a limited area of the organization until it is proven to be fully functional; only then can the conversion to the new system across the entire organization take place.

pivot table   Spreadsheet tool for reorganizing and summarizing two or more dimensions of data in a tabular format.

podcasting   Publishing audio broadcasts via the Internet so that subscribing users can download audio files onto their personal computers or portable music players.

portal   Web interface for presenting integrated personalized content from a variety of sources. Also refers to a Web site service that provides an initial point of entry to the Web.

portfolio analysis   An analysis of the portfolio of potential applications within a firm to determine the risks and benefits, and to select among alternatives for information systems.

post-implementation audit   Formal review process conducted after a system has been placed in production to determine how well the system has met its original objectives.

prediction markets   An analysis of the portfolio of potential applications within a firm to determine the risks and benefits, and to select among alternatives for information systems.

predictive analytics   The use of data mining techniques, historical data, and assumptions about future conditions to predict outcomes of events, such as the probability a customer will respond to an offer or purchase a specific product.

price discrimination   Selling the same goods, or nearly the same goods, to different targeted groups at different prices.

price transparency   The ease with which consumers can find out the variety of prices in a market.

primary activities   Activities most directly related to the production and distribution of a firm's products or services.

primary key   Unique identifier for all the information in any row of a database table.

privacy   The claim of individuals to be left alone, free from surveillance or interference from other individuals, organizations, or the state.

private cloud   A proprietary network or a data center that ties together servers, storage, networks, data, and applications as a set of virtualized services that are shared by users inside a company.

private exchange   Another term for a private industrial network.

private industrial networks   Web-enabled networks linking systems of multiple firms in an industry for the coordination of trans-organizational business processes.

process specifications   Describe the logic of the processes occurring within the lowest levels of a data flow diagram.

processing   The conversion, manipulation, and analysis of raw input into a form that is more meaningful to humans.

product differentiation   Competitive strategy for creating brand loyalty by developing new and unique products and services that are not easily duplicated by competitors.

production   The stage after the new system is installed and the conversion is complete; during this time the system is reviewed by users and technical specialists to determine how well it has met its original goals.

production or service workers   People who actually produce the products or services of the organization.

profiling   The use of computers to combine data from multiple sources and create electronic dossiers of detailed information on individuals.

program-data dependence   The close relationship between data stored in files and the software programs that update and maintain those files. Any change in data organization or format requires a change in all the programs associated with those files.

programmers   Highly trained technical specialists who write computer software instructions.

programming   The process of translating the system specifications prepared during the design stage into program code.

project   Planned series of related activities for achieving a specific business objective.

project management   Application of knowledge, tools, and techniques to achieve specific targets within a specified budget and time period.

project portfolio management software   Helps organizations evaluate and manage portfolios of projects and dependencies among them.

protocol   A set of rules and procedures that govern transmission between the components in a network.

prototype   The preliminary working version of an information system for demonstration and evaluation purposes.

prototyping   The process of building an experimental system quickly and inexpensively for demonstration and evaluation so that users can better determine information requirements.

public cloud   A cloud maintained by an external service provider, accessed through the Internet, and available to the general public.

public key encryption   Uses two keys: one shared (or public) and one private.

public key infrastructure(PKI)   System for creating public and private keys using a certificate authority (CA) and digital certificates for authentication.

pull-based model   Supply chain driven by actual customer orders or purchases so that members of the supply chain produce and deliver only what customers have ordered.

push-based model   Supply chain driven by production master schedules based on forecasts or best guesses of demand for products, and products are "pushed" to customers.

query language   Software tool that provides immediate online answers to requests for information that are not predefined.

radio-frequency identification (RFID)   Technology using tiny tags with embedded microchips containing data about an item and its location to transmit short-distance radio signals to special RFID readers that then pass the data on to a computer for processing.

Rapid Application Development (RAD)   Process for developing systems in a very short time period by using prototyping, fourth-generation tools, and close teamwork among users and systems specialists.

rationalization of procedures   The streamlining of standard operating procedures, eliminating obvious bottlenecks, so that automation makes operating procedures more efficient.

real options pricing models   Models for evaluating information technology investments with uncertain returns by using techniques for valuing financial options.

record   A group of related fields.

recovery-oriented computing   Computer systems designed to recover rapidly when mishaps occur.

referential integrity   Rules to ensure that relationships between coupled database tables remain consistent.

relational DBMS   A type of logical database model that treats data as if they were stored in two-dimensional tables. It can relate data stored in one table to data in another as long as the two tables share a common data element.

Repetitive Stress Injury (RSI)   Occupational disease that occurs when muscle groups are forced through repetitive actions with high-impact loads or thousands of repetitions with low-impact loads.

Request for Proposal (RFP)   A detailed list of questions submitted to vendors of software or other services to determine how well the vendor's product can meet the organization's specific requirements.

responsibility   Accepting the potential costs, duties, and obligations for the decisions one makes.

responsive Web design   Ability of a Web site to automatically change screen resolution and image size as a user switches to devices of different sizes, such as a laptop, tablet computer, or smartphone. Eliminates the need for separate design and development work for each new device.

revenue model   A description of how a firm will earn revenue, generate profits, and produce a return on investment.

richness   Measurement of the depth and detail of information that a business can supply to the customer as well as information the business collects about the customer.

risk assessment   Determining the potential frequency of the occurrence of a problem and the potential damage if the problem were to occur. Used to determine the cost/benefit of a control.

Risk Aversion Principle   Principle that one should take the action that produces the least harm or incurs the least cost.

router   Specialized communications processor that forwards packets of data from one network to another network.

routines   Precise rules, procedures and practices that have been developed to cope with expected situations.

RSS   Technology using aggregator software to pull content from Web sites and feed it automatically to subscribers' computers.

SaaS (Software as a Service)   Services for delivering and providing access to software remotely as a Web-based service.

safe harbor   Private self-regulating policy and enforcement mechanism that meets the objectives of government regulations but does not involve government regulation or enforcement.

sales revenue model   Selling goods, information, or services to customers as the main source of revenue for a company.

Sarbanes-Oxley Act   Law passed in 2002 that imposes responsibility on companies and their management to protect investors by safeguarding the accuracy and integrity of financial information that is used internally and released externally.

scalability   The ability of a computer, product, or system to expand to serve a larger number of users without breaking down.

scope   Defines what work is and is not included in a project.

scoring model   A quick method for deciding among alternative systems based on a system of ratings for selected objectives.

search costs   The time and money spent locating a suitable product and determining the best price for that product.

search engine   A tool for locating specific sites or information on the Internet.

search engine marketing   Use of search engines to deliver in their results sponsored links, for which advertisers have paid.

search engine optimization (SEO)   the process of changing a Web site's content, layout, and format in order to increase the ranking of the site on popular search engines, and to generate more site visitors.

Secure Hypertext Transfer Protocol (S-HTTP)   Protocol used for encrypting data flowing over the Internet; limited to individual messages.

Secure Sockets Layer (SSL)   Enables client and server computers to manage encryption and decryption activities as they communicate with each other during a secure Web session.

security   Policies, procedures, and technical measures used to prevent unauthorized access, alteration, theft, or physical damage to information systems.

security policy   Statements ranking information risks, identifying acceptable security goals, and identifying the mechanisms for achieving these goals.

Semantic Web   Ways of making the Web more "intelligent," with machine-facilitated understanding of information so that searches can be more intuitive, effective, and executed using intelligent software agents.

semistructured decisions   Decisions in which only part of the problem has a clear-cut answer provided by an accepted procedure.

senior management   People occupying the topmost hierarchy in an organization who are responsible for making long-range decisions.

sensitivity analysis   Models that ask "what-if" questions repeatedly to determine the impact of changes in one or more factors on the outcomes.

sentiment analysis   Mining text comments in an e-mail message, blog, social media conversation, or survey form to detect favorable and unfavorable opinions about specific subjects.

server   Computer specifically optimized to provide software and other resources to other computers over a network.

service level agreement (SLA)   Formal contract between customers and their service providers that defines the specific responsibilities of the service provider and the level of service expected by the customer.

service-oriented architecture   Software architecture of a firm built on a collection of software programs that communicate with each other to perform assigned tasks to create a working software application

shopping bot   Software with varying levels of built-in intelligence to help electronic commerce shoppers locate and evaluate products or service they might wish to purchase.

six sigma   A specific measure of quality, representing 3.4 defects per million opportunities; used to designate a set of methodologies and techniques for improving quality and reducing costs.

smart card   A credit-card-size plastic card that stores digital information and that can be used for electronic payments in place of cash.

smartphone   Wireless phone with voice, text, and Internet capabilities.

sniffer   Type of eavesdropping program that monitors information traveling over a network.

social bookmarking   Capability for users to save their bookmarks to Web pages on a public Web site and tag these bookmarks with keywords to organize documents and share information with others.

social business   Use of social networking platforms, including Facebook, Twitter, and internal corporate social tools, to engage employees, customers, and suppliers.

social CRM   Tools enabling a business to link customer conversatins, data, and relationships from social networking sites to CRM processes.

social engineering   Tricking people into revealing their passwords by pretending to rrbe legitimate users or members of a company in need of information.

social graph   Map of all significant online social relationships, comparable to a social network describing offline relationships.

social networking sites   Online community for expanding users' business or social contacts by making connections through their mutual business or personal connections.

social search   Effort to provide more relevant and trustworthy search results based on a person's network of social contacts.

social shopping   Use of Web sites featuring user-created Web pages to share knowledge about items of interest to other shoppers.

sociotechnical design   Design to produce information systems that blend technical efficiency with sensitivity to organizational and human needs.

sociotechnical view   Seeing systems as composed of both technical and social elements.

software-defined networking (SDN)   Using a central control program separate from network devices to manage the flow of data on a network.

software localization   Process of converting software to operate in a second language.

software package   A prewritten, precoded, commercially available set of programs that eliminates the need to write software programs for certain functions.

spam   Unsolicited commercial e-mail.

spoofing   Tricking or deceiving computer systems or other computer users by hiding one's identity or faking the identity of another user on the Internet.

spyware   Technology that aids in gathering information about a person or organization without their knowledge.

SQL injection attack   Attacks against a Web site that take advantage of vulnerabilities in poorly coded SQL (a standard and common database software application) applications in order to introduce malicious program code into a company's systems and networks.

storage area network (SAN)   A high-speed network dedicated to storage that connects different kinds of storage devices, such as tape libraries and disk arrays so they can be shared by multiple servers.

strategic information system   Information system that changes the goals, operations, products, services, or environmental relationships of an organization to help gain a competitive advantage.

strategic transitions   A movement from one level of sociotechnical system to another. Often required when adopting strategic systems that demand changes in the social and technical elements of an organization.

streaming   A publishing method for music and video files that flows a continuous stream of content to a user's device without being stored locally on the device.

structure chart   System documentation showing each level of design, the relationship among the levels, and the overall place in the design structure; can document one program, one system, or part of one program.

structured   Refers to the fact that techniques are carefully drawn up, step by step, with each step building on a previous one.

structured decisions   Decisions that are repetitive, routine, and have a definite procedure for handling them.

structured knowledge   Knowledge in the form of structured documents and reports.

Structured Query Language (SQL)   The standard data manipulation language for relational database management systems.

subscription revenue model   Web site charging a subscription fee for access to some or all of its content or services on an ongoing basis.

supply chain   Network of organizations and business processes for procuring materials, transforming raw materials into intermediate and finished products, and distributing the finished products to customers.

supply chain execution systems   Systems to manage the flow of products through distribution centers and warehouses to ensure that products are delivered to the right locations in the most efficient manner.

supply chain management systems   Information systems that automate the flow of information between a firm and its suppliers in order to optimize the planning, sourcing, manufacturing, and delivery of products and services.

supply chain planning systems   Systems that enable a firm to generate demand forecasts for a product and to develop sourcing and manufacturing plans for that product.

support activities   Activities that make the delivery of a firm's primary activities possible. Consist of the organization's infrastructure, human resources, technology, and procurement.

switch   Device to connect network components that has more intelligence than a hub and can filter and forward data to a specified destination.

switching costs   The expense a customer or company incurs in lost time and expenditure of resources when changing from one supplier or system to a competing supplier or system.

system testing   Tests the functioning of the information system as a whole in order to determine if discrete modules will function together as planned.

systems analysis   The analysis of a problem that the organization will try to solve with an information system.

systems analysts   Specialists who translate business problems and requirements into information requirements and systems, acting as liaison between the information systems department and the rest of the organization.

systems design   Details how a system will meet the information requirements as determined by the systems analysis.

systems development   The activities that go into producing an information systems solution to an organizational problem or opportunity.

systems life cycle   A traditional methodology for developing an information system that partitions the systems development process into formal stages that must be completed sequentially with a very formal division of labor between end users and information systems specialists.

T lines   High-speed data lines leased from communications providers, such as T-1 lines (with a transmission capacity of 1.544 Mbps).

tablet computer   Mobile handheld computer that is larger than a mobile phone and operated primarily by touching a flat screen.

tacit knowledge   Expertise and experience of organizational members that has not been formally documented.

tangible benefits   Benefits that can be quantified and assigned a monetary value; they include lower operational costs and increased cash flows.

taxonomy   Method of classifying things according to a predetermined system.

teams   Teams are formal groups whose members collaborate to achieve specific goals.

teamware   Group collaboration software that is customized for teamwork.

technology standards   Specifications that establish the compatibility of products and the ability to communicate in a network.

technostress   Stress induced by computer use; symptoms include aggravation, hostility toward humans, impatience, and enervation.

telepresence   Telepresence is a technology that allows a person to give the appearance of being present at a location other than his or her true physical location.

Telnet   Network tool that allows someone to log on to one computer system while doing work on another.

test plan   Prepared by the development team in conjunction with the users; it includes all of the preparations for the series of tests to be performed on the system.

testing   The exhaustive and thorough process that determines whether the system produces the desired results under known conditions.

text mining   Discovery of patterns and relationships from large sets of unstructured data.

token   Physical device similar to an identification card that is designed to prove the identity of a single user.

Total Cost of Ownership (TCO)   Designates the total cost of owning technology resources, including initial purchase costs, the cost of hardware and software upgrades, maintenance, technical support, and training.

Total Quality Management (TQM)   A concept that makes quality control a responsibility to be shared by all people in an organization.

touch point   Method of firm interaction with a customer, such as telephone, e-mail, customer service desk, conventional mail, or point-of-purchase.

trade secret   Any intellectual work or product used for a business purpose that can be classified as belonging to that business, provided it is not based on information in the public domain.

transaction costs   Costs incurred when a firm buys on the marketplace what it cannot make itself.

transaction cost theory   Economic theory stating that firms grow larger because they can conduct marketplace transactions internally more cheaply than they can with external firms in the marketplace.

transaction fee revenue model   An online e-commerce revenue model where the firm receives a fee for enabling or executing transactions.

transaction processing systems (TPS)   Computerized systems that perform and record the daily routine transactions necessary to conduct the business; they serve the organization's operational level.

transborder data flow   The movement of information across international boundaries in any form.

Transmission Control Protocol/Internet Protocol (TCP/IP)   Dominant model for achieving connectivity among different networks. Provides a universally agree-on method for breaking up digital messages into packets, routing them to the proper addresses, and then reassembling them into coherent messages.

transnational   Truly global form of business organization with no national headquarters; value-added activities are managed from a global perspective without reference to national borders, optimizing sources of supply and demand and local competitive advantage.

Trojan horse   A software program that appears legitimate but contains a second hidden function that may cause damage.

tuple   A row or record in a relational database.

Unified communications   Integrates disparate channels for voice communications, data communications, instant messaging, e-mail, and electronic conferencing into a single experience where users can seamlessly switch back and forth between different communication modes.

unified threat management (UTM)   Comprehensive security   management tool that combines multiple security tools, including firewalls, virtual private networks, intrusion detection systems, and Web content filtering and anti-spam software.

uniform resource locator (URL)   The address of a specific resource on the Internet.

unit testing   The process of testing each program separately in the system. Sometimes called program testing.

UNIX   Operating system for all types of computers, which is machine independent and supports multiuser processing, multitasking, and networking. Used in high-end workstations and servers.

unstructured decisions   Nonroutine decisions in which the decision maker must provide judgment, evaluation, and insights into the problem definition; there is no agreed-upon procedure for making such decisions.

user interface   The part of the information system through which the end user interacts with the system; type of hardware and the series of on-screen commands and responses required for a user to work with the system.

user-designer communications gap   The difference in backgrounds, interests, and priorities that impede communication and problem solving among end users and information systems specialists.

Utilitarian Principle   Principle that assumes one can put values in rank order and understand the consequences of various courses of action.

utility computing   Model of computing in which companies pay only for the information technology resources they actually use during a specified time period. Also called on-demand computing or usage-based pricing.

value chain model   Model that highlights the primary or support activities that add a margin of value to a firm's products or services where information systems can best be applied to achieve a competitive advantage.

value web   Customer-driven network of independent firms who use information technology to coordinate their value chains to collectively produce a product or service for a market.

virtual company   Organization using networks to link people, assets and ideas to create and distribute products and services without being limited to traditional organizational boundaries or physical location.

Virtual Private Network (VPN)   A secure connection between two points across the Internet to transmit corporate data. Provides a low-cost alternative to a private network.

Virtual Reality Modeling Language (VRML)   A set of specifications for interactive three-dimensional modeling on the World Wide Web.

virtual reality systems   Interactive graphics software and hardware that create computer-generated simulations that provide sensations that emulate real-world activities.

virtualization   Presenting a set of computing resources so that they can all be accessed in ways that are not restricted by physical configuration or geographic location.

Voice over IP (VoIP)   Facilities for managing the delivery of voice information using the Internet Protocol (IP).

war driving   Technique in which eavesdroppers drive by buildings or park outside and try to intercept wireless network traffic.

Web 2.0   Second-generation, interactive Internet-based services that enable people to collaborate, share information, and create new services online, including mashups, blogs, RSS, and wikis.

Web 3.0   Future vision of the Web where all digital information is woven together with intelligent search capabilities.

Web beacons   Tiny objects invisibly embedded in e-mail messages and Web pages that are designed to monitor the behavior of the user visiting a Web site or sending e-mail.

Web browser   An easy-to-use software tool for accessing the World Wide Web and the Internet.

Web hosting service   Company with large Web server computers to maintain the Web sites of fee-paying subscribers.

Web mining   Discovery and analysis of useful patterns and information from the World Wide Web.

Web server   Software that manages requests for Web pages on the computer where they are stored and that delivers the page to the user's computer.

Web services   Set of universal standards using Internet technology for integrating different applications from different sources without time-consuming custom coding. Used for linking systems of different organizations or for linking disparate systems within the same organization.

Web site   All of the World Wide Web pages maintained by an organization or an individual.

Wi-Fi   Standards for Wireless Fidelity and refers to the 802.11 family of wireless networking standards.

Wide Area Network (WAN)   Telecommunications network that spans a large geographical distance. May consist of a variety of cable, satellite, and microwave technologies.

wiki   Collaborative Web site where visitors can add, delete, or modify content, including the work of previous authors.

WiMax   Popular term for IEEE Standard 802.16 for wireless networking over a range of up to 31 miles with a data transfer rate of up to 75 Mbps. Stands for Worldwide Interoperability for Microwave Access.

Windows   Microsoft family of operating systems for both network servers and client computers. The most recent version is Windows Vista.

Windows 8   Most recent Microsoft Windows operating system, which runs on tablets as well as PCs, and includes multitouch capabilities.

Wintel PC   Any computer that uses Intel microprocessors (or compatible processors) and a Windows operating system.

wireless sensor networks (WSNs)   Networks of interconnected wireless devices with built-in processing, storage, and radio frequency sensors and antennas that are embedded into the physical environment to provide measurements of many points over large spaces.

wisdom   The collective and individual experience of applying knowledge to the solution of problems.

wisdom of crowds   The belief that large numbers of people can make better decisions about a wide range of topics or products than a single person or even a small committee of experts (first proposed in a book by James Surowiecki).

World Wide Web   A system with universally accepted standards for storing, retrieving, formatting, and displaying information in a networked environment.

worms   Independent software programs that propagate themselves to disrupt the operation of computer networks or destroy data and other programs.

Index

Name Index

A
Ahmadinejad, Mahmoud, 336
Allen, Reedy and Padma, 587
Archer, Michael, 109
Assante, Michael, 336

B
Barney, Jay, 557
Beane, Billy, 483, 484
Bharara, Preet, 587
Bloomberg, Michael, 586-588
Boger, Joshua, 447
Boire, Ron, 110
Brin, Sergey, 301
Brynjolfsson, Erik, 181

C
Camara, Amy, 557
Carpenter, Jake Burton, 526
Castro, George, 332
Clark, Denise, 15-18
Claypool, Alan, 561, 562
Columbus, Christopher, 38
Connor Christopher, 15-29
Cui, Jean, 448

D
Daines, David, 557
D'Ambrosio, Lou, 109, 110
Dean, Jeff, 471
DePodesta, Paul, 483

E
Elli, Alberto, 15-30

F
Fayol, Henri, 488
Filo, David, 301
Flynn, John, 578
Ford, Bill, Jr., 134
Ford, Henry, 89
Friedman, Thomas, 38

G
Gates, Bill, 89
Gosling, James, 219-220

H
Hassenfeld, Henry, 15-17
Hassenfeld, Herman, 15-17
Hassenfeld, Hilal, 15-17
Hunt, Neil, 235
Hyman, Nev, 460

J
Jackson, Eric, 39

James, Bill, 483
Jobs, Steve, 89

K
Kant, Immanuel, 161
Kern, Frank, 561
Kim, Jong Pyo, 555

L
Lautenbach, Marc, 561
Lucas, Tom, 15-29, 15-30, 15-31

M
Mason, Andrew, 401
Matejicek, Christian, 278
McConnell, Mike, 336-337
McCormick, Matt, 428
McDonald, Bob, 84
McIntosh, Madeline, 148
Metcalfe, Robert, 204
Mintzberg, Henry, 489
Moore, Gordon, 201
Myhrvold, Nathan, 443

N
Ng, Andrew Y., 471

O
Obama, Barack, 337
Orwell, George, 176
Oxley, Michael, 339

P
Page, Larry, 301
Page, Mark, 587
Palmisano, Sam, 561
Pincus, Mark, 512
Pitt, Brad, 483
Pontefract, Dan, 72
Porter, Michael, 124
Price, Mark, 460

R
Ratliff, John, 39
Rockefeller, Jay D., 164
Rudin, Ken, 512

S
Sarbanes, Paul, 339
Schultz, Howard, 130
Sheets, Don, 39
Simon, Herbert, 487
Soloway, Robert, 181
Sullivan, Jim, 110

T
Thompson, William C., 587
Torvalds, Linus, 219

U
Ubert, Kevin, 526

W
Wallace, Sanford, 181
Weiss, Larry, 561
Witte, Michele, 264

Y
Yach, David, 175
Yadati, Chandrasekhar A., 15-29, 15-30
Yang, Jerry, 301

Z
Zagat, Tim and Nina, 443, 444
Zuckerberg, Mark, 188

Organizations Index

A
Accenture, 586-588
Activision Blizzard, 513
Adku, 401
Advanced Micro Design (AMD), 38
Aetna, 68
AIC, 525
AKM Semiconductor, 15-4
Albassami, 469-470
Alcatel-Lucent, 209, 434
Alcoa, 372
Allot Communications, 352
Alta Vista, 117
Amazon Merchant Platform, 415
Amazon, 75, 127, 128, 133-134, 140, 147, 148, 165, 177, 200, 202, 214-215, 225, 234, 236, 249, 302, 305, 333, 352, 403, 412, 414, 415, 420, 434
AMD, 207
America Online (AOL), 168, 174
American Airlines, 140
American Bar Association (ABA), 161
American Management Association (AMA), 296
American Medical Association (AMA), 161
American National Insurance Company (ANCO), 525
Ancestry.com, 419
Ann Taylor, 138
Anthem Group, 213
Apache Software Foundation, 255
Apple Inc., 39, 40, 43, 44, 89, 117, 123, 127, 128, 140, 147, 148, 165, 170, 171, 172, 173, 177, 207, 220, 318, 412, 415, 419, 433, 473, 15-3-15-4
Armani Exchange, 434
Association for Computing Machinery (ACM), 161

Subject Index

INTEGRATING BUSINESS WITH TECHNOLOGY

By completing the projects in this text, students will be able to demonstrate business knowledge, application software proficiency, and Internet skills. These projects can be used by instructors as learning assessment tools and by students as demonstrations of business, software, and problem-solving skills to future employers. Here are some of the skills and competencies students using this text will be able to demonstrate:

Business Application skills: Use of both business and software skills in real-world business applications. Demonstrates both business knowledge and proficiency in spreadsheet, database, and Web page/blog creation tools.

Internet skills: Ability to use Internet tools to access information, conduct research, or perform online calculations and analysis.

Analytical, writing and presentation skills: Ability to research a specific topic, analyze a problem, think creatively, suggest a solution, and prepare a clear written or oral presentation of the solution, working either individually or with others in a group.

Business Application Skills

BUSINESS SKILLS	SOFTWARE SKILLS	CHAPTER
Finance and Accounting		
Financial statement analysis	Spreadsheet charts	Chapter 2*
	Spreadsheet formulas Spreadsheet downloading and formatting	Chapter 10
Pricing hardware and software	Spreadsheet formulas	Chapter 5
Technology rent vs. buy decision Total Cost of Ownership (TCO) analysis	Spreadsheet formulas	Chapter 5*
Analyzing telecommunications services and costs	Spreadsheet formulas	Chapter 7
Risk assessment	Spreadsheet charts and formulas	Chapter 8
Retirement planning	Spreadsheet formulas and logical functions	Chapter 11
Capital budgeting	Spreadsheet formulas	Chapter 14 Chapter 14*
Human Resources		
Employee training and skills tracking	Database design Database querying and reporting	Chapter 13*
Job posting database and Web page	Database design Web page design and creation	Chapter 15
Manufacturing and Production		
Analyzing supplier performance and pricing	Spreadsheet date functions Database functions Data filtering	Chapter 2
Inventory management	Importing data into a database Database querying and reporting	Chapter 6
Bill of materials cost sensitivity analysis	Spreadsheet data tables Spreadsheet formulas	Chapter 12*
Sales and Marketing		
Sales trend analysis	Database querying and reporting	Chapter 1

Customer reservation system	Database querying and reporting	Chapter 3
Improving marketing decisions	Spreadsheet pivot tables	Chapter 12
Customer profiling	Database design Database querying and reporting	Chapter 6*
Customer service analysis	Database design Database querying and reporting	Chapter 9
Sales lead and customer analysis	Database design Database querying and reporting	Chapter 13
Blog creation and design	Blog creation tool	Chapter 4

Internet Skills

Using online software tools to calculate shipping costs	Chapter 1
Using online interactive mapping software to plan efficient transportation routes	Chapter 2
Researching product information and evaluating Web sites for auto sales	Chapter 3
Using Internet newsgroups for marketing	Chapter 4
Researching travel costs using online travel sites	Chapter 5
Searching online databases for products and services	Chapter 6
Using Web search engines for business research	Chapter 7
Researching and evaluating business outsourcing services	Chapter 8
Researching and evaluating supply chain management services	Chapter 9
Evaluating e-commerce hosting services	Chapter 10
Using shopping bots to compare product price, features, and availability	Chapter 11
Using online software tools for retirement planning	Chapter 12
Redesigning business processes for Web procurement	Chapter 13
Researching real estate prices	Chapter 14
Researching international markets and pricing	Chapter 15

Analytical, Writing and Presentation Skills*

BUSINESS PROBLEM	CHAPTER
Management analysis of a business	Chapter 1
Value chain and competitive forces analysis Business strategy formulation	Chapter 3
Formulating a corporate privacy policy	Chapter 4
Employee productivity analysis	Chapter 7
Disaster recovery planning	Chapter 8
Locating and evaluating suppliers	Chapter 9
Developing an e-commerce strategy	Chapter 10
Identifying knowledge management opportunities	Chapter 11
Identifying international markets	Chapter 15

*Dirt Bikes Running Case on MyMISLab

REVIEWERS AND CONSULTANTS

CONSULTANTS

 AUSTRALIA
Robert MacGregor, *University of Wollongong*
Alan Underwood, *Queensland University of Technology*

CANADA
Wynne W. Chin, *University of Calgary*
Len Fertuck, *University of Toronto*
Robert C. Goldstein, *University of British Columbia*
Rebecca Grant, *University of Victoria*
Kevin Leonard, *Wilfrid Laurier University*
Anne B. Pidduck, *University of Waterloo*

GERMANY
Lutz M. Kolbe, *University of Göttingen*
Detlef Schoder, *University of Cologne*

GREECE
Anastasios V. Katos, *University of Macedonia*

HONG KONG
Enoch Tse, *Hong Kong Baptist University*

INDIA
Sanjiv D. Vaidya, *Indian Institute of Management, Calcutta*

ISRAEL
Phillip Ein-Dor, *Tel-Aviv University*
Peretz Shoval, *Ben Gurion University*

MEXICO
Noe Urzua Bustamante, *Universidad Tecnológica de México*

NETHERLANDS
E.O. de Brock, *University of Groningen*
Theo Thiadens, *University of Twente*
Charles Van Der Mast, *Delft University of Technology*

 PUERTO RICO,
Commonwealth of the United States
Brunilda Marrero, *University of Puerto Rico*

SOUTH AFRICA
Daniel Botha, *University of Stellenbosch*

SWEDEN
Mats Daniels, *Uppsala University*

 SWITZERLAND
Andrew C. Boynton, *International Institute for Management Development*
Walter Brenner, *University of St. Gallen*
Donald A. Marchand, *International Institute for Management Development*

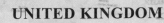 **UNITED KINGDOM**

 **ENGLAND**
G.R. Hidderley, *University of Central England, Birmingham*
Christopher Kimble, *University of York*
Jonathan Liebenau, *London School of Economics and Political Science*
Kecheng Liu, *Staffordshire University*

 SCOTLAND
William N. Dyer, *Falkirk College of Technology*

UNITED STATES OF AMERICA
Tom Abraham, *Kean University*
Evans Adams, *Fort Lewis College*
Kamal Nayan Agarwal, *Howard University*
Roy Alvarez, *Cornell University*
Chandra S. Amaravadi, *Western Illinois University*
Beverly Amer, *Northern Arizona University*
John Anderson, *Northeastern State University*
Rahul C. Basole, *Georgia Institute of Technology*
Jon W. Beard, *University of Richmond*
Patrick Becka, *Indiana University Southeast*
Michel Benaroch, *Syracuse University*
Cynthia Bennett, *University of Arkansas at Pine Bluff*
Nancy Brome, *Southern NH University*
Kimberly Cass, *University of Redlands*
Jason Chen, *Gonzaga University*
Edward J. Cherian, *George Washington University*
P. C. Chu, *Ohio State University, Columbus*
Kungwen Chu, *Purdue University, Calumet*
Richard Clemens, *West Virginia Wesleyan College*
Lynn Collen, *St. Cloud State University*
Jakov Crnkovic, *SUNY Albany*
John Dalphin, *SUNY Potsdam*
Marica Deeb, *Waynesburg College*
William DeLone, *American University*
Cindy Drexel, *Western State College of Colorado*
Warren W. Fisher, *Stephen F. Austin State University*
Sherry L. Fowler, *North Carolina State University*
William B. Fredenberger, *Valdosta State University*
Bob Fulkerth, *Golden Gate University*
Mark A. Fuller, *Baylor University*
Minnie Ghent, *Florida Atlantic University*
Amita Goyal, *Virginia Commonwealth University*
Bobby Granville, *Florida A&M University*